S0-EXQ-326

Photo by
Sharin Smelser

Neil J. Smelser is University Professor of Sociology at the University of California, Berkeley, where he has taught since 1958. He has written numerous books and articles in sociological theory, economic sociology, sociology of education, social movements, and the methodology of comparative analysis in the social sciences. He is also a graduate of the San Francisco Psychoanalytic Institute.

Eugene Garfield, Editor-in-Chief of the **Contemporary Classics in Science** series, is the Founder and President of the Institute for Scientific Information.

Contemporary Classics in the Social and Behavioral Sciences

Contemporary Classics in Science

EUGENE GARFIELD, *Editor-in-Chief*

This volume is one of a series published by ISI Press®. The series is designed to bring together analyses of papers that have been designated Citation Classics because they are influential and widely quoted.

Books published in this series:

Contemporary Classics in the Life Sciences
Volume 1: Cell Biology
Volume 2: The Molecules of Life

Contemporary Classics in Clinical Medicine

Contemporary Classics in Plant, Animal, and Environmental Sciences

Contemporary Classics in Physical, Chemical, and Earth Sciences

Contemporary Classics in Engineering and Applied Science

Contemporary Classics in the Social and Behavioral Sciences

Contemporary Classics in Science

Contemporary Classics in the Social and Behavioral Sciences

Compiled by Neil J. Smelser

With a Foreword by Robert K. Merton

Preface by Eugene Garfield

ISI PRESS®

Philadelphia

Published by

ISI PRESS® **A Subsidiary of the Institute for Scientific Information®**

3501 Market Street, Philadelphia, Pennsylvania 19104 U.S.A.

© 1987 ISI Press

Library of Congress Cataloging-in-Publication Data

Contemporary classics in the social and behavioral sciences.

(Contemporary classics in science)
Includes bibliography and indexes.
1. Social sciences. 2. Psychology. I. Smelser, Neil J. II. Series.
H35.C7724 1987 300 87-21164

ISBN 0-89495-069-X

All rights reserved. No part of this publication may be reproduced, stored in a retrieval system, or transmitted, in any form or by any means, including electronic, mechanical, photographic, or magnetic, without prior written permission of the publisher.

Printed in the United States of America
92 91 90 89 88 87 86 7 6 5 4 3 2 1

H
35
.C7724
1987

Contents

Foreword vii

Preface xi

Introduction xvii

1. Measurement 1
   - Perception and recall / 3
   - Behaviors / 9
   - Affects / 15
   - Attitudes and attributes / 19
   - Personality and adjustment / 25
2. Statistics, Design, and General Methodology 31
   - Association and regression analysis / 33
   - Types of techniques / 42
   - Design issues / 51
   - General and philosophical issues / 58
3. Biological Bases of Behavior 61
   - Areas of the brain and behavior / 63
   - Brain mechanisms and behavior / 69
4. Perception, Audition, and Cognition 75
   - Perception / 77
   - Audition and speech perception / 87
   - Memory and recall / 91
5. Behaviorism and Neo-behaviorism 103
   - General exposition and critique / 105
   - Reinforcement process / 110
   - Study of specific behaviors / 114
6. Cognitive Processes 133
   - Information and information processing / 135
   - Learning / 141
   - Higher cognitive processes / 159
   - Intelligence / 170

278820

7. Development, Personality, and Disturbance 173
Development / 175
Personality / 194
Disturbances / 201
8. Social Psychology 215
General / 217
Attitudes / 218
Attribution / 223
Interaction and groups / 231
Psychological effects of social situations / 242
9. Psychotherapy 247
General / 249
Reports on specific methods / 257
Evaluation of therapies / 270
10. Sociology 277
Theoretical studies and issues / 279
Organizational analysis / 288
Class, race, and mobility / 295
Social problems / 302
11. Economics 307
Novel perspectives / 309
Efficiency studies / 317
Behavior of prices / 320
12. Law and Political Science 323
Constitutional issues / 325
Power / 329
Public policy / 331
13. Miscellaneous 333

Index of Authors 345
Index of Subjects 349
Index of Institutions 358

Foreword

The first commentary on a *Citation Classic*® in the Social and Behavioral Sciences edition of *Current Contents*® appeared on New Year's Day, 1979. The article, by S. Schachter and J. Singer,[1] had been cited some 430 times in the 15 years after its publication in 1962, roughly 40 times as often as the average article in a source journal covered by the *Science Citation Index*® and *Social Sciences Citation Index.*® I found myself doubly interested in that commentary, which now re-appears on page 160 of this volume. First, it had been written by Stanley Schachter, a colleague at Columbia University. Second, a succession of this kind of commentary promised to provide abbreviated cases of what had long seemed to me worth having: "candid chronicles" of how scientific inquiries had been "carried out, full of the particulars of intellectual and social influences, chance encounters with data and ideas, errors, oversights, departures from the original design of inquiry, and all the other kinds of episodes that turn up in investigations but are seldom recorded in the published report."[2] Not, of course, that any one short piece could set out such full particulars; rather, that from the aggregate of them, as with the 300-or-so gathered up in this volume, one might get a sense of the range and diversity of those episodes that had not before been recorded on this scale.

In effect, then, these several hundred accounts provide capsule biographies of the work that went into papers and books that have elicited enough explicit attention by peers to emerge as *Citation Classics.* They tell, in brief compass, how the research came to be; report problems encountered in getting the work into print; and reflect on what the authors take to be the reasons for that work having received widespread notice. These short, and sometimes pithy, accounts thus supply the sort of contextual information that has been systematically screened out of scientific or scholarly publications by institutionalized editorial conventions. Those conventions, as they have evolved over the centuries, call for restricting accounts in the usual journals to what are defined as "the essentials": the design of inquiry, the technical procedures employed, the findings, and their implications. But not how the inquiry actually proceeded. The mores of scientific and scholarly publication therefore lead authors to write up their research in logically coherent (and preferably cogent) rather than biographically descriptive and analytical fashion.

All this is institutionalized by having editors and referees, themselves socialized in the standards of what is appropriate for the scant and expensive space of journals and for the scarce time of their research-bent readers, see to it that published books and articles are limited to what are defined as cognitive essentials. Authors are to supply only the materials required by peers to assess and to draw upon the fruits of their research. They are only to justify their knowledge-claims but not to tell, as best they can, how they found themselves going about the research being reported. Scientists and scholars are forbidden to "digress" into what Hans Reichenbach called "contexts of discovery" and made to confine themselves to "contexts of justification."[3]

Still, many of us continue to be interested in the contexts of discovery, in learning how a scientific or scholarly inquiry came to be and how it actually proceeded. That interest is evidenced by public response to the occasional autobiographies by scientists and scholars and the more numerous biographies about them. Of course, the individual commentaries on *Citation Classics* cannot substitute for full-scale efforts to reconstruct the course of a piece of research, to say nothing of a lifework. But in the aggregate, these vignettes (as Joshua Lederberg describes them in the Foreword to *Contemporary Classics in the Life Sciences*[4]) do provide a composite set of impressions of the diverse ways in which the researches began and then were carried out.

A goodly number of the vignettes give clues to the genealogy of the ideas central to their research. There are sketches of mentors, collaborators, and of research microenvironments. About a quarter of these *Citation Classics* are reported as having originated during graduate student days or as having drawn immediately upon the intellectual capital accumulated then. Reflecting on their choice of problem, a number of authors refer to dominant cognitive contexts—ideas that were "in the air" or a "major shift of paradigm"—while others refer to social contexts or movements (such as civil rights, feminism, and anti-poverty) as having led to their focus of research attention.

Every so often, authors declare that the *Citation Classic,* although their most cited work, is not their best work. These spontaneous judgments correspond to a pattern identified by Harriet Zuckerman in her study of Nobel laureates in the United States.[5] Asked to appraise their prize-winning work, nearly half of them maintained that though it had merit, "the research cited for their award was not the best they had done." Interestingly enough, the various reasons given for such personal assessments are much alike in both populations of scientists.

The vignettes also provide an inventory of authors' speculations about the bases for their articles or books having been cited so frequently. These cover a wide range. Works are said to have brought a new field of research into being or, in complementary style, to have filled a conspicuous gap in a fairly well-defined field of research. Other tentative explanations refer to the same array of cognitive and social contexts that were reported to have led to their own foci of research attention. The authors of critical review articles or new research procedures often speculate that these were singled out for peer attention because they happened to come along just when they were needed for the field to get on with research on problems, both old and new.

These personal accounts and interpretations are just that: retrospections and reflections of a kind ordinarily excluded from scientific or scholarly reports. As such, they hold an interest all their own.

Robert K. Merton
Columbia University

REFERENCES

1. **Schachter, S. & Singer, J.** Cognitive, social and physiological determinants of emotional state. *Psychol. Rev.* 69:379–99, 1962.
2. **Merton, R.K.** *Social theory and social structure.* 3rd enlarged ed. New York: The Free Press, 1968, p. 7.
3. **Reichenbach, H.** *The rise of scientific philosophy.* Berkeley and Los Angeles: University of California Press, 1951, p. 231.
4. **Lederberg, J.** Foreword. *Contemporary classics in the life sciences.* Philadelphia: ISI Press, 1986. 2 vols.
5. **Zuckerman, H.** *The scientific elite: Nobel laureates in the United States.* New York: The Free Press, 1977, pp. 210–11.

Preface

For almost 20 years I've been writing about Citation Classics, my term for highly cited papers and books that are classics in their fields. In 1977 we began publishing in *Current Contents®* (*CC®*) the feature "This Week's Citation Classic"—an invited 500-word commentary by the author of a Citation Classic. Over 2,300 autobiographical commentaries have appeared so far. In requesting these commentaries, we asked authors of Citation Classics to describe their research, its genesis, and circumstances that affected its progress and publication. We encouraged them to include the type of personal details that are rarely found in formal scientific publication, such as obstacles encountered and by-ways taken. We also asked that they mention the contributions of co-authors, any awards or honors they received for their research, and any new terminology arising from their work. Finally, we asked them to speculate on the reasons for their paper or book having been cited so often.

Contemporary Classics in the Social and Behavioral Sciences is the seventh volume to appear in the series "Contemporary Classics in Science." The commentaries collected here include all those published in *CC/Social & Behavioral Sciences* from 1979 to 1984. The first six volumes in the series cover the life sciences (in two volumes); clinical medicine; and plant, animal, and environmental sciences; physical, chemical, and earth sciences; and engineering and applied sciences.

Although I have previously described how we choose a paper or book as a Citation Classic,[1,2,3] it is useful to review these procedures in order to make the purpose of this monographic series clear. Not every scientific publication that deserves the designation "classic" is included in this series, which is limited to *Citation* Classics. There are other types of classics, including those that are rarely or only occasionally cited. More about these later. Our primary criterion for inviting a researcher to contribute a commentary is the number of citations that a particular work has accumulated.

We begin the selection process in gross terms by singling out the 300,000 papers and books most cited in our *Science Citation Index®* (*SCI®*) and *Social Sciences Citation Index®* (*SSCI®*) files (which presently span the years 1955 to 1985 and 1966 to 1985, respectively). We do not, however, rely solely on the highest number of citations in the entire population of publications, but make our selections by fields, in some of which, such as ecology, engineering, or mathematics, 100 citations or even fewer may qualify a work as a Citation Classic.

Searching for Citation Classics, therefore, is like fishing with nets. We seine the waters of the scientific literature in search of the biggest fish in a school. The big fish are the relatively few papers and books with the highest number of citations *in their field.* Now it's plain that the biggest fish in one school will be dwarfed by even the smallest fish in another school. So, too, the number of citations necessary to make a work a Citation Classic in radio astronomy, with its much smaller population of researchers and papers, is smaller than the number giving a work status as a Citation Classic in biochemistry. Realizing that one discipline is more populated than another, we have used different nets when searching different waters. In the Sea of Biochemistry we expect to encounter many giant fish, since in these waters the population of published papers is so great. The net we select has a wide mesh that captures only the big fish and allows the little ones to swim through. But the net we drop into the Bay of Radio Astronomy has a much smaller mesh and is designed to catch the largest of the relatively small fish found there. The mesh of the nets corresponds to the different thresholds of citation frequency we set depending on the fields in which we are searching for Citation Classics.

Along with the initial search for Citation Classics in terms of absolute and relative frequency of citation, we extend the search by creating a separate file for each journal to identify the most-cited papers published in that journal. If one assumes that a journal uniquely defines a field or specialty, then the list of most-cited papers for that journal will include many of the classics for that field. We have found that many classics were published in the first volumes of a specialty journal associated with the emergence of the then new field. But we have also found that the classic paper for a new field was sometimes published in a multidisciplinary journal such as *Nature* or *Science.* Thus, the most-cited paper published in a specialty journal may have been cited only 50 times, whereas the primordial paper for the same field may have appeared in *Nature* and received 100 citations. In cases such as these, we ask both the author of the paper published in the multidisciplinary journal and the author of the paper published in the specialty journal for commentaries. Not surprisingly, we often find that both papers were written by the same author(s).

We are further refining our selection process by relying increasingly on research-front data derived from co-citation analysis.[4] An analysis of most-cited, or core, papers in a research front provides a more sensitive classification of subjects than does citation analysis by journal.

Furthermore, and as a supplement to analytical methods, we ask for nominations from *CC* readers of works which they believe may qualify as Citation Classics.

* * * * *

We emphasize that this collection represents only a sample from the larger group we have identified as Citation Classics. About half of the authors invited to write commentaries actually do so. It follows, then, that the omission of a paper in this volume in no way signifies that it is not a Citation Classic. In the recent series of essays in *CC* devoted to the 1,000 most-cited papers in the *SCI* from 1961 to 1982, I identified papers for which we have received and published a *Citation Classics®* commentary.[5] In Appendix A of Volume One I provided a sampling of 100 most-cited works for which we have not yet received a commentary. I hope that some of the authors of these Citation Classics will put pen to paper to reminisce and interpret the citation impact of their research. Still, a remarkable number of Nobel laureates and other scientists I have described as *of Nobel class* have contributed commentaries. These are balanced by many from hundreds of other scientists who have received rather little formal recognition for their contributions.

* * * * *

Finally, a word about those classics I have reported as rarely or only occasionally cited. I have taken to describing these papers and books as uncited classics, and there are many reasons for a classic work having few or no citations. I have already described how a relatively low citation count can qualify a work as a classic when weighed against its companions in other fields, and how we use a flexible, composite, and, we hope, intelligent algorithm to compensate for this problem. It is most difficult, however, to compensate for the lifetime citation counts of papers and books published as long as 50 years ago or even more recently than that. We know that most older works receive fewer citations since typically most citations are received in the first decade after publication. Moreover, the exponential growth of the literature has changed the significance of any fixed threshold. In 1955 we processed 80,000 papers in about 600 journals in the *SCI,* whereas in 1985 we indexed about 600,000 from 3,000 journals in the natural and physical sciences. These numbers reflect the rapid expansion of modern science, which in turn affects the size of bibliographies and the potential for citation impact.

Furthermore, a recognized classic work may fail to be a Citation Classic because it has suffered what Robert K. Merton terms "obliteration by incorporation": "the obliteration of the source of ideas, methods, or findings, by their incorporation in currently accepted knowledge."[6,7] Thus, some works are no longer cited because their substance has been absorbed in the literature.[8] Just as neologisms and eponyms become part of scientific language, obliterated works become the common knowledge within a field, and explicit citation to them is viewed as unnecessary or pedantic. Quite often, a classic work is cited for a few years, excites rapid advances in its subject, and is then superseded by reviews or other papers containing new information. For a variety of reasons including little understood citation behavior, the primordial work is not mentioned; it nevertheless remains classic. On such matters I urge the reader to examine Joshua Lederberg's pithy remarks on obliteration in connection with the discovery that DNA is involved in the genetic transformation in bacteria.[9] The commentary published by Maclyn McCarty[10] on that milestone paper will be included in a future volume in this series for the life sciences.

* * * * *

I have always believed that these commentaries contribute to future historiography by preserving important biographical and behind-the-scenes information, otherwise generally unavailable. Working scientists reading this book will learn about unfamiliar aspects of otherwise familiar and classic research. These commentaries provide grist for the mill of historians and sociologists of science. They also help sensitize students and the public to the diverse nature and methods of science. The publication of these commentaries in this collected form adds to their value. Perhaps, too, the appearance of this book will stimulate other scientists to write *Citation Classics* commentaries. Since this is a continuing monographic series, their contributions will always be welcome.

Eugene Garfield
Institute for Scientific Information

REFERENCES

1. **Garfield E.** *Citation Classics*—four years of the human side of science. *Essays of an information scientist.* Philadelphia: ISI Press, 1982. Vol. 5. p. 123–34.
2. ———. The 100 most-cited papers ever and how we select *Citation Classics. Ibid.,* 1985. Vol. 7. p. 175–81.
3. ———. *Contemporary Classics in the Life Sciences:* an autobiographical feast. *Ibid.,* 1986. Vol. 8. p. 410–5.
4. ———. ABCs of cluster mapping. Parts 1 & 2. Most active fields in the life and physical sciences in 1978. *Essays of an information scientist.* Philadelphia: ISI Press, 1981. Vol. 4. p. 634–49.
5. ———. The articles most-cited in the *SCI,* 1961–1982. Pts. 1–5. *Ibid.,* 1985. Vol. 7. p. 175–81; 218–27; 270–6; 306–12; 325–35. Pts. 6–8. *Ibid.,* 1986. Vol. 8. p. 132–9; 187–96; 311–9. Pts. 9–10. *Current Contents.* (8):3–12; (16):3–14, 1986.
6. **Merton R K.** *Social theory and social structure.* New York: Free Press, 1968. pp. 27–9, 35–8.

7. ———. Foreword. (Garfield E) *Citation indexing—its theory and application in science, technology, and humanities.* New York: John Wiley & Sons, 1979. p. vii–xi.
8. **Garfield E.** The "obliteration phenomenon" in science—and the advantage of being obliterated. *Essays of an information scientist.* Philadelphia: ISI Press, 1977. Vol. 2. p. 396–8.
9. **Lederberg J.** Foreword. (Garfield E) *Ibid.,* 1977. Vol. 1. p. xiv.
10. **McCarty M.** *Citation Classic.* Commentary on Avery O T, MacLeod C M & McCarty M. Studies on the chemical nature of the substance inducing transformation of pneumococcal types. Induction of transformation by a desoxyribonucleic acid fraction isolated from pneumococcus Type III. *J. Exp. Med.* 79:139–58, 1944. *Current Contents/Life Sciences* 28(50):26, 16 December 1985.

Introduction*

Background: The Behavioral and Social Sciences

The intellectual range and diversity of those sciences and other areas of study and application that we call "behavioral and social" is enormous. The five academic disciplines that are customarily regarded as "core" to the enterprise are anthropology, economics, political science, psychology, and sociology. In addition, a great deal of work done in history, geography, psychiatry, and law falls under its rubric. The same can be said for new or specialized interdisciplinary areas such as demography, public choice, artificial intelligence, and management and decision science. The behavioral and social sciences overlap at one extreme with the humanities (historical investigations, philosophy of science, and the sociology of literature, for example) and at the other with the biophysical sciences (psychophysics, health and behavior, sociobiology).

This listing of subject matters suggests how diverse the behavioral and social sciences are. That diversity becomes even more evident when we acknowledge that each of the various disciplines is broken into numerous subdisciplines (in economics, for example, there are consumption economics, labor economics, theory of the firm, international economics, econometrics, and many more). Moreover, each of the disciplines and subdisciplines has a multiplicity of paradigms and perspectives, which sometimes conflict with one another (examples in psychology are operant conditioning, learning theory, gestalt psychology, and psychoanalytic psychology, with numerous

* More than the usual consulting help was given to me by Gardner Lindzey, Director of the Center for Advanced Study in the Behavioral Sciences in Palo Alto, in organizing this volume and planning the Introduction. He helped me greatly in areas of psychology which are beyond my range of command, and made numerous general suggestions which proved wise and found their way into the Introduction. I regard him as a silent, valuable, only feebly acknowledged (by this footnote), and unpaid co-author. N.J.S.

subdivisions within each). When this diversity is appreciated, it becomes difficult to regard the behavioral and social sciences as any kind of entity.

(A word is in order on the somewhat awkward label, "behavioral and social." A common-sense and approximate rendition of this distinction would be to acknowledge that many scientists, mainly but not exclusively psychologists, focus primarily on discrete items and patterns of behavior with the individual, while many other scientists study relations among individuals, and the organization of these relations into larger systems such as organizations, institutions, and cultures. Some, though by no means all, feel it important that they are identified as either "behavioral" or "social" because they believe that their focus is sounder and more promising scientifically. At the same time, it is difficult to sustain any adequate or consistent analytical distinction between the two foci. Certainly they do not distinguish disciplines from one another, because some economists, sociologists, and political scientists study "behavior" (e.g., spending behavior, voting behavior) as much as psychologists do, and some psychologists study social-relational qualities in experimental small groups. Furthermore, the domains clearly overlap empirically, for much of what we describe as "behavior" is social in character, and the study of the working of social structures invariably involves the investigator in studying the discrete behavior of those who populate them.)

One final aspect of the diversity of the behavioral and social sciences that should be noted is the tremendous diversity of their publication outlets. These include university and commercial presses, both of whose publications shade over into an indistinct area between scientific and popular books; a proliferation of journals of different degrees of specialization, which also merge with "intellectual" and popular magazines; and a great number of internationally based publications outlets (e.g., UNESCO, Organization for Economic Co-operation and Development).

One consequence of all these kinds of diversity is that it is a gargantuan if not impossible task to record in a truly representative or accurate way the scientific and scholarly trends in the behavioral and science literature. Authors of textbooks try to do this; various kinds of specialized journals *(Journal of Economic Literature, Sociological Abstracts)* also try; and another effort is the use of citation indices, of which this volume is an example. Each of these kinds of efforts is bound to be imprecise, selective, or wanting in some other way, perhaps especially so in the behavioral and social sciences, given their broad scope, diversity of subject-matter and approach, and heterogeneity of types of publications.

Perhaps it is a kind of silent belief that these kinds of measures, including citations, are limited in various ways that accounts for the fact that behavioral and social scientists have not made as much effort as, for example, life scientists and historians of science to make *scientific* use of citations, that is, to use them as empirical bases for tracing dominant strands of theory and research in their own fields. Behavioral and social scientists certainly make some *practical* use of citation indices, as, for example, when an academic and his or her department chair build up a dossier for his or her promotion or advancement. (Even that subject—the relations between scholars' citation histories and their career trajectories—could be made the subject of disciplined inquiry.) Be all that as it may, it still appears the case that citation indices and their scientific use are less developed and salient in the behavioral and social sciences than they are elsewhere. For that reason ISI Press is to be commended for venturing into this area, difficult as it is.

Determinants of Citation and Their Consequences: Some Speculations

What is it that determines whether a given book or article in the behavioral and social sciences will be cited frequently, infrequently, or not at all? At the outset we should acknowledge the most obvious and perhaps the most important answer: the evident importance of its contribution to the ongoing scientific tradition within which it is placed. This importance can be of several sorts: the book or article may constitute a decisive challenge to and/or significant modification of a major theoretical paradigm or an accepted set of empirical findings; it may report a study so well designed and executed that it constitutes a decisive consolidation of heretofore-unclear findings; or it may introduce a novel and powerful technique or mode of design that finds applications in many other lines of research. The importance of this answer lies in the logic of scientific inquiry and the dynamics of accumulation of scientific knowledge. Above and beyond this, there are no doubt a number of other factors that affect the rates and patterns of citation in various fields. Let me speculate on some of these:

(1) Size of the discipline and its publication base. The behavioral and social sciences differ considerably by size. Psychology is by far the largest, having approximately twice as many faculty members in American universities as economics, sociology, and political science (in that order). Anthropology is a little more than half of these three, and, of course, the subspecialties (e.g., demography) and interdisciplinary groups (e.g., cognitive science) are smaller still. The size of a discipline is reflected, more or less, in the numbers of publications produced by it. Unless very careful efforts are made to generate carefully corrected weights to publications by discipline, some will be represented better than others. This observation may constitute a hint as to why psychology is so extremely overrepresented in this volume, and why studies by anthropologists are almost not to be found. It would not contribute much, however, to explaining the fact that political science, a sizable discipline, is represented by only a few selections.

(2) The intellectual coherence of a discipline and its subdisciplines. It is sometimes asserted that the paradigmatic variations within economics and psychology are less pronounced than they are in anthropology, political science, and sociology; because of this—and because of the solidity of quantitative measurement in those traditions—these two fields are generally regarded as more "scientific" in their theories and methods. (By another standard, the other three might be seen as richer, more diverse and more interesting.) The implication of this phenomenon—if it is so—is that psychology and economics would be more likely to have a more definite understanding of what kinds of research is "central" to their fields and subfields, and therefore would have greater agreement on what is to be cited when carrying out a research project in a tradition or subtradition of inquiry. This would concentrate the citation rates in psychology and economics, and disperse them in anthropology, political science, and sociology. This observation makes a great deal of sense in accounting for the dominance of psychology in the rates of citation recorded in this book, but it does little to explain why economics is so little represented. Current efforts on the part of the ISI staff to unify the *Social Sciences Citation Index* with the *Arts and Humanities Citation Index* will certainly cast a wider net for much-cited publications in some disciplines, especially history.

(3) The "culture" of citing behavior in the various disciplines. In psychology, the dominant tradition is to give a coherent summary of contributions to the particular area of research up to this point, and to indicate how the reported research relates it. This means many citations in the introductory "review of the literature" section of most articles in the psychological journals. By contrast, many of us who have served as dissertation advisors in sociology, political science, and history have advised the student-authors of those dissertations to pare the traditional "review of the literature" sections mandatory in dissertations on the grounds that they are generally boring to the readers of the books that these dissertations will become. This tends to reduce the ultimate numbers of published citations, and affect the rate. If one were to do a citation index of the dissertations, the citation rates would undoubtedly be higher than in the books. This observation may also say something about why psychology is so represented in this book.

(4) Closely related, the degree to which a discipline is a "journal" discipline or a "book" discipline. All the disciplines have a number of learned journals as avenue for publication, but they differ in the degree to which they rely on these as opposed to books. Psychology is primarily a "journal" discipline (with books limited mainly to texts, readers, and some monographs). Economics is somewhat less so, though more than anthropology, political science, and sociology. Typically, journal articles are more focused in their terms of reference (and therefore in citations), whereas books tend to be more dispersed in their reference to relevant ideas and research traditions (and therefore less concentrated in their citation patterns). Again, this helps us with reference to the great representation of psychology in this book, but leaves economics in a somewhat mysterious status. The present efforts of the staff of the Institute for Scientific Information to implement procedures for incorporating well-cited books as well as articles will work toward a greater degree of representativeness.

(5) The particular methodology employed by the selectors of books and articles in which the citations are counted. It is my understanding that this process, as utilized by the Institute for Scientific Information, has become increasingly rationalized and representative, but in the period in which many of the citations leading to inclusion in this volume (mainly the 1960s and 1970s), the methodology was much less systematically thought through. It is well known that if one changes one's methodology for identifying indices over time, the quantitative representation of those indices will change. Another, perhaps accidental, ingredient of the citation-index articles which constitute this book lies in the fact that the authors of the highly cited contributions—varying as they do in how busy they are, as to whether they are alive or dead, and whether if the former their requested substitutes will respond to the call—also vary in the degree to which they are willing or able to respond to the request to write a selection that would have appeared in this book. (I can report personally that, upon being asked to write about a very famous and highly cited book of a deceased mentor and colleague, I declined on the grounds that I had written about him on other occasions and that I was impossibly overburdened at the time of the request; as a result, his work does not appear in this book.) Staff members of the ISI inform me that this factor of self-selection in responding to requests to write down their own reflections about much-cited articles and books is one of the most important variables in determining whether those publications will appear in "This Week's Citation Classic."

Such are some of the reflections that may help to account for the particular characteristics of this book, and for some of the limitations of the citation-index method of investigation.

Some Themes Revealed by Citation Patterns

The remarks I have made thus far have been cautionary with regard to the uses of citation indices. To correct any misconceptions that may have arisen from this emphasis, I would like now to give an indication of a number of genuine trends and changes in direction of research that have occurred in the past two decades or so, and which are quite accurately reflected in the Citation Classics represented in this book. Among these are:

- The persistence of widely cited research in the area of operant conditioning and other behaviorist traditions, despite their apparent overshadowing by the perspectives associated with cognitive psychology. This may be accounted for by the fact that the former traditions maintain a strong cadre of people who work and publish in them, and a sizable reservoir of specialized journals which report and cite their research.
- The apparent "takeover" of interest in psychotherapy by the behavior modification perspective (related historically and intellectually to the tradition of operant conditioning); if another range of literature were consulted, we might observe a similar "takeover" of the psychotherapeutic perspectives by a diversity of approaches emphasizing biochemical and psychopharmacological perspectives.
- The dominance of the "attribution" perspective in social psychology.
- The continuing dominance of the formal-organizational (e.g., bureaucratic), and stratificational (e.g., social class, ethnic group) perspectives in sociology.
- The appearance of significant parametric modifications of classical and neoclassical economics: modifications stressing variations in information, decision-making, organizational strategies and structures, economic motivation, and institutional behavior.
- The continuing preoccupation with and innovations in explicitly methodological issues. It is often asserted (but never has been proved) that the behavioral sciences are methodologically more self-conscious than other sciences, and that this assertion is often (invidiously) connected with another assertion, namely, that this preoccupation reflects less than full confidence on the part of the former that they are as mature as the latter. In any event, it remains the case that methodological innovations are an important source of citation in the behavioral and social sciences, and if one were to give advice to a young man or woman in the field, it would be to invent an important technique that would be widely emulated, and thereby cited in the literature. This is not to demean the importance of methodological innovations, of course, but to suggest one of the reasons that methodological innovations find an important place in this book.

I would like to call readers' attention to the diversity of styles represented in authors' commentaries on their own Citation Classics. Some seem unabashedly confident at the time of the original article or book that it would create a splash in their fields; others seem to have a disingenuous "gee whiz" reaction, as though they couldn't believe this could happen to them; still others, apparently hesitant to boast, fish around for seemingly improbable reasons why their contributions made it so big. All this diversity reflects, I suppose, the great human ambivalence, even—or especially—among scholars, toward putting oneself forward and taking credit.

How This Book Was Organized

The volume begins with two chapters that are methodological in character. Chapter 1 deals with issues of measurement, and this has been broken down into measurement questions in five topical areas—perception and recall, specific behaviors, affects, attitudes and attributes, and personality and adjustment. Chapter 2 deals with statistical techniques, design, and general methodology. Under this rubric four types of citation classics are listed—those dealing with association and regression analysis, specific types of techniques, issues of research design, and general and philosophical issues in the behavioral and social sciences.

The bulk of contents of the volume are found in Chapters 3–9, all of which deal with psychology, as this field is broadly conceived. Beginning with the biological boundaries of psychology, Chapter 3 deals with the biological bases of behavior, and virtually all of the articles are classifiable under the headings of areas of the brain and behavior on the one hand, and brain mechanisms. Chapter 4 deals with perception, audition, and memory and recall mainly. For lack of a better title, Chapter 5 is called "Behaviorism and Neo-behaviorism," and includes first a series of general expository and critical articles, second a number of selections on the process of reinforcement, and finally, laboratory studies of specific types of behavior.

Chapter 6 turns to cognitive processes, and includes selections on information and information processing, learning, and higher cognitive processes. Development, personality, and personality disturbance are the subject matter of Chapter 7. Under the first heading selections are listed under the headings of the development of language, abilities, adaptation, and longer developmental sequences. Next comes a set of selections on personality. And under the heading of "disturbances" I have divided these into childhood disturbances and disturbance syndromes. Chapter 9 deals with social psychology, and contains general selections, followed by studies of attitude, attribution, interaction and groups, and the psychological effects of social situations. Finally, Chapter 9 deals with the applied fields of psychiatry, psychoanalysis, and clinical psychology; it contains a series of general selections, reports on the development of new therapeutic methods, and the evaluation of different types of therapy.

The volume concludes with three chapters that are organized around social-science disciplines. Chapter 10 contains selections mainly from sociology, and the subtopics are, in order, theroretical studies and issues, the analysis of formal organizations, stratification or the class-race-mobility syndrome, and social problems, especially crime. Economics is covered in Chapter 11; the first section deals with selections that have brought novel perspectives to bear on the field, and these are followed by sections on efficiency studies and studies of the behavior of prices. The final substantive chapter, 12, deals with law and political science, and deals with constitutional issues, the analysis of power, and issues of public policy. A miscellaneous Chapter 13 contains a few selections that defied categorization, no matter how hard the editor labored.

By what process did I come up with these chapter headings and subheadings? Reconstructing, I think it is possible to specify several criteria that were employed:

- Inductive. It was necessary to let the materials speak for themselves, as it were, and a large number of clusters (for example, attribution studies in social psychology) naturally emerged.
- Deductive. Any editor of a volume of this sort has accumulated knowledge and impressions about disciplines, subdisciplines, and traditions of research. This also served as a guide in grouping selections.
- Arbitrary. It is important to stress that in all likelihood another editor would have divided the pie differently. For example, I put those selections dealing with educational processes under "learning," and as a result a separate subheading for "education" does not appear; some of the selections under "psychiatry, psychoanalysis, and clinical psychology" could have been reclassified under "applied behavioral psychology," and so on.
- Chapter continuity. The grouping was also influenced by the fact that the editor did not want to have chapters that were extremely long, or chapters that contained only a handful of selections.

Looking over the volume as a whole, I think it is possible to identify two types of what might be called "casualties." The first are whole disciplines and major traditions on research in the behavioral sciences that are not represented. Anthropology and history are virtually unseen and political science provides only a few selections. The same can be said for special lines of research in demography, sociology of medicine, comparative kinship, and dozens of others. It is impossible to reconstruct the dynamics that led to these results, but it has to be some combination of the peculiarity of citation patterns in these areas of inquiry and the methodology of selecting the journals and books in which the citations were counted. The second type of casualties are those that result from classification decisions on the part of the compiler. As indicated, there are a number of selections on education in the volume, but as a separate category education does not exist; linguistics is also present, mainly under the heading of acoustical studies, but it is also not visible as a heading. The editor takes full responsibility for this second type.

Chapter

1

Measurement

Perception and recall / 3–8

Behaviors / 9–14

Affects / 15–18

Attitudes and attributes / 19–24

Personality and adjustment / 25–30

 CC/NUMBER 39
SEPTEMBER 28, 1981

Jensen A R & Rohwer W D, Jr. The Stroop color-word test: a review.
Acta Psychologica **25**:36-93, 1966.
[University of California, Berkeley, CA]

The Stroop test is based on the differences between the speeds of (a) reading color names, (b) naming colors, and (c) naming the colors of words that are printed in incongruous colors, e.g., RED printed in green, yellow, or blue. It presumably measures a person's susceptibility to interference effects in various mental functions, especially learning and memory. The article reviews the results of the test's extensive uses in research on mental abilities, cognitive style, personality, and drug effects. [The *Social Sciences Citation Index®* (*SSCI®*) **indicates that this paper has been cited over 160 times since 1966.]**

Arthur R. Jensen
Institute of Human Learning
University of California
Berkeley, CA 94720

July 17, 1981

"At first, I was quite surprised to learn that this review article has become a *Citation Classic*. But on second thought, I should have seen it coming, as it is one of the only two of my articles (out of some 200) for which I have continuously received reprint requests over more than ten years after its publication. The other article, 'How much can we boost IQ and scholastic achievement?,' was also a *Citation Classic*.[1]

"In the early 1960s, I was using the Stroop test in my research on individual differences in susceptibility to intrinsic interference effects in various kinds of learning and memory. To my graduate-student research assistant at the time, William Rohwer, I assigned the task of compiling a complete bibliography on the Stroop. (Rohwer has since become a well-recognized psychologist in his own right and is now a full professor at Berkeley.) This literature was inordinately scattered throughout the world's psychological journals, some of them quite obscure, and in many unpublished research reports. Our compulsion for thoroughness eventually led us to all of these, through library searches, correspondence with researchers who had used the test, and notices in journals. While in England on a Guggenheim Fellowship, I tracked down the remaining few recondite references in the superb libraries of the British Psychological Society and the British Museum, and then wrote my review. I regarded the effort merely as an adjunct to my own research and as a service to other researchers using the Stroop. Its frequent citation suggests that it has fulfilled its purpose quite well. An updated review is in order. I would imagine that the number of studies involving the Stroop has more than tripled since our 1966 review. The considerable interest in the Stroop test is probably the result of its great simplicity and the fact that it shows significant (but usually modest) correlations with a host of other psychological variables and drug effects.

"John Ridley Stroop originally devised the color-word test and demonstrated some of its interesting properties as his psychology PhD thesis. He published only one other article[2] on the test, and then dropped completely out of sight in psychological and scientific circles. I had great difficulty trying to trace him in 1964. Professional organizations could offer no leads, nor could George Peabody College, where he had obtained his PhD. But finally I found him in Nashville, Tennessee, where for many years he had been professor of bible in the David Lipscomb College. He had long been out of touch with the psychological literature and was utterly unaware that his test had become quite famous and widely used. When later I sent him a reprint of our review, his laconic reply, scribbled on a postcard, was: 'Glad to know others have found the test useful. J.R. Stroop.'

"Today I phoned Lipscomb College with the hope of being able to tell Stroop that the review of his test had become a *Citation Classic*. The dean of the college informed me that Stroop died on September 1, 1973, at the age of 76."

1. **Jensen A R.** How much can we boost IQ and scholastic achievement? *Harvard Educ. Rev.* **39**:1-123, 1969. [Citation Classic. *Current Contents* (41):16, 9 October 1978.]
2. **Stroop J R.** Studies of interference in serial verbal reactions. *J. Exp. Psychol.* **18**:643-62, 1935.

This Week's Citation Classic

CC/NUMBER 48
NOVEMBER 29, 1982

Posner M I & Mitchell R F. Chronometric analysis of classification. *Psychol. Rev.* **74**:392-409, 1967.
[Department of Psychology, University of Oregon, Eugene, OR]

This paper sought to extend the method of reaction time analysis, first developed by F.C. Donders[1] for isolation of internal mental processes, to the operations involved in matching, naming, and classifying visual and auditory stimuli. [The *Science Citation Index®* (*SCI®*) and the *Social Sciences Citation Index®* (*SSCI®*) indicate that this paper has been cited in over 280 publications since 1967.]

Michael I. Posner
Department of Psychology
University of Oregon
Eugene, OR 97403

September 29, 1982

"The paper had two origins. At the University of Wisconsin I had been trying to measure the time to switch attention from vision to audition. In tasks involving identity, cross modality pairs required systematically longer times than intramodality pairs, but this was not the case when other classifications were used. Why did it take longer to determine if a visual and auditory 3 were the same than it did for two visual or two auditory 3s? The second experiment began for a different reason but it led us (by this time I had moved to the University of Oregon and Ron Mitchell was working with me) to ask how quickly people could classify pairs of visual letters as 'same' when they were either exactly identical, 'AA,' or identical only in having a common overlearned response, 'Aa.' The extra time required for 'Aa' was about 80 millisec or just about the same increase in reaction time as the cross modal pairs over the intramodal ones. We speculated that matches could be made either based on the identity of physical codes or upon the lookup of a learned name code.

"From that point on, the paper really wrote itself. It was simply necessary to run controls providing evidence that we could separate the time course of matching based on exact identity (physical identity) from that based on learning (name identity). The key was the fact that pairs like 'Ab' had times like 'AA' pairs when people were instructed to match on a physical basis and like 'Aa' pairs when people were required to match on name identity. Pairs like 'Aa' took no longer for 'different' responses with physical identity instructions than did pairs like 'Ac.'

"The paper received a cool reception from the journal to which I sent it. It simply didn't fit with the then dominant mathematical models that usually were published in the *Psychological Review.* I was asked to fit the data with exotic functions and otherwise to make it appear more 'theoretical.'

"However, the paper had a strong impact once it was published and many readers seemed to appreciate its simplicity. It has been highly cited for two reasons. First, it has been used as an example of the general coding approach to mental representations. Second, the methods have been used to study the codes of short-term memory, individual differences in availability of names, laterality, effects of brain injury, and a number of other issues. To me it helped direct my thinking toward the isolation of internal mental operations by experiment and later to understanding their neural bases.

"A major error I made in its format was to present the reaction times in terms of tree diagrams. That led readers to believe that these processes were strictly serial while, in fact, they were not. After 15 years of trying to correct this error, it still appears in textbooks. The written word never seems to catch up with a good picture. I have recently published a paper in this field."[2]

1. **Donders F C.** On the speed of mental processes. *Acta Psychol.* **30**:412-30, 1969.
(Originally published in *Netherland. Arch. Genees Natuur.* **4**:117-45, 1869.)
2. **Posner M I.** Cumulative development of attentional theory. *Amer. Psychol.* **37**:168-79, 1982.

CC/NUMBER 36
SEPTEMBER 7, 1981

Oltman P K. A portable rod-and-frame apparatus.
Percept. Mot. Skills **26**:503-6, 1968.
[Psychol. Lab., Dept. Psychiat., State Univ. New York Downstate Medical Center, Brooklyn, NY]

The paper presents a description of a portable version of Witkin's Rod-and-Frame Test and data indicating that it is a valid substitute for the standard apparatus. [The *Social Sciences Citation Index*® (*SSCI*®) **indicates that this paper has been cited over 135 times since 1968.]**

Philip K. Oltman
Division of Educational Research and Evaluation
Educational Testing Service
Princeton, NJ 08541

July 2, 1981

"The Rod-and-Frame Test (RFT) is one of the key measures of the cognitive style construct of field-dependence-independence. During the test, observers view a tilted square frame which takes up most of the visual field, and an adjustable rod which tilts on the same center as the frame. They are asked to adjust the rod to the gravitational vertical, and these adjustments vary greatly. Some, termed field independent, are quite accurate; others, termed field dependent, are influenced by the tilt of the frame and think the true vertical is tilted more or less in the direction of frame tilt. The significance of these differences between individuals in the extent of their susceptibility to contextual influences is most recently reviewed in Witkin, Goodenough, and Oltman.[1] The late Herman A. Witkin discovered this dimension, and most of his life's work was devoted to exploring its manifestations in a wide variety of psychological areas.

"My contribution in the cited paper was to develop a portable version of the RFT apparatus. The 'standard' darkroom version of the test requires a light-tight room and bulky equipment. I was interested in developing a desk-top apparatus which would be formally similar to the standard version, but which could easily be taken into the field. Apparently many others have felt a similar need, for the portable RFT has since been used in hospitals, schools, and even in remote jungle and arctic settings.

"I built the first prototype during the summer of 1966 in my backyard in Brooklyn, New York, while working at Downstate Medical Center. I needed some validation data, and offered to pay the participants in a doctoral student's dissertation if he would help administer both the standard and portable versions of the RFT. He agreed, although his interest was not in field dependence but in small group dynamics. He had a rather complicated and ingenious design, which manipulated a number of parameters of the usual conformity situation. As it turned out, none of his manipulations had any effect, but the RFT saved the day. It was very neatly related to a typology of styles of conformity which he observed in his data, and his work was often cited by us in later papers as an example of the influence of field dependence on interpersonal behavior. As we used to say of such situations, 'If the soufflé collapses, serve it anyway and call it a mousse.'

"During a family visit to Hong Kong, my wife and daughter visited John Dawson's department at the University of Hong Kong. There sat one of the portable RFTs, which was owned by the department, which at that time was part of the philosophy department. It was marked 'Phil. Department,' and my daughter exclaimed, 'Oh, does Phil work here too?'

"Over the years, the field-dependence-independence dimension has been related to phenomena in many areas of psychology, including education, interpersonal behavior, personality, psychopathology, lateralization of function of the brain, and even patterns of EEG activity. Over these years, our motto might have been 'My rod and my frame, they comfort me,' because of the usefulness of the dimension in generating new hypotheses for research. While there has been controversy (mostly, I think, coming from people who are too field independent to show any effect on the RFT themselves), the steadily increasing flow of articles and dissertations indicates the robustness of the phenomenon that now honors the memory of our beloved Hy Witkin."

1. **Witkin H A, Goodenough D R & Oltman P K.** Psychological differentiation: current status. *J. Personal. Soc. Psychol.* **37**:1127-45, 1979.

This Week's Citation Classic

Shepard R N. The analysis of proximities: multidimensional scaling with an unknown distance function, I &II.
Psychometrika **27:**125-40, 219-46, 1962.
[Bell Telephone Laboratories, Murray Hill, NJ]

A computer-based method of 'nonmetric' multidimensional scaling is described (Part I) and applied to empirical data (Part II). Knowledge, of merely the rank order of the n(n-1)/2 measures of similarity or 'proximity' between n objects, interpreted as n points in a coordinate space, permits a generally unique determination of the dimensionality of the space and the metric configuration of the points. [The *Science Citation Index*® *(SCI*® *)* **and the** *Social Sciences Citation Index*™ *(SSCI*™*)* **indicate that these papers have been cited over 445 times since 1962.]**

Roger N. Shepard
Department of Psychology
Stanford University
Stanford, CA 94305

May 31, 1979

"I have always regarded the development reported in this paper as one of my most original and significant accomplishments. It was largely responsible, I'm sure, for my later election to the presidency of the Psychometric Society and it, along with just two other of my contributions, was singled out for specific mention in the citation of the Distinguished Scientific Contribution Award that the American Psychological Association bestowed on me in 1976.

"The other two contributions referred to in that award were my computer generation of a paradoxical sequence of endlessly rising tones,[1]and my recent demonstrations of the analog character of 'mental rotation.'[2] I mention these two other developments because all three shared two notable circumstances: (a) In each case the basic idea came (typically just upon awakening) in a flash of geometrical intuition that carried great conviction, even though verification had to await a major effort of computer programming and experimental investigation; (b) In each case the empirical results, when finally obtained, surpassed even my own highest expectations. In the case of nonmetric multidimensional scaling, it was the precision with which metric structure could be recovered from purely ordinal proximity data that exceeded my fondest dreams.

"The idea of representing objects (such as colors, sounds, shapes, faces, word meanings, etc.) as points in space, in such a way that the distances between the points represented the perceived similarities between the objects, had occurred to me while I was an undergraduate student in 1951. But it was not until ten years later, when I gained access to the powerful computing facilities at the Bell Telephone Laboratories, that I conceived of an iterative process for reconstructing the implied spatial configuration even when the form of the monotone function relating similarity and distance was completely unknown.

"After a period of trial-and-error adjustment of the parameters of the iterative process, success came with dramatic suddenness on March 17, 1961. According to the computer log, it was at precisely 2.33 p.m. EST on that day that the iterative process first converged to a stationary configuration, revealing a remarkably exact recovery of an underlying test configuration. The excitement of that moment was rivaled only by the birth of my daughter on the very next day. Since then my daughter has developed into a fine young woman; and, thanks in part to the subsequent contributions of my mathematical colleague Joseph Kruskal, nonmetric multidimensional scaling is now finding wide application throughout the cognitive, behavioral, and biomedical sciences."[3]

1. **Shepard R N.** Circularity in judgments of relative pitch.
J. Acoust. Soc. Amer. **36:**2346-53, 1964.
2. **Shepard R N & Metzler J.** Mental rotation of 3-dimensional objects.
Science **171:**701-3, 1971.
3. **Kruskal J B.** Multidimensional scaling by optimizing goodness of fit to a nonmetric hypothesis.
Psychometrika **29:**1-27, 1964.

Kruskal J B. Multidimensional scaling by optimizing goodness of fit to a nonmetric hypothesis. *Psychometrika* **29**:1-27, 1964.
[Bell Telephone Laboratories, Murray Hill, NJ]

This paper presented the first widely-used method and computer program to implement the statistical model known as multidimensional scaling (MDS). It introduced 'monotonic regression' as a tool to perfect a method for nonmetric MDS. [The *Social Sciences Citation Index* ™ *(SSCI™)* **and the** *Science Citation Index® (SCI®)* **indicate that this paper has been cited over 635 times since 1964.]**

Joseph B. Kruskal
Bell Telephone Laboratories
Murray Hill, NJ 07974

August 29, 1979

"It is especially gratifying that a paper in statistics should receive the recognition of being frequently cited, since workers in other subjects often find statistics forbidding. The reason for this recognition is that this paper, in concert with papers by Roger Shepard and Warren Torgerson, helped introduce something which is quite unusual in statistics: a widely usable new statistical model called multidimensional scaling.[1,2]

"In the early 50s Torgerson emphasized the value of generalizing ordinary (psychophysical) scaling to the multidimensional case, and called attention to a forgotten method by which the procedure could be carried out numerically. In the early 60s Shepard made substantial advances and provided some strikingly interesting applications which attracted wide interest. A few years later, I provided further improvements in rationale and methodology, and made available the first computer program for MDS which was to receive wide use.

"The idea of MDS is basically quite simple. Suppose we have selected several objects belonging to a single domain, such as colors, facial expressions, brands of soap, political parties in Holland, or Slavic languages, to cite a few applications. By measuring experimentally how different each selected object is from every other, we obtain a dissimilarity for each *pair* of objects. Now we want to treat these dissimilarities as if they were spatial distances, though of course we must allow for experimental error, often quite substantial (and perhaps also for systematic distortion). Take some fixed low-dimensional space, such as a line, a plane, three-dimensional or even four-dimensional space. In the MDS model each object in the domain is represented by a point in the space. The central concept is that the experimental dissimilarities should 'agree with' the spatial distances among the points. In the simplest kind of metric MDS, 'agreement' means that each dissimilarity should be approximately equal to the corresponding spatial distance. More generally, 'agreement' means an (approximate) curvilinear relationship between dissimilarities and spatial distances. In nonmetric MDS we only assume that dissimilarities and distances should match approximately up to an arbitrary order-preserving relationship.

"MDS participates in the new emphasis on methods of data analysis which are *exploratory*. Its value is not helping to measure something accurately, nor in determining how accurate a measurement is. Instead, it helps provide insight into the relationships among the objects of the domain.

"MDS has found greatest use in psychology and such uses of psychology as marketing and candidate choice. The reason for this is that the concept of similarity (and dissimilarity) appears to be an integral part of people's thinking. It is easy to elicit reliable judgments of similarity by a variety of techniques. This approach greatly enriches the older approach to cognition and perception which relied heavily on judgments of single objects on various scales.

"Outside of psychology, MDS has found diverse applications, including the arrangement of the macromolecules which make up a ribosome, and the relationship among species based on the serum-antiserum reaction.

"One of the most important recent advances in MDS was the invention of the INDSCAL method by Carroll and Chang in 1970.[3] We now appear to be in the midst of a revived surge of interest centering on the analysis of three-way and many-way tables."

1. **Torgerson W S.** Multidimensional scaling: 1. Theory and method. *Psychometrika* **17**:401-19, 1952.
2. **Shepard R N.** Analysis of proximities: multidimensional scaling with an unknown distance function. I & II. *Psychometrika* **27**:125-39, 219-46, 1962.
3. **Carroll J D & Chang J J.** Analysis of individual differences in multidimensional scaling via an N-way generalization of Eckart-Young decomposition. *Psychometrika* **35**:283-319, 1970.

CC/NUMBER 19
MAY 7, 1979

Bousfield A K & Bousfield W A. Measurement of clustering and of sequential constancies in repeated free recall. *Psychol. Rep.* **19**:935-42, 1966.

When permitted to do so, subjects tend to impose their own sequential organization in recalling a list of randomly presented words. Theoretically derived formulas for measuring two manifestations of this phenomenon comprise the basic content of this study. [The *Science Citation Index®* *(SCI®* **) and the** *Social Sciences Citation Index* ™ *(SSCI™)* **indicate that this paper has been cited over 190 times since 1966.]**

Weston A. Bousfield
Department of Psychology
University of Connecticut
Storrs, CN 06268

March 15, 1978

"Research on organizational processes in recall had become extensive and there appeared to be a need for more refined quantitative measures of this phenomenon. The authors believed this requirement could best be met by basing the measures on assumptions derived from psychological theory. The theory advanced by Underwood and Schulz appeared to be the most suitable.[1]

"The study was the result of a son-father collaboration. The work was performed at the University of Connecticut. The son, the first author, was a 'pure' mathematician. The father, the second author, was a more or less 'pure' experimentalist. Their habits of thinking were very different, and the collaboration was difficult. It could never have been made without drawing heavily on a fund of mutual respect and affection. It was necessary to translate a psychological theory into a group of mathematically precise propositions. The report had to be written in a form acceptable to both parties. This was not easy. When finally completed, a different trouble arose. It was rejected, after a long interval, by the journal to which it was submitted on grounds that the theory was 'weak.' At any rate, the authors made several new basic modifications and it was readily accepted by *Psychological Reports.* The supply of 200 reprints was soon exhausted.

"Why the demand for this article? The formulas in the study were simple, up to date, and provided useful information. The authors hoped that for at least some of the readers, the steps involved in the derivation of the formulas were a useful model for the quantifications of psychological data.

"Two types of inferences are plausible. Genuine interdisciplinary collaboration must be spontaneous and not from arbitrary assignment. The second is that rejection of a paper by journal referees, while unpleasant, should not be discouraging when the authors are experienced, presumably competent, and confident of the validity of their work.

"The second of the authors knows a very able researcher who quit publications completely after experiencing the humiliation of rejection by journal referees. There are probably many others. Out of fairness it should be said that serving as a journal referee is in a sense, a labor of love—though not for the author of the article or the one making a research proposal. It is a nonremunerative and thankless undertaking. Perhaps a little charity is needed all around."

1. **Underwood B J & Schulz R W.** *Meaningfulness and verbal learning.* Chicago: Lippincott, 1960. 430 p.

This Week's Citation Classic™

Rathus S A. A 30-item schedule for assessing assertive behavior.
Behav. Ther. **4**:398-406, 1973.
[Montclair State College, NJ]

Studies of the reliability and validity of a schedule for measuring assertiveness are presented. Moderate to high test-retest reliability and split-half reliability are reported. Validity studies report moderate correlations between test scores and independent ratings of respondents' personality traits and assertive behavior. [The *Social Sciences Citation Index*® (*SSCI*®) indicates that this paper has been cited in over 285 publications since 1973.]

Spencer A. Rathus
Department of Psychology
St. John's University
Jamaica, NY 11439

March 20, 1984

"The apparent popularity of my assertiveness schedule and the frequent citation of the article in which it appeared have been two of the mysteries of my life. First, many of the items on the schedule were adapted from questions used by others, such as Joseph Wolpe and Arnold Lazarus.[1] In effect, I only quantified responses to these questions and validated their usefulness. Second, I put together the scale for use in my doctoral research on the efficacy of videotaped assertiveness-training models. To me, the videotaped treatment was the important feature of my research. The scale, by comparison, was an afterthought, and I submitted it for independent publication merely in hopes of building my *vita*.

"Yet I continue to receive dozens of requests each year for permission to use the scale from professionals and students in fields including psychology, psychiatry, social work, nursing, and sociology. I long ago lost track of the dissertations on, and other investigations of, the validity and reliability of the scale with this population and that population. It also turns out that there are a number of 'competing' scales and that investigators are infinitely concerned with the correlations among all these scales and what they might portend about assertiveness as it exists in the realm of forms. Whenever a study finds my scale lacking in some regard, there is sure to be a subsequent investigation that faults the faultfinder and reaffirms its essential validity.

"All this activity concerns a scale that I now recognize is confounded by the failure to differentiate between assertive behavior and aggressive behavior. (But, of course, others have by now used multivariate procedures to derive assertiveness and aggressiveness subscales, among many, many others.)

"All this activity concerns a scale for a field that lacks a single, definitive name and is now seen, by some, as a symptom of the excesses of the 'Me Decade.' As Richard M. McFall[2] aptly noted earlier in these pages, some have referred to the clinical art we have both researched as 'assertive training' while others, grammatical purists, have used the term 'assertion training.' Still other grammatical purists have prevailed on me and many others to join as a third force in nomenclature and use the term 'assertiveness training.' But do not be quick to place your cash on any of these; the focus of the field now seems to be shifting to something called 'social skills training'—which, in fact, I prefer. In assertive, er, assertion training, we usually encourage clients to speak their minds forcefully, to 'let it all hang out.' Social skills training is more complex and perhaps more socially appropriate. The socially skillful client sometimes keeps it in.

"In reviewing these paragraphs, I see that I have been assertive and not socially skillful about self-assertion. What can you expect from a PhD from the Me Decade? In recent years, I have managed to avoid all this empirical controversy by focusing on writing psychology textbooks. Now I stick to summarizing the controversies of others."

1. **Wolpe J & Lazarus A A.** *Behavior therapy techniques.* Oxford: Pergamon Press, 1966. 198 p.
2. **McFall R M.** Citation Classic. Commentary on *J. Abnormal Psychol.* 77:313-23, 1971.
Current Contents/Social & Behavioral Sciences **14**(23):22, 7 June 1982.

CC/NUMBER 18
APRIL 30, 1984

This Week's Citation Classic™

Galassi J P, DeLo J S, Galassi M D & Bastien S. The College Self-Expression Scale: a measure of assertiveness. *Behav. Ther.* **5**:165-71, 1974.
[Student Counseling Service, West Virginia University, Morgantown, WV]

The College Self-Expression Scale (CSES) is a 50 item self-report measure of assertiveness. The items tap three dimensions of assertiveness (positive, negative, and self-affirmation) in a variety of interpersonal contexts. Preliminary data concerning norms, reliability, and validity are presented. [The *Social Sciences Citation Index*® (*SSCI*®) indicates that this paper has been cited in over 140 publications since 1974.]

John P. Galassi
Human Development and
Psychological Services
School of Education
University of North Carolina
Chapel Hill, NC 27514

January 5, 1984

"Development of the College Self-Expression Scale (CSES) was stimulated both by my doctoral dissertation research and internship with their underpinnings in humanistic approaches and by postdoctoral institute training in behavioral approaches to counseling/psychotherapy. My doctoral research revealed that college students who sought personal counseling exhibited significantly more alienation and felt less able to influence their environment than those who either sought vocational-educational counseling or did not seek counseling. About the same time, I was introduced to the work of Joseph Wolpe by a fellow intern, William Minichiello, and became interested in a behavioral technique, assertion training, as an intervention for students who felt alienated and unable to express themselves. I enrolled in Wolpe's behavior therapy institute where I learned of the early experimental studies in assertion training by McFall and his colleagues and, most notably, by McFall and Lillesand, another *Citation Classic*.[1,2] However, I was not comfortable with McFall's reduction of assertion to simple refusal behavior and with his semiautomated analogue treatment. I viewed assertion more broadly as involving the ability to express a range of emotions and opinions, and I wanted to develop interventions more typical of those applied in college counseling.

"My interests were *clearly* in developing and researching interventions for nonassertive behavior and not in scale construction. However, an instrument to measure the broader assertion construct with which I was concerned seemed to be needed for college students. Sheila Bastien, a doctoral student in clinical psychology and a graduate assistant at the West Virginia University Student Counseling Service where I was employed, actually was the person who suggested that I develop an assertion scale. It was called a self-expression scale by my research team, which included James DeLo, Merna Galassi, and Bastien, in order to avoid cuing students that the scale was a measure of assertiveness.

"It took more than two years (largely due to manuscript backlog) for the article to appear in print from the time it was submitted for publication. During that time, the journal published the Rathus Assertion Scale,[3,4] and I worried that some of my originality had been anticipated and that the editor, Cyril Franks, might reverse his decision and decide not to publish another article about an assertion inventory. However, this was not the case. Unfortunately, the text of the article which appeared in print contained one scoring key misprint which I could not get corrected prior to publication. It stated that item 47 should be reverse scored, and it *should not be reverse scored.*

"The reason why the publication has been so highly cited is probably due to its timeliness. In the mid- and late 1970s, interest in both the research and practice of assertion training mushroomed. Assertion training was to the 1970s what sensitivity training was to the 1960s but with a greater empirical basis. Much of the research and practice was conducted with college students, and the article about the CSES simply appeared at the right time and in a visible journal."

1. **McFall R M & Lillesand D B.** Behavior rehearsal with modeling and coaching in assertion training. *J. Abnormal Psychol.* 77:313-23, 1971.
2. **McFall R M.** Citation Classic. Commentary on *J. Abnormal Psychol.* 77:313-23, 1971. *Current Contents/Social & Behavioral Sciences* **14**(23):22, 7 June 1982.
3. **Rathus S A.** A 30-item schedule for assessing assertive behavior. *Behav. Ther.* **4**:398-406, 1973.
4. **--------------.** Citation Classic. Commentary on *Behav. Ther.* **4**:398-406, 1973. *Current Contents/Social & Behavioral Sciences* **16**(17):16, 23 April 1984.

CC/NUMBER 51
DECEMBER 17, 1984

This Week's Citation Classic™

Thayer R E. Measurement of activation through self-report.
Psychol. Rep. **20**:663-78, 1967.
[California State College, Long Beach, CA]

Factor analyses involving self-ratings of activation states have yielded four factors, General Activation, Deactivation-Sleep, High Activation, and General Deactivation, that correlate substantially with physiological variables. Reliably predicted from self-ratings are diurnal sleep-wake cycles, day to evening variations, and differences in activation due to college exams. Theoretical issues relating to function and measurement of activation states are discussed. [The *Social Sciences Citation Index*® indicates that this paper, cited in over 150 publications, is among the 12 most cited for this journal.]

Robert E. Thayer
Department of Psychology
California State University
Long Beach, CA 90840

October 24, 1984

"This article was originally rejected for publication by a major psychology journal. The editor explained that even though the article was methodologically sound, it was not of sufficient interest for publication. Fortunately, that judgment proved incorrect. The article has now been reprinted in full and in part in a variety of books and journals, and its rate of citation continues to be high almost two decades after its original publication.

"I believe that these ideas have retained their importance, not only for psychologists, but also for a wider group of biological and behavioral scientists. Their importance arises from the hard evidence provided that psychophysiological activation or arousal states can be assessed at a number of levels of function; that is, arousal states that result in cardiovascular, respiratory, and skeletal-muscular changes also are identifiable through conscious awareness, and people can make meaningful self-ratings of these states. In fact, a point originally suggested in the article, that self-ratings may be better indications of global arousal states than are individual physiological measures, has now been supported by a wide variety of research in my laboratory and in others.[1] In this age of electronic sophistication of measurement, there is some satisfaction in the knowledge that it is still valuable to ask people how they feel.

"This article provided the theoretical measurement base (Activation-Deactivation Adjective Check List [AD ACL]) for evaluating an underlying dimension of behavior relating to intensity. In addition to being greatly impressed by the biological analyses of such scientists as Walter Cannon, Donald Hebb, Elizabeth Duffy, and Robert Malmo, I came to a personal understanding of the potential importance of the intensity continuum through self-observations that most days had predictable high and low periods. In some relationship to the elemental sleep-wakefulness cycle, I noted that my feelings of alertness and energy were high at times and low at others irrespective of situations and events. As an inveterate self-observer, I also noted that, among common emotions, mild states were related to strong reactions by an intensity continuum, and these differences seemed to affect all manner of behaviors. There was a predictability of response whatever the intense emotion. These initial self-observations have now been supported with a great deal of published research employing the AD ACL.

"The self-rating scales provided in the article have been translated into many foreign languages and continue to be widely used. However, as research progressed, it became increasingly clear that the original conceptualization of a unidimensional activation or arousal continuum had to be modified to a multidimensional model.[2,3] I believe that this model, which outlines a complex relationship between a general arousal dimension and a somewhat different type of preparatory-emergency arousal, is useful in accounting for a variety of everyday motivational circumstances relating to feelings of energy and tension."

1. **Thayer R E.** Activation states as assessed by verbal report and four psychophysiological variables. *Psychophysiology* **7**:86-94, 1970. (Cited 70 times.)
2. ----------------. Toward a psychological theory of multidimensional activation (arousal). *Motiv. Emotion* **2**:1-34, 1978. (Cited 30 times.)
3. ----------------. Factor analytic and reliability studies on the Activation-Deactivation Adjective Check List. *Psychol. Rep.* **42**:747-56, 1978. (Cited 20 times.)

CC/NUMBER 33
AUGUST 18, 1980

Kirk S A, McCarthy J & Kirk W D. *The Illinois test of psycholinguistic abilities.* Urbana, IL: University of Illinois Press, 1967. 136 p.

The ITPA is a diagnostic test of 12 linguistic, perceptual, and memory abilities which serve as measure of *intraindividual* difference in an individual child. This approach can lead to a program of remediation for children with learning disabilities. [The *Social Sciences Citation Index® (SSCI™)* indicates that this paper has been cited over 205 times since 1968.]

Samuel A. Kirk
Department of Special Education
University of Arizona
Tucson, AZ 85721

July 21, 1980

"In 1949 I was conducting an experiment on the effect of preschool experience on the mental and social development of young mentally retarded children. For this experiment I had selected three-, four-, and five-year-old children described by psychologists and pediatricians as mentally retarded. The children ranged in IQ from 37 to 80 on standardized intelligence tests.

"When we started working with these children we found that they differed so widely that the term mental retardation was not descriptive of their abilities or disabilities. One little girl with a recorded IQ of about 50 was legally blind but had good language and verbal communication. Another girl of about the same age and mental ability was unable to talk or understand language.

"Working from a psychological model of the communication process, my colleagues and I generated tests to measure responses which indicated the functioning of certain cognitive abilities. This work eventually turned out to be the Illinois Test of Psycholinguistic Abilities (ITPA).

"The abilities we wanted to isolate were both verbal and nonverbal. But we were also concerned with dimensions such as the processes of reception, expression, and an intermediate process of organizing symbols and concepts as well as levels of organization, i.e., the degree to which responses are automatic or require the rational translation of symbols into meaning and response.

"We had many false starts but by 1961, after ten years of research, we thought that we just might have something teachers, psychologists, and researchers could use. We wanted to turn it loose so that other people could do research on it, so we constructed 250 homemade kits and distributed them to those who would experiment with it. I do not know whether we were more surprised or pleased that the demand for this tool was so great. Workers in child development, education, and mental retardation were hungry for something that would diagnose children in such a way that would lead to remedial programs that would help teach children with intraindividual discrepancies. Thousands more kits had to be made, and although it was an experimental edition it was widely used for both clinical and research purposes. After considerable research by us and others we revised the test in 1968.

"The popularity and wide use of the test by teachers, speech pathologists, psychologists and others is both a boon and a danger. The ITPA was designed primarily for preschool and primary grade children, but it has been used inappropriately in research with fourth graders, high school students, and even prison inmates.

"In our article 'Uses and abuses of the ITPA,'[1] we have tried to note some of the misuses and misinterpretations that have occurred. It has been impossible to control the appropriate use of the ITPA as an instrument to *aid* clinicians, not *replace* clinicians, in assessing linguistic, perceptual, and memory behavior of young children.

"The ITPA measures and compares 12 abilities within a child (intraindividual differences) as opposed to classification tests comparing one child with another (interindividual differences).[2] This approach has educational relevance."

1. **Kirk S A & Kirk W D.** Uses and abuses of the ITPA. *J. Speech Hear. Disord.* **43**:58-75, 1978.
2. ---------------------------. *Psycholinguistic learning disabilities.* Urbana, IL: University of Illinois Press, 1971. 198 p.

CC/NUMBER 33
AUGUST 15, 1983

This Week's Citation Classic

Smith P C & Kendall L M. Retranslation of expectations: an approach to the construction of unambiguous anchors for rating scales. *J. Appl. Psychol.* **47**:149-55, 1963.
[Cornell University, Ithaca, NY]

Potential raters developed rating scales anchored by observed behaviors, scaled for dimension and level. Comparability across regional groups was indicated by scale reliabilities over .97. Attention to recorded observations and separation into dimensions should improve accuracy and facilitate constructive discussion with ratees. [The *Science Citation Index*® (*SCI*®) and the *Social Sciences Citation Index*® (*SSCI*®) indicate that this paper has been cited in over 170 publications since 1963, making it one of the most-cited papers published in this journal.]

Patricia C. Smith
Department of Psychology
Bowling Green State University
Bowling Green, OH 43403

May 12, 1983

"Recommending one treatment of employees over another requires comparison of results measured in different situations on comparable scales. Focusing on *observed behavior* rather than memory could foster comparability. Moreover, setting individual goals for improved performance requires supervisors to discuss actual *behavior* with employees. With the National League for Nursing, we developed Behaviorally Anchored Rating Scales (BARS), vertical graphic scales defined and anchored by scaled behavioral examples. Independent groups of head nurses defined dimensions to be rated, recalled examples they had experienced, and rated location of examples as anchors along the scales. High scale reliabilities showed comparability across regional groups. The resulting BARS, upon which new observations were to be noted and scaled, proved acceptable to users.

"Lorne Kendall recognized innovative features of the procedure and urged its publication. Other researchers were apparently attracted by potential accuracy of measurement. Some concentrated on minutiae of method while neglecting important note-taking, scaling, and discussion of observations.

"Unfortunately, Lorne did not live to see the happier outcomes we had anticipated: (1) An improved recommended procedure has now been published. (See Bernardin, La Shells, Smith, and Alvares;[1] Zedeck, Kafry, and Jacobs;[2] and Bernardin and Smith.[3]) (2) The advantages and disadvantages have been adequately researched. According to Jacobs, Kafry, and Zedeck,[4] the continued widespread use of BARS should be based upon subjective factors. BARS are acceptable to employees and raters (only, I have found, when management is trusted). Focus on observed behavior makes BARS more widely useful than other ratings—for disciplinary action, employee development, promotion, transfer, training, supervision, and job analysis. But they have *not* been shown to be superior in psychometric properties to other carefully constructed scales for assessment of overall performance. They have been expensive. Developing BARS is warranted only when management and organization are ready to use them fully. (3) They are being widely and justifiably used as research criteria. (4) Some researchers are at last generalizing the method to ratings in areas other than performance. (5) Others are finally attending to the *process* of observation, evaluation, and rating (Zedeck *et al.*[2]).

"Citations resulted from these developments. More citations will result from research on such unanswered questions as, can observations actually be made independent of selective perception? How do people combine evaluative data (with or without considering explicitly scaled observations) to yield summary evaluations? How many dimensions can various raters handle conceptually? Etc.

"Scales anchored by behavioral examples are probably here to stay, because of their acceptability to employees and management and usefulness for diagnosis and research. Procedures are being developed to simplify their construction, such as computer programs and grouping of jobs with similar dimensions. Emphasis will shift from minor psychometric issues to the importance of BARS in an accurate and constructive communication system."

1. **Bernardin H J, La Shells M D, Smith P C & Alvares K M.** Behavioral expectation scales: effects of developmental procedures and formats. *J. Appl. Psychol.* **61**:75-9, 1976.
2. **Zedeck S, Kafry D & Jacobs R.** Format and scoring variations in behavioral expectation evaluations. *Organ. Behav. Hum. Perform.* **17**:171-84, 1976.
3. **Bernardin H J & Smith P C.** A clarification of some issues regarding the development and use of Behaviorally Anchored Rating Scales (BARS). *J. Appl. Psychol.* **66**:458-63, 1981.
4. **Jacobs R, Kafry D & Zedeck S.** Expectations of Behaviorally Anchored Rating Scales. *Pers. Psychol.* **33**:595-640, 1980.

This Week's Citation Classic

Zuckerman M, Kolin E A, Price L & Zoob I. Development of a sensation-seeking scale. *J. Consult. Psychol.* **28**:477-82, 1964.
[Dept. Endocrinology and Reproduction, Albert Einstein Med. Ctr., Philadelphia, PA and Adelphi College, Garden City, NY]

A Sensation Seeking Scale (SSS) was developed to provide a measure of individual differences in optimal levels of stimulation and arousal. Factor analyses revealed a general factor, similar in males and females, running through diverse kinds of items. Reliability and initial validity studies are reported. [The *Social Sciences Citation Index*® (*SSCI*®) **indicates that this paper has been cited over 180 times since 1966.]**

Marvin Zuckerman
Department of Psychology
University of Delaware
Newark, DE 19711

August 31, 1981

"In the early-1960s I was working in the area of sensory deprivation (SD). Volunteers in these experiments were isolated from the world of external stimulation in dark, soundproof rooms or water tanks for periods ranging from one hour to two weeks. Some of the effects of the situation, such as anxiety and hallucinations, were found to be due to variations in the experimental conditions and the sets produced by the instructions and conditions. But a wide variety of individual reactions could not be entirely explained by these factors. Personality tests were given to subjects in an attempt to identify traits that made some persons more vulnerable to the effects of SD. I formulated a theory that there were individual differences in what constituted an *optimal level of stimulation* (OLS) or arousal, and that these differences played an important role in determining responses to SD.[1] Since there was no personality test specifically derived from the OLS construct, we developed the Sensation Seeking Scale (SSS). The cited article contains the first version of the test (subsequent forms were published in 1971 and 1978[2,3]).

"An experimental form was given to a large number of subjects and their responses were factor-analyzed to see if there was a common factor running through the items. The items expressed preferences for extremes of sensation, novel experiences, irregularity as opposed to routine, and enjoyment of risky activities or sports and exciting persons. A general factor was found that was very similar in males and females. A scale was formed on the basis of these analyses and its reliability was determined.

"The initial applications of the scale to the prediction of responses to SD produced mixed results, but high sensation seekers were generally more restless in SD or social isolation confinement situations. But other investigators found the test, and the theory behind it, useful in many other areas, such as research on drugs and sex. The test has been shown to be related to these phenomena as well as physical risk-taking, vocational interests and choices, and perceptual and cognitive styles.

"The earlier theory of sensation seeking had suggested a biological basis for the trait in the balance between strength of excitation and inhibition in the central nervous system. Beginning in the mid-1970s, studies by our group and others found a number of psychophysiological and biochemical correlates of the SSS.[4] Genetic studies using twins showed a high heritability for the trait. A recent book[5] has summarized all of the phenomenal and biological correlates of sensation seeking and the last chapter of this book presents a new biological model for the trait based on the pharmacology of the limbic reward systems.

"SD led us into sensation seeking, and a test designed for prediction of phenomena in a narrowly defined experimental situation has proven to have validity for much broader aspects of life experience. The idea that personality differences are rooted in biological traits is not new, but it is attracting increasing interest as a consequence of the new discoveries in neuropharmacology."

1. **Zuckerman M.** Theoretical formulations. (Zubek J P, ed.) *Sensory deprivation: fifteen years of research.* New York: Appleton-Century-Crofts, 1969. p. 407-32.
2. ------------------. Dimensions of sensation seeking. *J. Consult. Clin. Psychol.* **36**:45-52, 1971.
3. **Zuckerman M, Eysenck S & Eysenck H J.** Sensation seeking in England and America: cross-cultural, age, and sex comparisons. *J. Consult. Clin. Psychol.* **46**:139-49, 1978.
4. **Zuckerman M, Buchsbaum M S & Murphy D L.** Sensation seeking and its biological correlates. *Psychol. Bull.* **88**:187-214, 1980.
5. **Zuckerman M.** *Sensation seeking: beyond the optimal level of arousal.* Hillsdale, NJ: Erlbaum, 1979. 449 p.

This Week's Citation Classic

Geer J H. The development of a scale to measure fear.
Behav. Res. Ther. 3:45-53, 1965.
[Department of Psychology, State University of New York at Buffalo, NY]

A paper and pencil test to measure fears was developed using empirical item selection of self report data. The scale was validated by behavioral tests. The Fear Survey Schedule II was found to have excellent psychometric properties and to be related to other personality measures. [The *Science Citation Index®* *(SCI®)* **and the** *Social Sciences Citation Index® (SSCI™)* **indicate that this paper has been cited over 195 times since 1966.]**

James H. Geer
Department of Psychology
SUNY Stony Brook
Long Island, NY 11794

July 24, 1980

"The work on the Fear Survey II was one of the first projects that I undertook as a new faculty member at the State University of New York at Buffalo. I had worked on the original studies on Wolpe's systematic desensitization by Pete Lang and David Lazovik[1] at the University of Pittsburgh. That work and my dissertation research on cardiac conditioning led me to be interested in examining and testing a classical (Pavlovian) model of fear.

"The work thus far in that area had been based upon clinical experience or classical conditioning of autonomic responses using aversive unconditional stimuli. The data available seemed to suggest that classical conditioning provided a reasonably good fit to the data available on fear. There were, however, no data available directly testing the model on humans. It seems to me that such tests were both feasible and needed.

"I decided that one avenue of approach to these issues was to study individuals who had fears to determine whether or not their fears acted like conditioned responses. In order to follow that strategy I needed some way of identifying individuals who had fears so that they could be brought to the laboratory for study. A perusal of the literature made it clear that there was no available instrument that had been developed in a systematic manner that I could use to select fearful individuals. My first task was obvious, develop a psychometric instrument or test that would allow me to identify individuals who experienced a greater or lesser degree of fear. From that need to select populations for study, the Fear Survey Schedule II was born. I might note, parenthetically, the scale was named Fear Survey Schedule II since Akutagawa[2] had developed a fear survey several years earlier based upon his feeling as to what were the most common fears. There were 18 of 50 items in common between the two scales.

"Two points of interest about the scale are worth mentioning. First, when the paper that described this scale was originally submitted to one of the journals of the American Psychological Association, it was rejected with an offer to publish a brief one page note on the work. The journal editor in his letter of rejection said that he could not waste valuable journal space on the manuscript as psychologists would not be interested in viewing people as a 'bag of fears.' I presume that the study's inclusion as a *'Citation Classic'* vindicates my belief that the research was of interest and value.

"Finally, much of the interest and citation of the Fear Survey Schedule II has come from clinical interest and studies. This has always concerned me since I viewed the scale as a research tool that had no clinical validation. As we all know, however, once one publishes material he or she loses control over its application."

1. **Lang P J & Lazovik D.** The experimental desensitization of a phobia. *J. Abnorm. Soc. Psychol.* **66**:519-25, 1963.
2. **Akutagawa D.** *A study in construct validity of the psychoanalytic concept of latent test anxiety and test of a projection distance hypothesis.* University of Pittsburgh, 1965. Unpublished doctoral dissertation.

This Week's Citation Classic

Zuckerman M. The development of an affect adjective check list for the measurement of anxiety. *J. Consult. Psychol.* **24**:457-62, 1960.
[Institute of Psychiatric Research, Indianapolis, IN]

A test was developed to measure transient 'states' of anxiety, and another form was constructed to measure general levels of the affect (trait anxiety). The reliabilities of both forms were assessed and the sensitivity of the state form to the stress of classroom examinations was demonstrated. [The *Social Sciences Citation Index® (SSCI™)* indicates that this paper has been cited over 160 times since 1966.]

Marvin Zuckerman
Department of Psychology
University of Delaware
Newark, DE 19711

September 6, 1980

"In 1958 John I. Nurnberger, then director of the Institute of Psychiatric Research of the Indiana University Medical Center, asked me for a test that could be used to measure changes in anxiety. The test was needed for various studies being conducted at the Institute such as hypnotic induction of anxiety, changes during pregnancy, and changes produced by new tranquilizing drugs.

"The standard objective tests of anxiety being used then were designed to measure anxiety as a general trait. They asked subjects how they 'often' or 'usually' felt rather than how they felt at a given time. Such tests were bound to be insensitive to temporary changes in mood induced by suggestion or transient stress. Investigators doing experiments usually resorted to non-standardized, *ad hoc*, one-item self-ratings of dubious reliability and validity.

"I decided to develop a test which could be used to measure anxiety either as a state, a trait, or something intermediate such as a daily, weekly, or monthly level. The adjective check list lent itself to this kind of temporal specificity since the same items could be used for trait or state by a simple alteration of instructions: 'how do you generally feel'; or 'how do you feel now' or 'today.'

"This distinction between 'states' and 'traits' was first clearly formulated in this paper and elaborated in later work by myself and Charles D. Spielberger.[1, 2]

"The test was developed using the empirical method of item selection. Items that anxious patients responded to differently than normals, and that also showed changes in frequency of checking by normals in hypnotically suggested anxiety states, were incorporated in the test scale.

"The sensitivity of the test was demonstrated by giving it to a class of students on examination days, just prior to the exams, as well as on non-examination class sessions. Scores predictably rose prior to examinations and dropped on non–examination class days. The amount of increase on exam days was related to the grades students received on the exams.

"The test provided a standardized self-report method for assessing state anxiety which was widely employed by many investigators. A few years later we developed similar trait and state scales for depression and hostility[3] and these, together with the anxiety scale, were incorporated in a published test: The Multiple Affect Adjective Check-List.

"The frequent citation of this first study is not due solely to the wide utilization of this new method in research. The distinction between traits and states in assessment of emotions and motives was an idea whose time had arrived."

1. **Spielberger C D.** Theory and research on anxiety. (Spielberger C D, ed.) *Anxiety and behavior.* New York: Academic Press, 1966. p. 3-20.
2. **Zuckerman M.** The development of an affect adjectives check list for the measurement of anxiety. *J. Consult. Psychol.* **24**:457-62, 1960.
3. **Zuckerman M & Lubin B.** *Manual for the multiple affect adjective check list.* San Diego, CA: Educational and Industrial Testing Service, 1965. 24 p.

Templer D I. The construction and validation of a Death Anxiety Scale. *J. Gen. Psychol.* **82**:165-77, 1970.
[Department of Psychology, Washington University, St. Louis, MO]

The Death Anxiety Scale was developed and found to have good reliability, internal consistency, and freedom from response sets. Validation was carried out with college students and psychiatric patients. Minnesota Multiphasic Personality Inventory (MMPI) correlations were obtained and discussed. [The *Social Sciences Citation Index*® (*SSCI*®) indicates that this paper has been cited in over 150 publications since 1970, making it the 2nd most-cited paper published in this journal.]

Donald I. Templer
California School of
Professional Psychology
1350 'M' Street
Fresno, CA 93721

December 9, 1983

"This article was the product of my 1967 University of Kentucky doctoral dissertation. In the mid-1960s, death was a taboo topic, not only with the general public but with behavioral scientists and mental health professionals. Fortunately, my dissertation committee, Jesse G. Harris, Jr., chairman, Juris I. Berzins, Albert J. Lott, Frank A. Pattie, and E. Grant Youmans, were farsighted persons who were willing to participate in a pioneering adventure.

"As a psychology undergraduate and a clinical psychology graduate student, I was puzzled as to why psychologists said so little about death and its fear while saying so much about other important aspects of human existence such as aggression and sex. The small amount that had been written often relegated death anxiety to a phenomenon having roots in supposedly more basic entities such as castration anxiety. I can still vividly recall a very incisive comment of committee member Pattie in criticism of such a position. He said, 'Death is the ultimate castration.' The limited research on death anxiety was impeded by lack of an adequate published measuring instrument. So I proceeded to develop the Death Anxiety Scale for my dissertation.

"I am grateful for the cooperation of my early research subjects who were surprised at such a novel topic and yet regarded the research as a serious and legitimate undertaking worthy of their time.

"After I published the article, I expanded my focus to include the death anxiety resemblance of family members, and death anxiety level as a function of age, sex, religion, and personality and psychopathological variables.[1,2] I then developed my 'two-factor theory' for the determination of degree of death anxiety.[3] This conceptualization holds that death anxiety is a function of both psychological health and experiences pertaining to the matter of death. Within a few years, my scale was translated into a number of different languages and scores of students throughout the world were using it for doctoral dissertations. I tend to think that my most important theoretical and empirical death anxiety contributions were made after the scale was developed. However, I realize that I am best known for the scale and this one classic article. It is cited so much because it filled a methodological void at a time when thanatology was in its infancy. I happened to be at the right place at the right time and to have received excellent guidance from my dissertation committee. Other similar scales have been developed, but mine continues to dominate because of its psychometric soundness, and because I believe its content captures the essence of death anxiety as a universal experience."

1. **Templer D I, Ruff C M & Franks C M.** The relationship of age and sex to death anxiety. *Develop. Psychol.* **4**:108, 1971. (Cited 40 times.)
2. **Templer D I.** Death anxiety in religiously very involved persons. *Psychol. Rep.* **31**:361-2, 1972. (Cited 30 times.)
3. ----------------. Two-factor theory of death anxiety. *Essence* **1**:91-3, 1976.

This Week's Citation Classic™

McNair D M, Lorr M & Droppelman L F. *Manual for the profile of mood states.* San Diego, CA: Educational and Industrial Testing Service, 1971. 27 p.
[Depts. Psych., Boston Univ., MA; Catholic Univ. America, Washington, DC; and Univ. Tennessee, Knoxville, TN]

The series of studies described in the manual hypothesized and confirmed the existence of six mood or affective state factors. They also determined their internal consistency and test-retest reliability and their sensitivity for measuring the effects of brief psychotherapeutic and psychopharmacologic interventions. Norms were also obtained for psychiatric outpatients and normal individuals. [The *Science Citation Index*® (*SCI*®) and the *Social Sciences Citation Index*® (*SSCI*®) indicate that this book has been cited in over 380 publications since 1971.]

Douglas M. McNair
Department of Psychology
and
Clinical Psychopharmacology Laboratory
Boston University
Boston, MA 02215

June 12, 1984

"At the Outpatient Psychotherapy Research Laboratory at the Veterans Administration in Washington, DC, Maury Lorr, I, and others on the staff struggled long and hard in the late 1950s and early 1960s with the problems of detecting and measuring changes in symptoms and affective mood states. We were deeply interested in both early and long-term effects of psychotherapies and in the short-term effects of new and exciting pharmacologic treatments, especially in combination.

"Our initial mood measure, the Psychiatric Outpatient Mood Scale (POMS), was developed[1] and continually revised based on factor analytic studies of data from several large treatment outcome projects. After moving to Boston University in 1964, I continued work on the POMS, primarily with Leo Droppleman, and in continued collaboration with Lorr. Recognizing its generalizability to normals, we changed the name to Profile of Mood States, preserving the old acronym. We did additional factor analytic studies that resulted in revisions, identified an additional factor dimension, gathered the normative data for outpatients and normals, and added a number of validity studies. The resulting brief, easy to administer and score POMS is a set of 65 five-point adjective rating scales with a six oblique unipolar factor structure: tension-anxiety, depression-dejection, anger-hostility, fatigue, vigor, and confusion-bewilderment.

"I think it is cited so much because it met a widespread need for a sensitive measure of change and has been applied successfully in a host of treatment studies. Also its more general applicability has been recognized. To mention one example, mood profiles of groups of athletes—such as runners—have been identified and compared.[2]

"In the past few years, Lorr and I have worked on a bipolar factor version of the scale (POMS-BI). We think a problem that plagued us for years has been solved: why do factors on the POMS that seem semantically bipolar, such as vigor and fatigue, emerge from factor analysis as distinct unipolar factors? A research version of the POMS-BI and a preliminary manual are now available."[3]

1. **McNair D M & Lorr M.** An analysis of mood in neurotics. *J. Abnormal Soc. Psychol.* **69**:620-7, 1964. (Cited 220 times.)
2. **Morgan W P.** Test of champions: the iceberg profile. *Psychol. Today* **14**:92-3; 97-9; 102; 108, 1980.
3. **Lorr M & McNair D M.** *Manual for the profile of mood states, bipolar form (POMS-BI).* San Diego, CA: Educational and Industrial Testing Service, 1982. 7 p.

CC/NUMBER 15
APRIL 13, 1981

This Week's Citation Classic

Schaefer E S & Bell R Q. Development of a parental attitude research instrument. *Child Develop.* **29**:339-61, 1958.
[Natl. Inst. Mental Health, NIH, Public Health Serv., US Dept. Health, Education, and Welfare, Rockville, MD]

A review of theory and research that suggested parent attitudes influence child personality development provided a basis for development of 32 parent attitude concepts defined by short attitude scales, and analyses of reliabilities and correlations with maternal education. [The *Social Sciences Citation Index*® *(SSCI*™) **indicates that this paper has been cited over 130 times since 1966.]**

Earl S. Schaefer
Department of Maternal and Child Health
School of Public Health
University of North Carolina
Chapel Hill, NC 27514

March 18, 1981

"Theory and research on parent influence on child personality and psychopathology, especially reports of validity of parent attitude measures, motivated this collaboration with Richard Q. Bell during the early years of the Laboratory of Psychology at the National Institute of Mental Health. Initial acceptance of the Parental Attitude Research Instrument (PARI) might be attributed to the need for research methods for testing theories of parent-child relationships and to the multivariate conceptualization and measurement that improved upon earlier studies. Continuing use of PARI, despite low validity in research on parent influence on personality development, reflects the lack of research funding for development of improved family research methods. Apparently research methods as well as theories only become obsolete when superior methods and theories are developed. However, serendipitous findings that measures of childrearing and educational attitudes, beliefs, values, and behaviors might replace sociodemographic variables in the prediction of child intellectual development[1] have modified my earlier perception of PARI as a citation success but a scientific failure.

"The initial work of concept development and measurement facilitated development of other fruitful methods for research on parent-child relationships.[2] A circumplex model for parent behavior[3] and subsequent comprehensive configurational models[4] have integrated many multivariate analyses of parent behavior and child behavior. Investigators committed to development of improved theories, concepts, methods, and models through a process of conceptual differentiation and integration are needed to increase the fruitfulness of research on parents and children.

"Research on family environments and relationships among mother, father, child, and sibling has contributed to understanding of family influence on cognitive and social development. Yet investments in family research have not been commensurate with contributions of the family to health, education, and welfare of children and parents. More descriptive, longitudinal, and intervention research on family environments is needed to provide a knowledge base for the promising field of family-centered investment in human capital."[5]

1. **Schaefer E S & Edgerton M.** *Parent interview and sociodemographic predictors of adaptation and achievement.* Paper delivered at the American Psychological Association Meeting, September, 1979, New York, NY.
2. **Schaefer E S.** Children's reports of parental behavior: an inventory. *Child Develop.* **36**:413-24, 1965.
3. ------------------. A circumplex model for maternal behavior. *J. Abnormal Soc. Psychol.* **59**:226-35, 1959.
4. ------------------. Development of hierarchical, configurational conceptual models for parent behavior and child behavior. (Hill J, ed.) *Minnesota symposia on child psychology.* Minneapolis, MN: University of Minnesota Press, 1971. Vol. 5. p. 130-61.
5. **Schultz T W.** Investment in human capital. *Amer. Econ. Rev.* **51**:1-17, 1961.

CC/NUMBER 29
JULY 16, 1984

This Week's Citation Classic™

Wilson G D & Patterson J R. A new measure of conservatism.
Brit. J. Soc. Clin. Psychol. 7:264-9, 1968.
[University of Canterbury, New Zealand]

Previous tests of conservatism and authoritarianism are criticized on a number of grounds and the development of a new test which circumvents these deficiencies is described. The Conservatism Scale (C-Scale), which substitutes brief catch-phrases representing controversial issues for the wordy and leading statements of traditional questionnaires, is shown to be reliable, valid, and economical. [The *Science Citation Index*® (*SCI*®) and the *Social Sciences Citation Index*® (*SSCI*®) indicate that this paper has been cited in over 150 publications since 1968.]

Glenn D. Wilson
Department of Psychology
Institute of Psychiatry
London SE5 8AF
England

June 22, 1984

"Every Sunday night during my childhood, my grandparents would assemble at our house for an acrimonious game of cards. Granddad, in particular, was a martinet, and I became familiar with his rigid and predictable set of attitudes ranging across every social and political issue. Concepts like 'union,' 'fluoridation,' 'bearded students,' and 'contraceptive vending machines' were like a red flag to a bull, guaranteed to evoke a tirade. Any attempt at reasoned debate was futile and would only excite him further. From observation of Granddad and others, I became convinced that the emotional component of attitudes was central and that most of the arguments people use to support their cases are not so much rational as rationalizations.

"As an undergraduate at the University of Canterbury, New Zealand, in the early 1960s, I was impressed by the Adorno *et al.*[1] studies of authoritarianism, especially their idea that social attitude constellations served defensive personality functions. However, their questionnaires seemed to consist of clumsy, ambiguous, and leading statements and the bogey of acquiescence bias was beginning to be recognized.

"In 1965, my master's dissertation year, I shared an office with another student, John Patterson. We discussed the problems attitude researchers were having with their tests and hit upon the solution of paring the items down to seminal catch-phrases representing controversial issues that would evoke immediate emotional reactions. Keeping model conservatives (such as Granddad) in mind, as well perfect liberals (ourselves to a large extent), we compiled a pool of potentially suitable items. With a mixture of item analysis and considering criteria such as broad coverage of attitude areas, cross-cultural meaningfulness, and avoidance of ambiguity, we settled on a list of 50 items, half of which were scored in the conservative direction, and half liberal.

"When I proudly showed this test to the head of the department, he could not resist completing it himself. But having done so, with many a jocular comment, he put it aside, saying, 'That's good fun, but shouldn't you be getting on with your thesis?' Thereafter, we gathered our standardization data somewhat furtively with the help of friends, and wrote up the paper as an interim manual, duplicating it and providing our own covers. The writing was truly collaborative in that John and I sat together and agreed upon the wording of every sentence.

"In 1967, I took up my first academic appointment, at the Institute of Psychiatry in London. There I showed the C-Scale to Hans Eysenck, who, in contrast to my previous mentor, encouraged me to submit it for journal publication.

"The paper is widely cited because the scale has caught on with researchers as a quick, convenient, yet reliable and valid, social attitude measure that is relatively free of acquiescence and social desirability effects. In 1975, it was revised and a scoring system for subfactors such as religion/puritanism, militarism/punitiveness, ethnocentrism/intolerance, and anti-hedonism introduced.[2] It has been studied in connection with a wide variety of behaviours ranging from response to humour, art and poetry preferences, and name style to marital compatibility, effects of alcohol, and avoidance of walking under ladders. Translations have been made in many European and Oriental languages, permitting cross-cultural comparison of attitude patterns and their relation to demographic variables. There is a growing body of evidence to support the theory that high C-scores reflect a generalized aversion to uncertainty."[3,4]

1. **Adorno T W, Frenkel-Brunswik E, Levinson D J & Sanford R N.** *The authoritarian personality.* New York: Harper, 1950. 990 p. (Cited 1,770 times.)
2. **Wilson G D.** *Manual for the Wilson-Patterson Attitude Inventory (WPAI).* Windsor, England: National Foundation for Educational Research-Nelson, 1975. 71 p.
3. ---------------. *The psychology of conservatism.* London: Academic Press, 1973. 277 p.
4. ---------------. The catch-phrase approach to attitude and measurement. *Pers. Indiv. Differ.* To be published, 1985.

Sheehan P W. A shortened form of Betts' Questionnaire upon Mental Imagery. *J. Clin. Psychol.* **23**:386-9, 1967.
[Institute of Pennsylvania Hospital and University of Pennsylvania, Philadelphia, PA]

The cause of imagery within the *Zeitgeist* has continued to advance significantly since the 1960s, and measurement of imagery function is an essential part of the research endeavour. This paper reports on the measurement of imagery across different sensory modalities and offers a brief instrument which has good psychometric support. [The *Science Citation Index*® (*SCI*®) and the *Social Sciences Citation Index*® (*SSCI*®) indicate that this paper has been cited in over 165 publications, making it one of the most-cited papers for this journal.]

Peter W. Sheehan
Department of Psychology
University of Queensland
St. Lucia, Queensland 4067
Australia

July 20, 1984

"The research for this paper was part of work completed for my doctoral dissertation. It was supported by the National Institute of Mental Health (US) for study in Australia of the relationship between imagery, fantasy, and hypnosis. The project was a team effort, and this member of the team (under the direction of J.P. Sutcliffe) became very much interested in the function and nature of imagery. It was only later that I turned to research, just as energetically, on hypnosis. There were no real obstacles to the research, and cooperative effort obviously facilitated the work.

"The research can be placed relatively firmly within the *Zeitgeist* of the time. The cause of imagery was advancing. Francis Galton[1] began the emphasis in psychology on quantitative assessment of imagery and produced the first generally acknowledged method of measuring voluntary imagery ability. Galton's questionnaire was adapted by Betts,[2] but Betts' Questionnaire upon Mental Imagery was too long and so not particularly useful. The work reported in the above article aimed to provide a useful test that was brief, maintained measurement across sensory modalities (i.e., wasn't exclusively visual), and had good psychometric support.

"From a content analysis of citations that I have conducted, the major reason to emerge for the work being cited across time is clearly the perceived usefulness of the instrument for assessing individual differences in imagery ability. The most common fields of inquiry in which the work is cited for the purpose of measurement are imagery, hypnosis, experimental psychopathology, and clinical psychology (therapy). Not surprisingly, the earliest field where the work was cited was imagery. This extended into the fields of hypnosis and clinical abnormality in the early 1970s. The test began to be used heavily in the fields of special education and child psychology in the late 1970s, and interest broadened as far afield as art psychotherapy and parapsychology in the late 1970s. Currently, the scale is being used heavily in psychophysiological studies of conditioning and work investigating the effectiveness of cognitive therapy.

"With time, however, reasons for citation other than measurement emerged. The scale, for instance, has been studied extensively in its own right (e.g., what response sets affect performance on it?) and authors cite it because they are attempting to substantiate or refute original claims made about what the scale measures. The work is also cited frequently as relevant background material for the development of new scales and is used to train both subjects and practitioners in the employment of imagery skills. An update on the literature associated with measurement appears in a chapter by Ashton, White, and me.[3]

"While as a researcher I would not have chosen the work reported here as the most satisfying I have conducted, it is clearly the piece of research that has generated the most personal correspondence over the years. From postgraduate students to clinicians to established researchers, queries about the test have been steady over the 17 years since its construction. Psychology apparently needed a brief and easily administered test to tap individual differences in imagery ability, and perhaps it still does."

1. **Galton F.** *Inquiries into human faculty and its development.* London: Macmillan, 1883. 387 p.
2. **Betts G H.** *The distribution and functions of mental imagery.* New York: Teacher's College, Columbia University, 1909. 99 p.
3. **Sheehan P W, Ashton R S & White K D.** The assessment of mental imagery. (Sheikh A A, ed.) *Imagery: current theory, research and application.* New York: Wiley, 1983. p. 189-221.

CC/NUMBER 17
APRIL 28, 1980

This Week's Citation Classic

Harris D B. *Children's drawings as measures of intellectual maturity: a revision and extension of the Goodenough draw-a-man test.*
New York: Harcourt, Brace & World, 1963. 367 p.
[Pennsylvania State Univ., University Park, PA]

Reviews the extensive literature on children's drawings from the inception of research to date of publication, offers scales for assessing intellectual maturity of children aged three to 16 years, based on their human figure drawings, presents the standardization and norms for these scales, and discusses the psychology of children's drawings. [The *Science Citation Index®* **(***SCI®***) and the** *Social Sciences Citation Index®* **(***SSCI™***) indicate that this book has been cited over 330 times since 1963.]**

Dale B. Harris
Department of Psychology
College of Liberal Arts
Pennsylvania State University
University Park, PA 16802

January 31, 1980

"The Goodenough-Harris drawing test, a revision and extension of Florence Goodenough's Draw-a-Man test, was begun while I was at the University of Minnesota's Institute of Child Development and completed after I moved to Pennsylvania State University. The work was supported by small sums from the graduate schools of both universities. I did all the developmental work personally and used clerks only to assist in statistical work. In projects such as this, which represent the cut-and-try approach of the older measurement tradition, it is important that the researcher be completely immersed in the raw data, as many unexpected leads develop in the selection and tryout of items. Such a procedure is tedious, as all items and trial scales must be cross-validated on independently drawn samples of new material.

"Although the new scales were developed by more rigorous and psychometrically defensible procedures than Goodenough's original criteria, and indeed give finer gradations than that scale, I discovered renewed admiration for her original idea and the effectiveness of her quite simple analyses when tapping a powerful psychologic variable. The continued popularity of the test probably rests on its simplicity and inherent appeal to young children, its painstaking standardization, and its demonstrated utility.

"I came away from the project with several additional impressions: The effectiveness of stratification of samples by parental occupational status in controlling the distribution of intellectual ability in samples of children. The strong empirical evidence for common developmental features; yet, the infinite variety of ways in which children can express their ideas in drawings. The high correlation of this brief exercise with individual tests taking an hour or more (a finding repeatedly confirmed in subsequent research); yet, the hazard of using a single drawing in any serious assessment of ability. The dubious character of projective analyses based on single drawings of the human figure (see various critical reviews under my authorship in *Mental Measurements Yearbook*[1,2]); yet, the unquestionable fact that children do portray idiosyncratic personal features in their drawings. Here is a field rich in serendipity for the researcher open to discovery!

"Current research on children's drawings favors fine-grained analysis of the drawing act conducted under rigorous experimental controls, and usually ignores the interpretations and intentions of the child subjects as irrelevant. Yet anyone who has observed children draw and talked with them during or afterwards, must be convinced of the importance of *intention*. Child drawing *is* a form of communication, and invariably reflects a 'meaning!' The feature of my work which I most regret is that the data were necessarily gathered in groups, which precluded discussion of each child's work with its author. Intensive and fruitful research on children's drawings, I am convinced, in addition to simple tasks, should include more complex themes than the human figure (complex as that is!) and must include discussion of the products with their authors."

1. **Buros O K, ed.** *The seventh mental measurements yearbook.* Highland Park, NJ: Gryphon Press, 1972. 2 vols.
2. **Buros O K, ed.** *The eighth mental measurements yearbook.* Highland Park, NJ: Gryphon Press, 1978. 2 vols.

This Week's Citation Classic

Bem S L. The measurement of psychological androgyny.
J. Consult. Clin. Psychol. **42**:155-62, 1974.
[Department of Psychology, Stanford University, Stanford, CA]

A new masculinity-femininity scale is introduced that treats masculinity and femininity as two independent dimensions, thereby making it possible to characterize individuals not only as masculine or feminine, but also as 'androgynous'—that is, as having *both* masculine and feminine attributes. [The *Social Sciences Citation Index*® (*SSCI*®) indicates that this paper has been cited over 525 times since 1974.]

Sandra Lipsitz Bem
Department of Psychology
Cornell University
Ithaca, NY 14853

July 27, 1981

"I decided in the early 1970s to try to combine my personal, political, and scholarly interests by doing psychological research in the service of my feminist convictions. By that time, the women's liberation movement had made a whole generation of young Americans aware of the many ways that we, both men and women, had become locked into our respective sex roles. As women, we had become aware that we were afraid to express our anger, to assert our preferences, to trust our own judgment, to take control of situations. As men, we had become aware that we were afraid to cry, to touch one another, to own up to our fears and weaknesses.

"But there were very little data within psychology to give legitimacy to these experiential truths. Accordingly, I took for myself the feminist goal of trying to gather the relevant data, of trying to demonstrate empirically that traditional sex roles do restrict behavior in important human ways. More specifically, I began to do empirical research on the concept of psychological androgyny (from the Greek *andro*, male, and *gyne*, female), a concept that had not yet been conceptualized within the psychological literature.

"My research—which was done while I was on the faculty at Stanford University—was predicated on two basic assumptions: (a) that masculinity and femininity represent *complementary* domains of positive attributes and behaviors, and that it is therefore possible, in principle, for an individual to be both masculine and feminine, both instrumental and expressive, both agentic and communal; and (b) that for fully effective and healthy human functioning, masculinity and femininity must each be tempered by the other, and the two must be integrated into a more balanced, a more fully human, a truly androgynous personality.

"Before my empirical research on androgyny could be initiated, however, it was first necessary to develop a new type of masculinity-femininity scale, one that would not treat masculinity and femininity as opposite ends of a single dimension as most previous scales had done. The article that is honored here as a *Citation Classic* constituted the publication of that new scale, known as the Bem Sex Role Inventory (BSRI). In my view, this article has been cited as frequently as it has because so many other psychologists were also motivated by the women's liberation movement to take a feminist perspective in their research. For these psychologists, this first article in a series of articles on sex typing and androgyny[1] provided not only a provocative new concept, but a new methodology as well. (And there is nothing quite so effective as a new methodology for stimulating empirical research.)

"For my research on psychological androgyny—which included the development of the BSRI—I was awarded the 1976 Distinguished Scientific Award for an Early Career Contribution to Psychology from the American Psychological Association, the 1977 Distinguished Publication Award from the Association for Women in Psychology, and the 1980 Young Scholar Award from the American Association of University Women."

1. **Bem S L.** Gender schema theory: a cognitive account of sex typing. *Psychol. Rev.* **88**:354-64, 1981.

This Week's Citation Classic

Crowne D P & Marlowe D. A new scale of social desirability independent of psychopathology. *J. Consult. Psychol.* **24**:349-54, 1960.
[Ohio State University, Columbus, OH and College of Medicine, University of Kentucky, Lexington, KY]

A social desirability scale based on items reflecting a good-bad dimension and likely to be untrue of most people was developed. The content of this scale is relatively independent of psychopathology, and it appears to measure approval dependence and defensiveness. [The *Science Citation Index*® **(***SCI*®**) and the** *Social Sciences Citation Index*® **(***SSCI*®**) indicate that this paper has been cited in over 660 publications since 1961.]**

Douglas P. Crowne
Department of Psychology
University of Waterloo
Waterloo, Ontario N2L 3G1
Canada

February 24, 1983

"For many years, psychologists have recognized that personality tests are vulnerable to socially desirable responding. This vulnerability has been a problem of major proportion, limiting the predictive validity of personality tests and raising serious questions about discriminant validity when personality constructs have been defined by tests. A corrective approach has been to consider socially desirable responding as a source of error in tests and to take steps to eliminate it. The social desirability question may also be viewed from another perspective: as motivated and purposeful behavior, residing in the respondent's goals and beliefs about being evaluated.

"A number of years ago, our curiosity kindled by these contrasting views, David Marlowe and I set out to explore the tendency to give socially desirable personality test responses. As a descriptive account of test response distortion, the concept of social desirability had an intuitive plausibility about it, and it fitted rather neatly into an explanation that we thought bore some promise. That explanation was simply this: people describe themselves in favorable, socially desirable terms to achieve the approval of others. In a series of studies beginning in the summer of 1959, we developed a social desirability questionnaire and attempted first to test the implications of the concept of need for approval in personality testing. To do so, we had to establish that the need for approval was a valid inference from socially desirable test responses; we had to demonstrate that a presumed measure of an approval motive would predict approval-seeking behavior in situations other than testing. In the process, we moved a long way from the domain of personality tests to seek the predictive utility of the approval motive in experimental situations in the laboratory and in life situations outside.

"We began by defining a class of personality test items with two principal attributes: (1) a 'good-bad' (social desirability) dimension, and (2) quite likely to be true of most people or untrue of most people. Personal endorsement of 'good' items means claiming some very improbable things about oneself, and rejection of 'bad' items entails denial of common human frailties. We constructed our social desirability scale of such items and obtained the expected result. Respondents who characterized themselves in a socially desirable way on our test tended to produce scores in the 'normal,' 'adjusted' direction on other personality tests. We considered that what we had was an indirect measure of need for approval.

"In an extensive series of subsequent experiments,[1] we found that the tendency to avoid self-criticism in favor of stereotypically acceptable self-evaluation is associated with behavior far transcending the test situation. In our experimental analysis of social desirability, we found that persons who respond to personality tests in a socially desirable manner are more conforming, cautious, and persuasible, and their behavior is more normatively anchored, than persons who depict themselves with greater frankness. Approval-dependent persons also have a problem with aggression, tending to repress hostility, and they also engage in self-protective measures to avert anticipated threats to self-esteem.

"Our initial research burgeoned into a continuing program of studies by ourselves and others. I believe the success of the scale we developed and the concept it represents resulted from the fact that this approach to social desirability brought the whole problem of dissimulation on personality tests into the domain of personality itself and made self-characterization an interesting variable in its own right. Social desirability would no longer be simply a noisome technical obstacle in personality assessment. Thus, the real achievement of the research was to see that the problem lay in understanding self-evaluative behavior and not in the fallibility of tests. For a report of recent work in the field see *The Experimental Study of Personality*."[2]

1. **Crowne D P & Marlowe D.** *The approval motive: studies in evaluative dependence.* New York: Wiley, 1964. 233 p.
2. **Crowne D P.** *The experimental study of personality.* Hillsdale, NJ: Lawrence Erlbaum Associates, 1979. 254 p.

This Week's Citation Classic

Holtzman W H, Thorpe J S, Swartz J D & Herron E W. *Inkblot perception and personality: Holtzman Inkblot Technique.* Austin, TX: University of Texas Press, 1961. 417 p.

The Holtzman Inkblot Technique was developed and standardized on both normal and abnormal populations. This book describes the test construction and provides detailed information on reliability and validity for a wide variety of clinical and research applications. [The *Social Sciences Citation Index®* **(***SSCI*™**) indicates that this book has been cited over 200 times since 1966.]**

Wayne H. Holtzman
The Hogg Foundation
for Mental Health
University of Texas
Austin, TX 78712

March 9, 1981

"As a young graduate student in psychology 33 years ago, I was fascinated by Hermann Rorschach's method of assessing personality and psychopathology by analysis of a person's response to inkblots. Although firmly established as a leading clinical instrument for psychodiagnosis, the Rorschach technique was badly in need of scientific evaluation. By 1954 I was convinced that a totally new approach employing modern methods of test construction, standardization, and validation was the only way to overcome the serious weaknesses inherent in the Rorschach.

"After experimenting with thousands of inkblots, the stimulus materials comprising the Holtzman Inkblot Technique were finally completed and reproduced. Each of the two parallel forms is comprised of 45 inkblots with two identical practice blots for the initial warm-up period. The subject gives only one response to each blot, indicating what he sees, where he sees it, and what about the blot suggests that percept to him. A standardized scoring system of 22 variables dealing with the form, color, shading, content, and a variety of other dimensions was developed with a high degree of interscorer reliability.

"Initial standardization data were obtained from carefully defined samples of subjects in mental hospitals, schools for retarded children, colleges, elementary and secondary schools, and by door-to-door sampling of normal adults. Collecting, scoring, coding, and analyzing nearly 100,000 inkblot responses for almost 2,000 individual protocols proved to be a formidable task indeed. It would have been a hopeless task had it not been for the highly competent psychologists working with me on the research team, in particular, Joseph Thorpe, Jon Swartz, and Wayne Herron.

"The advent of highspeed computers made it possible to compute extensive statistics bearing upon reliability, validity, and normative tables for interpretation. Special computer programs were devised for diagnostic purposes; group methods of administration were developed to provide more cost-effective methods of personality assessment for many populations; and arrangements were made for final publication and distribution of the test materials by the Psychological Corporation.

"No other projective technique has been so rigorously developed and standardized, and this accounts for its frequent citation. The original book has been translated into several foreign languages[1,2] and has gone through three subsequent printings. Additional books have been published more recently on the Holtzman Inkblot Technique and its applications.[3,4] An annotated bibliography containing nearly 500 references is available upon request."[5]

1. **Holtzman W H, Thorpe J S, Swartz J D & Herron E W.** *Interpretación de manchas de tinta.* Mexico City: Editorial Trillas, 1971. 445 p.
2. **Hartmann H A, von Rosenstiel L & Neumann P.** *Lehrbuch der Holtzman-Inkblot Technik (HIT).* Bern, Switzerland: Verlag Hans Huber, 1977. 4 vols.
3. **Holtzman W H, Diaz-Guerrero R & Swartz J D.** *Personality development in two cultures.* Austin, TX: University of Texas Press, 1975. 427 p.
4. **Hill E.** *The Holtzman Inkblot Technique.* San Francisco: Jossey-Bass, 1972. 313 p.
5. **Swartz J D, Witzke D M, Holtzman W H & Bishop C.** *Holtzman Inkblot Technique: annotated bibliography.* Austin, TX: Hogg Foundation for Mental Health, 1978. 213 p.

Overall J E & Gorham D R. The brief psychiatric rating scale. *Psychol. Rep.* **10**:799-812, 1962.

The Brief Psychiatric Rating Scale (BPRS) is an instrument originally developed to characterize psychopathology and to measure change in clinical psychopharmacology research. It permits the recording of severity of 18 (originally 16) distinct signs and symptoms of psychopathology based on clinical interview of a patient. [The *Science Citation Index®* *(SCI®)* **and the** *Social Sciences Citation Index™* *(SSCI™)* **indicate that this paper was cited a total of 533 times in the period 1963-1977.]**

John E. Overall
Department of Psychiatry
& Behavioral Science
University of Texas Medical Branch
Galveston, TX 77550

January 10, 1978

"In 1959, I joined the staff of the Veterans Administration Central Neuropsychiatric Research Laboratory as a new Ph.D., having recently completed a one-year NSF postdoctoral fellowship in the L. L. Thurstone Psychometric Laboratory at the University of North Carolina. I had the good fortune to be assigned an office adjoining that of the senior clinical psychologist, Donald R. Gorham, who became my friend and champion in getting a research career underway. Everyone at the VA Central NP Lab was given the title of 'Chief' of something or other. I was Chief of Criterion Development, which implied that my job was to create and evaluate instruments for use in the VA multi-hospital cooperative studies in psychiatry. The big issue at that time was whether drugs really were of value in treatment of psychiatric disorders.

"It is fitting, after all these years, to be able to say that Don Gorham was really the father of the Brief Psychiatric Rating Scale (BPRS). He had the clinical experience and the practical awareness to recognize the need, and need created the BPRS. I was eager to apply my newly learned psychometric knowledge and to fulfill my role as Chief of Criterion Development, and we had extraordinary clinical data from previous VA cooperative studies with which to work.

"The BPRS has been a success primarily because it filled a need at a particular period in the development of psychiatry as a rational science. The need was for an instrument that could be used on a broad scale to evaluate treatment effects while at the same time imposing minimum additional burden on over-worked psychiatric staff. It has often been suggested that the success of the BPRS has been due to judicious use of the word 'brief' in the title. In about 1968, a major boost was given the BPRS when it was designated as one standard bit of data to be collected in most NIMH grant-supported clinical drug studies for several succeeding years. If any credit at all is due the present writer, it is for permitting the course of my career to be largely determined by a simple contribution that was so lightly considered at the time."

CC/NUMBER 23
JUNE 8, 1981

This Week's Citation Classic

Wing J K, Birley J L T, Cooper J E, Graham P & Isaacs A D. Reliability of a procedure for measuring and classifying "present psychiatric state." *Brit. J. Psychiat.* **113**:499-515, 1967.
[MRC Social Psychiatry Res. Unit, and Bilateral Diagnostic Study, Inst. Psychiat., Maudsley Hosp., London; and Cane Hill Hosp., Coulsdon, Surrey, England]

The Present State Examination and associated techniques provide a means of describing and classifying psychiatric disorders so that the results of research into causes, epidemiology, treatment, and prognosis, carried out in different parts of the world, can be more precisely compared. [The *Science Citation Index*® (*SCI*®) **and the** *Social Sciences Citation Index*® (*SSCI*®) **indicate that this paper has been cited over 185 times since 1967.]**

J.K. Wing
Institute of Psychiatry
Social Psychiatry Unit
Medical Research Council
De Crespigny Park
Denmark Hill
London SE5 8AF
England

May 6, 1981

"The fact that psychiatrists tend to use a common terminology (systematised in the International Classification of Diseases) promises a substantial degree of agreement about categories such as paranoia, schizophrenia, affective psychosis, anxiety state, and obsessional neurosis. But every schoolboy knows that no two psychiatrists can agree. At least, that was the case in the late 1950s and there were two good reasons for the opinion. First, several studies had shown appallingly poor reliability. Second, the conceptual, not to say ideological, approaches adopted by different groups of psychiatrists ensured that terms like 'schizophrenia' had many different connotations. Nevertheless, several quite reliable scales for rating behaviour had been constructed and this suggested that progress could be made even, perhaps, in rating the presence or absence of subjectively experienced 'symptoms.'

"My own education and predilections had led me to be suspicious of the inordinate and largely unsupported claims of psychoanalysis, on the one hand, and of the organic schools, on the other. The only way to test these and other theories seemed to be to devise a means of describing the 'phenomena' precisely and reliably and then to construct rules by which they could be classified.

"The first requirement was met by constructing a Present State Examination (PSE) which covered most of the symptoms likely to be experienced by people with functional psychotic and neurotic disorders in a flexible, but standardised, clinical interview. The 1967 paper reported the results of several years of testing the third, fourth, and fifth editions of the schedule. Since then, much experience has been gained in large international studies[1] and in smaller research projects. The PSE is now in its ninth revision and has been translated into 30 languages. It has been used extensively for purposes of clinical description and measurement of change.

"The second requirement was met by constructing an algorithm (the CATEGO program) which classified PSE symptoms and thus provided a reference classification on the basis of which research studies could be compared, no matter where in the world they were conducted. Other elements have been added—a Syndrome Check List for rating past episodes and an Etiology Schedule for adding information about possible causes.[2]

"With all its imperfections, the system has clearly met a need. The latest innovation has been to devise a means (the Index of Definition) of defining a threshold above which sufficient symptoms are present to allow a descriptive classification to be made. This allows a crude comparison between the results of population surveys in different parts of the world and a comparison, for example, of the severity and concomitants of depression in a community and in a hospital sample.[3]

"Other workers have developed similar techniques and, in due course, the advantages of each will need to be combined insofar as this does not also combine their limitations. The ideas behind the PSE/ID/-CATEGO system, however, have so far stood the test of time."[4]

1. **World Health Organization.** *Schizophrenia: an international follow-up study.* New York: Wiley, 1979. 438 p.
2. **Wing J K, Cooper J E & Sartorius N.** *Measurement and classification of psychiatric symptoms: an instruction manual for the PSE and CATEGO program.* New York: Cambridge University Press, 1974. 233 p.
3. **Wing J K, Bebbington P, Hurry J & Tennant C.** The prevalence in the general population of disorders familiar to psychiatrists in hospital practice. (Wing J K, Bebbington P & Robins L N, eds.) *What is a case? The problem of definition in psychiatric community surveys.* London: Grant McIntyre, 1981.
4. **Wing J K.** *Reasoning about madness.* New York: Oxford University Press, 1978. 265 p.

This Week's Citation Classic

Katz M M & Lyerly S B. Methods for measuring adjustment and social behavior in the community: I. Rationale, description, discriminative validity and scale development. *Psychol. Rep.* **13**:503-35, 1963.
[Psychopharmacology Service Ctr., Natl. Inst. Mental Health, Rockville, MD and Human Ecology Fund]

The development of measures for assessing adjustment and characterizing patterns of disturbed behavior is described. The major characteristics are the translation of psychopathology into everyday language, and the use of the relative to measure social behavior. The scales are applied to the long-term evaluation of psychiatric treatments. [The *Science Citation Index*® *(SCI*®) **and the** *Social Sciences Citation Index*® *(SSCI*®) **indicate that this paper has been cited over 200 times since 1963.]**

Martin M. Katz
Department of Psychiatry
and Behavioral Sciences
George Washington University
Medical Center
Washington, DC 20037

July 16, 1981

"In the late 1950s, psychotropic drugs for the treatment of schizophrenia were already in extensive use in the Western world, despite the fact that hard evidence on effectiveness was very sparse. Hospital trials of their efficacy with its chronic forms left little doubt that the drugs were having a favorable impact on this disorder.

"Questions remained, however, as to specificity and effectiveness with the acute forms of schizophrenia. The National Institute of Mental Health was commissioned by Congress to initiate trials to evaluate their effectiveness. As a young psychologist with limited experience in research on treatment and on the effects of chemicals on behavior, I was a recruit to this small interdisciplinary group. The study of drug efficacy was to be national in scope; involve nine hospitals, private and public; and eventually become a landmark effort in psychiatric research. There were a number of technical problems, however, to be solved before such an effort could be launched. One major gap was a technique which measured the durability of effects on certain critical symptoms, and the nature of the impact on the patient's capacity to function in the community. Our director asked me to develop a method to assess the patient's social and personal adjustment in the community following discharge. Strangely enough, no method suitable for standardization across the range of mental disorders actually existed at that time.

"Although partial to the challenge of developing psychological methods, this was not an area that interested me greatly. On the other hand, I was interested in developing procedures for cross-cultural research, which would make it possible to determine whether symptoms which represent psychopathological behaviors in one culture appear in the same form (or are part of the same basic disorder) in another very different culture. This interest would appear to be very different in quality than that required to assess the social adjustment of formerly hospitalized mental patients. One major requirement of each of these tasks was, however, the same. The behavioral descriptions must, in both cases, be done by a 'lay' person, an observer who would not be influenced by or have biases based on formal theories of psychopathology. The cross-cultural method required translating complex 'symptoms' into everyday language and reporting behaviors in the most concrete of terms. The social adjustment method required using a reporter who could closely observe the patient's behavior over weeks, in the community itself. Thus, (1) a close relative or friend from within that community, or cultural context, would have to be the source of the information; and (2) the inventory of behaviors would have to be free of jargon—precise and concrete in its content.

"As one might expect, with the increase in the type and number of drugs and psychotherapies over the past 20 years, a method which utilizes lay people to assess adjustment has great practical value.[1] Thus, this application of the method has become very popular. Recently, however, the reasons responsible for my early enthusiasm for the task have taken hold. Its format gave it a special advantage in the study of ethnocultural variations in deviant and normal behavior in Hawaii, which has led to some important insights.[2] Currently, the scales are in a World Health Organization cross-national study of the psychosocial determinants, including the role of family perception, in the development of severe mental disorders."

1. **Waskow I E & Parloff M B.** *Psychotherapy change measures.* Washington, DC: US Government Printing Office, 1973. 327 p. DHEW publ. no. (ADM) 74-120.
2. **Katz M M, Sanborn K O, Lowery H A & Ching J.** Ethnic studies in Hawaii: on psychopathology and social deviance. (Wynne L C, Cromwell R L & Mathysse S, eds.) *The nature of schizophrenia: new approaches to research and treatment.* New York: Wiley, 1978. p. 572-85.

This Week's Citation Classic

Kiresuk T J & Sherman R E. Goal attainment scaling: a general method for evaluating comprehensive community mental health programs. *Community Ment. Health J.* **4**:443-53, 1968. [Hennepin County Mental Health Ctr., Hennepin County General Hosp., Minneapolis, MN]

A psychometric method featuring individualized scaled expected treatment outcomes was proposed as a method to evaluate mental health treatment and programs. A formula combined the actual outcomes in a standardized outcome score that reflected relative importance and intercorrelation of the scales. [The *Science Citation Index*® (*SCI*®) and the *Social Sciences Citation Index*® (*SSCI*®) indicate that this paper has been cited in over 220 publications since 1968.]

Thomas J. Kiresuk
Minneapolis Medical Research Foundation
Hennepin County Medical Center
Minneapolis, MN 55415

May 9, 1983

"This article was written by a clinical psychologist (Kiresuk) and a biometry graduate student (Sherman) at the Hennepin County Medical Center with the guidance of the head of biometry, Byron W. Brown, Jr., at the University of Minnesota. The collaborative result addressed the realities of treatment and program administration within the framework of biometric research standards.

"Three factors probably account for the frequency of citation.

"The idea of goal setting has a self-evident quality and is widely utilized. Traceable to mid-nineteenth-century German formulations of 'intentionality,' there are derivatives in many clinical,[1] academic, and industrial fields.[2] Goal attainment scaling (GAS) was accepted by several groups: in medicine, perhaps because of congruence with the concept of prognosis (Hippocrates); by service providers, as a means of facilitating treatment and making evaluation closer to the actual agenda of treatment; by advocates of individualization, resisting prefabricated criteria for outcome; Bayesian sympathizers with their emphasis on prior beliefs, conditional probabilities, and their commitment to specific research and treatment outcomes; and by policy and administration figures because of congruence with concurrent methods of administrative guidance and accountability.

"At the time of publication, there was enormous pressure to evaluate services. Federal and local legislation, public sentiment, shrinking resources, and a wave of reformist sentiment favoring advocacy of consumer and special population groups all combined to ensure a demand for practically any form of evaluation technology.

"The philosophy of the National Institute of Mental Health Services Delivery Branch, led by Howard Davis, emphasized knowledge transfer and utilization of information to promote potentially useful innovations in service delivery. A four-year grant to develop and disseminate GAS was one of several projects funded in the pursuit of this philosophy.

"These factors led to widespread knowledge of GAS and many implementations.[3] A later book attempted to bring order to the variety of interpretations, 200 bibliographic references, common disputes, implementation and maintenance methods, validity, reliability, and psychometric status.[4]

"Originally, Sherman and I were naive with regard to the overall field of evaluation, especially developments in sociology, educational psychology, public policy, and administration. Complete novices in knowledge transfer and utilization, we were led by the hand by Susan Salasin, project manager, a specialist in the field.

"Unanticipated problems included defense against criticism that could be leveled at all psychological measures; implementations often led into larger issues of organizational change;[5] studies of durability and costs of adoption focused on GAS but not on other measures; and the popularity of GAS led to problems in definition and quality control.

"The influence of this article led, in part, to the 1979 Evaluation Research Society Myrdal Prize for Human Service Delivery. The method helped make treatment accessible to measurement by converting a common form of thinking into a reliable and valid measure of change. Potential facilitation of treatment outcome and organizational performance were unanticipated benefits that could lead to further research and citations."[2,6]

1. **Mintz J & Kiesler D.** Individualized measures of psychotherapy outcome. (Kendall P & Butcher J N, eds.) *Handbook of research methods in clinical psychology*. New York: Wiley, 1981. p. 491-534.
2. **Locke E A, Shaw K N, Saari L M & Latham G P.** Goal setting and task performance: 1969-1980. *Psychol. Bull.* **90**:125-52, 1981.
3. **Kiresuk T J, Lund S H & Larsen N E.** Measurement of goal attainment in clinical and health care programs. *Drug Intel. Clin. Pharm.* **16**:145-53, 1982.
4. **Smith A.** Goal attainment scaling: assessment of the outcome of mental health treatment. (McReynolds P, ed.) *Advances in psychological assessment*. San Francisco: Jossey-Bass, 1981. Vol. 5. p. 424-59.
5. **Kiresuk T J & Lund S H.** Goal attainment scaling: a medical-correctional application. *J. Med. Law* **1**:227-51, 1982.
6. ------------------------------. Goal attainment scaling. (Atkisson C C, Hargreaves M J & Sorenson J E, eds.) *Evaluation of human service programs*. New York: Academic Press, 1978. p. 341-70.

This Week's Citation Classic

Holmes T H & Rahe R H. The Social Readjustment Rating Scale.
J. Psychosom. Res. **11**:213-18, 1967.
[Department of Psychiatry, University of Washington School of Medicine, Seattle, WA]

The Social Readjustment Rating Scale was composed of 43 life events derived from clinical studies. The technique of subjective magnitude estimation was applied to generate the amount of change in adjustment required by each item. [The *Science Citation Index*® (*SCI*®) **and the** *Social Sciences Citation Index*® (*SSCI*®) **indicate that this paper has been cited in over 1,015 publications since 1967.]**

Thomas H. Holmes
Department of Psychiatry and
Behavioral Sciences
University of Washington
Seattle, WA 98195

June 10, 1982

"In 1963 at the University of Washington, Eugene Galanter, who was chairman of the department of psychology and a former student of the late S.S. Stevens, delivered a seminar on psychologic scaling to the faculty of the department of psychiatry. He spent considerable time talking about the technique of subjective magnitude estimation. At this point we already had the Schedule of Recent Experience (SRE), comprised of a series of life change events which correlated with the time of onset of illness.[1,2] The idea immediately took form to apply the objective magnitude estimation technique to these items. Richard H. Rahe, a psychiatric resident in my laboratory, collaborated with me. We constructed a questionnaire for assigning a magnitude of change to each of 43 items which had been revised from the original listing. These items included death of spouse, divorce, trouble with the boss, change in sleeping habits, retirement, and vacation. Marriage as a social event was used as the module to which each of the other 42 life events was compared. The means of each item, derived from the responses of 394 subjects, were arranged in rank order and constituted the Social Readjustment Rating Scale.

"In November 1966 this article was rejected by the editor of *Psychosomatic Medicine.* It was then submitted to the *Journal of Psychosomatic Research*, was promptly accepted by the editor, Denis Leigh, and appeared in that journal in 1967.

"The designation of 'life change events' as a Medical Subject Headings term used by MEDLARS signaled its coming of age as a research field. For a decade, life change events research had been indexed under the more general heading of 'stress, psychological.' But in 1977 the National Library of Medicine recognized the need for a separate index term to accommodate the growing number of publications and to facilitate information retrieval in the future. That expectation of continued research and interest in the field is well founded, judging from our own experience. The fact that inquiries come from researchers in non-medical as well as medical disciplines is additional testimony to the growth and expansion of the field.

"As with the publication of Darwin's *The Origin of Species*, the publication of the Social Readjustment Rating Scale came at just the right time. The critical notions contained in *The Origin of Species* had existed for at least a generation. Darwin brought it all together in his brilliant treatise. The critical themes in the Social Readjustment Rating Scale have been much in evidence for the past 50 years. The scale achieved a major breakthrough and brought together in one dynamic formulation the essence of a fragmented area of science. Certainly the Social Readjustment Rating Scale is an *idea* whose time has come."[3]

1. **Hawkins N G, Davies R & Holmes T H.** Evidence of psychosocial factors in the development of pulmonary tuberculosis. *Amer. Rev. Tuberc. Pulmonary Dis.* **75**:768-80, 1957.
2. **Rahe R H, Meyer M, Smith M, Kjaer G & Holmes T H.** Social stress and illness onset. *J. Psychosom. Res.* **8**:35-44, 1964.
3. **Petrich J, Hart C A & Holmes T H.** Recent life events and illness onset. (Day S B, ed.) *Life stress.* New York: Van Nostrand Reinhold, 1982. p. 109-20.

Chapter

2

Statistics, Design, and General Methodology

Association and regression analysis / 33–41

Types of techniques / 42–50

Design issues / 51–57

General and philosophical issues / 58–60

CC/NUMBER 24
JUNE 11, 1979

Kaiser H F. The varimax criterion for analytic rotation in factor analysis. *Psychometrika* **23**:187-200, 1958. [University of Illinois, Urbana, IL]

The varimax criterion for analytic rotation in factor analysis determines a factor matrix, representing uncorrelated factors, where the variance of the squared loading of a column of the factor matrix is maximized, summed over columns. In a special case the solution is invariant under the addition or subtraction of variables. [The *Science Citation Index®* *(SCI®)* **and the** *Social Sciences Citation Index™ (SSCI™)* **indicate that this paper has been cited over 725 times since 1961.]**

Henry F. Kaiser
School of Education
University of California
Berkeley, CA 94720

January 12, 1978

"The varimax criterion was developed in early 1955, when I was a graduate student in education at the University of California, Berkeley. At that time I was supposed to be studying for that awful anachronism, the Ph.D. qualifying examination in German.

"I had earlier developed the quartimax criterion, but was 'scooped' in publication by Carroll;[1] Wrigley and Neuhaus;[2] Saunders;[3] and Ferguson.[4] What was wrong with the quartimax criterion as a mathematical explication of Thurstone's simple structure was soon apparent: it applied the criterion to the rows of the factor matrix when what should have been done was to apply the criterion to the columns of the factor matrix. This produced varimax. It was originally developed from Carroll's point of view, and thus would have been dubbed 'covarimin,' but it was not obvious that the method would converge computationally in this form. More personally, I was miffed at Carroll, who did not answer my letter about what I had done, while Professor Wrigley, whose lead I ultimately followed, was most generous in correspondence.

"Not being good at mathematics, I was aided in the development by a simple computational paradigm I had devised for Jacobi's method for the algebraic eigenproblem, with which I needed only simple 13th grade calculus.

"Saunders suggested that the criterion should be applied to a factor matrix in which the rows had been normalized. This was crucial, for it gave better results subjectively, and, more importantly, allowed me to prove a theorem regarding the invariance of the varimax solution under the addition or subtraction of variables in a simple case. This invariance theorem is overlooked by those who use varimax. Its widespread use comes primarily from its almost always giving 'nice' results from the viewpoint of scientific interpretability.

"In succeeding years I have tried to improve varimax, without success. Most of these efforts have been 'trans-varimax,' to use Saunders' terminology. Varimax is robust under overfactoring while trans-varimax solutions are not, and the number of factors in a factor analysis seems to defy a definitive solution.

"Varimax has been a tough act to follow. It was my first paper, and none of the more than 100 papers I have written subsequently has had nearly the impact."

1. **Carroll J B.** An analytical solution for approximating simple structure in factor analysis. *Psychometrika* **18**:23-38, 1953.
2. **Neuhaus J O & Wrigley C.** The quartimax method: an analytical approach to orthogonal simple structure. *Brit. J. Statist. Psychol.* **7**:81-91, 1954.
3. **Saunders D R.** An analytic method for rotation to orthogonal simple structure. Princeton, NJ: Educational Testing Service Research Bulletin No. 53-10, 1953.
4. **Ferguson G A.** The concept of parsimony in factor analysis. *Psychometrika* **19**:281-90, 1954.

This Week's Citation Classic

Cattell R B. The scree test for the number of factors.
Multivariate Behav. Res. **1**:245-76, 1966.
[University of Illinois, Urbana-Champaign, IL]

The problem of when to stop factoring in the use of factor analysis has been variously conceived. This paper names five features of a test for a number of factors that would be appropriate if factors are to be considered as real influences rather than merely statistical derivatives. It shows by numerically made-up examples that if the principal axis factors are plotted in succession there is a sharp point on the curve where the descent suddenly becomes linear. [The *Science Citation Index*® **(***SCI*®**) and the** *Social Sciences Citation Index*® **(***SSCI*®**) indicate that this paper has been cited in over 350 publications since 1966.]**

Raymond B. Cattell
Department of Psychology
University of Hawaii at Manoa
Honolulu, HI 96822

November 20, 1982

"During the 1940s and 1950s, it had been an uphill fight trying to convince psychologists that factor analytic designs of experiment would open the door upon which they had beaten in vain with the classical bivariate type of instrument. I soon discovered that part of their reluctance was a general belief that factor analysts could not agree among themselves in their results. These sources of disagreement arose from psychologists looking at the same correlation matrix and taking out quite different numbers of factors, as well as from failure to achieve an objective technique in rotation. The first problem was particularly serious, and it seemed to me that until this difficulty was met, the whole object of factor analysis, namely, to reach objectively the dimensions of personality or anything else, was vitiated.

"I had given much thought to theoretical approaches to this problem,[1-3] which I had hoped would have solved it for us. I decided to attack the problem in a bold or brutal empirical fashion. That is to say, I made out—backstage as it were—a number of imaginary studies with different numbers of factors in them, with quite particular loadings, from which I generated a correlation matrix such as an experimenter would normally start with. This putting of a model into a literal numerical form I have since been calling *plasmode*. I then factored these correlation matrices in the way one normally would and began to look for various signs in the principal axis 'latent roots' extracted, and various other characteristics, to see if I could find anything that would have told me that I had the number of factors which I knew the problem contained (from backstage). To my delight, a very simple finding presented itself, namely, that if I plotted the principal components in their sizes, as a diminishing series, and then joined up the points all through the number of variables concerned, a relatively sharp break appeared where the true number of factors ended and the 'detritus,' presumably due to error factors, appeared. From the analogy of the steep descent of a mountain till one comes to the scree of rubble at the foot of it, I decided to call this the *scree* test.

"It seemed that from the point of practical operations in factor analysis the problem was solved, but it could well have been that with very different data and circumstances from my own examples the rule would be found not to work, so I began groping for a theoretical basis. The second half of the article describes my consideration of certain alternative possible theoretical bases for this effect.

"This article is actually one of half a dozen in which I have felt forced to try to get a solution without the aid of a professional statistician. An undue number of psychologists seem to find what I want to write on these occasions to be too statistically recondite for them to pursue, and most statisticians feel that my disregard of the proper sequences of statistical exposition justifies their professional contempt. Nevertheless, as the number of citations shows, and as I know from correspondence, psychologists and others have found the scree test extremely useful and in most cases quite reliable.[4] One welcomes the new advance into practicable programs for factor number by the maximum likelihood method, which has come about in the last decade and solves several other problems."

1. **Kaiser H T.** The application of electronic computers to factor analysis. *Educ. Psychol. Meas.* **20**:141-51, 1960.
2. **Thurstone L L.** *Primary mental abilities.* Chicago: University of Chicago Press, 1938. 121 p.
3. **Bartlett M S.** Tests of significance in factor analysis. *Brit. J. Psychol. Stat. Sect.* **3**:77-85, 1950.
4. **Hakstian A R, Rogers W T & Cattell R B.** The behavior of number-of-factors rules with simulated data. *Multivariate Behav. Res.* **17**:193-219, 1982.

This Week's Citation Classic

CC/NUMBER 26
JUNE 25, 1979

Goodman L A & Kruskal W H. Measures of association for cross classification. *J. Amer. Statist. Ass.* **49**:732-64, 1954.

In examining a cross classification, how might one usefully measure its degree of association? Our 1954 paper proposed a number of then non-traditional methods, all characterized by operational interpretability in probabilistic terms. Subsequent papers examined distribution theory and statistical inference. [The *Science Citation Index®* (*SCI®*) and the *Social Sciences Citation Index™ (SSCI™)* indicate that this paper has been cited over 330 times since 1961.]

Leo A. Goodman & William H. Kruskal
Department of Statistics
University of Chicago
Chicago, IL 60637

March 17, 1978

"In the early 1950s, as young faculty members at the University of Chicago, we had separate conversations with senior colleagues there about statistical treatment of data that were naturally arranged as cross classifications of counts. One of us talked to Bernard Berelson (then Dean of the Graduate Library School and later the President of the Population Council), who was at that time dealing with extensive cross classifications related to voting behavior. For example, he might have a number of cross classifications of intended vote against educational level for different sections of a city.

"The other conversations were with the late Louis Thurstone (a major figure in the field of psychometrics and in particular in the development of factor analysis), who also was dealing with multiple cross classifications in the context of the relationship between various personal characteristics (e.g., leadership ability) and results from various psychological tests.

"In both cases the investigator had substantial numbers of cross classifications and needed a sensible way to reduce the data to try to make it coherent. One promising approach was felt to be replacement of each cross classification by a single number that measured in a reasonable way the degree of association between the characteristics corresponding to the rows and columns of the tabulated cross classification.

"Thus, the two of us were independently thinking about the same question. We discovered our mutual interest during a conversation at a party—we think that it was a New Year's Eve party at the Quadrangle (Faculty) Club—and the paper grew out of that interaction.

"We knew something of the existing literature on measures of association for cross classifications, and as we studied it further we recognized that most suggested measures of association were formal and arbitrary, without relevant interpretations—or without interpretations at all. Our contribution was to suggest a number of association measures that have interesting interpretations and to provide a simple taxonomy for cross classifications. As an example of the latter, we emphasized the importance of knowing whether or not the categories of a classification have or have not a natural ordering.

"Since cross classifications occur throughout science, since our emphasis on interpretation was perhaps novel, and since our work was quickly incorporated into textbook expositions, citations to the paper became numerous. We continued work on the topic, digging more deeply into its history and fields of application, and treating at length the relevant approximate sampling in an effort to contribute some new approaches and to effect some changes in statistical thinking and practice.[1]

"One of us[2] also developed an interest in ordinal measures of association beyond cross classifications as such. The other[3] was led to extensive research in the analysis of multi-way cross classifications, leading to what have come to be known as log-linear model theory and methodology. Another outgrowth, we dare to hope, of our paper has been fresh general concern with descriptive statistics from the viewpoint of finding usefully interpretable characteristics of populations and samples."

1. **Goodman L A & Kruskal W H.** Measures of association of cross classifications. IV: Simplification of asymptotic variances. *J. Amer. Statist. Ass.* **67**:415-21, 1972.
2. **Kruskal W H.** Ordinal measures of association. *J. Amer. Statist. Ass.* **53**:814-61, 1958.
3. **Goodman L A.** The multivariate analysis of qualitative data: interactions among multiple classifications. *J. Amer. Statist. Ass.* **65**:226-56, 1970.

This Week's Citation Classic

CC/NUMBER 24
JUNE 15, 1981

Costner H L. Criteria for measures of association. *Amer. Sociol. Rev.* **30**:341-53, 1965. [University of Washington, Seattle, WA]

General rules and definitions are specified for measures of association interpretable in terms of the proportional reduction in prediction error made possible by statistical association. Measures thus interpretable are identified. Implications for choice of measures and for interpreting results are examined. [The *Science Citation Index*® (*SCI*®) **and the** *Social Sciences Citation Index*® (*SSCI*®) **indicate that this paper has been cited over 175 times since 1965.]**

Herbert L. Costner
Department of Sociology
University of Washington
Seattle, WA 98195

May 11, 1981

"Confession, they say, is good for the soul, and herein I confess. In the summer of 1964, the University of Washington provided me salary support to complete the analysis of some data I had collected. Early in the summer, I was asked by a graduate student to write a brief statement on how to interpret measures of association, to be included in a student handbook for users of a multi-purpose statistical computer program. I agreed to write such a statement, thinking that it would be quickly done because it would be nothing more than a summary of ideas featured in a course I had recently taught. But as I attempted to write a succinct statement that would make sense to those who had never taken the course, I found that it was not as easy as I had thought. Writing the statement for the student handbook and subsequently expanding and revising it into the paper as it appeared in print became an obsession that I could not lay aside, and I spent a good part of the summer on it. The designation of this paper as a *Citation Classic* has emboldened me to make this belated confession to the University that I did not use the time supported that summer to complete the project described in my request.

"The basic idea of this paper did not originate with me. As indicated in the paper, Guttman had briefly outlined the idea of an error-reduction interpretation for measures of association in 1941;[1] Goodman and Kruskal emphasized the use of 'probabilistic models of predictive activity' for measures of association in their 1954 paper.[2] My paper expressed these in a different way and introduced an awkward acronym (PRE for Proportional Reduction in Error).

"I assume this paper has been frequently cited because of its simplicity, and because it helped make sense out of a bewildering array of measures that yield different numerical values for the same data. The awkward acronym may also be partly responsible for the frequent citation since that abbreviation encapsulated the basic idea and may have made it easier to grasp and recall. I have an aversion to acronyms and would not have used one except that comments on my early draft suggested that an abbreviation would make the paper more readable. The acronym now seems to appear more frequently than citations to its source.

"There are two errors in the paper which I feel obliged to mention. First, my statement that Somers's d_{yx} did not lend itself to a PRE interpretation was incorrect, as Somers demonstrated in a note published in 1968.[3] The second error was an error in judgment. In the closing paragraphs of the paper I anticipated that emphasizing the PRE interpretation would 'diminish our inclination to conceive of associations between two variables as varying in degree only' because such an interpretation requires one to recognize explicitly the rule for predicting one variable from the other. My anticipation was unduly optimistic. We still seem to give undue attention to the degree of association *per se*, whereas it is the nature and 'shape' of the linkage between variables that is of greater substantive importance. If I were writing the paper with today's hindsight, I would make that point more strongly and request that it be printed entirely in italics."

1. **Guttman L.** Supplementary study B-1: an outline of the statistical theory of prediction. (Horst P.) *The prediction of personal adjustment.* New York: Social Science Research Council, 1941. Bulletin 48. p. 261-2.
2. **Goodman L A & Kruskal W H.** Measures of association for cross classifications. *J. Amer. Statist. Assn.* **49**:732-64, 1954. [Citation Classic. *Current Contents/Social & Behavioral Sciences* (26):14, 25 June 1979.]
3. **Somers R H.** On the measurement of association. *Amer. Sociol. Rev.* **33**:291-2, 1968.

This Week's Citation Classic

CC/NUMBER 38
SEPTEMBER 20, 1982

Zellner A. An efficient method of estimating seemingly unrelated regressions and tests for aggregation bias. *J. Amer. Statist. Assn.* **57**:348-68, 1962. [University of Wisconsin, Madison, WI]

This paper describes a special multivariate statistical regression model that is useful in analyzing economic and other types of data. Statistical estimation and testing methods for the model are developed and applied. The relations of the new methods to older methods are set forth. [The *Science Citation Index®* (*SCI®*) **and the** *Social Sciences Citation Index®* (*SSCI®*) **indicate that this paper has been cited in over 385 publications since 1962.]**

Arnold Zellner
Graduate School of Business
University of Chicago
Chicago, IL 60637

July 9, 1982

"In graduate work in economics and econometrics at the University of California, Berkeley, Ivan Lee and George Kuznets stimulated my interest in multivariate statistical models used in econometrics. The available models seemed very complicated and not appropriate for analyzing certain kinds of important types of micro-data. Thus, after completing my graduate work, I began to attempt to develop simpler models and methods while at the University of Washington, Seattle. In a 1958 paper, published in 1961,[1] I hit on the idea of algebraically representing a multi-equation model in single-equation form. This basic, simple idea that occurred to me late one rainy night in Seattle permits an easy interpretation of multi-equation models and an adaption of single-equation statistical inference procedures to apply to multi-equation problems. In my 1961 paper that considered traditional multivariate regression models, each dependent variable is a linear function of the same set of independent variables, a situation common in the physical sciences in which one sets the values of a set of independent variables and observes multiple responses. The model that I analyzed in my 1962 paper allowed dependent variables to depend on different sets of independent variables, a situation commonly encountered in analyses of micro-data in economics. It was surprising to me that this type of model had not been analyzed in the statistical literature and that the statistical estimation and testing techniques that I developed were very different from those for the traditional regression model. The model considered involved m regression equations, $\mathbf{y}_\alpha = X_\alpha \beta_\alpha + \mathbf{u}_\alpha$, $\alpha = 1,2,\ldots,m$, that seem unrelated (and hence the term, 'seemingly unrelated regressions'). In fact, taking account of the correlation of the error terms across equations led to new estimates that are asymptotically more efficient than usual least squares estimates and appropriate test statistics for testing hypotheses.

"Much of the work on my paper was done while I was Fulbright visiting professor at The Netherlands School of Economics (now Erasmus University) in 1960-1961. P.J.M. van den Bogaard and H. Theil provided stimulating comments on my work, much of it done during evenings in our house on a Dutch polder ten miles south of Rotterdam.

"On my return to the US in 1961, friends inquired about the finite sample properties of my estimation technique which led to my 1963 paper[2] providing some exact finite sample properties. Subsequent developments are summarized in Srivastava and Dwivedi.[3] My paper and later work based on it were probably important in my election to fellowship in several professional organizations. The economics profession displayed an encouraging and receptive attitude toward my work for which I am very grateful.

"As regards why my paper is frequently cited, the following are possible factors. (1) My estimation and testing procedures were and are directly applicable to a number of important applied economic problems. (2) My model is a rich one that has served as a basis for a number of useful extensions. (3) My emphasis on simplicity with respect to exposition and analysis apparently appealed to many. (4) A.H. Stroud and I developed a computer program in 1962 that permitted ready use of my statistical estimation and testing techniques.[4] Over the years, the program has been improved and widely distributed. (5) I have consulted with many colleagues and students on applications of my techniques. They have been most appreciative."

1. **Zellner A.** Econometric estimation with temporally dependent disturbance terms. *Int. Econ. Rev.* **2**:164-77, 1961.
2. --------------. Estimators for seemingly unrelated regression equations: some exact finite sample results. *J. Amer. Statist. Assn.* **58**:977-92, 1963.
3. **Srivastava V K & Dwivedi T D.** Estimation of seemingly unrelated regression equations: a brief survey. *J. Econometrics* **10**:15-32, 1979.
4. **Stroud A H & Zellner A.** *Program for computing efficient regression estimates and associated statistics.* Unpublished manuscript. Madison, WI: Department of Economics, University of Wisconsin, 1962.

CC/NUMBER 7
FEBRUARY 15, 1982

This Week's Citation Classic

Farrar D E & Glauber R R. Multicollinearity in regression analysis: the problem revisited. *Rev. Econ. Statist.* **49**:92-107, 1967.
[Sloan School of Management, Massachusetts Institute of Technology, and Harvard Business School, Cambridge, MA]

This paper reviews the nature of multicollinearity among independent or predictor variables in regression analysis. It develops certain statistical measures which may be used to determine the presence of multicollinearity in a set of independent variables and, if present, the variables most seriously affected and the pattern of interdependence among them. [The *Science Citation Index*® **(***SCI*®**) and the** *Social Sciences Citation Index*® **(***SSCI*®**) indicate that this paper has been cited over 215 times since 1967.]**

Donald E. Farrar
Benham Management Corporation
755 Page Mill Road
Palo Alto, CA 94304

December 3, 1981

"This paper was the first scholarly project I undertook on completing my doctoral dissertation. It grew out of my exposure to regression analysis and to standard multiple regression computer programs as a young economist in the early-1960s, together with my interest at the time in factor analysis as a technique for analyzing sets of highly interdependent variables in other empirical studies.

"Certain statistics which I did not understand, such as the determinant of the correlation matrix of independent variables and diagonal elements of the inverse correlation matrix, were produced routinely by standard multiple regression computer programs at the time. I was told they helped to diagnose multicollinearity among independent variables, but did not understand how or why. In an effort to understand this witchcraft, Robert Glauber and I immersed ourselves in the literature on distributional properties of closely related multivariate statistics, until finally we were able to develop transformations of the variables of interest (determinant and diagonal elements of inverse correlation matrix) which we could interpret and whose distributional properties were known. We then added additional statistics through which one could identify patterns of interdependence among multicollinear variables.

"The paper has become something of a classic over the years for a number of reasons. First, multicollinearity is an important and ubiquitous problem faced by any economist in applying the most fundamental of econometric tools, multiple regression analysis. Our paper was the first which attempted to help practitioners understand and deal with the problem. Second, the statistics we proposed for diagnostic purposes were easily available by-products of standard calculations performed routinely by computers during the course of regression computations. Hence, they were easily and economically obtained and were incorporated in a number of standard computational routines. And third, the paper was reasonably well written. It is capable of being understood by most of the persons who would have an interest in the subject.

"I am not sure which of the above reasons is most important. I believe that being first in an important field helps. I'd also guess that most persons read the paper after encountering the statistics it suggests in reams of computer output rather than the other way around. And, perhaps, the exposition also helped.

"As a matter of passing interest, I recall that the paper was turned down by at least one journal and was accepted only grudgingly by the *Review of Economics and Statistics*, where it was the last rather than the lead article in the issue which carried it. I also recall that a senior colleague of my coauthor did not like the paper, as it was not sufficiently Bayesian to satisfy his tastes. As a result, Glauber gave serious consideration at the last minute to withdrawing his name from the paper. Publication was not particularly important at the time for junior faculty at the Harvard Business School, but disapproval of one's work by a senior professor could be.

"I always liked the paper, however, and am pleased that it has left its mark in the literature and in the computing centers where work in our profession is done. A more recent review in this field has been written by Belsley, Kuh, and Welsch."[1]

1. **Belsley D A, Kuh E & Welsch R E.** *Regression diagnostics: identifying influential data and sources of collinearity.* New York: **Wiley, 1980. 292 p.**

Chow G C. Tests of equality between sets of coefficients in two linear regressions. *Econometrica* **28**:591-605, 1960.
[Cornell University, Ithaca, NY]

Having estimated a linear regression with p coefficients, one may wish to test whether m additional observations belong to the same regression. This paper presents systematically the tests involved, relates the prediction interval (for $m=1$) and the analysis of covariance (for $m>p$) within the framework of general linear hypothesis (for any m), and extends the results to testing the equality between subsets of coefficients. [The *Science Citation Index*® (*SCI*®) and the *Social Sciences Citation Index*® (*SSCI*®) indicate that this paper has been cited in over 605 publications since 1960.]

Gregory C. Chow
Econometric Research Program
Department of Economics
Princeton University
Princeton, NJ 08544

November 8, 1984

"The research took place while I was an assistant professor at the School of Industrial Management (now the Sloan School) of the Massachusetts Institute of Technology in 1958. I had completed my PhD dissertation at the University of Chicago in 1955 and published it as a book.[1] In 1958, A.C. Harberger of the University of Chicago solicited a contribution from me to the volume *The Demand for Durable Goods*, which was being edited by him and would be published by the University of Chicago Press.[2] I decided to investigate whether the statistical demand functions, estimated by using annual data up to 1953 and reported in the 1957 book, had remained stable in the years from 1954 to 1957. The statistical test developed was reported in the cited article.

"Later on, a test of equality of regression coefficients became known as the 'Chow test' in the econometrics literature. If there are sufficient observations to estimate all the parameters in two separate regressions, a test of the equality between the regression coefficients using the analysis of covariance was well known in 1958, as I pointed out in the 1960 article. However, in my problem, there were not enough observations to estimate a second regression using the data from 1954 to 1957, and a test for this case was not well known. Furthermore, a second approach to testing the stability of regression coefficients is to use the predictions based on one regression and examine whether the observations generated by a second regression model for a different time period or different set of circumstances fall within the prediction intervals of the first regression. I showed the relationship between this prediction interval approach and the analysis of covariance approach.

"This article has been cited often not because of its contribution to statistical theory, but because of the wide applicability of the methods presented. An important objective in science is to provide hypotheses that will yield accurate predictions. If economic relations are to yield good predictions, they should remain stable over time. This testing of the temporal stability of economic relations is an important problem in applied economics. My article may have stimulated the interest of economists in the question of stability of economic relations. The article was motivated by an important applied problem and its practical relevance explains its popularity.

"A recent article covering the same topic is 'Generalized Chow tests for structural change: a coordinate-free approach' by Jean-Marie Dufour."[3]

1. **Chow G C.** *Demand for automobiles in the United States: a study in consumer durables.* Amsterdam: North-Holland, 1957. 110 p.
2. --------------. Statistical demand functions for automobiles and their use for forecasting. (Harberger A C, ed.) *The demand for durable goods.* Chicago: University of Chicago Press, 1960. p. 147-78.
3. **Dufour J M.** Generalized Chow tests for structural change: a coordinate-free approach. *Int. Econ. Rev.* **23**:565-76, 1982.

This Week's Citation Classic

CC/NUMBER 34
AUGUST 23, 1982

Cohen J. Multiple regression as a general data-analytic system.
Psychol. Bull. **70**:426-43, 1968.
[New York University, New York, NY]

Techniques are presented for using multiple regression and correlation analysis as a versatile and powerful data-analytic procedure that generalizes the analysis of variance and covariance. These include the representation of nominal scales and methods for handling interactions, curvilinearity, missing data, and covariates. [The *Science Citation Index*® **(***SCI*®**) and the** *Social Sciences Citation Index*® **(***SSCI*®**) indicate that this paper has been cited in over 480 publications since 1968.]**

Jacob Cohen
Department of Psychology
New York University
New York, NY 10003

June 8, 1982

"Having flunked calculus in my freshman year at City College of New York, my vocational goal of teaching high school math (as well as further math training) was abandoned. Twelve years and one world war later, I was a full-fledged clinical psychologist PhD (1950) and all that remained of my earlier aspirations was a fascination with quantitative research methods. I drifted into teaching and research consulting in statistics and psychometric theory, and fiddling with methodological problems in the social and behavioral sciences. Without formal mathematical training, all I could do was make intuitive leaps and check them out numerically. Proofs were (and still largely are) beyond me.

"Multiple regression/correlation analysis (MRC), I had been taught, was a method for relating a group of variables to a single variable, and was largely used in psychotechnological applications, e.g., for predicting college grade point average from entrance examination scores; the resulting regression equation was used as a selection tool to aid in college admission decisions. My intuition and idea fragments wrested from barely comprehended technical publications led me to see MRC as potentially of far wider applicability. During the early-1960s, stumbling along, I constructed an MRC-based general data-analytic system which encompassed the analysis of variance and covariance as special cases. I had 'discovered' the general linear model. (An advantage of lack of training is the excitement of making such 'discoveries.') I prepared the article and sent it to some experts in the field for review. Their responses were detailed and conscientious, but not encouraging. They found the exposition 'fuzzy' and 'nonrigorous,' and objected most strongly to those of its aspects of which I was most proud. Since I did not understand all they wrote, I could not be sure, but as far as I could tell, they were not challenging the validity of the MRC system I presented, but rather its style, which certainly differed from theirs. With some trepidation, I nevertheless sent the manuscript off to *Psychological Bulletin* which, luckily, accepted it.

"I believe that part of the reason it has been so highly cited lies at the heart of the difference between the experts and me. The article was addressed to an audience of researchers and provided them with methods they could intelligently apply. What was 'fuzzy' and 'nonrigorous' in the mathematical-statistical framework of the experts was conceptually clear and intuitively accessible to behavioral scientists. There is an obvious object lesson here in scientific communication.

"The rash of reprint requests encouraged me to write (with a newly acquired wife) a textbook that expanded on the system[1] which has also been successful; we are currently winding up a second edition which features a causal models outlook.

"Unregenerate, I have recently completed a multivariate generalization of MRC called set correlation.[2] It had a similar reception from some of the experts who saw preprints. (Indeed, it was rejected by *Psychological Bulletin.*) This gives me reason to hope that some day it too will be a *Citation Classic*!"

1. **Cohen J & Cohen P.** *Applied multiple regression/correlation analysis for the behavioral sciences.* Hillsdale, NJ: Lawrence Erlbaum Associates, 1975. 490 p.
[The *SSCI* indicates that this book has been cited in over 535 publications since 1975.]
2. **Cohen J.** Set correlation as a general multivariate data-analytic method. *Multivariate Behav. Res.* **17**:301-42, 1982.

This Week's Citation Classic

CC/NUMBER 1
JANUARY 5, 1981

Draper N R & Smith H. *Applied regression analysis.* New York: Wiley, 1966. 407 p. [University of Wisconsin, WI and Proctor & Gamble Company]

This book provides a complete course on regression analysis, both linear and nonlinear, for the practitioner. While down-to-earth and practical, it also presents the necessary theory in such a way that readers without matrix knowledge can learn it en route. [The *Science Citation Index® (SCI®)* **and the** *Social Sciences Citation Index® (SSCI™)* **indicate that this book has been cited over 2,760 times since 1966.]**

Norman R. Draper
Department of Statistics
University of Wisconsin
Madison, WI 53706

December 1, 1980

"In 1962, the chemical division of the American Society for Quality Control asked Harry Smith (then with Proctor and Gamble, Cincinnati, and now at Mount Sinai School of Medicine, New York City) to prepare a short course on applied regression analysis with another instructor, chosen from a university. After making enquiries behind the scenes, Harry asked me to do it with him when we met at a research conference that summer. We had actually never met before, but knew much about each other through mutual contacts and the 'old boy' network consisting of North Carolina graduates. (Harry's 1954 PhD is from North Carolina State, Raleigh, and my 1958 PhD is from the University of North Carolina, Chapel Hill.)

"We hit it off immediately. Early correspondence shows that we originally intended to use an existing text but found none fully satisfactory, so we were soon writing up notes to hand out instead. Our first two-day industrial course was given in Rochester, New York, on October 18 and 19, 1964. By that time, the course notes were extensive and Andy Ford, a Wiley editor, was assuring us that the manuscript would make 'an eminently attractive book for our Wiley Statistics Series.' Our manuscript was submitted in February 1965 and, after the usual review process followed by revisions, was published in August 1966.

"I felt reluctant to use the book as a statistics department course text at Wisconsin, at first. However, when another department put forward a course proposal based on it, there was no alternative! The course (Statistics 333: Applied Regression Analysis) has proved popular among PhD students in other departments who wish to use regression analysis on data obtained as part of their thesis work. At one time, this was rare. However, with the advent of powerful computers, more and more regression analyses are being performed routinely in theses.

"A second edition has been in preparation for some time; it will be published in February 1981.[1] The first edition had 407 pages; the new edition has much new material and many additional exercises and has over 700 pages.

"The success of the first edition and the reason it is widely cited is (we have been told) due to the commonsense and down-to-earth presentation coupled with our personal opinions (clearly designated as such) of what to do in cases of doubt. We have tried to maintain those features in the second edition. We hope the book will continue to prove useful to those who must work with regression data."

1. **Draper N R & Smith H.** *Applied regression analysis.* New York: Wiley, 1981. In press.

CC/NUMBER 40
OCTOBER 1, 1984

This Week's Citation Classic™

Granger C W J & Hatanaka M. *Spectral analysis of economic time series.* Princeton, NJ: Princeton University Press, 1964. 299 p.
[Department of Economics, University of Nottingham, England]

Spectral analysis essentially decomposes a stationary series into a number of uncorrelated components, each associated with a different frequency. The relevant importance of each component can be measured by variance, and these variances plotted against frequency give the spectrum. A number of economic hypotheses can be tested by looking at the shape of this curve. The approach can be extended to bivariate situations and multivariate and nonstationary series. The book concludes with two substantial applications, including an analysis of leading indicators. [The *Science Citation Index*® (*SCI*®) and the *Social Sciences Citation Index*® (*SSCI*®) indicate that this book has been cited in over 330 publications since 1964.]

C.W.J. Granger
Department of Economics
University of California
La Jolla, CA 92093

August 3, 1984

"In 1959, while at the University of Nottingham, I won a Harkness Fellowship to study at an American university of my choice. I wrote to several and had a reply from Oskar Morgenstern at Princeton University inviting me to join a new time series project he was just starting. On arrival at Princeton, I found that the project was essentially just Michio Hatanaka and me, although some others soon joined us. Apparently Morgenstern's coauthor of the *Theory of Games and Economic Behavior*,[1] the eminent mathematician John Von Neumann, had insisted that economists should be using Fourier techniques when analyzing their data. It was immediately clear that he had Fourier transform ideas in mind, that is, the use of frequency decompositions, which gives rise to spectral techniques.

"The mathematics underlying single series was quite well known by 1960, but we were extremely fortunate that the very well-known Princeton statistician, John Tukey, had recently extended the ideas to pairs of series, which gave potentially more interesting interpretations.[2] He taught us in an unconventional manner. We started with some data, of exchange rates, and were told to perform a certain calculation. Once this was completed, he told us how to interpret the results. It was left up to us to work out the underlying mathematics.

"The sum of the calculations, interpretations, and mathematics became the book. A mathematical chapter was followed by one concentrating on interpretation using as little mathematics as possible. The book finished with two application chapters prepared by Hatanaka. Throughout, we tried to discuss the weaknesses of the techniques as well as their strengths. The one difficult concept that had to be developed was a usable definition of causality, so that the phase diagram in the cross-spectrum could be interpreted.

"The actual book was written on the top floor of a building at Princeton facing Nassau Hall, which housed Morgenstern's Econometrics Research Program, and which was without air conditioning, during three summers. I am unclear if the lack of comfort had any effect on the style used in the book.

"I believe that the book was a success, and thus widely cited, because there was a growing dissatisfaction with classical econometric approaches, which largely ignored the time series aspect of economic data. Spectral methods were viewed as a promising new viewpoint and were widely used until the time domain modeling methods of Box and Jenkins appeared in 1970.[3]

"The book is still in print, sells about 100 copies a year, and has total sales of over 5,000, which is remarkable for such a narrow, technical topic.

"See reference 4 for a recent publication in this field."

1. **Von Neumann J & Morgenstern O.** *Theory of games and economic behavior.* New York: Wiley, 1967. 641 p.
2. **Tukey J W.** *Exploratory data analysis.* Reading, MA: Addison-Wesley, 1977. 688 p.
3. **Box G E P & Jenkins G M.** *Time series analysis: forecasting and control.* San Francisco, CA: Holden-Day, 1970. 553 p.
4. **Granger C W J & Newbold P.** *Forecasting economic time series.* New York: Academic Press, 1977. 333 p.

This Week's Citation Classic™

Morrison D G. On the interpretation of discriminant analysis.
J. Market. Res.—Chicago **6**:156-63, 1969.
[Graduate School of Business, Columbia University, New York, NY]

Discriminate analysis is a commonly used statistical technique in the social sciences. While this procedure is appropriate for many classification problems, it has the potential to be misinterpreted. This article helps clarify the interpretation issues involved. [The *Science Citation Index*® (*SCI*®) and the *Social Sciences Citation Index*® (*SSCI*®) indicate that this paper has been cited in over 175 publications since 1969.]

Donald G. Morrison
Graduate School of Business
Columbia University
New York, NY 10027

May 31, 1984

"During my early years (1966-1968) at Columbia University, I taught some courses that involved discriminant analysis. Such issues as small sample sizes, no holdout sample, differing costs of misclassification, unequal group sizes, and the general effectiveness of the analysis were discussed. The students asked where they could read about these topics. I could think of no one article that discussed all of these issues clearly. Initially, I had no desire to write such an article. First of all, review or tutorial articles are not nearly as much fun to write as are articles on one's own original research. Second, this type of article usually carries very few academic brownie points. (I was nontenured at the time.) However, after being pestered for two years by these students and a few colleagues, I decided to write this nontechnical overview of discriminant analysis. Bob Ferber, the editor of the *Journal of Marketing Research*, was particularly helpful in improving the original manuscript.

"My target audience was the then fairly small group of serious quantitative marketing researchers in industry and academia. By 1971 or so, the article appeared to have met the needs of this targeted group. By 1972, I basically had forgotten about the paper.

"As 1973 and 1974 rolled around, a curious thing happened. I started to get an enormous number of papers to referee from disciplines such as sociology, psychology, demography, medicine, and business-related areas such as finance and accounting. All of these articles used—or misused—discriminant analysis and all of them referenced my paper. After looking at the references, the editors must have selected me as the 'methodology' referee. I refereed most of these papers early on, but gradually I had to start sending some back unrefereed.

"My original target market for this paper—the quantitative marketeers—could not have made my paper a *Citation Classic*. The probably small number of other social scientists who read and referenced the paper added additional citations. However, it is my guess that the social scientists who referenced my paper because other social scientists did are the ones who pushed my paper over the top. I wonder how many nonmarketing social scientists who currently cite my paper actually read it?

"Parts of my paper are still up-to-date, i.e., those dealing with Bayes's theorem and common sense. Neither of these ideas will ever become obsolete. However, the statistical issues are now much better addressed through various resampling procedures such as jackknifing and bootstrapping (see reference 1 and the numerous references therein.)

"Finally, there is an interesting moral to this story. I was reluctant to write the article. I did write it out of a somewhat altruistic attitude of 'service to the community.' The result is that I have received far more recognition from this one article than from anything else I have written. Leo Durocher was wrong!"

1. **Efron B.** *The jackknife, the bootstrap and other resampling plans.* Philadelphia: SIAM, 1982. 92 p.

This Week's Citation Classic™

Lykken D T. Statistical significance in psychological research. *Psychol. Bull.* **70**:151-9, 1968.
[University of Minnesota, Minneapolis, MN]

It was argued that a statistically significant finding, confirming a direction prediction based on a psychological theory, is usually an insignificant event. Replicability is the real desideratum. Three types of replication were identified and their importance discussed in terms of examples from the literature. [The *Science Citation Index*® (*SCI*®) and the *Social Sciences Citation Index*® (*SSCI*®) indicate that this paper has been cited in over 175 publications since 1968.]

David T. Lykken
Mayo Hospital
University of Minnesota
Minneapolis, MN 55455

July 1, 1984

"This paper was turned down by the journal to which it was first sent because the editor found its style too racy and polemical. I believe that psychology in the twentieth century is a shambling sort of enterprise attempting to become a scientific discipline and is beset by many difficulties, some of its own making. My intention in this paper was to point out one of these self-imposed obstacles that had become institutionalized as part of our research tradition. When one is attacking a tradition, it is hard to avoid polemics; when one is pointing out a blind spot, it is natural to wave one's arms about.

"The flaw I had in mind was the use of statistical significance as a kind of scientific shibboleth. Since the null hypothesis is almost always false, one has a fifty-fifty chance of confirming most theoretical predictions, no matter how fatuous one's theory or illogical one's reasoning. Moreover, statistically significant findings are frequently not true and, as Darwin himself pointed out, false facts are far more mischievous than false theories. R.A. Fisher explained in 1929 that replicability, not statistical reliability, is the real desideratum.[1]

"Psychologists trained at the University of Minnesota in the 1950s had a tendency, which I later overcame, to believe that scientists should be guided by philosophers of science. I was surprised at the time to discover that philosophers of science had not analyzed the important concept of replication. My own amateur analysis, which distinguished between 'literal,' 'operational,' and 'constructive' replication, still seems to me to be valid and useful.

"I think the article was popular because it said what many psychologists already believed and wanted to pass on to their students. The research strategy based on a series of overlapping studies in which each replicates and extends the one preceding has recently been advocated again by Muller, Otto, and Benignus."[2]

1. **Fisher R A.** The statistical method in psychical research. *Proc. Soc. Psychical Res.* **39**:189-92, 1929.
2. **Muller K, Otto D & Benignus V.** Design and analysis issues and strategies in psychophysiological research. *Psychophysiology* **20**:212-18, 1983.

This Week's Citation Classic

Dawes R M & Corrigan B. Linear models in decision making.
Psychol. Bull. **81**:95-106, 1974.
[University of Oregon and Oregon Research Institute, Eugene, OR]

Optimal linear prediction outperforms intuitive prediction of skilled clinicians—e.g., in psychology, medicine, and business. Nonoptimal linear models based on such judges' own predictions also outdo them. We demonstrated that linear models with *random* weights—correctly oriented—do as well as clinicians and unit weighted models outperform them. [The *Science Citation Index*® (*SCI*®) and the *Social Sciences Citation Index*® (*SSCI*®) indicate that this paper has been cited in over 245 publications since 1974.]

Robyn M. Dawes
Department of Psychology
University of Oregon
Eugene, OR 97403

November 29, 1982

"As a first-year graduate student in the (neoanalytic) clinical psychology program at Michigan, I read Paul Meehl's book on statistical versus clinical prediction.[1] I was impressed that—in numerous studies involving the prediction of human outcomes—optimal linear (multiple regression) models of relevant input variables outperform clinicians.

"Moving to the University of Oregon and the (old) Oregon Research Institute in 1967, I became involved with the work of Lew Goldberg, Paul Hoffman, Sarah Lichtenstein, Len Rorer, and Paul Slovic on linear modeling of clinical experts. They had discovered an apparent paradox—that linear models not only outperform clinicians at predicting actual outcomes, but that they predict these clinicians' own predictions as well; see, for example, Goldberg's *Citation Classic*.[2] That made sense when clinicians were viewed as imperfect mediators between input and output, introducing unreliability by their inconsistency, and invalidity by the degree to which the linear model predicting their judgments was not optimal for predicting the output. Unreliability could be removed by replacing the clinician's actual judgments with a (necessarily consistent) linear model of those judgments, a replacement termed 'bootstrapping.' It worked. Prediction improved. See Goldberg[3] or Dawes.[4]

"But were clinicians necessary at all? The efficacy of bootstrapping was demonstrated by comparing the model of the clinician to the clinician, but what would happen if we compared that model to some other model with appropriately oriented weights? (If such a model did as well, then the clinicians were good for *nothing but* choosing the variables, and their orientation.)

"I occasionally had a crazy idea—that some cynic might take one of our data sets, standardize the variables, add them together in some arbitrary way, and outperform our 'bootstrap judges.' One day my programmer, Corrigan, had slack time and asked for something to do. 'Well, for the last couple of years I've had a crazy idea that....' In four data sets (involving such outcomes as final psychiatric diagnosis and graduate success), we (Corrigan) chose tens of thousands of random weights in the right direction (determined *a priori*); linear composites based on these weights performed as well as did those with weights based on clinicians' judgments. Unit weights did better.

"Talking about our results before they were published was fun. (There was time to talk because *Psychological Review* rejected our paper before *Psychological Bulletin* made it a lead article.) Many people didn't believe random weights would work until they tested them out on their own data sets (phone calls and letters, 'My god, you were right!'). The reason random and unit weights work is that they can be expected to yield results highly correlated with those based on optimal weights—whatever those happened to be. (Weight optimization involves a 'flat maximum.') That can be demonstrated mathematically—as was later done by John Castellan, Ward Edwards, Hillel Einhorn, Robin Hogarth, Dettof von Winterfeldt, and Howard Wainer—and as early as 1938 by S.S. Wilkes.[5] Had we not been dumb enough to use data sets, however, the results would probably have gotten little publicity. Our naiveté made this work a 'classic.'"

1. **Meehl P E.** *Clinical versus statistical prediction: a theoretical analysis and a review of the evidence.* Minneapolis, MN: University of Minnesota Press, 1954. 149 p.
2. **Goldberg L R.** Simple models or simple processes? Some research on clinical judgments. *Amer. Psychol.* **23**:483-96, 1968. [Citation Classic. *Current Contents/Social & Behavioral Sciences* **13**(10):18, 9 March 1981.]
3. ------------------. Man versus model of man: a rationale, plus some evidence for a method of improving on clinical inferences. *Psychol. Bull.* **73**:422-32, 1970.
4. **Dawes R M.** A case study of graduate admissions: application of three principles of human decision making. *Amer. Psychol.* **26**:180-8, 1971.
5. **Wilkes S S.** Weighted systems for linear functions of correlated variables when there is no dependent variable. *Psychometrika* **8**:23-40, 1938.

This Week's Citation Classic

NUMBER 16
APRIL 16, 1979

Johnston J. *Econometric Methods,*
New York: McGraw Hill, 1971 (1963) 437 p.

An exposition of the methods used by economists in the statistical estimation and testing of economic models is described. Major topics are linear regression model, including the complications due to autocorrelation, heteroscedasticity, multicollinearity, and lagged variables; and identification and estimation of simultaneous equation models. [The *Science Citation Index®* *(SCI®)* **and the** *Social Sciences Citation Index™ (SSCI™)* **indicate that this paper has been cited over 435 times since 1963.]**

Jack Johnston
School of Social Sciences
University of California
Irvine, CA 92717

September 8, 1978

"Econometrics involves the application of mathematical and statistical methods to the formulation, estimation, and testing of economic models. Scientifically the subject is still in its infancy, but the last quarter century has seen an explosive growth, facilitated by the ever increasing abundance and power of modern computers, and spurred on by the desire of governments and businesses to gain increased understanding and control of the economic environment in which they function.

"This development did not come easily. It was hindered by two factors, one general and one specific. The general factor, which still persists, is the wide ranging nature of the intellectual demands on the econometrician in that he must have competence in economic theory, mathematics, and statistics and computing. He must also have a keen appreciation of the defects and limitations of his data and an understanding of the institutional realities of the economic or social system that is the focus of his analysis. The specific factor was that classical statistical methods were basically geared to the experimental sciences and thus inappropriate in several crucial respects for observational rather than experimental situations. The first fundamental steps in the required theoretical development were mostly made at the Cowles Commission in Chicago in the years after World War II. By the mid-fifties the stage was set for the first real flowering of the subject. The only difficulty was that only a handful of professional economists at that time had any real grasp of the subject.

"In 1957/58, as an assistant professor at Harvard University, I was teaching a course in quantitative methods for graduate economists. The following year I moved to the University of Wisconsin at Madison with one of America's most distinguished econometricians (Guy H. Orcutt, now of Yale). I had presumed that he would teach the graduate course in econometrics there, but to my horror I found myself charged with that responsibility. Horror is not an overstatement, for I had no strong professional base in econometrics. I had never taken a formal course in mathematical statistics, even as an undergraduate, nor indeed had I ever had the chance to take a graduate level course in any subject. To crown it all, the five graduate students in the class were outnumbered by Wisconsin economics professors, including Orcutt himself, ranged like an intellectual Mafia in the back row. This turned out to be a stimulating set of circumstances. The notes prepared for those three weekly lectures throughout the year were the basis for the first edition of *Econometric Methods.*

"The publishing decision was almost equally unusual. There was no outline, no table of contents, no specimen chapters. Over an indifferent sherry in a Madison bar the late Marty Hogan, then of the McGraw Hill Chicago office, asked some questions about the course, and on his next visit proffered a draft contract. The main reason, I am sure, for whatever success the book may have had is that my ignorance and lack of formal graduate training put me closer to the mind and difficulties of the average student than would have been the case had I been the fortunate product of a high-powered graduate school. The disadvantage, of course, is that the ignorance of the author shows through here and there in both editions, as discerning students in many countries have reminded me. I sincerely hope their comments will continue and help make the third edition, on which I am currently working, better than its predecessors."

This Week's Citation Classic

CC/NUMBER 22
MAY 28, 1979

Nunnally J C. *Psychometric theory.* New York: McGraw Hill, 1967, 640 p.
[University of Chicago, Chicago, IL]

The book is intended to be a comprehensive text on psychometric theory, substantive findings in the area, and related methods of statistical analyses. It was specifically intended for graduate students in their second year of training in psychology, education, and other behavioral sciences. However, it has also proved to be useful to people in various disciplines such as engineering, various medical specialties, and other areas. [The *Science Citation Index*® (*SCI*®) and the *Social Sciences Citation Index*™ (*SSCI*™) indicate that this book has been cited over 425 times since 1967.]

Jum C. Nunnally
Department of Psychology
Vanderbilt University
Nashville, TN 37240

July 28, 1979

"Of course I am extremely gratified that *Psychometric Theory* has been adopted so widely throughout the behavioral sciences and purchased by so many professional people; also, I am quite flattered that the book is being listed as a 'Citation Classic.' My original motivation for writing it springs from the same source as that of so many authors—namely, I could not find a comprehensive textbook for the graduate course in psychometric theory that I had been teaching for over ten years. Many of the topics that come under the heading of psychometric theory are highly technical, difficult for the average graduate student to understand, and the major methods and theories are scattered throughout dozens of different journals. Consequently, both in self-defense and in an effort to help befuddled graduate students understand a very wide variety of topics which are essential to their professional development, I made an effort to bring all of the major theories and methods together in one comprehensive text. The book covers the gamut of what I consider to be the most important topics in psychometric theory for graduate students and practicing behavioral scientists.

"Although a large part of psychometric theory concerns mathematical methods, I realized that the average graduate student would not understand complex mathematical treatments of the topic. Consequently, I made every effort to 'talk out' the mathematical aspects of the problem rather than present detailed mathematical derivations. At the same time, I made every effort to 'load' the book with references to technical articles and monographs where the more mathematically minded person could obtain an in-depth understanding of the mathematical arguments. I think that this effort to 'talk out' the mathematical arguments has been one of the major reasons that the book has been popular with students and professional people. A second feature of the book which I think has added to its popularity is that I made every effort to give interesting examples whenever possible and made efforts in other ways to create interest in what would otherwise be a very dry, unpalatable topic for most readers.

"Because a decade had passed between the first edition of the book (1967) and when I began revising it,[1] I found that there was a massive amount of literature which I needed to master before I could adequately write the second edition. It actually took me longer to revise the book than it did to write the original one. I suspect that the sheer amount of work which an effort of this kind requires has discouraged any other person in psychology from trying to put together a thoroughly comprehensive coverage of the field of psychometrics. For the benefit of anyone who wants to try his hand at writing a book that covers this much technical ground in an understandable and palatable way, let me wish him good luck."

1. **Nunnally J C.** *Psychometric theory.* New York: McGraw Hill, 1978. 701p.

CC/NUMBER 35
AUGUST 31, 1981

This Week's Citation Classic

Edwards W, Lindman H & Savage L J. Bayesian statistical inference for psychological research. *Psychol. Rev.* **70**:193-242, 1963.
[University of Michigan, Ann Arbor, MI]

The definition of probability as a measure of the opinions of ideally consistent people, the topic of this paper, has many consequences. Bayesian statistical inference specifies how opinions should be changed in the light of new information. Topics covered include specific distributions, the principle of stable estimation, the likelihood principle, and paradoxes that result from comparing a sharp null hypothesis with a diffuse alternative. [The *Social Sciences Citation Index*® *(SSCI*®) **indicates that this paper has been cited over 200 times since 1966.]**

Ward Edwards
Social Science Research Institute
Department of Psychology
and Industrial and Systems Engineering
University of Southern California
Los Angeles, CA 90007

July 6, 1981

"When L.J. (Jimmie) Savage moved from the University of Chicago to the University of Michigan in the early 1960s, I was tickled pink; I consider the first half of his book, *The Foundations of Statistics*,[1] to be the finest combination of wisdom with good writing that I have yet seen. I knew a little of Bayesian thinking, thought its impact would be enormous, and wanted to know more. So I asked Harold Lindman, then a graduate student, to prepare a draft on the topic for the other graduate students. He did—and I found myself looking at a topic too important for casual treatment. So I rewrote Harold's draft, and showed the result to Savage. He, in his gentle but painfully explicit way, showed me a subset of my intellectual and expositional errors. I asked him if he would be willing to cooperate with me in fixing the draft up, and he said yes.

"That was the beginning of the most exciting year of my life. One piece at a time, we took my draft, analyzed its intellectual and verbal deficiencies, and Jimmie helped me to understand where the truth lay. I then went home, and tried my hand at writing down what I had just finished learning, and in a day or so the cycle started again. Every page of the manuscript passed through my typewriter at least 13 times before we were both satisfied. In the process, I developed an intuition about such ideas as the likelihood principle sufficiently strong so that I could suggest new lines of thought to Jimmie, with perhaps a .600 batting average.

"Toward the end, the three of us began to understand that a special effort was leading to a special result. No previous paper had done a good job of presenting the Bayesian point of view to those not already steeped in statistics. That, of course, is why it has become a *Citation Classic*. To this day, I know of no better presentation of the justification for use of uniform priors. Of course, numerous books have by now made the Bayesian ideas far more accessible, to psychologists and others. Authors include Phillips,[2] Hays and Winkler,[3] and Novick and Jackson.[4]

"Savage died of a very premature heart attack a few years later. I cannot even imagine what statistics (or my life) would be like if he had fulfilled his years. He was then, and remains, the most creative, most profound, and gentlest man I have ever known."

1. **Savage L J.** *The foundations of statistics.* New York: Dover, 1972. 310 p.
2. **Phillips L D.** *Bayesian statistics for social scientists.* New York: Thomas Y. Crowell, 1974. 363 p.
3. **Hays W L & Winkler R L.** *Statistics: probability, inference and decision.* New York: Holt, Rinehart & Winston, 1970. Vol. II.
4. **Novick M R & Jackson P H.** *Statistical methods for educational and psychological research.* New York: McGraw-Hill, 1974. 456 p.

CC/NUMBER 28
JULY 12, 1982

This Week's Citation Classic

Greenhouse S W & Geisser S. On methods in the analysis of profile data. *Psychometrika* **24**:95-112, 1959.
[Biometry Branch, Natl. Institute of Mental Health, NIH, Bethesda, MD]

Methods are presented for analyzing repeated measurements on a variable, or a battery of tests, given to subjects in one or more groups. Approximate procedures based on classical analysis of variance are presented and exact, generalized multivariate methods are also discussed. [The *Science Citation Index®* **(***SCI®***) and the** *Social Sciences Citation Index®* **(***SSCI®***) indicate that this paper has been cited in over 295 publications since 1961.]**

Samuel W. Greenhouse
Department of Statistics
George Washington University
Washington, DC 20052

February 2, 1982

"Seymour Geisser joins me in expressing our pleasure in learning that our 1959 paper is now a *Citation Classic*. Each of us was aware that our procedures were being applied because of the many letters and calls we received over the years. In preparing for this statement, I reread the paper. I must say it reads very well and is quite lucid in its exposition. I believe we have the then-editors of *Psychometrika* to thank for this in that, contrary to editorial strictures currently imposed, they did not demand that we shorten the paper. The pace of the exposition and the examples presented made it possible for any interested reader to apply the methods we were describing.

"Geisser and I were in a statistical research and consulting section of the Biometry Branch of the National Institute of Mental Health. We were confronted with a number of repeated measurement problems brought to us by psychologists, psychiatrists, and other social scientists in the intramural program of the institute. Being unhappy with the lack of rigor and the too specialized methods then available in the literature, we attacked the problem from scratch. Since both Geisser and I had received some special training in multivariate analysis, it was not too difficult to solve the theoretical issues which we published[1] a year prior to the publication of the paper in *Psychometrika*. I am sure familiarity with our procedures was greatly facilitated and enhanced when shortly thereafter our work was included in several statistical textbooks, put into a number of computer programs, and reprinted in a book of readings[2] in educational research.

"It is interesting to note that many designs of a similar nature have appeared in research fields other than the social sciences, particularly in biomedical research. Our proposed techniques for analyzing these data would clearly be applicable. Indeed, such uses have already been made in these other fields. Recently, I reviewed a paper generalizing our techniques to multifactors observed on the same individual. (This paper has not been published as yet.) Actually, Geisser published a paper wherein he considered two factors each observed a repeated number of times on each individual[3] and wrote another paper involving Latin square designs.[4]

"As far as I am aware, these methods have not been superseded by any better procedure and are as applicable today, given that the assumptions hold, as they were 20 years ago."

1. **Geisser S & Greenhouse S W.** An extension of Box's results on the use of the F distribution in multivariate analysis. *Ann. Math. Statist.* **29**:885-91, 1958.
[The *SCI* and the *SSCI* indicate that this paper has been cited in over 145 publications since 1961.]
2. **Collier R O & Hummel T J,** eds. *Experimental design and interpretation, readings in educational research.* Berkeley, CA: McCutchan, 1977. p. 211-33.
3. **McHugh R, Sivanich G & Geisser S.** On the evaluation of personality changes as measured by psychometric test profiles. *Psychol. Rep.* **9**:335-44, 1961.
4. **Geisser S.** The Latin square as a repeated measurements design. (Neyman J, ed.) *Proceedings of the Fourth Berkeley Symposium on Mathematical Statistics and Probability, 20 June-30 July 1960, Berkeley, CA.* Berkeley, CA: University of California Press, 1961. Vol. 4. p. 241-50.

CC/NUMBER 12
MARCH 24, 1980

This Week's Citation Classic

Rao C R. *Linear statistical inference and its applications.* New York: Wiley, 1965. 522 p. [Indian Statistical Institute, New Delhi, India]

This is a comprehensive treatise on statistical inference presented in a logically integrated and practical form. In addition, there is an adequate discussion of results in matrix algebra and foundations of probability needed for a rigorous treatment of statistical inference. [The *Science Citation Index® (SCI®)* **and the** *Social Sciences Citation Index™ (SSCI™)* **indicate that this book has been cited over 1,220 times since 1965.]**

C. Radhakrishna Rao
Department of Mathematics
and Statistics
University of Pittsburgh
Pittsburgh, PA 15260

February 8, 1980

"In 1952 I wrote the book *Advanced Statistical Methods in Biometric Research* with the objective of providing an integrated approach to advanced statistical theory and applications.[1] Of special interest in the book is a discussion of multivariate statistical methods developed by the Indian School of Statisticians for applications in biology, psychology, and related disciplines. I was glad to see that this book was on the list of 72 'highly cited works in applied mathematics during 1961-1972.'[2]

"The success of *Advanced Statistical Methods* encouraged me to write a more comprehensive text to introduce statistical inference to theoretically oriented mathematical statisticians, while emphasizing the need to keep in touch with practical problems which only can provide stimulus for basic research in and enrichment of statistical methodology. This was the motivation for writing *Linear Statistical Inference (LSI).*

"I was exposed to statistics when the subject was still in its initial stages of development and there were no standard books on the subject describing the major trends of research and current controversies. I thought it was a good idea to write a book for my own understanding of the newly emerging science. I wanted the book to be useful to those who wished to study statistics in all its logical, mathematical, and computational aspects and not confine themselves to narrow areas of specialization or be unduly influenced by advocates of particular modes of statistical inference. It was difficult to write a book with such a mission in view.

"However, I was gratified to see that *LSI* was well received; it was translated into the Russian, German, Japanese, and Czech languages and a cheap edition was brought out for sale in developing countries. I have received numerous letters mentioning that a particular lemma in the text or an isolated result mentioned in 'Complements and Exercises' has been useful in solving problems. The book contains a wide variety of results in matrix algebra and probability useful in research in mathematical statistics. Besides comprehensiveness, there are several novel features such as the unified theories of linear models and multivariate normal distribution including the case when the variance-covariance matrix is singular. This was possible through the use of generalized inverse of matrices, to which I have made extensive contributions, and density free approach in studying properties of random variables. Surprisingly, the unified approach is simpler, more elegant, and intuitive. 'It removes the mathematical trees and allows us to see the statistical wood.' It makes the study of statistics more interesting and provides the necessary inspiration for research.

"*LSI* is a comprehensive source for reference for all research workers as it provides a logically documented account of all aspects of statistical inference both in theory and applications. This, I think, accounts for its high citation.

"I have discussed numerous practical examples in my book involving the testing of a hypothesis. But one thing I may not like to do for obvious reasons is to test my wife's claim that the book is frequently cited because it was dedicated to her."

1. **Rao C R.** *Advanced statistical methods in biometric research.* New York: Wiley, 1952. 390 p.
2. **Garfield E.** Highly cited works in mathematics. Part 2. "Applied" mathematics. *Current Contents* (48):5-9, 28 November 1973. (Reprinted in: **Garfield E.** *Essays of an information scientist.* Philadelphia: ISI Press, 1977. Vol. 1. p. 509-13.)

Goldberg L R. Simple models or simple processes? Some research on clinical judgments. *Amer. Psychol.* **23**:483-96, 1968.
[Univ. Oregon and Oregon Research Inst., Eugene, OR]

This article reviewed the literature on the reliability and validity of clinical judgments, presented the rationale and procedures for regression analyses of the judgment process, described three such studies of professional decision-making, and presented preliminary results from an intensive attempt to teach clinical inference. [The *Social Sciences Citation Index*® *(SSCI*™) **indicates that this paper has been cited over 150 times since 1968.]**

Lewis R. Goldberg
College of Arts and Sciences
Department of Psychology
University of Oregon
Eugene, OR 97403

February 20, 1981

"When Jerry S. Wiggins wrote what is now considered to be the major textbook in personality assessment, he dedicated it 'To ORI: The people and the concept;' in the preface he praised '...the stimulating intellectual atmosphere which prevails at that institution.'[1] The place to which he referred was the Oregon Research Institute, which during the first decade of its existence (1960 to 1970) was probably as exciting a setting to pursue scientific problems as any in the world. Many of the leading scientists in the field of judgment and decision-making either worked at ORI (Paul Hoffman, Paul Slovic, Leonard Rorer, Gordon Bechtel, Sarah Lichtenstein, Robyn Dawes, and Baruch Fischhoff) or visited frequently (e.g., Ward Edwards, Kenneth Hammond, Adriaan de Groot, Nancy Hirschberg Wiggins, Amos Tversky, and Daniel Kahneman).

"My article was a paean to that institution. It reflected our mutual sense of discovery, and reviewed the literature we had produced, plus that of many others. Mostly, however, it was an account of our experimental *failures*—failures to demonstrate the complexities of human judgments that we and others assumed must characterize this important process.

"The founder of ORI, Hoffman, had published a seminal paper on judgment[2] in which he argued for the use of linear multiple regression analysis to study the way individuals use information in making their judgments or predictions. Since the previous anecdotal literature was filled with speculations about the complex interactions to be expected when professionals process clinical information, we had naively expected to find that the simple linear combination of cues would not be highly predictive of individuals' judgments, and consequently that we would soon be in the business of devising highly complex mathematical expressions to represent an individual's judgmental strategy. Alas, it was not to be: '...in study after study our initial hopes went unrealized; the accuracy of the linear model was almost always at approximately the same level as the reliability of the judgments themselves, and—no doubt because of this—the introduction of more complex terms into the basic equation rarely served to significantly increase the cross-validity of the new model.' My article may have been so highly cited because it made these ideas and findings widely available to psychologists in a nontechnical manner.

"Also reported in my article were the preliminary results from an extensive study by Leonard G. Rorer and myself on the learning of clinical inferences. What we learned was that intensive training with knowledge of outcomes (i.e., feedback) was not a sufficient condition for complex clinical learning to occur. Both types of findings eventually forced us, as well as investigators elsewhere, to consider the role of simplifying strategies (or heuristics) in complex decision-making.[3]

"One such heuristic that was soon discovered has been called 'availability': when people have to estimate the frequency of an event, they typically rely on the ease with which instances spring to mind. Use of such a tactic is not unreasonable, but under some circumstances it can lead us astray (e.g., the frequency of more striking or memorable events gets overestimated). So it is with me: had someone asked me to estimate which of my publications was the most frequently cited, I'd certainly have selected another!"[4]

1. **Wiggins J S.** *Personality and prediction: principles of personality assessment.* Reading, MA: Addison-Wesley, 1973. p. iii-iv.
2. **Hoffman P J.** The paramorphic representation of clinical judgment. *Psychol. Bull.* **57**:116-31, 1960.
3. **Tversky A & Kahneman D.** Judgment under uncertainty: heuristics and biases. *Science* **185**:1124-31, 1974.
4. **Goldberg L R.** Man versus model of man: a rationale, plus some evidence, for a method of improving on clinical inferences. *Psychol. Bull.* **73**:422-32, 1970. [The *Social Sciences Citation Index*® (*SSCI*™) indicates that this paper has been cited over 110 times since 1970.]

This Week's Citation Classic

Roenker D L, Thompson C P & Brown S C. Comparison of measures for the estimation of clustering in free recall. *Psychol. Bull.* **76**:45-8, 1971. [Kansas State University, Manhattan, KS]

Five measures of clustering are compared and their relative strengths and weaknesses evaluated. A new measure of clustering (ARC score) is proposed which is free of the limitations of previous measures and which is invariant with respect to irrelevant characteristics of recall. [The *Science Citation Index*® **(***SCI*®**) and the** *Social Sciences Citation Index*® **(***SSCI*®**) indicate that this paper has been cited in over 185 publications since 1971.]**

Daniel L. Roenker
Department of Psychology
Western Kentucky University
Bowling Green, KY 42101

December 17, 1982

"In the fall of 1969, I enrolled for my first semester of graduate work at Kansas State University. Having expressed an interest in the area of human memory, I enrolled in a seminar entitled 'Organizational Processes in Memory.' The seminar was taught by Chuck Thompson and Sam Brown. At the time, the organization of recall from memory was a critical topic because it was generally believed that the analysis of recall patterns was an effective way to understand the structure and processes of the human memory system. Two particular organizational phenomena had been isolated and were receiving considerable attention in the literature. The first of these was the phenomenon of clustering. If subjects were given a list of words to remember and these words fell into several conceptual categories, then subjects tended to recall the words in categorical groupings, even though not specifically instructed to do so. The second organizational phenomenon was termed subjective organization. In this case, when subjects were given a list of unrelated words to remember, they tended to recall the words in a specific order which stabilized over successive recall attempts.

"One of the requirements of the course was the preparation and presentation of a paper dealing with some issue or phenomenon in the area of organizational processes. The issue of the measurement of organization struck me as an area which I might be able to handle. A review of the literature showed that the available measures of organization, particularly clustering, had numerous problems. The primary problem that most of the measures suffered from was the fact that it was difficult to compare the amount of clustering under different experimental conditions. As a result, I attempted to develop a measure which was free of this problem as well as several others. An initial measure was proposed to the class which alleviated the problems associated with previous measures. However, it turned out to have a set of unique problems all its own. After much discussion with Chuck and Sam, a second measure (the ARC measure reported in the article) was developed. The following semester was devoted to preparing an article for publication.

"After the article had been submitted, we received word from the journal that another article on the same topic had been received at the same time. The editor requested that we exchange papers and each critique the other's measure. As a result, the article appeared with a companion article by Frankel and Cole[1] in the same issue of the journal.

"As to why the article has been cited so often, I'm not really sure. I would like to think that it is because the measure we proposed was a relatively sensitive measure of the phenomenon. A recent application of the measure may be found in an article by Masson and McDaniel."[2]

1. **Frankel F & Cole M.** Measures of category clustering in free recall. *Psychol. Bull.* **76**:39-44, 1971. [The *Social Sciences Citation Index* (*SSCI*) indicates that this paper has been cited in over 85 publications since 1971.]
2. **Masson M E J & McDaniel M A.** The role of organizational processes in long-term retention. *J. Exp. Psychol.—Hum. Learn. Mem.* **7**:100-10, 1981.

This Week's Citation Classic™

Scott W A. Reliability of content analysis: the case of nominal scale coding. *Public Opin. Quart.* **19**:321-5, 1955.
[Institute for Social Research, University of Michigan, Ann Arbor, MI]

This paper suggests an improved method of reporting the extent of interobserver agreement in assigning overt or verbal behavioral items to a set of categories. It was developed specifically for standard survey research coding operations, but it can be used in a wide variety of research situations to measure the reliability of classifying a large number of responses into nominal scale categories. The requirements are that the categories be mutually exclusive and that observations be duplicated on a random sample of the total set of responses being studied. [The *Science Citation Index*® (*SCI*®) and the *Social Sciences Citation Index*® (*SSCI*®) indicate that this paper has been cited in over 185 publications since 1955—one of the most cited for this journal.]

William A. Scott
Department of Psychology
Australian National University
Canberra 2600
Australia

July 24, 1984

"This was only my fourth experience, as a student, in publishing in a professional journal. I was quite surprised to learn that the article had attracted attention nearly 30 years later (see, for example, reference 1). Perhaps this is because it was an early attempt to confront a practical problem faced by investigators who found it appropriate to use open questions in their research. Also, it is shorter, more sharply focused, and more interestingly written than many of my subsequent papers. Perhaps it was easier for the relevant audience to understand than others' more complex treatments of the problem.

"We no longer have much occasion to use nominal-scale measures, but instead prefer to construct multiple-item summative scales to represent variables anticipated in advance. If responses are coded after the interview, we typically use a small number of categories that can readily be encompassed within some simple theoretical framework. Then we convert a nominal scale of *k* categories into *k* dichotomous variables. It is thus possible to represent the level of coding reliability for each category separately, using the intraclass correlation or *phi* coefficient.

"The preparation of this paper was encouraged in the stimulating environment of the University of Michigan's Survey Research Center, where I worked with colleagues and supervisors who had a marvelous capacity for giving ideas to each other, without concern for copyright. I still can't distinguish many of my own ideas from those of Steve Withey, George Belknap, Gerry Gurin, Libby Douvan, and Warren Miller, and this may account for my attitude toward plagiarism: it would be very annoying if someone tried to steal my last idea.

"The selection of *Public Opinion Quarterly* as an outlet stemmed from my previous experience publishing in that journal. Under encouragement from Ron Lippit, I had submitted a manuscript that grew out of a first-year graduate paper, reporting practical experience in the military government of Japan.[2] For 18 months I heard nothing, then back came a beautifully edited, shortened article in galley proofs. One hardly expects such assistance nowadays. It helped me adopt Don Campbell's advice in the face of many subsequent delays in production: 'Science is timeless.'

"I have recently learned of a PhD thesis in mathematics dealing with the *kappa* statistic[3-5] (*kappa* is a close relative of the *pi* statistic which I proposed). The eminent statistician who told me about it couldn't see how *kappa* was worth a thesis. But it seems it may have been worth four pages. As my paper was presented in the journal's section on 'Living Research,' it is gratifying to see that the baby has survived so long.

"On the occasion (sometime in the 1950s) of its radio broadcast of the 'Song of the Wood-Dove' from Arnold Schönberg's *Curre-Lieder*, the New York Philharmonic invited the composer to comment. His reply went something like this: 'As I wrote this piece 50 years ago, your performance of it now gives me hope that, 50 years hence, your eminent orchestra might get around to playing something I am writing today.' That's not such bad encouragement, after all!"

1. **Craig R T.** Generalization of Scott's index of intercoder agreement. *Public Opin. Quart.* **45**:260-4, 1981.
2. **Scott W A.** The information meeting as an instrument of social change in occupied Japan. *Public Opin. Quart.* **16**:160-78, 1952.
3. **Cohen J.** A coefficient of agreement for nominal scales. *Educ. Psychol. Meas.* **20**:37-46, 1960. (Cited 645 times since 1960.)
4. **Fleiss J L.** Measuring nominal scale agreement among many raters. *Psychol. Bull.* **76**:378-82, 1971. (Cited 120 times.)
5. **Landis J R & Koch G G.** The measurement of observer agreement for categorical data. *Biometrics* **33**:159-74, 1977. (Cited 75 times.)

CC/NUMBER 27
JULY 2, 1979

This Week's Citation Classic

Rosenthal R. *Experimenter effects in behavioral research.* New York, NY: Appleton-Century-Crofts, 1966. 464 p.

Within the context of a general discussion of the unintended effects of scientists on the results of their research, this work reported the growing evidence that the hypothesis of the behavioral scientist could come to serve as self-fulfilling prophecy, by means of subtle processes of communication between the experimenter and the human or animal research subject. [*The Science Citation Index*® (*SCI*®) **and the** *Social Sciences Citation Index* ™ *(SSCI*™*)* **indicate that this book has been cited over 740 times since 1966.**]

Robert Rosenthal
Department of Psychology
and Social Relations
Harvard University
Cambridge, MA 02138

January 10, 1978

"This work was published 10 years after I had unnecessarily, playfully, and compulsively re-analyzed statistically the data of my UCLA doctoral dissertation on the Freudian defense mechanism of projection. That re-analysis suggested strongly that my hypothesis or expectation about how the subjects should respond had somehow been communicated to the subjects so that my hypothesis might have become a self-fulfilling prophecy.

"The next few years were given over in part to a series of experiments showing that, far more often than could be expected if the null hypothesis were true, experimenters obtained results from their subjects that were in line with the hypotheses or expectations that we had randomly assigned to the experimenters we were studying. These 'experimenter expectancy effects' were obtained in studies of human and animal learning, in studies of personality and ability, in studies of reaction time and psychophysical judgments, and in studies of person perception and everyday life situations.

"The first few studies of this type met with a rather chilly reception, and unpublished manuscripts dominated both my desk and my curriculum vitae. In due course, after I moved from the University of North Dakota to Harvard University, those manuscripts were published.

"It's hard to be sure why this work is cited frequently but in most cases it seems due to three lines of implication; the first is methodological, the other two are substantive. The methodological implications of the work have to do with a variety of controls for the expectancy effects of the experimenter including increasing the number of experiments, observing the behavior of experimenters, analyzing experimenters for order effects and for computational errors, developing selection and training procedures, developing a new profession of data collector, maintaining blind and minimal contact, and employing expectancy control groups.[1,2]

"A second line of implication has to do with the everyday life occurrence of interpersonal expectation effects. Thus, not only do experimenters' expectations for their subjects' behavior actually affect that behavior, but teachers' expectations for the intellectual performance of their pupils can also come to serve as self-fulfilling prophecies.[3]

"Finally, the third line of implication has to do with the subtle processes of communications by which experimenters, teachers, and employers unintentionally communicate their expectations to their subjects, pupils, and employees. This line of implication is fascinating to me. For the last few years my colleagues (Judith A. Hall, M. Robin DiMatteo, Miron Zuckerman, Bella DePaulo, Dane Archer, and Peter L. Rogers) and I have been studying the related problem of measuring sensitivity to nonverbal communication in various channels such as tone of voice, body movements, and facial expression. The next few years may well be devoted to studying how a receiver's ability to decode nonverbal cues in various channels coupled with a sender's ability to encode nonverbal cues in various channels leads to certain kinds of interpersonal outcomes when experimenters, teachers, doctors, and employers interact with subjects, pupils, patients, and employees. It should be fun."

1. **Rosenthal R. & Rosnow R L** (eds.). *Artifact in behavioral research.* New York, NY: Academic Press, 1969. 400 p.
2. **Rosenthal R. & Rosnow R L** *The volunteer subject.* New York, NY: Wiley-Interscience, 1975. 266p.
3. **Rosenthal R & Jacobson L.**, *Pygmalion in the classroom.* New York, NY: Holt Rinehart & Winston, 1968. 240 p.

NUMBER 45
NOVEMBER 5, 1979

This Week's Citation Classic

Kirk R E. *Experimental design: procedures for the behavioral sciences.* Belmont, CA: Brooks/Cole Publishing Co., 1968. 577 p. [Baylor Univ., Psychol. Dept., Waco, TX]

A detailed coverage of the designs and statistical techniques that have the greatest potential use in behavioral and educational research is provided. Extensive coverage is given to multiple comparison procedures, trend analysis, measures of strength of association, and the relative efficiency of designs. Complex experimental designs are seen as combinations of two or more simpler building block designs. [The *Science Citation Index® (SCI®)* **and the** *Social Sciences Citation Index™ (SSCI™)* **indicate that this paper has been cited over 1,365 times since 1968.]**

Roger E. Kirk
Department of Psychology
Baylor University
Waco, TX 76703

October 2, 1979

"I started the first draft of *Experimental Design: Procedures for the Behavioral Sciences* in the spring of 1963. It was published in October, 1968—three and one-half years later than I had anticipated. I discovered during the process that authoring a book requires a major commitment of time and energy. But even if I had looked to an eight or ten year commitment it would not have deterred me, because by 1963 I was convinced that I had found something important to say about the design and analysis of experiments. At the time, I was teaching a two-semester graduate course on design and changing texts every other year. The students in my classes, behavioral science and education majors, were bright but mathematically unsophisticated. In a typical class only six percent had taken courses beyond college algebra. The textbooks available to me belonged to one of two categories: the excellent mathematically-oriented books that carried a calculus prerequisite, and the once-over lightly ones that emphasized rule of thumb procedures and covered only the most elementary designs. Books in the first category were not appropriate for my students, and I was not satisfied with those in the second. I saw a need for something in between, a readable book that covered both elementary and complex experimental designs without glossing over underlying assumptions or omitting important algebraic proofs. Since *Experimental Design* has become one of the most widely cited books in its field, such a need apparently existed.

"I had always assumed that authors write Chapter 1 first, Chapter 2 second, and so on. But I found myself writing Chapter 4 first, Chapter 8 second, and Chapter 7 third. Chapter 1 was written last. The three substantive contributions in the book which I consider the most important were: (1) development of my classification system for experimental designs accompanied by an abbreviated nomenclature, (2) identification of three designs—the completely randomized, randomized block, and Latin square designs—as building blocks from which all complex designs can be constructed, and (3) a more extensive treatment of multiple comparison procedures along with recommendations for their use. At least one reviewer did not share my enthusiasm for the 'simpler' nomenclature. He wrote, 'The author has a penchant for acronyms (who would guess that YBIB-t was a Youden square balanced incomplete block design?)...that would make the most imaginative Department of Defense official green with jealousy.'[1]

"*Experimental Design* contains numerous elements of personal significance. The book jacket, for example, sports the colors of Ohio State University, my alma mater, and the square matrix on the cover was inspired by the one on the dust jacket of *The Design of Experiments,* the classic text by Sir Ronald Fisher, that introduced me to the field."

1. **Taylor P A.** Review of *Experimental design: procedures for the behavioral sciences by* Roger E. Kirk. *Educ. Psychol. Meas.* **29**:218-21, 1969.

NUMBER 13
MARCH 26, 1979

This Week's Citation Classic

Orne M T. On the social psychology of the psychological experiment: with particular reference to demand characteristics and their implications. *Amer. Psychol.* **17**:776-83, 1962.

An effort was made to analyze the psychological experiment as a unique social form of interaction, emphasizing that the subject is not merely a passive responder to stimuli but an active participant whose perception of the total situation may profoundly affect his behavior. [The *SCI®* indicates that this paper has been cited over 740 times since 1962.]

Martin T. Orne
Department of Psychiatry
University of Pennsylvania
Philadelphia, PA 19139

April 7, 1978

"To systematically study man's behavior, it is necessary to carefully control the circumstances, which is often possible only in a psychological experiment. Yet it seemed to me that the experiment itself changes the circumstances of observation. I felt it would be necessary to examine the effects of being in an experiment in order to make inference from those circumstances to a larger life situation. It seemed naive to assume that human subjects respond only to those aspects of the experiment that we define as stimuli. Rather, they, as well as the experimenter, realized that there was a larger purpose in an experiment and that their perception of this larger purpose would affect how they perceived what was happening in the microcosm of the experiment and could dramatically alter their response. In a number of demonstrations it was possible to show how powerful the experimental setting is and how different some observations obtained in that setting would be from those obtained in another setting.

"This paper reported work done at the Massachusetts Mental Health Center, Boston. It appeared at a time when there was an increasing dissatisfaction with the naive behavioral approach. The observations affected all research with human subjects, and I proposed procedures for assessing the extent to which being in an experiment is likely to affect a subject's behavior. This explains why the paper became widely cited. It also helped focus attention on the subject as an active, thinking individual rather than as a passive responder. To the extent that this and other papers resulted in a concern with these issues, their purpose was served. Unfortunately, this work has also been used as the basis for criticizing all experimental research in psychology and as an argument to abandon such efforts. I cannot share this view since I would not have been concerned about analyzing the nature of the psychological experiment if it were not an essential tool to elucidate psychological processes.

"It appears to me that the difficulties with psychological experiments can best be conceptualized by assuming that in all studies there are two experiments: the one which the investigator intends and the one which the subject perceives. The ecological validity of the inferences drawn from any given experiment will largely depend upon how closely the experiment the subject perceives approximates the one the experimenter intends. We cannot assume the nature of the relationship, and our methodology must concern itself with assessing it empirically.

"Though I remain convinced that progress in science depends upon the merit of our hypotheses and the validity of our methodology, I also believe that methodological progress is most likely to follow from a concern with doing vigorous research on substantive issues. The 1962 paper evolved from the day-to-day efforts to systematically study the nature of hypnosis and assure that findings would generalize beyond the laboratory. We continue to innovate in our methodological approach, not as an abstract effort, but because it appears necessary to do so in order to obtain answers to specific substantive questions.

"The study of man will never be an easy matter. It will inevitably be complicated by the fact that our subjects, like ourselves, have purposes and motives, overt and hidden, that extend beyond the experimental situation but affect what they do in the experimental context. Such difficulties should not, however, cause us either to abandon experimental research nor to close our eyes to the problem. Rather, we need to recognize that a meaningful body of knowledge about how man thinks, acts, and experiences can only be created by developing techniques which permit systematic observations despite the fact that our subjects are, in varying degrees, inevitably active participants in the enterprise being studied."

Schaie K W. A general model for the study of developmental problems. *Psychol. Bull.* **64**:92-107, 1965.
[West Virginia University, Morgantown, WV]

Conventional longitudinal and cross-sectional methods are shown to be a special case of a general model for research on behavioral change over time. The complete model requires consideration of the components of age, time, and cohort differences. New research strategies are proposed that involve optimal combinations of the cross-sectional and longitudinal methods into sequential designs. [The *Social Sciences Citation Index*® (*SSCI*®) indicates that this paper has been cited in over 320 publications since 1966.]

K. Warner Schaie
Department of Individual
and Family Studies
College of Human Development
Pennsylvania State University
University Park, PA 16802

September 12, 1984

"As an undergraduate student of R.D. Tuddenham at the University of California at Berkeley, in 1951, I had become interested in changes in the adult development of psychometric intelligence. This interest led to a dissertation at the University of Washington, under the direction of C.R. Strother, that involved a cross-sectional study of the primary mental abilities from early adulthood into old age.[1] I was fortunate enough to obtain access to one of the earliest Health Maintenance Organizations (Group Health Cooperative of Puget Sound), from the membership of which I obtained my dissertation sample. Some years later, while preparing to teach a seminar on adult development, I became alerted to research findings suggesting that the steep linear age decrement in intelligence reported in cross-sectional studies (including my own) seemed contradicted by findings of longitudinal studies following the same individuals over time.[2] I consequently decided to do a follow-up of my cross-sectional study to permit comparison of cross-sectional and longitudinal data in the same population, as well as drawing a new sample from the same population. This initial follow-up actually led to what is now one of the major longitudinal studies of adult psychological development, now in its 28th year.[3]

"Results of our initial follow-up replicated the steep cross-sectional age differences, while showing much less pronounced age changes within individuals, not reaching significance until the late 1960s. This discrepancy led to theoretical analyses that showed the longitudinal and cross-sectional approaches to be special cases of a more general model for the study of change over time. Specifically, it became clear that cross-sectional data confounded age and cohort differences, while longitudinal data confounded age and time-of-measurement (period) effects. Thus, data obtained via the two methods can only agree if cohort and period effects are of trivial magnitude. A third method was then identified and named *time-lag* that compares samples of individuals of the same age at different points in time (e.g., college classes). This method, however, also confounds cohort and time-of-measurement effects.

"The general model specifies the three components of age, cohort (year of birth), and time of measurement (period). It was shown that similar to the relation of temperature, volume, and pressure in physics, specification of any two components would determine the third. As in physics, one might, however, be interested in any of the three different combinations of two components. This led to the introduction of what are now called *sequential methods* of developmental data collection and data-analysis strategies, including the *cohort-sequential*, *time-sequential*, and *cross-sequential* paradigms.[4] I have recently begun to show that the remaining dependencies can be addressed by redefining the general developmental model in noncalendar terms."[5]

1. **Schaie K W.** Rigidity-flexibility and intelligence: a cross-sectional study of the adult life span from 20 to 70 years. (Whole issue.) *Psychol. Monogr.* **72**(9), 1958. 26 p.
2. **Owens W A, Jr.** Age and mental abilities: a longitudinal study. *Genet. Psychol. Monogr.* **48**:3-54, 1953.
3. **Schaie K W.** The Seattle Longitudinal Study: a twenty-one year exploration of psychometric intelligence in adulthood. (Schaie K W, ed.) *Longitudinal studies of adult psychological development.* New York: Guilford Press, 1983. p. 64-135.
4. ----------------. Quasi-experimental designs in the psychology of aging. (Birren J E & Schaie K W, eds.) *Handbook of the psychology of aging.* New York: Van Nostrand Reinhold, 1977. p. 39-58.
5. ----------------. Historical time and cohort effects. (McCloskey K A & Reese H W, eds.) *Life-span developmental psychology: historical and generational effects.* New York: Academic Press, 1984. p. 1-15.

CC/NUMBER 47
NOVEMBER 22, 1982

This Week's Citation Classic

Gergen K J. Social psychology as history.
J. Personal. Soc. Psychol. **26**:309-20, 1973.
[Department of Psychology, Swarthmore College, Swarthmore, PA]

Theories of social behavior are not, as traditionally argued, subject to empirical correction and progressive refinement across time. Patterns of human conduct are, for the most part, historically contingent, thus rendering behavioral theory vulnerable to historical decay. Dissemination of theory may also hasten such decay. [The *Social Sciences Citation Index*® (*SSCI*®) **indicates that this paper has been cited in over 190 publications since 1973.]**

Kenneth J. Gergen
Department of Psychology
Swarthmore College
Swarthmore, PA 19081

September 22, 1982

"Although many of the ideas in this paper were developed while I was a graduate student, and later presented to seminars at Harvard University, at the time I saw little promise of publication. Not only did most of the important journals in the field discourage reflexive scrutiny, but my ideas were at variance with the traditionally accepted beliefs and all the more unlikely to be accepted from a fledgling scholar. It was not until I had published a sizable number of more traditional articles, and had thus gained membership in an elite organization, the Society for Experimental Social Psychology, that the door was opened to publishing my ideas. A presentation at a society meeting prompted the editor of the most central journal in the discipline to ask if I would submit a piece for possible publication. Many months after submission of the requested article, the editor indicated that he could find no one willing to review the piece. Later, when he agreed to publish, the article was placed at the end of the journal. In spite of its obscure positioning, however, the immediate result was somewhat staggering. Unlike anything I had written within the traditional mold, I received hundreds of reprint requests, letters of both support and disapproval, papers that extended or attacked the thesis, and many invitations to speak. On the other hand, the journal editor seemed to feel that he had made an error. He accepted only one paper[1] on the issues raised by my paper, a biting defense of traditional empiricism. This piece was allowed to exceed my own in length and was featured as a lead article. Response from me and all others was then barred as a matter of editorial policy. His stance was later adopted by his colleague, an editor of a second major journal. In this case, my extension of the initial article, an invited address to the American Psychological Association, was denied publication after it had passed peer review on the apparent grounds that it would damage the reputation of the field. This article was subsequently published in a European journal.[2]

"In spite of these various problems, the issues I have raised concerning the character of the science and its potential have become the focal point for several international symposia, special sections in other periodicals, interviews, and books. Many others are now engaging in reevaluation and one is able to recognize a significant movement to reconceptualize the nature of the science. Many of the critical issues surrounding this movement are now featured in my recent book, *Toward Transformation in Social Knowledge*.[3] There appear to be a number of reasons for the widespread interest in the initial article. First, the arguments represented an attack on the long prevailing understandings of the discipline. Their impact was enhanced by the fact that for ten years I had contributed actively to this tradition; in effect, I was not an outsider. In addition, the fact that the article appeared in the major periodical of the field seemed to give it positive sanction. However, the article also seemed to speak either directly or indirectly to the concerns of a broad number of investigators, particularly in the younger ranks, who had unexpressed doubts about the traditional cast of the discipline. It seemed to capture a certain aspect of a then unarticulated *Zeitgeist*."

1. **Schlenker B R.** Social psychology and science. *J. Personal. Soc. Psychol.* **29**:1-15, 1974.
2. **Gergen K J.** Experimentation in social psychology: a reappraisal. *Eur. J. Soc. Psychol.* **8**:507-27, 1978.
3. --------------. *Toward transformation in social knowledge*. New York: Springer-Verlag, 1982. 272 p.

CC/NUMBER 29
JULY 18, 1983

This Week's Citation Classic

Price D J D. *Little science, big science.*
New York: Columbia University Press, 1963. 119 p.
[Yale University, New Haven, CT]

This book contains four introductory lectures on quantitative methods in the analysis of historical and modern science: 1. Prologue to the science of science (exponential and logistical growth of scientific publication and manpower); 2. Galton revisited (productivity distributions, laws of Lotka and Zipf); 3. invisible colleges and the affluent scientific commuter (multiple discovery and authorship, Bradford's law, half-lives of papers); 4. political strategy for big scientists (saturation, language distribution, emergence of Japanese science, big science phenomena). [The *Science Citation Index*® *(SCI*®) **and the** *Social Sciences Citation Index*® *(SSCI*®) **indicate that this book has been cited in over 690 publications since 1963.]**

Derek J. de Solla Price
History of Science
Yale University
New Haven, CT 06520

May 18, 1983

"In 1949, I was at Raffles College (now the University of Singapore) when their new library, not yet built, received a complete set (1662-1930s) of the *Philosophical Transactions of the Royal Society of London*. I took the beautiful calf-bound volumes into protective custody and set them in ten-year piles on the bedside bookshelves. For a year I read them cover to cover, thereby getting my initial education as a historian of science. As a side product, noting that the piles made a fine exponential curve against the wall, I counted all the other sets of journals I could find and discovered that exponential growth, at an amazingly fast rate, was apparently universal and remarkably long-lived. In 1950, to mark my transition from physics and mathematics to the history of science, and from Asia back to Europe, I gave a paper on this topic to the International Congress for the History of Science in Amsterdam.[1,2] It passed totally unnoticed, and was very ill-received when I entered Cambridge for a second PhD in the new field. It went over like a lead balloon on a couple more trials, but I included it as the last lecture in an inaugural lecture series when I finally got a chair and a department at Yale University, and it was published in *Science since Babylon* in 1961.[3]

"Although most of my time was then given to straight history of science, mainly in ancient astronomy and scientific instrumentation, the exponential growth business needled me a lot, and I began to pursue other quantitative researches about science, stimulated much by Robert Merton's writings in the sociology of science, by Eugene Garfield's new book on citation indexing, and by rereading Desmond Bernal's books which had prepared my mind for the initial sensitivity that led me to this field in the first place. A few months after *Science since Babylon* hit the bookstores, I was asked if I would like to expand that last lecture into a new series for the Pegram lectures at Brookhaven. The series met with an enthusiastic reception from the physicists who were very interactive while I lived there working out the weekly lectures and writing them up for publication as I went along as I had done for the Yale lectures before. I ladled into those lectures all the half-baked results I had collected together in this non-field over the past several years, and tried to give the whole thing some measure of coherence. It was, apparently, an immediate success, and sold quite well among the scientists, remaining totally alien to the historians and historians of science. *Little Science, Big Science* became a success and a *Citation Classic*, I think, because just at that time there were two new fields emerging as part of the academic explosion of the 1960s, the sociology of science and library science (as distinct from library trade schools). Those two fields seemed to react almost alchemically with my offbeat development of quantitative methods in what was to become science of science or scientometrics; my book was accepted as one of the prime sources for the techniques and results.

"For recent reports of work in this field the reader should refer to the journal *Scientometrics* and *Essays of an Information Scientist*.[4] Also, a major book has appeared in Russian, but is not yet available in an English edition."[5]

1. **Price D J D.** Quantitative measures of the development of science. *Arch. Int. Hist. Sci.* **14**:85-93, 1951.
2. --------------. Quantitative measures of the development of science. *Actes du VI Congrès International d'Histoire des Science*, 1950, Amsterdam. Paris: Herman & Cie, 1951. p. 413-21.
3. --------------. *Science since Babylon*. New Haven, CT: Yale University Press, 1961. 149 p.
[The *SCI* and the *SSCI* indicate that this book has been cited in over 200 publications since 1961.]
4. **Garfield E.** *Essays of an information scientist*. Philadelphia: ISI Press, 1983. 5 vols.
5. **Haitun S D.** *Naukometriya*. Moscow: Akademiya Nauk, 1983. 344 p.

CC/NUMBER 27
JULY 7, 1980

This Week's Citation Classic

Kaplan A. *The conduct of inquiry: methodology for behavioral science.* San Francisco, CA: Chandler, 1964. 428 p.
[University of Michigan, Ann Arbor, MI]

Methodology for the behavioral sciences is not essentially different from that for other sciences. The task is not more closely to imitate physics or any other science but to do better what the behavioral sciences now do. The 'hard' and 'soft' styles need not strive to replace, but rather to improve, one another. [The *Social Sciences Citation Index® (SSCI™)* **indicates that this book has been cited over 740 times since 1966.]**

Abraham Kaplan
Department of Philosophy
University of Haifa
Mount Carmel, Haifa 31 999
Israel

December 30, 1979

"This book was written chiefly at the Center for Advanced Study at Wesleyan University (Connecticut). It was prompted by my distress at the outcome of the logical positivist tradition in which I had been trained. Though the philosophy championed science and scientific method, in practice its logic made for sterility and its positivism for superficiality.

"The philosophy was at fault because of its remoteness from actual scientific practice. It analysed such 'scientific generalizations' as 'all crows are black' and debated whether the belief was justified that the sun will rise tomorrow. My undergraduate major in laboratory chemistry, a hobby of observational astronomy, and a long interest in the history of science made me sympathetic to a more realistic pragmatism—for instance, in the spirit, if not in the conceptual structure, of John Dewey's *Logic: The Theory of Inquiry,*[1] the title I consciously echoed.

"The book has been translated into Spanish, Portuguese, and Hebrew; various sections and whole chapters have been reprinted in a half-dozen collections—of social science rather than of philosophy. I take this to be relevant to the frequency of its citation: I have tried to replace the judgmental posture of many philosophers of science by critical analysis in a more accepting vein.

"Acceptance has not prevented me from identifying common shortcomings, like 'the law of the instrument' (give a small boy a hammer and he will find that everything he runs into needs pounding) and 'the drunkard's search' (he hunts for his door key not where he dropped it but under the street-lamp, because it's lighter there).

"Formal requirements can be discerned only in substantive contents. Some of these contents were familiar to me because of personal association over the years with a variety of behavioral scientists. Some years spent consulting for the mathematics division of the Rand Corporation preserved and sharpened a sense of the power of abstraction as well as the importance of concreta.

"Science is not merely a set of propositions; it is the work of scientists and is localized in their belief in these propositions. Its growth depends above all on their belief in the worth of what they are doing. Behavioral scientists have good reason for such a belief."

1. **Dewey J.** *Logic: the theory of inquiry.* New York: H. Holt, 1938. 546 p.

Chapter

3

Biological Bases of Behavior

Areas of the brain and behavior / 63–68

Brain mechanisms and behavior / 69–73

This Week's Citation Classic

NUMBER 6
FEBRUARY 5, 1979

Kimble D P. Hippocampus and internal inhibition.
Psychol. Bull. **70**: 285-95, 1968.

Behavioral effects of hippocampal lesions are reviewed in a theoretical framework which suggests that the intact hippocampus is important in allowing animals to alter their behavior when environmental contingencies change. The hippocampus is proposed to interact with brainstem and thalamic arousal systems in these situations. [The *Science Citation Index*® *(SCI*® *)* **and the** *Social Sciences Citation Index*™ *(SSCI*™*)* **indicate that this paper has been cited 217 times since 1969.]**

Daniel Porter Kimble
Department of Psychology
University of Oregon
Eugene, OR 97403

January 18, 1978

"I first became interested in the hippocampus in the late 1950s as a graduate student at the University of Michigan. Robert Isaacson came in one day very excited about a recent report by Wilder Penfield and Brenda Milner concerning two neurological patients who displayed an amnesia for recent events, without either gross dementia or longer term amnesia. Penfield and Milner suggested that hippocampal destruction was responsible for this syndrome. Not having access to such patients, Isaacson persuaded Robert Y. Moore (now at the University of California School of Medicine at La Jolla) to show us how to locate and aspirate the hippocampus in laboratory rats. Using this approach, I completed my disseration with Isaacson (now at the University of Florida), examining several different behavioral effects of hippocampal lesions in rats. It soon became apparent that while there were some interesting behavioral changes, the recent memory loss seen in the human patients was not obvious in our animals.

"I came to the University of Oregon in 1963, where I was aided greatly by the stimulation and collaboration of my wife Reeva and several outstanding graduate students. These included Gary Coover, Ernie Greene, Linda Gummow, Carolyn Harley, Robert Kirkby, and Don Stein. We soon found ourselves struggling to find some conceptual framework into which to fit our various results as well as those of others. In several experiments we had been impressed by the dramatic persistence of the rats which had undergone hippocampal ablations to carry out previously learned tasks even when reward was no longer given. For example, we discovered that our lesioned rats would continue to run rapidly to an empty goal box which had previously contained water even after 100 or more consecutive unrewarded trials. Normal rats or rats with brain lesions restricted to the neocortex which overlies the hippocampus, would cease responding to such 'extinction' situations in less than 25 trials. In rereading Pavlov on experimental extinction it occurred to me to relate our findings to the theoretical notions of Pavlov, using his term of 'internal inhibition.' The final theoretical idea that went into the Bulletin paper was Magoun and Morruzzi's concept of the brainstem reticular formation and its thalamic connections as 'arousal' mechanisms. I proposed that the hippocampus might exert some inhibitory effects on those arousal systems.

"In the decade since publication, many experimenters have enlarged the possibilities concerning hippocampal functions, and, of course, our own ideas have changed too, although the exact role of the hippocampus in behavior remains speculative. The paper concluded: 'If the present formulation is useful for further research and speculation on hippocampal function, it will have served its primary purpose.' I am encouraged by the citation data to believe that this has happened."

CC/NUMBER 30
JULY 23, 1984

This Week's Citation Classic™

Douglas R J. The hippocampus and behavior. *Psychol. Bull.* **67**:416-42, 1967.
[Department of Psychiatry, Stanford Medical Center, CA]

The behavioral effects of hippocampal damage are reviewed, and it is concluded that they form a coherent pattern indicating the loss of a single underlying function. It is suggested that this function is akin to Pavlov's 'internal inhibition.' [The *Science Citation Index*® (*SCI*®) and the *Social Sciences Citation Index*® (*SSCI*®) indicate that this paper has been cited in over 540 publications since 1967.]

Robert J. Douglas
Department of Psychology
University of Washington
Seattle, WA 98195

May 22, 1984

"There are four reasons why this is a highly cited paper. First, it genuinely is an excellent paper. Second, it is a convenient reference to a whole era of research. Third, it appealed to a large group of prolific investigators. Finally, the time of publication was so 'ripe' that at least three other people were writing similar papers when mine appeared. Five of my other articles have been cited more than a hundred times each, but all lacked one or more of these factors and thus fell far short of the present paper in citations.[1-5] When I sat down to begin writing this paper, I knew that a 'classic' was about to be born, and the paper virtually 'wrote itself.' This was possible only because I happened to be at the right place at the right time when 'everything happened.' I worked simultaneously for both Bob Isaacson and 'Mac' McCleary.

"Although both labs were in Mason Hall at the University of Michigan, I was the only one who regularly commuted between Bob's top floor empire and Mac's basement dungeon. While the basic idea relating the hippocampus to inhibition was mine (I wrote it down in 1959), its elaboration owed much to Mac's brilliant analysis of avoidance behavior, Bob's insistence that Pavlov had the answer, and the data and ideas of students such as Dan Kimble, Dave Olton, Carol Van Hartesveldt, and many others. I could have written the paper in 1962, but I always assumed that Bob or Dan would review our work. Five years later, when I was in Pribram's lab at Stanford, I was overwhelmed by an urge to do the job myself.

"Although the paper revolves about theories, these were very rare because of the anti-theoretical climate of the times. As a result, I was forced to invent them just to spice up the discussion. One such space-filler, the 'working memory hypothesis,' has proved to be surprisingly viable. Of more significance, however, was the one idea I deliberately omitted. In my doctoral research, I had rediscovered 'spatial orientation' and realized that much, if not all, of the data could be explained in those terms. But at that time, the idea was considered to be 'crazy' and I was afraid to even mention it. Needless to say, O'Keefe and Nadel[6] and Olton[7] made the idea 'respectable,' and it has dominated the field in recent years.

"Finally, I am living proof that there is no causal relationship between citations and any other known measure of success. I have not received a single honor or award for this paper or any of the others that have elicited a total of over 1,750 citations. The latter are, however, an ample reward in and of themselves."

1. **Douglas R J & Isaacson R L.** Hippocampal lesions and activity. *Psychon. Sci.* **1**:187-8, 1964. (Cited 130 times.)
2. **Douglas R J.** Cues for spontaneous alternation. *J. Comp. Physiol. Psychol.* **62**:171-83, 1966. (Cited 130 times.)
3. **Douglas R J & Pribram K H.** Learning and limbic lesions. *Neuropsychologia* **4**:197-220, 1966. (Cited 160 times.)
4. **Douglas R J.** Pavlovian conditioning and the brain. (Boakes R A & Halliday M S, eds.) *Inhibition and learning.* London: Academic Press, 1972. p. 529-53. (Cited 120 times.)
5. **Isaacson R L, Douglas R J & Moore R Y.** The effect of radical hippocampal ablation on acquisition of avoidance response. *J. Comp. Physiol. Psychol.* **54**:625-8, 1961. (Cited 205 times.)
6. **O'Keefe J & Nadel L.** *The hippocampus as a cognitive map.* Oxford: Clarendon Press, 1978. 570 p.
7. **Olton D.** Spatial memory. *Sci. Amer.* **236**:82-98, 1977.

This Week's Citation Classic

NUMBER 10
MARCH 5, 1979

Kimura D. Cerebral dominance and the perception of verbal stimuli. *Can. J. Psychol.* **15**:166-71, 1961.

When different words are presented simultaneously to the two ears, report is more accurate for the ear opposite the cerebral hemisphere in which speech is represented. For most people, the left hemisphere is dominant for speech, and consequently the right ear is more accurately reported. [The *Science Citation Index®* **(*SCI®*) and the** *Social Sciences Citation Index™* **(*SSCI™*) indicate that this paper has been cited 260 times since 1961.]**

Doreen Kimura
Department of Psychology
University of Western Ontario
London, Ontario, Canada N6A 5C2

January 18, 1978

"Although I am rather fond of this paper, I have long since left the field of dichotic listening, and had lately begun to feel that I had finally lived down my association with it!

"This research formed part of my doctoral dissertation in psychology at McGill University. I was working with Dr. Brenda Milner at the Montreal Neurological Institute on the role of the temporal lobes in perception and memory, and I wanted a demanding test of speech perception. Dr. Woodburn Heron suggested that I use the dichotic listening technique devised by Donald Broadbent in England. This consisted in presenting two different digits to the two ears simultaneously, three such pairs in succession, after which the subject reported all the digits he could, in any order he liked.[1] Broadbent had used this method to study certain features of attention span.

"Accordingly, Dr. Heron and I got together to make a tape. Money for apparatus was not plentiful and we had to make do with a very imperfect stereophonic tape recorder, and a rather crude method of marking the tapes, which unfortunately left a bit of noise on them. All in all, the final tape was not an elegant piece of work, but I got around the problem of possible asymmetry in the channels by simply counterbalancing channels over ears. Many people have written for a copy of this early tape, and I have embarrassedly explained that they would be better off making their own.

"When I played the tape to neurological patients, I found, as expected, that patients with damage to the left half of the brain were impaired in reporting the words accurately, compared to patients with right-hemisphere damage. But a more intriguing finding was that most patients, regardless of the locus of their damage, reported more words accurately from the right ear than from the left. Broadbent had not reported any such ear differences in his studies, and when I asked other people who were using the dichotic listening task whether they got a right-ear effect in normal subjects, they assured me they did not, and that it must be some kind of artifact.

"Still, the effect was so strong in patients that I decided to test a small group of normal subjects, and sure enough, they also showed a significant right-ear superiority. I thought the effect might be due to the fact that the right ear had better connections with the opposite left hemisphere, which processes speech in most people (crossed pathways are commonly predominant in the nervous system). It followed that in patients who had speech represented in the right hemisphere, the left ear ought to be more accurate; and that, in fact, turned out to be true, when I looked at a small group of patients with right-hemisphere speech.

"These ear asymmetries are not due to sensory properties of the ears but to their central nervous system connections. I subsequently showed that, if melodic patterns (more dependent on the right hemisphere), were dichotically presented to normal subjects, the left ear would be favoured, in the same people who favoured the right ear for speech material.[2]

"The reason this paper became so popular is that it provided a technique for studying functional brain asymmetry in normal persons, whereas previously this could only be studied in patients with nervous system damage. By systematically varying certain characteristics of the stimuli presented to the two ears, and studying the ear differences, one could make inferences about characteristics of specialization of function in left and right hemispheres. This general principle holds also for visual and possibly tactual, modalities."[3]

REFERENCES

1. **Broadbent D E.** The role of auditory localization in attention and memory span. *J. Exp. Psychol.* **47**:191-6, 1954.
2. **Kimura D.** Left-right differences in the perception of melodies. *Quart. J. Exper. Psychol.* **14**:335-8, 1964.
3. **Kimura D.** Dual functional asymmetry of the brain in visual perception. *Neuropsychologia* **4**:275-85, 1966.

This Week's Citation Classic

NUMBER 11
MARCH 12, 1979

Teitelbaum P & Epstein A N. The lateral hypothalamic syndrome: recovery of feeding and drinking after lateral hypothalamic lesions. *Psychol. Rev.* **69**:74-90, 1962.

After bilateral lateral hypothalamic damage in rats, eating and drinking are abolished. Recovery occurs gradually, in behavioral stages that reveal: (a) eating recovers before drinking; (b) peripheral stimuli (taste of food, dry mouth) can motivate ingestion, but central regulation may still be absent; (c) later, central control systems appear to recover separately. [The *Science Citation Index®* *(SCI®)* **and the** *Social Sciences Citation Index™(SSCI™)* **indicate that this paper has been cited over 345 times since 1963.]**

Philip Teitelbaum
Department of Psychology
University of Illinois Urbana-Champaign
Champaign, IL 61820

January 30, 1978

"As a psychology graduate student at Johns Hopkins under Eliot Stellar's direction, I was trying to produce hypothalamic obesity. We failed at first, so we varied our lesion placements. Several animals refused to eat and drink until they died. I dismissed it as surgical trauma. Later, Anand and Brobeck localized a hypothalamic area controlling feeding.[1] Our aphagic animals' lesions were always at the coordinates they specified. We felt like kicking ourselves for missing an obviously important finding.

"But our failure had a silver lining. Believing the animals merely debilitated, I tried coaxing them to eat. Earlier, while cleaning the department's rat colony (my assistantship), I used to stop, munch chocolate bars, and offer the rats some. I soon discovered that shortly before my break, many rats were lined up at the front of each cage, all waiting for their treat. Later, I remembered this when trying to tempt aphagics to eat. Nevertheless, it was a thrill to see a rat, being kept alive by tube-feeding, refusing ordinary food and water for two months postoperatively, suddenly gobble up bits of chocolate.

"Strangely, such rats ate Hershey's milk chocolate, but refused Nestle's. Naively, I wrote to Hershey's describing our findings, asking for their formula, so that I could isolate the essential ingredient that induced our rats to eat. No answer. Years later, through the intervention of Charles King, father of Fred King, a fellow graduate student, I eventually got a letter from someone at Hershey's, gently informing me that the formula for their milk chocolate was their most closely guarded secret.

"A few years later, at the University of Pennsylvania, Alan Epstein and I (both of us had been students of Eliot Stellar's and we were old friends from Hopkins) joined our common interests in hunger and thirst. By then, there was controversy about the effects of lateral hypothalamic damage. We realized that such damage produced a syndrome that changed rapidly with recovery. Both hunger and thirst were affected but they recovered at different rates.

"Stages of recovery are now a standard method for operationally defining both the degree of disorganization and the progress of recovery after such damage. This is one reason for our paper's wide citation. Others are: (1) In late recovery, when such animals eat relatively normally, we found separable deficits in subcomponents of hunger and thirst. In part, Epstein's later work on angiotensin and thirst grew from this. (2) The dopaminergic nigrostriatal bundle, implicated in Parkinsonism, is also involved in the lateral hypothalamic syndrome.[2] This has linked two huge areas of research.

"The syndrome still fascinates me. It is gratifying that it interests others as well."

References

1. **Anand B K & Brobeck J R.** Hypothalamic control of food intake in rats and cats. *Yale J. Biol. Med.* **24**:123-40, 1951.
2. **Ungerstedt U.** Aphagia and adipsia after 6-hydroxydopamine induced degeneration of the negro-striatal dopamine system. *Acta Physiol. Scand. Suppl.* **367**:95-122, 1971.

Valenstein E S, Cox V C & Kakolewski J W. Reexamination of the role of the hypothalamus in motivation. *Psychol. Rev.* 77:16-31, 1970.
[Fels Research Institute, Yellow Springs, OH]

Evidence challenging the prevailing view of discrete hypothalamic 'motivation centers' was presented. It was shown that: (1) identical hypothalamic stimulation evoked different behaviors following environmental changes; (2) individuals tended to respond idiosyncratically to stimulation; (3) motivational states such as hunger could not explain evoked behavior; and (4) anatomical specificity for evoking different behaviors had been exaggerated. [The *Science Citation Index*® (*SCI*®) and the *Social Sciences Citation Index*® (*SSCI*®) indicate that this paper has been cited in over 175 publications since 1970.]

Elliot S. Valenstein
Neuroscience Laboratory
University of Michigan
Ann Arbor, MI 48109

November 22, 1983

"It will be recalled that W.R. Hess[1] had observed that electrical stimulation at some hypothalamic sites made cats eat voraciously. Later, Greer[2] used electrical stimulation to demonstrate a hypothalamic 'drinking center' in rats and his report was soon followed by a succession of brief publications describing hypothalamic 'centers' not only for eating and drinking, but also for aggression, sex, hoarding, and other behaviors. Although the list kept increasing, there were few serious attempts to study the behavior that was evoked.

"In reviewing this literature, we were impressed by the anatomical overlap of what was presumed to be 'separate' motivational systems. Our first study clearly demonstrated that if animals were given the opportunity, they usually displayed several different behaviors when stimulated. It began to appear that much of the specificity was in the interest of previous investigators. We became most anxious to explore further.

"Our laboratory was in the Fels Research Institute where Verne Cox and I had recently been joined by Jan Kakolewski. These were heady times! When we had an idea for an experiment, we usually continued discussing it as we pushed furniture into the hall to create a 'temporary' lab. Typically, we were operating on animals in an 'assembly line' on the same day. Antioch University undergraduates kept records, and handed us shaved, numbered, and anesthetized animals. After operating, we passed the animals to other students who were thrilled to be allowed to close the incisions. Usually, we were collecting data only a few days after our 'inspiration.'

"We soon completed several studies that questioned whether stimulation actually made animals hungry or thirsty as had been claimed. For example, animals that ate during stimulation usually switched from eating to another behavior rather than to eating a normally acceptable, but different, food. Or animals that drank would continue to lick empty water bottles when stimulated with no evidence of the behavior extinguishing. When we had accumulated a significant amount of histological data, we were forced to question the anatomical specificity others claimed. It also became clear that some animals were predisposed to display the same evoked behavior when aroused by stimulation at different sites. These results and others required a reexamination of hypothalamic function.

"The response to our article was enthusiastic, but bimodal. Many felt that an analysis of evoked behavior was long overdue and were pleased to see 'electrode phrenology' criticized. Others decided, however, that our approach was heuristically sterile and characterized it as 'Lashlian equipotentiality' theory in new clothes. Although the phenomena we described proved easy to replicate, the controversy has continued. Perhaps it's due to rose-colored glasses, but I believe our conclusions have gained support. Briefly, over the ensuing years, different types of evidence have indicated that stimulated animals are not hungry or thirsty; the same behavior was shown to be evoked after moving the electrode; arousal by such nonspecific stimuli as tail-pinch could also evoke several different behaviors.[3,4] The importance of individual predisposition has also been confirmed by additional studies. Recently, Guy Mittleman and I have found that animals that eat or drink during hypothalamic stimulation show the most ingestive behavior when aroused by other means than brain stimulation. We are not claiming, however, that we have a method for selecting animals that are arrested at Freud's 'oral stage' of development."

1. **Hess W R.** *The functional organization of the diencephalon.* New York: Grune & Stratton, 1957. 180 p.
2. **Greer M A.** Suggestive evidence of a primary "drinking center" in hypothalamus of rat. *Proc. Soc. Exp. Biol.* **89**:59-62, 1955.
3. **Valenstein E S.** The interpretation of behavior evoked by brain stimulation. (Wauquier A & Rolls E T, eds.) *Brain-stimulation reward.* Amsterdam: North-Holland, 1976. p. 557-75.
4. ------------------. Brain mechanisms of reinforcement. (Sweet W H, Obrador S & Martin-Rodriguez J, eds.) *Neurosurgical treatment in psychiatry, pain, and epilepsy.* Baltimore, MD: University Park Press, 1977. p. 27-49.

This Week's Citation Classic

NUMBER 14
APRIL 2, 1979

Hebb D O. Drives and the CNS (conceptual nervous system). *Psychol. Rev.* **62**:243-54, 1955.

Psychological evidence puts human motivation on a continuum of arousal, from deep sleep to strong emotion. Optimal levels for adaptive behavior are in the middle of the continuum. [The *Science Citation Index®* *(SCI®)* **and the** *Social Sciences Citation Index™* *(SSCI™)* **indicate that this paper has been cited over 380 times since 1964.]**

Donald Olding Hebb
RR 1 Chester Basin
Nova Scotia BOJ 1KO

February 7, 1978

"This paper was mainly concerned with the behavioral meaning of the arousal system or ARAS (ascending reticular activating system) recently discovered by G. Moruzzi and H.W. Magoun.[1] This was one of an exciting series of physiological developments offering a new basis for understanding brain and mind. Earlier ones were incorporated in my book, *Organization of Behavior,* but not this one, for it was reported only in the year my book was published, 1949.[2]

"The title of the paper was a little joke. B.F. Skinner, who thinks that psychology should have nothing to do with the brain, had had his joke earlier. He said that for psychology CNS stands for 'conceptual' (instead of central) nervous system. Perhaps he was right; at the best, neurophysiology still has a long way to go; but if we have to conceptualize the nervous system, let's conceptualize it as well as we can. And perhaps Skinner's own views were more affected than he knew by an earlier nervous system. So what I proposed to do was to bring Skinner's CNS, and mine, up to date.

"Behavior at the time was mostly regarded as a matter of stimulus and response controlled by reward and punishment, and the new physiological information was changing all that. The brain was no longer inert unless stimulated from outside. The higher animal especially might then be intrinsically motivated, not solely by biological drives (hunger, pain, sex). But now Moruzzi and Magoun added a further point. Spontaneous activity of the cortex is unorganized and without behavioral effect, unless there is also arousal, a maintained excitation from ARAS. This in turn depends on a background of varied, nonspecific sensory stimulation. So motivation required sensory stimulation after all.

"We were then concluding our 'sensory deprivation' experiments, at McGill University which were really experiments on boredom. The subjects were only deprived of variety in their sensory input. The intense need that developed to escape the monotony was very enlightening. There is a continuum of arousal, from deep sleep to strong emotion. At low levels, any action moderately raising the level of arousal is supported by ARAS, and the subject acts as if seeking excitement. At high levels we may suppose that support is too great and makes conflicting reaction tendencies nullify one another. Now any act that lowers arousal will be supported, so the subject escapes from or avoids the situation that causes the high excitement.

"This theoretical scheme made sense of the anomalous fear-seeking behavior of mountain-climbing (and roller-coasters), and the attraction of puzzles and intellectual games like bridge and chess, as escapes from boredom. On the other side of the coin, it made intelligible the impaired thought and action in crisis situations ('paralysis of terror'), and perhaps also fainting at watching a surgical operation. Such phenomena were well-known but omitted from the textbooks, presumably for lack of the rationale that ARAS could now provide. Unlike Skinner, I think 'neurologizing' can be a stimulant."

1. **Moruzzi G & Magoun H W.** Brain stem reticular formation and activation of the EEG. *EEG Clin. Neurophysiol.* **1**:455-73, 1949.
2. **Hebb D O.** *Organization of behavior.* New York: Wiley, 1949. 335 p.

This Week's Citation Classic

NUMBER 43
OCTOBER 22, 1979

Carlton P L. Cholinergic mechanisms in the control of behavior by the brain. *Psychol. Rev.* **70**:19-39, 1963.
[Squibb Institute for Medical Research, New Jersey]

A number of experimental results cohere in suggesting that brain-acetylcholine acts to inhibit nonrewarded behaviors. This activity thereby provides a kind of 'guidance system' by which irrelevant behaviors are eliminated from the animal's goal-directed repertoire of responses. [The *Science Citation Index®* *(SCI®)* and the *Social Sciences Citation Index ™ (SSCI™)* indicate that this paper has been cited over 300 times since 1963.]

Peter L. Carlton
Department of Psychiatry
Institute of Mental Health Sciences
Rutgers Medical School
Piscataway, NJ 08854

August 6, 1979

"Shortly after I had received my Ph.D., about 20 years ago, I was employed at the Squibb Institute for Medical Research. The situation was an uncomfortable one because, although I knew something about behavior, I knew nothing about drugs. Fortunately, the Institute then supported a basic research program of which I was a part. Thus, I was able to set out on a course of remediation under the superb tutelage of the late B.N. Craver. That period at the Institute was, in effect, a postdoctoral experience that could not have been duplicated elsewhere.

"I soon came to realize that, of the many classes of drugs, the anticholinergics were among the best understood because the role of acetylcholine in the peripheral nervous system had been well worked out. It occurred to me that if it could be assumed that the peripheral rules about the anticholinergics applied to the brain, it might be possible to use these drugs as tools to understand some of the normal brain mechanisms that control behavior. That is, if it were possible to attenuate the actions of brain-acetylcholine and observe the behavioral consequences, it might be possible to infer the role of acetylcholine when its function was not attenuated. The logic was the same as that in neurology where the effects of a lesion permit inferences about function when the lesion is absent. The fundamental difference was that I was thinking in terms of chemically defined, not anatomically defined, systems in the brain.

"About two years later I had learned a great deal about general pharmacology and had a vast collection of data on the anticholinergics that I did not understand. At that time I reread an article by E. Hearst[1] for what must have been the fourth or fifth time. Hearst had found that the normal decline in responding due to nonreward did not occur when anticholinergics were given. Thus, acetylcholine might be required for nonreward to have its impact on behavior. Furthermore, it dawned on me that this simple idea could account for the otherwise confusing array of data I had on hand. Those data and that idea were the basis of this paper.

"In retrospect, I am both gratified and disappointed by the attention the paper has ultimately received. On the positive side, the most important idea that drugs can be used as analytical tools for understanding behavior has apparently made its impact; the effects of the anticholinergics are certainly better understood; some anatomical bases for the chemically defined processes have been elucidated. On the negative side, a great deal of the research that the paper engendered has been directed at testing something called 'Carlton's theory' when there is, in fact, no theory to be tested at a purely behavioral level. The paper embodies a very circumstantial conjecture that can only be evaluated by direct measurement of acetylcholine activity, independently of the behavioral effects themselves. That process of evaluation has not been undertaken."

1. **Hearst E.** Effects of scopolamine on discriminated responding in the rat. *J. Pharmacol. Exp. Ther.* **126**:349-58, 1959.

This Week's Citation Classic™

Vanderwolf C H. Limbic-diencephalic mechanisms of voluntary movement. *Psychol. Rev.* **78**:83-113, 1971.
[University of Western Ontario, London, Canada]

Studies of the role of the diencephalon and hippocampal formation in behavior are discussed in relation to the concept that activity in ascending reticulocortical mechanisms is closely linked to voluntary movement. The importance of Jackson's concept of levels of function[1] is emphasized. [The *Science Citation Index*® (*SCI*®) and the *Social Sciences Citation Index*® (*SSCI*®) indicate that this paper has been cited in over 210 publications since 1971.]

C.H. Vanderwolf
Department of Psychology
University of Western Ontario
London, Ontario N6A 5C2
Canada

November 3, 1983

"When I arrived at McGill University in 1958, D.O. Hebb suggested that I work on the medial thalamus. I found that rats with large lesions of this region could not avoid a painful shock by running away although they could escape readily. As training continued, the rats began to squeal immediately prior to the shock (as if in fear), even though they did not move. If shock was omitted, the rats would often run away suddenly after a long initial delay. These observations made a great impression on me. The fact that the thalamic lesions interfered with the initiation of running, but not with vocalization, recalled Jackson's distinction between 'voluntary' and 'automatic' movements.[1]

"One day, over a beer, I described this work to Woody Heron who suggested that we could record from the medial thalamus at his lab at McMaster University, and look for a relation to motor activity. We discovered that rhythmical 'theta waves' occurred in both the medial thalamus and hippocampus during locomotion but were not ordinarily present during alert immobility or grooming behavior.[2] Since I suspected that the thalamic waves might be generated in the hippocampus, I began a detailed study of hippocampal activity in relation to movement.[3] The term rhythmical slow activity (RSA) was introduced because the editor (C. Ajmone Marsan) of *Electroencephalography and Clinical Neurophysiology* **insisted that waves with a frequency up to 12 Hz could not be 'theta waves.' The term 'RSA' has since come into widespread use.**

"The *Psychological Review* **paper summarized what I had learned (including extensive references to the unpublished work of two able graduate students, Brian Bland and Ian Whishaw) and related it to the control of voluntary movement. It received two unenthusiastic reviews. I thought the criticisms were not entirely justified and the editor (C.N. Cofer) obtained a third review (from Steve Glickman as I learned later) which recommended publication.**

"I think the paper is cited mainly because it contains a description of the relation between hippocampal slow waves and behavior. Many people regarded the idea that the hippocampus plays a role in the control of movement as not merely wrong but slightly crazy. However, the observations have been confirmed repeatedly and serve as the basis for further work on both the hippocampus and neocortex."[4-6]

1. **Taylor J,** ed. *The selected writings of John Hughlings Jackson*. London: Staples Press, 1958. 2 vols.
2. **Vanderwolf C H & Heron W.** Electroencephalographic waves with voluntary movement. Study in the rat. *Arch. Neurol.* **11**:379-84, 1964.
3. **Vanderwolf C H.** Hippocampal electrical activity and voluntary movement in the rat. *Electroencephalogr. Clin. Neuro.* **26**:407-18, 1969. (Cited 210 times.)
4. **Vanderwolf C H & Robinson T E.** Reticulocortical activity and behavior: a critique of the arousal hypothesis and a new synthesis. *Behav. Brain Sci.* **4**:459-514, 1981.
5. **Vanderwolf C H.** The role of the cerebral cortex and ascending activating systems in the control of behavior. (Satinoff E & Teitelbaum P, eds.) *Handbook of behavioral neurobiology*. New York: Plenum Press, 1983. Vol. 6. p. 67-104.
6. **Robinson T E,** ed. *Behavioral approaches to brain research*. New York: Oxford University Press, 1983. 352 p.

CC/NUMBER 16
APRIL 16, 1984

This Week's Citation Classic™

Bakan P. Hypnotizability, laterality of eye-movements and functional brain asymmetry. *Percept. Mot. Skills* **28**:927-32, 1969.
[Michigan State University, East Lansing, MI]

The direction of lateral eye movement upon reflection in answering a question is related to hypnotizability. Leftward eye movement is related to greater hypnotizability. Lateral eye movement and hypnotizability are related in terms of functional asymmetry of the cerebral hemispheres. [The *Social Sciences Citation Index*® (*SSCI*®) indicates that this paper has been cited in over 185 publications since 1969.]

Paul Bakan
Department of Psychology
Simon Fraser University
Burnaby, British Columbia V5A 1S6
Canada

February 20, 1984

"In 1968, I was awarded the Thomas Welton Stanford Fellowship to work in E.R. Hilgard's Laboratory for Hypnosis Research at Stanford University. My interest at that time was in investigating correlates of the lateral eye movements associated with the beginning of reflective thought after a person is asked a question. It had earlier been shown that the direction of those lateral eye movements was characteristic for each individual and that a person could be classified as a right or left mover. It was suggested that left movers were more subjectively oriented than right movers.[1] Since highly hypnotizable subjects had also been described as subjectively oriented,[2] I decided to test the hypothesis that left movers were more hypnotizable than right movers. This hypothesis was confirmed and the results were reported in my 1969 paper.

"In considering an explanation of this result, I felt that there might be a relationship between my results and brain laterality. Functional asymmetry of the right and left cerebral hemispheres was then an area of growing interest, especially in light of reports of the results of split-brain surgery. My search of the literature on eye movements revealed that lateral eye movements are contralaterally controlled, i.e., right hemisphere stimulation leads to left eye movements and left hemisphere stimulation leads to right eye movements. In my paper, I proposed that the characteristic direction of lateral eye movements in individuals was a reflection of relative hemispheric dominance, or hemisphericity. I interpreted the right-left eye movement typology as a left-right hemisphere typology, with right movers considered as left hemisphere people and left movers as right hemisphere people. The behavior of the right mover is related to greater reliance on left hemisphere functioning and that of the left mover to greater reliance on right hemisphere functioning. The association between hypnotizability and left eye movements was due, I concluded, to a greater reliance of hypnotizable people on the right hemisphere. The theory also suggests a possible localization of hypnotizability in the right hemisphere of the brain.

"The high citation count for this paper is due to several factors. The interpretation of the right-left eye movement typology in terms of a left-right hemisphere typology was congruent with the explosive interest in brain laterality. Individual differences in behavior could now be seen as differences in lateral hemispheric organization. An easily observable eye movement response became available as an indication of hemisphericity.[3] The paper suggested a possible localization of hypnotizability in the right hemisphere and provided a simple indicator of hypnotizability. More generally, the work served as a bridge between the interest in states of consciousness and brain laterality. The paper has stimulated a large body of research tending to support the theoretical position. Subsequent work on CLEMS (the acronym I use for conjugate lateral eye movements) has been the subject of several reviews."[4-6]

1. **Day M E.** An eye-movement phenomenon relating to attention, thought and anxiety. *Percept. Mot. Skills* **19**:443-6, 1964. (Cited 110 times.)
2. **Hilgard J R.** *Personality and hypnosis.* Chicago: University of Chicago Press, 1979. 309 p.
3. **Bogen J E, DeZure R, Ten Houten W D & March J E.** The other side of the brain. IV: the A/P ratio. *Bull. LA Neurological Soc.* **37**:49-61, 1972. (Cited 90 times.)
4. **Bakan P.** Two streams of consciousness: a typological approach. (Pope K S & Singer J L, eds.) *The stream of consciousness: scientific investigations into the flow of human experience.* New York: Plenum Press, 1978. p. 159-86.
5. **Ehrlichman H & Weinberger A.** Lateral eye movements and hemispheric asymmetry: a critical review. *Psychol. Bull.* **85**:1080-101, 1978. (Cited 95 times.)
6. **Gur R & Gur R.** Correlates of conjugate lateral eye movements in man. (Harnad S, Doty R W, Goldstein L, Jayne S J & Krauthamer G, eds.) *Lateralization in the nervous system.* New York: Academic Press, 1977. p. 261-84.

CC/NUMBER 44
NOVEMBER 3, 1980

This Week's Citation Classic

Groves P M & Thompson R F. Habituation: a dual-process theory. *Psychol. Rev.* 77:419-50, 1970.
[Dept. Psychobiology, Univ. California, Irvine, CA]

A series of experiments characterizes neurons in the spinal cord that could produce the simple forms of learning, habituation, and sensitization. A dual-process theory is developed in which the plasticity of a behavioral response to an iterated sensory stimulus may be accounted for by interacting populations of interneurons in the spinal cord and brain. [The *Science Citation Index*® *(SCI*®*)* **and the** *Social Sciences Citation Index*® *(SSCI*™*)* **indicate that this paper has been cited over 275 times since 1970.]**

Philip M. Groves
Department of Psychiatry
School of Medicine
University of California
La Jolla, CA 92093

July 28, 1980

"Graduate studies in psychobiology at the University of California at Irvine were just beginning in the late 1960s, where the experimental work described in this publication was carried out. I feel very fortunate to have been one of the early students in the psychobiology program there. I had tried several areas of research in psychobiology before settling on studies of the cat spinal cord, in part because it was exhilarating to work on a classic problem in the study of behavior with a preparation of such significance in the history of the neurosciences. You thought that you could actually experience the feelings of Sherrington and the many other historical figures who had studied the spinal cord and used it to discover and to solve important issues of the day in brain research. This work fit into the scheme of things and seemed to be contributing to a line of conceptual and empirical development with a rich history and a certainty that others who followed you would be equally rewarded.

"Of course, the reasons that this publication has been cited frequently do not have much to do with the experimental work, and I think that the experiments that I do now are probably a lot better. One certainly hopes that one's experimental work will get better after being at it for more than a decade. But this paper provided an experimental and conceptual framework for understanding the neural substrates of these simple forms of learning which seems to have applicability across particular experimental preparations and different levels of analysis. It represented a simple model and theoretical scheme for understanding how changes in the activity of certain nerve cells could lead to similar changes in behavior. It also accounted for a wider domain of behavioral plasticity than had been the case in previous attempts. But most importantly, it fit into the history of work on the phenomena of habituation and sensitization. In fact, a frequently cited paper by Richard F. Thompson and the late W. Alden Spencer published in 1966,[1] had already predicted such an account, based upon experimental work published by Spencer, Thompson, and Nielson that same year.[2-4] Indeed, the theoretical and experimental setting for my thesis work, and the formal direction given the field by this publication in 1970, were more the work of Thompson, with whom I took my degree, than myself. A remarkably similar experimental and theoretical analysis of the neural mechanisms underlying these simple forms of learning was developed at about the same time by Eric Kandel and his associates using an invertebrate model system, as described elegantly in his recent text.[5] I am pleased to have been a contributor to a problem of longstanding interest in biological psychology and the neurosciences."

1. **Thompson R F and Spencer W A.** Habituation: a model phenomenon for the study of neuronal substrates of behavior. *Psychol. Rev.* **173**:16-43, 1966.
2. **Spencer W A, Thompson R F & Nielson D R, Jr.** Response decrement of flexion reflex in the acute spinal cat and transient restoration by strong stimuli. *J. Neurophysiology* **29**:221-39, 1966.
3. --. Alterations in responsiveness of ascending and reflex pathways activated by iterated cutaneous afferent volleys. *J. Neurophysiology* **29**:240-52, 1966.
4. --. Decrement in ventral root electrotonus and intracellularly recorded post-synaptic potentials produced by iterated cutaneous afferent volleys. *J. Neurophysiology* **29**:253-74, 1966.
5. **Kandel E R.** *Cellular basis of behavior: an introduction to behavioral neurobiology.* San Francisco: W. H. Freeman, 1976. 727 p.

CC/NUMBER 34
AUGUST 20, 1979

This Week's Citation Classic

Thompson R F & Spencer W A. Habituation: a model phenomenon for the study of neuronal substrates of behavior. *Psychol. Rev.* **73**:16-43, 1966.
[University of Oregon Medical School, Eugene, OR]

The behavioral process of *habituation* was shown to exhibit nine defining properties. The hindlimb flexion reflex of acute spinal cat was shown to be a good model for analysis of the mechanism of habituation—which appears to be a form of synaptic depression at interneurons. [The *Science Citation Index*® *(SCI®)* and the *Social Sciences Citation Index™ (SSCI™)* indicate that this paper has been cited over 275 times since 1966.]

Richard F. Thompson
Department of Psychobiology
University of California
Irvine, CA 92717

To the Memory of
W. Alden Spencer, MD
1931-1977

June 7, 1979

"My pleasure in having our article selected as a 'Citation Classic' is clouded by the tragic and untimely death of my colleague, W. Alden Spencer. I can imagine no scientific tribute that would have pleased Spencer more than to know that our initial paper on habituation has been identified as one that has 'left its mark on the progress of the whole of science.'

"Under the circumstances, a brief personal commentary is in order. Spencer and I became very close friends when we were undergraduates together at Reed College. We then followed somewhat different career lines—Alden obtained an MD and postdoctoral research in neurophysiology, and I obtained a PhD in physiological psychology and postdoctoral research in neurophysiology. We later joined forces as faculty members at the University of Oregon Medical School, Alden in physiology and I in psychiatry and medical psychology. Our collaborative effort extended over a period of several years in the 1960s.

"Our plan was to utilize simplified neuronal systems as models of phenomena of behavioral plasticity. We selected the hindlimb flexion reflex of acute spinal cat as a model. An elementary but important form of behavioral plasticity, *habituation*, is very prominent in this preparation. Slow rates of cutaneous stimulation (e.g., 1/sec. to 1/5 secs.) produce a pronounced decrease in flexion reflex amplitude that requires a period of many minutes to recover—a form of learning not to respond. There were perhaps three major contributions of our work.

"First, characterization of the process of habituation. This is a general definitional issue. There was lack of agreement on the properties and definitions of behavioral habituation and the literature was often contradictory. We surveyed the behavioral literature in detail and identified some nine consistent parametric features relating to stimulus and training variables that characterized habituation. These properties have come to be accepted in the field as the detailed definition of habituation.

"Second, use of simplified neuronal systems as models of behavioral plasticity. This is an epistemological issue. How does one decide that response change or plasticity in a given simplified neuronal system is a good model of the general behavioral process? We were able to show, using the criteria noted above, that our spinal model system was in fact a good model of the process of habituation.

"Third, analysis of neuronal mechanisms of habituation. In simplified systems, it is possible to use 'strong inference'—to eliminate possible mechanisms. We ruled out decrement at sensory input, motor output, and the motor neurons themselves. The process was located in interneurons. We suggested that the mechanism involved synaptic depression occurring presynaptically at (interneuron) axon terminals. More recent studies from several laboratories using monosynaptic models of habituation have consistently supported this general mechanism."[1]

1. **Castellucci V F & Kandel E R.** A quantal analysis of the synaptic depression underlying habituation of the gill-withdrawn reflex in *Aplysia*. *Proc. Nat. Acad. Sci. US* **71**:504-8, 1974.

Chapter

4

Perception, Audition, and Cognition

Perception / 77–86

Audition and speech perception / 87–90

Memory and recall / 91–101

CC/NUMBER 35
AUGUST 30, 1982

This Week's Citation Classic

White M J. Laterality differences in perception: a review.
Psychol. Bull. **72**:387-405, 1969.
[Victoria University of Wellington, Wellington, New Zealand]

This paper summarizes much of the work in visual laterality published up to 1969 and evaluates the merits of explanatory hypotheses based on a functional trace-scanning mechanism and on structural factors such as cerebral dominance. [The *Science Citation Index*® (*SCI*®) **and the** *Social Sciences Citation Index*® (*SSCI*®) **indicate that this paper has been cited in over 240 publications since 1969.]**

Murray J. White
Department of Psychology
Victoria University of Wellington
Wellington
New Zealand

June 30, 1982

"When I wrote this paper (1968) I was three years into a four-year, part-time PhD at Victoria University of Wellington. The person who got me interested in visual perception had resigned in 1964, our chairman unexpectedly died in 1965, and I went through three changes of supervisors between 1965 and 1969; none of these knew very much about perception. There were eight of us on the staff and it was tacitly understood that PhD candidates could expect a minimum of informed supervision. If nothing else, the situation encouraged a certain independence of mind.

"The choice of visual laterality phenomena as a PhD topic was fortuitous. I wanted to research something in the area of human perception and, at the time, the department's total resources consisted of one locally built tachistoscope. It was a chance reading of Heron's 1957 paper which got me involved in the area.[1] The problem itself seemed tractable and had not been worked to death. The literature was of a manageable size and the available theory was conceptually simple. The seven experiments I did for my dissertation attempted to answer some of the questions raised in the review paper. The most general of these concerned the relative contribution of a hypothetical trace-scanning mechanism and structural components, such as cerebral dominance, to visual laterality effects. I was fortunate in getting the literature review (the present paper) and five of the seven experiments accepted for publication before my oral examination.

"I had no idea then about how popular the topic, especially the left-brain right-brain aspect, would become in the next ten years. I don't claim any responsibility for this burgeoning interest and I am at a loss to explain the forces which have stimulated countless psychologists, neurologists, philosophers, and literati, and resulted in thousands of publications—papers, books, and colloquia. For all this effort, however, the business of perceptual laterality and hemispheric specialization still does not fit comfortably within any currently accepted model of human behavior. This is partly because too many people have detected a passing bandwagon and have jumped on, grimly determined to cover as many miles as possible before the axles break; in short, a classic example of data-driven research where sensible theory has lagged far behind empirical data. Of course there are exceptions and I should here cite two recent examples of fine scholarship written by my friends Mike Corballis and Ivan Beale.[2,3]

"Why is my paper frequently cited? Most probably because it critically appraises the relevant literature published up to 1969, thereby serving as a source document, and because it makes the useful conceptual distinction between functional and structural determinants of laterality. Honours and awards? My early publications in this area were instrumental in my being made the first Sir Thomas Hunter Awardsman of the New Zealand Psychological Society (1972), a Fellow of the same society (1975), and a Fellow of the British Psychological Society (1978)."

1. **Heron W.** Perception as a function of retinal locus and attention. *Amer. J. Psychol.* **70**:38-48, 1957.
2. **Corballis M C.** Laterality and myth. *Amer. Psychol.* **35**:284-95, 1980.
3. **Corballis M C & Beale I L.** *The psychology of left and right.* Hillsdale, NJ: Lawrence Erlbaum Associates, 1976. 227 p.

CC/NUMBER 21
MAY 21, 1979

This Week's Citation Classic

Sperling G. The information available in brief visual presentations. *Psychological Monogr.* **74**:1-29, 1960.

When a subject looks at a briefly flashed array of a dozen or so letters, he typically reports seeing more letters than he can remember. This paper introduces a method of partial report to demonstrate that the subject has a very short-term visual memory of the array and to measure the decay of this memory during the half-second following the exposure. [The *Science Citation Index® (SCI®)* and the *Social Sciences Citation Index ™(SSCI™)* **indicate that this paper has been cited over 455 times since 1960.]**

George Sperling
Bell Laboratories
Murray Hill, NJ 07974
and
New York University
New York, NY 10003

June 16, 1978

"When observers view a few rows of letters that are flashed very briefly, they enigmatically insist that they have seen more than they can remember immediately afterwards. The apparently simple question: 'What did you see?' requires the observer to report both what he remembers and what he has forgotten! To clarify this conundrum, I developed a new version of the long-forgotten method[1] of partial report. The observer is required to report only one row; at a precisely defined time after the exposure, the observer is given a randomly selected cue (e.g., a high, middle, or low frequency tone) indicating which row. When the cue occurs within a few tenths of a second after the exposure, reports are almost perfectly accurate; longer delays result in a precipitous loss of accuracy. From the accuracy of his reports, one can infer the number of letters that are *visually available* to the observer (his short-term visual memory) and the decay of this availability with time.

"Before turning to psychology in graduate school, I had studied physical sciences. My ambition was to find ways to use the inferential methods of atomic physics to make inferences about internal mental states. For example, when an observer is asked to report all he can from a briefly viewed visual display, his report is said to define his 'span of apprehension.' Previously, this span had been regarded as an irreducible, basic characteristic of the observer. My research showed that the report that defined the span of apprehension was itself the outcome of the complex interplay of more elementary processes. Like the atom, the span had been split. Many new procedures and concepts followed. In my own follow-up work, I introduced the method of visual-noise masking to measure the rate of transfer of information from very short-term visual memory to a more durable form. I proposed short-term auditory memory as one of the longer-term repositories, and I measured the rate of subvocal rehearsal—a process that maintains information.[2] In the new cognitive psychology that has emerged over the last two decades, it is (as I had hoped) the style rather than the specific content of my research that has had the greatest influence.

"An interesting sidelight is that the research for the paper was carried out during the summer after I had been failed by Harvard's Department of Social Relations and therefore was not permitted to conduct the research project I originally had planned. I transferred to Harvard's Department of Psychology and did this short-term memory study as an alternative summer project."

1. **Külpe O.** Versuche über abstraktion. *Bericht über den ersten Kongress für experimentelle Psychologie.* Leipzig: Barth, 1904. p. 56-68.
2. **Sperling G.** A model for visual memory tasks. *Human Factors* **5**:19-31, 1963.

CC/NUMBER 10
MARCH 5, 1984

This Week's Citation Classic™

Bamber D. Reaction times and error rates for "same"-"different" judgments of multidimensional stimuli. *Percept. Psychophys.* **6**:169-74, 1969.
[Stanford University, CA]

Subjects judged whether two letter strings were the same or different. A model assuming serial letter comparison that terminates upon finding a mismatch explained the reaction times of 'different' judgments. However, 'same' reaction times increased too little with string length to fit this model. [The *Social Sciences Citation Index*® (*SSCI*®) indicates that this paper has been cited in over 175 publications since 1969.]

Donald Bamber
Research Office
Veterans Administration
Medical Center
St. Cloud, MN 56301

January 13, 1984

"Which should be quicker: determining that two stimuli are the same or determining that two stimuli are different? It is reasonable to expect judgments of sameness to be slower than judgments of difference. After all, to verify that two stimuli are the same, it is necessary to compare all their features. However, to verify that two stimuli are different, it often suffices to compare only some of their features. Surprisingly, the opposite is found empirically. Judgments of sameness are typically faster than judgments of difference.

"While a graduate student at Stanford University, I became intrigued by this phenomenon of fast 'same' judgments and decided to investigate it in my doctoral dissertation (which became the basis of this *Citation Classic*™). In my dissertation experiment, subjects viewed one row of letters followed by another and indicated whether the two rows were the same or different by pressing one of two response keys. The two rows contained equal numbers of from one to four letters and could either be the same or could differ at any possible combination of letter positions.

"I used the resulting reaction-time data to test a model in which subjects compare corresponding letters from the two rows one pair at a time. If a mismatching pair is found, the 'different' key is pressed. If all the pairs are found to match, the 'same' key is pressed. This model gave a good fit to the 'different' reaction times with the comparison time for a matching letter pair estimated at 60 msec. The 'same' reaction times were faster than the 'different' reaction times and did not fit the model at all. In particular, lengthening the two rows by one letter increased 'same' reaction times by only 25 msec instead of the expected 60 msec. To account for these results, I proposed a model in which a fast and a slow letter comparison process operate simultaneously and respectively generate the 'same' and 'different' judgments.

"I see two reasons why this paper has been frequently cited. First, it described intriguing results which, if anything, added to the mystery of fast 'same' judgments. Second, the two-process model is often discussed in papers on same-different judgment.

"Models of same-different judgment have become more sophisticated since the time of this paper. Loosely based upon Link's choice-reaction-time theory,[1] some models[2,3] have attempted with moderate success to predict not only the means of reaction times but also their distributions together with the proportions of incorrect responses."

1. **Link S W.** The relative judgment theory of two choice response time. *J. Math. Psychol.* **12**:114-35, 1975. (Cited 40 times.)
2. **Krueger L E.** A theory of perceptual matching. *Psychol. Rev.* **85**:278-304, 1978. (Cited 95 times.)
3. **Ratcliff R.** A theory of order relations in perceptual matching. *Psychol. Rev.* **88**:552-72, 1981.

This Week's Citation Classic

Breitmeyer B G & Ganz L. Implications of sustained and transient channels for theories of visual pattern masking, saccadic suppression, and information processing. *Psychol. Rev.* **83**:1-36, 1976.
[Univ. Houston, TX and Stanford Univ., CA]

Response interactions within and between long-latency sustained and short-latency transient visual pathways provide a basis for theoretically integrating a host of neural and perceptual studies relevant to our understanding of forward or backward visual masking, visual response (iconic) persistence, motion and pattern perception, saccadic suppression, and the spatial guidance of visual selective attention. [The *Science Citation Index*® **(***SCI*®**) and the** *Social Sciences Citation Index*® **(***SSCI*®**) indicate that this paper has been cited in over 190 publications since 1976.]**

Bruno G. Breitmeyer
Department of Psychology
University of Houston
Houston, TX 77004

April 26, 1983

"In 1971, two Stanford University graduate colleagues, Bruce Bridgeman and Sybille Sukale-Wolf, had separately completed dissertations on metacontrast which became part of the grist for a seminar on visual masking offered that year by Leo Ganz. Participation in this seminar was complemented by my concurrent dissertation work on motion perception.

"In this context, stroboscopic motion and metacontrast masking assumed prime importance. Literature reviews revealed that both phenomena can be generated when two stimuli are flashed in spatiotemporal proximity. In his classical study on stroboscopic motion, Wertheimer[1] noted the occasional loss of visibility of either stimulus at onset intervals yielding optimal stroboscopic motion, indicating that metacontrast masking might accompany stroboscopic motion and produce this loss of visibility.

"Subsequent work, in part conducted in my laboratory,[2,3] confirmed and quantified this limited yet clear relation between metacontrast and stroboscopic motion. This relation revealed a puzzle which, in my opinion, was not adequately explained by the then extant theories of visual masking. For perception of stroboscopic motion to occur, activity generated by the first stimulus somehow must span a temporal interval and *integrate* with the activity generated by the second stimulus. However, during metacontrast suppression, the pattern component of the first stimulus does not persist and integrate with that of the second; on the contrary, the first pattern seems to be actively suppressed by, i.e., temporally *segregated* from, the second stimulus.

"This existence of separate motion-integrative and pattern-segregative components in stroboscopic motion and metacontrast led me, in line with Saucer's[4] suggestion, to conjecture the existence of at least two types of visual channels: one responsive to rapid motion; the other, to a static or slowly moving pattern. This distinction seemed also to fit with accumulating studies of the spatiotemporal response properties of fast-conducting transient and slow-conducting sustained visual pathways. This evidence, in conjunction with Singer and Bedworth's[5] finding of their mutual inhibitory interactions, provided the basic elements for a theoretical approach to a wide variety of visual phenomena.

"Initially, the approach was to apply to an account of metacontrast, paracontrast, and other types of backward and forward masking. Spurred by helpful discussions with Naomi Weisstein and Ethel Matin, I sought the collaboration of Ganz in extending the approach to other visual phenomena. During the summer of 1975, we completed a manuscript describing the basically simple assumptive context of our theoretical approach and the broad range of phenomena to which it can apply, including a more recent extension to explanations of visual behavior in extralaboratory, natural settings.[6] In my opinion, besides extensively integrating neurophysiological and neuroanatomical results and concepts with perceptual ones, it is this combination of simplicity and especially the broad range of explanatory applicability appealing to a correspondingly wide range of vision research interests which is responsible for the article's numerous citations."

1. **Wertheimer M.** Experimentelle Studien über das Sehen von Bewegung. *Z. Psychol.* **61**:161-265, 1912.
2. **Breitmeyer B, Love R & Wepman B.** Contour masking during stroboscopic motion and metacontrast. *Vision Res.* **14**:1451-6, 1974.
3. **Breitmeyer B, Battaglia F & Weber C.** U-shaped backward contour masking during stroboscopic motion. *J. Exp. Psychol.—Hum. Percep. Perf.* **2**:167-73, 1976.
4. **Saucer R T.** Processes of motion perception. *Science* **120**:806-7, 1954.
5. **Singer W & Bedworth N.** Inhibitory interaction between X and Y units in cat lateral geniculate nucleus. *Brain Res.* **49**:291-307, 1973.
6. **Breitmeyer B G.** Unmasking visual masking: a look at the "why" behind the veil of the "how." *Psychol. Rev.* **87**:52-69, 1980.

This Week's Citation Classic

NUMBER 8
FEBRUARY 19, 1979

Swets J A, Tanner W P Jr & Birdsall T G. Decision processes in perception. *Psychol. Rev.* **68**: 301-40, 1961.

The human observer is regarded as a rational decision-maker, one appropriately influenced by stimulus probabilities and response utilities in acting on sensory data. A new analytical technique isolates the effects of such decision variables to yield pure measurements of sensory capacity. [The *Science Citation Index®* **(***SCI®* **) and the** *Social Sciences Citation Index™ (SSCI™)* **indicate that this paper has been cited 289 times since 1961.]**

John A. Swets
Bolt Beranek and Newman Inc
50 Moulton Street
Cambridge, MA 02138

January 27, 1978

"This paper proposed and supported a new theory of human sensory discrimination. The theory carried with it a solution to a long-standing analytical problem in psychophysics, the discipline concerned with the measurement of sensory capacity.

"Spike Tanner and I were graduate students in psychology at the University of Michigan in the early 1950s, whose common interests included mathematical approaches to the study of sensory processes. In pursuit of this interest we teamed up with two graduate students in engineering, Wes Peterson and Ted Birdsall, who were studying electronic sensing devices. Tanner, in his late 30s at the time, died this past summer after an influential teaching and research career in Ann Arbor. Birdsall too remained at Michigan and continues, on the side, to co-author articles with psychologists.

"The dominant sensory theory over the years was that human discrimination capacity is determined, in an all-or-none fashion, by a physiological threshold. But also apparent through the history of psychophysics was a view that sensory information is continuous, and that an observer must therefore deliberately select a criterion amount of apparent difference for reporting the existence of a physical difference. A related concern was that this criterion might be so variable as to confound attempts at precise and reliable sensory measurement. The key analytical insight of our engineer colleagues was that a particular transformation of the 'operating characteristics,' as developed in statistical theory, serves to separate whatever response criterion might be adopted for or by a sensor (receiver, observer) from that sensor's fundamental capacity to discriminate. The 'receiver operating characteristic' provides independent measures of sensory capacity and the extra-sensory criterion.

"The difficulties we experienced in publishing the paper probably resulted from the strong suggestion that a venerable theory be discarded, with the proposed replacement seeming to come from left field. In any event, it is wryly amusing in the present context to recall that the paper spent five years in the review process of one journal before it was submitted to the journal that published it.

"The admission that the paper dealt with a problem in psychophysics would have suggested to psychologists at the time that the paper would receive very few citations even if it were tremendously influential in its field, because that field was quite generally viewed as a dustbowl in psychology. According to William James, indeed, its literature was thorough, subtle, and dreadful, and it all amounted to 'just *nothing*.' However, the demonstration that the human observer runs his sensory inputs through a rational decision process on the way to response, in even the simplest discrimination task, seemed to stir a wider interest—e.g., among the budding cognitive psychologists of the day. Moreover, with a solution available, the existence of 'the criterion problem' became more evident in other traditional areas of psychology, as in the study of memory.

"In more recent years, another line of extrapolation has appeared. It happens that the fundamental analytical problem turns up in a variety of practical settings in which an evaluation is sought of the performance of a man, machine, or man-machine system. Though the statistical ideas might have traveled a more direct route, their use in psychology has been credited in their applications to industrial monitoring and quality control, information retrieval systems, forensic situations, aspects of transportation, and medical diagnosis.

CC/NUMBER 10
MARCH 10, 1980

This Week's Citation Classic

Howard I P & Templeton W B. *Human spatial orientation.* London: Wiley, 1966. 533 p. [Univ. Durham, Durham, England]

This book is about how people perceive the direction and orientation of things. Early chapters review the relevant physiology of vision, eye movements, kinesthesis, the vestibular system, and auditory localization. Middle chapters review behavioral studies on gravitational, geographical, and egocentric orientation. End chapters review the behavioral consequences of distorting sensory inputs, with a chapter on the behavioral effects of weightlessness. [The *Science Citation Index®* (*SCI®*) **and the** *Social Sciences Citation Index™* (*SSCI™*) **indicate that this book has been cited over 305 times since 1966.]**

Ian P. Howard and W.B. Templeton
Department of Psychology
York University
Downsview, Ontario
Canada

August 24, 1979

"In 1961 we were working on the perception of the visual vertical and decided to write a short review paper on this topic because no such review existed. Our search through the literature soon revealed an extensive earlier German literature. We also began to receive a flood of reports sponsored by the American space programme. Our review became a journal monograph supplement. It soon became apparent that visual orientation to gravity concerns kinesthesis and the vestibular system just as much as vision, and no adequate review of these topics existed at the time. Our monograph supplement became a small book.

"At about this time the translation into English of the work of Erisman and Kohler in Austria was leading to a revival of interest in the behavioral effects of upside-down vision.[1] It was becoming generally recognized that the problem of how people adapt to an upside-down world is one of a larger set of problems having to do with distortions of vision and other senses. Our small book became larger. In moments of euphoria we planned to write a multivolume work on all aspects of space perception. In moments of fatigue and despair we wondered why we were writing at all rather than doing experiments. The idea of confining ourselves to the orientation aspects of space perception, leaving out distance and movement perception, finally emerged and, after four years, we had a manuscript which we called complete.

"In retrospect we can see that the attempt to be comprehensive interfered with the smooth flow of ideas, and our efforts to cover the literature caused us to ignore the obvious implications of very recent work, especially the work of Hubel and Wiesel on the physiology of orientation detectors.[2] We were nevertheless pleased with the good reception that the book received.

"The second author, Templeton, died suddenly in September, 1979. The first author is just completing a sequel to the 1966 volume entitled *Human Visual Orientation.*[3] There has been more published work on this topic since 1966 than there had been up to that time. In order to encompass this new material only one percent of the references in the new book are to pre-1966 publications. The most that any writer of such a book can hope is that it will help to shorten the time it takes for the book to become out of date.

"The book has been cited often because it is the only detailed review of human spatial orientation. We have been pleased to note that our suggestions for further research have been acted upon."

1. **Kohler K.** The formation and transformation of the perceptual world. Monograph No. 12. *Psychol. Issues* **3**:1-175, 1964.
2. **Hubel D H & Wiesel T N.** Receptive fields of single neurones in the cat's striate cortex. *J. Physiology* **148**:574-91, 1959.
3. **Howard I P.** *Human visual orientation.* London: Wiley, 1982.

This Week's Citation Classic

Poulton E C. The new psychophysics: six models for magnitude estimation. *Psychol. Bull.* **69**:1-19, 1968.
[Applied Psychology Research Unit, Cambridge, England]

Six pictorial models describe the effects on numerical magnitude judgments of the experimenter's choices of the independent variables. The effects are more compatible with a learned calibration theory of numerical magnitude judgments than with a simple transducer theory. Transfer effects within and between experiments are also described. [The *Social Sciences Citation Index*® *(SSCI™)* **indicates that this paper has been cited over 135 times since 1968.]**

E.C. Poulton
Medical Research Council
Applied Psychology Unit
Cambridge CB2 2EF
England

April 28, 1981

"This review had its beginning when I worked as a research fellow under S.S. Stevens at Harvard in 1953-1954. Smitty Stevens and Didi Stone, later to become his second wife, met my young family and me at the boat in Boston during Thanksgiving, and drove us to the temporary accommodations they had arranged for us. Stevens then took me to the Psychological Laboratories in the basement of Memorial Hall, and got me to make numerical magnitude judgments of loudness. I came away feeling that I had been brainwashed.

"Soon I found myself playing Stevens's role, getting the graduate students to judge loudness using numbers. As I tried out one idea after another, the graduate students became resistant to my frequent requests to them to serve as observers. Their judgments ceased to be affected by my innovations. They were skeptical of the validity of the kind of experiments that I was conducting on Stevens's behalf. To make any sense, I realized that I needed large numbers of uninitiated observers. After what appeared to be an almost unbearable delay, I obtained the volunteer services of a student practical class at Harvard, and later of students from the Harvard Summer School. When I left after 11 months as a research fellow, I had discovered to my cost most of the biases that affect numerical magnitude judgments.

"I returned to the other Cambridge, and tried to forget my unfortunate experiences. Then in 1959, Dick Warren, who was visiting Cambridge, suggested that we should collaborate. He had just published his physical correlate theory of numerical magnitude judgments.[1] The theory states that judgments of loudness and brightness are based on judgments of the apparent distance of the source of the sound or light. Together we invaded the Junior Combination Rooms of the Cambridge colleges at about the time of Hall Dinners in the evening. We collected two, or at most four, judgments of the lightness of grey papers from each student. We used separate groups of 50 undergraduates for each data point. When Warren returned to the US, John Webster and then Derek Simmonds took his place. Our results clearly demonstrate the biases in magnitude judgments, which were often obscured at Harvard by transfer from prior experiments of a similar kind.

"In July 1966 I reviewed our findings in a talk entitled 'The New Pseudophysics.' But the editor of *Psychological Bulletin* refused to accept this title. I suppose my 1968 review is often cited because it represents the first extensive criticism of Stevens's work that is accompanied by experimental evidence to support it.

"One of the reviewers suggested that my review should be extended to cover category rating as well as magnitude judgments. The composite review he asked for was delayed until 1979.[2] It describes six main biases in quantifying judgments. The biases occur, either separately or combined in various ways, in every kind of quantitative judgment. My forthcoming book[3] describes how the biases occur in the quantitative judgments of everyday life, and shows how Stevens[4] soon made use of the biases to obtain the results he wanted."

1. **Warren R M.** A basis for judgments of sensory intensity. *Amer. J. Psychol.* **71**:675-87, 1958.
2. **Poulton E C.** Models for biases in judging sensory magnitude. *Psychol. Bull.* **86**:777-803, 1979.
3. ----------------. *Bias in judgment.* San Francisco: Academic Press. Expected date of publication, 1982.
4. **Stevens S S.** *Psychophysics: introduction to its perceptual, neural, and social prospects.* New York: Wiley, 1975. 329 p.

CC/NUMBER 4
JANUARY 24, 1983

This Week's Citation Classic

Berry J W. Temne and Eskimo perceptual skills. *Int. J. Psychol.* **1**:207-29, 1966.
[University of Edinburgh, Scotland]

Cultural and ecological characteristics of two populations (agricultural Temne in West Africa and hunting Eskimo in Baffin Island) were analysed; these provided a basis for predicting differential development of spatial-perceptual and related skills. Testing with two samples in each field area confirmed these predictions. [The *Social Sciences Citation Index*® (*SSCI*®) **indicates that this paper has been cited in over 155 publications since 1966.]**

J.W. Berry
Psychology Department
Queen's University
Kingston, Ontario K7L 3N6
Canada

October 18, 1982

"An interest in psychological and cultural differences among human populations was stimulated early while growing up as an English Canadian in a predominantly French Canadian milieu, and was nurtured later by travels as a teenage merchant seaman to Africa and the Arctic. After undergraduate courses at Sir George Williams University with J.W. Bridges (who appeared to ignore the conventional distinction between psychology and anthropology), I was given the opportunity by James Drever at the University of Edinburgh to attempt a rather freewheeling doctoral thesis comparing peoples from these two contrasting culture areas. The choice of perception as a focus for these studies derived in part from a century of anecdotal and ethnocentric observations concerning the 'sensory prowess of savages,' and in part from my own prior experience of the contrasting life-styles and survival strategies of Arctic hunters and African farmers.

"Fieldwork was conducted under anything but 'standard laboratory conditions': some test data were collected under extremes of temperature and humidity (in steamy and dripping huts during tropical torrents, and in igloos while sitting on a bear rug to separate flesh from ice). In contrast, the paper itself was typed in a camper van mired in a beach in southern Spain. Somehow, such a strange collection of material found its acceptance in the new IUPS journal whose mandate was to internationalize psychology.

"Why the paper has been cited is not at all clear to me. There are some factors which seem to provide some positive indications, but others which suggest that it should have been ignored. On the citation side, there are two possible reasons: one is that the study was one of the first to try to demonstrate the existence of specific psychological characteristics of differing peoples, based upon an analysis of the 'ecological demands' of carrying out a life under varying conditions; this enabled a functional or adaptive approach to the differences found, rather than one based upon notions of intellectual deficit. (In fact, on some spatial-perceptual tasks, no differences were found in comparison to a Scottish control sample, thus further questioning the appropriateness of a global deficit-type interpretation.) Another factor is that the 1966 study was one of the first of a long series by myself[1] and others, rather than a one-shot study; this generated a cumulative research domain (one which became aligned with the cognitive style work of H.A. Witkin[2]) leading inevitably to citation by researchers in the field.[3]

"On the 'ignoring' side, the paper was published in the first volume of a new journal, in a field (cross-cultural psychology) which was not fully established or accepted by psychology, by a novice researcher who as a matter of personal preference has published outside the 'mainstream' of psychology. This profile does not suggest that the paper would even be read, never mind cited! However, continuing interest in the work suggests that the approach taken in this early paper may have created two distinct citation advantages over other psychological studies: interdisciplinary and international attention which is paid to work done by Western researchers may be directly proportional to the 'universality' (in the anthropological sense) of the topic; it may be that culture-bound research in psychology may be on its way out."

1. **Berry J W.** *Human ecology and cognitive style: comparative studies in cultural and psychological adaptation.* New York: Sage/Halsted, 1976. 242 p.
2. **Witkin H A & Berry J W.** Psychological differentiation in cross-cultural perspective. *J. Cross-Cult. Psychol.* **6**:4-87, 1975.
3. **Triandis H C, Lambert W W, Berry J W, Lonner W J, Heron A, Brislin R & Draguns J,** eds. *Handbook of cross-cultural psychology.* Boston: Allyn and Bacon, 1980. 6 vols.

Exline R, Gray D & Schuette D. Visual behavior in a dyad as affected by interview content and sex of respondent. *J. Personal. Soc. Psychol.* **1**:201-9, 1965. [University of Delaware, Newark, DE]

Male and female interviewers asking only personal or impersonal questions while gazing attentively at interviewees received more mutual gazes from women than from men. Data replicated and extended earlier findings of sex differences in mutual gaze. All interviewees gazed less on personal questions and looked more when listening than speaking. [The *Social Sciences Citation Index*® **(***SSCI*®**) indicates that this paper has been cited over 155 times since 1966.]**

Ralph V. Exline
Department of Psychology
University of Delaware
Newark, DE 19711

May 21, 1981

"This study represents a line of research which grew out of a serendipitous observation made in a study designed for another purpose. Before coming to the University of Delaware, where my studies of social gaze behavior originated and continue, I had found that women in discussion groups were better than men in judging interpersonal attraction within the group. Given the evidence that women, on the average, scored higher on tests of affiliation motives than did men, I decided to compose like-sex groups, homogeneous as to high or low affiliation, to test the prediction that affiliation differences rather than sex explained accuracy in judging interpersonal attraction.

"Results were interesting and complex, but, more important, we observed a striking, unanticipated discussion phenomenon. Regardless of sex, members of high affiliation groups appeared to look long into each other's line of regard while low affiliators appeared to avoid each other's gaze. In affiliative groups it was as if several pairs of searchlights focused upon the speaker, who, in turn, would slowly traverse the group as he/she talked, engaging in mutual looks with first one and then another of his/her listeners. In contrast, mutual gaze in nonaffiliative groups was sporadic—looks would flicker here and there, a gaze caught and held would soon be broken by either speaker or listener. The contrast was so marked I embarked on a series of studies designed to explore systematically the phenomenon of social visual attention—the looks, glances, stares, glares, and gaze avoidances which characterize the interaction of specified kinds of persons, in specified roles, and in specified situations.

"The cited study was a follow-up of my initial study of gaze behavior[1] in which sex, affiliation motive, and the competitiveness of the situation were found to affect differentially the amount of mutual gazing. It generalized the earlier found sex differences in gaze from like-sex to cross-sex interaction; it demonstrated that, on the whole, one gives less social visual attention when speaking than when listening to another; it suggested that gaze avoidance could well be a way of 'distancing' oneself from another (see Argyle and Cook's development of this point in their discussion of Argyle's affiliative conflict theory in *Gaze and Mutual Gaze*[2]); and it strongly suggested that the observed sex differences were indeed a function of person-oriented personality attributes—possibly stemming from socialization practices.

"Why has this study been frequently cited? Perhaps readers had already experienced the relevance and power of social gaze behavior in their personal lives, and this early study showed that it could be investigated in experiments. The study suggested that gaze could be reliably measured, appearing to connect or separate people, and to lend itself to precise experimental manipulation.[3] In addition, the research appealed to those interested in integrating verbal and nonverbal aspects of interpersonal communication.[4] Finally, the article appeared in an important, widely read journal."

1. **Exline R V.** Explorations in the process of person perception: visual interaction in relation to competition, sex, and need for affiliation. *J. Personality* **31**:1-20, 1963.
2. **Argyle M & Cook M.** *Gaze and mutual gaze.* London: Cambridge University Press, 1976. 210 p.
3. **Ellsworth P C.** Direct gaze as a social stimulus. (Pliner P, Krames L & Alloway T, eds.) *Advances in the study of communication and affect.* New York: Plenum Press, 1975. Vol. 2. p. 53-76.
4. **Exline R V & Fehr B J.** Applications of semiosis to the study of visual interaction. (Siegman A W & Feldstein S, eds.) *Nonverbal behavior and communication.* Hillsdale, NJ: Lawrence Erlbaum Associates, 1978. p. 117-58.

This Week's Citation Classic

Dale E & Chall J S. A formula for predicting readability.
Educ. Res. Bull. **27**:11-20; 37-54, 1948.
[Bureau of Educational Research, Ohio State Univ., Columbus, OH]

By providing a list of 3,000 familiar words we enable the analyst to make use of two factors in readability levels: 1) the semantic and frequency levels of the words, and 2) the length of the sentence which governs its complexity. [The *Science Citation Index*® (*SCI*®) **and the** *Social Sciences Citation Index*® (*SSCI*®) **indicate that this paper has been cited in over 355 publications since 1961.]**

Edgar Dale
Academic Faculty of Educational
Foundations and Research
Ohio State University
Columbus, OH 43210

April 19, 1982

"The study on readability which Jeanne Chall of Harvard and I completed in 1948 had its roots in the long past. When I was teaching in Winnetka, Illinois (1924-1926), Carlton Washburne, superintendent of schools, and Mabel Vogel, research assistant, were working on their readability formula which appeared in 1928.[1]

"I became interested in developing a technique for finding the grade levels of instructional materials. This was when new materials were being rapidly developed and teachers were concerned about reading grade levels. The vocabulary was sometimes too hard for the readers, and less commonly too easy.

"My doctoral dissertation, *Factual Basis for Curriculum Revision in Arithmetic with Special Reference to Children's Understanding of Business Terms*,[2] disclosed that in studying specific technical fields glossaries were necessary. I developed a list of 2,276 business words and tested 200 of the important ones by a multiple-choice test.

"When Chall was enrolled in the graduate school at Ohio State University she studied the possibility of determining readability levels by scaling paragraphs. Her 1947 master's thesis was entitled *Graded Reading Paragraphs in Health Education, Readability by Examples*. We now had two major causes of reading difficulty· the words used and the sentence length.

"Fortunately, we had already compared the vocabulary of children before entering the first grade prepared by the Child Study Committee of the International Kindergarten Union with E. L. Thorndike's most frequent thousand words.[3] This was reported in an article entitled 'A comparison of two word lists.'[4]

"Irving Lorge next used the Dale list of 769 common words in his readability studies and added a factor of sentence length.[5] Edward W. Dolch took the Dale list of 769 words and added 231 words obtained by interviewing samples of children early in the first grade, thus making a list of 1,000 words.[6] Clarence Stone removed 173 words and added 173 making a list of 1,000 words.[7] George Spache first used the Stone list, then added 361 words and removed 87 words, making a total of 1,041 words.[8]

"Another early readability study was by myself and Ralph Tyler. Our formula was described in an article entitled 'A study of the factors influencing the difficulty of reading materials for adults of limited reading ability.'[9]

"After exploring the use of the Dale 769 list we concluded that it was satisfactory for early reading but had weaknesses when used with the upper grades. The 3,000 word list was then developed which was more broadly applicable.

"It is likely that the next extensive research on readability levels will be a semantic approach using the familiarity scores on each word. These data will be found in *The Living Word Vocabulary*, a list of 44,000 words with their scores.[10]

"The data available on readability levels suggest: more critical use of readability formulas, better exchange of results of appraisals, and more use of the formula in preparing readable materials at or near the sixth grade level."

1. **Vogel M & Washburne C W.** An objective method of determining grade placement of children's reading material. *Elem. Sch. J.* **28**:373-81, 1928.
2. **Dale E.** *Factual basis for curriculum revision in arithmetic with special reference to children's understanding of business terms.* PhD thesis. Chicago, IL: University of Chicago, 1929.
3. **Thorndike E L.** *The teacher's word book.* New York: Teacher's College, Columbia University, 1921. 134 p.
4. **Dale E.** A comparison of two word lists. *Educ. Res. Bull.* **10**:484-9, 1931.
5. **Lorge I.** Predicting readability. *Teach. Coll. Rec.* **45**:404-19, 1944.
6. **Dolch E W.** *Problems in reading.* Champaign, IL: Garrard Press, 1948. 373 p.
7. **Stone C R.** Measuring difficulty of primary reading material: a constructive criticism of Spache's measure. *Elem. Sch. J.* **57**:36-41, 1956.
8. **Spache G D.** *Good reading for poor readers.* Champaign, IL: Garrard Publishing Company, 1974. p. 201-4.
9. **Dale E & Tyler R W.** A study of the factors influencing the difficulty of reading materials for adults of limited reading ability. *Lib. Quart.* **4**:384-412, 1934.
10. **Dale E & O'Rourke J.** *The living word vocabulary.* Chicago: World Book-Childcraft International, 1981. 682 p.

This Week's Citation Classic™

CC/NUMBER 36
SEPTEMBER 3, 1984

Massaro D W. Preperceptual images, processing time, and perceptual units in auditory perception. *Psychol. Rev.* **79**:124-45, 1972.
[Department of Psychology, University of Wisconsin, Madison, WI]

A theoretical account of the auditory recognition process is given in terms of the information in a preperceptual image and the time it is available for perceptual processing. Necessary distinctions are drawn between auditory detection, recognition, and short-term memory. [The *Science Citation Index*® (*SCI*®) and the *Social Sciences Citation Index*® (*SSCI*®) indicate that this paper has been cited in over 140 publications since 1972.]

Dominic W. Massaro
Program in Experimental Psychology
University of California
Santa Cruz, CA 95064

July 18, 1984

"When I was notified that a publication of mine was identified as one of the most-cited items in its field, my first terrifying thought was that I was citing my own work too frequently. This is not the case for the paper in question, however, since most of my research areas after the cited paper have been 'something completely different,' to steal a phrase from Monty Python.

"As a graduate student and a postdoctoral fellow, I was impressed with the information-processing framework as a heuristic for psychological inquiry. Performance in any domain could be conceptualized as involving a set of processing stages, and it is important to isolate and define the nature of the information and the operations performed on it at each stage of processing. This paradigm has major implications for experiment and theory. The primary one in my mind was that it served as an organizational framework to relate disparate areas of investigation previously believed to be concerned with fundamentally different psychological questions.

"My interest in auditory perception evolved from my thesis research on memory for pitch, a situation chosen to eliminate the possibility of subvocal rehearsal during the forgetting interval. It became apparent that memory performance was as much dependent upon 'perception' as memory, and this realization clarified previous studies of verbal memory.[1] I pursued the study of auditory perception utilizing many of the concepts developed in the visual information-processing area[2] and quickly discovered the widely different approaches to the study of the problem. The approaches ranged from the highly sensory orientation of psychoacoustics to the study of the auditory modality in memory tasks. The goal of the cited paper was to review the relevant literature across these areas and to provide a single theoretical account of phenomena rarely related to one another.

"Why choose such a project for a Wisconsin summer after a long, cold winter's first year of teaching? Although we had a gigantic garden on our new country land, weeding wasn't a problem and there was much time for library research. (There seems to be less time for such endeavors today.) The project and its apparent success provided a model for employing a similar organization for a textbook.[3]

"The frequent citation of the publication is probably due to the value of the information-processing framework for clearly expressing psychological facts and to the paper capturing the state of the art for the following decade. Although some of the central themes have since been hotly debated, criticized, and supported, the endeavor has been healthy and progressive. The most encouraging outcome has been the general success of the theoretical framework even when extended beyond its original domain."[4-6]

1. **Massaro D W.** Perceptual processes and forgetting in memory tasks. *Psychol. Rev.* **77**:557-67, 1970. (Cited 35 times.)
2. ----------------. Preperceptual auditory images. *J. Exp. Psychol.* **85**:411-17, 1970. (Cited 65 times.)
3. ----------------. *Experimental psychology and information processing*. Chicago, IL: Rand McNally, 1975. 651 p. (Cited 115 times.)
4. **Cowan N, Suomi K & Morse P A.** Echoic storage in infant perception. *Child Develop.* **33**:984-90, 1982.
5. **Kallman H J & Massaro D W.** Backward masking, the suffix effect and preperceptual storage. *J. Exp. Psychol.—Learn. Mem. Cogn.* **9**:312-27, 1983.
6. **Watson C S & Kelly W J.** The role of stimulus uncertainty in the discrimination of auditory patterns. (Getty D J & Howard J H, Jr., eds.) *Auditory and visual pattern recognition.* Hillsdale, NJ: Erlbaum, 1981. p. 37-59.

CC/NUMBER 47
NOVEMBER 19, 1979

This Week's Citation Classic

Crowder R G & Morton J. Precategorical acoustic storage (PAS). *Percept. Psychophys.* **5**:365-73, 1969.
[Dept. Psychology, Yale University, New Haven, CT]

This paper describes a system of sensory memory for the auditory modality. It occurred at a time when the visual sensory memory system was well established but no corresponding auditory store had yet been proposed formally. The main applications of the precategorical acoustic storage hypothesis (PAS) are to experiments on presentation modality in immediate memory and to experiments showing interference with immediate memory by a redundant stimulus suffix. [The *Science Citation Index®* *(SCI®)* **and the** *Social Sciences Citation Index™* *(SSCI™)* **indicate that this paper has been cited over 175 times since 1969.]**

Robert G. Crowder
Department of Psychology
Yale University
New Haven, CT 06520

April 17, 1979

"The preparation of this paper owes entirely to the fact that John Morton spent 1967-1968 visiting at Yale. But it was the English psychologist R. Conrad who was responsible in a more basic way. Independently of Morton, I had been interested for several years in a discovery by Conrad in the late 1950s—that producing a redundant prefix immediately before recall of an immediate memory list hurts recall for that list. (Perhaps the British postal and telecommunications system should be thanked, for they supported Conrad's work.) When I met Morton in 1967, I had just published a paper showing that if the redundant item is presented at the end of the memory list, spoken by the tester rather than by the person being tested, the effect is quite different.[1] In this case, with a suffix presented at the end of the list, performance is again damaged, but only for the last item or two in the list.

"Meanwhile, at the Medical Research Council's Applied Psychology Research Unit in Cambridge, Morton had become aware through contact with Conrad that visual and auditory presentation of memory lists do not yield the same result; rather, the auditory mode gives better performance on the last few items in the list. This observation fit with expectations of a large theoretical model[2] Morton had been working on for explaining certain relationships between memory, perception, and language (the *logogen* model). He, too, had just finished a study showing a selective interference effect on the last portion of memory lists.[3]

"When we saw how neatly Morton's model seemed to handle the results of both of our experiments, we spent several months testing further implications of the PAS notion. The most important of these was that a spoken suffix following visual presentation of the list should not affect performance. The paper was drafted while Morton was still in New Haven and then revised later by correspondence. We were pleased that it gave us the opportunity to tie together a large number of experimental findings in the literature about short-term memory as well as to lay down Morton's views on the roles of audition and articulation in memory.

"A particular emphasis that I pushed was the intimate relation between perception and memory coding. This emphasis on coding analysis seems to have anticipated the more recent interest in 'levels of processing' that has developed with a disillusionment about distinguishing short and long-term memory stores. We said, for example, '...linguistic materials go through a somewhat stereotyped progression of perceptual stages...."What is learned" by the *S* in an experiment may then be said to depend on how far into such perceptual processing the materials have passed at the termination of stimulus presentation.'

"I wish these more systematic aspects of the paper had had more impact and that our estimate that PAS could last about two seconds had had less impact. The time estimate was pure conjecture, and there was then no evidence (nor is there now) to prefer it over some other figure of the same order of magnitude. Yet, the two-second conjecture seems to be our most frequently cited statement.

"The PAS hypotheses have survived almost a decade of experimental tests reasonably well. The revisions that have been suggested by subsequent work largely have been to elaborate the original assumptions rather than to change them fundamentally. For me, the most important of these elaborations have been, first, to show the relation of PAS to different classes of speech sounds, and, second, to discover the type of backward masking that is responsible for the suffix effect."

1. **Crowder R G.** Prefix effects in immediate memory. *Can. J. Psychol.* **21**:450-61, 1967.
2. **Morton J.** Selective interference in immediate recall. *Psychonom. Sci.* **12**:75-6, 1968.
3. **Morton J.** The interaction of information in word recognition. *Psychol. Rev.* **76**:165-78, 1969.

This Week's Citation Classic

CC/NUMBER 3
JANUARY 19, 1981

Studdert-Kennedy M & Shankweiler D. Hemispheric specialization for speech perception. *J. Acoust. Soc. Amer.* **48**:579-94, 1970.
[Haskins Labs., New Haven, CT; Queens College, City Univ. New York, Flushing, NY; and Univ. Connecticut, Storrs, CT]

The results of a dichotic listening study are interpreted as evidence that, whereas the general auditory system common to both hemispheres can extract the auditory parameters of a speech signal, the dominant hemisphere alone is specialized for the extraction of phonological information from those parameters. [The *Science Citation Index® (SCI®)* **and the** *Social Sciences Citation Index® (SSCI™)* **indicate that this paper has been cited over 250 times since 1970.]**

Michael Studdert-Kennedy
and
Donald Shankweiler
Haskins Laboratories
270 Crown Street
New Haven, CT 06510

December 23, 1980

"Our work sprang directly from the demonstration by Kimura[1] (1961, and several later papers) that, if different spoken digits are presented to left and right ears simultaneously, those presented to the right ear are more accurately recalled than those presented to the left. Kimura interpreted her results as reflecting left hemisphere specialization for language processes, and stronger contralateral than ipsilateral pathways from ears to hemispheres.

"We saw in her method an opportunity to test the hypothesis that the human capacity for language, typically vested in the left hemisphere, includes a specialized capacity for perceiving the phonetic structure of speech. We therefore chose as our materials pairs of consonant-vowel-consonant nonsense syllables, differing from each other by a single consonant or vowel. The results confirmed those of our previous study in demonstrating a right-ear advantage for a purely phonetic, or phonological, task.

"We therefore proposed as a working hypothesis that, whatever else the left cerebral hemisphere is specialized for, it alone has the capacity to perform phonological analysis of the speech signal. The right nondominant hemisphere's capabilities for perceiving speech are based on a holistic strategy of pattern recognition without recourse to phonology. We are no longer convinced by all the arguments we made in the paper, but our general conclusion still seems to be correct. Subsequent work with split-brain patients by Levy[2] and Zaidel[3] has given it new underpinnings.

"Our paper has perhaps been cited so often because it served as an example of a carefully controlled and analyzed dichotic study. Dichotic studies themselves engendered interest because they offered a novel, benign, and noninvasive way to explore lateralization of function in the human brain.

"Although the flow of dichotic research continues unabated, we feel a certain disaffection with the approach. As a method of studying brain function, dichotic listening has been hard to tame, and we are plagued by questions that threaten its validity. How should we best measure the ear advantage? How are we to interpret variability of response in different tasks with the same materials? Why do individuals differ so widely?

"We stressed in our paper a methodological *caveat* that is still not sufficiently appreciated: perceptual asymmetry scores do not give a direct measure of asymmetry of brain processing. The ear asymmetry depends not only on material-specific and task-specific cerebral competencies, but also on the unequal representation of each ear in the two sides of the brain. Both sets of factors may vary, perhaps independently, and we still do not know how to partition their effects. If dichotic listening is to fulfill its early promise as a valid measure of lateralized perceptual processes, we need to renew our efforts to establish its validity for speech localization against the criteria of intracarotid sodium amytal injection and the newer measures of cerebral metabolism."

1. **Kimura D.** Cerebral dominance and the perception of verbal stimuli. *Can. J. Psychol.* **15**:166-71, 1961.
2. **Levy J.** Psychobiological implications of bilateral symmetry. (Dimond S J & Beaumont J G, eds.) *Hemisphere function in the human brain.* New York: Halsted Press, 1974. p. 121-83.
3. **Zaidel E.** Lexical organization in the right hemisphere. (Buser P A & Rougeul-Buser A, eds.) *Cerebral correlates of conscious experience.* Amsterdam: Elsevier/North Holland, 1978. p. 177-97.

CC/NUMBER 14
APRIL 7, 1980

This Week's Citation Classic

Liberman A M, Cooper F S, Shankweiler D P & Studdert-Kennedy M. Perception of the speech code. *Psychol. Rev.* **74**:431-61, 1967.
[Haskins Laboratories, New York, NY]

The phonemic segments (consonants and vowels) of speech are encoded in such a way that a single acoustic cue carries information in parallel about successive phonemes. This reduces the rate at which discrete sound segments must be perceived, but at the price of a peculiar relation between acoustic cue and phoneme: cues vary with context, and there are, in these cases, no commutable acoustic segments of phonemic size. Phoneme perception therefore requires a special decoder. [The *Science Citation Index® (SCI®)* **and the** *Social Sciences Citation Index™ (SSCI™)* **indicate that this paper has been cited over 415 times since 1967.]**

A.M. Liberman
Haskins Laboratories
270 Crown Street
New Haven, CT 06510

January 31, 1980

"The paper's publication coincided with the rising influence of modern linguistics on psychology and with a revived interest among psychologists in the biological foundations of human cognitive capacities, thus accounting for its frequent citation.

"Our work began with our inability, just after World War II, to solve a practical problem: how to convert print to sound in a reading machine for the blind. Initially, we assumed that, just as consonants and vowels are represented in writing by discrete letters of an optical alphabet, so are they represented in speech by an alphabet of sounds. We therefore created devices to transform each letter into an arbitrary but distinctive pattern of sound, expecting that our blind subjects would learn this acoustic alphabet much as they had, in our view, learned the equally alphabetic sounds of natural speech. In the event, they did not. We were slow to appreciate the significance of this failure, but we finally saw that it might be impossible for a human being ever to learn to make efficient use of an arbitrary alphabet of sounds, however distinctive each sound might be. That led us, naturally enough, to ask: what is special about speech that makes it work so well?

"The answer we offered in our 1967 paper was that speech is not an acoustic alphabet (or cipher) but a peculiar, and peculiarly efficient, code. From a functional point of view, the speech code matches the special requirements of linguistic communication to properties of the vocal and auditory systems that evolved long before language. The chief formal characteristic of the code is that successive consonant and vowel segments are restructured (i.e., encoded) for overlapping and near simultaneous transmission. Since that characteristic of speech follows from the way it is articulated—or, more properly, co-articulated—we came to appreciate that the key to the code is in its manner of production: in speech the processes of perception and production are somehow intimately linked.

"The greatest change in our thinking since the 1967 paper is in our recognition that research on speech opens broad and inviting vistas. We are ever more persuaded that speech is a grammatical code, exhibiting close formal and functional resemblances to the codes of phonology and syntax. In that sense—and, we think, in every other—speech is an integral part of language. It is also the part most accessible to scientific investigation. We hope, therefore, to use it increasingly as a window on language, believing that for many purposes it will afford a better view than we can get at other levels.

"Having been invited to say here what could hardly be said in a formal scientific publication, we would point out that a full six years elapsed between the beginning of the work and the first publication of results. There are, we suppose, few institutions that would have given young investigators so much time. We are therefore grateful to the very small and very independent laboratory that did."

This Week's Citation Classic

Anderson J R & Bower G H. *Human associative memory.*
Washington, DC: Winston & Sons, 1973. 524 p.
[Yale Univ., New Haven, CT and Stanford Univ., Stanford, CA]

The book described an associative theory of human memory, embodied in a computer simulation that made a wide range of predictions about sentence memory and other verbal learning phenomena. The theory dealt successfully with organizational phenomena thought to disconfirm associative theories. [The *Science Citation Index*® (*SCI*®) and the *Social Sciences Citation Index*™ (*SSCI*™) indicate that this book has been cited over 320 times since 1973.]

John R. Anderson
Department of Psychology
Carnegie-Mellon University
Pittsburgh, PA 15213

August 8, 1979

"The book reflects the culmination of a four year collaborative relationship between myself and Gordon Bower. When I arrived at Stanford University as a graduate assistant to Gordon Bower, there was an ongoing research program concerned with organizational and imaginal factors in various memory tasks. As we tried to become precise, even quantitative, in fitting organizational theory to free recall data, its differences from associationistic models of free recall seemed to evaporate, frankly, because neither theory had been formulated with any real precision up to that time. It became clear that what was needed was a theory of memory that was both general and precise.

"The outcome of rather intensive ruminations and discussions was the theory for human associative memory (HAM) that was proposed in the book. This was first worked out in detail in a long 'dissertation proposal' in which I had several goals: To present an associative theory of sentence memory, to report evidence relevant to it, to relate the theory to the historical tradition of associationism, and to indicate how a few standard 'verbal learning' phenomena might be interpreted in terms of this approach. That document formed the basic outline for the book. I wrote the language parser and question-answerer of HAM as LISP code. The proposal and computer simulation led to a productive set of discussions and experiments, many of which are scattered throughout the book.

"In the spring of 1972 the collaborative writing of the book began. Each day was filled with hours of fruitful discussions followed by our individual writing efforts. In these discussions we came to adopt characteristic roles—I as the proposer, interpreter, and defender of HAM, and Gordon Bower as the critic, provider of more problems, and the demander of greater generality. However, like most fruitful interchanges, ours were freewheeling, and we adopted various roles as the occasion demanded. The discussions and writing turned out to be both personally and intellectually the most gratifying moments of our collaboration.

"Since that time HAM has been subject to considerable experimentation and discussion. It has been found to be wrong on some points and controversial on others. I was bothered by the fact that HAM did not say much about how memories were used in thought. This led to the development of the ACT model[1] which has a production system for mental procedures which interfaced this procedural component with a memory model derived from HAM. Gordon Bower was bothered by the fact that HAM does not address the issues of how large bodies of text material are processed, how large knowledge structures are organized in memory, and how these large structures are used to interpret text. This led him to an interest in story comprehension, scripts and schemata, and reconstructive memory processes.[2]

"Still HAM is very much with us and has important influences on our thinking about these new problems. In HAM we find many concepts and analyses that we can use as foundations for our new endeavors. Shortly, a revised edition of the book will appear.[3] This edition is an attempt to focus on those aspects of the HAM theory that still seem relevant for the 1980s."

1. **Anderson J R.** *Language, memory, and thought.* Hillsdale, NJ: Lawrence Erlbaum Associates, 1976. 546 p.
2. **Bower G H, Black J B & Turner T J.** Scripts in memory for text. *Cog. Psychol.* **11**:177-220, 1979.
3. **Anderson J R & Bower G H.** *Human associative memory: revised edition.* Hillsdale, NJ: Lawrence Erlbaum Associates. In press, 1980.

CC/NUMBER 50
DECEMBER 10, 1979

This Week's Citation Classic

Craik F I M & Lockhart R S. Levels of processing: a framework for memory research. *J. Verb. Learn. Verb. Behav.* **11**:671-84, 1972.
[University of Toronto, Toronto, Ontario, Canada]

The authors suggest that human memory be viewed as the record of mental operations carried out primarily for the purposes of perception and comprehension. The operations are performed at various levels of processing, where 'deeper' levels involve greater semantic analysis and are associated with longer-lasting memory traces. [The *Science Citation Index*® *(SCI*®*)* **and the** *Social Sciences Citation Index* ™ *(SSCI*™*)* **indicate that this paper has been cited over 590 times since 1972.]**

Fergus I. M. Craik
Department of Psychology
University of Toronto
Toronto, Canada

September 7, 1979

"In the 1960s, human memory was thought about principally in terms of stores that were characterized as holding different kinds of information for various lengths of time. The generally accepted model was one in which the sense organs fed information into associated sensory memory stores. The information was then transferred to a limited-capacity short-term memory and finally into a permanent long-term memory. Researchers were concerned with such problems as the capacity of the various stores, their coding characteristics, and the mechanism of information transfer between the stores.

"Robert Lockhart and I had both been involved with these types of questions in Sydney and London respectively, but since coming to Toronto we had both developed serious reservations about the continuing usefulness of the stores metaphor. Presumably, different experimental techniques should yield the same values of capacity, decay rate, and so on, but they did not; perhaps the data could be reinterpreted within a rather different conceptual framework. Lockhart and I found that we held very similar views on one such alternative framework in which discrete stores were replaced by a continuum of processing varying from shallow sensory analyses to deeper, semantic analyses. We postulated that memory was the record of the operations carried out during perception and comprehension, and that deeper levels of processing were associated with longer-lasting memory traces.

"At that time our colleague, Endel Tulving, was editor of the *Journal of Verbal Learning and Verbal Behavior* and he asked us to write up the ideas for the last issue under his editorship, December 1972. So Lockhart and I worked on the article in the early summer of that year, by turns being praised, threatened, and cajoled by Tulving in order to meet his publication deadline! In fact Endel Tulving gave us a great deal of help during the writing and editing process and it is pleasant to be able to record our appreciation of his efforts.

"It seems likely that the article has attracted some attention because memory researchers were unhappy with the notion of memory stores and were looking for a more process-oriented account of remembering and forgetting. The ideas that Lockhart and I put forward were very much in the air at the time, to the extent that quite a few people told us later that they were just about to write a similar article. Indeed, one person—Laird Cermak—had already set down a parallel set of ideas in his textbook on memory.[1] More recently, the levels of processing viewpoint has come in for a good deal of criticism on the grounds of its lack of predictive power. Over the next few years it will be interesting to see whether the Craik and Lockhart framework can nevertheless lead to a fuller *understanding* of memory processes."

1. **Cermak L S.** *Human memory: research and theory.* New York: Ronald Press, 1972. 294 p.

This Week's Citation Classic

Brown R & McNeill D. The "tip of the tongue" phenomenon.
J. Verb. Learn. Verb. Behav. **5**:325-37, 1966.
[Harvard University, Cambridge, MA]

In a 'tip of the tongue' state (unable to recall a word well known), one can recall much about the word (e.g., length in syllables, first and last letters). The kinds of information recalled provide clues to the mode of organization of the mental lexicon. [The *Social Sciences Citation Index*® (*SSCI*®) indicates that this paper has been cited in over 200 publications since 1966.]

Roger Brown
Department of Psychology and
Social Relations
Harvard University
Cambridge, MA 02138

November 8, 1982

"This experiment was inspired by a passage from William James[1] in which he considers the seeming paradox that when one cannot recall a word, the gap in memory which, described as a gap, should be empty of content is, nevertheless, singularly definite in its ability to identify words that are almost correct and confident to reject words that are far from being correct. We invented a procedure that would fairly often precipitate 'tip of the tongue' (TOT) states and a way of collecting information from persons in the throes of that state and were able to resolve James's paradox by showing that the empty gap always has a generic shape.

"We read definitions of fairly uncommon words to large numbers of potential subjects (e.g., 'a navigational instrument used in measuring angular distances, especially the altitude of sun, moon, and stars at sea') and when one fell into a TOT seizure (unable to recall *sextant* but certain he knew the word and, in fact, it was just on the tip...), we asked him to guess the first letter and number of syllables and to report all the candidate words that came to mind (e.g., *secant, sexton, astrolabe, compass, sextet, protractor*). Prospecting for TOTs in this way, we obtained 360 instances across many subjects and many words. Analysis of the full data showed that a person in a TOT state has quite a lot of information about the missing target word: number of syllables, location of primary stress, and some constituent letters, especially those at the beginning and end of the word (a bowed serial position effect in general). The information recalled, though short of the full target word, was sufficient to reject bad matches and resonate to near-fits. From the very canonical character of this abstract recall, it was possible to formulate hypotheses about both word perception and the organization of what we may call the mental lexicon.

"The basic findings of the TOT experiment have proved to be highly replicable and the method adaptable to the discovery of additional information.[2] Some of the fascination of the TOT state derives surely from the feeling that in this state the mind is very near the surface. It was an entertaining experiment to do and is, furthermore, an enduring source of pleasure because as one's memory for names grows worse, the loss is compensated by increased opportunity to study the associative structure of memory."

1. **James W.** *The principles of psychology*. New York: Holt, 1893. Vol. I.
2. **Rubin D C.** Within word structure in the tip-of-the-tongue phenomenon. *J. Verb. Learn. Verb. Behav.* **14**:392-7, 1975.

 CC/NUMBER 36
SEPTEMBER 6, 1982

Peterson L R & Peterson M J. Short-term retention of individual verbal items.
J. Exp. Psychol. **58**:193-8, 1959.
[Indiana University, Bloomington, IN]

Marked forgetting of a single syllable was found within seconds after one presentation. Forgetting progressed at differential rates depending on amount of controlled rehearsal. Short-term retention was indicated as a factor in the acquisition process. [The *Science Citation Index®* (*SCI®*) **and the** *Social Sciences Citation Index®* (*SSCI®*) **indicate that this paper has been cited in over 625 publications since 1961.]**

Lloyd R. Peterson
Department of Psychology
Indiana University
Bloomington, IN 47405

June 17, 1982

"My graduate research with rats involved the study of the effects of short delays between a tone and the delivery of food. Having become aware of the importance of brief intervals of time, when I turned as an assistant professor at Indiana University to do research on human memory, I was struck by its neglect of short retention intervals. Classical methods examined recall of a list of words many minutes or hours after learning. I suspected that forgetting must occur during the learning itself, as one forgets one word while thinking about others.

"My wife and I planned studies of forgetting of a single verbal item, and she carried them out. It was surprisingly difficult for a college student to remember three letters while counting backward for three to 18 seconds after one presentation. Time was required to retrieve an item much as in long-term memory. Contrary to a speculation that rehearsal merely postponed the onset of forgetting,[1] we found that the forgetting curve starting at the end of the last rehearsal had an asymptote dependent on the number of rehearsals. The evidence linked short-term retention with the acquisition process.

"An associate editor accepted our manuscript for publication with the proviso that several graphs be condensed into one table to save space. This eliminated the key graph showing differential forgetting as a function of rehearsal. Because tables are seldom studied, textbook authors tend to miss the heart of the article. Typically, they reproduce the figure showing a plunging retention curve after one presentation and ignore the effects of rehearsal. Even the description of the figure is often faulty in implying the curve represents all that could be recalled. Our article explained that the figure was limited to recalls having a latency less than the mean for all recalls, the objective being to fit a stimulus fluctuation model to the data. Total amount recalled was displayed cumulatively in another graph.

"Appreciation of the article's theoretical implications owes much to Arthur Melton, the senior editor, who discussed it in a well-known address to the American Association for the Advancement of Science.[2] Three factors appear to underlie its continuing citation. First, the experiments emphasized temporal process characteristics of short-term memory rather than traditional capacity limitations. Second, the article suggested a neglected theoretical relationship between short-term memory and learning. Third, it described a simple method for measuring short-term retention by which experimenters could readily explore the implications of the first two factors. Continuing controversy over a number of issues keeps the memory of the article alive."[3]

1. **Brown J.** Some tests of the decay theory of immediate memory. *Quart. J. Exp. Psychol.* **10**:12-21, 1958.
2. **Melton A W.** Implications of short-term memory for a general theory of memory. *J. Verb. Learn. Verb. Behav.* **2**:1-21, 1963.
3. **Lewis D J.** Psychobiology of active and inactive memory. *Psychol. Bull.* **86**:1054-83, 1979.

CC/NUMBER 13
MARCH 26, 1984

This Week's Citation Classic™

Tversky B. Pictorial and verbal encoding in a short-term memory task. *Percept. Psychophysics* **6**:225-33, 1969.
[Hebrew University, Jerusalem, Israel]

The encoding modality, pictorial or verbal, of schematic faces was manipulated by subjects' expectations of the retrieval task, either face or name recognition, and verified by faster 'same' reaction times to the expected modality and slower 'different' reaction times to similarity along the expected modality. [The *Science Citation Index*® (*SCI*®) and the *Social Sciences Citation Index*® (*SSCI*®) indicate that this paper has been cited in over 150 publications since 1969.]

Barbara Tversky
Department of Psychology
Stanford University
Stanford, CA 94305

February 16, 1984

"In the 1960s, under the direction of Arthur Melton and Paul Fitts, the Human Performance Center (HPC) of the psychology department of the University of Michigan was a lively place. There were new ideas, new questions, new measures, and new paradigms; the field of information processing was wide open. Photocopying was new and cheap, so reprints and preprints were readily available from enormous filing cabinets. If you listened to the buzzing, you could hear: 'Melton says short-term memory (STM) and long-term memory (LTM) are just ends of a continuous phenomenon,' 'Conrad and Wickelgren claim STM is acoustic but LTM is semantic,' 'Sternberg showed that STM is scanned serially and exhaustively,' 'Neisser showed that with practice, memory scanning is parallel,' and so on. Issues waiting to be explored and settled. HPC was bustling with graduate students, undergraduates, young faculty, old faculty, short-term visitors, and long-term visitors. The names on the reprints and preprints appeared in real life to share their wisdom and inspire more experiments.

"Of all the issues buzzing in the background, the one that captured my attention was the claim that STM is acoustic (or articulatory or verbal). Since STM was the gateway to LTM, that implied that memory for sights and sounds and smells was verbal description. I set out to find evidence for pictorial encoding in STM. In order to do so, I needed stimuli that could be represented pictorially or verbally, and a way to tell them apart. Faces and names seemed appropriate, where pictorial similarity of the faces and verbal similarity of the names could be varied orthogonally. I induced subjects to encode pictorially by giving a pictorial test ('Did you just see this person?') or verbally by giving a verbal test ('Was that so-and-so?'). In the experiments that were never sent for publication, I looked for pictorial or verbal errors of memory depending on task expectations. Although I found them, they were not very numerous, so I turned to a young measure gaining in popularity, reaction time. That worked, providing a useful demonstration of flexible pictorial or verbal encoding of the same stimuli in accordance with task demands.

"Although the fields of picture memory and imagery have since burgeoned, the issues are still with us in the guise of the so-called propositional-imagery debate. This is a war between dualists, who maintain that there are imaginal and linguistic representations in memory, and unitarians, who maintain that propositions represent both verbal and pictorial events. By now, the agnostics have entered the field, declaring the dispute undecidable in principle. Of course, there is only one underlying representation, and that representation is neural. But I believe that there is a level of analysis where it makes sense to talk about different *kinds* of representations, and where different and interesting consequences of such representations can be demonstrated (for a cogent review, see Shepard and Podgorny[1]).

"It seems to me that the bias that led psychologists in the 1960s to posit that STM is acoustic and rehearsal is verbal is the same bias that leads psychologists in the 1980s to maintain that knowledge is represented in propositions. When we think about thinking, we think we are thinking in words."

1. **Shepard R N & Podgorny P.** Cognitive processes that resemble perceptual processes. (Estes W K, ed.) *Handbook of learning and cognitive processes. Volume 5. Human information processing.* Hillsdale, NJ: Lawrence Erlbaum, 1978. p. 189-237.

CC/NUMBER 25
JUNE 18, 1984

This Week's Citation Classic™

Slamecka N J. An examination of trace storage in free recall.
J. Exp. Psychol. **76**:504-13, 1968.
[University of Vermont, Burlington, VT]

The question was whether, after the study of a list of verbal items, the stored memory traces of the words have formed direct connections to each other, or whether they have not. It was concluded that they have not. [The *Social Sciences Citation Index*® (*SSCI*®) indicates that this paper has been cited in over 140 publications since 1968.]

Norman J. Slamecka
Department of Psychology
University of Toronto
Toronto, Ontario M5S 1A1
Canada

May 8, 1984

"This work was started in my days at the University of Vermont, as a modest effort aimed at demonstrating the correctness of the prevailing associationistic doctrine of the time, namely, that memorization of a verbal list entails the forming and strengthening of direct associative bonds among the words on the list. The only original contribution anticipated was the relatively simple method to be employed for the demonstration. After studying a list, an experimental group would be given some of the words free, to use as retrieval cues for recall of the remaining ones. A control group, given no cues, would try to recall the entire list. Both groups were then to be scored on the very same items, those not given free. It was clearly expected that the experimental condition would show superior performance because of activation of some otherwise inaccessible associative links, these being stimulated by the presence of the free words.

"Accordingly, I sent my graduate assistant, Ed Coppage, to collect the initial data on this straightforward exercise. In the face of our compelling preconceived expectations, we were annoyingly disappointed to find that the experiment failed to show any advantage for the cued group, and worse, that it revealed a small but significant inhibitory effect in that condition. Thinking that this first outcome was only a matter of bad luck which would not persist across subsequent replications, we returned to the laboratory to carry out a series of variations on this experiment, always keeping the same basic design. We manipulated the proportion of free words given, the type of material comprising the lists, and access to short-term memory. All told, we conducted six separate experiments and each one told the same empirical story, namely, that provision of free words did not aid memory performance. I had no choice but to conclude that the classical theoretical portrayal of memory traces as being joined by direct associative links was wrong.

"It so happened that Endel Tulving came to give a talk at Vermont just when I had completed writing the report of this work. Maintaining a firm grip on his lapel, I regaled him with these findings in my office until 11 o'clock that night. He endured this with exemplary fortitude and, as I found out later, harbored some silent scepticism about the meaning of the whole thing until further work by me[1,2] and independent efforts by others[3,4] extended the tenor of the initial findings, and led to a theoretical picture of a hierarchical storage structure. The original publication doubtless attracted interest because of the beguiling simplicity of the method, and the then counterintuitive nature of the findings. A recent overview of this work is in Roediger and Neely."[3,5]

1. **Slamecka N J.** Testing for associative storage in multitrial free recall. *J. Exp. Psychol.* **81**:557-60, 1969.
2. ------------------. The question of associative growth in the learning of categorized material. *J. Verb. Learn. Verb. Behav.* **11**:324-32, 1972.
3. **Roediger H L.** Inhibition in recall from cueing with recall targets. *J. Verb. Learn. Verb. Behav.* **12**:644-57, 1973.
4. **Rundus D.** Negative effects of using list items as recall cues. *J. Verb. Learn. Verb. Behav.* **12**:43-50, 1973.
5. **Roediger H L & Neely J H.** Retrieval blocks in episodic and semantic memory. *Can. J. Psychol.* **36**:213-42, 1982.

Thomson D M & Tulving E. Associative encoding and retrieval: weak and strong cues. *J. Exp. Psychol.* **86**:255-62, 1970.
[Department of Psychology, Yale University, New Haven, CT]

To-be-remembered words were presented for study in the presence of weakly associated cue words. Recall of to-be-remembered words was facilitated when these weakly associated words were provided as retrieval cues. No facilitation of recall occurred where strong normative associated words were provided as retrieval cues. It was concluded that the effectiveness of retrieval cues depends on the format of the to-be-remembered information at the time of its storage. [The *Science Citation Index*® (*SCI*®) and the *Social Sciences Citation Index*® (*SSCI*®) indicate that this paper has been cited in over 170 publications since 1970.]

D.M. Thomson
Department of Psychology
Monash University
Clayton, Victoria 3168
Australia

April 27, 1984

"The research reported in this paper was conceived by me with two objectives in mind: to illuminate memory processes and as a means of launching an attack on Endel Tulving. In 1967, I had resigned a well-paid job and, with my wife and children, moved from Australia halfway around the world to undertake graduate studies in social psychology at the University of Toronto. On arriving in Toronto, I was stunned to learn that I had been shanghaied into memory research. My initial meeting with the person assigned as my supervisor, Tulving, exacerbated my resentment and anger. I was subjected to a comprehensive oral quiz on memory research. My humiliation was complete when, at the conclusion of the interview, Tulving informed me that on a 0 to 10 scale I was somewhere about -3. I left Tulving's room determined to master the area and to puncture his arrogant mien.

"I read widely on different aspects of memory and then critically examined all of Tulving's publications. In one of his papers,[1] which then was about to be published, I found what I thought was the means of achieving my goals. In the paper, it was implicitly denied that cues strongly associated to the information to be remembered would be effective in retrieving the information. For the next three months, I avoided Tulving while I designed and ran experiments that would surely reveal his foolishness. It is history that the experimental findings provided convincing support for Tulving's claim. The findings of this research formed the basis of this paper, the first of three[2,3] published by Tulving and me reporting findings in support of the encoding specificity principle. The effectiveness of a retrieval cue varies directly with the extent it matches the format of the to-be-remembered information stored in memory.

"Perhaps predictably, the reactions of my academic colleagues passed through two phases. In the first phase, both the results and the theory were fiercely disputed; and in the second phase, my colleagues asserted, just as vehemently, that both the results and the theory were obvious and trite.

"In my judgment, the reason why this paper had the impact it did was that the position it espoused more accurately described memory than previous explanations. Whereas previously researchers had examined memory as a function of encoding events or as a function of retrieval events, this paper treated encoding and retrieval as interrelated and integrated processes. My current research in this area indicates that the validity of the encoding specificity principle extends to memory for objects and persons.[4]

"Cognizance of these latter findings has been taken in the recommendation of the Australia Law Reform Commission with respect to identification procedures."

1. **Tulving E & Osler S.** Effectiveness of retrieval cues in memory for words. *J. Exp. Psychol.* 77:593-601, 1968. (Cited 150 times.)
2. **Tulving E & Thomson D M.** Retrieval processes in recognition memory: effects of associative context. *J. Exp. Psychol.* **87**:116-24, 1971. (Cited 160 times.)
3. ----------------------------------. Encoding specificity and retrieval processes in episodic memory. *Psychol. Rev.* **80**:352-73, 1973. (Cited 600 times.)
4. **Thomson D M, Robertson S L & Vogt R.** Person recognition: the effect of context. *Hum. Learn.* **1**:137-54, 1982.

CC/NUMBER 50
DECEMBER 12, 1983

This Week's Citation Classic

Broadbent D E. The role of auditory localization in attention and memory span. *J. Exp. Psychol.* **47**:191-6, 1954.
[Applied Psychology Research Unit, Medical Research Council, Cambridge, England]

This paper reported a series of experiments on the efficiency with which people could understand one of two speech messages, presented from the same or different locations. A second group of experiments showed a short-lasting memory that could temporarily hold unselected material, and allow later response. [The *Science Citation Index*® (*SCI*®) and the *Social Sciences Citation Index*® (*SSCI*®) indicate that this paper has been cited in over 200 publications since 1961.]

Donald E. Broadbent
Department of Experimental Psychology
University of Oxford
Oxford OX1 3UD
England

October 31, 1983

"As technology expanded in the 1940s and 1950s, people were increasingly expected to work in artificial environments. That applied particularly to the military, where gunnery systems or air traffic control problems might require the same person to monitor, and sometimes to respond to, numerous speech messages arriving by loudspeaker or headphones. The Royal Navy, and later the Royal Air Force, asked for advice on ways of improving performance. The request ended up at the Medical Research Council's Applied Psychology Unit in Cambridge, England, where I was working as a newly fledged BA. So I spent quite a lot of time looking at ships and control towers, as well as talking to the people who worked in them. Obviously there were problems of speech quality, and of masking of one voice by another. There seemed also, however, to be difficulties that arose when the man was 'overloaded' with work.

"To research this problem meant getting some of the newfangled tape recorders; more, it would obviously be useful to have one which carried two independent messages on different tracks. We therefore got by special order what must have been almost the first stereo tape recorders in Britain. I then settled down to see how multiple messages could best be presented: mixed, separated into different places, stereo separated, or perhaps one on one earphone and the other on another. Almost all ways of marking two competing messages as localised improved performance, but there was more to it than a reduction in acoustic masking. What we were getting was a selective mechanism, picking some of the input signals for response and discarding others.

"Academic theory of the time did not give much space to such concepts, but tried to work directly with stimulus-response, or at least stimulus-experience links. While this paper had a big practical effect, the main reason for it being cited is probably because it was an early step in the move to theories of internal information processing. Interestingly, it seems to be rarely remembered that the paper itself showed that the selectivity was *not* peripheral, but would work with stereo. Further, it followed an unselective memory system. Much debate on just these points has raged since, and the field of 'attention' is now so extended that it is dividing into separate special groups working in subfields.[1] In the past decade, the emphasis has shifted toward visual rather than auditory performance, because techniques of stimulus control are better. The paper remains relevant as an example of the way in which practical problems can reveal a weak point in academic theorising."

1. **Broadbent D E.** Task combination and selective intake of information. *Acta Psychol.* **50**:253-90, 1982.

This Week's Citation Classic

Sachs J S. Recognition memory for syntactic and semantic aspects of connected discourse. *Percept. Psychophys.* **2**:437-42, 1967.
[Bell Telephone Labs., Murray Hill, NJ]

This paper demonstrated that the original wording of a sentence is typically remembered only for a very brief time. When a semantic interpretation has been made, the meaning but not the exact linguistic form is stored. [The *Social Sciences Citation Index*® *(SSCI™)* **indicates that this paper has been cited over 220 times since 1967.]**

J. S. Sachs
Department of Communication Sciences
University of Connecticut
Storrs, CT 06268

August 28, 1980

"This paper was based on my PhD dissertation research carried out at the University of California at Berkeley. I had long been intrigued by language processing, including the phenomenon of an 'auditory echo' of what one had just heard or said. This example of short-term memory is most startlingly apparent when one suddenly realizes that one has said something incorrectly.

"Most memory studies using verbal material at that time seemed to be based upon the assumption that the stimulus as perceived is stored in memory, with the 'trace' of the stimulus gradually fading with time or due to interference from previous and subsequent experience. Typically, experiments required subjects to learn lists or pairs of lists of words or nonsense syllables that appeared one at a time, briefly, in the window of a 'memory drum.' Serving as a subject in such experiments for many hours at Berkeley, and earlier as an undergraduate at Northwestern University, convinced me that, although such experiments were convenient to run, the rote memory process had little resemblance to memory in most everyday life contexts. I suspected that at least in language, but probably more generally, a dramatically recoded perception, rather than the original one, was stored in memory.

"My experiment demonstrated that the specific wording of an utterance is forgotten within seconds after it is heard. In contrast, the meaning of that utterance can be retained for a very long period. The 'auditory echo' that allows one to rehear an error is transient and fragile. Later, I showed that this phenomenon applies not only to aural language but also to text that is read.[1]

"I believe that this work is cited so often for two reasons. First, it provided a method for studying memory for language and for changes in meaning that was much less cumbersome than other methods such as scoring accuracy of recall. Also, my study was cast in a theoretical context that was consistent with the developing *Zeitgeist:* a view of memory (all memory, not just for language) in terms of levels of processing. According to this view, incoming stimuli are recoded, and various aspects of the material may be retained, recast, or cast aside in processing.

"In addition to its contribution to a basic understanding of language processing and memory, this study had practical implications; for example, in the weighing of the credibility of legal testimony. Clearly, if an attorney asks a witness, 'What exactly did the defendant tell you. . . ?', the witness's answer is unlikely to be an exact quotation, although it *may* be an accurate paraphrase.

"In recent years I have turned my attention to how children acquire their first language. In view of the considerable demands that retaining the form of an utterance has for adults, the processing demands upon infants who are learning their first language can be seen to be extraordinary."

1. **Sachs J S.** Memory in reading and listening to discourse. *Mem. Cognition* **2**:95-100, 1974.

This Week's Citation Classic

Tulving E & Pearlstone Z. Availability versus accessibility of information in memory for words. *J. Verb. Learn. Verb. Behav.* 5:381-91, 1966.
[University of Toronto, Canada]

Information stored in memory is accessible to retrieval only under special conditions. Inability to recall learned material, therefore, does not necessarily mean that the information has been lost; it may only reflect the inadequacy of retrieval cues. This paper describes an experimental demonstration of these facts. [The *Science Citation Index® (SCI®)* **and the** *Social Sciences Citation Index™ (SSCI™)* **indicate that this paper has been cited over 255 times since 1966.]**

Endel Tulving
Department of Psychology
University of Toronto
Toronto, Ontario

April 5, 1978

"This paper owes its existence to a student who questioned a routine statement I made in my memory seminar one day early in 1963. The statement was to the effect that people remember many things they cannot recall even when they try very hard and are given a lot of time for it. The sceptical student wanted to know what kind of evidence was available for the statement, and I had to admit that it was a self-evident truth that did not require any laboratory results for its support. Such an unscientific attitude did not please the members of the seminar. In an attempt to convince them, I did a simple demonstration experiment on the spot, the nine students in the seminar serving as subjects.

"The Tulving and Pearlstone paper describes a much more extensive and tightly controlled version of the original classroom demonstration. The results of a large experiment provided massive data in support of the conclusion that recall of studied material depends critically on both the conditions of storage and the conditions of retrieval: large variations in the amount recalled can occur when either of these two sets of conditions is held constant.

"Neither our experimental findings nor attendant theoretical speculations were novel, the distinction between what we called 'availability' and 'accessibility' of memory information—corresponding to the distinction between storage and retrieval—having appeared in various disguises at various times in history. But we may have been among the first to combine data and theory in a reasonably convincing package. Since the paper appeared relatively early in the *zeitgeist*-driven period of growing interest in the interaction between storage and retrieval processes in memory, it frequently serves as a convenient reference for some of the basic facts pertaining to the distinction. An interesting observation is that although 'availability' and 'accessibility' are generally identified with our paper, another term we introduced, 'retrieval cue,' widely used in contemporary psychological literature on memory, suffered absolutely instant obliteration.

"Zena Pearlstone was my research assistant. She tested over 900 high-school students as subjects in the experiment and helped to collate and analyze the data. Some time after completing this Herculean task, she left Toronto and also the field of experimental psychology. She now lives in New Jersey, and is on the verge of receiving her Ph.D. in art history. I have continued working on problems of memory. Almost all of my research over the past 15 years has its roots in the Tulving and Pearlstone experiment and the lessons it taught us."

CC/NUMBER 17
APRIL 25, 1983

This Week's Citation Classic

Mandler J M & Johnson N S. Remembrance of things parsed: story structure and recall. *Cognitive Psychol.* 9:111-51, 1977.
[University of California, San Diego, La Jolla, CA]

An analysis is presented of the structure of simple stories, couched in the form of a grammar, consisting of rules defining story units and their relationships. Experience with this structure creates a schema that guides encoding and retrieval. Reanalyses of Bartlett's[1] protocols and new developmental data support the formulation. [The *Social Sciences Citation Index*® *(SSCI*®) **indicates that this paper has been cited in over 190 publications since 1977.]**

Jean M. Mandler
Department of Psychology
University of California
La Jolla, CA 92093

February 28, 1983

"When I began work on cognitive development at the University of California, San Diego, in the early-1970s, I wanted to study how complex, naturalistic kinds of materials are processed. Most of my work at that time was on memory for scenes. I wanted to extend this kind of work to the verbal realm, and that old standby—lists of words—simply would not do. Stories seemed to be excellent materials. I was familiar with Piaget's[2] claim that children have difficulty in recalling stories in their proper order. From my observation of children, this finding seemed odd. The clue as to what might be wrong came when I examined the stories he had used. I tried to retell one of them one day and botched it. This (not surprisingly) suggested to me that there was something odd about the story, not the child. But how could one characterize what was wrong with the story?

"At about this time Dave Rumelhart was working on the notion of a story schema.[3] When I heard him talk about it in one of our departmental seminars, I realized that this sort of analysis could be used not only to differentiate well-structured stories from poorly structured ones, but also to express the ways in which one recall protocol differed from another. What a boon for developmental research! We might be able to say not just that adults remember more than children, but to characterize the qualitative differences, if any, in their recall.

"So, using Rumelhart's work as a base, Nancy Johnson and I began to develop our *story grammar.* We spent many months trying to formulate a simple and workable, yet comprehensive, set of rules to describe the typical forms of folktales and other stories from the oral tradition. In the process, we found (as had linguists before us) that the same forms occurred repeatedly in the stories of many cultures. Something looking very much like a universal type of structure began to emerge, but one that had psychological, as well as linguistic, significance.

"The *Citation Classic* described the rules of the grammar and showed that six-year-olds recall stories in ways very similar to adults. Later work showed that when stories are poorly structured, children indeed have trouble in sequencing their recall, but so do adults.[4] People from other cultures also recall stories in the same way—the universals are not just in the form of the texts, but in how they are processed as well.[5]

"This paper has been highly cited for several reasons. The ability to relate a text's structure in a detailed fashion to the way in which it is understood and remembered was new, and led to a great deal of research by developmental, cognitive, and educational psychologists. The ideas espoused in the paper (and in the more recent expansions[6,7]) also fit in well with the growing interest in schema theory in general, which probably contributed to the article's popularity. Its title may have helped too!"

1. **Bartlett F C.** *Remembering.* Cambridge, England: Cambridge University Press, 1932. 317 p.
2. **Piaget J.** *The language and thought of the child.* London: Routledge & Kegan Paul, 1960.
3. **Rumelhart D E.** Notes on a schema for stories. (Bobrow D G & Collins A, eds.) *Representation and understanding: studies in cognitive science.* New York: Academic Press, 1980. p. 211-36.
4. **Mandler J M.** A code in the node: the use of a story schema in retrieval. *Discourse Process.* 1:14-35, 1978.
5. **Mandler J M, Scribner S, Cole M & DeForest M.** Cross-cultural invariance in story recall. *Child Develop.* 51:19-26, 1980.
6. **Johnson N S & Mandler J M.** A tale of two structures: underlying and surface forms in stories. *Poetics* 9:51-86, 1980.
7. **Mandler J M & Goodman M S.** On the psychological validity of story structure. *J. Verb. Learn. Verb. Behav.* 21:507-23, 1982.

Chapter

5

Behaviorism and Neo-behaviorism

General exposition and critique / 105–109

Reinforcement process / 110–113

Study of specific behaviors / 114–132

This Week's Citation Classic

NUMBER 30
JULY 23, 1979

Ferster C B & Skinner B F. *Schedules of Reinforcement.*
Englewood Cliffs, NJ: Prentice-Hall, 1957, 741 p.
[Indiana Univ. Med. Ctr., Bloomington, IN and Harvard Univ., Cambridge, MA]

Intermittent reinforcement, an important condition of action, was studied by altering the schedule by which a pigeon's peck at an illuminated disc produces brief access to food. Far from falling short of the ideal of inevitable reinforcement, it constitutes an important condition of action. The control proved to be orderly and systematic, demonstrable in the individual and a highly reproducible baseline for the study of other biological variables. [The *Science Citation Index®* *(SCI®)* **and the** *Social Sciences Citation Index™* *(SSCI™)* **indicate that this paper has been cited over 1180 times since 1961.]**

C. B. Ferster
Department of Psychology
American University
Washington, DC 20016
and
B.F. Skinner
Harvard University
Cambridge, MA 02138

July 31, 1978

"The research was a playful experience. No thought was given to publication during its first three years, major energy going into the discoveries of orderliness and control which fortunately came in an abundant harvest almost weekly. When a variable was altered the results were visible in the individual organism without elaborate statistical processing. The cumulative recorder which processed the data in visual summary form was crucial, allowing us to see the overall pattern and details of rate changes over a 10-hour day experimental session at a glance. Until a recorder was designed which could operate reliably for thousands of hours and millions of pecks, a considerable portion of my time was spent servicing them. Eventually, almost a billion pecks were recorded.

"We opposed the, then, current emphasis on formally designed experiments, theory testing, and statistics. Yet the results were reliable and reproducible because we repeated the experiments, implicitly in systematic replications. We avoided theoretical discussion, in the sense of hypothetical accounts. The end result was a highly theoretical statement, imbedded in the classification system that ordered the hundreds of schedules we studied and the myriads of systematic relations among them. Each successive experiment became a starting point for another, so that by the end of the 5-year program, the basic types of schedule control had been replicated over and over again in multiple, mixed, tandem, chained, and concurrent schedules. Instrumentation, an important contributor to the level of control and the novel experimental arrangement, was achieved easily and naturally because the laboratory had its own small shop and a custom of stocking parts and gadgets from the war surplus catalogues that were prevalent then. We purchased good quality relays at 25 cents each. Skinner served as a model for my own instincts to gadgeteering and the Harvard machine shop, with its skilled staff, stood behind us. Perhaps the workable conception of instrumentation, reliable enough to carry out a large number of experiments concurrently, automatically, and reliably, was as crucial a factor in the research program as any other.

"We discovered that the magnitude of control that exposed our phenomena was of the order of 6-12 hour experimental sessions as compared with the much briefer periods previously used. The availability of a predictable, steady stream of behavior, representing fundamental psychological processes, provided baselines for evaluating variables of interest to neighboring fields of biology such as, physiology, neurochemistry, pharmacology nutrition, and even exploration of outer space."

This Week's Citation Classic

CC/NUMBER 26
JUNE 30, 1980

Barker R G. *Ecological psychology: concepts and methods for studying the environment of human behavior.* Stanford, CA: Stanford University Press, 1968. 242 p.

Empirical evidence is presented that behavior settings constitute the relevant environment of human molar behavior. Methods of identifying and describing behavior settings are given in detail, and a theory of the relationship between behavior settings and behavior is developed. [The *Social Sciences Citation Index*® *(SSCI™)* indicates that this book has been cited over 305 times since 1968.]

Roger G. Barker
P.O. Box 98
Oskaloosa, KS 66066

May 30, 1980

"This book had its beginning in the early 1940s on a passenger train of the Illinois Central Railroad. As an assistant professor at the University of Illinois, I was assigned to teach a class in child psychology at the state college in Carbondale. I was young and eager to bring to Little Egypt the truth about children from the laboratories and clinics where I had been trained. The I.C. train south passed through many small towns. They fascinated me. To my laboratory-conditioned eyes they were activity cages walled in by miles of almost uninhabited space so that most of the behavior of the towns' children occurred within the cage walls. As I observed the towns week after week, the awful truth dawned upon me that although I was well informed about the behavior of children when confronted with tests and experiments devised by scientific investigators, I knew no more than a lay person about the situations and conditions the towns provided their children and how the children behaved.

"I began to see that I was a defective child psychologist, and formed the intention to investigate the environments of children and their behavior in the community cages where they live their lives far removed from psychologists' laboratories and clinics. Almost a decade passed before the opportunity arose to establish a field station to do this at the University of Kansas in cooperation with Herbert F. Wright. We soon discovered that behavior comes not only in the form of stable, discriminable patterns of the *individual* behavior of Tom, Dick, and Harry, but also as stable, discriminable patterns of *extra-individual* behavior in connection with Bethels service station, the high school boys basketball game, and the city council meeting, and that these entities constitute the environment of individual behavior which I first sought on the trip to Carbondale. This book is about behavior settings.

"Our first report[1] appeared well before the great surge of interest in the environment. The present book was published near the beginning of the widespread concern for the built environment and probably accounts for the extent of the citations, for it provided a toehold of methods and theory for architects, town planners, community experts, and so forth. In recent years we[2] and others[3] have extended and modified the methods and theory of behavior setting research."

---

1. **Barker R G & Wright H F.** *Midwest and its children: the psychological ecology of an American town.* New York: Harper and Row, 1955. 532 p.
2. **Barker R G & Schoggen P.** *Qualities of community life: methods of measuring environment and behavior applied to an American and an English town.* San Francisco: Jossey-Bass, 1973. 562 p.
3. **Wicker A W.** *An introduction to ecological psychology.* Monterey, CA: Brooks/Cole, 1979. 228 p.

Rescorla R A. Pavlovian conditioning and its proper control procedures. *Psychol. Rev.* **74**:71-80, 1967.
[University of Pennsylvania, Philadelphia, PA]

A novel conception of the conditions producing Pavlovian conditioning was proposed. The implications of this proposal for the choice of controls for nonassociative effects and for the notion of inhibition were discussed. [The *Science Citation Index*® (*SCI*®) and the *Social Sciences Citation Index*® (*SSCI*®) indicate that this paper has been cited in over 405 publications since 1967.]

Robert A. Rescorla
Department of Psychology
University of Pennsylvania
Philadelphia, PA 19104

October 7, 1983

"This article was one of several which signaled a change which has taken place in thinking about Pavlovian conditioning in the last several decades. It suggested that the contingency between a conditioned stimulus (CS) and unconditioned stimulus (US), rather than their simple pairing (or contiguity), is responsible for their becoming associated. The notions of contingency and contiguity had not explicitly been separated in Pavlovian conditioning although they are conceptually quite distinct. An animal which is sensitive to contingencies evaluates not only the number of times the CS and US jointly occur but also the degree to which they occur separately from each other. Attention to the latter part of the CS/US relation makes the animal a much more sophisticated assessor of its experiences. It suggests a sensitivity to the degree to which the CS signals or provides information about the US rather than simply to their joint occurrences.

"The notion of contingency had two important consequences. First, it suggested a novel control procedure for 'nonassociative effects' in conditioning, the 'truly random control.' With that procedure, the CS and US occur independently of each other in time, resulting in a zero contingency. Second, it naturally generated a class of CS/US relations which had received little attention in American views of Pavlovian conditioning: inhibitory relations. In inhibitory relations, the contingency between the CS and US is *negative*. Consequently, this view helped encourage the exploration of a new set of CS/US relations.

"I think that this paper has proved influential both because it suggested a new theoretical view of conditioning which proved very heuristic and because it proposed some new methodology. Those interested in understanding the learning process theoretically were interested in the former aspect. But the fact that conditioning is broadly applied in the study of other psychological issues led others to be interested in the methodological features of the paper.

"Both the theoretical and methodological aspects of the paper have received more sophisticated treatment since the time of this paper. We now have available several quite successful theories of Pavlovian conditioning in the context of which this paper is better understood.[1]

"My writing of this paper had quite a practical local impetus. I was in the process of writing my dissertation on Pavlovian fear conditioning, in which I described experiments which employed the truly random control procedure. I realized that there was a need to discuss the theoretical basis of using that novel control, but found the required lengthy discussion out of place in the dissertation itself. Consequently, I wrote this paper as a source to which I could refer. Of course, this paper has proved of much more inherent interest than has my dissertation."

1. **Rescorla R A & Holland P C.** Behavioral studies of associative learning in animals. *Annu. Rev. Psychol.* **33**:265-308, 1982.

CC/NUMBER 46
NOVEMBER 15, 1982

Baer D M, Wolf M M & Risley T R. Some current dimensions of applied behavior analysis. *J. Appl. Behav. Anal.* **1**:91-7, 1968.
[Dept. Human Development, Univ. Kansas, Lawrence, KS]

The emerging field of applied behavior analysis is best defined according to its seven most functional characteristics: it should be behavioral, applied, analytic, technological, conceptually systematic, effective, and generalizable. This analysis of the new field reveals its origin in the laboratory-based experimental analysis of behavior, and emphasizes the special characteristics that make it research into application rather than nonanalytic application. [The *Science Citation Index*® (*SCI*®) **and the** *Social Sciences Citation Index*® (*SSCI*®) **indicate that this paper has been cited in over 535 publications since 1968.]**

Donald M. Baer
Department of Human Development
University of Kansas
Lawrence, KS 66045

September 22, 1982

"In 1966, a new doctoral training program began at the University of Kansas to see what the experimental analysis of behavior (often identified with operant conditioning) could do if applied to real-life personal and social problems ranging from idiosyncratic maladjustments to public education. The best way to do that was from a university base and as a training program, because this application had to be done in the form of research questions at every step of its progress.

"The question was not, 'Does the experimental analysis of behavior have relevance and application to these problems?' but rather was, 'Can the experimental analysis of behavior be made to have relevance and applicability to these problems?' These applications would not be automatic, obvious, or simple; they would require a great deal of integrated, step-by-step research that would vary from the laboratory methods in which most of us had been socialized. It was to be research into every aspect of these applications amenable to research, and it was to exemplify the logic (but not very often the laboratory technology) of the experimental analysis of behavior.

" 'Some current dimensions of applied behavior analysis' was written partly as an act of self-instruction in what we were just discovering, and partly to insure that a field defined as research into a certain logic of application never stopped being research; if it did, it might slide as a whole into the easy trap of nonanalytic application. In our opinion, the invalidity of then current psychological application was both manifest and painful; we meant to see if it was possible to do much better with a new logic, and if so, to begin making the indicated technology, and if not, to quit. We were not clinicians, but we were willing to produce clinicians—eventually, if the data allowed. 'Some current dimensions...' was a description of how the necessary data might be gathered, and what a field gathering that kind of data could be like.

"Significantly, it was published in the first number of the new *Journal of Applied Behavior Analysis*, a journal that had to be created then because we could rarely convince existing journals to include our work in their current contents. The Society of the Experimental Analysis of Behavior, which existed primarily to publish the *Journal of the Experimental Analysis of Behavior*, agreed to create the new journal partly because of intellectual sympathy and partly because its established journal, while admiring our new applications of its distinctive logic, still could not abide our typically noninstrumented data.

"The article has been cited often essentially as an act of agreement—as a way of joining the field, and identifying data as a contribution to it. Writing the article was itself an experiment: to see who would agree, who would join, and what would happen. Its original title was an unthinking 'The current dimensions....' The prudence of changing 'the' to 'some' is seen in two successive presidential addresses of the Association for Behavior Analysis[1,2] debating how much of its prescription is still good, and exactly what behavior it prescribes for behavior-analytic researchers."

1. **Michael J L.** Flight from behavior analysis. *Behav. Analyst* **3**:1-22, 1980.
2. **Baer D M.** A flight of behavior analysis. *Behav. Analyst* **4**:85-91, 1981.

CC/NUMBER 17
APRIL 26, 1982

This Week's Citation Classic

Bowers K S. Situationism in psychology: an analysis and a critique. *Psychol. Rev.* **80**:307-36, 1973. [University of Waterloo, Ontario, Canada]

The methodological and epistemological assumptions of behaviorism are highly problematic when applied to a study of personality. The virtues of an alternative approach to personality are stressed, whereby the environment and the person are seen as reciprocally interactive with each other. [The *Social Sciences Citation Index®* **(***SSCI®***) indicates that this paper has been cited over 280 times since 1973.]**

Kenneth S. Bowers
Department of Psychology
University of Waterloo
Waterloo, Ontario N2L 3G1
Canada

February 15, 1982

"I began to write this paper on my sabbatical at Stanford University in 1970-1971, but the issues had been steeping in my mind since graduate school. I wanted very much to redress what I considered a misguided application of behavioral psychology to personality—a trend that I considered both wrongheaded and philosophically naive.

"The fact that the paper was actually begun at Stanford is ironic, since the position that I was criticizing was for the most part a Stanford creation. I recall with mixed feelings my reluctance to discuss my ideas with people there. Partly, I did not wish to feel any personal responsibility or loyalty to people whose position I was attempting to dismantle, and partly, it was due to a presentiment that the full realization of my ideas might be adversely affected by premature exposure of them. I think I made the right decision, but I regret the missed opportunity to thrash out some of the fundamental issues of personality and behavior with people who were highly influential in the field. Ironically, the paper was recommended for publication in *Psychological Review* (with considerable revision) by one of my unconsulted Stanford adversaries—after being rejected by more sympathetic referees from *Psychological Bulletin.*

"I derived great pleasure in formulating my arguments in as convincing prose as I could muster, and I would often spend hours trying to express a single idea in a manner that appealed to my aesthetic sense. To illustrate, I recall trying to communicate the essence of interactionism in a way that would strike the right balance between accuracy and memorability. Just as I was about to give up for the evening, the sentence came to me with a rush of excitement that I can still recapture: *'Situations are as much a function of the person as the person's behavior is a function of the situation.'* The phrasing looks pretty simple once written, but it was a damn elusive idea to express the first time. I have been gratified that it is one of the most frequently quoted sentences from the paper.

"I am less enthusiastic about being cited for showing that the variance due to the environment by person interaction exceeds the sum of the main effects variance across 11 studies employing an anova design. In fact, my chief regret about the paper is that I did not see clearly at the time that the only similarity between statistical and psychological interaction was the word 'interaction.' I have since corrected myself,[1] and other contributors to this same anthology have also advanced a more psychological notion of interaction (see, for example, Magnusson[2]). Another regret is that my thinking was not at the time informed by the seminal work of Jack Block, whose 1971 book, *Lives through Time,*[3] is a genuine masterpiece of empirical and conceptual investigation in the field of personality. Perhaps students of personality will someday fully appreciate and assimilate this extraordinarily prescient work.

"Despite these regrets, I remain pleased with the paper, and if it helps to liberate the study of personality from the bondage of methodological behaviorism, I will have succeeded in my goal."

1. **Bowers K S.** There's more to Iago than meets the eye: a clinical account of personal consistency. (Magnusson D & Endler N S, eds.) *Personality at the crossroads: current issues in interactional psychology.* Hillsdale, NJ: Lawrence Erlbaum Associates, 1977. p. 65-81.
2. **Magnusson D.** *Toward a psychology of situations: an interactional perspective.* Hillsdale, NJ: Lawrence Erlbaum Associates, 1981. 488 p.
3. **Block J & Haan N.** *Lives through time.* Berkeley, CA: Bancroft, 1971. 313 p.

This Week's Citation Classic

Barrish H H, Saunders M & Wolf M M. Good behavior game: effects of individual contingencies for group consequences on disruptive behavior in a classroom. *J. Appl. Behav. Anal.* **2**:119-24, 1969. [University of Kansas, Lawrence, KS]

An applied behavior analysis was used to study the effects of a 'Good Behavior Game' in which a contingency was arranged for disruptive behavior of each child while the consequence of the child's behavior was shared by all members of his team as a group. [The *Social Sciences Citation Index*® (*SSCI*®) **indicates that this paper has been cited over 130 times since 1969.]**

Harriet H. Barrish
Executive Building
4121 West 83rd Street
Prairie Village, KS 66207

February 18, 1982

"We were honored to learn that this publication has been selected as a *Citation Classic*. The setting of our study was the fourth-grade classroom of a rural, midwestern, public elementary school. As a graduate student, I had expressed interest to my adviser, Montrose Wolf, in applications of behavioral techniques to problems in an educational setting. He suggested contacting Muriel Saunders, who was the wife of another graduate student in our department and also a fourth-grade teacher. After observing Saunders's classroom, I proposed the applied research presented in our article. Saunders's utilization of other team games to encourage learning and the enthusiastic responsiveness of her students suggested the basic format to me. Wolf provided many hours of invaluable collaboration, critique, and support. The research represents one of those 'wished for' theses which for the most part progressed rather smoothly.

"After having been employed by a school system, having been in private practice for a number of years during which I frequently collaborated with educators, and having taught graduate student educators, I have often been struck by a point of particular interest and sometimes amusement which is one of the issues represented by our article; namely, science seems to have the ability to sometimes take what has been extensively used for many years by educators, to modify, systematize, and research it, and then to call it a significant and sometimes new scientific contribution to the field. While our 'Good Behavior Game' has been appealing to psychologists and educators alike, it is not unusual to have an educator indicate surprise at our reported technique since some educators have used team games to stimulate learning and enthusiasm for years. Generally, I think we have much to learn as scientists by being good observers of skilled professionals in many disciplines and then exploring these skills and techniques scientifically so that they can be taught to benefit more people.

"I personally think that our article has been highly cited for a number of reasons. First, it represents one example of the impact of applied behavioral psychology in general to the field of education and the consequent mutual benefit.[1] Second, it has had scientific appeal because of explicit methodology which offers potential for replication by colleagues.[2,3] Third, and similarly, its explicit methodology allows the classroom teacher to understand how to precisely implement the game. Fourth, it has professional appeal to educators who have frequently used team games with good response from students. Fifth, and finally, it has perhaps provided both an impetus and bridge for psychologists and educators who have preferred to shift behavioral interventions to specifically, rather than incidentally, increasing on-task behaviors with consequent increases in learning."

1. **Becker W C**, ed. *An empirical basis for change in education: selections on behavioral psychology for teachers.* Chicago: Science Research Associates, 1971. 522 p.
2. **Harris W V & Sherman J A.** Use and analysis of the "good behavior game" to reduce disruptive classroom behavior. *J. Appl. Behav. Anal.* **6**:405-17, 1973.
3. **Medland M B & Stachnik T J.** Good-behavior game: a replication and systematic analysis. *J. Appl. Behav. Anal.* **5**:45-51, 1972.

 CC/NUMBER 15
APRIL 14, 1980

Herrnstein R J. On the law of effect. *J. Exp. Anal. Behav.* **13**:243-66, 1970.
[Harvard Univ., Cambridge, MA]

The 'law of effect' refers to the strengthening of behavior by reinforcement (i.e., reward). Experimental findings indicate that each behavior's strength is directly proportional to its level of reinforcement and inversely proportional to the total reinforcement concurrently obtained. [The *Science Citation Index*® *(SCI*®*)* **and the** *Social Sciences Citation Index*™ *(SSCI*™*)* **indicate that this paper has been cited over 260 times since 1970.]**

R.J. Herrnstein
Department of Psychology
and Social Relations
William James Hall
Harvard University
Cambridge, MA 02138

January 31, 1980

"It has long been known that the strengths of behavioral alternatives depend on the reinforcement associated with them. This principle was embodied in E.L. Thorndike's 'law of effect,'[1] in B.F. Skinner's concept of 'operant conditioning,'[2] and in other theories of behavior. Though the principle was widely accepted in qualitative form, there was no general quantitative expression to cover the large variety of settings in which behavioral strength could be shown to depend on reinforcement. My article proposed that each behavior's strength (as measured, for example, by its average rate of occurrence during a specified observation period) is directly proportional to its own level of reinforcement and inversely proportional to the total reinforcement concurrently obtained from all sources. The empirical literature was shown to fit this simple principle, and the accumulating evidence has continued to support it. Its simplicity, generality, and at least approximate validity no doubt explain the frequency with which the article has been cited.

"My interest in the quantification of the law of effect started in 1954, during my second year as a graduate student at Harvard University. After some unsuccessful experiments, a particular procedure using pigeons started to yield orderly results in 1958. Pigeons allocated the proportion of pecking at each of two response-keys so as to equal the proportion of reinforcements obtained by pecking that key. The matching of proportions of responses to reinforcements was first published by me in 1961 and has since been more or less substantiated in over one hundred experiments on a variety of species including human beings.[3] The occasional, and usually minor, deviations from the 'matching law' (as the finding is commonly called) have themselves been related to the underlying formulation of the law of effect.

"During the early 1960s, I sought a version of the law of effect applicable not just to proportions of responses (as in the original matching law) but to absolute rates of responding as well. The solution given in the 1970 article first occurred to me on 10 December 1965. It is easy to show mathematically that response rate should be a hyperbolic function of its own reinforcement if my equation is right and if all sources of reinforcement besides those associated with the response in question are held constant. The predicted hyperbolic relationship has been approximately confirmed in several score experiments on various species including human beings.

"Present work on the matching law is directed less at its empirical accuracy than at its relation to other, possibly more fundamental, behavioral processes. The law of effect articulates with optimal foraging in biology and utility maximization in economics, each dealing with the control of behavior by its consequences. Several new theories by various workers have attempted to unify these concepts, but at this writing no final conclusion can be drawn."

1. **Thorndike E L.** *Animal intelligence.* New York: Macmillan, 1911. 297 p.
2. **Skinner B F.** *The behavior of organisms.* New York: Appleton-Century, 1938. 457 p.
3. **Herrnstein R J.** Relative and absolute strength of response as a function of frequency of reinforcement. *J. Exp. Anal. Behav.* **4**:267-72, 1961.

CC/NUMBER 5
FEBRUARY 1, 1982

This Week's Citation Classic

Rotter J B. Generalized expectancies for internal versus external control of reinforcement. *Psychol. Monogr.* **80**:1-28, 1966.
[University of Connecticut, Storrs, CT]

The effects of reinforcement on preceding behavior depend in part on whether or not the reinforcement is perceived as contingent on the person's behavior. Acquisition and performance differ in chance versus skill situations. Stable individual differences in expectancies for internal versus external control of reinforcement in the same situations can be validly measured. [The *Social Sciences Citation Index®* (*SSCI®*) **indicates that this paper has been cited over 2,735 times since 1966.]**

Julian B. Rotter
Department of Psychology
University of Connecticut
Storrs, CT 06268

December 2, 1981

"This monograph, published in 1966, was an analysis of work begun many years earlier, first as part of my graduate students' research and then as a four-year project supported by the Air Force Office of Scientific Research. The dissertations of E. Jerry Phares[1] and William James[2] were important starts in test construction and initial data gathering, and two colleagues and co-investigators of the research grant, Melvin Seeman and Shepherd Liverant, made important conceptual as well as empirical contributions. The forced choice personality test (I-E Scale) that was presented in the monograph was the fifth revision of a test which first appeared in Phares's dissertation and was revised in James's dissertation.

"By my own estimate, the most important reason for the interest in internal versus external control of reinforcement was the 'real world' sociopolitical concerns of psychologists and other social scientists of the times and the implications of the work for applied problems. It is interesting that my own original interest was theoretical; that is, a discovery that changes in expectancies were *systematically* predictable from whether or not the person perceived his or her own actions as the cause of rewards or if he or she saw rewards as not contingent on his or her own behavior. However, by the time this monograph was published the country was involved in the Vietnam War, the student revolution, the black riots, Watergate, and the assassinations. Interest in social action ran high and there was a great deal of disillusionment accompanying people's awareness of their inability to control events important to their lives. Social scientists' interests often reflect their sociopolitical concerns. Many of these problems, such as social action taking behavior in blacks, response to political appeals, efficiency in the practice of psychotherapy, and the effectiveness of self-treatment regimes in medical rehabilitation had potentially important applications and had a special appeal.

"A word should be said about the form of publication. Some of the research reported in the monograph was previously published, some was in press or being prepared for publication, some was only available in the form of unpublished theses and dissertations, and some data were presented only in the monograph. The totality added up to more than the sum of the parts. Without the monograph, most readers would have seen only a small part of the data and perhaps would have been interested but not overly impressed. It seems to me that programmatic research suffers when it is published only piecemeal, so that the reader does not get in one place and at one time the overview of history, theory, empirical data, and potential applications.

"If this analysis is true, it follows that less publications of individual, isolated, nontheoretical articles and more publications of programmatic empirical-theoretical articles and monographs might increase the rate at which stable, major increments in knowledge occur in psychology. More recent work in the field has been published by H.M. Lefcourt[3] and me."[4]

1. **Phares E J.** *Changes in expectancy in skill and change situations.* PhD dissertation. Columbus, OH: Ohio State University, 1955.
2. **James W H.** *Internal versus external control of reinforcements as a basic variable in learning theory.* PhD dissertation. Columbus, OH: Ohio State University, 1957.
3. **Lefcourt H M,** ed. *Research with the locus of control construct. Vol. 1. Assessment methods.* New York: Academic Press, 1981.
4. **Rotter J B.** Some problems and misconceptions related to the construct of internal versus external control of reinforcement. *J. Consult. Clin. Psychol.* **43**:56-67, 1975.

This Week's Citation Classic

CC/NUMBER 32
AUGUST 10, 1981

Katkin E S & Murray E N. Instrumental conditioning of autonomically mediated behavior: theoretical and methodological issues. *Psychol. Bull.* **70**:52-68, 1968. [Dept. Psychology, State Univ. New York, Buffalo, NY]

This paper reviews the empirical literature on instrumental conditioning of autonomic responses and raises a number of questions concerning the theoretical mechanisms by which such conditioning occurs. It concludes that voluntary control of autonomic functions cannot be understood within the context of operant theory. [The *Social Sciences Citation Index*® **(***SSCI*®**) indicates that this paper has been cited over 125 times since 1968.]**

Edward S. Katkin
Department of Psychology
State University of New York
Buffalo, NY 14226

June 4, 1981

"This paper emerged from the frustration that the late Neil Murray and I experienced in trying to replicate the first few experimental reports of operant autonomic conditioning that were emanating from Shapiro's[1] laboratory at Harvard and Kimmel's[2] at Florida. After poring over the few reports of the phenomenon that existed at the time (this was before N.E. Miller[3] hit the scene with his dramatic—and not so replicable—reports on curarized rats), we decided with great anxiety that our data were OK, but that the discrepancy between our laboratory and the others was a result of interpretation rather than experimentation. The phenomenon of acquired autonomic control was an incontrovertible fact, but the proper theoretical explanation of its mechanism, we felt sure, was entirely beyond empirical resolution. The only thing we felt confident about was that the then popular tendency to describe the phenomenon as instrumental conditioning was unwarranted *on the basis of the available evidence.*

"Neil and I went into a frenzy of writing in the spring of 1967, but no sooner had we finished our first (enormously overwritten) draft of the paper when Kimmel's[4] review of the field appeared in the *Psychological Bulletin*! We were stunned. Although we had written a paper that was entirely different in theme and purpose from Kimmel's, we felt sure that the *Bulletin* would not publish two reviews of the same literature within a year. Panicky, we wrote to the editor to tell him of our plight, and to inquire if we should proceed to polish (i.e., reduce the shameful glut of words) the manuscript for submission, or just forget the entire affair and return to clinical psychology from whence we had come.

"The editor encouraged us to submit the paper, and we did. Shortly thereafter we received a letter of rejection, along with a scathing denunciation by an anonymous reviewer, in which our intellect, integrity, training, and academic credentials were called into question. The review was so unprofessional and so clearly *ad hominem* that we were convinced at first that it was a practical joke, but it was not. Had the anonymous reviewer merely written a coherent rejection, we might have buried the paper and contented ourselves with trying to persuade our friends and students of the wisdom of our view, safe from the scrutiny of the outside world, but the reviewer had declared war on us. He demanded a reply! We requested from the journal an additional, independent review of the paper. We received a thoughtful (i.e., positive) review the second time around, and the paper was published (after more reductions) and widely read. Among the many readers of the paper, needless to say, there have been some who have called into question our intellect, integrity, training, and academic credentials.

"The high frequency with which this paper has been cited is undoubtedly related to its role in the subsequent development of theory and practice in biofeedback, for which I apologize.

"During the 1970s, literally hundreds of papers appeared in the areas of self-regulation and biofeedback. An annual volume on consciousness and self-regulation serves to summarize much of this research."[5]

1. **Shapiro D, Crider A B & Tursky B.** Differentiation of an autonomic response through operant reinforcement. *Psychon. Sci.* **1**:147-8, 1964.
2. **Kimmel H D & Baxter R.** Avoidance conditioning of the GSR. *J. Exp. Psychol.* **68**:482-5, 1964.
3. **Miller N E & DiCara L.** Instrumental learning of heart rate changes in curarized rats: shaping and specificity to discriminative stimulus. *J. Comp. Physiol. Psychol.* **63**:12-19, 1967.
4. **Kimmel H D.** Instrumental conditioning of autonomically mediated behavior. *Psychol. Bull.* **67**:337-45, 1967.
5. **Schwartz G E & Shapiro D**, eds. *Consciousness and self-regulation: advances in research and theory.* New York: Plenum, 1978. Vol. 2.

This Week's Citation Classic

CC/NUMBER 9
MARCH 2, 1981

Milgram S. Behavioral study of obedience.
J. Abnormal Soc. Psychol. **67**:371-8, 1963.
[Yale University, New Haven, CT]

A simple procedure is devised for studying obedience. A person comes to the laboratory and, in the context of a learning experiment, is told to give increasingly severe shocks to another person (who is actually an actor). The purpose of the experiment is to see how far a subject will proceed before refusing to comply with the experimenter's instructions. Twenty-six of 40 subjects administered the highest shocks on the generator. [The *Social Sciences Citation Index*® **(*SSCI*™) indicates that this paper has been cited over 255 times since 1966.]**

Stanley Milgram
Department of Psychology
Graduate School and University Center
City University of New York
New York, NY 10036

February 9, 1981

" 'Behavioral study of obedience' was the first published account of a series of studies I had undertaken at Yale University on the response of individuals to destructive authority. It was not easy to publish the paper. It was submitted first to the *Journal of Abnormal and Social Psychology* (*JASP*) and was duly rejected, then to the *Journal of Personality*, which also turned it down. I decided to abandon the paper and began to write an expanded account of the experimental program. But some months later, in an unusual twist, the editor of *JASP* spontaneously recalled the initially rejected paper and published it.

"The responses to 'Behavioral study of obedience' were strong and varied. The first wave consisted of a score of congratulatory letters from social scientists around the country. The media, also, evidenced immediate interest, which I attempted to discourage. When *The New York Times* indicated they would publish an account, I telegrammed its science writer, Walter Sullivan: 'I do not wish to have the experiment generally publicized at this time because publicity will interfere with further research. The experiment only works if the subject does not know what it is about....' But the *Times* published its account anyway.

"The next response to the paper was an attack on its ethics and method, which appeared in *American Psychologist*.[1] Thus, we can see that behind the simple quantification of citations lie many complexities. The citation count gives a measure of the impact of a paper, but it is only a starting point for an analysis of its reception.

"The paper failed in several respects. First, whereas I had hoped that the experimental paradigm it presented would be widely used as a general tool for the study of obedience, it became more a subject of citation than replication. Second, the controversies surrounding the experiment tended to deflect attention from the substantive issues of obedience to authority.

"The paper was superseded by a fuller analysis of obedience, especially in two works: 'Some conditions of obedience and disobedience to authority'[2] (173 citations) and the book, *Obedience to Authority*[3] (186 citations). Yet the original paper has had an unusual durability, and continues to be reprinted in anthologies of psychology, political science, education, sociology, and readings of English prose. We may ask why.

"First, the paper is brief, simple, and seeks to apply scientific methods to the analysis of a human issue of compelling interest. Conceived in a scientific framework, it nonetheless contains significant dramatic elements. Finally, the very polarization of opinion which the paper provoked contributed to its longevity, as controversy leads to engaging and potentially instructive discussion, which many instructors have come to appreciate. This was an unanticipated consequence of a paper which, first and foremost, was intended as a clear report of what I had observed in the laboratory.

"In expanded form, the work was awarded the annual Socio-Psychological Award of the American Association for the Advancement of Science. A follow-up book, translated into several languages, was nominated for a National Book Award."

1. **Baumrind D.** Some thoughts on ethics of research: after reading Milgram's "Behavioral study of obedience." *Amer. Psychol.* **19**:421-3, 1964.
2. **Milgram S.** Some conditions of obedience and disobedience to authority. *Hum. Relat.* **18**:56-76, 1965.
3. -------------. *Obedience to authority: an experimental view.* New York: Harper and Row, 1974. 224 p.

This Week's Citation Classic

Bolles R C & Woods P J. The ontogeny of behaviour in the albino rat. *Anim. Behav.* **12**:427-41, 1964. [Department of Psychology, Hollins College, VA]

Litters of rat pups with their mothers were observed systematically every few hours around the clock from birth through the age of weaning. The different patterns of behavior are described, and the results are analyzed in terms of their functional significance. [The *Science Citation Index*® (*SCI*®) **and the** *Social Sciences Citation Index*® (*SSCI*®) **indicate that this paper has been cited over 150 times since 1964.]**

Robert C. Bolles
Department of Psychology
University of Washington
Seattle, WA 98195

June 2, 1981

"I have always believed in the idea that experimenters should look at their animals. While there is much to be said for automatic recording devices in terms of reliability and objectivity, machines have certain limitations. They tend to restrain rather than encourage new kinds of data. A machine is great if you know beforehand exactly what it is to do, but the human eyeball is the instrument of choice if you want to observe a new phenomenon, and particularly if you want to gain a new understanding of it. So I started looking at my experimental animals. I had watched them grooming themselves.[1] Following the lead of the late Dalbir Bindra,[2] I had watched them in their living cages to determine the effects of deprivation on general arousal.[3] And I had learned a lot about the organization of the rat's behavior by watching them mate, eat, explore, and run around.

"Paul Woods was already at Hollins College when I got there, and he found such an approach quite congruent with his own thinking. The idea of simply looking at baby rats growing up was his. Woods was the developmental psychologist in the department. So we started watching baby rats. We observed them as unobtrusively as possible, i.e., with minimal intervention. We developed the techniques as we went along. It was a lot of fun—full of discovery. Even the day and night ritual became fun. Almost every day one of us would say to the other, 'Hey, you know what I saw last night?' So Woods and I taught each other what to watch for and how to record it. Actually, I like to think that those little animals taught us both how to collect the data.

"Soon we had mountains of data, and we set about writing it up. We worked out tables and graphs. We analyzed it in terms of age trends and by circadian cycles. We looked at everything chronologically and categorically. And with great confidence we broke out all the data in terms of postures, reflex figures, and functional categories. We also had a bit of evidence for early learning, and bits more on all sorts of phenomena.

"The wide citation of the paper reflects, I think, that we did have quite a variety of new data. We had noted a lot of things that simply had not been noted before, and we had a little of everything. Part of it, too, was that animal developmental psychology was a relatively new field then. It was just coming into its own and just beginning to establish its own methods of study. We had thought that some fairly substantial body of normative data would be useful, and we were right. For more recent work in the field, see *Ontogeny of Learning and Memory*."[4]

1. **Bolles R C.** Grooming behavior in the rat. *J. Comp. Physiol. Psychol.* **53**:306-10, 1960.
2. **Bindra D & Blond J.** A time-sample method for measuring general activity and its components. *Can. J. Psychol.* **12**:74-6, 1958.
3. **Bolles R C.** Effect of food deprivation upon the rat's behavior in its home cage. *J. Comp. Physiol. Psychol.* **56**:456-60, 1963.
4. **Spear N E & Campbell B A,** eds. *Ontogeny of learning and memory.* New York: Lawrence Erlbaum, 1979. 321 p.

CC/NUMBER 47
NOVEMBER 24,1980

Catania A C & Reynolds G S. A quantitative analysis of the responding maintained by interval schedules of reinforcement. *J. Exp. Anal. Behav.* **11**:327-83, 1968. [New York Univ., Bronx, NY and Univ. California San Diego, La Jolla, CA]

By studying how pigeons' pecking depended on varying times between peck-produced food deliveries, we were able to design schedules that generated relatively constant rates of pecking over extended periods. Such schedules provide useful baselines for assessing how drugs and other variables affect behavior. [The *Social Sciences Citation Index*® *(SSCI*™) **indicates that this paper has been cited over 210 times since 1968.]**

A. Charles Catania
Department of Psychology
University of Maryland Baltimore County
Catonsville, MD 21228

and

George S. Reynolds
Department of Psychology
University of California
La Jolla, CA 92037

October 10, 1980

"George Reynolds and I began this research while we were both graduate students working in B.F. Skinner's pigeon laboratory at Harvard University. Ferster and Skinner[1] had developed the subject matter of reinforcement schedules there. Responding is maintained by its reinforcers or consequences, as when a pigeon's pecking persists if it occasionally produces access to grain. Rate of responding and its patterning in time depend on the schedule, an arrangement determining which responses produce reinforcers. We systematically examined variable-interval (VI) schedules, in which responses become eligible to produce reinforcers at varying times after some event. This schedule is important because responding need not interact with the delivery of reinforcers: as long as response rate exceeds some minimum value, response rate does not affect reinforcement rate. The implications were practical as well as theoretical, in that VI schedules had become schedules of choice for generating behavioral baselines.

"We set up two experimental chambers using available electromechanical equipment. The successive occasions on which responses could produce VI reinforcers were usually arranged by punched tapes driven past a sensing switch. Our main technical innovations were substituting a stepping motor for the continuous tape drive, so we could synchronize our recording circuitry with the intervals on the punched tape, and designing our schedules explicitly in terms of reinforcement probability as a function of elapsed time. Because session durations varied with schedule parameters, one of our more difficult problems was that of ordering the values studied for different pigeons so that all could be run within the available time. Daily sessions, from June 1960 through May 1962, included weekends and holidays.

"We submitted and then withdrew our first manuscript in 1961, after deciding that one comprehensive paper was preferable to several short ones. In successive drafts, we condensed theory and expanded empirical content, and several revisions and editorial reviews culminated in the published monograph supplement. Most citations were probably to the second of two appendices, which provided a rationale and a simple formula for constructing VI schedules that generated constant response rates. Our schedule finitely approximated the output of a random generator. As solid-state devices and dedicated computers gradually replaced electromechanical equipment, the instrumentation of such schedules became routine. Our monograph also demonstrated how momentary and overall response rates were jointly determined by momentary and overall reinforcement rates. Those functional relations have entered into a variety of mathematical accounts of reinforced behavior. We acknowledge that our technical appendices are fast becoming obsolete, but are pleased by the continuing citation of our empirical findings. Skinner had left us free to select our own research directions, and we regard those opportunities to conduct our own research as crucial aspects of our early careers. We mainly regret that few such rewarding laboratory environments exist these days for us and for our students."

1. **Ferster C B & Skinner B F.** *Schedules of reinforcement.* New York: Appleton-Century-Crofts, 1957. 741 p.

This Week's Citation Classic

Dunham P J. Contrasted conditions of reinforcement: a selective critique.
Psychol. Bull. **69**:295-315, 1968.
[Dalhousie University, Halifax, Nova Scotia, Canada]

Simultaneous or successive exposure to two different magnitudes of reward enhances the value of the larger magnitude and reduces the value of the smaller magnitude when compared to either magnitude presented alone. These phenomena have traditionally been called contrast effects, and this paper critically reviewed the methods and theory concerned with contrast effects in the context of research concerned with animal learning and motivation processes. [The *Social Sciences Citation Index*® (*SSCI*®) **indicates that this paper has been cited over 120 times since 1968.]**

Philip J. Dunham
Department of Psychology
Dalhousie University
Halifax, Nova Scotia B3H 4J1
Canada

May 26, 1981

"During the period between 1950 and 1970 there were a number of phenomena which emerged as 'hot' topics of research for psychologists interested in animal learning and motivation. With the aid of hindsight, I tend to clump these phenomena together under the general label of neo-Hullian research. They originally attracted attention because they challenged the predictions of the grand S-R learning theories of the first half of this century— Hullian theory in particular. Long after our enchantment with such grand theories had worn thin, the phenomena seemed to persist and each attracted a constellation of 'miniature theories' and special methods devoted almost exclusively to each phenomenon. Contrast effects are a prime example, and students of this literature will recognize other labels such as the partial reinforcement phenomenon, the overlearning extinction phenomenon, the delay of reward phenomenon, etc., as similar 'hot' topics.

"In 1966, I had taken my first job as an assistant professor in Canada. I had completed a dissertation that year on contrast phenomena, and decided that my first task upon arriving here in Halifax would be to write a critical review of the contrast literature which covered the existing theoretical ideas and the methodological variations. This paper was the result, and I remember celebrating the editorial decision in the Lord Nelson Beverage Room— Halifax's finest in those days (believe it or not, women were not permitted in public taverns and ale was served by the quart).

"Ironically, I also recall that the paper served to plant the first seeds of disenchantment with this area of research in my mind. I felt that the Hullian and neo-Hullian theoretical roots from which contrast phenomena had emerged no longer provided the most viable approach to thinking about behavior, and my interests gradually shifted away from contrast effects and related phenomena. My other theoretical efforts over the past decade are a record of this gradual shift in interest[1-3]—although I still celebrate at the Lord Nelson where ale is now served by the pint and women are permitted!

"In spite of my different interests, it pleases me to know that the first major paper I wrote in my academic career has become a *Citation Classic*. I suspect that there are two reasons for the frequent citations the paper receives. First, it is a review article, and they tend to be more frequently cited than experimental papers. Second, the timing was fortuitous. I suspect that interest in contrast phenomena was at its very peak when the paper appeared and has gradually declined since that time."

1. **Dunham P J.** Punishment: method and theory. *Psychol. Rev.* **78**:58-70, 1971.
2. ----------------. The nature of reinforcing stimuli. (Honig W K & Staddon J, eds.) *Handbook of operant behavior.* New York: Prentice-Hall, 1977. p. 98-124.
3. ----------------. Crustacean sex pheromones. *Biol. Rev.* **53**:555-83, 1978.

This Week's Citation Classic

Davison G C. Systematic desensitization as a counterconditioning process. *J. Abnormal Psychol.* **73**:91-9, 1968.
[State Univ. New York, Stony Brook, NY]

If systematic desensitization derives its effectiveness from a counterconditioning process, then disrupting the pairing of relaxation with imaginal aversive stimuli should significantly reduce the efficacy of the procedure in eliminating unrealistic fears. The experiment reported here supported that hypothesis. [The *Social Sciences Citation Index®* *(SSCI™)* **indicates that this paper has been cited over 170 times since 1968. Of these, 37 occurred within two years of publication.]**

Gerald C. Davison
Department of Psychology
University of Southern California
Los Angeles, CA 90007

January 7, 1981

"True to the Chance Theory of Life, I went to Stanford in 1962 to specialize in social psychology, only to switch to physiological and finally to settle on clinical. This happened because I learned there for the first time of an approach to clinical psychology that aligned itself epistemologically (and spiritually) with general experimental psychology. The idea that one could be an experimentalist *and* a clinician was new to me, though it should not have been, had I been well-read in the history of clinical psychology. I doubt I would have elected clinical otherwise.

"The basic idea of this dissertation study was fairly simple. If systematic desensitization was effective because of counterconditioning (i.e., enabling people to substitute a fearless response for a fearful one), then disrupting the presumed necessary pairing of fear with relaxation should significantly reduce its potency.

"For several months my entire life had been organized around the pleasant drive from Stanford to Foothill Junior College in Los Altos Hills, where some good-natured instructors had given me access to a pool of undergraduates willing to expose themselves to something they found loathsome and frightening. My world was defined by a storage closet, a reclining chair for subjects to relax in, and a tape recorder to provide standardized instructions. It was exhilarating, and became even more so when, after treatment, most of the desensitization subjects—having learned to tolerate images of holding a nonpoisonous snake without becoming anxious—actually approached the creature they had been unable to get close to prior to the treatment. Control subjects did not fare so well. I was frankly surprised and delighted to see this happen under reasonably controlled laboratory conditions.

"My dissertation, on which the article was based, became known in behavior therapy circles rather quickly, perhaps because there had been till that time few persuasive demonstrations of applying learning principles to the amelioration of psychological suffering. The experiment was also an early example of how one could dismantle a therapy procedure to examine its theoretical underpinnings. I believe too that my study gladdened the hearts of those who wanted to believe that clinical psychology could be truly scientific.

"It was not long afterward that people, including myself, began to critique what I had done, nor did many years pass before I began to doubt the implications of the study and of the conditioning bases of behavior therapy generally. No matter. It was good to have been a true believer in graduate school and for a year or two thereafter. And it is certainly immensely gratifying to know that this article has been referred to so often by colleagues, even though many of the more recent citations are, I believe, critical in nature."[1,2]

1. **Kazdin A E & Wilcoxon L A.** Systematic desensitization and nonspecific treatment effects. A methodological approach. *Psychol. Bull.* **83**:729-58, 1976.
2. **Borkovec T D & O'Brien G T.** Methodological and target behavior issues in analogue therapy outcome research. (Hersen M, Eisler R M & Miller P M, eds.) *Progress in behavior modification.* New York: Academic Press, 1976. p. 133-72.

This Week's Citation Classic

Azrin N H, Hutchinson R R & Hake D F. Extinction-induced aggression. *J. Exp. Anal. Behav.* **9**:191-204, 1966. [Anna State Hospital, Anna, IL]

Extinction of conditioned responses had been shown to produce a variety of emotional effects. The present experiments revealed that extinction also produced physical aggression and showed its relationship to such factors as the number of food reinforcements, satiation, social history, history, and response requirements. [The *Social Sciences Citation Index*® (*SSCI*™) **indicates that this paper has been cited over 145 times since 1966.]**

Nathan H. Azrin
Department of Psychology
Nova University
Fort Lauderdale, FL 33314

April 30, 1981

"I had been studying shock avoidance behavior with animals in a series of studies since my doctoral dissertation at Harvard in 1956 and continued these studies at Anna State Hospital in Illinois. I was surprised when I discovered[1] that the pain-shock caused rats to attack each other and that other physically aversive events such as heat and a physical blow did the same. What about aversive events which were not physically painful? Would they also cause this violent attack? Much anecdotal and correlational evidence suggested that psychologically aversive events caused an emotional reaction such as frustration at not achieving a goal. These two lines of evidence suggested that the sudden discontinuation of food reinforcement of a conditioned response (extinction) might cause physical aggression. My principal research focus was on the effects of reinforcement on the conditioned response, but these emotional nonspecific effects of reinforcers were so great and so fascinating that I was obliged to study them in their own right.

"The initial discovery in this experiment, that extinction did cause physical aggression, was so surprising and important that I delayed publication until I completed additional experiments to isolate possible artifacts and to determine its parameters.

"The results reported in this study showed that this physical aggression was caused by the sudden termination of a strong reinforcer and did not depend on a conditioned response, or a history of aggression over the reinforcer. Perhaps most important was the objective manner in which the aggression was measured without the need of subjective rating scales or interpretation, thereby permitting scientific study in quantitative terms of this phenomenon. The vague notion that frustration may produce aggression was now established with a laboratory animal model which allowed scientific study of its specific causes. The two coauthors of this study have continued to study the emotional states caused by extinction or by pain.

"More recently, my research has been primarily in the area of developing psychological treatments for behavioral problems, including aggression. Awareness of the extinction-induced aggression relation has led me to devise training and treatment procedures in which aversiveness is minimized.[2] I believe the study has been cited so often because other applied psychologists have been similarly influenced by these results in addition to the intrinsic value in understanding the causes of aggression and the effects of conditioning procedures."

1. **Ulrich R E & Azrin N H.** Elimination of undesired escape from footshock. *J. Exp. Anal. Behav.* **5**:72, 1962.
2. **Webster D R & Azrin N H.** Required relaxation: a method of inhibiting agitative-disruptive behavior of retardates. *Behav. Res. Ther.* **11**:67-78, 1973.

CC/NUMBER 32
AUGUST 6, 1979

This Week's Citation Classic

Ulrich R E & Azrin N H. Reflexive fighting in response to aversive stimulation. *J. Exp. Anal. Behav.* **5**:511-20, 1962.
[Illinois Wesleyan University, Anna State Hospital, Bloomington, IL]

The basic emphasis of this paper was that stereotyped fighting would occur between some paired animals as a reflex type reaction to electric shock prior to any specific conditioning. [The *Science Citation Index®* **(***SCI®***) and the** *Social Sciences Citation Index™* **(***SSCI™***) indicate that this paper has been cited over 245 times since 1962.]**

Roger E. Ulrich
Western Michigan University
Kalamazoo, MI 49001

March 31, 1978

"This study was my Ph.D. dissertation with Nate Azrin as my advisor and director of the Behavioral Research Laboratory in which it was conducted. The Lab was greatly concerned with the study of various aversive control strategies. Thus, the discovery that aggression occurred as a consistent and unlearned response side effect to aversive stimulation was of special importance, especially since operant conditioning people were beginning more and more to take the findings of the lab out into applied settings via the fledgling behavior modification movement. This study was of interest in another way; it emphasized the power of genetic input in the face of the Skinnerian bias toward environmental determinants. Also, the political and social climate was such that aggression was becoming an issue both domestically and internationally.

"Following this paper, I entered into a ten year period of dedicated analysis of the causes of aggression. It was secretly hoped that a better understanding of how to control man's aggression would follow. When I told my Mennonite mother what we had found in my dissertation research she said, 'Well, we know that. Dad always told us to stay away from wounded animals on the farm since they were more inclined to be aggressive.'

"In short, this study was a rediscovery of a well known fact now put to careful scientific analysis. From where do the roots of aggression come? If unconditioned, then how does the environment affect it? The area of study was and still is emotion-laden. We were hurting animals and animal protection groups were concerned. Still,the hope existed that we could shed some light on the issue of controlling man's aggression toward his fellow man. In 1973, I finally came to the conclusion that if the control of human aggression was the touchstone upon which this research was based, we were looking in the wrong place. I still was in no way enlightened in that area to the extent that I could offer meaningful advice to people who questioned me in relation to aggression. Indeed, my own anger was often uncontrollable in spite of my discoveries and laboratory knowledge. Thus one spring, in response to my department chairman's question, 'What is the most innovative thing that you have done professionally during the past year?' I replied, 'Dear Dave, I've finally stopped torturing animals.'

"I personally learned a great deal from the research, about the politics of science, governmental funding, and also myself as I moved from the university laboratory out into an experimental community which showed me that objective science was just another interesting illusion."

This Week's Citation Classic

CC/NUMBER 26
JUNE 29, 1981

Ropartz P. The relation between olfactory stimulation and aggressive behaviour in mice. *Anim. Behav.* **16**:97-100, 1968.
[Lab. Psychophysiol., Univ. Louis Pasteur, Strasbourg, France]

In order to demonstrate the likely role of olfactory cues in the aggressive behaviour in mice, the level of aggression of male mice was measured in three situations: (a) natural conditions, (b) after the males had been artificially scented, and (c) after removing their olfactory bulbs. [The *Science Citation Index*® (*SCI*®) **and the** *Social Sciences Citation Index*® (*SSCI*®) **indicate that this paper has been cited over 120 times since 1968.]**

P. Ropartz
Laboratoire de Psychophysiologie
Université Louis Pasteur
67000 Strasbourg
France

April 4, 1981

"Since 1966, I had been working on olfaction and social behaviour in domestic mice. It seemed to me reasonable to suspect the role of olfactory cues in the aggressive behaviour of male mice. I was sincerely amazed that nobody had had this idea before me!

"Two techniques were used: the first one, the removal of olfactory bulbs, was not an original one; it was used in rats, for example, by Karli's team in Strasbourg.[1] It was in this laboratory that I learned this surgical method.

"The second one was more original. I had to find an artificial scent in order to mask the natural odours of male mice. As this artificial scent had to be vaporized on each encounter every day, I was afraid of the odour which would be expanded in my experimental room (it was also my *bureau* and I possess a 'good nose!'). I decided to buy a good French perfume for the mice as well as for my nose.

"I went to a perfumer in Strasbourg and asked for 'Diorling' by Dior. The young sales woman blushed and glanced at me as if I were funny. I had told her: 'I would like to buy a very good perfume: it is for mice (in French mice is one of the nicknames for young girls)...for mice *à poils* (in French *à poils* means with fur and *à poil* means naked.)' She called for the *patron*!

"A few months later, when the experiments were finished, I offered the remainder of the perfume to my wife. I don't know why but she did not accept!

"I encountered some difficulties in publishing this paper in an international journal. This is frequently the case when a paper comes from France. The referees didn't find any scientific failure. But, they did find errors in my usage of English. They didn't know that the translation had been done by an English ethologist! Additional work in this field appeared in *Olfaction and Taste*.[2]

"Finally if this paper has been highly cited, it is perhaps because it was the evidence of an evident phenomenon!"

1. **Karli P & Vergnes M.** Rôle du rhinencéphale dans le contrôle du comportement d'agression interspécifique rat-souris. *J. Physiol.-Paris* **55**:272-3, 1963.
2. **Ropartz P & Haug M.** Olfaction and aggressive behaviour in female mice. (Denton D A & Coghlan J P, eds.) *Olfaction and taste*. New York: Academic Press, 1975. Vol. 5. p. 411-12.

Scott J P. Agonistic behavior of mice and rats: a review. *Amer. Zool.* **6**:683-701, 1966. [Dept. Psychol., Bowling Green State Univ., Bowling Green, OH]

This is a general review paper concerning the agonistic behavior of the two mammalian species most commonly used in research on aggression and is organized around a multifactorial theoretical framework which was the basis for the later development of a more highly integrated polysystemic theory. [The *Science Citation Index® (SCI®)* **and the** *Social Sciences Citation Index® (SSCI™)* **indicate that this paper has been cited over 150 times since 1966.]**

J.P. Scott
Center for Research on Social Behavior
Bowling Green State University
Bowling Green, OH 43403

February 18, 1980

"In the early 1940s I, along with Benson Ginsburg and others, originated the use of the house mouse for research on aggression. The suitability of this species lay chiefly in the fact that it was easy to elicit among mice the kind of injurious and often fatal violence that is of primary concern in human affairs.

"The paper under discussion is the second of two review papers that followed up research in this field. The first[1] pointed out that causes of fighting could be found on any level of organization from the genetic to the ecological, and this theme was expanded in a later book.[2]

"This second paper was originally presented as a summary of a symposium organized by R.E. Ulrich. I am pleased to hear that it has been often cited, but I can only surmise the reasons. Among others it was reprinted in Southwick's book of readings on *Animal Aggression* and hence is easily accessible to both zoologists and psychologists.[3] Also, I would like to think that it is cited because it is a well-written critical review of then current research, covers an extensive field, and indicates new areas that needed to be explored. It also helped to put to rest the issue of spontaneous internal stimulation of fighting.

"Its title includes the term 'agonistic behavior,' a concept that I had originated and which has since become widely accepted. Defined as behavior that is adaptive in situations of conflict between members of the same species, it is a much more precise and analytically useful concept than the term aggression, whose meaning has become so widely extended as to make it almost useless as a research tool.

"If I were to write a similar paper today I would have to chronicle extensive progress that has been made in fields that were barely mentioned in it. For example, there is now an extensive literature on agonistic responses to odorous stimuli in mice.[4] Methods of inducing serious fighting in rats have been developed by several experimenters, and the Blanchards[5] have demonstrated that it is organized so as to minimize serious injury. Fighting among females has now been seriously studied: in mice by Ebert and Hyde,[6] and in the rat by the Blanchards.[7] Notable advances have been made in the field of endocrinology, especially the organizing effect of testosterone in neonatal mice.[8]

"The one serious shortcoming of the paper is that it was based on a multifactorial theory of behavior and only foreshadows the theoretical framework which I have since developed into a polysystemic theory.[9] The same theme is extended to include the evolution of agonistic behavior in a forthcoming paper."[10]

1. **Scott J P & Fredericson E.** The causes of fighting in mice and rats. *Physiol. Zool.* **24**:273-309, 1951.
2. **Scott J P.** *Aggression*. Chicago: University of Chicago Press, 1958. 148 p.
3. -----------. Agonistic behavior of mice and rats: a review. (Southwick C H, ed.) *Animal aggression*. New York: Van Nostrand Reinhold, 1970. p. 103-28.
4. **Kessler S, Harmatz P & Gerling S A.** I. Strain differences in the capacity of male urinary odors to elicit aggression. *Behav. Genet.* **5**:233-8, 1975.
5. **Blanchard R J, Fukunaga K, Blanchard D C & Kelley M S.** Conspecific aggression in the laboratory rat. *J. Comp. Physiol. Psychol.* **89**:1204-9, 1975.
6. **Ebert P D & Hyde J S.** Selection for agonistic behavior in wild female *Mus musculus. Behav. Genet.* **6**:291, 1976.
7. **Blanchard R J, Kleinschmidt C J, Fukunaga-Stinson C & Blanchard D C.** Defensive attack behavior in male and female rats. *Anim. Learn. Behav.*, in press.
8. **Whitsett J M, Bronson F H, Peters P J & Hamilton T H.** Neonatal organization of aggression in mice: correlation of critical period with uptake of hormone. *Hormone Behav.* **3**:11-21, 1972.
9. **Scott J P.** Violence and the disaggregated society. *Aggress. Behav.* **1**:235-60, 1975.
10. -----------.The evolution of function in agonistic behavior. (Brain P F & Benton D, eds.) *A multidisciplinary approach to aggression research.* Amsterdam: Elsevier/North Holland, 1981. p. 129-157.

This Week's Citation Classic

Terrace H S. Discrimination learning with and without "errors."
J. Exp. Anal. Behav. **6**:1-27, 1963.
[Columbia University, New York, NY]

Discrimination of color can be learned without responses to S- ('errors') if training begins early in conditioning, with S+ and S- differing with respect to brightness, duration, and wavelength. The brightness and duration differences are faded out progressively leaving only the difference in wavelength. [The *Social Sciences Citation Index*® (*SSCI*®) indicates that this paper has been cited over 185 times since 1966.]

H.S. Terrace
Department of Psychology
Columbia University
New York, NY 10027

July 4, 1981

"Watching a pigeon learn to discriminate two colors without making any errors came as a rude but pleasant surprise during my first graduate school project on animal learning. I was actually pursuing a different problem based on work I had done during the previous summer for H.M. Jenkins (then at Bell Labs, Murray Hill, New Jersey). Jenkins speculated that, during discrimination learning, errors functioned as a source of intermittent reinforcement. He tested this hypothesis by comparing resistance to extinction after three types of training: continuous reinforcement, intermittent reinforcement, and successive discrimination. For each subject given intermittent reinforcement, non-reinforcement occurred on those trials in which a matched subject from the discrimination group made an error. Jenkins's hypothesis was clearly confirmed: the continuous reinforcement group showed significantly less resistance to extinction than the intermittent reinforcement and discrimination groups.[1]

"When I returned to Harvard I began to study this effect parametrically by varying the number of errors that occurred to S-. Quite arbitrarily I decided first to minimize (as opposed to maximize) the number of errors needed to learn a successive red-green discrimination. I started training with a simple discrimination (red *vs.* no color) shortly after the pigeon was trained to peck the response key, and faded slowly to the more difficult red-green discrimination. The first three subjects made no errors during their first session. To my amazement they continued to perform perfectly, that is, to respond to S+ and not respond to S-, during 30 subsequent sessions.

"I decided that 'errorless discrimination learning' was a more interesting dissertation topic than a parametric variation of a well-documented phenomenon. My dissertation research, the basis of my article 'Discrimination learning with and without "errors,"' opened a new area of research stimulus control. Originally, this work was cited because it challenged a widely held assumption that 'extinction is the hallmark of discrimination learning.'[2] Subsequent research showed that certain widely observed 'by-products' of discrimination learning do not occur following errorless learning, for example, behavioral contrast, the peak shift, inhibitory stimulus control, drug induced responding to S-, and escape from S-. I hypothesized that these phenomena were direct consequences of the frustration caused by emitting unreinforced responses to S-.[3]

"Because the 'fading' procedure I used to establish errorless learning was conceptually similar to the programs used in teaching machines and because pigeons who learned to discriminate without errors seemed less frustrated than those who learned with errors, B.F. Skinner, my dissertation advisor, cited my results as evidence for the efficacy of programmed instruction. Other researchers demonstrated that the fading techniques I introduced proved successful in training children as well as animals.[4] However, my theory that errorless learning resulted in a neutral S-, one that evoked no conditioned inhibition, turned out to be an oversimplification. As is the case with so many interesting phenomena in psychology, multiple causation, involving factors that I did not anticipate, proved to be the rule."

1. **Jenkins H M.** The effect of discrimination training on extinction. *J. Exp. Psychol.* **61**:111-21, 1961.
2. **Keller F S & Schoenfeld W N.** *Principles of psychology: a systematic text in the science of behavior.* New York: Appleton-Century-Crofts, 1950. 431 p.
3. **Terrace H S.** By-products of discrimination learning. (Bower G H, ed.) *The psychology of learning and motivation.* New York: Academic Press, 1972. Vol. 5. p. 195-265.
4. **Schreibman L & Koegel R L.** A guideline for planning behavior modification programs for autistic children. (Turner S M, Calhoun K S & Adams H E, eds.) *Handbook of clinical behavior therapy.* New York: Wiley, 1981. p. 500-26.

Staddon J E R & Simmelhag V L. The "superstition" experiment: a reexamination of its implications for the principles of adaptive behavior. *Psychol. Rev.* **78**:3-43, 1971.
[Duke Univ., Durham, NC and Scarborough Coll., Univ. Toronto, Canada]

The paper describes two kinds of behavior of hungry pigeons given periodic brief access to food: *interim activities,* **that occur just after food, and the** *terminal response,* **that occurs in anticipation of food. The paper offers a view of reinforcement as** *selection* **to account for them and for a number of other anomalous results. [The** *Social Sciences Citation Index®* (*SSCI*™) **indicates that this paper has been cited over 200 times since 1971.]**

J.E.R. Staddon
Departments of Psychology and Zoology
Duke University
Durham, NC 27706

January 20, 1981

"The experimental part of this paper was based on Virginia Simmelhag's University of Toronto MA thesis. The experiment, begun in 1966, was strictly of the 'what if?' variety normally regarded as unfundable by any responsible granting agency. The experiment was originally done to see if pigeons exposed to aperiodic (i.e., *variable-time*) food deliveries would show the same kinds of stereotypy as that demonstrated with periodic (i.e., *fixed-time*) food by B.F. Skinner in 1948.[1] (They do.)

"Skinner's famous account was anecdotal and had never been formally replicated—possibly because of behavioristic distrust of observational data. Virginia and I were familiar with ethological methods of recording behavior in one-second time bins and decided that this might be an appropriate method here. The results were strikingly reliable: pigeons (and, in later work, rats[2] and golden hamsters[3]) partition the fixed time between food deliveries into two periods, an *interim* period just after food, when food is never available, and a *terminal* period, when food is probable. During the interim period they engage in vigorous but non-food-related activities, during the terminal period they engage in food-related activities which, for pigeons at short interfood intervals, usually include pecking. The terms *interim* and *terminal* have passed into general use.

"Our results nicely complemented experiments by Brown and Jenkins and Williams and Williams which showed that key pecking in pigeons (the prototypical operant response) could be induced and maintained by a classical conditioning procedure, even in the face of opposing instrumental contingencies (*autoshaping* and *automaintenance*).[4,5] These results, and others on so-called 'schedule-induced' behaviors, had been the cause of a 'crisis' in the field. Our paper provided a unified account which pointed out the two-part nature of reinforced learning: a process of *behavioral variation* that generates behavior and allows animals to sample their environment, and an opposed process of *selection* that picks out effective variants. The conventional concept of 'reinforcement' corresponds only to the second, selective process. Autoshaping involves the first process, hence it is not surprising that it fails to fit the usual reinforcement account. The timeliness of the paper in explaining these anomalies probably accounts for its success.

"We argued that the partitioning of the interfood interval into interim and terminal periods is a result of built-in processes for the efficient allocation of behavior. Optimality analyses of operant behavior are now an active research area.[6]

"The first version of the paper was a short, mostly experimental report. A couple of paragraphs in the *Discussion* appeared cryptic to reviewers and their interest prompted me to greatly expand the theoretical part to explain the numerous anomalies to which I have alluded. Virginia's level-headed criticism restrained and simplified these theoretical excursions."

1. **Skinner B F.** "Superstition" in the pigeon. *J. Exp. Psychol.* **38**:168-72, 1948.
2. **Staddon J E R & Ayres S.** Sequential and temporal properties of behavior induced by a schedule of periodic food delivery. *Behaviour* **54**:26-49, 1975.
3. **Anderson M C & Shettleworth S J.** Behavioral adaptation to fixed-time food delivery in golden hamsters. *J. Exp. Anal. Behav.* **25**:33-49, 1977.
4. **Brown P L & Jenkins H M.** Auto-shaping of the pigeon's key-peck. *J. Exp. Anal. Behav.* **11**:1-8, 1968.
5. **Williams D R & Williams H.** Auto-maintenance in the pigeon: sustained pecking despite contingent non-reinforcement. *J. Exp. Anal. Behav.* **12**:511-20, 1969.
6. **Staddon J E R,** ed. *Limits to action: the allocation of individual behavior.* New York: Academic Press, 1980. 320 p.

 NUMBER 3
JANUARY 15, 1979

Amsel A. The role of frustrative nonreward in noncontinuous reward situations. *Psychol. Bull.* **55**: 102-19, 1958.

This paper presents a conceptualization of the role of frustrative factors in the invigoration of behavior, the development of learned persistence, and the formation of discriminations. The theory describes how goal-incentive mechanisms, defined by Pavlovian conditioning and the hypothetical feedback stimuli from such conditioning, mediate approach and avoidance responding. Some sample data are presented to show the correspondence of the theory to phenomena that occur when a rat learns under a schedule of intermittent reinforcement. [The *Science Citation Index®* **(***SCI®***) and the** *Social Sciences Citation Index™ (SSCI™)* **indicate that this paper was cited 550 times in the period 1961-1977.]**

Abram Amsel
The University of Texas at Austin
Austin, TX 78712

February 13, 1978

"This paper was the second in a series of theoretical articles defining and developing the concept of frustration in learning theory. An earlier paper had been rejected in 1951 by the major theoretical journal in our field, because the editor felt there was 'no point patching up Hull's theory.' I had proposed that adding a 'frustration-inhibition' factor to Hull's two-factor theory of inhibition would bring it more into line with its Pavlovian antecedents and with Kenneth W. Spence's influential theory of discrimination learning. Because such a factor would depend on classical conditioning of frustration, it seemed to me necessary first to identify the requisite Pavlovian unconditioned response of frustration to the unconditioned stimulus of nonreinforcement. This led to a large number of experiments in our laboratory and elsewhere—the first with Jacqueline Roussel in 1952—to establish an indicant of primary unconditioned frustration, the so-called frustration effect (FE). In the 1958 *Bulletin* article, I returned to an examination of the presumed mechanisms of conditioned frustration.

"An outline of the theory introduced in this paper, and developed in subsequent ones, jumped out at me in a laboratory at Newcomb College, Tulane University as I watched rats running an alley for food under a schedule of intermittent reinforcement. In such schedules, studied earlier by L. G. Humphreys and B. F. Skinner, reward is given or withheld quasi-randomly for the same response. I observed that on this (as compared with a consistent-reward) schedule subjects appear at first to approach vigorously even though reward is given only on half the trials, and nonrewards appear to have little effect. In a second stage they react emotionally when reward is withheld; and in a third stage emotional, conflict-like behavior occurs in anticipation of the goal. The conflict disappears in a fourth stage, and the animal returns to vigorous and consistent approach. The nub of the theory is that overcoming the emotional conflict of the third stage and getting to the fourth depends on a counterconditioning mechanism which makes animals more resistant to extinction—persistent.

"This early version of the theory provided an integration of the frustration effect, the partial reinforcement effect, and the appearance and disappearance of emotional effects of frustration in discrimination learning. My guess is that this paper has been cited so frequently because the explanatory scope of the theory has been expanded since its publication. Going from less to more molar examples, the theory has been addressed to some suggested neurophysiological and pharmacological correlates of frustration and persistence; to other behavioral phenomena, such as simultaneous positive and successive negative contrast, Pavlovian induction, the formation of behavioral rituals, and the emission of ultrasonic calls in extinction by infant rats; and to psychopathic persistence, aggression, and regression."

Rozin P & Kalat J W. Specific hungers and poison avoidance as adaptive specializations of learning. *Psychol. Rev.* 78:459-86, 1971. [Univ. Pennsylvania, Philadelphia, PA]

It is argued that learning mechanisms differ in different situations, and are adapted, through evolution, to deal with particular problems faced by the organism. This point of view is illustrated by an analysis of the type of learning in specific hungers and poison avoidance. [The *Social Sciences Citation Index®* (*SSCI™*) indicates that this paper has been cited over 230 times since 1971.]

Paul Rozin
Department of Psychology
University of Pennsylvania
Philadelphia, PA 19104
and
James W. Kalat
Department of Psychology
North Carolina State University
Raleigh, NC 27650

January 3, 1980

"In the 1930s and 1940s, Curt Richter and others demonstrated that rats deficient in particular nutrients would select foods that were rich in these nutrients. Rozin was attracted to this problem in the early 1960s because the phenomenon was simple, easy to obtain, and biologically significant. Furthermore, it seemed unlikely that all specific hungers could be explained either as innate mechanisms or as trial-and-error learning; some unknown principle had to be involved.

"Work done by Rozin at the University of Pennsylvania, largely in collaboration with Willard Rodgers and later with Kalat, led to explanations involving the rat's natural suspicion of new foods, its pattern of sampling dietary choices, and two new principles of learning, which were most clearly demonstrated by John Garcia. The 1971 paper offered an explanation of specific hungers, linked them to poison-avoidance, and reviewed the literature on taste-aversion learning.

"We proposed a modification in the prevalent view that all learning could be accounted for by a few general processes, and argued for the position stated in the abstract. This represented an extension of the ethological tradition into the domain of American learning theory, and was reinforced by papers with a similar message, at about the same time, by Bolles, Garcia, Seligman, and Shettleworth. There was, however, resistance to these ideas. One of the editorial reviews of our 1971 paper began: '...I am unable to find a single new idea of any power in this ridiculously overblown hodge-podge of a manuscript.' (We are grateful that the *Psychological Review* editor felt otherwise.) It has been our general experience that the more novel a paper, the easier it is to criticize and the harder to publish. Some of our favorite pages from the manuscript for this paper, speculating on the evolution of intelligence, were severely cut in the editorial process. Rozin eventually published these ideas in an expanded form in an invited chapter, because he doubted that they would survive the editorial process of any standard journal.[1]

"Starting from nothing, taste-aversion learning has, in the last decade, become an overcrowded area. This accounts for many of the citations of our paper and our shift of interests to other, less studied problems. The relation between specialized and general mechanisms of learning remains controversial,[3] but we believe that, partly as a result of this paper, there is now a greater sensitivity to biological context in the study of learning."

1. **Rozin P.** The evolution of intelligence and access to the cognitive unconscious. (Sprague J A & Epstein A N, eds.) *Progress in psychobiology and physiological psychology, 6.* New York: Academic Press, 1976. p. 245-80.
2. ----------. The significance of learning mechanisms in food selection: some biology, psychology and sociology. (Barker R, Best M & Domjan M, eds.) *Learning mechanisms in food selection.* Waco, TX: Baylor University Press, 1977. p. 557-83.
3. **Kalat J W.** Biological significance of food-aversion learning. (Milgram N W, Krames L & Alloway T M, eds.) *Food aversion learning.* New York: Plenum, 1977. p. 73-103.

This Week's Citation Classic

Crespi L P. Quantitative variation of incentive and performance in the white rat. *Amer. J. Psychol.* **55**:467-517, 1942. [Princeton University, Princeton, NJ]

The study addressed first the influence of different amounts of incentive upon level of performance and distribution of effort within performance (speed gradients). Explored secondly were the effects of shifts of incentive amounts. A theory of emotional drive was elaborated to account for observed 'depression' and 'elation' effects. [The *Social Sciences Citation Index®* (*SSCI®*) **indicates that this paper has been cited over 175 times since 1966.]**

Leo P. Crespi
Office of Research
US International
Communication Agency
Washington, DC 20547

August 31, 1981

"It's a pleasure to comment on the genesis of the present study, if only to correct a misapprehension on the part of M.E. Bitterman[1] that it was a repetition of an earlier study by M.H. Elliott.[2] In fact, the present inquiry was independently conceived along quite different lines. The Elliott study was concerned with *qualitative* change of reward. My study was concerned with the effect upon performance of quantitative variation in the amount of the *same* reward. The Elliott study said nothing about amount of reward and introduced the possible confounding effects of unknown changes in appetitive drive. The present study held drive constant to study the influence of carefully calculated gradations of the same incentive.

"The inspiration for the present study was an earlier inquiry into gambling behavior among white rats.[3] This was conceived of as a comparative approach, without cultural overlays, to a possible philogenetic propensity to gamble or not to gamble on the attainment of rewards. In this connection, some of my fellow graduate students at Princeton accused me of promoting rodent roulette or vice in mice.

"This study involved the choice between a constant-goal of a certain amount of food and a gamble-goal of a lesser or greater amount. The preliminary indications were inconclusive and were not further pursued because I became interested in the more general question of the influence of quantitative variation of incentive on performance. I was struck by the fact that hundreds of animal experiments had been done without specifying the magnitude of a factor of possible considerable influence.

"This interest motivated the present study, which indicated at the outset that amount of incentive was indeed a major influence in performance and could readily explain some apparent conflicts in the animal literature as to the true shape of the speed of locomotion gradient in a runway.

"But more interesting were the results of shifts in incentive amounts after rats had established a level of performance for a given magnitude. Those shifted downward ran more slowly than rats started at the lower level; rats shifted upward ran faster than those started at the upper level. I dubbed these effects 'depression' and 'elation' and elaborated a hypothesis of emotional drive to account for them—a theory to which O.H. Mowrer has subscribed.[4]

"The psychological fraternity rechristened these phenomena, as described in my thesis and subsequently elaborated,[5] the 'Crespi effect' and subjected them to no little attention because they posed a major challenge to Thorndikean laws of effect and to Clark Hull's comprehensive theory of animal behavior.

"In consequence, among others, one of Hull's students, Kenneth Spence, had a group of graduate assistants explore every possibility of explaining away these apparent departures from Hull's conceptions. He was led, to my mind unconvincingly, to argue that the elation effect was an artifact of training procedure rather than a true response to a shift in incentive.

"In any event, the Crespi effect has continued to draw attention and has been applied so far afield as in the design of a dietary regimen for overweight adults. Later experiments have been reported in *The Psychology of Animal Learning.*"[6]

1. **Bitterman M E.** Thorndike and the problem of animal intelligence. *Amer. Psychol.* **24**:444-53, 1969.
2. **Elliott M H.** The effect of change of reward on the maze performance of rats. (Brown W, Tolman E C & Jones H E, eds.) *University of California publications in psychology.* Berkeley, CA: University of California Press, 1932. Vol. IV. p. 19-30.
3. **Crespi L P.** *Gambling behavior: a comparative approach. I. Constant-goal vs. gamble-goal in the albino rat.* Paper delivered at the eleventh annual meeting of the Eastern Psychological Association. 5-6 April 1940, Atlantic City, NJ.
4. **Mowrer O H.** *Learning theory and behavior.* New York: Wiley, 1960. p. 261-3. [Citation Classic. *Current Contents/Social & Behavioral Sciences* **12**(5):16, 4 February 1980.]
5. **Crespi L P.** Amount of reinforcement and level of performance. *Psychol. Rev.* **51**:341-57, 1944.
6. **Mackintosh N J.** *The psychology of animal learning.* London: Academic Press, 1974. 730 p.

This Week's Citation Classic

Falk J L. Production of polydipsia in normal rats by an intermittent food schedule. *Science* **133**:195-6, 1961.
[Dept. Nutrition, Harvard Univ. School of Public Health, Boston, MA]

Marked, chronic overdrinking (polydipsia) was produced in all rats reduced in body weight and receiving most of their daily food ration under a variable-interval one-minute schedule of food-pellet availability. [The *Science Citation Index*® (*SCI*®) **and the** *Social Sciences Citation Index*® (*SSCI*®) **indicate that this paper has been cited over 270 times since 1961.]**

John L. Falk
Department of Psychology
Rutgers University
New Brunswick, NJ 08903

March 4, 1982

"In 1959, I was a National Institutes of Health postdoctoral fellow at the department of nutrition in the laboratory of Jean Mayer, who generously allowed me complete research freedom. I had begun a study to determine whether rats given bilateral, ventromedial hypothalamic lesions would increase their lever-pressing behavior when this behavior was reinforced intermittently by the delivery of food pellets. A possible change in the relation between food-pellet ingestion and water intake also was of interest, so drinking was measured by a lick-detecting drinkometer. To my surprise, before I had a chance to inflict the planned brain lesions, the rats all revealed a severe and persistent polydipsia (overdrinking) during each of their daily, intermittent feeding sessions. Fortunately, having done dissertation work in water balance with Lawrence I. O'Kelly at the University of Illinois, I knew that rats drinking one-half their body weights in water in about three hours every day was unprecedented. After all, they were not deprived of water at any time, and the imposed constraint on food intake always decreases water intake in rats under other circumstances. It became evident that food-deprived animals obtaining small food portions spread out over time (within certain limits) is a sufficient condition for the production of polydipsia.

"While the article suggested that this curious behavioral effect might be useful for physiological studies in which a continuous, self-imposed diuresis needed to be maintained, it excited little technical or theoretical interest in water balance circles. The spectacle of an animal persistently self-administering loads of water far in excess of its requirements on a chronic basis is more than those with a theoretical commitment to equating ingestion with homeostatic function can bear. Research, however, was stimulated in those who used the technique to induce animals to ingest drug solutions in order to study the variables initiating and maintaining excessive drug intake.[1]

"A second line of investigation has implications for behavior theory. Many studies have demonstrated not only that the polydipsia is not species specific, but that other kinds of behavior can become excessive under intermittent food-schedule conditions (e.g., aggression, activity, pica, escape).[2] Furthermore, intermittent schedules of commodities and activities other than food also can induce behavioral excesses.[3,4] This research has given rise to the term 'schedule-induced behavior' or 'adjunctive behavior' to distinguish its source and maintenance as different from classically or operantly conditioned behavior. It is gratifying to see that a lucky observation of a postdoctoral fellow has grown into a vigorous area of inquiry.

"Citation of the paper has been frequent perhaps for three reasons: it presents a useful technique, an interdisciplinary theoretical puzzle, and an exemplar of the environmental roots of excessive behavior."

1. **Gilbert R M.** Schedule-induced self-administration of drugs. (Blackman D E & Sanger D J, eds.) *Contemporary research in behavioral pharmacology.* New York: Plenum Press, 1978. p. 289-323.
2. **Falk J L.** The nature and determinants of adjunctive behavior. *Physiol. Behav.* **6**:577-88, 1971.
3. -----------. The origin and functions of adjunctive behavior. *Anim. Learn. Behav.* **5**:325-35, 1977.
4. -----------. The environmental generation of excessive behavior. (Mulé S J, ed.) *Behavior in excess: a guide to the volitional disorders.* New York: Free Press, 1981. p. 313-37.

CC/NUMBER 21
MAY 24, 1982

Greenspoon J. The reinforcing effect of two spoken sounds on the frequency of two responses. *Amer. J. Psychol.* **68**:409-16, 1955.
[Indiana University, Bloomington, IN]

The primary objective of this research was to determine if verbal responses were modifiable in a manner similar to nonverbal responses. The results indicated that verbal behavior could be investigated as a legitimate phenomenon in and of itself. [The *Social Sciences Citation Index®* **(***SSCI®***) indicates that this paper has been cited over 160 times since 1966.]**

Joel Greenspoon
Department of Psychology
University of Texas
of the Permian Basin
Odessa, TX 79762

March 4, 1982

"The impetus for this research, which was a part of my doctoral dissertation at Indiana University, came from two major sources, a course in verbal behavior taught by B.F. Skinner and the nondirective therapy of Carl Rogers. Skinner presented the position that verbal behavior was governed by the same principles as nonverbal behavior though there was little research to support his position. Rogers contended that the passivity of the counselor meant that the counselor didn't directly manipulate the client's verbal behavior. The research tended to support Skinner's position but refute Rogers's.

"I spent a considerable amount of time devising the method of investigation. I tried several different methods, but didn't think that any of them were very good in providing the answers to the questions that I was asking. One day I was running a college sophomore using one of these methods. When we were finished, he suggested that I simply ask subjects to say individual words. I tried his suggestion and it worked beautifully and that was the method I used.

"A major technical problem involved recording the entire procedure. At that time tape recorders were beginning to appear on the market, but there were no continuous hour tapes. Since each session lasted for approximately one hour, I needed to record for the entire hour. The only device available was a wire recorder. I soon became convinced that the wire recorder was invented by a sadist. The wire was very thin and became easily entangled in unbelievable snarls. Since I had to transcribe all the words from each wire, I was never home free on any one subject until I had completed the transcribing. There were several occasions when the wire became so entangled during the transcription that I could not complete it. When this happened I would have to run another subject to replace the lost one. There were occasions when I had wire strewn all over the office in an effort to salvage a subject.

"My initial effort to publish the research was rebuffed by an editor who completed his very critical review of the article with the comment that he didn't believe that there was very much interest in this kind of research. Shortly thereafter a former student of mine had an article based on my research accepted by the same editor.[1]

"I believe that several factors contributed to the frequent citation of this research. It opened the way for the experimental investigation of verbal behavior as a phenomenon rather than an epiphenomenon, resulting in the development of the term verbal conditioning. The research also contributed to the development of behavior modification since it suggested that verbal behavior was subject to the same variables as nonverbal behavior, and many behavior problems involve verbal behavior. The research also raised anew the issue of the role of awareness in human learning, an issue that remains unresolved at the present time. More recent work in the field has been reported."[2-4]

1. **Sidowski J B.** Influence of awareness of reinforcement on verbal conditioning. *J. Exp. Psychol.* **48**:355-60, 1954.
2. **Das J P.** *Verbal conditioning and behavior.* New York: Pergamon Press, 1969. 163 p.
3. **Greenspoon J & Brownstein A J.** Awareness in verbal conditioning. *J. Exp. Res. Personal.* **2**:295-308, 1967.
4. **Greenspoon J.** Verbal conditioning and clinical psychology. (Bachrach A J, ed.) *Experimental foundations of clinical psychology.* New York: Basic Books, 1962. p. 510-53.

This Week's Citation Classic

Dember W N & Earl R W. Analysis of exploratory, manipulatory, and curiosity behaviors. *Psychol. Rev.* **64**:91-6, 1957.
[University of Michigan, Ann Arbor, MI]

Exploration, manipulation, and curiosity are classified in the category of attention. Two determinants of attention, temporal and spatial change, are identified and symbolically represented in Coombsian terminology. Stimuli arouse attention through their ability to increase the perceiver's level of complexity. [The *Social Sciences Citation Index*® (*SSCI*®) indicates that this paper has been cited in over 150 publications since 1966.]

W.N. Dember
Department of Psychology
University of Cincinnati
Cincinnati, OH 45221

October 15, 1982

"This article was one of several products of a close collaboration with Robert W. Earl when we were graduate students in psychology at the University of Michigan in the early- and mid-1950s. We both worked in Edward L. Walker's lab on the phenomenon of spontaneous alternation behavior in rats. In essence, if rats enter one arm of a T-maze on a given trial, they are highly likely to enter the other arm on the next trial, at least until differential reinforcement leads to their consistently choosing one of the arms. We saw conventional rewards as transforming an inherent pattern of variability into one of stereotypy. We began to think of animals and people as being highly responsive to stimulus change, and stimulus change in turn as underlying a variable we dubbed complexity. Calling on the measurement theory of Clyde H. Coombs, we noted that organisms as well as stimuli could be assigned a complexity measure. An organism's complexity, the ideal, corresponds to the value of the most complex stimulus which the organism can comfortably process. An organism will prefer to interact with stimuli closest to the ideal, generating an inverted U-shaped preference function.

"During that period, our thinking was honed by hours of discussion and sometimes dispute with Walker. Only much later did I come to realize that Walker's resistance was intended not only to get us to think more clearly but also to strengthen our resolve to prove him wrong.

"The *Citation Classic* was initially written in an effort to clarify our ideas for an undergraduate student who wished to do her senior thesis[1] under my direction. I wrote a draft over one weekend; Earl revised and improved it. In a fit of grandiosity, we submitted it to *Psychological Review* and were stunned and delighted when we learned that it had been accepted for publication. A direct test of the theory, actually completed before the theory took final form, was also published.[2] For his dissertation,[3] Earl applied the theory to the choices made by adolescent boys of puzzles to work on, and also added the vital concept of the pacer stimulus—that is, a stimulus just a little more complex than the ideal. It is pacers, we believe, that make the world interesting by providing a vehicle for increasing one's complexity.

"Earl and I were fortunate in subsequent years to have had a number of superb graduate students who further tested and extended the theory. We also were gratified to find our mentor, Walker, developing and testing his own version of the theory, and recently telling the complexity story in considerable detail and with great charm.[4]

"The ideas expressed in our article were 'in the air.' We synthesized them and presented them in a simple, formal manner. I believe our notions caught on and were cited because they appeared at the right time in the right place, were broadly applicable, and were essentially correct."

1. **Dember W N & Millbrook B A.** Response by rats to the greater of two brightness changes. *Psychol. Rep.* **2**:465-7, 1956.
2. **Dember W N, Earl R W & Paradise N.** Response by rats to differential stimulus complexity. *J. Comp. Physiol. Psychol.* **50**:514-18, 1957.
3. **Earl R W.** *Problem-solving and motor skill behaviors under conditions of free-choice.* PhD dissertation. Ann Arbor, MI: University of Michigan, 1957.
4. **Walker E L.** *Psychological complexity and preference: a hedgehog theory of behavior.* Monterey, CA: Brooks/Cole, 1980. 569 p.

Amsel A. Frustrative nonreward in partial reinforcement and discrimination learning: some recent history and a theoretical extension. *Psychol. Rev.* **69**:306-28, 1962.
[Univ. Toronto, Ontario, Canada]

The first part of this paper examined the history and current status of the concept of frustrative nonreward in behavior theory. The second part was a frustration-theory account of the effect of prediscrimination treatments on subsequent discrimination learning. [The *Science Citation Index*® (*SCI*®) and the *Social Sciences Citation Index*® (*SSCI*®) indicate that this paper has been cited in over 450 publications since 1962.]

Abram Amsel
Department of Psychology
University of Texas
Austin, TX 78712

October 14, 1983

"As I wrote originally, this paper was an extension of the application of frustration theory[1,2] to discrimination learning. It was designed to deal with variations in the rate at which discriminations between stimuli are formed as a function of the reinforcement history of these stimuli. For example, if response to the to-be-positive stimulus has been reinforced continuously and to the to-be-negative stimulus intermittently, discrimination will be retarded relative to a history of both stimuli being continuously reinforced. I had worked out a number of such predictions in some detail and based them on frustration-theory assumptions and some principles taken from N.E. Miller's analysis of conflict.

"As it was finally published, the paper included a kind of preface—the 'recent history' referred to in the title. This is how it happened. In 1961, Leon Festinger published a paper[3] in which he applied the concept of cognitive dissonance to the partial reinforcement extinction effect. The idea, taken from his theory of cognitive dissonance, is that rats, as well as humans, 'come to love that for which they have suffered.' To demonstrate this point, Festinger employed a runway with a start box, mid box, and end box arrangement so that the rats could be delayed in the mid box before being allowed to run and find food in the end box. Dissonance produced in the empty mid box was said to have induced 'some extra preference' for something about the empty mid box.

"Richard Solomon, then editor of the *Psychological Review*, found Festinger's idea about extra attractiveness (later extended in a monograph by Lawrence and Festinger[4]) very similar to some work his student, James Olds, had done for his doctoral degree at Harvard University.[5] (Olds later became famous for his work on electrical stimulation of the brain.) The finding was that delayed reward in children constitutes 'practice at wanting' and that such practice increases the value of the reward. Solomon was also struck by the similarity of Festinger's ideas, and particularly of his runway with its mid box, to earlier experimental and theoretical work of mine (e.g., see references 1 and 6) which had addressed the partial reinforcement extinction effect and in which a double-runway apparatus of essentially the same design as Festinger's was used to study the 'frustration effect.' During a visit to the University of Toronto, shortly after the appearance of Festinger's paper, Solomon invited me to write an article for the *Psychological Review* to 'set the record straight.'

"The paper extending the 1958 theory to prediscrimination experiences had by then been completed, but I agreed to add to it a brief historical introduction that would address the similarities and differences in approach among Festinger's, Old's, and my work on the dynamic properties of nonreinforcement. My thinking was that 'setting the record straight,' by itself, did not really constitute the kind of theoretical paper that would normally appear in the *Psychological Review*.

"In retrospect, putting these two kinds of things into a single paper was not a good idea, even though this combination may be a reason it is frequently cited. But, despite this frequent citation, I still think that the part of it in which I was most interested, the theory of prediscrimination effects, had less of an impact than it would have had it been published separately. I once had a paper returned to me by an editor whose referee remarked that the paper had 'only two or three ideas in it.' My advice is to write papers with just one idea—provided it is a good one."

1. **Amsel A** The role of frustrative nonreward in noncontinuous reward situations. *Psychol. Bull.* **55**:102-19, 1958.
2. --------------. Citation Classic. Commentary on *Psychol. Bull.* **55**:102-19, 1958. *Current Contents/Social & Behavioral Sciences* **11**(3):14, 15 January 1979.
3. **Festinger L.** The psychological effects of insufficient rewards. *Amer. Psychol.* **16**:1-11, 1961.
4. **Lawrence D H & Festinger L.** *Deterrents and reinforcement*. Stanford, CA: Stanford University Press, 1962. 180 p.
5. **Olds J.** *The growth and structure of motives: psychological studies in the theory of action*. Glencoe, IL: Free Press, 1956. 277 p.
6. **Amsel A & Roussel J.** Motivational properties of frustration: I. Effect on a running response in the addition of frustration to the motivational complex. *J. Exp. Psychol.* **43**:363-8, 1952.

CC/NUMBER 24
JUNE 11, 1984

This Week's Citation Classic™

Anger D. The dependence of interresponse times upon the relative reinforcement of different interresponse times. *J. Exp. Psychol.* **52**:145-61, 1956.
[Harvard University, Cambridge, MA]

Rats adjusted the time between their responses (interresponse times, IRTs) according to the relative reinforcement of different IRTs. Clear adjustment occurred when only certain IRTs were reinforced, and further evidence indicated adjustment was occurring during interval schedules, which favor reinforcement of certain IRTs. [The *Science Citation Index*® (*SCI*®) and the *Social Sciences Citation Index*® (*SSCI*®) indicate that this paper has been cited in over 245 publications since 1956.]

Douglas Anger
Department of Psychology
University of Missouri
Columbia, MO 65210

April 24, 1984

"When a response of an animal is reinforced with food on a ratio schedule, the animal responds at a higher rate than it does on an interval schedule. (Ratio schedules require a number of responses between reinforced responses; interval schedules require a time interval between.) My 1956 paper sought to clarify how a rat detects that subtle difference. Skinner[1] had mentioned that ratio schedules reinforce high response rates more than interval ones, and animals might discriminate that difference. One test of that possibility is to reinforce only certain response rates, or only certain interresponse times (IRTs), and measure whether rats change their response appropriately. (The term 'IRTs' was introduced in 1956.) Experiments in 1948 during my first semester as a Harvard University graduate student found that selective reinforcement of responses ending long IRTs slowed responses, even when slowing increased reinforcement frequency. After a diversion, I returned to this problem for a dissertation that became the 1956 paper. Further experiments confirmed the response adjustment to long-IRT reinforcement. They also showed that interval schedules quickly change behavior from an initial state with equal probability of different IRTs to unequal probabilities that roughly reflect the relative reinforcement of different IRTs by the schedule. Since interval schedules reinforce short IRTs less than ratio schedules, adjustment could be responsible for the lower response with interval schedules.

"The paper's citation frequency has probably been somewhat due to its theoretical significance: the demonstration that reinforcements can decrease as well as increase response, the suggestion of an inhibitory process, and evidence for IRT reinforcement mediating schedule effects. For a while, the paper stimulated investigations of IRT reinforcement effects with schedules, but the results were disappointing. No simple precise relation emerged, although a rough relation was found. As a result, other theories are dominant now and IRT analysis receives little attention. In my opinion, the evidence still indicates that differences in IRT reinforcement are an important source of the behavior differences controlled by schedules, but the relation is complex. The several different processes operating with schedules need clarification before the role of IRT reinforcement can be well defined.

"However, many more citations seem to have resulted from wide use of long-IRT reinforcement as a baseline for study of other factors: other treatment variables, drugs, physiological changes, etc. The procedure easily and reliably produces stable behavior whose sensitivity to variables is quite different from that of other common procedures. My paper has been a convenient initial one to reference for the procedure and its basic features. Though unexpected, that usefulness apparently did result from the attempt to show an unusual slowing or inhibitory effect of reinforcements. The 1956 study was published with no trouble; in contrast, a recent investigation[2] of a related problem encountered stiff resistance."

1. **Skinner B F.** *The behavior of organisms: an experimental analysis.* New York: Appleton-Century, 1938. 457 p.
2. **Anger D.** Reinforcement of inhibition. *J. Exp. Anal. Behav.* **39**:213-26, 1983.

Chapter

6

Cognitive Processes

Information and information processing / 135–140

Learning / 141–158

Higher cognitive processes / 159–169

Intelligence / 170–171

This Week's Citation Classic

CC/NUMBER 24
JUNE 16, 1980

Attneave F. *Applications of information theory to psychology: a summary of basic concepts, methods, and results.*
New York: Holt, Rinehart, and Winston, 1959. 120 p.
[University of Oregon, Eugene, OR]

The book contains an introduction to the concept of information as a quantifiable variable, detailed descriptions of procedures for the calculation of informational statistics, a review of psychological studies using information theory, and suggestions for further developments. [The *Social Sciences Citation Index® (SSCI™)* **indicates that this book has been cited over 355 times since 1966.]**

Fred Attneave
Department of Psychology
University of Oregon
Eugene, OR 97403

January 10, 1980

"In 1954 or 1955, when I was working on problems of shape and pattern perception for a remarkably tolerant and supportive Air Force laboratory, I set out to write a long review article on information theory for a series known as the Doubleday Papers in Psychology, which almost immediately became defunct when Doubleday was taken over by Random House. I put the manuscript away with only a little disappointment, since a major part of my motivation in writing it had been to clarify my own understanding of information measurement. It lay practically forgotten until a couple of years later when I happened to mention it to a representative of Holt, whose editors read it and decided that it was perhaps worth bringing out as a book.

"Information theory was new and exciting to a great many psychologists in the 1950s. The basic works of Wiener[1] and Shannon[2] in the late 1940s had an almost immediate impact on psychology. In 1949 Miller and Frick[3] showed how response sequences could be analyzed in informational terms, and in 1951 Garner and Hake[4] presented a method of multivariate informational analysis that had a generality far beyond its original application to absolute judgments. A small flood of studies—good, bad, and indifferent—ensued. In at least one area, that of unidimensional absolute judgments, it proved possible to specify a fairly definite performance limit in terms of the Shannon-Wiener information measure. More generally, human capacities showed little or no invariance in terms of bits. Even these negative findings had value in suggesting what people *were* doing: The bit was not a very good *psychological* unit, but Miller's 'chunk'[5] was.

"It is certainly true, however, that the enthusiasm for measuring everything possible in bits which developed during this period was excessive and ultimately counterproductive, fostering a view that 'information theory' was just a fad. This reaction was well under way by 1959 when my book appeared; thus the popularity of the book, in the original and in German and Japanese translations, was rather surprising. Perhaps I was fairly successful in emphasizing somewhat more basic and less faddish applications.

"The proposition that the function of the nervous system is to process information has been so widely assimilated that most psychologists would now accept it as a truism. The corollary is that information theory *in a sufficiently general sense* must be absolutely basic to psychology. MacKay[6] distinguished between structural information (logons) and selective information (bits), and current developments such as Leeuwenberg's[7] elegant system for evaluating the information in complex patterns indicate that the former is primary in psychological importance. The information theory pursued in the 1950s was simply too narrow, but the time may be approaching when a book on psychological applications of information theory far more profound than mine can be written."

1. **Wiener N.** *Cybernetics.* New York: Wiley, 1948. 194 p.
2. **Shannon C E & Weaver W.** *The mathematical theory of communication.* Urbana: University of Illinois Press, 1949. 125 p.
3. **Miller G A & Frick F C.** Statistical behavioristics and sequences of responses. *Psychol. Rev.* **56**:311-24, 1949.
4. **Garner W R & Hake H W.** The amount of information in absolute judgments. *Psychol. Rev.* **58**:446-59, 1951.
5. **Miller G A.** The magical number seven, plus or minus two: some limits on our capacity for processing information. *Psychol. Rev.* **63**:81-7, 1956.
6. **MacKay D M.** *Information, mechanism, and meaning.* Cambridge, MA: MIT Press, 1969. 196 p.
7. **Leeuwenberg E.** A perceptual coding language for visual and auditory patterns. *Amer. J. Psychol.* **84**:307-49, 1971.

This Week's Citation Classic™

Broadbent D E. *Perception and communication.*
London: Pergamon Press, 1958. 338 p.
[Applied Psychology Research Unit, Medical Research Council, Cambridge, England]

This book set out a model of human performance in terms of the processing of information, using the data available at the time. It particularly emphasised task combination and selective intake of information as methods of clarifying the nature of internal events. [The *Science Citation Index*® (*SCI*®) and the *Social Sciences Citation Index*® (*SSCI*®) indicate that this book has been cited in over 1,375 publications since 1958.]

Donald E. Broadbent
Department of Experimental Psychology
University of Oxford
Oxford OX1 3UD
England

March 27, 1984

"This book was written in odd evenings, in aircraft, on trains, and during weekends, while I was working during normal hours on human factors problems in Cambridge, England. At that time, those of us studying man-machine interfaces had a problem. We found we needed a particular kind of psychology to make sense of our results. But the academic journals were dominated by a different kind of thinking. As Paul Fitts showed, one could get an audience by starting a paper in the conventional language of stimulus and response (S-R), and then slowly modulating into a more useful vocabulary of information processing. With the increase of knowledge throughout the 1950s, however, this got harder and harder, because it meant doing the whole job within each paper; we needed some general statement of the whole background. I thought, therefore, that I would write a kind of survey of the scattered papers and technical reports that were being inspired by the newer language, point out that they were all coming from a consistent point of view, and relate them to the interests of the more dominant schools of psychology. The view itself, of course, had already been formulated by Craik, Bartlett, Fitts, Garner, and others.

"As luck would have it, many other people were discontented with the S-R associationist framework, and the book appeared just at the right moment to be used as a citation with which to club harmless behaviorists over the head. That probably is the reason for its frequent citation. In addition, some parts of the book could be read in a way that did not require *too* much of a change of mind in psychologists of a different tradition. It therefore won a few converts. The cost, however, was that it was often misquoted with approval. Bits of it (such as the problems of the word 'consciousness,' the reasons two tasks can often be done simultaneously, or the treatment of practice) escaped notice and can still be read with profit today.

"Since those innocent days, the world has become more complex, so that it is difficult to point to a single summary of the same entire area. The more academic aspects of cognitive psychology appear in texts such as that of Anderson,[1] more applied topics in books on specialised subjects,[2,3] and so on. One widespread view, which I support, is that the framework of the 1958 book now requires shifting to a different kind of simplistic conceptual framework."[4]

1. **Anderson J R.** *Cognitive psychology and its implications.* San Francisco: Freeman, 1980. 503 p.
2. **Davies D R & Parasuraman R.** *The psychology of vigilance.* London: Academic Press, 1982. 288 p.
3. **Hockey G R J**, ed. *Stress and fatigue in human performance.* New York: Wiley, 1983. 396 p.
4. **Broadbent D E.** Maltese Cross: a new simplistic model for memory. *Behav. Brain Sci.* In press, 1984.

This Week's Citation Classic

CC/NUMBER 8
FEBRUARY 22, 1982

Morton J. Interaction of information in word recognition.
Psychol. Rev. **76**:165-78, 1969.
[Applied Psychology Research Unit, Cambridge, England]

Quantitative predictions are made from a model of word recognition on the effects of word frequency on recognition, the interaction of stimulus and context information, and the effects of repeated presentation of stimuli. The relevance of the model for studies of memory is discussed. [The *Social Sciences Citation Index®* **(***SSCI®***) indicates that this paper has been cited over 205 times since 1969.]**

John Morton
Applied Psychology Unit
Medical Research Council
Cambridge CB2 2EF
England

December 4, 1981

"As a graduate student I looked at the effect of a Reading Efficiency Course. It became clear that slow readers often had skills that were not being used, such as knowledge of the structure of language which could be used to 'predict' what was being read. So I studied the role of context on word recognition and showed that less stimuli information was required for a word to be identified if the word fit into a context. From this, I conceived the idea of a 'unit' corresponding to each word, at which stimulus and contextual information could interact and I described its properties. This unit was later called a 'logogen,' following a suggestion at a conference by the physiologist Hallowell Davis (probably the most useful comment I have ever had at a conference!).

"My thesis was finished in 1961 and the material reached the journals in 1964. There wasn't much interest in the model I had developed and I did other things for a few years until I got interested in signal detection. I then realised that I could treat the model mathematically, which I did, and went on to write the cited paper which was a less technical version of the same thing together with a discussion of more general psychological implications for a wider audience. This paper was finished at Yale University, where I was spending the year working with Tex Garner. In the first draft I had spent a lot of space criticising other people. Tex advised me most emphatically to cut all that out and concentrate on the positive side of my own contribution. Incidentally, the qualitative aspects of the model formed the theoretical basis of another *Citation Classic*, in collaboration with Bob Crowder, whom I met at Yale that year.[1]

"The model turns out to have been far too simple in certain respects, but I found that out myself a few years later before anyone else did.[2] As it stood, the model made certain predictions which we falsified experimentally. So the model was changed, though the name, the Logogen Model, was carried over from the original. Now, the revised version is being used extensively for describing dyslexia and other results of brain damage.[3,4]

"I think the paper has been popular because it showed the utility of an information processing approach to psychological theory within which a model could be clearly expressed. In addition, in this and other papers, I showed how experimental results on a variety of human skills could be related by means of purely psychological models of the brain processes.

"There is a strong visual component to the expression of the model which I find useful in keeping track of its complexity but which has stimulated others to criticise 'this pre-occupation with boxes and arrows'—to quote a reviewer's comment on a recently submitted paper! However, the ideas have also been attacked seriously (as well as supported), which is healthy. Curiously, no one has challenged the quantitative aspects of the paper, which, I am sure, originally gave it respectability."

1. **Crowder R G & Morton J.** Precategorical acoustic storage (PAS). *Percept. Psychophys.* **5**:365-73, 1969. [Citation Classic. *Current Contents/Social & Behavioral Sciences* **11**(47):10, 19 November 1979.]
2. **Morton J.** Facilitation in word recognition: experiments causing change in the Logogen Model. (Kolers P A, Wrolstad M E & Bouma H, eds.) *Processing in visible language.* New York: Plenum, 1979. Vol. 1. p. 259-68.
3. **Morton J & Patterson K.** A new attempt at an interpretation. (Coltheart M, Patterson K E & Marshall J C, eds.) *Deep dyslexia.* London: Routledge and Kegan Paul, 1980. p. 91-118.
4. **Beauvois M F, Derouesne J & Saillent B.** Syndromes neuropsychologiques et psychologie cognitive. Trois exemples: aphasie tactile, alexie phonologique et agraphie lexicale. *Cah. Psychol.* **23**:211-46, 1980.

This Week's Citation Classic

CC/NUMBER 23
JUNE 9, 1980

Kagan J, Rosman B L, Day D, Albert J & Phillips W. Information processing in the child: significance of analytic and reflective attitudes.
Psychol. Monogr. **78**:1-37, 1964.
[Fels Research Inst., Yellow Springs, OH]

School age children differ in the time they take to evaluate the validity of their solutions in intellectual tasks with response uncertainty. This dimension, called reflection-impulsivity, is moderately stable over tasks and time. [The *Social Sciences Citation Index® (SSCI™)* **indicates that this paper has been cited over 285 times since 1966.]**

Jerome Kagan
Department of Psychology and
Social Relations
Harvard University
Cambridge, MA 02138

February 1, 1980

"The origin of this first set of investigations into the dimension called reflection-impulsivity was a set of sorting responses produced by adults in the Fels longitudinal sample.[1] I noted that those subjects who used concrete, descriptive bases for their grouping were more cautious and inhibited than the adults who used categorical or functional dimensions. We initiated a series of studies with children which indicated that the disposition to show long decision times and low error rates because the children examined all alternatives in a problem situation (called reflectivity), in contrast to fast decision times and high error rates (called impulsivity), was a moderately stable characteristic of school-age children. Subsequent to the 1964 monograph many other investigators have explored the implications of this construct because the psychological property of impulsivity has been popular among investigators concerned with syndromes of reading disability, learning disorder, and hyperactivity.[2] Additionally, the methods used to operationalize reflection-impulsivity are objective, reliable, relatively easy to implement, and require only a half-hour to administer.

"At the present time it appears that this disposition is predictive of quality of performance on selected academic subjects, reactivity to humor, and style of creativity. Our current interpretation is that socialization experiences that create anxiety over error predispose a child toward a reflective attitude. In general, across the period four through 10 years of age, children become more reflective and less impulsive as they come to appreciate the undesirable consequences of error. Japanese children appear to be socialized to avoid error more consistently than American children and develop a reflective attitude earlier than American children. Additionally, we believe that temperamental attributes which can be detected in the first two years of life, especially slow tempo of play and a high frequency of occurrence of the smile of assimilation during the first year, can predispose a child toward a reflective or an impulsive attitude depending upon socialization experiences related to attitude toward error. The complete corpus of data suggests that when a child or adult is solving a problem that contains response uncertainty, the probability of error can be influenced by the reflection-impulsivity disposition. Hence, investigators should take this attitude into account in their empirical work."

1. **Kagan J & Moss H A.** *Birth to maturity.* New York: Wiley, 1962. 381 p.
2. **Messer S B.** Reflection-impulsivity: a review. *Psychol. Bull.* **83**:1026-52, 1976.

This Week's Citation Classic

CC/NUMBER 28
JULY 14, 1980

Slovic P & Lichtenstein S. Comparison of Bayesian and regression approaches to the study of information processing in judgment.
Organ. Behav. Hum. Perform. **6**:649-744, 1971.
[Oregon Research Institute, OR]

Studies of information use in judgment and decision making have been conducted within two schools of research, which we have labeled the 'Bayesian' and the 'regression' approaches. This paper presents a review and comparative analysis of these two approaches. [The *Social Sciences Citation Index*® *(SSCI™)* **indicates that this paper has been cited over 230 times since 1971.]**

Paul Slovic
Decision Research
A Branch of Perceptronics
1201 Oak Street
Eugene, OR 97401

April 8, 1980

"By 1968, several hundred studies had investigated the ways that people use information to arrive at a judgment or decision. Most of this work was done within two different paradigms, one based on probability theory (in particular, Bayes' theorem), the other based on regression analysis. Although the two groups of researchers were interested in many of the same questions, there was virtually no communication between them. Sarah Lichtenstein and I were among the few who had worked within both paradigms. When David Summers and Leon Rappoport invited us to write a chapter comparing the two approaches for a book they were editing,[1] we eagerly agreed to do so.

"Our article defined the important substantive issues and took a stand on many of them. We urged researchers to shed the blinders imposed upon them by working within a single paradigm. We pointed out some important generalizations derived from both paradigms—that people respond in highly systematic ways to information; that intuitive judgment need not be mysterious but can be described by precise, quantitative models, and that people's insights into their own judgmental processes are often inaccurate. We asserted that difficulties of processing information often cause people to employ simplified mental strategies, many of which cause relevant data to be ignored or misused. Finally, we pointed out the need for decision aids to offset these shortcomings and described several promising aiding techniques.

"In retrospect, although we may have stimulated interest in judgment research, we failed to convince researchers to take a multi-paradigm approach. However, they did seem to heed another recommendation—that research should move towards more molecular analyses of information processing strategies. In recent years, many studies have shown how judgment processes are molded by the interaction between task demands and human cognitive limitations.[2,3]

"One of the judgmental strategies we described was anchoring and adjustment. We later used our own inability to forecast the completion date of this article as an example of anchoring bias:

On this date	*We promised it for this date*
September 16, 1968	June 1969
May 1969	end of July 1969
December 1969	end of January 1970
January 1970	end of June 1970
Draft sent	July 24, 1970

"Perhaps because other authors experienced similar problems, completion of the Rappoport and Summers book was delayed. We worried that our review might lose its timeliness. Generously, Rappoport and Summers allowed us to submit it to a journal, and Jim Naylor agreed to devote an entire issue of *Organizational Behavior and Human Performance* to the article. Sarah and I were pleased that our mentor, Ward Edwards, wrote a forward to the journal version, since his own highly influential review articles[4,5] had established the now burgeoning field of behavioral decision theory.

"We have probably sent out more than 5,000 reprints of the article. One professor, who requested many copies, later told us that he assigned it in its entirety the first week of the term to pare his overly large class down to manageable size."

1. **Rappoport L & Summers D A.** *Human judgment and social interaction.* New York: Holt, Rinehart & Winston, 1973. 403 p.
2. **Tversky A & Kahneman D.** Judgment under uncertainty: heuristics and biases. *Science* **185**:1124-31, 1974.
3. **Slovic P, Fischhoff B & Lichtenstein S.** Behavioral decision theory. *Annu. Rev. Psychol.* **28**:1-39, 1977.
4. **Edwards W.** The theory of decision making. *Psychol. Bull.* **51**:380-417, 1954.
5. ---------------. Behavioral decision theory. *Annu. Rev. Psychol.* **12**:473-98, 1961.

This Week's Citation Classic

Deutsch J A & Deutsch D. Attention: some theoretical considerations.
Psychol. Rev. **70**:80-90, 1963.
[Stanford University, Stanford, CA]

The selection of messages to which we attend from those to which we do not attend requires discrimination mechanisms of as great a complexity as those in normal perception. This presents a difficulty for Filter theory. Another mechanism is proposed that postulates the existence of a shifting reference standard which takes up the level of the most pertinent arriving signal. [The *Social Sciences Citation Index®* (*SSCI™*) **indicates that this paper has been cited over 180 times since 1966.]**

J.A. Deutsch and D. Deutsch
Department of Psychology
University of California
La Jolla, CA 92093

February 23, 1981

"At the time our paper was written, Broadbent had published his important book, *Perception and Communication.*[1] His book marked the real beginning of the modern era of cognitive psychology, a field which has been steadily expanding since. Among other theories proposed in that book, Broadbent put forward Filter theory to account for the phenomena of attention. Because of the assumed limited channel capacity of the central nervous system, some device was postulated that would reduce the information inflow from the senses and so prevent overload. Information was thought to be excluded from the central nervous system by a filter, which would admit only a single message, as defined by some fairly simple features such as a particular frequency range or spatial location. Such a theory endeavored to explain why we cannot listen effectively to two conversations at once, though both conversations are clearly audible, when attention is focused to each separately. The problem for Broadbent's theory, as the experimental work that it stimulated began to show, was that the filter screening the information flowing into the central nervous system seemed to be using very complex features to select the perceived message. For instance work by Anne Treisman[2] indicated that the selection process must use sophisticated criteria, such as transition probabilities in speech. It thus became necessary to postulate perceptual and mnemonic capabilities for the filter that were almost identical with those of the central nervous system. This suggested to us that perhaps it was after all the central nervous system that was doing the selecting underlying attention. Our theory therefore sought to explain how the central nervous system could select a perceptual stream after it had sorted and analyzed all the incoming information. The mechanism which we postulated compared the various arriving signals with a shifting reference standard which took up the level of the most pertinent arriving signal. Only the signal reaching the level of this reference standard switched in further processes, such as motor output, memory storage, and other correlates of awareness. In a sense the theory is somewhat paradoxical. Normally one would tend to assume that it is the process of perceptual analysis which coincides with a state of awareness. However in our theory we assume that this stage of awareness is only reached after a decision is made to deal with a percept that is already formed.

"The reason why our paper has been so widely cited is probably two-fold. The first is that it gave a clear alternative to Filter theory, and therefore stimulated a great deal of discussion and experimental work. The second is that it was written in a field which was small at the time but which has since expanded enormously. While the distinction between perceptual and attentional processes no longer seems as clear as it once was, many of the problems that were there when the paper was written are still with us and still challenge experimental ingenuity. A recent article in this field appears in the *Handbook of Perception.*"[3]

1. **Broadbent D E.** *Perception and communication.* London: Pergamon, 1958. 338 p.
2. **Treisman A M.** Contexual cues in selective listening. *Quart. J. Exp. Psychol.* **12**:242-8, 1960.
3. **Keele S W & Trammell-Neill W.** Mechanisms of attention. (Carterette E C & Friedman M P, eds.) *Handbook of perception: perceptual processing.* New York: Academic Press, 1978. Vol. 9. p. 3-48.

CC/NUMBER 47
NOVEMBER 19, 1984

This Week's Citation Classic™

Meyer D E & Schvaneveldt R W. Facilitation in recognizing pairs of words: evidence of a dependence between retrieval operations. *J. Exp. Psychol.* **90**:227-34, 1971.
[Bell Laboratories, Murray Hill, NJ, and State University of New York, Stony Brook, NY]

An experimental technique was introduced to investigate the mental processes whereby people recognize printed words and retrieve their meanings from semantic memory. Results of the technique, which involved measuring subjects' reaction times, provided early support for currently popular 'spreading-activation' models of human information processing. [The *Science Citation Index*® (*SCI*®) and the *Social Sciences Citation Index*® (*SSCI*®) indicate that this paper has been cited in over 200 publications since 1971.]

David E. Meyer
Department of Psychology
University of Michigan
Ann Arbor, MI 48104
and
Roger W. Schvaneveldt
Department of Psychology
and Computing Research Laboratory
New Mexico State University
Las Cruces, NM 88003

October 1, 1984

"Like other *Citation Classics*, our original article happened to come at the right time for having a significant impact. Experimental psychology had experienced a major paradigm shift during the 1960s, triggered by a confluence of new ideas from communications theory, computer science, and the formal study of language.[1] There was, in particular, a growing concern about the speed of mental processes and the mechanisms underlying human linguistic performance. Thus, the stage was already set for our research on word recognition.

"We each began participating in these developments as graduate students at the Universities of Michigan and Wisconsin. For example, our doctoral dissertations dealt, respectively, with semantic memory, (that is, the representation and retrieval of stored word meanings) and with choice reaction time.[2,3] However, the collaboration between us started rather unexpectedly.

"This chance event occurred at a meeting of the Psychonomic Society in San Antonio, Texas, during November 1970. There, one of us (DEM) presented a paper summarizing some of his new experiments on word recognition and reaction time that were conducted at Bell Laboratories.[4] Following the presentation, the other of us (RWS) came up and casually mentioned some related experiments that he was then conducting at the State University of New York, Stony Brook. It turned out that several studies in these two lines of investigation, although conceived independently, had very similar designs, results, and theoretical implications. We quickly hit it off professionally and personally and agreed to coauthor a joint report of our findings. The agreement led directly to the cited article. Upon receiving the article, David Grant, then-editor of the *Journal of Experimental Psychology*, accepted it without much question or fanfare.

"We continued working together for five more years before moving on to other positions. A number of additional papers were produced. These culminated in a 1976 *Science* article and a colloquium paper presented at a meeting of the American Association for the Advancement of Science.[5]

"There are probably several reasons for the impact that our work has had. It popularized a simple, yet informative, experimental technique for studying the temporal properties of mental processes in word recognition. The technique, called a 'lexical-decision' procedure, involved measuring how quickly people can decide whether rows of letters are English words or nonwords. We showed that such decisions are faster when one word (e.g., 'nurse') is preceded by another semantically related word (e.g., 'doctor'). The time course of this facilitation, and its interaction with other experimental factors such as the legibility of the stimuli, were easy to replicate and had important implications concerning the dynamics of information-processing mechanisms. Our experiments, therefore, paved the way for exploring various facets of memory organization and retrieval associated with semantic memory.

"Furthermore, our theorizing involved an intriguing metaphor drawn from neurophysiology. We hypothesized that word recognition can be characterized in terms of 'spreading activation' that flows through a complex network of nodes and branches. This hypothesis has since gained considerable favor among psychologists and other cognitive scientists, as evidenced by a current proliferation of spreading-activation models of human information processing."[6]

1. **Lachman R, Lachman J L & Butterfield E C.** *Cognitive psychology and information processing: an introduction.* Hillsdale, NJ: Erlbaum, 1979. 573 p.
2. **Meyer D E.** On the representation and retrieval of stored semantic information. *Cog. Psychol.* **1**:242-99, 1970. (Cited 125 times.)
3. **Schvaneveldt R W.** Effects of complexity in simultaneous reaction-time tasks. *J. Exp. Psychol.* **81**:289-96, 1969. (Cited 40 times.)
4. **Meyer D E & Ellis G B.** *Parallel processes in word recognition.* Unpublished paper presented to the Psychonomic Society. November 1970. San Antonio, TX.
5. **Meyer D E & Schvaneveldt R W.** Meaning, memory structure, and mental processes. *Science* **192**:27-33, 1976. (Cited 40 times.)
6. **McClelland J L & Rumelhart D E.** An interactive-activation model of context effects in letter perception. Part 1. An account of basic findings. *Psychol. Rev.* **88**:375-407, 1981.

CC/NUMBER 26
JUNE 25, 1984

This Week's Citation Classic™

Bower G H & Hilgard E R. *Theories of learning.* Englewood Cliffs, NJ: Prentice-Hall, 1981. 647 p. [Stanford University, CA]

This textbook reviews the major theories and systematic viewpoints regarding the psychology of learning and behavior. Historically significant positions are discussed and evaluated in relation to current research. Additional chapters on recent developments review new findings in conditioning, memory, school learning, neurophysiology, and computer modeling of learning. [The *Science Citation Index*® (*SCI*®) and the *Social Sciences Citation Index*® (*SSCI*®) indicate that all five editions of this book have been cited in over 655 publications since 1955.]

Gordon H. Bower
Department of Psychology
Stanford University
Stanford, CA 94305

May 25, 1984

"*Theories of Learning* is now in its fifth edition. Ernest Hilgard wrote the first two editions, published in 1948[1] and 1956;[2] I came aboard as a coauthor in the third edition (1966)[3] and assumed more responsibility for the book's contents in its fourth (1975)[4] and fifth (1981) editions. The first edition appeared when learning theory was the dominant orientation of the main movers of psychology, when Clark Hull, Edwin Guthrie, Wolfgang Kohler, Kenneth Spence, Edward Tolman, and B.F. Skinner were vigorous spokesmen for their view of psychology. In those days, theorizing in psychology was practically synonymous with theorizing about learning and behavior. The first edition of *Theories of Learning* summarized the conflicting perspectives in such a fair manner that it was immediately adopted by the field as the authoritative textbook. Had citation indices been computed in those days, the text would have been a *Citation Classic* from its inception. The book's balanced, authoritative nature was prototypic of the many insightful reviews for which Hilgard became famous professionally and for which he was recognized with the NAS Award for Scientific Reviewing given in 1984 by the National Academy of Sciences.[5] The award was established by Annual Reviews, Inc., and ISI®.

"Successive revisions of the book have followed the developments of the field. New material and chapters were added as theorists developed their positions in response to empirical results and arguments. As the field gradually changed its focus, to less emphasis on animal conditioning studies, new chapters were added on human memory, information processing, computer simulation and mathematical models of learning, and neurophysiology of learning and behavior. Since I participated in those research developments, Hilgard invited me to write chapters on them for the third edition. Although the text could be classified technically as a 'history' book, I have tried in the fourth and fifth editions to relate each historical position to still-active issues in recent research. I have been continually surprised at how easy it is, in modern debates, to detect issues that were foreseen and argued about by our forefathers. Besides updating each chapter, new editions also review and integrate recent developments, so that the text continues to have a contemporary flavor in its topics.

"Over its 36 years, *Theories of Learning* has been a highly recommended and used textbook. Solso[6] surveyed American and Canadian graduate psychology departments for their lists of recommended readings for students preparing for their PhD comprehensive or qualifying exams. *Theories of Learning* was among the few most frequently recommended readings in the 1979 survey. Moreover, it was the only psychology text that had been in this most recommended category throughout all previous, similar surveys of reading lists, conducted in 1971, 1966, 1958, and 1953. Thus, *Theories of Learning* has stood the test of time in a field that has been characterized by rapid scientific change. Perhaps the text has endured because it has changed with the times, while striving to be authoritative, balanced, and accurate. A sixth edition is currently being planned."

1. **Hilgard E R.** *Theories of learning.* New York: Appleton-Century-Crofts, 1948. 409 p.
2. ----------------. *Theories of learning.* New York: Appleton-Century-Crofts, 1956. 563 p.
3. **Hilgard E R & Bower G H.** *Theories of learning.* New York: Appleton-Century-Crofts, 1966. 661 p.
4. ---------------------------------. *Theories of learning.* Englewood Cliffs, NJ: Prentice-Hall, 1975. 698 p.
5. **Garfield E.** The 1984 NAS Award for Excellence in Scientific Reviewing: E.R. Hilgard receives sixth award for his work in psychology. *Current Contents* (24):3-6, 11 June 1984.
6. **Solso R.** Twenty-five years of recommended readings in psychology. *Amer. Psychol.* **34**:703-5, 1979.

This Week's Citation Classic

CC/NUMBER 29
JULY 16, 1979

Bandura A. *Principles of behavior modification.*
New York: Holt, Rinehart & Winston, 1969. 677 p.
[Stanford University, Stanford, CA]

This volume presents basic psychological principles governing human thought and behavior within the conceptual framework of social learning. This theory emphasizes the prominent roles played by vicarious, symbolic, and self-regulatory processes in psychological functioning. [The *Science Citation Index* **® (***SCI®* **) and the** *Social Sciences Citation Index* **™ (***SSCI™***) indicate that this book has been cited over 1215 times since 1969.]**

Albert Bandura
Department of Psychology
Stanford University
Stanford, CA 94305

June 15, 1978

"Theories of human behavior were undergoing major changes at the time I was writing this book. Interest in traditional psychodynamic approaches was declining as their deficiencies were becoming increasingly apparent. Behavioristic formulations emphasizing peripheral mechanisms were giving way to cognitively-oriented theories that explained behavior in terms of central processing of information. However, because of their major concern with internal mental operations, the information-processing models neglected the issue of how knowledge is converted to effective courses of action.

"The program of research I was pursuing at the time was aimed at broadening the scope of experimentation to human potentialities that were receiving comparatively little attention. The prevailing theories were concerned almost exclusively with how behavior is acquired and modified through direct experience. Our investigations focused on the determinants and processes by which human thought, affect, and behavior are markedly influenced by observing the behavior of others and its effects for them.

"People are not only perceivers, knowers, and actors. They are also self-reactors with a capacity for self-direction. Recognition of people's self-directing capacities provided the impetus for research on self-regulatory functions in which people serve as the principal agents of their own changes. These are only a few of the conceptual issues addressed in the volume.

"I have always subscribed to the view that the adequacy of a psychological theory should ultimately be judged by the power of the procedures it generates to effect psychological changes. A sizeable portion of this volume is therefore devoted to a discussion of how methods derived from principles of social learning can be used successfully to promote cognitive, emotional, and behavioral change.

"A responsible social science must concern itself not only with advancement of knowledge, but also with the social consequences of its applications. The ethical and value issues involved in the application of social learning procedures to achieve personal and social changes are examined in some detail. A psychological technology operates within the values, ideologies, and power structures of a social system. Major attention is devoted to institutional applications of psychological knowledge because it is at the institutional level that the value premises of psychological practices become most controversial.

"I suppose the reason for the sustained interest in this volume is that it provided a unified conceptual framework within which to study diverse psychological phenomena and it specified procedures for effecting change."

This Week's Citation Classic

CC/NUMBER 30
JULY 27, 1981

Mowrer O H. *Learning theory and personality dynamics.*
New York: Ronald Press, 1950. 776 p.
[University of Illinois, Champaign-Urbana, IL]

The 24 chapters comprising this book consist of a wide-ranging collection of previously published and unpublished papers, most of which had been well received. The topics covered range from 'Enuresis—a method for its study and treatment' to 'The life and work of Edgar Allan Poe.' [The *Social Sciences Citation Index*® (*SSCI*®) **indicates that this book has been cited over 285 times since 1966.]**

O. Hobart Mowrer
Department of Psychology
University of Illinois
Champaign, IL 61820

May 27, 1981

"My first 19 published papers dealt with vestibulo-ocular functions and spatial orientation. However, upon receiving an appointment at the Yale Institute of Human Relations in the fall of 1934, my interests shifted to the Institute's major objective, which was the integration of psychology, psychiatry, and the social sciences. The first paper I wrote and published in this new setting was entitled, 'A stimulus-response analysis of anxiety and its role as a reinforcing agent' and appears as Chapter 1 in *Learning Theory and Personality Dynamics* (*LTPD*). It was particularly concerned with the conceptual interrelationships between learning theory and psychoanalysis and generated a large number of researchable hypotheses. Most of the ensuing chapters represent avenues of inquiry which, in one way or another, were suggested by this first paper. These include animal and human research on the psychology of fear and expectancy, experimental analogues of psychoanalytic dynamisms, systematic learning theory, the development and function of language, personality theory, and the nature of psychopathology.

"One of the reasons *LTPD* has been widely cited and remained in print for more than 25 years is the diversity of empirical data and conceptual innovations it contains. It has also provided the foundation for much of the work I have reported in subsequently published books.[1-5]

"In many ways, the most interesting and important aspect of *LTPD* is the light it throws upon the intellectual ethos and excitement that prevailed at the Institute of Human Relations during the middle and late 1930s. In this period the Institute was the 'psychological capital' of the world, as indicated, for example, by the fact that between 1934 and 1940, six of the persons who were then graduate students, research fellows, or junior staff members were later to become presidents of the American Psychological Association. Yet, paradoxically, the Institute of Human Relations narrowly averted failure.

"The original plan was to establish the Institute by bringing together, in a rather elegant, specially constructed new building, distinguished senior members of the various disciplines which were to produce a kind of scientific and scholarly hybrid vigor by interaction and integration. However, the hoped-for symbiotic relationships did not develop until a special seminar was started, in which junior staff and graduate students, as well as the senior staff members, participated. This was precisely the leaven needed to activate the Institute's high potential and avoid what might otherwise have been a serious fiasco."

1. **Mowrer O H.** *Learning theory and behavior.* New York: Wiley, 1960. 555 p.
   [Citation Classic. *Current Contents/Social & Behavioral Sciences* (5):16, 4 February 1980.]
2. ----------------. *Learning theory and the symbolic processes.* New York: Wiley, 1960. 473 p.
3. ----------------. *The new group therapy.* Princeton, NJ: Van Nostrand, 1964. 262 p.
4. ----------------. *Morality and mental health.* Chicago: Rand McNally, 1967. 669 p.
5. ----------------. *Psychology of language and learning.* New York: Plenum Press, 1980. 294 p.

This Week's Citation Classic

CC/NUMBER 34
AUGUST 24, 1981

Bandura A & Walters R H. *Social learning and personality development.* New York: Holt, Rinehart & Winston, 1963. 329 p. [Stanford Univ., Stanford, CA and Univ. Waterloo, Ontario, Canada]

In this volume the explanatory principles of social learning are applied to major domains of social development. This conceptual scheme explains human behavior in terms of complex interactions of social, vicarious, and self-generated influences. [The *Social Sciences Citation Index*® (*SSCI*®) **indicates that this book has been cited over 985 times since 1966.]**

Albert Bandura
Department of Psychology
Stanford University
Stanford, CA 94305

July 6, 1981

"It is sometimes said that writing a book takes possession of the author. Walters and I found ourselves so completely possessed by this one that it would have astounded even the most devout exorcist. During a summer of self-imposed confinement we labored from dawn into the late hours of the night for days on end without a break. Three weary months later we emerged into the real world from this marathon writing session with the completed manuscript in hand. Even the mere thought of proofreading and revising what we had written under this taxing schedule was enough to send us to the Excedrin cabinet.

"At the time this book was written, theories about social development were undergoing major change. The conceptual system that had been in vogue for years was an amalgam of tenets of psychoanalytic and Hullian learning theory. Human behavior was viewed from this perspective as mainly the product of internal drives, often operating below the level of consciousness. The research that we and others were conducting at the time underscored the paramount role played by social, vicarious, and self-regulatory influences in human behavior. This work formed a solid basis for a reconceptualization of social development.

"Psychological theorizing and research on how behavior patterns are acquired had been essentially confined to learning through response consequences. As a result, the rudimentary form of learning by direct experience was exhaustively studied, but the more pervasive and powerful mode of learning through modeling was largely ignored. Learning would be exceedingly laborious, not to mention perilous, if people had to rely solely on the effects of their actions to inform them what to do. We rectified this prolonged neglect by giving observational learning the prominence it fully deserved.

"The same limited perspective was also reflected in behavioral theories about what regulates human behavior. Much of the empirical research was concerned with how actions are shaped and controlled by their external consequences. But external outcomes, influential as they often are, are not the sole determinants of human action.

"Theories that depicted behavior as the product of external rewards and punishments presented a truncated image of human functioning because people partly regulate their actions through self-evaluative consequences. Therefore, the development of self-reactive functions, which gives humans the capacity for self-direction, also figured prominently in our book. The various aspects of personality development—dependency, independence, aggression, sex, achievement, anxiety, empathy, morality, and psychopathy, to mention just a few—were explained in terms of complex interactions of external, vicarious, and self influences.

"I suppose one reason this book has been widely cited over the years is that it offered principles of broad explanatory power that are readily applicable to diverse psychological phenomena. A subsequent book provides a more detailed discussion of the major determinants and mechanisms of social learning and its pervasive impact on human functioning."[1]

1. **Bandura A.** *Social learning theory.* Englewood Cliffs, NJ: Prentice-Hall, 1977. 247 p.

CC/NUMBER 5
FEBRUARY 4, 1980

This Week's Citation Classic

Mowrer O H. *Learning theory and behavior.* New York: Wiley, 1960. 555 p. [University of Illinois, Champaign, IL]

This book is progressive, in both a logical and historical sense. It pushes stimulus-response (S-R) theory to its limits; then introduces emotions as secondary drives; and, to overcome remaining problems, posits such mental (cognitive) constructs as imagery and servomechanisms. [The *Science Citation Index®* *(SCI®)* **and the** *Social Sciences Citation Index™ (SSCI™)* **indicate that this book has been cited over 380 times since 1961.]**

O. Hobart Mowrer
Department of Psychology
University of Illinois
Champaign, IL 61820

December 14, 1979

"The book under consideration here, and its companion,[1] are the only publications which I have written specifically as books. The other ten published volumes are collections of articles or unpublished lectures (with a unifying theme), or edited compendiums.

"*Learning Theory and Behavior (LT&B)* was first adumbrated in a paper published 13 years earlier[2] and in a book published three years after that.[3] Research and theory refinement continued for the next six years. The writing and publication of this book and its companion volume took the remaining four years.

"The writing of *LT&B* was like picking ripe fruit. But publication involved rather astonishing circumstances. The final version of the manuscript was mimeographed, and a copy, with a cover letter, was submitted to a publisher who had excellently handled two earlier books for me. However, to my dismay, I got no response, despite follow-up letters, over a period of about six months. At that point I sent a copy to another company, and immediately received an encouraging reply. Soon letters of evaluation were forthcoming, with comments ranging from 'entire approach is wrong' to 'will be of enduring significance.'

"But no sooner had a contract been signed with this second company than the first publisher belatedly came to life and wrote expressing very active interest in the book. When, in reply, I explained what had transpired, a vice-president was dispatched to talk to me personally to try to get me to break this contract and let his company have the book!

"Shortly thereafter the book went into production, and I found I was dealing with a copy editor with a variety of crotchets, including a total intolerance for the word 'otherwise.' Also, the art department reworked entirely satisfactory illustrations in absolutely ludicrous ways. I protested, gently but firmly, and was invited to New York for a conference with the field editor and the vice-president in charge of production. When the editor and I entered the latter's office, he was already red-faced with anger and immediately released a volley of vituperation. I waited a few minutes for the storm to subside, but it didn't, so I picked up my briefcase and walked out.

"The story of how this seemingly hopeless impasse was eventually resolved is interesting but too complicated to be told here. Suffice it to say that when the book was published (quite handsomely, I thought), it was extensively and, on the whole, favorably reviewed and sold well for about a decade. It then was allowed to go out of print, and a reprint edition has sold very poorly. I was therefore rather amazed, but gratified, to receive a letter from ISI® announcing that this book 'has been identified as one of the most cited items in its field' and inviting me to prepare this commentary.

"Perhaps the most distinctive, and useful, feature of this highly cited book is that it turned out to be congruent with what is now called *general systems theory,* as indicated by the 24 references to 'feedback,' three to 'cybernetics,' but none to 'systems' (cf. 'integration')."

1. **Mowrer O H.** *Learning theory and the symbolic processes.* New York: Wiley, 1960. 473 p.
2. ----------------. On the dual nature of learning—a reinterpretation of conditioning and problem solving. *Harvard Educ. Rev.* **42**:3-32, 1947.
3. ----------------. *Learning theory and personality dynamics: selected papers.* New York: Ronald Press, 1950. 776 p.

This Week's Citation Classic

Trabasso T, Bower G H & Gelman R. *Attention in learning: theory and research.* New York: Wiley, 1968. 268 p.
[Univ. California, Los Angeles, and Stanford Univ., Stanford, CA]

A mathematical model for how we select and test various hypotheses about the categorization of objects is developed and tested. The model predicts the selective learning of attributes of objects where two or more attributes are relevant and redundant to the solution. This and other selective attention and learning effects are demonstrated. [The *Science Citation Index*® (*SCI*®) and the *Social Sciences Citation Index*® (*SSCI*®) indicate that this book has been cited over 275 times since 1968.]

Tom Trabasso
Department of Education
University of Chicago
Chicago, IL 60637

September 11, 1981

"In the 1960s there was a revival of interest in the psychological community in the process of attention. This issue had been addressed historically, notably by Lashley in his neurophysiological work in the 1930s and 1940s.[1] We revived Lashley's questions and provided a mathematical account for how one might selectively attend to and learn one stimulus aspect even though several were correlated with the identification of an object.

"In addition, learning theories which viewed the acquisition of associations as being gradual and continuous were undergoing a number of challenges, foremost among which were demonstrations that learning was abrupt, discontinuous, or 'all-or-none.' We had been successful in developing and testing a mathematical model for the learning of simple classifications which assumed all-or-none associations.

"Thirdly, the 1960s had witnessed a small explosion of stochastic models in psychology and the development of a subfield of mathematical psychology.

"Finally, the 1960s also witnessed the beginnings of cognitive psychology where complex mental operations were being studied with respect to, and as a result of, a growing acceptance of the computer both as a tool and as a metaphor. Our process assumptions stressed the human problem-solver as one who entertained and tested hypotheses about the aspects underlying classification. We considered and formalized, following Frank Restle's pioneering work,[2] a variety of schemes for hypothesis selection and testing within the framework of an all-or-none learning model.

"My interest in attention arose in graduate school at Michigan State University in the 1950s, when various models for attention, selective attention and orienting reflex activity in animals, and neurophysiological discoveries on arousal came to my notice. Restle had developed an all-or-none learning model which I tested in a dissertation. At the same time, Gordon Bower,[3] at Stanford University, independently developed an equivalent all-or-none learning model for simple associations. As I was writing my dissertation, Restle passed on chapters to Bower and a subsequent direct correspondence between Bower and me led to an extensive and productive postdoctoral collaboration.

"Near the end of my postdoctoral fellowship, we spent an evening speculating about selective learning effects. These speculations kept us up all night, generating intuitive ideas and formalizing them into models. The result was a 'position' paper which I carried with me to UCLA where I carried out a critical experiment on whether the likelihood of selectively learning one stimulus attribute or another or both could be predicted from knowledge of how fast learners learned on the basis of single attributes alone. The model yielded remarkably good quantitative predictions. Encouraged by this initial success, we explored the empirical implications of the model in detail, finding further confirmations.

"Rochel Gelman, a graduate student at UCLA, became a collaborative author as a result of her scholarship and contribution of original experiments to the book.

"The book's reception was immediate. Despite the fact that the concept of attention has broadened since our monograph's inception, the historical perspective contained in our book and its problem continue to be of interest, thus accounting for its high citation. For a source on recent work in the area of attention, the reader is referred to an annual series entitled *Attention and Performance*."[4]

1. **Lashley K S.** An examination of the continuity theory as applied to discrimination learning. *J. Gen. Psychol.* **26**:241-65, 1942.
2. **Restle F.** The selection of strategies in cue learning. *Psychol. Rev.* **69**:11-19, 1962.
3. **Bower G H.** Application of a model to paired-associate learning. *Psychometrika* **26**:255-80, 1961.
4. *Attention and performance.* Hillsdale, NJ: Erlbaum, 1977-1981. Whole series.

NUMBER 41
OCTOBER 8, 1979

This Week's Citation Classic

Gibson E J. *Principles of perceptual learning and development.* New York: Appleton-Century-Crofts, 1969. 537 p.

This book surveyed traditional and current theories of perceptual learning and presented the author's theory, that perceptual learning is a process of differentiation of distinctive features of objects, permanent features of the spatial layout and invariants of events. The theory is applied to phylogenetic development of perception over species and especially to development of perceiving objects, places, events, and pictorial and symbolic information in children. [The *Science Citation Index®* *(SCI®)* **and the** *Social Sciences Citation Index™(SSCI™)* **indicate that this book has been cited over 365 times since 1969.]**

Eleanor J. Gibson
Department of Psychology
Cornell University
Ithaca, NY 14853

September 6, 1979

"Learning by perceiving the world around us, its permanent properties, its furnishings and ongoing events has always been of interest to philosophers, and deservedly so. Where else has an adult acquired the information about his environment that permits him to act adaptively in it and upon it? Yet modern experimental psychologists generally ignored the problem, although their interests for many years were dominated by learning. Motor learning, verbal learning, affective learning, and simple contingency learning were studied intensively, but comprehensive books on learning never mentioned perceptual learning. Developmental psychology, a younger branch of the science than experimental psychology, was almost equally negligent, but for better reasons—no one had devised feasible, reliable methods for studying early perceptual development.

"It is gratifying, therefore, to see that the problems discussed in this book and the attempt to provide a framework for understanding them have had an impact. The book alone, however, was not responsible for the progress that has taken place since its publication in our knowledge of perceptual development. There is always an element of luck in the success of a book or a theory. There has to be an audience ready to listen and experimental progress depends on concomitant advances in technology. Fortunately, the theory and these factors appeared together at the right time. Psychologists were dissatisfied with S-R learning theory and were ready to pay attention to a theory of perceptual learning. At the same time, new methods of studying perception in infants were being worked out and a whole new field of research opened up.

"A third factor explains why this book is widely cited. It has an important field of application. While I was writing the book, I was conducting research on processes involved in learning to read. Reading was making a comeback as an area for scientific study. Granting agencies were generous with funds, and my own work made the connection between a theory of perceptual learning and learning to read.

"It is interesting to consider progress in the book's field since its publication. The theory of perceptual learning in adults has progressed scarcely at all. Work on reading has burgeoned. There has been a surge of research on perception in infants and very young children, accounting for many of the citations. I have recently directed my own research to this area, and I find that the theory generating my experiments is reflected more and more in work of others on similar problems. As we discover more about early development, it will be possible to refine the theory of perceptual development and to provide guidelines for applied work.

"A recent review of the subject can be found in *Review of Child Development Research.*"[1]

1. **Appleton T, Clifton R & Goldberg S.** The development of behavioral competence in infancy. *Review of child development research.* (Horowitz F D, ed.) Chicago: University of Chicago Press, 1975. Vol. 4, p. 101-85.

This Week's Citation Classic

Kintsch W. *Learning, memory, and conceptual processes.* New York: Wiley, 1970. 498 p. [Univ. Colorado, Boulder, CO]

This textbook describes the general methods and results of traditional verbal learning studies, followed by a discussion of the recent work on memory. Finally, discrimination and concept learning are considered, leading up to modern psycholinguistics. [The *Science Citation Index® (SCI®)* **and the** *Social Sciences Citation Index® (SSCI™)* **indicate that this book has been cited over 210 times since 1970.]**

Walter Kintsch
Department of Psychology
Muenzinger Building
University of Colorado
Boulder, CO 80309

January 8, 1980

"In the mid-1960s every psychology department had a course in 'learning' that started with Pavlovian conditioning, went from there to instrumental conditioning, and eventually wound up with human learning and memory. Indeed, a lot of psychology departments still have that course, but many don't any more. *Learning, Memory, and Conceptual Processes (LMCP)* was the first textbook designed to break with that tradition.

"Many experimental psychologists of my generation share a similarly convoluted course of professional development: we were trained as rat runners or pigeon trainers in graduate school, but in our first years out, we became dissatisfied with an enterprise that had lost its one-time vigor and promise. Something else seemed to be in the air: the gentle, alluring *Vorboten* of the great cognitive thaw disturbed our behaviorist cloisters (in my case, that was a rather beaten up rat lab). I quickly shifted from rats to dogs, raced through a developmental stage called 'verbal learning,' and then finally found what has been my passion ever since: memory and language!

"Thus, with the zeal of the convert, I started teaching my learning class that way at the University of California at Riverside, and, one hot summer, wrote out an outline for a book. The book was finally written in two basements: in a windowless one in the then Stanford psychology department where I spent a year as a visitor, and finally in another one when I moved to Colorado. I enjoyed it: they were two stimulating, exciting years, and I never had to interrupt my research work for the book writing.

"Of course, I was writing a book for a course that did not exist. But I was convinced the time had come for an exclusively human learning, cognitively oriented text. Fortunately, the publisher believed so, too, and we were, of course, both right. Today, the cognitive psychology course is at least as big as the learning course, and there is an entire flood of textbooks in this area.

"But *LMCP* was the first, was the groundbreaker. That is, of course, not the only reason why it gets cited frequently. It is comprehensive, detailed, and quite carefully done: most of the things it says are actually correct. Thus, some people seem to use it like a handbook.

"What I like best about *LMCP* is that it achieves a certain level of integration between the theoretical and the experimental aspects of psychology. I tried very hard to make clear the interplay and interdependence between the two. Experimental psychologists are extremely concerned (and skilled) about experimental methodology, but often quite casual about theoretical explanations. But theories that actually explain something are just as hard to come by as experiments that really demonstrate something.

"A second edition of *LMCP* was published in 1977, under the title *Memory and Cognition.*[1] The title change signifies a certain change in emphasis, and actually about two-thirds of the book was newly written. I think *Memory and Cognition* is an improvement: it is of course much more up-to-date, but it is also more clearly organized, and focused better on the significant issues of our field."

1. **Kintsch W.** *Memory and cognition.* New York: Wiley, 1977. 490 p.

This Week's Citation Classic

CC/NUMBER 8
FEBRUARY 25, 1980

Seligman M E P. On the generality of the laws of learning.
Psychol. Rev. 77:406-18, 1970.
[Dept. Psychology, Cornell Univ., Ithaca, NY]

Organisms are evolutionarily prepared to associate certain events with each other, unprepared for some associations, and contraprepared for others. The taste aversion literature challenges the general process learning assumption that all events are equally associable and obey common laws. The laws of learning may vary with preparedness and different physiological and cognitive mechanisms may underlie the dimension. [The *Science Citation Index*® *(SCI®)* **and the** *Social Sciences Citation Index* ™ *(SSCI™)* **indicate that this paper has been cited over 300 times since 1970.]**

Martin E.P. Seligman
Department of Psychology
University of Pennsylvania
Philadelphia, PA 19104

January 11, 1980

"Sauce béarnaise, an egg thickened tarragon-flavored sauce, used to be one of my favorite foods in the world. One evening, in 1966, I had sauce béarnaise on filet mignon. About six hours later I began to throw up and spent the next several hours retching. After that, sauce béarnaise tasted foul to me.

"How could such learning have taken place? At first glance it seemed to me like an instance of Pavlovian conditioning with the conditioned stimulus (CS) being the sauce; the unconditioned stimulus (US) being illness; the unconditioned response (UR), throwing up; and the conditioned response (CR), nausea and the foul taste of the sauce. But cursory examination of what I knew about Pavlovian conditioning suggested that my taste aversion violated five basic assumptions of general process learning theory. 1) Learning took place with a *six-hour delay* between CS and US, and this never occurs in the laboratory. 2) The learning was *selective*. Only the sauce, and not the filet mignon nor the white plates from which I ate, became aversive. 3) The phenomenon was *robust*. It has lasted 13 years. Normal Pavlovian conditioning, in contrast, extinguishes readily. 4) The phenomenon was *not cognitive*. I found out that the stomach flu was going around and therefore 'knew' that it wasn't the sauce that caused the illness. In spite of this cognition, my aversion remained. In contrast, having the relevant expectations that the CS will no longer be followed by the US is a clear instance of inhibitory conditioning within the Pavlovian laboratory. 5) It made good *evolutionary sense* that taste should be selectively associable with illness, whereas promiscuous Pavlovian conditioning makes no evolutionary sense at all.

"Within a few weeks after the sauce béarnaise phenomenon, John Garcia published his (truly) classic article upon which my review was parasitic. Garcia demonstrated that when rats were X-rayed following a compound CS of light, noise, and taste, they learned to stay away only from the taste, and learned no aversion to the light and the noise. He also showed such learning over very long delays.[1]

"My review was an attempt to highlight these developments in taste aversions and to integrate them into learning theory. In general, I intended it as an experimentally based attack on the *tabula rasa* principle. This was highly unpopular at the time, and Garcia, Paul Rozin, I, and others took considerable flak from traditional learning theorists. One major learning theorist said of Garcia's findings, 'They are no more likely to be true than you would find bird droppings in a cuckoo clock.'

"The claim that natural selection might have influenced associability itself did not fall on wholly deaf ears, however. Younger learning theorists, ethologists, and cognitive psychologists under Chomskian influence found the claim congenial, if a bit ill-defined.

"In spite of its high citation rate, I count the article a failure. I had hoped that a new research strategy might emerge in which investigators looked for *differences* between associations depending on the species, the niche, and the stimuli. But this has not happened. The research that followed this article has concentrated on the *similarities* across species and niches. Even though my review is often cited, it is usually to pay lip service to an evolutionary influence on learning, but it has not deeply influenced the research practices of the field. A more recent review of the subject has been prepared by A.W. Logue."[2]

1. **Garcia J & Koelling R.** Relation of cue to consequence in avoidance learning. *Psychonomic Sci.* **4**:123-4, 1966.
2. **Logue A W.** Taste aversion and the generality of the laws of learning. *Psychol. Bull.* **86**:276-96, 1979.

This Week's Citation Classic

CC/NUMBER 6
FEBRUARY 11, 1980

Harlow H F. The formation of learning sets. *Psychol. Rev.* **56**:51-65, 1949.
[Univ. Wisconsin, Madison, WI]

The concept of learning sets was designed to show that the original learning on any problem or any kind of problem is a slow belabored process. However, if many problems of a single type are done, the nature of the learning changes from trial and error to immediate insightful learning. [The *Science Citation Index*® **(***SCI*®**) and the** *Social Sciences Citation Index*™ **(***SSCI*™**) indicate that this paper has been cited over 310 times since 1961.]**

Harry F. Harlow
Department of Psychology
University of Arizona
Tucson, AZ 85721

January 2, 1980

"In the original research on learning sets we ran all of the problems for a predetermined number of trials. Six to be exact. The problem selected is that of object-quality discrimination learning. During the first 50-100 problems none of the subjects came close to mastering the test. However, as successive groups of 50 or 100 problems were presented, the nature of the learning changed and the percentage of correct responses on trial two rose from chance, i.e., 50% correct reponses, to 60, 70, 80, 90, and 95% correct. In other words, the information given by trial one was all that was required to make perfect or almost perfect responses on trials two, three, four, five, or six.

"Conventional learning theory of the Hull-Spence type assumed that all learning was made on a trial and error basis. This contrasted with the Gestalt theory hypothesis that learning was achieved suddenly or insightfully or that it was an 'ah-hah' experience. Thus the behaviorist trial and error learning theory and the Gestalt insight learning theory were at total odds.

"The learning set theory studies were designed to show that there were no real discrepancies between the trial and error learning theory and the Gestalt learning theory. When an animal learns a new kind of problem, he solves it according to a behaviorist learning theory model by slow painful plodding trial and error. However, if he has experience with a large number of problems of a single type or class the trial and error is replaced by the Gestalt learning theory model so that the individual problems are eventually solved insightfully.

"Thus trial and error learning theory and insight learning theory are merely two phases of a learning model, an initial phase and an ending phase.

"I believe my paper has been widely cited because learning sets describe the mechanisms by which complex learning problems are mastered by primate animals. After a time these problems are solved immediately or almost immediately."

CC/NUMBER 50
DECEMBER 15, 1980

This Week's Citation Classic

Mackintosh N J. Selective attention in animal discrimination learning.
Psychol. Bull. **64**:124-50, 1965.
[Oxford University, Oxford, England]

This paper attempted to bring the continuity-noncontinuity dispute up-to-date by reviewing data showing that animals do not learn equally about all stimuli present in a discrimination problem, and that the solution of such a problem must partly involve learning to attend to relevant cues and ignoring irrelevant ones. [The *Social Sciences Citation Index® (SSCI™)* **indicates that this paper has been cited over 245 times since 1966.]**

N.J. Mackintosh
Experimental Psychology
University of Sussex
Brighton BN 1 9QG
England

October 20, 1980

"I originally wrote this review as part of my PhD thesis, completed two years earlier under the supervision of Stuart Sutherland. Although I revised it extensively for publication, I can still detect the brash confidence of its origins. Perhaps that is why it became so popular.

"More probably, it simply appeared at the right time to capture a variety of converging interests. For opposition was growing from several directions to one of the central principles of traditional 'continuity' theory—the notion that all stimuli present at the moment of reinforcement will be associated with that reinforcer. My own interest had stemmed from the classic work of Lashley[1] and Krechevsky[2] on discrimination learning in rats. That work had long been dismissed in most textbooks which concluded that Spence[3] had won the continuity-noncontinuity dispute—even if some more recent work of Lawrence's[4] had suggested some new possibilities. I was not satisfied with that judgment and tried to show why in this article (which made no pretence to being a neutral review of the literature normally expected in *Psychological Bulletin*). But others were thinking along similar lines. Research on discrimination learning in young children and in retardates, or on so-called concept-learning in college students, was throwing up a number of related ideas. No one supposed that continuity theory would apply to such subjects, and the work of Zeaman and House[5] had already pointed the way to the theoretical stance I wanted to take.

"What I did not foresee was that many of the phenomena of discrimination learning that seemed to suggest the operation of a mechanism of selective attention would shortly be demonstrated in supposedly simpler conditioning paradigms. Kamin[6] reported, rather more convincingly than Lashley had ever been able to, that animals initially conditioned to one stimulus signaling the delivery of a reinforcer, would learn little or nothing about a second stimulus added to the first, when the compound continued to signal the same reinforcer. This seemed compelling evidence for the idea of selective attention: the animals were so busy attending to the first stimulus that they did not have time to attend to the second. Alas, life is rarely so simple.

"For the last ten years, most work on selective association has used simple conditioning paradigms and has tended to support Kamin's original conclusion that failure to learn about an added stimulus does not reflect an inability to attend to one stimulus while already attending to another, but rather that either the redundancy of the added stimulus or the predictability of the reinforcer renders one or the other of them ineffective. Rescorla and Wagner's[7] influential model of conditioning has made this second alternative popular. I have clung to the first[8]—no doubt because the idea has links with the more traditional theories of selective attention that I was discussing in this review."

1. **Lashley K S.** *J. Gen. Psychol.* **26**:241-65, 1942.
2. **Krechevsky I.** *Psychol. Rev.* **45**:107-33, 1938.
3. **Spence K W.** *J. Exp. Psychol.* **35**:253-66, 1945.
4. **Lawrence D H.** *J. Exp. Psychol.* **39**:770-84, 1949.
5. **Zeaman D & House B J.** The role of attention in retardate discrimination learning. (Ellis N R, ed.) *Handbook of mental deficiency: psychological theory and research.* New York: McGraw-Hill, 1963. p. 159-223.
6. **Kamin L J.** Predictability, surprise, attention, and conditioning. (Campbell B & Church R, eds.) *Punishment and aversive behaviour.* New York: Appleton-Century-Crofts, 1969. p. 279-96.
7. **Rescorla R A & Wagner A R.** A theory of Pavlovian conditioning: variations in the effectiveness of reinforcement and non-reinforcement. (Black A H & Prokasy W F, eds.) *Classical conditioning II.* New York: Appleton-Century-Crofts, 1972. p. 64-99.
8. **Mackintosh N J.** *Psychol. Rev.* **82**:276-98, 1975.

This Week's Citation Classic

Schmidt R A. A schema theory of discrete motor skill learning.
Psychol. Rev. **82**:225-60, 1975.
[Department of Physical Education, University of Southern California, Los Angeles, CA]

A theory of motor skill learning is presented, based on the idea that learners acquire abstractions (or schemas) about a class of actions rather than individual movements. Assumptions, constructs, and supporting evidence are discussed. [The *Science Citation Index*® **(***SCI*®**) and the** *Social Sciences Citation Index*® **(***SSCI*®**) indicate that this paper has been cited in over 155 publications since 1975.]**

Richard A. Schmidt
Department of Kinesiology
University of California
Los Angeles, CA 90024

April 14, 1983

"During my years at the University of Michigan in the early-1970s, I was influenced strongly by the work and theorizing of a former mentor at Illinois, Jack Adams. His 1971 theory[1] of the acquisition of motor responses, emphasizing feedback processes and the detection of one's own errors after a movement, motivated a great deal of my initial research and thinking. But, by 1973, I had decided that a number of aspects of his theory were wrong, particularly with respect to the learning of more rapid actions.

"At about the same time at Michigan, Dick Pew became impressed with some incidental findings of his graduate student Armstrong,[2] as well as Posner and Keele's[3] notions about abstraction processes in cognitive tasks. He began to discuss with me and others the idea that movements might be based on schemas—i.e., abstract representations of knowledge about actions. The idea, mentioned 40 years earlier by Bartlett,[4] was that the basis for action was not individual movements, but rather some abstract schema about a class of similar movements.

"The combination of my dissatisfaction with certain aspects of Adams's theory, together with the suggestions from Bartlett and Pew that actions may be represented by schemas, led me to consider how such schemas might be learned with practice. I borrowed heavily from Adams, but added extant concepts about motor programs, schemas, and recognition and recall memory to generate a different view of the processes in motor acquisition. In our recent review, Shapiro and I[5] argued that the theory still has a number of appealing features, but it is now clear that it must be modified in various ways to accommodate a number of recent findings.

"In viewing the reactions to the schema theory since 1975, I think that the idea was popular because it suggested a very different view of learning than had been present at the time, one which emphasized the acquisition of schemas rather than individual actions; and a variety of lines of evidence supported this view. Also, it seemed to help in the solution of some long-standing problems in motor behavior: how a nearly inconceivable number of possible movements might be represented, and how novel actions can occur. And many workers were attracted to its testable predictions, particularly those involved in practice variability and motor learning."

1. **Adams J A.** A closed-loop theory of motor learning. *J. Motor Behav.* **3**:111-50, 1971.
2. **Armstrong T R.** *Training for the production of memorized movement patterns.* Ann Arbor, MI: University of Michigan, Human Performance Center, August 1970. Technical Report No. 26.
3. **Posner M I & Keele S W.** On the genesis of abstract ideas. *J. Exp. Psychol.* **77**:353-63, 1968.
4. **Bartlett F C.** *Remembering*. Cambridge, England: Cambridge University Press, 1932. 317 p.
5. **Shapiro D C & Schmidt R A.** Schema theory: recent evidence and developmental implications. (Kelso J A S & Clark J E, eds.) *The development of movement control and coordination*. New York: Wiley, 1982. p. 113-50.

This Week's Citation Classic™

Gagné R M. *The conditions of learning.* New York: Holt, Rinehart and Winston, 1977. 339 p. [Florida State Univ., Tallahassee, FL]

This textbook reports and interprets research studies and theories of human learning, drawing implications relating them to instruction. Successive chapters describe in detail the internal and external learning conditions for five kinds of learning outcomes: (a) verbal information, (b) intellectual skills, (c) cognitive strategies, (d) motor skills, and (e) attitudes. [The *Social Sciences Citation Index*® (*SSCI*®) indicates that this edition of the book has been cited in over 105 publications since 1977. All three editions have been cited in over 875 publications.]

**Robert M. Gagné
Department of Educational Research
Florida State University
Tallahassee, FL 32306**

March 16, 1984

"While continuing the aims and themes of two previous editions,[1,2] this book reflects the shift in learning research and theory that has come with the surge of interest in cognitive psychology and information-processing conceptions. An information-processing model of learning and memory derived from that proposed by Atkinson and Shiffrin[3] provides a framework for discussion of the conditions of learning as they relate to instruction.

"In following developments in theories of learning and memory during the period of the early 1970s, I could not help being aware of the profound change in conceptualization of the processes of learning, and of the accompanying change in the nature of research questions raised and investigated. At the same time, studies of school curricula and my own observations of classroom behavior convinced me of the need to identify categories of learning outcomes which cut across the traditional subjects of the curriculum, such as mathematics, language, history, etc.

"The result of these occurrences, and my thinking about them, was the definition of five classes of learning outcomes: (a) verbal information, (b) intellectual skills, (c) cognitive strategies, (d) motor skills, and (e) attitudes.[4,5] Separate chapters of the book describe learning for each of these outcomes in terms of internal and external conditions. Internal conditions include motivational states and previously acquired knowledge and skills stored in long-term memory that are accessible for new learning. External conditions, when deliberately planned and instituted, make up a set of events collectively called instruction.

"The events of instruction are shown to be derivable from the information-processing model of learning and memory. According to this model, learning processes follow a stage-like progression from sensory registration to long-term storage and learner performance. Events of instruction, conceived as a set of stimuli which give support to internal learning processes, accordingly follow a similar progression. These events begin with gaining attention, followed by informing the learner of the learning objective, and proceed through the stages of stimulating recall of prior learning, presenting the stimulus, providing learning guidance, eliciting performance, providing feedback, assessing the performance, and enhancing retention and transfer. These instructional events form the basis for the design of instruction as described by myself and Briggs.[6]

"The systematic attempt to relate instruction to learning theory probably accounts for frequent references to this work. The two major themes of differential requirements for instruction associated with five different kinds of learned capabilities, on the one hand, and the delineation of instructional events, on the other, are woven together in a couple of ending chapters on analyzing requirements for learning and on designing instruction."

1. **Gagné R M.** *The conditions of learning.* New York: Holt, Rinehart and Winston, 1965. 308 p.
2. --------------. *The conditions of learning.* New York: Holt, Rinehart and Winston, 1970. 407 p.
3. **Atkinson R C & Shiffrin R M.** Human memory: a proposed system and its control processes. (Spence K W & Spence J T, eds.) *The psychology of learning and motivation.* New York: Academic Press, 1968. Vol. 2. p. 89-195.
4. **Gagné R M.** Domains of learning. *Interchange* **3**:1-8, 1972.
5. ---------------. Learning outcomes and their effects. *Amer. Psychol.* **39**:377-85, 1984.
6. **Gagné R M & Briggs L J.** *Principles of instructional design.* New York: Holt, Rinehart and Winston, 1979. 321 p.

This Week's Citation Classic™

Brophy J E & Good T L. *Teacher-student relationships: causes and consequences.* New York: Holt, Rinehart and Winston, 1974. 400 p.
[Univ. Texas, Austin, TX and Univ. Missouri, MO]

This book discusses methodological issues and presents substantive findings from research on the dynamics of teacher-student relationships. In particular, it focuses on how teachers develop beliefs, attitudes, and expectations about students in response to their individual personal characteristics or their group status (race, sex, socioeconomic status, achievement level), leading to differential patterns of dyadic teacher-student interaction. [*The Social Sciences Citation Index*® (*SSCI*®) indicates that this book has been cited in over 265 publications since 1974.]

Jere Brophy
Institute for Research on Teaching
College of Education
Michigan State University
East Lansing, MI 48824

March 16, 1984

"The research that led to this book had its roots in conversations that Tom Good and I had about *Pygmalion in the Classroom*,[1,2] shortly after we arrived as new faculty members at the University of Texas at Austin. We found ourselves fascinated by the *Pygmalion* experiment but interested in exploring teachers' naturally formed expectations about students (rather than expectations induced experimentally) and the processes (differential treatment of different students in similar situations) that might mediate any self-fulfilling prophecy effects of such expectations.

"To pursue this interest, we needed an observation system designed to record (separately for each student) the teacher's dyadic interactions with individual students. Most of the classroom observation research done prior to that time had focused on the teacher's interactions with the class as a whole, and had not considered contrasting patterns of interaction with different individuals or subgroups. Consequently, we had to devise what became known as the Brophy-Good Dyadic Interaction Observation System. Our first study using that system[3] showed that, compared to their treatment of low expectation students, teachers were more likely to praise high expectation students for correct answers, less likely to criticize them for failure, and more likely to try to elicit an improved response from them when they failed to answer correctly the first time.

"This first study was followed by several related studies done in collaboration with Carolyn Evertson, Teresa Harris Peck, Vern Jones, Jev Sikes, Sherry Willis, and other colleagues. Our interests in teachers' expectations expanded to include teachers' beliefs and attitudes, and to include student effects on teachers as well as teacher effects on students. In addition, as frequently happens in science, once a tool devised for a particular purpose is in existence, it can be used for other purposes as well. In this case, it quickly became obvious that our observation system could be used to study differential teacher behavior toward boys *vs.* girls, whites *vs.* blacks, and so on. Also, the system's focus on questioning and responding to students during recitation lessons eventually led to studies on such topics as how the nature of teacher-student interaction changes across grade levels and how teachers' instructional behaviors relate to student achievement.

"The book is cited frequently in part because it discusses several of our studies done in the early 1970s in some detail, but mostly because it systematically reviews the research on teacher expectations, teacher-student interaction, and related topics that emerged as active research areas in the late 1960s and have remained active since. The book remains a basic reference on the topics that it covers in detail and in general has stood the test of time well, although more recent reviews[4-6] indicate that interpretation of certain data needs to be supplemented by insights developed through more recent research on teacher effects, attribution theory, and other topics."

1. **Rosenthal R & Jacobson L.** *Pygmalion in the classroom: teacher expectation and pupils' intellectual development.* New York: Holt, Rinehart and Winston, 1968. 240 p.
2. **Rosenthal R.** Citation Classic. Commentary on *Pygmalion in the classroom: teacher expectation and pupils' intellectual development. Current Contents/Social & Behavioral Sciences* **12**(7):12, 18 February 1980.
3. **Brophy J & Good T.** Teachers' communication of differential expectations for children's classroom performance: some behavioral data. *J. Educ. Psychol.* **61**:365-74, 1970. (Cited 210 times.)
4. **Brophy J.** Research on the self-fulfilling prophecy and teacher expectations. *J. Educ. Psychol.* 75:631-61, 1984.
5. **Good T & Brophy J.** *Looking in classrooms.* New York: Harper and Row, 1984. 424 p.
6. **Cooper H & Good T.** *Pygmalion grows up: studies in the expectation communication process.* New York: Longman, 1982. 173 p.

CC/NUMBER 7
FEBRUARY 18, 1980

This Week's Citation Classic

Rosenthal R & Jacobson L. *Pygmalion in the classroom: teacher expectation and pupils' intellectual development.* New York: Holt, Rinehart & Winston, 1968. 240 p. [Harvard Univ., Boston, MA and South San Francisco Unified Sch. District, San Francisco, CA]

This work summarized the evidence that expectations held by behavioral researchers for the responses of their research subjects could come to serve as self-fulfilling prophecies. In addition, the results of the first experiment to demonstrate that teachers' expectations could affect the actual intellectual performance of their pupils is reported. [The ***Science Citation Index®*** **(*SCI®*) and the** ***Social Sciences Citation Index™*** **(*SSCI™*) indicate that this book has been cited over 700 times since 1968.]**

Robert Rosenthal
Department of Psychology
and Social Relations
Harvard University
Cambridge, MA 02138

January 2, 1980

"In 1963 I published a paper in the *American Scientist,* summarizing the evidence that experimenters' expectations might affect the responses obtained from their research subjects within the context of the psychological experiment.[1] I ended that paper by suggesting that the same type of self-fulfilling prophecy might operate in the classroom such that teachers' expectations for the intellectual performance of their pupils might actually affect those pupils' intellectual performance. Shortly after publication of this article I received a letter from a most unusual school principal, Lenore Jacobson. She wanted to know whether this suggestion (a) was part of the rhetoric of scientific writing (i.e., the 'suggestions for future research') or (b) was really going to get done. If it were to be the latter she knew of a school where the experiment could be conducted: hers.

"The results of our collaborative research were reported in this book and were greeted by an awesomely bimodal response: you loved it or you hated it. There were good reasons to love it and bad reasons to love it. The chief good reason to love it was that it was a well-designed and well-conducted study on an important question. The chief bad reason to love it was that it implied to the environmental theorists (of the origins of IQ differences) that 'genes don't matter;' it implied no such thing, of course. There were good reasons to hate it and bad reasons to hate it. The chief good reason to hate it was that you didn't think of it first. The chief bad reason to hate it was that it implied to the genetic theorists (of the origins of IQ differences) that 'genes don't matter;' it implied no such thing, of course. There were also some wonderfully inept statistical critiques of the *Pygmalion* research. This got lots of publications for the critics of our research including one whole book aimed at devastating the *Pygmalion* results, which only showed that the results were even *more* significant than Lenore Jacobson and I had claimed.

"In recent years there have been many replications of the *Pygmalion* effect and even more replications of the more general finding of interpersonal self-fulfilling prophecies. Altogether, 345 studies have been conducted and they show beyond doubt that interpersonal self-fulfilling prophecies not only occur, but that their average size of effect is far from trivial.[2] More recent work on *Pygmalion* effects has also led to the development of a four factor theory of the mediation of teacher expectancy effects and the development of instruments to measure pupils' sensitivity to the nonverbal cues emitted by their teachers.[3,4] The work goes on and it continues to be fun.

"This work may have been cited frequently because it addressed experimentally a question of both scientific importance and social relevance and because of the extreme praise and criticism it evoked."

1. **Rosenthal R.** On the social psychology of the psychological experiment: the experimenter's hypothesis as unintended determinant of experimental results. *Amer. Sci.* **51**:268-83, 1963.
2. **Rosenthal R & Rubin D B.** Interpersonal expectancy effects: the first 345 studies. *Behav. Brain Sci.* **1**:377-86, 1978.
3. **Rosenthal R.** *On the social psychology of the self-fulfilling prophecy: further evidence for Pygmalion effects and their mediating mechanisms.* Module 53. New York: MSS Modular Publications, Inc., 1974. 28 p.
4. **Rosenthal R, Hall J A, DiMatteo M R, Rogers P L & Archer D.** *Sensitivity to nonverbal communication: the PONS test.* Baltimore: Johns Hopkins University Press, 1979. 432 p.

This Week's Citation Classic

Carroll J B. A model of school learning. *Teach. Coll. Rec.* **64**:723-33, 1963.
[Harvard University, Cambridge, MA]

In giving a unified perspective on the variables, and their relationships, that affect a student's degree of achievement in school subjects, this paper pointed out that degree of learning is a function of the ratio of the time the student actually spends on learning to the time the student needs, both being in turn a function of aptitude and other variables. [The *Social Sciences Citation Index*® (*SSCI*®) indicates that this paper has been cited over 180 times since 1966.]

John B. Carroll
Department of Psychology
University of North Carolina
Chapel Hill, NC 27514

December 7, 1981

"This paper was a spin-off—a 'think piece' rather than a real research report—from a project on the measurement of foreign language aptitude. A more technical account was given elsewhere.[1] I had noticed that different people could achieve the same level of success, but took different amounts of time. I therefore concluded that aptitude could be defined in terms of the amount of time needed to learn—low aptitude people requiring more time than those of high aptitude. But I needed other variables to explain all my results satisfactorily.

"Probably the article would never have been written had not E.J. Shoben, Jr., then editor of the *Teachers College Record*, encouraged me to present my ideas in a form that might generalize to many types of school learning. It seems to have received little attention until Benjamin Bloom used its ideas in formulating what he called 'mastery learning.'[2] While my paper provided a basic theory, Bloom did much more than I to put my notions into research and development.

"Whether as a result of the original publication, or of Bloom's use of it, it seems to have had a large impact on the conduct of education and of educational research in America and abroad. The 'model' is regularly treated in standard texts on educational psychology, and thousands of teachers and teacher trainees must have become acquainted with it. It stimulated a number of major projects designed to improve instruction at various levels, for example, the Beginning Teacher Evaluation Study.[3] The article may have been one basis for my receiving several awards, such as the Edward Lee Thorndike Award for Distinguished Psychological Contribution to Education given to me by the American Psychological Association in 1970.

"I have often wondered why my article has had such appeal. I considered this question—along with a review of most of the citations that I found in the *Social Sciences Citation Index*® (*SSCI*®)—in a paper now in press.[4] As I stated there: 'The idea that learning takes time is so obvious as to be almost trivial....' Of only slightly more novelty is the proposition that variations in aptitude can be correlated with variations in the amount of time a student needs to master a task: teachers have always recognized differences between 'fast' and 'slow' learners. Yet, the implication of this proposition, that students should be allowed to proceed at their own rate in order to take the amount of time they need, has been the linchpin for all sorts of applications and interpretations of the model. Perhaps the model's appeal to educators in general lies in its suggestion that a radical revision of customary school practices in this regard was needed. Bloom's mastery learning concept added the suggestion that if all the elements of the model were properly orchestrated, all or nearly all students could master almost any task demanded in the school curriculum."

1. **Carroll J B.** The prediction of success in intensive foreign language training. (Glaser R, ed.) *Training research and education.* Pittsburgh: University of Pittsburgh Press, 1962. p. 87-136.
2. **Bloom B S.** Learning for mastery. (Whole issue.) *Evaluation Comment* **1**(2), 1968. 12 p.
3. **Denham C & Lieberman A,** eds. *Time to learn: a review of the Beginning Teacher Evaluation Study.* Washington, DC: US Government Printing Office, 1980. 246 p.
4. **Carroll J B.** The model of school learning: progress of an idea. (Fisher C W & Berliner D C, eds.) *Proceedings of a Conference on Instructional Time.* In press, 1982.

This Week's Citation Classic

NUMBER 5
JANUARY 29, 1979

Hall R V, Lund D & Jackson D. Effects of teacher attention on study behavior. *J. Appl. Behav. Anal.* **1**: 1-12, 1968.

It was demonstrated that if teachers gave attention to pupils when they engaged in appropriate classroom behavior and ignored them when they were disruptive or dawdled, study levels increased dramatically. When teachers discontinued giving attention for study, pupil study decreased until teachers attended to it once more. [The *Science Citation Index®* (*SCI®*) and the *Social Sciences Citation Index™* (*SSCI™*) indicate that this paper has been cited 355 times since 1969.]

R. Vance Hall
Juniper Gardens Children's Project
Department of Human Development and Family Life
University of Kansas
Kansas City, KS 66101

January 20, 1978

"This study was an extension of others my colleagues (e.g., Don Baer, Montrose Wolf, Todd Risley, Marcia Broden) and I had carried out at the University of Washington which had demonstrated that adult attention could increase desired behaviors of normal preschool children and older children with severe behavior and learning problems.

"One reason that it is frequently cited may be because it was probably the first study reported in which systematic reinforcement procedures were used in a regular school classroom. A number of prior reinforcement studies were carried out with deviant children in institutions and special classrooms, but few if any were with 'normal' students in a regular class.

"Another likely reason for its popularity is that the effects were immediate and dramatic, often increasing study behavior from about 25% to 75% in a few days. Similar dramatic decreases were observed if teacher attention was withdrawn. These data were graphed daily to provide excellent illustrations of the newly recognized single subject reversal design which helped launch the field of applied behavior analysis. Because it was applied, behavioral and analytic, it was selected as the lead article in the first issue of the *Journal of Applied Behavior Analysis.*

"Another factor was that the procedures which produced the dramatic changes were simple and easily implemented. Prior studies using Skinner's approaches often involved tangible rewards or complex token systems. This study demonstrated that naturally available consequences could be easily implemented to bring about behavior change. Furthermore, the teachers found that once the behavior was established it took no more time to attend to appropriate pupil behavior than it previously had for disruptive behavior.

"The studies pointed out that one of the most important factors distinguishing between effective teachers and parents and unsuccessful ones is that the former attend primarily to and provide feedback for appropriate, rather than inappropriate behavior.

"This study and the fifty or more which followed were carried out in a community research project in the inner-city of Kansas City, Kansas. Many project visitors have been amazed to find our offices in two locations, the basements of a church and a liquor store.

"One anecdote occurred as one of the teachers began to come by the desk of a heretofore disruptive third grader to comment on his work and praise his efforts. A classmate leaned across his desk and said, 'Robbie, what you doin' over there that so special anyway?'

"Another concerns a co-author, Deloris Jackson, a paraprofessional observer from the community where the study was conducted. Both she and Diane Lund, a graduate student, contributed substantially to the development of the observation codes and other study aspects. Deloris chuckled on receiving a number of letters addressed to Dr. Jackson and on being invited to join various professional associations because of her contributions to the field."

NUMBER 4
JANUARY 22, 1979

This Week's Citation Classic

Battig W F & Montague W E. Category norms for verbal items in 56 categories: a replication and extension of the Connecticut category norms. *J. Exp. Psychol. Monograph Suppl.* 80: No. 3, Part 2, 1969. 46 p.

The article presents responses to 56 conceptual category labels (e.g., fruit, weapon) in order of frequency of occurrence for 442 students from the Universities of Maryland and Illinois. Also included are additional data such as which responses are given first, and numbers of different responses for each category. The *Science Citation Index®* *(SCI®)* **and the** *Social Sciences Citation Index™ (SSCI™)* **indicate that this paper was cited 267 times in the period 1969 - 1977.]**

William F. Battig
Institute for the Study of
Intellectual Behavior
University of Colorado
Boulder, CO 80309

January 13, 1978

"This paper is actually no more than an extended replication of the unpublished University of Connecticut category norms of Cohen, Bousfield, and Whitmarsh. This kind of normative information clearly does not fit the usual image of a major scientific contribution, but may well exceed more original theoretical publications in its usefulness to scientists for actual research purposes. Moreover, our project did require over three years of hard work by many people, especially Janis Gregory and Diane Ray.

"I suspect the widespread citation of this monograph can best be understood as analogous to generally useful new instruments or research materials in other sciences. Other possible reasons include: (1) An encouraging editor (David A. Grant) willing to publish these norms in full in a high-quality journal, thereby giving them wide circulation and visibility at minimal cost; and (2) Their publication at an ideal time when research on semantic aspects of information-processing and memory was becoming a major topic of research interest. These norms have had other unexpected uses, such as a children's game of 'personality analysis' where e.g., Judy (ranking 5th among girls names) is characterized by corresponding 5th-ranking members of other categories (e.g., garter snake, spider).

"Other than the above, these category norms may differ from numerous other similar normative projects because of our primary concern with making them as useful as possible for other researchers. Thus when co-author William Montague offered to collect parallel data at Illinois, we realized that geographical comparisons with our Maryland data would greatly increase the general usefulness of these norms. Ironically, we both subsequently moved West, Montague now being in San Diego.

"Even more ironically, we probably could not get research funding for this kind or normative project, nor could it be published today in those top-quality journals which once included such norms. I base this judgment upon our recent experience with an even larger 5-year normative scaling project which had to be published as a book.

"Both projects were possible only as secondary aspects of large and long-term research grants with other primary goals. Research funding agencies rarely if ever will consider direct research support for such normative projects, despite their demonstrable value, if not necessity, for any kind of research requiring verbal materials. Thus the honor of our monograph being designated as a citation classic is especially appreciated. If it helps in any way to remedy the still tremendous need throughout the behavioral sciences for more normative projects of this kind, our research and its frequent citations will have made an especially significant scientific contribution."

NUMBER 1
JANUARY 1, 1979

This Week's Citation Classic

Schachter S & Singer J. Cognitive, social and physiological determinants of emotional state. *Psychol. Rev.* **69**:379-99, 1962.

These experiments independently manipulated physiological and situational determinants of emotional state. It was demonstrated that neither physiological nor psychological explanations alone could account for the experimental facts and an interactional view of emotion was proposed. [The *Science Citation Index®* *(SCI®)* **and the** *Social Sciences Citation Index™* *(SSCI™)* **indicate that this paper was cited 432 times in the period 1962-1977.]**

Stanley Schachter
Columbia University in the City of New York
Department of Psychology
New York, NY 10027

December 20, 1977

"When W. B. Cannon (1929) wrote his devastating and brilliant critique of the James-Lange theory of emotion,[1] he would have been wise to follow the example of that great teacher of philosophy, Morris Raphael Cohen. At the end of a course in which he had demonstrated what was wrong with virtually every philosopher who had lived, Cohen was begged by his students to tell them what was right, what they should believe. 'When Hercules cleaned out Augeias' stables,' Cohen responded, 'they didn't ask him to fill them up again.'

"Unlike Cohen, Cannon chose to offer his own theory—the so-called thalamic theory of emotion—a view which in the long run proved no more useful than had James' theory. Where James had equated emotion with visceral, peripheral, physiological processes, Cannon equated emotion with processes and structures in the central nervous system. Though these theories differed in the locus they assigned to emotional states, both theories agreed that emotion was to be understood in physiological terms.

Singer and I demonstrated that no purely physiological theory of emotion could possibly cope with all of the existing data. In our experiments, precisely the same physiological state—the state of sympathetic arousal induced by an injection of adrenalin—could be labeled by the subject as any of a variety of emotional states or indeed as no emotional state at all, depending largely on cognitive and situational manipulations. It was our conclusion that to be predictively useful, any physiologically based formulation of emotion must specify the fashion in which physiological processes interact with stimulus, cognitive and situational factors. Since such a message is likely to be popular with social scientists, the high citation rate of this study in psychological and sociological discussions of emotion, always a popular topic, is hardly surprising.

"Probably the other reason this article proved so popular was the realization that emotion is a special case and that the point of view of these studies could be generalized to bodily states other than those characteristic of intense emotions. This has proved particularly true of the physiological changes induced by the psychoactive drugs.

"More surprisingly, we were able to demonstrate that the set of naturally occurring physiological symptoms characteristic of food deprivation (e.g., gastric motility, hypoglycemia, etc.) are by no means invariably labeled as 'hunger' and that there are major individual differences in which physiological changes are associated with the desire to eat. This finding has proven useful in understanding obesity and other forms of pathological eating and drinking behavior."

REFERENCE

1. **Cannon W B.** *Bodily changes in pain, hunger, fear and rage.* Harper Torchbooks, 1963. 404 p.

This Week's Citation Classic

CC/NUMBER 35
AUGUST 29, 1983

Olson D R. Language and thought: aspects of a cognitive theory of semantics. *Psychol. Rev.* 77:257-73, 1970.
[Ontario Institute for Studies in Education, Toronto, Canada]

My attempt was to show that semantics was less a matter of the structure of dictionaries than it was a matter of cognition, the language user's knowledge of the world. The meaning of a word, I argued, expressed speakers' knowledge of objects and events relative to a context of alternatives. I illustrated my hypothesis by showing how meaning marked both the object or event *and* its context of excluded alternatives. [The *Social Sciences Citation Index*® (*SSCI*®) indicates that this paper has been cited in over 155 publications since 1970.]

David R. Olson
Centre for Applied Cognitive Science
Ontario Institute for
Studies in Education
Toronto, Ontario M5S 1V6
Canada

June 8, 1983

"When psycholinguistics burst onto the field in the 1960s, it restricted its concerns to the psychological processes directly related to the linguistic structure *per se*—studies of syntactic transformation and semantic relations, as, for example, represented in dictionaries. At the same time, there coexisted a thriving cognitive psychology which offered some understanding of perceptual and conceptual problems which bore little or no relation to the structure of language.

"My paper was an attempt to put the two fields together. I tried to show that the categories of perception—which I treated as knowledge of objects and events relative to a context of alternatives—characterized both perception and language. Semantics was, in my view, not the study of dictionaries or even mental dictionaries, but rather the study of concepts, schemata, and knowledge. My paper was widely cited, I suspect, because it was one of the first to give the cognitive process such a central place in the understanding of language. In that my paper argued that language was not an autonomous system, it was taken as somewhat anti-Chomskian. I pursued this issue in a review paper published seven years later with the title 'From utterance to text.'[1] In the years after my paper, I was delighted to see what I believed to be this hypothesis in new forms in the writing of John Macnamara,[2] Katherine Nelson,[3] and Rosch and Mervis,[4] all of whom characterized this knowledge and its role in language acquisition and semantic development even more clearly than I had. I continue to believe that the most interesting problem in psychology and in psycholinguistics is the relation between language and thought, a problem that has taken a new step in recent theories of speech acts and mental states following on the work of J.L. Austin,[5] John Searle,[6] and Z. Vendler.[7]

"What I failed to recognize sufficiently at the time was that even if language may take some of its meaning from cognition, language is, as Annetta Karmiloff-Smith[8] puts it, a 'problem space' in its own right. Cognition may provide access to language but language has its own structure which the child must sort out.

"The one insight in the paper which I have never been able to advance is what I took to be a radical discontinuity between the perception of an event and the meaning of a word designating that event, namely, that words carry in them not only designations but their 'contrast sets.' I wrote: 'There is more information in an utterance than in the perception of an event out of context.' I think that problem could be stated in such a way as to show why language learning is so crucial to cognitive development.

"It is that perceptual categories and cognitive structures tend to reflect personal experience; an event is perceived and categorized relative to the immediate context of alternatives—we see a block as round in one context and white in the other. But words reflect cultural experience; words indicate those objects relative to the alternatives the language community has chosen to mark out for us. Thus, perceptually, an object x identifies only that x in its perceptual context; linguistically, an object x is identified relative to the set of alternatives from which it is traditionally differentiated in that culture. Thus, in learning language, as Whorf[9] and Wittgenstein[10] both suggested, we are learning to see the world in a way common to members of a particular social group."

1. **Olson D R.** From utterance to text: the bias of language in speech and writing. *Harvard Educ. Rev.* **47**:257-81, 1977.
2. **Macnamara J.** The cognitive basis of language learning in infants. *Psychol. Rev.* **79**:1-13, 1972.
3. **Nelson K.** Concept, word and sentence: interrelations in acquisition and development. *Psychol. Rev.* **81**:267-85, 1974.
4. **Rosch E & Mervis C G.** Family resemblances: studies in the internal structure of categories. *Cog. Psychol.* **7**:573-605, 1975.
5. **Austin J L.** *How to do things with words.* Oxford, England: Clarendon Press, 1962. 166 p.
6. **Searle J R.** *Intentionality: an essay in the philosophy of mind.* Cambridge, England: Cambridge University Press, 1983. 278 p.
7. **Vendler Z.** Say what you think. (Cowan J L, ed.) *Studies in thought and language.* Tucson, AZ: University of Arizona Press, 1970.
8. **Karmiloff-Smith A.** Language development after five. (Fletcher P & Garman M, eds.) *Language acquisition: studies in first language development.* Cambridge, England: Cambridge University Press, 1979. p. 307-23.
9. **Whorf B L.** *Language, thought, and reality: selected writings.* Cambridge, MA: Technology Press of Massachusetts Institute of Technology, 1956. 278 p.
10. **Wittgenstein L.** *Philosophical investigations.* Oxford, England: Basil Blackwell, 1953. 232 p.

NUMBER 12
MARCH 19, 1979

Paivio A. Mental imagery in associative learning and memory. *Psychol. Rev.* **76**:241-63, 1969.
[University of Western Ontario, London, Ontario, Canada]

Imagery and verbal symbolic processes are operationally distinguished in terms of stimulus attributes and experimental procedures, and their effects considered in relation to associative learning and memory. Imagery was manipulated by varying the image-evoking value of memory material and by instructions to use imagery as a mediator; verbal processes, by varying verbal meaningfulness of items and instructions to use verbal mediators. Experimental tests substantiated the explanatory and heuristic value of the imagery concept. [The *Science Citation Index®* *(SCI®)* **and the** *Social Sciences Citation Index ™ (SSCI™)* **indicate that this paper has been cited over 300 times since 1969.]**

Allan Paivio
Department of Psychology
University of Western Ontario
London, Ontario, Canada N6A 5C2

February 2, 1978

"This paper summarized an experimental-theoretical research program that had a very specific and personal beginning. Around 1950, before returning to graduate studies in psychology, I became familiar with mnemonic techniques that made use of overlearned 'memory pegs' and visual imagery as memory aids. The idea was introduced, without reference to imagery, in a co-authored paper in 1956, which reported asymmetrical order effects in the learning of sequences of English adjectives and nouns.[1] Nouns seemed to function as good 'conceptual pegs' for their modifiers. In the early 1960s, I began to explore the role of imagery in such learning and progressively expanded the research to include other tasks. The informal theoretical ideas developed gradually into a general theory of memory and cognition in which both imagery and verbal mechanisms assume equal importance. The approach was first reported in an invited address to the Canadian Psychological Association in 1967. The 1969 article grew out of that talk and was motivated partly by the positive response from some of my colleagues and partly by my own feeling that such a report might be timely. Accordingly, I devoted much of my writing time during the ensuing months to the paper. I have always been grateful that I did so because research in the areas it covered moved so quickly that it would not have attained whatever influence it had as part of the evolving *Zeitgeist*.

"The frequent citations may reflect the fact that the research approach contrasted successfully with an orientation that had dominated certain areas of psychology for several decades. As a result of the rote memory tradition that began in Germany and the behavioristic revolution in North America, higher mental phenomena tended to be interpreted primarily in terms of verbal processes. The argument was that perceptual information must be quickly translated into a linguistic code or it will be forgotten, that associative verbal learning involves the formation of direct or indirect (verbally mediated) connections between words, and that thinking similarly goes on mainly in the form of inner speech. Ignored and even suppressed during that era was the much older idea that learning, memory, and thought might go on in a nonlinguistic form, sometimes experienced as visual imagery.

"The 1969 article re-emphasized the theoretical importance of imagery, and showed how the concept could be experimentally manipulated so that its effects could be distinguished from those of verbal mechanisms. The empirical approach adapted the operational procedures of the verbal tradition to concepts and phenomena that seemed to be more relevant to the emerging cognitive psychology of the 1960s. The success and relevance of the research program, impinging perhaps on a persistent though suppressed fascination with the mentalistic concept of imagery, may be among the reasons why the article has been cited as often as it has."

REFERENCE

1. **Lambert W E & Paivio A.** The influence of noun-adjective order on learning. *Can J. Psychol.* **10**:9-12, 1956.

CC/NUMBER 23
JUNE 6, 1983

This Week's Citation Classic

Kosslyn S M & Pomerantz J R. Imagery, propositions, and the form of internal representations. *Cognitive Psychol.* 9:52-76, 1977.
[Johns Hopkins University, Baltimore, MD]

What is the nature of the internal representations that underlie the experience of 'mental imagery'? In the first part of this paper we summarize Pylyshyn's[1] arguments that image representations are not qualitatively distinct from 'propositional' representations (e.g., as are used in storing the meaning of sentences). In the second part we criticize these arguments and present arguments supporting the plausibility of imagery's being a distinct form of representation. Finally, in the third part we review classes of imagery findings, and compare and contrast imagery and propositional accounts for the results. [The *Social Sciences Citation Index*® **(***SSCI*®**) indicates that this paper has been cited in over 150 publications since 1977.]**

Stephen M. Kosslyn
Department of Psychology
and Social Relations
Harvard University
Cambridge, MA 02138

April 5, 1983

"If you are asked to describe the shape of a beagle's ears, to decide whether a mouse is larger than a hamster, or to report the number of windows in your living room, you probably will experience 'seeing' the object or objects 'in your mind's eye' when answering. The introspection that you can 'see' with a mind's eye was contrary to the theoretical biases of the early computer-oriented psychologists, who believed that all information is stored using 'mental descriptions.' Images convey information by *resembling* what they stand for, whereas descriptions are strings of symbols whose meaning is arbitrarily assigned. It is most straightforward to program a computer to store information using descriptions, and many researchers assumed that the mind is like that too. In 1973, Zenon Pylyshyn wrote a paper entitled 'What the mind's eye tells the mind's brain: a critique of mental imagery,'[1] in which he claimed that the experience of imagery really says nothing about the way the information is stored, and argued that all information in the mind is stored in terms of descriptions—including the information underlying mental imagery. This was music to the ears of many computer-inspired cognitive psychologists at the time.

"However, upon reflection, it seemed clear to us that there were holes in Pylyshyn's arguments. In particular, it was clear that a 'mental picture' need not be a *real* picture (which would require eyes to view, and would probably be rather uncomfortable up there in the head): for example, in computers one can store pictures as configurations of points in an array.

"Thus, Pylyshyn's *in principle* objections to mental images provided the motivation for the paper James Pomerantz and I wrote. When I arrived at Johns Hopkins University in 1974, I met Jim and discovered that we shared similar biases with regard to mental imagery. I had written a very rough draft of some of the paper when I was still a graduate student, and showed it to him. He immediately suggested excellent improvements and I suggested a collaboration.

"The paper was 'completed' at the beginning of 1975. It was subsequently submitted to the *Psychological Bulletin*, where it was rejected, and then to the *Psychological Review*, where it was also rejected. Then we tried the journal *Cognitive Psychology*, which went easier on us—asking us to make numerous changes and finally deciding to accept it.

"The paper has been widely cited for three reasons, I believe. First, the summary of arguments and counterarguments helps to define a basic issue in the study of the mind. Second, it summarizes data that bear on that issue, and provides concrete examples of how data can be interpreted from two very different points of view—demonstrating that the problem of studying mental representation is more difficult than many of us had initially believed. Third, the issue seems central to computational models of mental representation, and this topic currently is fashionable—in part because it is a point of contact between psychology and artificial intelligence.

"The paper formed the foundation of chapter two of *Image and Mind*,[2] which further developed the arguments in light of the debate that continued after the paper was published. A consideration of the issues in the paper led to research that in turn led to my receiving the 1983 Award for Initiatives in Research from the National Academy of Sciences."

1. **Pylyshyn Z W.** What the mind's eye tells the mind's brain: a critique of mental imagery. *Psychol. Bull.* **80**:1-24, 1973. [Citation Classic. *Current Contents/Social & Behavioral Sciences* **14**(42):22, 18 October 1982.]
2. **Kosslyn S M.** *Image and mind.* Cambridge, MA: Harvard University Press, 1980. 500 p.

This Week's Citation Classic

Pylyshyn Z W. What the mind's eye tells the mind's brain: a critique of mental imagery. *Psychol. Bull.* **80**:1-24, 1973.
[Univ. Western Ontario, London, Ontario, Canada]

This paper presents a critique of contemporary research which uses the notion of a *mental image* as a theoretical construct to describe one form of memory representation. It is argued that an adequate characterization of 'what we know' requires that we posit abstract mental structures to which we do not have conscious access and which are essentially *conceptual* and *propositional*, rather than sensory or pictorial, in nature. [The *Social Sciences Citation Index*® (*SSCI*®) indicates that this paper has been cited in over 210 publications since 1973.]

Zenon W. Pylyshyn
Centre for Cognitive Science
University of Western Ontario
London, Ontario N6A 5C2
Canada

August 20, 1982

"This was a much more painful paper to write than might appear. It started off as a criticism of some of the claims I heard graduate students making about the theoretical significance of experimental results involving mental imagery. I had the impression that they really did believe that there were pictures in the head that we examined when we created mental images. Of course everyone denied that this is what they actually believed.

"As I discussed this problem with various people at colloquia and conferences I discovered that the equivocation about the nature of mental images was extremely deep-seated and pervasive. Almost everyone I spoke to was prepared to admit that, though they themselves did not take the picture view literally, the person in the next office did fall prey to that error. The trouble was that nobody seemed to be exempt from the conceptual trap. I have to confess that I had trouble with it myself. During my first attempts at writing the paper I was plagued with doubts about my own coherence, so powerful is the subjective impression that imaging is a species of 'looking' at some mental object. It was certainly true of the reviewers of the manuscript I finally submitted to one journal: they rejected it with arguments that showed that they were precisely the 'straw men' that I was arguing against. The universal response to my arguments was (and, indeed, still is) to deny that any right-thinking person took the picture view seriously and to insist that the correct way to interpret the findings was *X*. But when I looked closely at *X* I found that it was either the picture view in very flimsy disguise or it was not explanatory at all (i.e., it was merely a *name* for the general capacity to reason about visual phenomena—as in the case of the phrase 'second-order isomorphism').

"My claim, that the theoretical construct required to *explain* the phenomena surrounding mental imagery had almost none of the characteristics associated with pictures, met with enormous and widespread resistance. I soon realized that what was at stake was a serious misunderstanding of what one had access to through conscious introspection. When you introspect and you see an image of a large heavy green tree-shaped thing there is *nothing* in your head that has any of the properties 'large,' 'heavy,' 'green,' or 'tree-shaped'—those are properties of the thing you are thinking *about*. Failure to keep this point in mind has been the central weakness of two decades of theorizing about mental images and, as far as I can see, is still true today (see my 1981 paper for a discussion of this as it applies to more modern research[1]).

"It is this conceptual slipperiness of the idea of imagery that contributed both to the popularity of the paper and to the fact that it is so widely misunderstood. People cite it mainly because it represents a critique of a view about which they have some lingering uneasiness—and it came out at a time when the interest in imagery was so strong that nobody was bothering to be the least bit critical except the doctrinaire behaviorists. The best way to put it is that psychologists found the paper tantalizing without being convinced. Some were impressed enough to have serious doubts about the interpretation of at least some of the claims of imagery research (such as that long-term memory consists of an indexed store of pictures). But most citations look something like, 'Images have been shown to have some property *P*—but see Pylyshyn, 1973, for a contrary view.'

"I have to confess that I find it wearisome to be associated with the argument about imagery, even though it has played a central role in shaping my career and my current interest in related philosophical questions.[2] In one sense the intuition that people have when they claim that there is something special about thinking imaginally must be true. The problem is that nobody has been able to give any coherent story about what the special thing is. In the process of trying to do so, however, psychologists have uttered more silly things per page than in almost any other area of psychology. So while I keep doggedly pursuing the more fashionable alternative proposals (e.g., see my papers of 1978[3] and 1981[1]), I believe there is something in research that will eventually provide clues to the nature of the mind. In the meantime it seems to be telling us more about the problems of interpreting experimental regularities."

1. **Pylyshyn Z W.** The imagery debate: analogue media versus tacit knowledge. *Psychol. Rev.* **88**:16-45, 1981.
2. ------------------. Computation and cognition: issues in the foundations of cognitive science. *Behav. Brain Sci.* **3**:111-32, 1980.
3. ------------------. Imagery and artificial intelligence. (Savage W, ed.) *Perception and cognition: issues in the foundations of psychology*. Minneapolis: University of Minnesota Press, 1978. p. 19-55.

This Week's Citation Classic

CC/NUMBER 36
SEPTEMBER 8, 1980

Bieri J, Atkins A L, Briar S, Leaman R L, Miller H & Tripodi T. *Clinical and social judgment: the discrimination of behavioral information.* New York: Wiley, 1966. 271 p.
[Dept. Psychol., Univ. Texas; Dept. Psychol., Yeshiva Univ., NY; School of Soc. Welfare, Univ. Calif., Berkeley; and Brooklyn Col., City Univ., NY]

This book considers the judgment process in relation to two aspects of personality, the cognitive complexity of the judge and ability to process information. The relationship of these factors to phenomena of anchoring, situational influences, and affect, are discussed in the context of empirical research. [The *Social Sciences Citation Index*® *(SSCI™)* **indicates that this book has been cited over 225 times since 1966.]**

James Bieri
Department of Psychology
University of Texas
Austin, TX 78712

August 12, 1980

"The research reported in this book was an intensely collaborative effort and a product of a stimulating and creative research group that I was privileged to lead for six years at the Columbia University School of Social Work. Our work brought together two major currents at that time, information theory in experimental psychology, and clinical judgment in applied psychology. Both of these were integrated within a cognitive structure approach to personality functioning, specifically within the concept of cognitive complexity. The frequent citation of this volume is largely due to the discussion it contains of cognitive complexity, both in terms of theory and assessment methods. There is a continuing interest in cognitive complexity in clinical, personality, and social psychology, as well as in many applied fields such as education, child development, management, and business.

"I first published a paper on cognitive complexity in 1955,[1] in which I was setting forth ideas that had been stimulated by my graduate work with the late George A. Kelly in personal construct theory. The 50s and 60s were heady years for cognitive research and it was natural to apply these ideas to the problem of clinical judgment. The extra ingredient, that of information theory, was provided when I struck up a friendship with a colleague at Columbia, an assistant professor named William J. McGill. Bill was later to become president of Columbia University, but in those days our talks centered around the application of information theory to clinical judgment. Bill had already made notable contributions to the development of information theory, and the many talks we had on this topic were very important to me. His influence and involvement in this book were substantial, and I wish to thank him again for his creative assistance in all phases of our research.

"Ours was truly an interdisciplinary group. In addition to McGill, an experimental psychologist, and me, a clinical psychologist, my coauthors formed a varied and stimulating intellectual group. Robin Leaman had completed graduate work in perceptual psychology, and she acted as an integrator for all our efforts with her astute, insightful contributions. Alvin Atkins was trained in social psychology, while Scott Briar, Henry Miller, and Tony Tripodi were in social work. With the exception of Leaman, all the coauthors obtained doctorates under my supervision, and their efforts are fundamental in this book. Atkins is responsible for much of the work on anchoring effects, while Briar was concerned with situational influences on judgment. Both Miller and Tripodi had strong interests in the cognitive and information processing aspects of our work. This scholarly mix provided a fount of intellectual stimulation and personal friendship that was unmatched in my research work before or since that time. I believe our work and the interest it has generated underscores the fruitfulness of collaborative work across disciplines in today's increasingly compartmentalized intellectual world."

1. **Bieri J.** Cognitive complexity/simplicity and predictive behavior. *J. Abnorm. Soc. Psychol.* **51**:263-68, 1955.

CC/NUMBER 14
APRIL 4, 1983

This Week's Citation Classic

Tversky A & Kahneman D. Judgment under uncertainty: heuristics and biases. *Science* **185**:1124-31, 1974.
[Department of Psychology, Hebrew University, Jerusalem, Israel]

The paper describes three judgmental heuristics—representativeness, availability, and anchoring—that are commonly used to estimate probability, frequency, and values. The heuristics are highly economical and usually effective, but they also produce predictable biases. [The *Social Sciences Citation Index*® (*SSCI*®) **indicates that this paper has been cited in over 420 publications since 1974.]**

Amos Tversky
Department of Psychology
Stanford University
Stanford, CA 94305
and
Daniel Kahneman
Department of Psychology
University of British Columbia
Vancouver, British Columbia V6T 1W5
Canada

February 3, 1983

"The research reviewed in this paper began in 1969 when Daniel Kahneman invited Amos Tversky to discuss potential applications of research on judgment and decision making in a seminar on applied psychology. Immediately after the seminar we started a conversation about errors of judgment, their causes and consequences, which led to an extensive professional collaboration and a close personal friendship lasting more than 13 years. The research was sparked by the realization that intuitive predictions and judgments under uncertainty do not follow the laws of probability or the principles of statistics. Instead, people appear to rely on a limited number of heuristics and evaluate the likelihood of an uncertain event by the degree to which it is representative of the data generating process, or by the degree to which its instances or causes come readily to mind. These hypotheses were formulated very early in conversations between us but it took many years of research and thousands of subject hours to study the role of representativeness, availability, and anchoring, and to explore the biases to which they are prone.

"We spent the better part of 1973 writing the paper and then revising it again and again in an attempt to summarize our research on heuristics and biases in judgment under uncertainty. To our pleasant surprise, the paper reached many readers outside psychology and it has been reprinted in several volumes of readings in economics, public policy, statistics, and cognitive science. It was widely cited because it suggested a new approach to the study of subjective probability.

"The approach to the study of judgment that is reflected in the paper is characterized by (1) a comparison of intuitive judgment to normative principles of probability and statistics, (2) a search for heuristics of judgment and the biases to which they are prone, and (3) an attempt to explore the theoretical and practical implications of the discrepancy between the psychology of judgment and the theory of rational belief. This approach has become one of the foci of judgment research during the last decade. It was criticized by some who found the theory too vague and the phenomena too elusive; it has also generated a substantial body of empirical research. Much of this work has been reprinted and summarized in a recent book, *Judgment under Uncertainty: Heuristics and Biases*.[1] We have received the Distinguished Scientific Award of the American Psychological Association for our research on judgment and decision making."

1. **Kahneman D, Slovic P & Tversky A,** eds. *Judgment under uncertainty: heuristics and biases.* Cambridge: Cambridge University Press, 1982. 555 p.

CC/NUMBER 34
AUGUST 25, 1980

This Week's Citation Classic

Newell A & Simon H A. *Human problem solving.* Englewood Cliffs, NJ: Prentice-Hall, 1972. 920 p. [Carnegie-Mellon University, Pittsburgh, PA]

The human problem solver can be viewed as an information processing system that manipulates symbolic structures. Studies in three domains—elementary logic, chess, and puzzles—show this in combined experimental and theoretical detail. These are integrated into a general theory of human problem solving. [The *Social Sciences Citation Index® (SSCI™)* **indicates that this book has been cited over 360 times since 1972.]**

Allen Newell
Department of Computer Science
Carnegie-Mellon University
Pittsburgh, PA 15213

July 16, 1980

"By general accord, a revolution happened in the scientific study of man in the mid-1950s, shifting the view to man as an active processor of symbolic information. The scope of that revolution is indicated by the names associated with it, who made pathbreaking, complementary, but distinct contributions: Broadbent, Chomsky, Miller, Newell and Simon, Tanner and Swets. Our work on the logic theory program for proving theorems in a heuristic manner on a computer (1956), followed by the work on the general problem solver (1958), was one strand of that revolution. It was associated with both the initiation of the field of artificial intelligence and the application of those ideas to human psychology. *Human Problem Solving* provided a full scale presentation of that work and the stream of research that followed (and has hardly yet abated).

"Little surprise is occasioned by the book being highly cited. The work itself has been the source of continued acts of recognition, for example: the American Psychological Association Scientific Contribution Award to Simon (1971) and the Association of Computing Machinery A.M. Turing Award jointly to Newell and Simon (1975).

"One interesting question, perhaps, is why it took 17 years to write the thing. We claimed (and had) a first outline in 1956. Another question might be why the thing is so long (920 pages). We have yet to find anyone who has really read it thoroughly from cover to cover. (A number of planted gems of wisdom have never caused the slightest ripple at the surface.)

"The answers to these two questions are intertwined. Artificial intelligence research differs stylistically from experimental psychology, raising questions of whether computer simulations are relevant to psychology, are metaphorical, or what. Early on we became convinced that we did not want to write the natural book, which would have been a melange of various artificial intelligence programs (some with data, some without), with relevant lessons for psychology. Thus the title became shorn of all references to computers to just *Human Problem Solving,* and many interesting programs (even those with data) were shucked aside. The book became severely limited (to problem solving, out of all cognitive functions), it became data heavy, and it became tightly integrated. Alas, it also became a treatise instead of a textbook. The aim was to make the case that *psychology* was being done, not something that could be pigeon-holed as associated with computers. We relied on protocol data on individuals, and it seemed necessary to include this in the book. The combination of all these new goals and the insistence on data throughout caused a complete reworking of the book. Thus the delay, thus the size.

"Whether the strategy we adopted was ultimately successful is hard to say. Pigeon-holing still went on. The book would have reached more widely if cast as a textbook. And on. But those are the woulds and coulds of another world than the one that happened."

CC/NUMBER 15
APRIL 12, 1982

Kuethe J L. Social schemas. *J. Abnormal Soc. Psychol.* **64**:31-8, 1962. [Johns Hopkins University, Baltimore, MD]

When people place representations of human figures on a field, their responses are organized rather than scattered or random. For example, children are associated with women, and women with men. This technique permits the study of both generic and specific social schemata in different populations. [The *Social Sciences Citation Index*® (*SSCI*®) indicates that this paper has been cited over 150 times since 1966.]

James L. Kuethe
Department of Educational Psychology and Statistics
State University of New York
Albany, NY 12222

February 9, 1982

"My development of this technique for studying social cognition had its roots in observations that human behavior in certain social contexts is much more predictable than most psychology textbooks would lead us to believe. For example, I could ask 100 strangers at bus stops for the time and expect every one of them to glance at his watch and respond. Many social scientists have confined their investigations to phenomena that require carefully controlled conditions and powerful analyses in order to demonstrate an effect. I have long been interested in those social behaviors that are so pervasive that they appear 'obvious' and are seldom studied. I like Heider's statement, 'The veil of obviousness that makes so many insights of intuitive psychology invisible to our scientific eye has to be pierced.'[1]

"What I needed was a technique that would allow subjects to organize social stimuli under conditions of minimal constraint. I wanted the free expression of social predilections which suggested a projective measure, but at the same time I wanted to avoid the subjective scoring typical of such techniques. The solution came during a visit to an elementary school classroom. The teacher had a flannel board on which the children could place objects cut from felt. The nap permits the cutouts to adhere anywhere they are placed and with any orientation. In addition, when the objects are removed the field is again clear and ready for a new construction. This was just what I needed! A visit to a department store and an expenditure of less than $5.00 for felt provided the 'apparatus' for a series of studies.

"Paper dolls were used as templates to cut out representations of men, women, and children which subjects placed on a large felt field stretched on my office wall. They were instructed, 'Place them in any way you want to.' As predicted, the subjects (in this study, male undergraduates at Johns Hopkins University) did not place the figures at random but instead employed specific high commonality social schemata. A child figure was placed next to a woman figure and nonhuman figures were not allowed to separate a male-female pair of figures. (By the way, the tables appearing in this *Citation Classic* article were composed by photographing the actual stimulus sets with high contrast film and then superimposing the frequencies with which each configuration was used.)

"The second part of the study demonstrated the pervasive nature of these schemata. Using a reconstruction technique, subjects attempted to accurately replace pairs of figures after viewing them with a fixed separation. Subjects erred in replacing male-female pairs too close together while the replacements of neutral stimuli were relatively accurate. This showed that under some conditions social schemata function as response sets. The technique has been extended in a series of subsequent investigations.[2-4]

"I believe that this study has received many citations because of the versatility of the technique and the fact that although it is projective, the relative distances of the placements can be objectively measured. Other investigations use different stimuli with different populations to test hypotheses unrelated to my initial purpose."

1. **Heider F.** *The psychology of interpersonal relations.* New York: Wiley, 1958. 322 p.
2. **Kuethe J L.** The pervasive influence of social schemata. *J. Abnormal Soc. Psychol.* **68**:248-54, 1964.
3. ------------. Prejudice and aggression: a study of specific social schemata. *Percept. Mot. Skills* **18**:107-15, 1964.
4. **Kidder S J & Kuethe J L.** Children's parental schemata as related to reading achievement. *Percept. Mot. Skills* **40**:971-3, 1975.

NUMBER 38
SEPTEMBER 17, 1979

Witkin H A, Dyk R B, Faterson H F, Goodenough D R & Karp S A.
Psychological differentiation: studies of development.
Potomac, MD: Lawrence Erlbaum Associates, 1974. 418 p.
(Originally published: New York: Wiley, 1962.)
[Dept. Psychiat., State Univ. New York, Coll. Med., New York, NY]

The theory which guided this research conceives of the development of differentiation as an organism-wide process, and proposes, accordingly, that greater or lesser differentiation is likely to characterize an individual's psychological functioning in diverse domains. This expectation of self-consistency in behavior across domains was substantially confirmed in studies which examined people's perceptual, intellectual, and personality functioning. [The *Science Citation Index*® *(SCI®)* **and the** *Social Sciences Citation Index*™ *(SSCI™)* **indicate that this book has been cited over 1,045 times since 1962.]**

Herman A. Witkin*
Division of Psychological Studies
Educational Testing Service
Princeton, NJ 08541

March 3, 1978

"This book was the second major installment in the story of a program of research which began in the early 1940s. The first major installment appeared in 1954.[1] Additional pieces of the story have been told in a number of journal articles published between the inception of the program and now. While its specific content inevitably changed as the program unfolded, it has remained a constant objective of our work to arrive at a more holistic conception of the individual's psychological life.

"Perhaps the main reason for the frequent citation of *Psychological Differentiation* is its relevance to the concerns of many of the specialties in psychology. The theoretical framework it proposed sought to bring together a variety of psychological domains, often considered in isolation from each other; accordingly, it contains constructs which have broad applicability. The lead construct, differentiation, is a large piece of the psychological pie and it is salient in the conception of psychological development as well. The search for self-consistency in behavior, prompted by the holistic emphasis of the theoretical framework, led to the identification of pervasive dimensions of psychological functioning. Among these, the field-independent and field-dependent cognitive styles (which are tendencies toward greater or lesser autonomy of external referents in information processing) have shown themselves, in a particularly impressive way, not to respect the boundaries into which the psyche has traditionally been divided.

"A second possible reason for the use made of our work by others is that it has produced a variety of standardized tests of cognitive styles. Measures from these tests provide objective 'tracer' indicators of the more general differentiation dimension of which cognitive styles are a part. The availability of these tests has considerably facilitated research on differentiation.

"The constructs, dimensions, and methodology which emerged from our work have contributed to its use by others in areas as diverse as interpersonal behavior, learning and memory, defense mechanisms, socialization practices, cultural differences in development, dreaming, psychopathology, and cerebral lateralization. The demonstration, in some of these investigations, that our theoretical formulations and the dimensions of individual functioning we identified are useful in conceptualizing behavior in real-life situations has given impetus to research on practical applications. Represented in that research has been work on the role of psychological differentiation in academic and vocational choices, alcohol addiction, driving safety, patients' progress in psychotherapy, teacher effectiveness, and learning disabilities.

"The program of research is still going on. As has been true throughout its life, its guiding theory is continuing to undergo change and its empirical underpinning to expand, thanks in no small measure to the labors of the many who have taken up this line of work. It has been a recurrent experience on this long march that an observation we made at an earlier time acquired a fresh meaning in the light of an alteration in the theoretical perspective. We have not infrequently felt, as T.S. Eliot put it in his *Four Quartets,* that 'the aim of all exploring is to arrive where we started and know the place for the first time.' "[2]

1. **Witkin H A, Lewis H B, Hertzman M, Manchover K, Meissner P B & Wapner S.** *Personality through perception.* New York: Harper, 1954. 571 p.
2. **Elliot T S.** *Four quartets.* New York: Harcourt, Brace & Co., 1943. 39 p.

*We regret to report Dr. Witkin's untimely death on July 8, 1979. (See *NY Times* 11 July 1979, p. B12.)

CC/NUMBER 13
MARCH 31, 1980

This Week's Citation Classic

Wallach M A & Kogan N. *Modes of thinking in young children: a study of the creativity-intelligence distinction.* New York: Holt, Rinehart & Winston, 1965. 357 p. [Duke Univ., Durham, NC and Educational Testing Service, Princeton, NJ]

This book succeeded in finding creativity tests which were strongly correlated with one another and virtually uncorrelated with standard measures of intelligence. These results gave empirical support to the belief that creativity is a human characteristic quite different from intelligence. [The *Science Citation Index®* (*SCI®*) **and the** *Social Sciences Citation Index™* (*SSCI™*) **indicate that this book has been cited over 345 times since 1965.]**

Michael A. Wallach
Department of Psychology
Duke University
Durham, NC 27706

January 30, 1980

"The limitations of conventional intelligence tests have long been suspected, but attempts to demonstrate those limitations empirically have not been easy to come by. The major appeal of this book has been that it succeeded in such an attempt. It argued that previous work had failed to provide convincing evidence because too wide a range of different functions had been included under 'creativity,' at least some of which overlap with intelligence. Also, the purported measures of creativity had been administered under test-like conditions, whereas exercise of creativity calls for more relaxed, game-like circumstances. The book showed: (1) Tasks could be defined which, on their face, looked relevant to creativity—tasks concerning the readiness of a person's flow of ideas and the uniqueness of the ideas produced. (2) These tasks could be administered under relaxed, game-like conditions. (3) Productivity and uniqueness of ideas, assessed under game-like circumstances, not only was consistent across different kinds of tasks, but virtually unpredictable from results on intelligence tests. I believe the book has been highly cited because it systematically demonstrated ways to assess creativity as distinct from intelligence.

"The unfinished business remaining from where the book left off was considerable. First, the book proposed two necessary characteristics for making creativity tests independent from intelligence tests—namely, they should concern ideational flow and they should be administered under game-like rather than test-like circumstances. In the book, however, these two characteristics had been varied jointly. The basic outcome in work since has been to show that, contrary to what we first thought, administration context does not seem to matter. Ideational fluency tests give individual differences that are essentially independent of intelligence whether administered in game-like or test-like contexts.[1]

"The second major area of unfinished business concerned the crucial question of what the ideational fluency tests have to do with creative achievements in real life. Extensive research by various investigators in the years following the book has addressed this question. Results suggest that intelligence tests not only fail to predict ideational fluency but also fail to predict these real-life accomplishments. Ideational fluency tests, in turn, may do a little better than intelligence tests at such predictions, but, in fact, do not predict well enough to serve as useful proxies for the real-world achievements themselves. Tests of ideational fluency are subject to many sources of variance besides what they may have in common with the display of real-life creativity, for example, a tendency to please a test administrator by trying harder to come up with more ideas. What best predicts creative achievements in the world is earlier achievements of similar kinds.[2,3] Intelligence tests do have striking limitations, therefore, but to find out more about creativity we seem best advised to study real-life accomplishments themselves and the conditions that bring them about."

1. **Wallach M A.** *The intelligence/creativity distinction.* Morristown, NJ: General Learning Press, 1971. 32 p.
2. -----------------. Tests tell us little about talent. *Amer. Sci.* **64**:57-63, 1976.
3. -----------------. Psychology of talent and graduate education. (Messick S & Associates, eds.) *Individuality in learning.* San Francisco: Jossey-Bass, 1976. p. 178-210.

CC/NUMBER 43
OCTOBER 27, 1980

This Week's Citation Classic

Hudson L. *Contrary imaginations.* New York: Schocken, 1966. 181 p.
[King's College, Cambridge, England]

In an educational system that encourages early specialisation, clever young men with a 'convergent' bias of ability move towards the physical sciences, while those with a 'divergent' bias move towards the humanities. [The *Social Sciences Citation Index®* *(SSCI™)* **indicates that this book has been cited over 225 times since 1966.]**

Liam Hudson
Department of Psychology
Brunel University
Uxbridge, Middlesex UB8 3PH
England

July 11, 1980

"*Contrary Imaginations* was my first book, and was written very much in isolation. No one else in Cambridge in the mid-1960s was much interested in the problems of human intelligence, beyond the production of yet another IQ test, and my comrades in the psychological laboratory were persuaded, in any case, that it was a topic best suited to the second-rate. I worked on my own, too, from choice; Fenland winters being cold and damp, I often did so in bed.[1]

"This isolation provided the research which *Contrary Imaginations* summarises with one of its redeeming virtues: beyond the freedom to be cheerfully rude about other, more august workers in the field, it enabled me to see that the statistical sandcastles they habitually built with their data had led them to overlook some very simple truths indeed. Chief among these was the fact that, in a classroom of fairly clever 16 year olds, the correlations between tests of different sorts of mental ability are close to zero. Students who are good at one sort of test are often relatively weak at others. This discovery, made quite naively, was given special point when my professor, Oliver Zangwill, gave me Getzels and Jackson's courageous *Creativity and Intelligence* to review.[2] Trying out their open-ended tests for myself, I found to my surprise that they effected a neat separation, not so much between the creative and the non-creative, as between students specialising in the physical sciences and those specialising in the humanities. In the English school system at that time, 'convergers,' i.e., those with high IQs, but relatively little taste for tests of free association, were flowing into mathematics, physics, and chemistry, while 'divergers,' those with the reverse bias of ability, were gravitating towards disciplines like English literature and history. On the strength of this lucky find, I was able to build a more general account of the ways in which the two 'Two Cultures' of C.P. Snow were systematically recruiting young people with biases of ability and temperament that could only serve to widen and perpetuate the gulf that already existed between them.

"When it came out in 1966, *Contrary Imaginations* was seen among the staid as mildly subversive. It contained, for example, the occasional joke. The Cambridge University Press declined to publish it; although fortunately for me, both Methuen and Penguin were happy to snap it up.[3,4] It has been used since, I think, as a reference point by people who suspect that generalisations about human intelligence put about by experts are sometimes less dispassionate than they seem: that they are often motivated by a desire to foster the conventional (and readily measurable) academic virtues and to penalise the more antic. It is a text for pluralists, in other words. Also for those who are sceptical of statistical abstractions and who dislike jargon."

1. **Hudson L.** *The cult of the fact.* New York: Harper & Row, 1972. 189 p.
2. **Getzels J W & Jackson P W.** *Creativity and intelligence.* New York: Wiley, 1962. 293 p.
3. **Hudson L.** *Contrary imaginations.* London: Methuen, 1966. 181 p.
4. ------------. *Contrary imaginations.* Harmondsworth, England: Penguin, 1967. 205 p.

Chapter

7

Development, Personality, and Disturbance

Development
- Language / 175–178
- Abilities / 179–182
- Adaptation / 183–189
- Developmental sequences / 190–193

Personality / 194–200

Disturbances
- Childhood disturbances / 201–208
- Disturbance syndromes / 209–214

CC/NUMBER 26
JUNE 28, 1982

This Week's Citation Classic

Brown R. *A first language: the early stages.* Cambridge, MA: Harvard University Press, 1973. 437 p.

Stage I child speech is made up of contentives expressing a small set of semantic relations primarily by word order. In Stage II the little words and inflections which modulate meanings with respect to number, person, tense, definiteness, etc., evolve in an order of increasing derivational complexity. [The *Social Sciences Citation Index*® **(***SSCI*®**) indicates that this book has been cited over 710 times since 1973.]**

Roger Brown
Department of Psychology and Social Relations
Harvard University
Cambridge, MA 02138

February 1, 1982

"In the fall of 1962, we began a longitudinal study of the development of English as a first language in the preschool years of three children whom we called Adam, Eve, and Sarah. The principal data of the study were periodic transcriptions of the spontaneous speech of child and mother in conversation at home. These children were fortunate in their amanuenses: Adam had Ursula Bellugi (now research professor at the Salk Institute for Biological Studies); Eve had Colin Fraser (now university lecturer at Cambridge); and Sarah had Courtney Cazden (professor of education at Harvard). During the first year of the project, a group of students of the psychology of language met each week to discuss the state of the children's construction processes as of that date. The idea was that the members of the seminar would, from close study of the week's protocols, devise deft little experiments that would choose among hypotheses suggested by the naturalistic data. The children's acquisition processes were, of course, too fast for us. By the time we were ready to pose question 'A,' they were always 'on beyond Zebra.'

"It turned out, however, that a great deal could be learned from meticulous records of spontaneous speech in combination with answers to simple questions. No one at the start had any way of knowing how much because the methods of analysis were all still to be invented. They are, basically, adaptations to the problem of child speech of the methods of distributional analysis devised by anthropological linguists for discovering the structure of exotic tongues never before explicitly recorded. We felt ourselves to be in not dissimilar circumstances.

"In the years of data collection we reported on many subsystems of English grammar (e.g., early negatives, modal auxiliaries, tag questions) and it was not until data collection was over that I felt the full force of an expectation that there should be a report of the stages of English as a whole. *A First Language* was my response to that expectation. I think the book has been often cited because the inductive games one plays with child speech have proved captivating to many scientists and because nature has so arranged matters that many things discovered to be true of three children are true of all children learning English, and a few things may be true of children learning whatever language. The book caused me to be given the G. Stanley Hall Award in developmental psychology and the David H. Russell Award of the National Council of Teachers of English.

"For an excellent review of the field, see *Language Acquisition*[1] by Jill and Peter de Villiers."

1. **de Villiers J G & de Villiers P A.** *Language acquisition.* Cambridge, MA: Harvard University Press, 1978. 312 p.

CC/NUMBER 48
NOVEMBER 30, 1981

This Week's Citation Classic

Fraser C, Bellugi U & Brown R. Control of grammar in imitation, comprehension, and production. *J. Verb. Learn. Verb. Behav.* **2**:121-35, 1963. [Harvard University, Cambridge, MA]

The familiar assertion that, in language development, understanding precedes production was examined by testing the mastery of grammatical contrasts by three-year-olds. Production proved consistently less advanced than comprehension, which was consistently less advanced than imitation. The relevance of these findings for alternative conceptions of imitation, comprehension, and production was considered. [The *Social Sciences Citation Index*® **(*SSCI*®) indicates that this paper has been cited over 220 times since 1966.]**

Colin Fraser
Social and Political Sciences Committee
University of Cambridge
Cambridge CB2 3RQ
England

September 3, 1981

"Just as developmental psycholinguistics was beginning its own development, I had the good fortune that my very first job, in 1960, was as research associate at MIT on a new project of Roger Brown, on the young child's acquisition of syntax. Almost straightaway we started exploratory work looking for patterning in the speech of two-year-olds.[1] In 1961, Ursula Bellugi joined us and, in 1962, the three of us embarked on the study of Adam, Eve, and, subsequently, Sarah, which culminated in Roger's very fine book a decade later.[2] The present paper represents a slight digression undertaken during 1961-1962.

"We had started with the working assumption that we would detect the beginnings of syntax if we recorded the speech of children just starting to produce two- and multi-word utterances. I may have been the first of us to worry aloud about our starting point, though our paper was so consistently a joint endeavour that that could be hazy recollection enhancing self-importance; the main reason my name appears first was that it was my turn.

"Anyway, we realised that if anything like a grammar of a two-year-old's production was going to be discoverable, we should also be thinking about a possible grammar of comprehension which might be developing in the one-year-old. Viable ways of systematically documenting the comprehension of a one-year-old did not suggest themselves, but we remained attracted to the possibility of exploring comprehension and its relation to production. Pairs of drawings of minimally different grammatical contrasts gave us a technique and a focus. Eventually, piloting convinced us that three-year-olds were the youngest children we could reliably get through our testing procedures. Before then, however, the three of us, and a few interested others, had spent many sessions relating our likely operationalizations to alternative conceptions of comprehension, production, and imitation, painstakingly locating grammatical contrasts which could be unambiguously illustrated, commissioning and rejecting artist's drawings of the contrasts, and occasionally wondering if we were really doing anything of value.

"That this work should have become a *Citation Classic* is a pleasantly surprising tribute to an exceedingly enjoyable, as well as stimulating, three-way partnership. To have done full justice to our collaboration, however, the paper would have had to have been much funnier.

"As for reasons for the popularity of our paper, it was the first attempt within the new developmental psycholinguistic 'paradigm' to tackle the largely ignored issues of young children's comprehension of speech. Although our procedures and materials were open to criticism—all three tasks, for example, have problematic features—they produced very regular data and were relatively easily modified, making them attractive to others. They, and our paper, did not become obsolete as quickly as one might have hoped, because of inherent difficulties in advancing the study of young children's comprehension. Providing valid data about intrinsically unobservable processes remains a demanding task. A greater range of possibilities is now available,[3] but on many relevant issues[4] the volume of work on early comprehension remains dwarfed by that on speech production."

1. **Brown R & Fraser C.** The acquisition of syntax. (Cofer C N & Musgrave B S, eds.) *Verbal behavior and learning: problems and processes.* New York: McGraw-Hill, 1963. p. 158-97.
2. **Brown R.** *A first language: the early stages.* Cambridge, MA: Harvard University Press, 1973. 437 p.
3. **Cocking R R & McHale S.** A comparative study of the use of pictures and objects in assessing children's receptive and productive language. *J. Child Lang.* **8**:1-13, 1981.
4. **Wells C G & Robinson W P.** The role of adult speech in language development. (Fraser C & Scherer K R, eds.) *Advances in the social psychology of language.* Cambridge: Cambridge University Press. To be published, 1982.

This Week's Citation Classic

Meichenbaum D H & Goodman J. Training impulsive children to talk to themselves: a means of developing self-control.
J. Abnormal Psychol. 77:115-26, 1971.
[University of Waterloo, Waterloo, Ontario, Canada]

The efficacy of a self-instructional (SI) training program was examined in two studies. The training program taught the impulsive child to talk to himself, initially overtly and then covertly. Relative to placebo and assessment control groups, the SI training group demonstrated improvement across tasks and over time. [The *Social Sciences Citation Index*® (*SSCI*®) **indicates that this paper has been cited over 270 times since 1971.]**

Donald H. Meichenbaum
Department of Psychology
University of Waterloo
Waterloo, Ontario N2L 3G1
Canada

March 1, 1982

"Several lines of investigation gave impetus to the design of this study. On the one hand a number of studies suggested that children who had problems with self-control were evidencing a 'mediational' deficit or an inability to use their own language to guide and control their nonverbal behavior. The impulsive and hyperactive child was described as someone who did not 'stop, look, and listen.'[1] Although a number of treatment approaches ranging from behavior modification to pharmacological intervention were being employed with children who had self-control problems, there was increasing concern about the limitation of these approaches in terms of generalization and durability of treatment effectiveness.

"It was within this context that a cognitive-behavioral self-instructional (SI) training program was developed. A training program designed to teach impulsive children a set of problem-solving skills or 'how to think' when confronted by academic and social situations was developed with Joseph Goodman, a graduate student at the University of Waterloo.

"The format of the training was influenced by the developmental theory and research of the Soviet psychologists L. Vygotsky[2] and his student, A.R. Luria.[3] They suggested that children become socialized by first responding to the instructions of an adult or older sibling and then internalizing those instructions in an abbreviated fashion as a form of inner speech. With age and task proficiency those self-verbalizations drop out of the child's repertoire.

"An analogy could be drawn to the following adult example. Consider for a moment how you learn a motor skill such as driving a stick-shift car or skiing. At the outset you likely talk to yourself in an intentional manner, but with proficiency these verbalizations drop out of your repertoire until your plan or the automaticity of your act is interrupted. At that point you likely talk to yourself once again. The SI training program was designed along these lines. Impulsive children were encouraged to talk to themselves, initially aloud and then covertly. They were then assessed on a variety of measures of self-control.

"Although the results of this initial study were at best encouraging, the study provided a powerful paradigm for interventions. In the last ten years we have learned a great deal about how to teach impulsive children, as well as a variety of other populations, how to talk to themselves.[4] These procedures have now been applied to a host of populations ranging from adult psychotic patients to athletes, from retarded children to uncreative college students. We have learned how an SI training program can supplement other forms of interventions and what are the limitations of the procedures.[5] Our study has been cited so often because it pointed the direction for future cognitive-behavioral interventions. The study contributed to a shifting *zeitgeist* whereby psychological interventions were becoming more cognitive. Behavior modification was going cognitive as was psychology in general. This study fit the new mold."

1. **Douglas V.** Stop, look and listen: the problem of sustained attention and impulse control in hyperactive and normal children. *Can. J. Behav. Sci.* **4**:259-76, 1972.
2. **Vygotsky L.** *Thought and language.* Cambridge: MIT Press, 1962. 168 p.
3. **Luria A R.** *The role of speech in the regulation of normal and abnormal behavior.* New York: Liveright, 1961. 148 p.
4. **Meichenbaum D.** *Cognitive-behavior modification: an integrative approach.* New York: Plenum Press, 1977. 305 p.
5. **Meichenbaum D & Asarnow J.** Cognitive-behavioral modification and metacognitive development: implications for the classroom. (Kendall P & Hollon S, eds.) *Cognitive-behavioral interventions: theory, research and procedures.* New York: Academic Press, 1979. p. 11-36.

This Week's Citation Classic

Reese H W. Verbal mediation as a function of age level. *Psychol. Bull.* **59**:502-9, 1962. [University of Buffalo, Buffalo, NY]

Performance in many tasks can be 'mediated' (facilitated or suppressed) by verbal behavior such as naming the stimuli presented. Preschool children often fail to exhibit predicted mediational effects, thus exhibiting 'mediational deficiency' (failure to use potential mediators). Older children exhibit mediational deficiency in some situations. [The *Social Sciences Citation Index*® **(*SSCI*®) indicates that this paper has been cited over 165 times since 1966.]**

Hayne W. Reese
Department of Psychology
West Virginia University
Morgantown, WV 26506

September 2, 1981

"The hypothesis that the mediating effect of words on behavior is deficient in an early stage of concept formation was suggested by Margaret Kuenne in the *Journal of Experimental Psychology* in 1946,[1] but it was ignored because experimental psychology at that time dealt with animals and college students rather than children, and developmental psychology had not yet become experimental. I mentioned her hypothesis in my master's thesis in 1955, but I did not recognize its developmental significance until later. On February 11, 1960, I addressed a seminar at McMaster University on behavioristic theories of cognition, and discussed Kuenne's hypothesis as a possible explanation of why parrots can talk but not think—a problem for these theories mentioned by Dollard and Miller.[2] Later that month, the hypothesis was independently revived by Kendler, Kendler, and Wells,[3] but with respect to stages of ontogeny rather than of concept formation. I began a review of the literature, and as a sort of pilot study decided to reanalyze my master's thesis data after dividing the samples into younger and older preschoolers. I had not made any age split in the thesis, but I discovered that I had matched the experimental groups on median age and consequently the study provided not merely pilot data but a particularly convincing test in that the data were collected five years before the outcome was predicted. The results supported the hypothesis. The literature review had become too long to serve as the introduction to the report of the results, and therefore I submitted it for separate publication. It was accepted without revision (except for changing 'these *Ss*' learning' to 'the learning of these *Ss*') and eventually became the *Citation Classic* under discussion here.

"The impact of the paper may be attributable to its timing. Experimental child psychology had only recently emerged as a distinct movement—the *Journal of Experimental Child Psychology* began publication in 1964—and although age differences in learning were already well established, the mediational deficiency hypothesis was the movement's first developmental principle with enough scope to be generally interesting. It led to much research, and production and mediational deficiency (John H. Flavell's[4] refinements of my general term) are still active and fruitful topics of investigation. Recent reviews have been published by Kendler[5] and Zivin."[6]

1. **Kuenne M K.** Experimental investigation of the relation of language to transposition behavior in young children. *J. Exp. Psychol.* **36**:471-90, 1946.
2. **Dollard J & Miller N E.** *Personality and psychotherapy; an analysis in terms of learning, thinking, and culture.* New York: McGraw-Hill, 1950. 488 p.
3. **Kendler T S, Kendler H H & Wells D.** Reversal and nonreversal shifts in nursery school children. *J. Comp. Physiol. Psychol.* **53**:83-8, 1960.
4. **Flavell J H.** Developmental studies of mediated memory. (Reese H W & Lipsitt L P, eds.) *Advances in child development and behavior.* New York: Academic Press, 1979. Vol. 5. p. 181-211.
5. **Kendler T S.** The development of discrimination learning: a levels-of-functioning explanation. (Reese H W & Lipsitt L P, eds.) *Advances in child development and behavior.* New York: Academic Press, 1979. Vol. 13. p. 83-117.
6. **Zivin G,** ed. *The development of self-regulation through private speech.* New York: Wiley, 1979. 369 p.

This Week's Citation Classic

Hess R D & Shipman V C. Early experience and the socialization of cognitive modes in children. *Child Develop.* **36**:869-86, 1965.
[University of Chicago, Chicago, IL]

Many studies document a correlation between children's achievement and SES of their families, but mediating processes are obscure. Variations in mother-child interaction among three groups drawn from different SES backgrounds are described. We argue that social environment affects family interaction in ways that influence school achievement. [The *Social Sciences Citation Index*® (*SSCI*™) **indicates that this paper has been cited over 250 times since 1966.]**

Robert D. Hess
School of Education
Stanford University
Stanford, CA 94303

April 28, 1981

"Writing an article is a bit like rearing a child—one does one's best but the results sometimes depend on circumstances beyond one's control. This paper was timely and presented data not available in the mid-1960s. We are surprised and pleased that it continues to be referenced.

"The article came from research motivated, in part, by issues raised during the 'War on Poverty' of the early 1960s. It was an attempt to analyze social and economic deprivation as conditions that shape family interaction and regulate the development of school-relevant skills in young children. It is related, conceptually, to analyses of the influence of family background on cognitive development and achievement in school.

"There was an unusual excitement in the mid-1960s in this sort of research. Much of the empirical work on early learning of school-related skills was conducted in nursery schools attached to universities and thus represented data from upper middle, often academic, families. We knew very little about interaction and cognitive development in low income families and even less about Black families. Given the political and social context, the work had a particular relevance. There was a general sense of educational injustice and discrimination against Blacks and against the poor in the US. A spirit of crusade was in the air; we were exhilarated by the relevance of our research to social problems. Unfortunately, the high hopes we had for amelioration of educational inequality haven't been fulfilled. Things haven't changed much. Fortunately, the theoretical issues and data of this article are not limited to a particular population or social climate.

"This paper was one of several prepared from a study of cognitive environments of urban Black children.[1] The study was intended to provide specific information about family environments that could be used in planning intervention programs for children from low-income communities. Our colleagues on this project were Jere Brophy and Roberta Bear.

"The article was originally one of four papers prepared for a symposium presented at the AAAS meetings in Montreal in 1964. It would probably not have been written without the occasion of a symposium. The data presented are preliminary and do not include results that we obtained later that seem to confirm our hypothesis of a connection between social class and school achievement through early socialization in the family setting.[2] Its popularity comes, we suspect, from the attractiveness of family interaction research and the heightened interest in the 1960s in social reform through early intervention. It was this social and political climate that produced Head Start and other national programs of early education. We like to think that the article deserves such widespread recognition, but we suspect that it was a matter of saying something useful at the right place and the right time. More recent work in the field is to appear in *Families as Learning Environments for Children*."[3]

1. **Hess R D & Shipman V.** Cognitive elements in maternal behavior. (Hill J P, ed.) *Minnesota symposia on child psychology.* Minneapolis, MN: University of Minnesota Press, 1967. Vol. 1. p. 57-81.
2. **Hess R D.** Maternal behavior and the development of reading readiness in urban Negro children. (Douglass M P, ed.) *Claremont reading conference thirty-second yearbook.* Claremont, CA: Claremont University Center, 1968. p. 83-99.
3. **Hess R D, Holloway S D, Price G G & Dickson W P.** Family environments and acquisition of reading skills: toward a more precise analysis. (Laosa L M & Sigel I, eds.) *Families as learning environments for children.* New York: Plenum. In press, 1981.

CC/NUMBER 51
DECEMBER 17, 1979

This Week's Citation Classic

Hunt J M. *Intelligence and experience.* New York: Ronald, 1961. 416 p.

This book assembled the evidence against the beliefs that intelligence is essentially fixed and that development is predetermined by each individual's heredity. The evidence supported plasticity in development and suggested that, once the adaptive interaction between young individuals and their environmental circumstances are better understood, it should be possible to increase the average level of intelligence within the population substantially, as then and now measured, by something like 30 points of IQ. [The *Science Citation Index*® (*SCI*®) **and the** *Social Sciences Citation Index*™ (*SSCI*™) **indicate that this book has been cited over 490 times since 1961.]**

J. McVicker Hunt
Department of Psychology
University of Illinois
Champaign, IL 61820

October 12, 1979

"The first draft of this book was originally written in the summer of 1957 as a chapter for an intended book on behavioral science and child rearing. I undertook the latter book because I learned while serving as director of the Institute of Welfare Research at the Community Service Society of New York that the counsel given to parents by professional people varied radically. When I suggested that someone should examine the literature of the behavioral sciences for empirical evidence relevant to assertions about child rearing, Donald Young, then executive director of the Russell Sage Foundation, agreed and encouraged me to do it with Sage support.

"Because of my background in psychopathology and personality development in the theoretical terms of a synthesis of behaviorism with psychoanalysis, I had expected to focus on the emotional and motivational aspects of psychological development. But, I was committed to a serious scrutiny of the investigative literature. That scrutiny greatly altered my beliefs about what is important in early experience,[1] demonstrated for me the inadequacy of the drive theory shared by Hullian behavior theory and psychoanalysis,[2] and reversed my beliefs that the rate of cognitive development is largely set by heredity and that intelligence is fixed.

"When it became evident that the chapters of the intended book were each approaching book length, I focused, in the spring of 1960, with support from the Commonwealth Fund, on revising and elaborating the chapter on the development of intelligence which I defined as the adaptive abilities, habits, knowledge, and skills which can be observed and measured. My task was to focus the evidence against the beliefs in fixed intelligence and predetermined development and to indicate the implications. In *The Children's Cause*, G.Y. Steiner has credited this book with a share of the influence on the decision of Presidents Kennedy and Johnson to launch Project Head Start.[3] Subsequent research, some of it my own,[4] has shown the empirical 'range of reaction' to rearing conditions to be even greater than I had expected. The new evidence thereby fortifies the thesis of this book, yet arguments based on evidence from 'heritability' indices from such as Arthur Jensen sustain the old debate over the relative potency of heredity and environment."

1. **Hunt J M.** Developmental psychology: early experience. *Annu. Rev. Psychol.* **30**:103-43, 1979.
2. **Hunt J M.** Intrinsic motivation and its role in psychological development. *Nebr. Symp. Motiv.* **13**:189-282, 1965.
3. **Steiner G Y.** *The children's cause.* Washington, DC: Brookings Institution, 1976. 265 p.
4. **Hunt J M, Mohandessi K, Ghodssi M & Akiyama M.** The psychological development of orphanage reared infants: interventions with outcomes (Tehran). *Genet. Psychol. Monogr.* **94**:177-226, 1976.

This Week's Citation Classic

MacKinnon D W. The nature and nurture of creative talent.
Amer. Psychol. **17**:484-95, 1962.
[University of California, Berkeley, CA]

The meaning of creativity is explored. Three nationwide samples of architects, differing in levels of creativeness, are described in terms of assessment findings and revealed life history correlates of creativity. The implications of the research findings for the nurturing of creative potential are discussed. [The *Science Citation Index*® (*SCI*®) **and the** *Social Sciences Citation Index*® (*SSCI*®) **indicate that this paper has been cited over 195 times since 1962.]**

Donald W. MacKinnon
Department of Psychology
University of California
Berkeley, CA 94720

October 13, 1981

"It was from Henry A. Murray at the Harvard Psychological Clinic that I first experienced the excitement of studying persons and their lives. And it was again with Murray on the assessment staff of the Office of Strategic Services during World War II that I became fascinated by the problem of what in the person and what in the life history makes an individual become a highly effective person.

"The question was stirred by finding again and again that candidates of the most extraordinary effectiveness had had in childhood and adolescence the kinds of frustrations, deprivations, and traumatic experiences that would have led us in the light of the then accepted theory of personality to predict that they would have become crippled personalities.

"I returned to my academic post with a strong desire to establish through research a more adequate formulation of the development process by which potentialities of human development are realized.

"The chance to do this came with the establishment of the Institute of Personality Assessment and Research on the Berkeley campus of the University of California in 1949, thanks to a grant from the Rockefeller Foundation. The expressed purpose of the institute was to develop further the assessment method not for purposes of selection but for basic research into problems of personality development and dynamics with special focus on the characteristics of effective persons and the life history determinants of their effectiveness.

"I had the privilege of directing the institute for 21 years (1949-1970) in its studies of highly effective persons in a variety of fields—writers, architects, research scientists, mathematicians, *et al.*

"The research reported in this paper, like all of my best research, had been done as a member of a collective, the other members of which in our creativity studies were Frank Barron, Kenneth H. Craik, Richard S. Crutchfield, Harrison G. Gough, Wallace B. Hall, and Ravenna M. Mathews.[1-3]

"The kind of research that is described in the paper requires a home-like building in which staff and assessers live together during assessments that run for several days. We were fortunate to have as our institute a fraternity house remodeled to meet the needs of an assessment center. Bringing highly creative persons to our institute for study from all over the US was an expensive operation made possible by a grant from the Carnegie Corporation of New York.

"I believe there are several reasons why the paper has been so highly cited. It was written in English, not psychological jargon. It reports on a topic of wide interest, creativity, appealing to laypersons as well as to scientists in many fields. It was given prominence as one of the series of Walter Van Dyke Bingham lectures on 'the discovery of the talented' sponsored by the American Psychological Association. It has been frequently reprinted in 'collections' of papers and in 'readings' for students. Recent papers in this field have been published by myself and F. Barron and D.M. Harrington."[4,5]

1. **Barron F.** The creative writer. *California Monthly* **72**:11-14; 38-9, 1962.
2. **Gough H G & Woodworth D G.** Stylistic variations among professional research scientists. *J. Psychology* **49**:87-98, 1960.
3. **Helson R & Crutchfield R S.** Creative types in mathematics. *J. Personality* **38**:177-97, 1970.
4. **MacKinnon D W.** Sigmund Freud, Carl Jung, and Otto Rank: some implications of their work for the understanding of creativity. (Gryskiewicz S S, ed.) *Creativity week II, 1979 proceedings.* Greensboro, NC: Center for Creative Leadership, 1980. p. 4-26.
5. **Barron F & Harrington D M.** Creativity, intelligence and personality. *Annu. Rev. Psychol.* **32**:439-76, 1981.

This Week's Citation Classic™

Stein A H & Bailey M M. The socialization of achievement orientation in females. *Psychol. Bull.* **80**:345-66, 1973.
[Pennsylvania State University, University Park, PA]

The literature on females' achievement-related behavior was reviewed by examining the effects of sex role expectations, parental socialization practices, and related personal dispositions such as anxiety about failure and locus of control. The hypothesis that affiliation is a primary goal of females' achievement striving was challenged. [The *Social Sciences Citation Index*® (*SSCI*®) indicates that this paper has been cited in over 175 publications since 1973.]

Aletha C. Huston
Department of Human Development
University of Kansas
Lawrence, KS 66045

January 9, 1984

"The mid-1960s, when I finished graduate school, was an exciting time of national ferment about poverty, racism, and equal opportunity. One hypothesis proposed by educators and social critics of the time was that boys' academic motivation was impaired because they considered school a feminine environment. That notion seemed overly simple to me. Instead, I proposed that children learn to view some areas of school achievement as feminine and others as masculine, and that the motivation of both genders in particular domains of school achievement is affected by these sex role concepts.

"This line of reasoning led to a series of studies investigating the development of sex role concepts about achievement and the effects of such concepts on achievement behavior.[1,2] That work provided the scholarly roots of this *Citation Classic*™. But the social movements of the early 1970s played an equally important role in the final product. The women's movement brought an awareness of females' 'disadvantage' in education and ultimate achievement. Social scientists also began to recognize that most psychological theories applied more accurately to men than to women, partly because the theories were formulated about men in the first place. That was certainly true of McClelland's[3] classic early work on achievement motivation which was confined almost entirely to males, partly because initial studies failed to confirm the theory for females.

"At Pennsylvania State University, a group of women graduate students organized a seminar on the psychology of women, and one of them, Peggy Bailey, worked closely with me. We wrote this review of the literature, attempting some theoretical formulations about female achievement orientations. One of the most controversial aspects of the paper is a challenge to the widespread belief that females' achievement efforts are motivated primarily by the need for affiliation or for social approval. We concluded instead that females' achievement efforts are often focused on different content domains than those of males; one of those content domains is social skill.

"This research has been widely cited because it was part of a major reorientation of personality theory by scholars interested in females. It was followed in the journal by Constantinople's[4] seminal challenge to the assumptions underlying previous measures of femininity and masculinity. The psychology of women as a field was born in that period. Research on sex-typing since that time bears the stamp of new ways of conceptualizing the processes involved."[5]

1. **Stein A H.** The effects of sex-role standards for achievement and sex-role preference on three determinants of achievement motivation. *Develop. Psychol.* 4:219-31, 1971. (Cited 35 times.)
2. **Stein A H, Pohly S R & Mueller E.** The influence of masculine, feminine, and neutral tasks on children's achievement behavior, expectancies of success, and attainment values. *Child Develop.* **42**:195-207, 1971. (Cited 60 times.)
3. **McClelland D C, Atkinson J W, Clark R A & Lowell E L.** *The achievement motive.* New York: Appleton-Century-Crofts, 1953. 384 p. (Cited 900 times.)
4. **Constantinople A.** Masculinity-femininity: an exception to a famous dictum? *Psychol. Bull.* **80**:389-407, 1973. (Cited 235 times.)
5. **Huston A C.** Sex typing. (Mussen P H & Hetherington E M, eds.) *Handbook of child psychology. Volume 4. Socialization, personality, and social development.* New York: Wiley, 1983. p. 387-467.

CC/NUMBER 29
JULY 19, 1982

This Week's Citation Classic

Bowlby J. *Attachment and loss. Volume I. Attachment.* London: Hogarth Press; New York: Basic Books, 1969. 428 p.

Attachment theory is a way of conceptualizing the propensity of children to remain in proximity to a mother-figure, behaviour formerly conceived of as 'dependency.' Organized cybernetically, the behaviour is activated by pain, hunger, fatigue, and anything frightening and terminated by sight, sound, or touch of the attachment figure. It is associated with strong emotion and postulated to promote the child's safety. [The *Social Sciences Citation Index®* **(*SSCI®*) indicates that this book has been cited in over 905 publications since 1969.]**

John Bowlby
Tavistock Clinic
120 Belsize Lane
London NW3 5BA
England

March 4, 1982

"Working as a child psychiatrist before World War II, I was struck by the high incidence of seriously disrupted mother-child relationships during the early years of delinquent and psychopathic children, and published a monograph on the subject.[1] I then spent five years as an army psychiatrist.

"When I returned to child psychiatry, at the Tavistock Clinic, I set up a small unit to research the effects on young children of separation from mother. In the course of the project, James Robertson, then my research assistant, made naturalistic observations of the responses of children between the ages of one and four years before, during, and after stays in residential nurseries and hospitals. These observations led to our generalization of the responses as those of protest, despair, and detachment. I also wrote a report for the World Health Organization entitled *Maternal Care and Mental Health*,[2] in which the ill-effects of maternal deprivation are described.

"A principal problem was how to understand the intense anxiety and distress observed during and after these separations, and hence how to conceptualize the tie the disruption of which was clearly responsible.

"In the early-1950s, it was widely held that a child becomes interested in his mother only because she feeds him. Two kinds of drive were postulated, primary and secondary. Food is thought of as primary; the personal relationship, referred to as dependency, as secondary. Since this does not fit the facts, I cast around for an alternative. A friend mentioned Lorenz's work on the following response of goslings.[3] This led me to study ethology.

"In July 1957 I presented a paper[4] in which an early version of attachment theory was proposed. This was followed by further papers applying ethological principles to problems of personality development and psychopathology. By the early-1960s, however, it was clear that these papers were inadequate and I began drafting what I believed would be a single volume to be called *Attachment and Loss*. In the writing it became a trilogy, with the second and third volumes entitled *Separation: Anxiety and Anger*[5] and *Loss: Sadness and Depression*.[6] In writing these volumes I benefitted enormously from contributions made by colleagues; for *Attachment*, those of Mary Ainsworth were invaluable.[7]

"*Attachment* has been translated into Italian, German, Japanese, Spanish, French, and Portuguese (in preparation).

"I believe *Attachment* has become a *Citation Classic* because it presents a new paradigm for understanding the socioemotional development of children, adolescents, and adults; has promoted fruitful research, notably in developmental psychology, ethology, and psychiatry; and has provided guidelines for practice to the caring professions.

"For a recent evaluation of attachment theory see Rajecki and others.[8]

"For my work in this field I have received the G. Stanley Hall Medal of the American Psychological Association (1974), and the Distinguished Scientific Contributions Award from the Society for Research in Child Development (1981)."

1. **Bowlby J.** *Forty-four juvenile thieves: their characters and home life.* London: Bailliere, Tindall & Cox, 1946. 56 p.
2. ------------. *Maternal care and mental health.* Geneva: World Health Organization, 1952. 194 p.
3. **Lorenz K.** Der Kumpan in der Umvelt des Vogels. *J. Orn. Berlin* **83**:137-213; 289-413, 1935. [English translation: Companionship in bird life. (Schiller C H, ed.) *Instinctive behavior: the development of a modern concept.* New York: International Universities Press, 1957. p. 83-128.]
4. **Bowlby J.** The nature of the child's tie to his mother. *Int. J. Psychoanal.* **39**:350-73, 1958.
5. ------------. *Attachment and loss. Volume II. Separation: anxiety and anger.* London: Hogarth Press; New York: Basic Books, 1973. 456 p. [The *SSCI* indicates that this book has been cited in over 390 publications since 1973.]
6. ------------. *Attachment and loss. Volume III. Loss: sadness and depression.* London: Hogarth Press; New York: Basic Books, 1980. 472 p.
7. **Ainsworth M D S.** *Infancy in Uganda: infant care and the growth of attachment.* Baltimore, MD: Johns Hopkins Press, 1967. 471 p.
8. **Rajecki D W, Lamb M E & Obmascher P.** Towards a general theory of infantile attachment: a comparative review of aspects of the social bond. *Behav. Brain Sci.* **3**:417-64, 1978.

CC/NUMBER 38
SEPTEMBER 19, 1983

This Week's Citation Classic

Allen K E, Hart B, Buell J S, Harris F R & Wolf M M. Effects of social reinforcement on isolate behavior of a nursery school child. *Child Develop.* **35**:511-18, 1964.
[Developmental Psychology Laboratory, University of Washington, Seattle, WA]

Using a ten-second observational sampling system, the nursery-school teachers of a four-year-old demonstrated that systematic and discriminative timing of their attention resulted in desirable changes in the child's social interactions with peers. Random post-checks throughout the school year indicated the changes were durable. [The *Science Citation Index*® (*SCI*®) and the *Social Sciences Citation Index*® (*SSCI*®) indicate that this paper has been cited in over 200 publications since 1964.]

K. Eileen Allen
Department of Human Development
and Family Life
University of Kansas
Lawrence, KS 66045

July 15, 1983

"Ann was a four-year-old in the Developmental Psychology Laboratory Preschool at the University of Washington, where I was head teacher. The other teachers and I were concerned about her: instead of playing with other children, she withdrew from them, clung to adults, and displayed disturbing tic-like behaviors. Giving her increased amounts of nurturing support—a traditional approach—only made the problem worse. Finally, we consulted with Mont Wolf, a research associate working with the preschool staff. The consultation led to a collaborative study showing that teachers, by differentially timing their interactions with a child, could produce dramatic changes.

"What made this study a landmark? It defied tradition. First, it was a pioneer effort at Single N research in a naturalistic setting: 'little old nursery-school teachers' (as we were described by one psychologist) carried out exacting experimental work while conducting an exemplary preschool program. 'Collecting data on the hoof'—recording observations as we worked with children—is a term I coined that was widely associated with these studies. Second, it was among the first studies to detail an experimentally rigorous approach to analyzing a child's social-emotional responses. We broke ground by rejecting Freudian psychodynamics and maturational determinism. Instead, we defined children's reactions operationally and so were able to quantify and then record them in a ten-second time-sampling observation system that produced a high degree of interrater reliability.

"The traditional child-development people scorned us as heretics—as experimentalists tampering with the fragile psyches of little children. But others received our study enthusiastically, partly because it appeared just when the application of Skinnerian methods to clinical and educational problems was causing a great stir. Since the appearance of this first study, our heresy has become an orthodoxy: it and the many studies that followed have been widely reprinted, stimulating replications and methodological elaborations in the US and abroad.

"For the authors, this pioneering work became the springboard for many years of research, application, and dissemination. For example, my own first text[1] presents behavioral procedures as the common base for an interdisciplinary team approach to treating developmental problems. (In 1980, this text received an award of excellence from the American Medical Writers Association.) Two other texts[2,3] are practical translations of applied research of the Edna A. Hill Child Development Laboratory Preschools at the University of Kansas, where I have been a member of the faculty since 1974. Now—nearly 20 years and goodness knows how many children since Ann and that first study—Betty Hart (the second author of the early study) and I have distilled even further what children and our research have taught us; in this latest effort,[4] we describe how to arrange what we believe to be the optimum learning environment for young children."

1. **Allen K E, Holm V A & Schiefelbusch R L**, eds. *Early intervention: a team approach.* Baltimore, MD: University Park Press, 1978. 489 p.
2. **Allen K E & Goetz E M**, eds. *Early childhood education: special problems, special solutions.* Rockville, MD: Aspen Systems Corp., 1982. 349 p.
3. **Goetz E M & Allen K E**, eds. *Early childhood education: special environmental, policy and legal considerations.* Rockville, MD: Aspen Systems Corp., 1983. 341 p.
4. **Allen K E & Hart B.** *The early years—arrangements for learning.* Englewood Cliffs, NJ: Prentice Hall. To be published, 1984.

CC/NUMBER 52
DECEMBER 27, 1982

This Week's Citation Classic

Peterson D R. Behavior problems of middle childhood.
J. Consult. Psychol. **25**:205-9, 1961.
[University of Illinois, IL]

A procedure for assessing children's behavior disorders was developed by recording the presenting problems of children at a psychological clinic, selecting the most common problems, ordering those into a checklist, factor analyzing ratings, and examining the descriptive properties of the problem patterns that emerged. [The *Social Sciences Citation Index*® (*SSCI*®) indicates that this paper has been cited in over 170 publications since 1966.]

Donald R. Peterson
Graduate School of Applied and
Professional Psychology
Rutgers University
New Brunswick, NJ 08903

November 3, 1982

"In the 1950s, a group of us at the University of Illinois began to study parent-child relationships. We wanted to examine the ways parents treated their children and what those conditions had to do with the problems children displayed. Methods then available for assessing children's problems were primitive, and I took as my part of the project the task of designing better instruments. We tried several procedures—a battery of objective tests, an orally administered questionnaire, and some new projective techniques. The objective tests were a complete flop, awkward to administer and uncorrelated with any of the criteria we studied. The questionnaire and the other tests failed too. Of all the measures we tried, the only one that stood the test of further research was the behavior problem checklist. When I finished the report of its development, I thought I had done a workmanlike job, but saw nothing special about it.

"I still feel that way. I suppose the checklist is used as much as it is because it offers an economical way to get reasonably dependable information about something that matters. The instrument was carefully constructed. It started from the problems children actually displayed rather than any theory. My Minnesota empiricism might have had something to do with that. The factors that emerged were efficient and stable. My work with Ray Cattell had taught me how important those matters were. Of its kind, it was, and I believe still is, the best instrument available.

"Later, as I thought more about the assessment of human problems, the limitations of procedures like these began to glare in my mind. Behavior, I came to believe, could only be understood in its social context. The very concept of 'trait' was questionable. An entirely new approach to assessment, directed toward the study of functional process and the linkage of assessment with change, seemed the way to go. I expressed these ideas in a book[1] and in the process repudiated my 'classic' checklist procedure and all others like it. I did no further research along the earlier lines, and I suspect the checklist would have sunk into oblivion if it had not been for Herb Quay, one of my colleagues in the original work on parent-child relationships, a collaborator in the study of delinquency, and a lifelong friend. Quay refused to go along with my exclusive Functionalism. He continued to use the checklist in his own research, developed it further, and encouraged his students to do likewise.

"By now, I have come around to the view that there is, after all, a place in psychology for trait concepts and carefully designed measures of personality, although I still maintain that the study of process and change[2] is more useful than any personality 'snapshots' can be. Quay and I recently collaborated on a manual for the checklist[3] and are currently revising the procedure to suit the problems of the 1980s and the facts we now know about them."

1. **Peterson D R.** *The clinical study of social behavior.* New York: Appleton-Century-Crofts, 1968. 254 p.
[The *SSCI* indicates that this book has been cited in over 100 publications since 1968.]
2. ----------------. Functional analysis of interpersonal behavior. (Anchin J C & Kiesler D J, eds.)
Handbook of interpersonal psychotherapy. New York: Pergamon Press, 1982. p. 149-67.
3. **Quay H C & Peterson D R.** *Manual for the behavior problem checklist.* (Manuscript.)
New Brunswick, NJ: Graduate School of Applied and Professional Psychology, Rutgers University, 1979. 20 p.

CC/NUMBER 6
FEBRUARY 8, 1982

This Week's Citation Classic

Warren J R. Birth order and social behavior. *Psychol. Bull.* **65**:38-49, 1966.
[College Student Personnel Institute, Claremont, CA]

Eminence, college attendance, intellectual achievement, and social responsiveness are more common among firstborn than later children. Schizophrenia, alcoholism, and delinquency are more common among the later born. Yet the evidence for those assertions is confused, and their implications are more cloudy still. [The *Science Citation Index*® **(***SCI*®**) and the** *Social Sciences Citation Index*® **(***SSCI*®**) indicate that this paper has been cited over 190 times since 1966.]**

Jonathan R. Warren
Educational Testing Service
Berkeley, CA 94704

December 3, 1981

"While at the University of Nebraska in the early-1960s I was struck with the seriousness of purpose of the eldest sons coming from the farm to the College of Agriculture. Schachter's book[1] had recently appeared and sharpened my interest in the psychological effects of birth order and in the mechanisms that produced them. At a College of Agriculture seminar, I learned that rotifers, microscopic water animals, became less robust with increasing age of the mother. Since then, biochemical changes in human mothers have been found to be associated with age and number of pregnancies. Physiological origins of birth order effects cannot be dismissed, although current explanations tend to focus on family structure and intrafamilial relationships. This interplay of influences represented by a deceptively simple and easily observed concept may account for the appeal of birth order as a topic of study. Further, like sex, age, and birth date, everyone has it, and like birth date can attribute mystical powers to it, such as those of the seventh son of a seventh son. Benjamin Franklin took great satisfaction in being the youngest son of a youngest son for five generations. Daughters in those days had no apparent importance.

"People are intrigued on learning that Rhodes scholars show the expected overrepresentation of firstborns, no one from the seventh through twelfth birth positions, and then abruptly two thirteenth children. They then recall eminent people such as Samuel Taylor Coleridge who were thirteenth children. But while Coleridge was his father's thirteenth child, he was his mother's tenth. Myth gives greater weight to birth order counted from the father, as with the seventh son of a seventh son. Modern theory, such as that suggested by the rotifers, gives greater weight to the order counted from the mother.

"Birth order is a concept in which physiological, psychological, and social influences merge, making its study both complicated and potentially revealing. The age of the mother, the number of previous pregnancies, the spacing between children, the order of the sexes among siblings, the greater tendency for later born to be raised by single parents, and the density of the family structure in terms of age, may all contribute to the effects of birth order. Zajonc[2] has proposed that birth order affects intellectual achievement through the greater proportion of less mature persons in large families. While currently the most widely discussed theory in the birth order literature, the evidence is mixed.

"The attention given in the cited article to the complexity of birth order may account for its frequent citation. I would like to believe that it had influenced people to respect that complexity, yet only a few of the hundreds of studies of the past decade have done so. Are the schizophrenogenic properties of a late order of birth due to the physiological and biochemical environment of a heavily used uterus or to the social environment of a large family? And through what mechanism does either influence act? Recent advances in the analysis of data organized into ordered categories make questions like these more tractable than they have previously been."

1. **Schachter S.** *The psychology of affiliation: experimental studies of the sources of gregariousness.* Stanford, CA: Stanford University Press, 1959. 141 p.
2. **Zajonc R B.** Family configuration and intelligence. *Science* **192**:227-36, 1976.

Schooler C. Birth order effects: not here, not now! *Psychol. Bull.* **78**:161-75, 1972.
[National Institute of Mental Health, Bethesda, MD]

A review of published and unpublished birth order data reveals almost no reliable evidence for birth order effects among men living in the US in the mid-1960s, and only a marginal increase in such evidence when such restrictions in time, place, and sex are removed. [The *Social Sciences Citation Index*® (*SSCI*®) indicates that this paper has been cited in over 150 publications since 1972.]

Carmi Schooler
Laboratory of Socio-Environmental Studies
National Institute of Mental Health
9000 Rockville Pike
Bethesda, MD 20205

January 6, 1984

"At the National Institute of Mental Health in the early 1960s, I was involved in investigating the effects of social interaction on the functioning of chronic schizophrenics. One of the approaches I took was to modify social psychological experiments that had been done with normal subjects in ways that I hoped would explain the nature of schizophrenics' aversion to social interaction. An especially logical candidate for modification was Schachter's[1] experiment on affiliative behavior. Since his findings seemed to indicate that later-born individuals were less affiliative when anxious, it was a natural extension to test the possibility that schizophrenics are likely to be later-born.

"At about the same time, I worked with William Caudill on a study of symptom patterns in Japanese mental patients. Caudill predicted that Japanese culture would interact with birth order to produce different symptom patterns. Several papers I wrote in the mid-1960s supplied confirmatory evidence for both strands of thought. However, subsequent more carefully controlled analyses on better samples did not replicate the earlier findings. In addition, the more I thought about it and the more I read, the more likely it began to appear that my original findings were due to the absence of controls for such relevant factors as social class and changing trends in family size. As my doubts mounted, I decided to search the literature thoroughly to see whether there were any reported birth order effects that would hold up to reasonable scrutiny. 'Birth order effects: not here, not now!' was the result.

"In that paper I concluded, 'The general lack of consistent findings...leaves real doubt as to whether the chance of positive results is worth the heavy investment needed to carry out any more definitive studies. On the other hand, I suspect that...investigators, including myself, will not be able to resist the temptation of taking a cheap bet on a long shot by collecting birth order data on their subjects as they pursue studies more central to their interests.' (p. 174) The fact that the article has been cited often enough to become a *Citation Classic*™ attests to the irresistibility of the temptation. Whether the bet has paid off is another matter. Zajonc and Markus received the 1975 AAAS Social Psychology Award for their confluence model of birth order effects on intellectual functioning.[2] On the other hand, in 1982 after extensively reviewing the evidence, Galbraith concluded, 'The contribution to date of the confluence models to understanding intellectual development (and the birth order puzzle) may best be described as 'Not here, not yet.'[3] (p. 173)"

1. **Schachter S.** *The psychology of affiliation: experimental studies of the sources of gregariousness.* Stanford, CA: Stanford University Press, 1959. 141 p.
2. **Zajonc R B & Markus G B.** Birth order and intellectual development. *Psychol. Rev.* **82**:74-85, 1975.
3. **Galbraith R C.** Sibling spacing intelligence and the confluence model. *Develop. Psychol.* **18**:151-73, 1982.

CC/NUMBER 48
NOVEMBER 26, 1984

This Week's Citation Classic™

Marcia J E. Development and validation of ego identity status.
J. Personal. Soc. Psychol. **3**:551-8, 1966.
[State University of New York, Buffalo, NY]

Four ways of resolving the late adolescent identity crisis, described by Erik Erikson, were identified and some of their empirical implications determined. 'Identity Achievement' and 'Moratoriums' were cognitively flexible under stress. 'Foreclosures' were authoritarian and set unrealistically high goals. 'Identity Diffusions' had difficulty thinking under stress. [The *Social Sciences Citation Index*® (*SSCI*®) indicates that this paper has been cited in over 185 publications since 1966.]

James E. Marcia
Simon Fraser University
Department of Psychology
Burnaby, British Columbia V5A 1S6
Canada

September 13, 1984

"This study was an attempt to integrate the scientific spirit permeating my graduate work at Ohio State University with the rich clinical experience of my psychoanalytically oriented internship at Massachusetts Mental Health Center. It was done in order to meet the immediate demands of completing a doctoral dissertation.

"As part of my internship, I was assigned a 16-year-old boy for psychodiagnostics. His test protocol looked 'schizophrenic'; however, three months later, he was discharged in complete remission. That outcome wasn't consistent with my fledgling understanding of schizophrenia. My supervisor, Dave Guttman, was teaching a seminar for Erik Erikson at Harvard and suggested that I read 'Identity and the life cycle'[1] in order to understand identity diffusion. I found Erikson's theory to be a useful link between academic scientific psychology and clinically relevant but untested psychoanalytic propositions. I decided to do my dissertation on the most singular aspect of Erikson's theory: ego identity.

"I presented my first attempt at a research design to Julian Rotter's research team; it went badly. A second fared better, although a good friend and fellow graduate student, Jay Efran, warned me that trying to validate a construct as complex as identity was, even if possible, not practical. Doug Crowne was willing to act as my chairman in the dubious enterprise.

"By interviewing 20 male college students, I found exceptions to the original dichotomy of identity versus identity diffusion. Two types of identity were formed—Identity Achievement, exhibited by those who had made their own choices, and Foreclosure, exhibited by those who had merely followed parental dictates. Similarly, two types of identity diffusion were seen—Moratoriums, shown by those who were struggling and concerned, and Identity Diffusion, shown by those who were floundering and unconcerned.

"The next task was to construct and establish the reliability of an identity status interview and scoring manual, as well as an overall measure of identity—the Ego Identity Incomplete Sentence Blank. Four pilot studies later, I was ready to choose some dependent variables for validating the new identity status constructs. These were concept attainment under stressful conditions (necessitating a fifth pilot study), resistance to self-esteem manipulation, authoritarianism, and level of aspiration. The results of these studies both confirmed the high-low identity distribution and established some discriminant validity for the individual statuses. Although the Foreclosure status didn't emerge as distinctly as I had hoped, George Kelly suggested that I not drop it, which was good advice in light of subsequent research findings.

"I think that the appeal of the identity status approach, aside from its established validity, is its usefulness for understanding such a complex psychological process as identity development and its translatability into clinical work. While the interview method requires time and training, it allows the researcher an in-depth look at his/her subjects and their individual developmental pathways. It is a method that respects both the researcher's skill and the subject's complexity.

"My current research and that of my students involves expansion of the identity status constructs[2] as well as the development of measures of other Eriksonian stages."

1. **Erikson E H.** Identity and the life cycle. (Whole issue.) *Psychol. Issues* **1**(1), 1959. 171 p. (Cited 355 times since 1959.)
2. **Marcia J E.** Identity in adolescence. (Adelson J, ed.) *Handbook of adolescent psychology.* New York: Wiley, 1980. p. 159-87.

This Week's Citation Classic

CC/NUMBER 16
APRIL 20, 1981

Bell R Q. A reinterpretation of the direction of effects in studies of socialization. *Psychol. Rev.* 75:81-95, 1968.
[Child Research Branch, Natl. Inst. Mental Health, Rockville, MD]

The effects of children on parents can no longer be dismissed as a logical but implausible interpretation of nondirectional associations found between parent and child behaviors. A model for explaining existing findings as due to child effects is presented. [The *Social Sciences Citation Index*® (*SSCI*™) **indicates that this paper has been cited over 170 times since 1968.]**

Richard Q. Bell
Alcohol, Drug Abuse, and
Mental Health Administration
10 C 24 Parklawn Building
5600 Fishers Lane
Rockville, MD 20857

March 30, 1981

"It was in a teasing and provocative mood that I set out to write this paper for presentation at a conference on socialization in 1964, one that would be attended by some of the leading scientists who had spent their entire careers studying correlations between child and parent behaviors in order to find evidence of parent effects on children. For each of the few consistent correlations that had come out of over 40 years of research, I supplied a plausible explanation consisting of an effect of children on parents. I was completely surprised at the response to my paper when it was presented. Instead of setting off a wave of criticism and rebuttal, I received very favorable reactions, comments to the effect that the corrective viewpoint was long overdue.

"The paper was held up for three years waiting for a book on the conference to materialize. I finally withdrew it and sent it to the *Psychological Review*. I expected a bitter battle with reviewers, but the paper was quickly accepted with only minimal changes. By that time it had undergone several revisions as a result of reactions from many colloquium audiences. I had put the hypotheses into the context of a model which would accommodate parents' expectations for their children, their values, and attitudes. The model would explain a lot of existing findings, and later generated new hypotheses,[1] research designs,[2] and a way of accommodating reciprocal effects.[3]

"At the time I submitted that first paper the model was just beginning to convince me too! It was no longer a logical exercise. However, even I had been subject to the extreme and illogical cultural compulsion of American psychology to see the environment as all powerful (in this case, the parents). Thus I needed the three year delay to perfect my argument, and time to reassure myself that I was right. The environmentalism was illogical because it caused us to overlook the fact that the child is a potent part of the environment for the parent!

"The paper came out at a time when there was dissatisfaction with the existing unproductive approach. The typical expedient study had consisted in identifying children with different characteristics, then interviewing or observing their parents in order to see what they had done to produce these characteristics. The field was ready to move on with the more difficult task of experimentally altering or in other ways varying parent and child behavior to test hypotheses in a more definitive way. It is this which accounts for the paper's frequent citation."

1. **Bell R Q & Harper L V.** *Child effects on adults.* New York: Halsted Press, 1977. 253 p.
2. **Bell R Q.** Parent, child, and reciprocal influences: new experimental approaches (introduction to a symposium). *J. Abnormal Child Psychol.* In press, 1981.
3. ----------. Parent, child, and reciprocal influences. *Amer. Psychol.* **34**:821-6, 1979.

CC/NUMBER 27
JULY 4, 1983

This Week's Citation Classic

Bronfenbrenner U. Toward an experimental ecology of human development. *Amer. Psychol.* **32**:513-31, 1977. [Cornell University, Ithaca, NY]

The proposed theoretical perspective emphasizes using rigorously designed naturalistic and planned experiments for studying development in the actual environments, both immediate and more remote, in which people live. The evolving reciprocal relation between person and environment through life is conceptualized and operationalized in systems terms. [The *Social Sciences Citation Index*® (*SSCI*®) **indicates that this paper has been cited in over 175 publications since 1977.]**

Urie Bronfenbrenner
Department of Human Development
and Family Studies
Cornell University
Ithaca, NY 14853

April 28, 1983

"The ideas presented in this article have their origins in both manifest and latent content. In the former sphere, I am most indebted to my first teacher in psychology, Frank S. Freeman (who taught, as I do now, at Cornell University). Freeman's course and text, *Individual Differences*,[1] presented an interactionist view that was decades ahead of its time, and perhaps still of ours.

"It was also Freeman who enrolled me in a one-student course in which he assigned several works then quite alien to the psychology curriculum, including the three chapters by Lewin, Piaget, and Freud published in the first *A Handbook of Child Psychology*.[2] In the fourth edition of this same handbook, Ann Crouter and I[3] show that the complex multilevel conceptions of organism-environment interaction I set forth in the original article, and the volume that followed,[4] stem from the revolutionary ideas of these paradigm makers, and the subsequent transformations of their ideas in empirical work. The designation of my 1977 article as a *Citation Classic* pays honor to these paradigm makers and their equally creative interpreters. For what I did was to synthesize the emerging paradigms, both explicit and implicit, into a larger whole—a system of systems within systems, like a set of nested Russian dolls.

"In my work I have tried to show that research based on such more differentiated conceptions reveals the hitherto unrecognized power of environments to shape the course of human growth and—paradoxically—the power of human beings to adapt to, modify, and create the very environments that shape their development.

"This orientation also has roots in personal experiences: emigrating from Russia as a child, I entered school not knowing a word of English. My classmates—mostly Irish, Italians, and blacks from poor families living in a neighborhood integrated by poverty—initiated me into the world of American childhood, quite different from that of my family. The effort to integrate these 'two worlds of childhood'[5] is not difficult to detect in my research, teaching, and theory building. The effort was given new direction when a year later we moved to rural upstate New York to live on the grounds of a state institution for the then called 'feebleminded,' where my father was a neuropathologist. A superb diagnostician, he also had a PhD in zoology, and was a field naturalist at heart. The institution and its setting offered a rich biological and social terrain for his observant eye.

"It was in this third world of my childhood that my father took me on innumerable walks, through the wards, shops, and farmland—where he preferred to see and talk with his patients—and then beyond the barbed wire fence into the woods and hills that began at our doorstep. Wherever we went, he would point to the functional interdependence between living organisms and their surroundings.

"These early experiences may provide a key to an understanding of the nature and origin of the research paradigms developed and described in my recent work. These experiences may also explain why the paradigms are now being cited and applied in contemporary research. As investigators move beyond the laboratory and the testing room into the sequence of varied multiple settings that actually shape our lives, we need theoretical frameworks that permit the systematic analysis of these settings and their interrelations. It is gratifying to know that my effort to provide such a framework is proving useful to my colleagues."

1. **Freeman F S.** *Individual differences: the nature and causes of variations in intelligence and special abilities.* New York: H. Holt, 1934. 355 p.
2. **Murchison C,** ed. *A handbook of child psychology.* Worcester, MA: Clark University Press, 1931. 711 p.
3. **Bronfenbrenner U & Crouter A.** The evolution of environmental models in developmental research. (Mussen P H, ed.) *A handbook of child psychology.* New York: Wiley, 1983.
4. **Bronfenbrenner U.** *The ecology of human development: experiments by nature and design.* Cambridge, MA: Harvard University Press, 1979. 330 p.
5. ------------------------. *Two worlds of childhood: U.S. and U.S.S.R.* New York: Russell Sage Foundation, 1970. 190 p.

This Week's Citation Classic

Kagan J & Moss H A. *Birth to maturity: a study in psychological development.* New York: Wiley, 1962. 381 p.
[Fels Research Institute, Yellow Springs, OH and National Institute of Mental Health, Rockville, MD]

An analysis of the intra-individual stability of motivational and behavioral properties from birth through mid-adulthood revealed minimal preservation of most qualities from the behaviors coded prior to school entrance but moderately significant preservation from age ten through adulthood. [The *Social Sciences Citation Index*® (*SSCI*®) **indicates that this book has been cited over 460 times since 1966.]**

Jerome Kagan
Department of Psychology
and Social Relations
Harvard University
Cambridge, MA 02138

November 24, 1981

"The research report contained in *Birth to Maturity* began with an invitation in 1956 from Lester W. Sontag, the director of the Fels Research Institute, to assume responsibility for evaluating the adult subjects who were members of the Fels longitudinal population and integrating that information with the extensive data that had been gathered on each person from their infancy through late adolescence. After reading excerpts from the individual records I became convinced that this project provided an unusual opportunity to learn more about the genesis of personality, and in January 1957, I began the work. Howard Moss, who had just received his degree from Ohio State University, joined me as a collaborator. He took responsibility for quantification of the longitudinal records while I interviewed the adults and, with Moss as well as John and Beatrice Lacey, administered a battery of experimental procedures designed to evaluate characteristics concerned with the adult's hierarchy of motives and conflicts.

"The generalizations revealed by the analysis of the extensive corpus of data have influenced, directly or indirectly, most of my subsequent research.[1] This project became the major incentive for the subsequent investigations of reflection-impulsivity as well as the study of tempo of play in young children.[2] One of the most surprising relations in the corpus was the discovery that the only psychological characteristic quantified during the first three years of life that had any predictive power for future behavior was the variable Moss and I called passivity. I now think it should have been labeled 'inhibition in the face of uncertainty.' The most inhibited infant boys retained that characteristic through adolescence and adulthood. The most recent research in my laboratory indicates that this temperamental dimension is robust and related to biological qualities of the infant. It may be that 20 years after *Birth to Maturity* my colleagues and I will finally clarify the meaning of the relationships that puzzled us so many years ago.

"The popularity of *Birth to Maturity*, which won the Hofheimer Prize of the American Psychiatric Association, is due, I think, to the fact that it was the first extensive report on the degree of continuity and discontinuity in human development, a theme of major interest to both psychologists and parents. Additionally, some of the work's major conclusions were in accord with the presuppositions of the psychological community; namely, there is preservation of individual differences from childhood to adulthood but that local sex role standards and the social class of the child's family would affect the degree of preservation. When a scientist's conclusions match the *a priori* beliefs of the community, the work is generally not given as critical a review as generalizations that violate consensus. When, a decade after *Birth to Maturity*,[3] I suggested that there might be minimal preservation of the individual qualities of infants, that statement generated considerably more resistance. A general reference which provides a review of this field has been published."[4]

1. **Kagan J.** A psychologist's account at mid-career. (Krawiec T S, ed.) *The psychologists.* New York: Oxford University Press, 1972. Vol. 1. p. 137-66.
2. ----------. *Change and continuity in infancy.* New York: Wiley, 1971. 298 p.
3. **Kagan J & Klein R E.** Cross-cultural perspectives on early development. *Amer. Psychol.* **28**:947-61, 1973.
4. **Kagan J & Brim O G.** *Constancy and change in human development.* Cambridge: Harvard University Press, 1980. 754 p.

CC/NUMBER 33
AUGUST 13, 1984

This Week's Citation Classic™

Vaillant G E. *Adaptation to life*. Boston: Little, Brown, 1977. 396 p.
[Harvard University, Cambridge, MA]

The lives of college men, selected for health and prospectively followed for three decades, are examined. The powerful associations between ego mechanisms of defense, mental health, and maturity are analyzed. Defense mechanisms are validated by behavioral and psychobiographical methods rather than by metapsychological inference. [The *Social Sciences Citation Index*® (*SSCI*®) indicates that this book has been cited in over 255 publications since 1977.]

George E. Vaillant
Department of Psychiatry
Dartmouth Medical School
Hanover, NH 03756

June 16, 1984

"During my psychiatric residency, I became interested in the natural healing processes that could be observed in mentally ill adults who were followed for decades. Because of this interest, I welcomed the chance to study the extensive dossiers of 268 'normal' college sophomores, selected for mental health, who had been prospectively followed for three decades. These life records had been assembled by the staff of the Harvard Study of Adult Development (HSAD) under the successive directorships of Clark Heath and Charles McArthur. Although I had had no experience in the initiation of longitudinal studies, I had devised certain methods for harvesting them. These methods included keeping the data analysis as simple as possible, paying attention to global outcome variables, and setting greater store by how people behaved than by what they said or how they performed on pencil and paper tests.

"As a way of organizing the HSAD data, I studied the ego mechanisms of defense used by the men in their efforts to master difficulties in their lives. Although selected for mental health and favored by social privilege, these men had all met severe difficulties. By taking a longitudinal approach—by focusing on life course—I made their invisible defenses apparent by 'triangulation' of biography, autobiography, and creative (pathologic) product. In other words, by contrasting the objective biographical facts of their lives both with subjective autobiographical statements and with odd or unusual behaviors, it was possible to obtain better consensual validation of defense choice than had been previously achieved by others. I then correlated individual defense choice with age, with psychopathology, and with adult success at working and loving. This produced an empirically derived hierarchy of defenses. By studying the men's lives over time, it was possible to see one defense evolve into another; it was even possible to see personality disorder evolve into creative adaptation.

"I suspect that the book's frequent citation in part reflects increased popular interest in adult development. However, because the book is limited to one sex, one social class, and one birth cohort, its value in this area is limited. Since then, I have replicated the findings in a cohort of inner city men.[1,2] I hope that the book is also cited because it elucidates the importance and clinical validity of defenses and because it helps to rescue the Freudian baby from being discarded with its bathwater. In 1978, a reviewer for *Contemporary Psychology* (vol. 23, p. 538) wrote, 'Psychologists scientifically or professionally concerned with human development will find little in the way of evidence or insight in Vaillant's offering.' I am glad that the book's frequent citation suggests that this judgment was too harsh. I am also glad that the scientific community appears to value a work that insists that the brain is affected by the heart."

1. **Vaillant G E & Milofsky E.** Natural history of male psychological health: IX. Empirical evidence for Erickson's model of the life cycle. *Amer. J. Psychiat.* **137**:1348-59, 1980.
2. **Vaillant G E.** *The natural history of alcoholism*. Cambridge, MA: Harvard University Press, 1983. 359 p.

This Week's Citation Classic

Baltes P B. Longitudinal and cross-sectional sequences in the study of age and generation effects. *Hum. Develop.* **11**:145-71, 1968.
[Universität des Saarlandes, Federal Republic of Germany and West Virginia University, Morgantown, WV]

Cross-sectional, longitudinal, and cohort-sequential research designs for the study of human development are presented and discussed. Particular attention is paid to Schaie's general developmental model. Schaie's model is critically evaluated and a modified strategy (cross-sectional and longitudinal sequences) is proposed. The role of generational change in human development is stressed. [The *Social Sciences Citation Index*® *(SSCI*™*)* **indicates that this paper has been cited over 165 times since 1968.]**

Paul B. Baltes
Max Planck Institute for
Human Development and Education
Lentzeallee 94, D-1 Berlin 33
Federal Republic of Germany

April 16, 1981

"This article is the outcome of a fruitful dialectical relationship between one of my mentors, K. Warner Schaie, and myself. While I was a graduate exchange student from Germany at the University of Nebraska during 1963-1964, Schaie was my sponsor and mentor. During that time, Schaie wrote his influential article on the general developmental model.[1] The dialectic resulted from the fact that I was very much impressed with the importance of Schaie's work, but at the same time had emerging disagreements with the specifics of his proposal.

"After returning to Germany to complete my doctorate (1967), I decided to focus in my dissertation on developmental research design including an assessment and reformulation of Schaie's model. This occurred with long-distance encouragement from Schaie, although he continued, as is true for most dialectical arguments, to vehemently disagree with my felt need to modify his proposals. The present article is a partial summary of my dissertation work. Since then, the dialectic has progressed and together we have tried to present a shared view in which we spell out both our commonalities and our differences.[2]

"A contingency accentuated further the intellectual dialogue. In 1968, Schaie attracted me as a faculty member to West Virginia's department of psychology. There, we developed our personal and professional friendship further, while the public assumed us to be mortal scientific enemies. This resulted in a number of amusing experiences at meetings where colleagues, especially graduate students, noticed with much surprise that Schaie and Baltes were friendly colleagues who enjoyed their intellectual conflict as a mutually enhancing condition.

"What is the gist of the reformulation offered in the article? First, the role of cohort effects in cross-sectional age studies was emphasized supporting the basic premise for Schaie's proposals. Second, Schaie's work was put into a larger context and, in addition, it was described in a perhaps more readable fashion than was true for his original article. Third, it was shown that Schaie's model promised more than it could deliver. While it is important to chart the age-development of successive cohorts, Schaie's simultaneous effort at causal explanation of age and cohort variation was a less than persuasive recipe. The primary value of cohort-sequential strategies is in descriptive identification of the fact that age-development can differ among cohorts. This can be best accomplished by what I have called 'cross-sectional and longitudinal sequences.' Explaining the why and how of age and cohort variation is a separate matter and should be approached in various ways depending on theory and content.[3]

"Why has this article received much attention? One reason is surely that it deals with the basics of methodology in developmental psychology. Showing how cultural change jeopardizes the age-based interpretation of cross-sectional studies, the bread and butter of many developmentalists, is a serious matter. Furthermore, the lively dialectic among some of the innovators and their integral colleague-friends (such as Riegel and Nesselroade) was bound to help the cause.[4] Additionally, several concurrent trends in neighboring fields provided a supportive context. This is particularly true for sociology, where the interplay between individual development and social change has been equally emphasized (e.g., Elder, Riley).[5,6] Sequential methodology plays a crucial role in such a venture. Finally, despite my own certainty about the matter, the dialectic is far from settled. There is more work (and citing!) to be done."

1. **Schaie K W.** A general model for the study of developmental problems. *Psychol. Bull.* **64**:92-107, 1965.
2. **Schaie K W & Baltes P B.** On sequential strategies in developmental research: description or explanation? *Hum. Develop.* **18**:384-90, 1975.
3. **Baltes P B, Cornelius S W & Nesselroade J R.** Cohort effects in developmental psychology. (Nesselroade J R & Baltes P B, eds.) *Longitudinal research in the study of behavior and development.* New York: Academic Press, 1979.
4. **Riegel K F.** Dialectics of human development. *Amer. Psychol.* **31**:689-700, 1976.
5. **Elder G H, Jr.** Age differentiation and the life course. *Annu. Rev. Sociol.* **1**:165-90, 1975.
6. **Riley M W, Johnson W & Foner A, eds.** *Aging and society (vol. 3): a sociology of age stratification.* New York: Russell Sage Foundation, 1972. 652 p.

CC/NUMBER 46
NOVEMBER 12, 1984

This Week's Citation Classic™

Adorno T W, Frenkel-Brunswik E, Levinson D J & Sanford R N. *The authoritarian personality.* New York: Harper & Row, 1950. 990 p.
[Columbia University, New York, NY and University of California, Berkeley, CA]

In this comprehensive five-year study, seven investigators used objective tests, interviews, and projective techniques in demonstrating that personality processes, especially unconscious ones, had a major role in the determination of anti-Semitism and a broad pattern of related beliefs and attitudes—a pattern that came to be called authoritarianism. [*The Social Sciences Citation Index* (*SSCI*®) indicates that this book has been cited in over 1,800 publications since 1966.]

R. Nevitt Sanford
65 Roble Road
Berkeley, CA 94705

September 10, 1984

"In January 1943, I was asked by the Provost of the University of California at Berkeley if I could use $500, from an anonymous donor, for a study of anti-Semitism. I certainly could, not only because I wanted to join the scientific attack on Fascism but because I saw a chance to carry on the kind of psychoanalytically oriented research on personality in which I had been trained under Henry Murray at the Harvard Psychological Clinic. I immediately recruited one of my graduate students, Daniel Levinson, a highly talented kindred spirit.

"We began by constructing a scale for measuring anti-Semitism. This we administered, together with a personal-data questionnaire, to groups of students, and by early fall we were giving talks on anti-Semitism before community groups and had a paper ready for publication.[1] This led to more funds becoming available, making it possible for Else Frenkel-Brunswik to join us. Within a year, we had ready for publication a paper that embodied most of the kinds of findings and interpretations that were to be embodied in our book.[2]

"By that time, our work had come to the attention of Max Horkheimer, an associate of the American Jewish Committee. He saw to it that we were adequately funded and enabled Theodore Adorno to join our group.

"Our book has been hailed as a 'classic'—and severely criticized both for its theory and for its methods. After 30 years, it was still available in hardcover, and two paperback editions had appeared. It has been translated into German, French, and Italian. A book about our book was published in 1954.[3] In 1982, an abridged edition appeared.[4] I think it was mainly because of this book that the International Society of Political Psychology established its Nevitt Sanford Award and made me its first recipient.

"The criticism that rolled over our work came both from people who approved of our approach but worried about our methods and from people desiring to discredit the whole thing. Our F scale became a special object of criticism. There were heroic but unsuccessful efforts to improve it or to produce less far-out substitutes for it. These studies were far outnumbered, however, by those in which this scale was used successfully to predict performance on other instruments and overt behavior in various situations.

"It is rare that as many as four senior scientists collaborate for five years or longer. We had our problems—not the least those deriving from pride of authorship—but were held together by the conviction that our important work had to be published at whatever cost and by our agreement that it be presented as a collective enterprise. Unfortunately for me, this last constraint required that authors' names be listed in alphabetical order. Thus, over the years, when friends and relatives have wanted to look up a work that they knew was my labor of love for seven years, they could not find it in the library. Such is life in academia."

1. **Levinson D J & Sanford R N.** A scale for the measurement of anti-Semitism. *J. Psychology* **17**:339-70, 1944.
2. **Frenkel-Brunswik E & Sanford R N.** Some personality factors in anti-Semitism. *J. Psychology* **20**:271-91, 1945.
3. **Christie R & Jahoda M,** eds. *Studies in the scope and method of "The authoritarian personality."* Glencoe, IL: Free Press, 1954. 279 p.
4. **Adorno T W, Frenkel-Brunswik E, Levinson D J & Sanford R N.** *The authoritarian personality, abridged edition.* New York: Norton, 1982. 493 p.

CC/NUMBER 7
FEBRUARY 13, 1984

This Week's Citation Classic™

Snyder M. Self-monitoring of expressive behavior.
J. Personal. Soc. Psychol. **30**:526-37, 1974.
[Lab. for Research in Social Relations, Dept. Psychology, Univ. Minnesota, Minneapolis, MN]

A psychological construct of self-monitoring (self-observation and self-control) of expressive behavior and self-presentation was proposed, and the development of a reliable and valid measure of differences between individuals in these self-monitoring propensities was described. [The *Social Sciences Citation Index*® (*SSCI*®) indicates that this paper has been cited in over 170 publications since 1974.]

Mark Snyder
Department of Psychology
University of Minnesota
Minneapolis, MN 55455

January 5, 1984

"The gaps and contradictions between the public selves that we allow other people to see and the more private self that only we are allowed to know have been the focal points of my explorations into the nature of the self. Many people, I have found, have much in common with the state of affairs described by W.H. Auden: 'The image of myself which I try to create in my own mind in order that I may love myself is very different from the image which I try to create in the minds of others in order that they may love me.'

"This creating of images in the minds of others, this acting in ways designed to control the impressions conveyed to others, is no doubt practiced to some extent by most people. But for some people it is almost a way of life. These are the people who are particularly sensitive to the ways they express and present themselves in social situations, and who possess the ability to carefully observe their own performances and to skillfully adjust these performances in order to create and maintain appearances particularly suited to their current situations. I call such persons 'high self-monitoring individuals' because of the great extent to which they are engaged in *monitoring* or controlling the *selves* that they project to others in social circumstances. In marked contrast to these individuals, low self-monitoring individuals are not so concerned with constantly assessing the social climate around them. Instead, low self-monitoring individuals tend to express what they think and feel, rather than mold and tailor their self-presentations and social behavior to fit the situation.

"To identify high self-monitoring individuals and low self-monitoring individuals, I have developed a 25-item Self-Monitoring Scale that measures how concerned people are with the impressions they make on others, as well as their ability to control the impressions that they convey to others in social situations. High self-monitoring individuals, in their endorsement of Self-Monitoring Scale items, claim, 'When I am uncertain how to act in a social situation, I look to the behavior of others for cues' and 'In different situations and with different people, I often act like very different persons.' Low self-monitoring individuals, by contrast, in their item endorsements, claim, 'My behavior is usually an expression of my true inner feelings, attitudes and beliefs' and 'I would not change my opinions (or the way I do things) in order to please someone or win their favor.'

"In the cited article, I presented diverse sources of converging evidence for the reliability and validity of this measure of self-monitoring. This research, which had been the subject of my doctoral dissertation at Stanford University, received the Society of Experimental Social Psychology's Dissertation Award in 1973. This research also was the beginning of a long-term, and continuing, series of programmatic investigations of the ways in which self-monitoring propensities are reflected in the lives that individuals actually live. Self-monitoring propensities profoundly influence individuals' views of themselves and their social worlds, their behavior in social contexts, and the dynamics of their relationships with other people. Perhaps it is the intimate interweaving of self-monitoring processes into the fabric of social life that accounts, at least in part, for the frequent citation of this article in which the self-monitoring construct was first introduced.

"Theory and research on self-monitoring (almost 200 investigations of self-monitoring have been reported) is reviewed in a 1979 contribution to *Advances in Experimental Social Psychology*.[1] Current emphases of self-monitoring researchers are the role of self-monitoring in close and intimate relationships, the influence of self-monitoring on choices of occupational and professional situations, applications of self-monitoring to concerns in clinical and counseling psychology, and investigations of the developmental origins of self-monitoring propensities."

1. **Snyder M.** Self-monitoring processes. *Advan. Exp. Soc. Psychol.* **12**:85-128, 1979.

This Week's Citation Classic

NUMBER 37
SEPTEMBER 10, 1979

Rokeach M. *The open and closed mind: investigations into the nature of belief systems and personality systems.* New York: Basic Books, 1960. 447 p.

A structural theory about the organization of belief systems, and about the general properties of authoritarianism and intolerance, regardless of political, religious, or scientific content is presented. Measures of general authoritarianism (dogmatism scale) and intolerance (opinionation scale) are derived and employed in various investigations carried out by the author and many collaborators that were designed to test construct validity and to shed further light on the organization and processes of belief and thought. [The *Science Citation Index® (SCI®)* **and the** *Social Sciences Citation Index ™ (SSCI™)* **indicate that this book has been cited over 1,295 times since 1961.]**

Milton Rokeach
Department of Sociology and
Social Research Center
Washington State University
Pullman, WA 99164

January 17, 1979

"Speaking personally, *The Open and Closed Mind* grew out of my need to better understand and thus to better resist continuing pressures during my earlier years on my intellectual independence, on the one side from orthodox religion and on the other side from orthodox Marxism-Leninism. Speaking scientifically, the work was first conceived during my graduate days in Berkeley where I had the good fortune to come into close contact with several of the authors of *The Authoritarian Personality*—Else Frenkel-Brunswik, Daniel Levinson, and Nevitt Sanford.[1] My approach differed, however, from theirs, in being more cognitive, more experimental, and by emphasizing structure rather than content. It reflected a convergence of several theoretical orientations to which I had been exposed—psychoanalysis, Maslow's theory of motivation, and the cognitive Gestalt orientations of Levin, Asch, Krech, and Crutchfield.

"I can think of several possible reasons why my book has made the 'most cited' list. First, it generated a good deal of research concerning the controversial issue as to whether it is similarity of belief rather than race or ethnicity that is the main psychological determinant of social discrimination. Second, my dogmatism scale has been widely employed as a measure of individual differences in closed-mindedness. The *SSCI™* shows that different kinds of journals in psychology, sociology, education, political science, religion, and communication have published papers employing this scale. And possibly third, the book may have succeeded (as I had hoped) in being socially as well as theoretically relevant.

"Building on this work I attempted in later works[2,3] to concentrate on the role that attitudes and values play within belief systems, their relation to social action, their antecedents, and long-term cognitive and behavioral consequences. As a result, I am now persuaded that values are the most important components of belief systems, relevant at all levels of social analysis, and thus of central concern across all the social sciences. I believe that social scientists should therefore devote more of their efforts than they presently do to the further development of theory and research on individual and supra individual values.

"My long-lasting interest in the antecedents and consequents of organization and change in belief systems has provided me with a framework broad enough to pursue many other theoretical and applied interests, some of which go against the mainstream of contemporary social psychology. Most gratifying, though, are the frequent citations to my work across several social science disciplines, suggesting that I have succeeded to some extent in realizing my ambition to become interdisciplinary in my thinking and research."

1. **Adorno T W, Frenkel-Brunswik E, Levinson D J & Sanford R.** *The authoritarian personality.* New York: Harper, 1960. 990 p.
2. **Rokeach M.** *Beliefs, attitudes, and values.* San Francisco: Jossey-Bass, Inc., 1968. 214 p.
3. **Rokeach M.** *The nature of human values.* New York: Free Press, 1973. 438 p.

This Week's Citation Classic

NUMBER 15
APRIL 9, 1979

Lefcourt H M. Internal-external control of reinforcement. A review. *Psychol. Bull.* **65**:206-20, 1966.

When causes for performance outcomes are attributed to external forces, people generally become less alert and resourceful. Persons who habitually attribute outcomes to fate, chance, or others often appear apathetic and more vulnerable to stressors than 'internals' who cognitively prepare themselves for challenges. [The *Science Citation Index® (SCI®)* **and the** *Social Sciences Citation Index™ (SSCI™)* **indicate that this paper has been cited over 310 times since 1966.]**

Herbert M. Lefcourt
Department of Psychology
University of Waterloo
Waterloo, Ontario,
Canada N2L 3GI

January 7, 1978

"My interest in the locus of control construct derived from a convergence of experience and academic instruction. At Ohio State University when I was a graduate student, research was focused on perceptions of causality. During my clinical internship at a hospital for narcotic addicts, I became privy to the pervasive helplessness among urban blacks which seemed to predetermine continued failure and despair. My early research dealt with despair via perceptions of causality with the hypothesis that disbelief in personal efficacy resulted in failure to recognize available opportunities and presaged a dearth of positive experiences. Over the years many data have been reported which support these contentions. The *Psychological Bulletin* article was among the first reviews of this research and filled a void at the right moment. The popularity of the article probably derives from its timeliness.

"Many others have witnessed something akin to the apathy I found among black drug addicts. The inability to manage one's day as one wishes gives everyone at least a taste of helplessness, when causes for outcomes are beyond one's personal means. To obtain a seat on a subway or to avoid a mugging through selection of one's route may be residual efforts at maintaining a semblance of control. For some, such successes may comprise their day's highlight and have helped to make them aware of their efforts to maintain control. This 'awareness' has been heightened greatly by the social movements of the last decade in which the terms 'powerlessness' and 'alienation' became almost trite explanations for much of today's malaise.

"Given the popularity of terms akin to locus of control, it has become difficult to save the construct from conceptual fuzziness that can result with popularization. Consequently, I have written a book, *Locus of Control,*[1] in which I have tried to preserve the meaning of the construct while exploring its relevance to given social problems.

"Due perhaps to my lengthy involvement with the construct, I have come to believe that locus of control is a major determinant of what I refer to as vitality. When people believe that outcomes flow from their actions, then behavior becomes more purposive and, to others, they seem to be that much more alive. Support for this contention, which comprises the conclusion of my book has been found in research and, of equal importance, in the writings of great authors. It is comforting to find support from the likes of James Fenimore Cooper, who records the momentary shifts in vitality reflected in Deerslayer's face and body as he shifts in his beliefs regarding his efficacy."

REFERENCE

1. **Lefcourt H M.** Locus of control: current trends in theory and research. Hillsdale, NJ: Lawrence Erlbaum Assoc., 1976. 211 p.

This Week's Citation Classic

CC/NUMBER 41
OCTOBER 10, 1983

Haan N, Smith M B & Block J. Moral reasoning of young adults: political-social behavior, family background, and personality correlates.
J. Pers. Soc. Psychol. **10**:183-201, 1968.
[Institute of Human Development, University of California, Berkeley, CA]

During the 1960s, activists of various bents and nonactivists were compared with one another with respect to their political-social views, moral maturity, and personalities and family backgrounds. Active protesters were found to be morally more mature, energetic personalities from liberal families. [The *Social Sciences Citation Index*® (*SSCI*®) indicates that this paper has been cited in over 195 publications since 1968.]

Norma Haan
Institute of Human Development
University of California
Berkeley, CA 94720

August 29, 1983

"In the fall of 1964, students who had worked on civil rights in the South returned to the Berkeley campus of the University of California to find new regulations banning campus political activity. They had intended to recruit others to augment their efforts so the now famous Free Speech Movement was born. Some four months of debate, anger, new agreements, and broken agreements ensued before definitive civil disobedience and a massive arrest occurred. I and my colleagues, Jeanne H. Block and M. Brewster Smith, recognized a target of research opportunity, not only in the Berkeley students' protest but also in the spreading activism of San Francisco State University students and the more social service-oriented commitments of young people who were becoming Peace Corps volunteers. Our foci were the differences—personal, social, and moral—among activists of various commitments and between activists and nonactivists. What kind of people act with respect to societies' injusticr others merely deplore? Nonetheless, the social thrust of the 1960s also provided these young people with hope and impetus. For instance, some Berkeley students who were not arrested argued with us about the research plan. They declared their failure to be arrested was no fault of their own! The police wouldn't let them in the building.

"The paper described here probably became famous (or infamous) because it addressed the activists' central claims of their morality, assertions that were doubted and countered by conservatives of the older generation and various media personnel.[1]

"Nevertheless, in a sample of 517 and with the measures we used (Kohlberg's definition of morality[2]), principled students were more often activists than were morally conventional students. Principled activists were also distinctive in their demographic status, organizational activity, self and ideal views, family background, and so forth. They seemed more independent, vigorous, radical, and aggressive. In other words, the activists were not simply morally benighted nor could they be facilely understood as neurotically rebellious or misled.

"As the study proceeded, activists became less willing to comply with our depersonalized methods of collecting data. One night we found ourselves in a crowded, sweaty living room explaining to some 50 San Francisco State University students that the 'reality' we sought was still valid although different than the reality of their individual lives, which they thought was a much better target for our research.

"The findings were subsequently replicated[3] but also disputed.[1] In 1974, interest in this report became so sufficient that it was reproduced in the Bobbs-Merrill Report Series in Psychology."

1. **Lipset S M.** The activists: a profile. *Public Interest* (13):39-51, 1968.
2. **Kohlberg L.** A cognitive-developmental approach to socialization. (Goslin D, ed.) *Handbook of socialization.* New York: Rand McNally, 1969. p. 347-480.
3. **Fishkin J, Keniston K & MacKinnon C.** Moral reasoning and political ideology. *J. Pers. Soc. Psychol.* **27**:109-19, 1973.

This Week's Citation Classic™

Herzberg F, Mausner B & Snyderman B B. *The motivation to work.* New York: Wiley, 1959. 157 p.
[Dept. Psychology, Western Reserve Univ., Cleveland, OH and Dept. Psychology, Beaver College, Glenside, PA]

The book describes the original research leading to the development of motivation-hygiene theory. It suggests that there are no antonyms for affective states. In this instance, job satisfaction and job dissatisfaction are separate continua produced by different sets of job factors. [The *Social Sciences Citation Index®* (*SSCI®*) indicates that this book has been cited in over 795 publications since 1966.]

Frederick I. Herzberg
Graduate School of Business
University of Utah
Salt Lake City, UT 84112

March 13, 1984

"In 1950, I received my PhD in psychology. I was offered a fellowship to attend the Graduate School of Public Health at the University of Pittsburgh. My major was to be in industrial mental health under the direction of an industrial psychiatrist from McGill University in Canada by the name of Graham Taylor. Unfortunately, I soon discovered that the concepts of industrial mental health were really a restatement of the concepts of mental illness that I had previously studied in clinical and abnormal psychology. Reflecting this disappointment, I entitled my Public Health Practice thesis *Mental Health Is Not the Opposite of Mental Illness*. **After receiving my master's degree in public health, I took a job as research director for Psychological Services of Pittsburgh. A local industrialist came to see me after a nasty labor relations disturbance and asked me plaintively, 'What do people want from their jobs?' I answered him in typical academic fashion, 'Sir, I don't know but if you give me enough money I will find out.'**

"I followed up on my School of Public Health thesis by designing a study to test the hypothesis that job satisfaction and job dissatisfaction were separate concepts. The result was the book, *The Motivation to Work*, **which led to a fundamentally different approach to the study of people's affective states. This is the twenty-fifth anniversary of the publication of** *The Motivation to Work*. **The original study has produced perhaps more replications than any other research in the history of industrial and organizational psychology. The new approach to viewing job attitudes was the beginning of many present-day concepts and applications of industrial and organizational psychology (e.g., job enrichment, quality control circles, quality of work life, cafeteria-style benefits, guaranteed annual wage, flextime, etc.).**

"Bernard Mausner and Barbara Snyderman were two senior members of my research staff. Both of them contributed significantly to the carrying out of the research and to the publication of *The Motivation to Work*.

"I have since published three major amplifications of motivation-hygiene theory: *Work and the Nature of Man*,[1] *The Managerial Choice*,[2] **and** *Herzberg on Motivation*."[3]

1. **Herzberg F I.** *Work and the nature of man.* New York: Crowell, 1966. 203 p.
2. ----------------. *The managerial choice.* Salt Lake City, UT: Olympus, 1982. 360 p.
3. ----------------. *Herzberg on motivation.* Cleveland, OH: Penton/IPC, 1983. 52 p.

This Week's Citation Classic

CC/NUMBER 20
MAY 19, 1980

Holland J L. *Making vocational choices: a theory of careers.* Englewood Cliffs, NJ: Prentice-Hall, 1973. 150 p. [Johns Hopkins University, Baltimore, MD]

A typology of six personality types, six corresponding occupational environments, and their interactions is offered as a tool for understanding work histories, vocational satisfaction, and achievement, and for organizing and interpreting personal and occupational data. [The *Science Citation Index®* *(SCI®)* **and the** *Social Sciences Citation Index®* *(SSCI™)* **indicate that this book has been cited over 260 times since 1973.]**

J.L. Holland
Department of Social Relations
Johns Hopkins University
Baltimore, MD 21218

February 25, 1980

"The origins of my typology are multiple. The key experiences are stretched over most of my work history, and I have noticed that I give different explanations on different days.

"My military experience (1942-46) as an induction interviewer led me to think that people fall into a relatively small number of types. Later my vocational counseling experience with college students, physically impaired, and psychiatric patients reinforced my belief that it is useful to see people as types. My counseling experience also made me anxious to find a way to organize occupational information so that the counseling assessment could be related more explicitly to occupations.

"The three versions of the theory are similar; each revision was an attempt to provide a theory that better complies with scientific standards of logic and evidence. Between revisions, I have listened to critics, friends, and the evidence. In all, I have had about 20 active collaborators who performed the necessary research, clarified my thinking, taught me something about the philosophy of science, and kept me from quitting when I became discouraged.

"It was easy to get discouraged. The first statement[1] resulted in a stalemate that a friendly journal editor resolved in my favor, but a critique was published simultaneously in the same journal. Psychologists had been burned by typologies and were in no mood for another. The 1966 statement, a book,[2] received more positive reviews (I finally had some evidence) and the 1973 statement generally received positive reviews.

"I attribute the current popularity and high citation of my delusional system to many things. (1) It is easy to comprehend and to apply to research or practical problems. This is occasionally a defect because some social scientists cannot believe that relatively simple formulations can be useful. (2) It has spawned some popular self-help devices (the Self Directed Search[3] and its multiple imitations). (3) It has provided a technical terminology that lends status to the typology—terms such as hexagonal model (a theory without a diagram cannot be science), congruency, and type. The types (Realistic, Investigative, Artistic, Social, Enterprising, Conventional) have also become part of the vocabulary of counselors and researchers. (4) The typology rests on considerable research evidence (300+ articles so far), and the theoretical ideas are often applied successfully to a wide range of practical problems. For example, the Canadian government has used the classification to reorganize their occupational classification for counseling purposes. And (5) the typology has become more immune to criticism as defects have been eliminated or softened in successive revisions. I hope to produce one more revision, for critics and friends continue to act as coauthors."

1. **Holland J L.** A theory of vocational choice. *J. Couns. Psychol.* **6**:35-45, 1959.
2. ---------------. *The psychology of vocational choice.* Waltham, MA: Blaisdell, 1966. 132 p.
3. ---------------. *Professional manual for the self directed search.* Palo Alto, CA: Consulting Psychologists Press, 1979. 96 p.

This Week's Citation Classic

Rimland B. *Infantile autism: the syndrome and its implications for a neural theory of behavior.* New York: Appleton-Century-Crofts, 1964. 282 p. [Personnel Measurement Res. Dept., US Naval Personnel Res. Lab., San Diego, CA]

Part I of this book is an integrated review of infantile autism, a rare mental disorder beginning in infancy. Part II presents autism as a cognitive defect and develops a neural theory of autism. Part III extends the theory of autism into a general theory of behavior. [The *Science Citation Index*® (*SCI*®) **and the** *Social Sciences Citation Index*® (*SSCI*™) **indicate that this book has been cited over 425 times since 1964.]**

Bernard Rimland
Institute for Child Behavior Research
4758 Edgeware Road
San Diego, CA 92116

April 23, 1981

"How curious! Here is a neural explanation of infantile autism written by a psychologist with no training in physiological psychology or child development!

"In earning my PhD in experimental psychology, I had carefully avoided such irrelevant courses as child psychology and physiological psychology. I did not encounter the word 'autism' until five years after my PhD. Our then two-year-old son, definitely planned and wanted, had been a source of pride and despair from the moment of birth. Physically perfect and startlingly alert, he had screamed so vigorously while still in the hospital that it was almost impossible to nurse him. At eight months, he suddenly began walking, and at one year he was clearly articulating whole sentences. But he never said mommy or daddy, and when not screaming, seemed lost in a perpetual daydream.

"My concern led me to the library, where I found the works of Leo Kanner. Kanner, in 1943, had first described several children *precisely* like mine.[1] I began to read voraciously, first for my own edification, then to produce a review paper. I found the field chaotic; a comprehensive review was needed to pull together what little was known. The level of scholarship was abysmal. Murky psychoanalytic interpretations masqueraded as truth. Authors built incoherent theories on dubious interpretations of isolated events, liberally misquoting each other in the process. The field was dominated by psychoanalysts like Bruno Bettelheim, who asserted confidently that autistic children were normal youngsters who had emotionally repudiated their unloving families. These theories, presented as fact, deterred biological research and added guilt and untold anguish to the heavy burdens already borne by the mothers of autistic children.

"My study expanded to include genetics, biochemistry, neurophysiology, and other fields. After five years, my wife observed that my 'paper' had become a book. I had to agree.

"In 1963, the Appleton-Century-Crofts Company announced its annual competition for a distinguished contribution to psychology. With misgivings, I submitted my work. To my delight and amazement, the judges 'unanimously and enthusiastically' awarded the first Century prize to *Infantile Autism*.

"The impact of the book was dramatic. In 1978, a national magazine[2] reported that 90 percent of the people in the field felt that Rimland had 'blown Bettelheim's theories to hell.' I have often been told that *Infantile Autism* was pivotal in redirecting the entire field of psychology from its morbid preoccupation with psychodynamics toward a more productive interest in biology. While my two main goals, exposing the psychogenic myth and encouraging biological research,[3] were realized, my attempt to clarify the muddled problem of diagnosing autism has had little success.

"Part III of *Infantile Autism*, the neural theory of behavior, has had an impact on such diverse fields as aesthetics, philosophy, political science, and artificial intelligence. Morse Peckham devoted an appendix of his book on aesthetics, *Man's Rage for Chaos*,[4] to this theory, and commented that the theory puts Schopenhauer's ideas in an entirely new light. Artist Elizabeth Willmott cited the neural theory extensively in her essay 'Creative relationships.'[5] Political scientist R.I. Wolfe credited the neural theory with giving him the key idea for his paper *War as a Surrogate*.[6] Biocyberneticist Harry Klopf presents, in his forthcoming book *The Hedonistic Neuron*,[7] an independently derived brain model strikingly similar to mine, including stimulus-seeking neurons and a brain stem reticular formation which serves functions crucial to intelligence and consciousness.

"A strange outcome for a story that started with a screaming infant!"

1. **Kanner L.** Autistic disturbances of affective contact. *Nerv. Child* **2**:217-50, 1943. [Citation Classic. *Current Contents/Social & Behavioral Sciences* (25):14, 18 June 1979.]
2. **Katz D R.** The kids with the faraway eyes. *Rolling Stone*, 8 March 1979, p. 48-53.
3. **Rimland B, Callaway E & Dreyfus P.** The effects of high doses of vitamin B_6 on autistic children: a double-blind crossover study. *Amer. J. Psychiat.* **135**:472-5, 1978.
4. **Peckham M.** *Man's rage for chaos: biology, behavior and the arts.* Philadelphia: Chilton, 1965. 339 p.
5. **Willmott E.** Creative relationships. *Structuralist* 7:23-34, 1967.
6. **Wolfe R I.** *War as a surrogate.* Paper delivered at the annual meeting of the Peace Research Society. 19 February 1973, San Francisco, California. 51 p.
7. **Klopf A H.** *The hedonistic neuron: a theory of meaning, learning and intelligence.* Washington, DC: Hemisphere Publishing. In press, 1981.

This Week's Citation Classic

Dunn L M. Special education for the mildly retarded—is much of it justifiable? *Except. Child.* **35**:5-22, 1968.
[Inst. on Mental Retardation and Intellectual Development, George Peabody Coll. for Teachers, Nashville, TN]

It was argued that the then prevalent practice should cease of labeling many disadvantaged children from the minority groups as mentally retarded because they scored a bit low on tests of intelligence. Instead of placing them in segregated special day classes, it was proposed that they remain *unlabeled* in the mainstream of education with special educators serving as resource teachers for all pupils with learning difficulties. [The *Social Sciences Citation Index*® (*SSCI*®) indicates that this paper has been cited in over 240 publications since 1968.]

Lloyd M. Dunn
Department of Special Education
University of Hawaii at Manoa
Honolulu, HI 96822

December 7, 1982

"There are two main reasons why this paper has been referenced and reprinted so often. One is explained by the quotation: 'Nothing is as powerful as an idea whose time has come.' The other is because of status. I was an active past-president of the professional organization in whose house organ the paper appeared. It was highlighted in the lead position in the first issue of the year. A reader could hardly overlook it. Perhaps there is a third reason. On rereading the article today, I find it to be quite ambiguous. Almost anyone could find something in it with which to agree, even though some special educators (school people who specialize in the education of handicapped children) were upset and threatened by it.

"There are two other, more important forces which, combined, swept 'mainstreaming' into the schools in a record, short seven-year period. *First*, parents from minority groups sought the relief of the courts against school people labeling their children as mentally retarded and so segregating them into special day classes. Time and again they won their cases. *Second*, in 1975, the federal government passed, and funded generously, 'The Education of All Handicapped Children Act' (Public Law 94-142) which mandated that all handicapped children be educated in the least restrictive environment appropriate to their needs.

"I am frequently asked three questions: 1. Are you sorry you stirred up such a hornet's nest? 2. Have the schools implemented your major suggestions? 3. Have you changed your views? The answer to the first question is 'no.' I still feel self-contained special schools and classes for the mildly retarded are primarily devices to enable the regular schoolteachers to transfer the pupils they consider to be 'misfits' out of sight and out of mind. Too, I still feel it is unethical to label minority group children as mentally retarded when they are disruptive in school, when they are slow learners, and especially when they obtain IQ scores in the 60s.

"The answer to the second question is a resounding 'no.' My main suggestion was that we stop classifying minority group children as mentally retarded when they do moderately poorly on intelligence tests because this label is not a badge of distinction. To a slight degree, this has happened. However, through PL 94-142, a new category was created known as 'learning disabilities.' Now, an even larger percentage of children who formerly would have been labeled educable mentally retarded are called learning disabled, certainly an improvement over mentally retarded. These so-called learning disabled pupils are then placed in the mainstream (regular class) but fished out once or twice a day, and placed in an aquarium (resource room), both for tutoring and to provide relief for the regular teacher and his or her more able charges. Empirical evidence indicates they achieve no more under this arrangement than if they were left unlabeled in the regular grades (see Semmel *et al.*, 1979[1]).

"The answer to the third question is a qualified 'yes.' Where I was most wrong in my article, in my current view, was in finding a place for so-called special educators in serving these mainstreamed children. I now think their talents would be better utilized if they focused solely on the moderately and severely handicapped. Full responsibility for the so-called mildly retarded/learning disabled, who are often disruptive males, should rest with regular and remedial educators who will need to do a better job than they have in the past of individualizing instruction for these pupils.

"For the best update on mainstreaming, I recommend the article 'Mainstreaming: perspectives on educating handicapped children in the public school.' "[1]

1. **Semmel M I, Gottlieb J & Robinson N M.** Mainstreaming: perspectives on educating handicapped children in the public school. (Berliner D C, ed.) *Review of research in education.* Washington, DC: American Educational Research Association, 1979. Vol. 7. p. 223-79.

Kanner L. Autistic disturbances of affective contact. *Nerv. Child* **2**:217-50, 1943.

Eleven children, discussed in this paper, present a previously unreported congenital infantile psychosis, now known universally as 'early infantile autism' or 'Kanner Syndrome.' It is characterized by extreme aloneness and a desire for the preservation of sameness, with a variety of behavioral (cognitive, affective) symptoms derived from them. [The *Science Citation Index (SCI®)* **and the** *Social Sciences Citation Index™ (SSCI™)* **indicate that this paper has been cited over 315 times since 1961.]**

Leo Kanner
4000 North Charles Street
Baltimore, MD 21212

July 27, 1978

"At the risk of being accused of unmitigated superstition, I do not hesitate to say that I seem to be endowed with serendipity, or 'the gift of finding unsought treasures.' I shall limit myself to the circumstances which brought about the inclusion of my 1943 paper on autism in Citation Classics.

"It was not a search for survival when in 1924 I accepted a job at the Yankton, South Dakota, State Hospital, offered to me on the recommendation of a postgraduate American student at the University of Berlin, whom I instructed in electrocardiography. Little did I know that, had I remained in Germany, I would have perished in the Hitler holocaust a few years later. A clear case of serendipity.

"My switch from cardiology to psychiatry served me well. A few published reports soon gave me a 'name' in the field. In 1928, Adolf Meyer had a place for me at his renowned Phipps Clinic. By 1930, an annex was put at my disposal at the adjacent pediatric hospital 'for the investigation of the rank and file of patients for the formulation of problems, the mastery of which would be made accessible as the psychopathological principles in dealing with children.' I did not realize that this was to mark the origin of academic child psychiatry as a psychobiologically oriented discipline *sui generis* rather than a miniature subdivision of the adult model. The resulting 'Children's Psychiatric Service' of the Johns Hopkins Hospital, of which I was the director, grew into a major clinical, research, and teaching center. Children were referred from everywhere. Governments and private foundations established special training fellowships.

"The first—plurilingual—*Journal of Child Psychiatry,* of which I was an associate editor, appeared in Switzerland in 1934. In 1935, I published 'the first textbook of child psychiatry in the English language.' It has since had several editions and many reprints. It has been translated into several languages, and is still the standard text.[1]

"In 1938, five-year-old Donald T., brought to my clinic from Forest, Mississippi, made me aware of a behavior pattern not known to me or anyone else theretofore. When I saw a few more children presenting similar characteristics, I reported in 1943 eleven cases in some detail in a now extinct journal, *The Nervous Child.* This is the article so frequently cited ever since.

"Interest in autism has become universal. The literature (books, monographs, periodicals, reprints) would fill many shelves. Television and lay magazines have not kept behind. As of now, there are in this country 102 chapters of the National Society for Autistic Children, spread over 34 states, and there are 66 Societies for Autistic Children in 31 countries all over the globe. Of course, there have been diagnostic quandaries, etiological eccentricities, and dogmatic claims from representatives of sectarian 'approaches.' But much progress has been, and more will be, made. All this started 40 years ago with Donald T., now a 45-year-old bank clerk, whose townspeople know him to be the first reported specimen of what many of my colleagues call 'the Kanner Syndrome.' How is that for serendipity?"

1. **Kanner L.** *Child psychiatry.* Springfield, IL: C. C. Thomas Publishing Co., 1935. 527p.

CC/NUMBER 52
DECEMBER 24-31, 1984

This Week's Citation Classic™

Moely B E, Olson F A, Halwes T G & Flavell J H. Production deficiency in young children's clustered recall. *Develop. Psychol.* **1**:26-34, 1969.
[Institute of Child Development, University of Minnesota, Minneapolis, MN]

Developmental changes in children's use of organization in recall were observed. Younger children showed a 'production deficiency,' whereby they failed to group items conceptually during study, although they were able to do so with simple training. By fifth grade, children employed a grouping strategy spontaneously. [The *Social Sciences Citation Index*® (*SSCI*®) indicates that this paper has been cited in over 130 publications since 1969.]

Barbara E. Moely
Department of Psychology
Tulane University
New Orleans, LA 70118

October 10, 1984

"This research was conducted while Fran Olson, Terry Halwes, and I were graduate students working with John Flavell at the University of Minnesota. Learning-theory accounts of developmental change in children's learning, put forth in the 1960s, characterized the young child as showing a 'mediation deficiency' in that potentially available skills or knowledge would not be employed appropriately in learning tasks. Mediation was used as an intervening variable to represent unspecified and unobserved cognitive activities occurring prior to response and varying with age. Flavell moved beyond this model to propose that the child might fail to demonstrate a given skill for several reasons: a production deficiency might occur, in which the appropriate mediator was not produced in the task situation, or the child might show a mediational deficiency, in which the mediating activity occurred but failed to influence task performance.

"This perspective led us to an interest in observing children's activities as they studied in preparation for recall, a design feature we implemented by modifying the traditional method of presenting the task. A free recall task was used to assess strategy use because of our interest in children's conceptual abilities and also because of the influence of James J. Jenkins and his colleagues at Minnesota, who were concerned at that time with the organizational structures influencing language knowledge and use.

"Our study gave strong support to the production deficiency hypothesis, in that children who used an organizational strategy during study did well in recall, while those who did not, although they possessed knowledge about the conceptual categories comprising recall lists, recalled less information in a less organized fashion. With brief instruction, these younger children could be induced to organize and showed concomitant increases in recall performance. Three aspects of the study caused it to be of interest to researchers at the time. First, the study showed striking age differences that fit the production deficiency model. Second, simple training procedures were found to have notable effects on young children's study and recall. Third, the study presented new methods for observing and quantifying the child's spontaneous study activities that were informative and easy to use.

"Visibility of the study was affected by its presentation in two major reviews of memory development by Flavell[1] and Hagen.[2] Cronbach[3] mentioned the study in his arguments against Jensen's[4] proposed conceptualization of industrial differences in learning. Work done more recently has elaborated our picture of children's use of organization and other recall strategies,[5] described the acquisition of metamemory skills implied by our findings,[6] extended training efforts to affect not only other memory strategies but also higher-order metacognitive skills,[7] and described memory development in special populations of developmentally delayed children."

1. **Flavell J H.** Developmental studies of mediated memory. (Reese H W & Lipsitt L P, eds.) *Advances in child development and behavior.* New York: Academic Press, 1970. Vol. 5. p. 181-211.
2. **Hagen J W, Jongeward R H, Jr. & Kail R V, Jr.** Cognitive perspectives on the development of memory. (Reese H W, ed.) *Advances in child development and behavior.* New York: Academic Press, 1975. Vol. 10. p. 57-101.
3. **Cronbach L J.** Heredity, environment, and educational policy. *Harvard Educ. Rev.* **39**:338-47, 1969. (Cited 25 times.)
4. **Jensen A R.** How much can we boost IQ and scholastic achievement? *Harvard Educ. Rev.* **39**:1-123, 1969. [See also: **Jensen A R.** Citation Classic. *Current Contents* (41):16, 9 October 1978.]
5. **Moely B E.** Organizational factors in the development of memory. (Hagen J W & Kail R V, Jr., eds.) *Perspectives on the development of memory and cognition.* Hillsdale, NJ: Erlbaum Associates, 1977. p. 203-36.
6. **Flavell J H & Wellman H M.** Metamemory. (Hagen J W & Kail R V, Jr., eds.) *Perspectives on the development of memory and cognition.* Hillsdale, NJ: Erlbaum, 1977. p. 3-33.
7. **Leal L, Crays N & Moely B E.** Training children to use a self-monitoring study strategy in preparation for recall: maintenance and generalization effects. *Child Develop.* (In press.)

Douglas V I. Stop, look and listen: the problem of sustained attention and impulse control in hyperactive and normal children. *Can. J. Behav. Sci.* **4**:259-82, 1972. [McGill University and Montreal Children's Hosp., Canada]

It is hypothesized that processes involving sustained attention and effort and inhibitory control account for the behavioral and cognitive deficits found in hyperactive children. It is also argued that therapeutic results obtained with stimulant medication result from its effect on these processes. [The *Science Citation Index*® (*SCI*®) and the *Social Sciences Citation Index*® (*SSCI*®) indicate that this paper has been cited over 165 times, making it the most-cited paper ever published in this journal.]

Virginia I. Douglas
Department of Psychology
McGill University
Montreal, Quebec H3A 1B1
Canada

September 5, 1984

"This paper was written after I joined the Department of Psychology at McGill University to help build its clinical training program. Since my new department was a bastion of physiological and experimental psychology, it is perhaps fortunate that I had chosen physiological psychology as a minor area of study during clinical training at the University of Michigan.

"When I developed an interest in childhood hyperactivity while working at the Montreal Children's Hospital, I found several of my colleagues at McGill interested in the questions I wanted to answer and ready to help. Although I had been warned that Donald Hebb, a world-renowned physiological psychologist, was 'anti-clinical,' he proved to be a gently ironic source of wisdom and perspective.

"Most of the work reported in the paper was carried out in collaboration with students in our clinical program, which combines service and research training. As our research expanded into the areas of learning, perception, cognition, memory, neuropsychology, and psychopharmacology, we drew on the ideas of a number of experimental psychologists, some of whom had made a strong impression on my students. These included D. Bindra, A. Amsel, E. Tulving, D. Berlyne, D. Broadbent, B. Milner, and J. Kagan.

"The paper was based on my presidential address to the Canadian Psychological Association and reflects an attempt to integrate our findings up to that time. I argued that the children's hyperactive and disruptive behaviors are accompanied by more subtle cognitive deficits involving the deployment of attention and effort and the inhibition of impulsive responding. I also argued that stimulant medication helps reduce these deficits. In 1980, the importance of attentional problems in the syndrome was recognized—and perhaps exaggerated—by the adoption of a new diagnostic label, 'attention deficit disorder,' by the American Psychiatric Association.

"Recently, the Canadian Psychological Association honored me with its Award for Distinguished Contributions to Psychology as a Profession. I used the occasion to review the research findings and theoretical biases that have made different observers focus on defects in processes governing attention, inhibitory control, arousal, response to reinforcement, stimulation-seeking behavior, or motor activity, and I argued that a comprehensive theory will have to account for the interrelated deficits emphasized in these different theories. I also stressed that many of the children's abilities are intact. Consequently, our research group has adopted the working hypothesis that we are dealing with a disturbance in self-regulation involving both facilitory and inhibitory processes.[1,2]

"I believe that the paper was heavily cited because I happened to begin work on hyperactivity just when investigators from several disciplines were developing an intense interest in the disorder. In addition, the children are both troubling and intriguing. Their thoughtless, impulsive behavior creates serious problems for themselves and society, and the fact that stimulant medication helps curb these tendencies raises perplexing theoretical and ethical issues. Because many of the children have good IQs, they elicit concern about wasted potential. Perhaps, too, they make us aware of the fine line that separates our behavior from theirs."

1. **Douglas V I & Peters K G.** Toward a clearer definition of the attentional deficit of hyperactive children. (Hale G A & Lewis M, eds.) *Attention and the development of cognitive skills.* New York: Plenum Press, 1980. p. 173-247.
2. **Douglas V I.** Attention and cognitive problems. (Rutter M, ed.) *Developmental neuropsychiatry.* New York: Guilford Press, 1983. p. 280-328.

CC/NUMBER 44
NOVEMBER 1, 1982

This Week's Citation Classic

Lovaas O I, Berberich J P, Perloff B F & Schaeffer B. Acquisition of imitative speech by schizophrenic children. *Science* **151**:705-7, 1966. [Dept. Psychology, Univ. California, Los Angeles, CA]

This paper reports a procedure and data on teaching imitative verbal behavior to two previously mute, autistic (schizophrenic) children. Imitation was defined as the teaching of a discrimination where the children's verbal responses became increasingly similar to their discriminative stimulus (the adults' verbal responses). The acquisition was positively accelerated. [The *Science Citation Index*® (*SCI*®) **and the** *Social Sciences Citation Index*® (*SSCI*®) **indicate that this paper has been cited in over 230 publications since 1966.]**

O. Ivar Lovaas
Department of Psychology
University of California
Los Angeles, CA 90024

April 30, 1982

"Autistic children evidence extreme social isolation and fail to develop affective attachments to other people. They typically have failed to develop language, show little or no play behavior, and are grossly deficient in self-help skills. They show limited or no affect such as anxiety, sadness or grief, etc. In a way they are people without the behavior of persons. The prognosis for such children is extremely poor and it is estimated that 99 percent of adult autistic persons are institutionalized. The etiology of the condition is not known.

"In formulating a treatment program for such children we chose a behaviorally based, educational program where we slowly built together behaviors, piece by piece, so as to make the children act more like normal people. We taught these children using explicit rewards, such as food, for appropriate behavior and explicit punishment, such as spanking, for inappropriate behavior; we used prompt and fading techniques, etc. The basic model for this kind of program derives from modern learning theory which goes as far back as Thorndike's work in 1898 and is the mainstay of American psychology.[1]

"There were two major challenges that faced us. The first one was whether this particular teaching/treatment intervention could in fact produce complex behavior changes such as language. The second big challenge concerned the children's own 'capacity' to learn complex behaviors, because most people in the field felt that the autistic children were damaged to such a severe degree, either organically or psychologically, that they could not acquire complex behaviors in the first place.

"We used the same conceptual framework which we had used in building simpler behaviors, specifically we followed a program known as discrimination learning. Much to our joy, the children acquired imitative verbal behavior. This was a major breakthrough in the program of treating autistic and other retarded children because the acquisition of language is so important in order to function as a more competent human being. We initially ran this program on two previously mute autistic children (Michael and Marty) and then replicated these procedures on a number of other disabled children as well. Once we had taught the children verbal imitation, we could teach the children to appropriately use this verbal behavior (as in grammar) as well as the meaning (semantics) of this newly acquired behavior.[2]

"There are certain limitations on these findings which are not immediately apparent in examining these data. The most important is that this kind of verbal behavior does not constitute meaningful language. Rather it is an essential first step. Meaning had to be taught separately at a later time. Secondly, there were large individual differences in the rate at which the children acquired verbal imitation. About half of the previously mute children, even after several years of training, struggled with their verbal expressions, while the other half of the children became truly skillful at imitation and in a way never stopped talking. We are not able to account for this variability at this time.

"I think the article is cited so often because it has been the aim of teachers, psychologists, and other professional people for a long time to help mute children talk, and this is the first time that such a program was successful. For example, the famous physician and educator Itard, who is considered the father of special education, worked with the Wild Boy of Aveyron (Victor), tried very hard to teach Victor speech, but failed in his attempts.[3] Many thought that Itard had failed to a significant degree in his program. It was hoped that acquisition of language on Victor's part would have revealed a great deal of 'innate' knowledge on Victor's part about God, what is right or wrong, space and time, and so on. Actually, Itard's work was very ingenious and much ahead of its time, and there are procedures which Itard developed which are still used some 150 years later. However, Itard did not have the advantage of drawing upon information from experimental psychology which has accrued since 1900. We had that advantage."

1. **Thorndike E L.** *Animal intelligence: an experimental study of the associative processes in animals.* New York: Macmillan, 1898. 109 p.
2. **Lovaas O I.** *The autistic child: language development through behavior modification.* New York: Irvington, 1977. 246 p.
3. **Lane H L.** *The Wild Boy of Aveyron.* Cambridge, MA: Harvard University Press, 1976. 351 p.

This Week's Citation Classic

Heston L L. Psychiatric disorders in foster home reared children of schizophrenic mothers. *Brit. J. Psychiat.* **112**:819-25, 1966.
[Univ. Oregon Med. Sch., Psychiat. Genet. Res. Unit, Maudsley Hosp., London, England]

Fifty persons whose mothers had schizophrenia were compared as adults with 47 controls whose mothers had no psychiatric history. All subjects were reared by adoptive or foster parents. Schizophrenia appeared in five persons born to schizophrenic mothers but in none of the controls, a highly significant difference. [The *Science Citation Index*® *(SCI*®*)* **and the** *Social Sciences Citation Index*® *(SSCI*™*)* **indicate that this paper has been cited over 230 times since 1966.]**

Leonard L. Heston
Psychiatry Research Unit
Mayo Memorial Building
University of Minnesota
Minneapolis, MN 55455

August 29, 1980

"This study had its beginning in 1962 when as a new resident in psychiatry, I made a clinical presentation to my faculty and several visiting physicians. The case presented was that of a paranoid schizophrenic whose father and two of his three siblings were also schizophrenic. I also presented a review of the genetic literature which I hoped would open for discussion the whole question of genetics and schizophrenia. The result was most disquieting. Most of the audience strongly held the view that schizophrenia was due to some catastrophic psychic trauma in early childhood, most likely produced by the mother. I was urged to forget genes and explore this possibility. However, I had become acquainted with the mother of my patient; she seemed to be an uncomplicated, basically optimistic person who was doing her very best to provide some semblance of family life. I thought that having a schizophrenic husband and three schizophrenic children was a heart wrenching burden, for which she had carried responsibility for many years. To accuse her of causing the illness of her children, even if this were done implicitly in 'therapy,' seemed mindlessly cruel. Moreover, the then current theories of the etiology of schizophrenia, the 'schizophrenic mother' and the 'double-bind' which I heard a lot about during the discussion of my case seemed *post hoc* and quite unsupported by evidence. I began to think through ways to resolve the issue and soon had decided to study adopted children. Doing this presented major problems of course, for example, locating persons who had been adopted years before, and indeed, federal granting agencies refused to support the project. 'Impossible to do,' was the verdict. But I did get the help and support of two of my teachers, George Saslow and Duane Denney, and the work was done.

"This study has been cited often for several reasons. It was one of the first to use adoptive children as experiment of nature and the methodology attracted attention. It also was often cited as proving a genetic contribution to schizophrenia. That was wrong. What was actually done was to eliminate the environment that had been thought to produce schizophrenia. Once that environment had been excluded it seemed to many that genes were the only cause left. Of course such views reflected extremely naive environmentalism or, less often, naive geneticism which ignored the extremely complex interplay between genes and environment. Psychiatry's notion of causality has become more sophisticated since this article was published and I like to think of that as one of the happy results of it."

CC/NUMBER 43
OCTOBER 24, 1983

This Week's Citation Classic

Vaughn C E & Leff J P. The influence of family and social factors on the course of psychiatric illness: a comparison of schizophrenic and depressed neurotic patients. *Brit. J. Psychiat.* **129**:125-37, 1976.
[Medical Research Council Social Psychiatry Unit, Inst. Psychiatry, London, England]

The main finding of Brown *et al.*[1] was replicated for two clinically different groups of psychiatric patients. The expressed emotion (EE) of a key relative was the best single predictor of symptomatic relapse, independent of all other factors investigated. Important additive effects between social influence and pharmacological treatments provided clear guidelines for clinical intervention. [The *Science Citation Index*® (*SCI*®) and the *Social Sciences Citation Index*® (*SSCI*®) indicate that this paper has been cited in over 215 publications since 1976.]

Christine E. Vaughn
Schizophrenia Research Unit
Prestwich Hospital
Manchester M25 7BL
England

October 4, 1983

"In 1971, I was a research assistant in the MRC Social Psychiatry Unit when I read my colleague George Brown's latest paper concerning the social environment and relapse in schizophrenia.[1] I was enormously excited by the clinical implications of the findings reported, especially the idea that the relationship between a highly critical, emotional family atmosphere and relapse might be moderated not only by phenothiazine medication but also by reduced contact between patient and relative. I wondered whether I might pursue this line of research for my dissertation, perhaps extending the work by comparing schizophrenic patients with patients from another diagnostic group.

"At first, only Julian Leff shared my enthusiasm for doing what essentially would be a replication of a replication. Eventually, however, it was agreed that he and I might carry out the proposed project if I somehow could streamline the main family interview used to rate relatives' expressed emotion (EE). The interview's great length was a major obstacle since I was to be responsible for all the family assessments. Fortunately, I was able to demonstrate that the production of criticism (the main EE component) was independent of the length of interview, thereby justifying the use of a carefully abbreviated interview schedule. Within weeks the study was under way in what I now realize were near perfect research conditions: full cooperation, few distractions, and no grant continuation applications to write!

"This paper has been highly cited for several reasons. It gave rise to a virtual 'EE industry' of international replications, concurrent validity studies, and clinical intervention programs. It received a lot of attention as did the definitive early papers of Brown *et al.*,[1,2] who first elucidated all the themes which appear in our later work. Undoubtedly we benefited from the progressive refinement of research methods over the years, and the verification of results by the repetition of studies over long periods. The controversial nature of some of our conclusions probably also contributed to the paper's impact. In particular, we made provocative statements about the role of medication in the prevention of relapse in schizophrenia, indicating that social rather than clinical factors accounted for medication failures. The implications for the management and rehabilitation of patients were obvious: pharmacological and social treatments must be prescribed together. Clinical support for this view comes from recent successful attempts to reduce relapse rates of high-risk schizophrenic patients through a combination of medication, mental health education, and specific family interventions.[3,4]

"Our results also went some way toward vindicating the much maligned family of the schizophrenic patient, although this aspect of the EE research regrettably tends to be overlooked. The depression data, interesting in their own right, demonstrated that the attitudes associated with relapse in schizophrenia were not specific to that disorder. Furthermore, psychophysiological experiments by Tarrier and Sturgeon have confirmed our impression that many relatives of schizophrenic patients usually exert a *positive* influence, aiding in the patient's recovery and making future relapses less likely."

1. **Brown G W, Birley J L T & Wing J K.** Influence of family life on the course of schizophrenic disorders: a replication. *Brit. J. Psychiat.* **121**:241-58, 1972.
[The *SCI* and the *SSCI* indicate that this paper has been cited in over 300 publications since 1972.]
2. **Brown G W, Monck E M, Carstairs G M & Wing J K.** Influence of family life on the course of schizophrenic illness. *Brit. J. Prev. Soc. Med.* **16**:55-68, 1962.
[The *SCI* and the *SSCI* indicate that this paper has been cited in over 145 publications since 1962.]
3. **Falloon I R H, Boyd J L, McGill C W, Razani J, Moss H B & Gilderman A M.** Family management in the prevention of exacerbation of schizophrenia. *N. Engl. J. Med.* **306**:1437-40, 1982.
4. **Leff J P, Kuipers L, Berkowitz R, Eberlein-Vries R & Sturgeon D.** A controlled trial of social intervention in the families of schizophrenic patients. *Brit. J. Psychiat.* **141**:121-34, 1982.

CC/NUMBER 49
DECEMBER 5, 1983

This Week's Citation Classic

Buchsbaum M S & Silverman J. Stimulus intensity control and the cortical evoked response. *Psychosom. Med.* **30**:12-22, 1968.
[Laboratory of Psychology and Adult Psychiatry Branch, Clinical Investigations, National Institute of Mental Health, Bethesda, MD]

Cortical evoked potentials (EPs) to light flashes of four intensities and performance on a kinesthetic figural after-effects (KFA) perceptual task were obtained from normal and nonparanoid schizophrenic subjects. Significant correlations were found between EP amplitude/intensity slopes and KFA. [The *Science Citation Index* (*SCI*®) and the *Social Sciences Citation Index*® (*SSCI*®) indicate that this paper has been cited in over 155 publications since 1968.]

Monte S. Buchsbaum
Department of Psychiatry
University of California
Irvine, CA 92717

August 26, 1983

"A hypothetical curve showing first increasing and then decreasing evoked potential (EP) amplitude with successive increases in stimulus intensity was first drawn on a napkin (like the famous declining Lauffer curve) at lunch in the National Institutes of Health (NIH) cafeteria in 1966. I had just arrived at the National Institute of Mental Health (NIMH) in David Shakow's laboratory of psychology. My spare moments during medical school had been spent in Enoch Callaway's laboratory at Langley Porter Neuropsychiatric Institute, learning the then fledgling EP methodology.

"The problem of experimentally characterizing the disturbed perceptual process in schizophrenia was beginning to be actively explored at this time. Julian Silverman had written a review article[1] (also highly cited[2]) relating problems in modulating sensory input to subtypes of schizophrenia. A particularly intriguing finding was the apparent sensory inhibition or 'reducing' in the kinesthetic figural after-effects (KFA) studies of Petrie.[3] Silverman, a psychologist; Robert Henkin, an endocrinologist interested in sensory abnormalities; and I discussed the need for a simple neurophysiological probe free from the need for the subject to follow complicated psychophysical instructions. Presentation of stimuli at various intensities seemed to me a simple way to observe departures from a linear response gradient. With the then state of the art four-channel Mnemotron CAT (computer of average transients) and a Grass photostimulator on hand, the four-intensity 'augmenting-reducing' paradigm was born. Later in the week, our first patient with schizophrenia showed EPs which decreased markedly as stimulus intensity increased—matching his 'reducing' perceptual style on Petrie's test.

"Why was this paper so highly cited? Its historical position in applying EPs to individual differences and consistency with perceptual theories of schizophrenia were important as was the technical ease with which other EP researchers could adopt the paradigm and replicate or refute. This strategy of examining individual differences in pain sensitivity allowed us to detect the subtle actions of naloxone on the endogenous opiate system,[4] to track the switch process in rapidly cycling manic-depressives,[5] and to examine multifactor vulnerability models in suicide and other disorders.[6-8]

"The multidisciplinary total research environment at NIH, the freedom of the Research Associate Program, and the strong interest of the intramural NIMH in new technologies were all factors in the success of this work."

1. **Silverman J.** The problem of attention in research and theory in schizophrenia. *Psychol. Rev.* **71**:352-79, 1964.
2. **Garfield E.** Highly cited articles. 19. Human psychology and behavior. *Essays of an information scientist.* Philadelphia: ISI Press, 1977. Vol. 2. p. 262-8. (Reprinted from: *Current Contents* (18):5-11, 5 May 1975.)
3. **Petrie A.** *Individuality in pain and suffering.* Chicago: University of Chicago Press, 1978. 170 p.
4. **Buchsbaum M S, Davis G C & Bunney W E, Jr.** Naloxone alters pain perception and somatosensory evoked potentials in normal subjects. *Nature* **270**:620-2, 1977.
5. **Buchsbaum M S, Post R M & Bunney W E, Jr.** Average evoked responses in a rapidly cycling manic depressive patient. *Biol. Psychiat.* **12**:83-99, 1977.
6. **Buchsbaum M S, Haier R J & Murphy D L.** Suicide attempts, platelet monoamine oxidase and the average evoked response. *Acta Psychiat. Scand.* **56**:69-79, 1977.
7. **Haier R J, Buchsbaum M S, Murphy D L, Gottesman I I & Coursey R D.** Psychiatric vulnerability, monoamine oxidase and the average evoked potentials. *Arch. Gen. Psychiat.* **37**:340-5, 1980.
8. **Buchsbaum M S.** Neurophysiological studies of reduction and augmentation. (Petrie A.) *Individuality in pain and suffering.* Chicago: University of Chicago Press, 1978. p. 141-57.

 CC/NUMBER 9
MARCH 3, 1980

Winokur G, Clayton P J & Reich T. *Manic depressive illness.* St. Louis, MO: C.V. Mosby, 1969. 186 p. [Washington Univ. Sch. Med., St. Louis, MO]

Manic-depressive illness is described using a classical disease model. Definition, epidemiology, symptoms, genetics, other etiologies, course of illness, and special factors (personality, suicide, occupational status, post-partum impact) are presented. The data base is a systematic clinical and family study. [The *Science Citation Index® (SCI®)* **and the** *Social Sciences Citation Index™ (SSCI™)* **indicate that this book has been cited over 330 times since 1969.]**

George Winokur
Department of Psychiatry
College of Medicine
University of Iowa
Iowa City, IA 52242

December 3, 1979

"In the middle 1960s Paula Clayton and I studied the family histories of 426 affectively ill inpatients. We were interested in heterogeneity within the rubric of broadly defined manic-depressive illness. On the basis of family differences, we separated two types of affective disorders, manic-depressive illness and depressive illness, the former showing a mania. It seemed to us that manic-depressive illness constituted the best example of a homogeneous disease in psychiatry. We decided to do a systematic clinical and family study in manic-depressive illness and, as is usually the case in a medical setting, we looked for somebody who would do the hard work. Ted Reich was a resident who was available and interested in research.

"We collected consecutive admissions of manic-depressive patients and conducted a follow-up and family study. After developing a simple structured interview (a far cry from the current complex systematic interviews), Reich traveled around interviewing both probands and family members. The field work was particularly interesting in that families were always trying to ply him with gifts and with various forms of nourishment. Whether this was a commentary on the families of bipolar patients or Reich is unknown.

"After the material was collected, it was clear that we had the only recent systematic study in the United States on manic-depressive illness. Interesting findings included a high degree of familial affective disorder, more affected females than males in the families, age of onset that was quite early in the probands, a strong suggestion of X-linkage in the genetic transmission of the illness, development of specific symptoms within the mania (i.e., short-lived hallucinations and delusions), and a follow-up which suggested the illness was serious in terms of morbidity and subsequent episodes.

"Our biggest problem was Ted Reich's flight of ideas which necessitated the imposition of deadlines but also enriched the book. Paula, Ted, and I interacted daily on the project and we remained very good friends.

"The reason for the book's success and frequent citation was that there was a concatenation of events in American psychiatry which made it reasonable to consider psychiatric problems as medical entities. The book is quite clearly based on the idea that the medical model is a useful concept, although at no time did any of us interact with each other on the basis of that particular term. The material was presented so that clinicians could understand the data. Manic-depressive illness looks like any illness in medicine. It has a time of onset, a specific clinical picture, and a circumscribed course. There is evidence for a genetic factor. Thus, the book was probably the first in recent times to go back to the old classical viewpoint in psychiatry. This was probably refreshing to a lot of people who for years had had psychiatric problems described to them in words that bore no relation to reality and had these illnesses attributed to a variety of theories, none of which were really testable."

CC/NUMBER 28
JULY 9, 1984

This Week's Citation Classic™

Chapman L J & Chapman J P. *Disordered thought in schizophrenia.* New York: Appleton-Century-Crofts, 1973. 359 p.
[Department of Psychology, University of Wisconsin, Madison, WI]

This book reviews the better-known theories of schizophrenic thought disorder, together with the research evidence for each theory. Methodological problems are a focus of this review. Research designs for testing hypotheses about differential deficit receive special attention. [The *Science Citation Index*® (*SCI*®) and the *Social Sciences Citation Index*® (*SSCI*®) indicate that this book has been cited in over 205 publications since 1973.]

Loren J. and Jean P. Chapman
Department of Psychology
University of Wisconsin
Madison, WI 53706

June 11, 1984

"This book is primarily concerned with schizophrenics' differential deficits, that is, their greater deficit on some kinds of tasks than on others. Most investigators of schizophrenics' disordered thought have studied differential deficits, rather than single deficits, because schizophrenics tend to do worse than normal subjects on almost every kind of task. When we wrote this book, we had been involved with research on schizophrenic thought disorder for almost ten years. We found ourselves puzzled by the many contradictory findings in the field. During a seminar discussion with graduate students, we began to suspect that some of our findings, as well as those of other investigators of differential deficit, might somehow reflect the patient's generalized deficit. We worked to explore this possibility in a systematic way. About this time, our eccentric dean was insisting that all important contributions to science are made through books rather than journal articles. We decided to cater to his whimsy, although by the time we finished the book we had left that school and its dean to move to the University of Wisconsin. The book is the result of several years of work and many discussions with graduate students. Fortunately, the National Institute of Mental Health supported its writing with a grant.

"The reason for this book becoming widely cited is, we believe, in part because of its treatment of theories of schizophrenic thought disorder, but more because of its treatment of methodological problems in the design of research on cognitive defect. We show in this book (as well as in a paper[1] published that same year) that generalized performance deficit in schizophrenia is easily mistaken for specific differential deficit because subjects with such generalized deficit show their greatest mean difference from normal subjects on tasks which have the greatest reliability and the greatest variance. These are tasks which tend—other things being equal—to be composed of items in the middle range of difficulty. The book shows that a surprisingly large number of research findings turn out to be artifacts of this principle. Both the book and an article[1] in the *Psychological Bulletin* discuss practical solutions that involve matching tasks on reliability and difficulty. A more recent article[2] offers a somewhat more general approach.

"The role of generalized poor performance as a potential artifact in studies of differential deficit has gradually become widely accepted in studies of schizophrenic thought disorder but has only recently begun to be recognized by investigators who deal with other content areas. It is, of course, equally important in many studies of other low scoring groups, such as children, brain damaged patients, and retarded persons, as well as in many studies in which accuracy scores vary as a function of either subjects or conditions. For example, we are currently studying similar psychometric issues in the related but somewhat more complicated psychometric problem of measuring the relative effectiveness of right and left hemisphere functioning."

1. **Chapman L J & Chapman J P.** Problems in the measurement of cognitive deficit. *Psychol. Bull.* **79**:380-5, 1973. (Cited 60 times.)
2. ------------------------------------. The measurement of differential deficit. *J. Psychiat. Res.* **14**:303-11, 1978.

This Week's Citation Classic

Bieber I, Dain H J, Dince P R, Drellich M G, Grand H G, Gundlach R H, Kremer M W, Rifkin A H, Wilbur C B & Bieber T B. *Homosexuality: a psychoanalytic study.* New York: Basic Books, 1962. 358 p.

This study demonstrated the influence of specific types of disordered parent-child relationships in the genesis of male homosexuality, particularly the salience of defective father-son inter-relatedness, and it identified a continuity of disturbed relations with other males in childhood and preadolescence. [The *Science Citation Index®* (*SCI®*) and the *Social Sciences Citation Index®* (*SSCI*™) indicate that this book has been cited over 300 times since 1962.]

Irving Bieber
132 East 72nd Street
New York, NY 10021

October 9, 1980

"In 1952 when I organized a psychoanalytic research team, I was research neuropsychiatrist at Memorial Hospital and Sloan Kettering Institute investigating with several others the psychological effects of cancer surgery, but for some time I had wanted to tap the reservoir of data that psychoanalysts are privy to. They gather vast amounts of detailed information about human behavior but with rare exceptions clinical reports are by single practitioners on individual cases or small samples.

"I recruited a research group from an organization to which I belong, the Society of Medical Psychoanalysts. Eight psychiatrists and an invited psychologist, each a practicing psychoanalyst, constituted the team. When we were ready to put our data together, a social psychologist-psychoanalyst joined us.

"The topic of homosexuality was chosen because it could be defined operationally, diagnosed without ambiguity, and it allowed for confidence that the syndrome was represented by the sample. We defined a homosexual as an adult who had repetitive sexual experiences with same-sex partners, and a heterosexual as a sexually active adult who did not participate in homosexual behavior. In all, 77 of about 100 Society members answered three questionnaires containing 500 items concerning 106 homo- and 100 heterosexual male analysands.

"The research group met weekly at my apartment for nine years. We designed the questionnaires, collected and assessed data, discussed inferences, and worked together in an atmosphere of congeniality and cooperation. The entire study cost about $5,000 but the labor was free, including the editing and a lot of typing. All royalties went to the Society for future research.

"The publication contributed initially by helping to break the silence about homosexuality in the media. The study successfully tapped the experience of many psychoanalysts, permitted a rigorous evaluation of theory and clinical process, documented specific parent-child patterns in the background of male homosexuals, emphasized the signal importance of the father in sexual outcome, and delineated developmental characteristics of the pre-homosexual child. Results of treatment showed that about one-third shifted to exclusive heterosexuality.

"In 1964 we received from the American Psychiatric Association the Hofheimer Award for Research, Honorable Mention, a category created for this study. Our work has provided a major data base for other investigators and several who used our questionnaire on non-patient homosexuals produced findings consistent with ours. A negative reception came from activist homosexual groups and others committed to the position that homosexuality is but one adaptation in the broad spectrum of normal sexuality. However, until solid evidence shows homosexuality to be other than an adaptation to pathological childhood experiences, our study stands."

This Week's Citation Classic

CC/NUMBER 48
DECEMBER 1, 1980

Marks I M. *Fears and phobias.* New York: Academic Press, 1969. 302 p.
[Inst. Psychiatry and Bethlem Royal and Maudsley Hospitals, London, England]

Fears and phobias trouble many people, and scientific observation and experiment in animals and men have demonstrated how this inborn response changes with maturation and learning. Abnormal fears can now be treated effectively by behavioral means. [The *Science Citation Index*® *(SCI*®*)* and the *Social Sciences Citation Index*® *(SSCI*TM*)* indicate that this book has been cited over 240 times since 1969.]

Isaac Marks
Institute of Psychiatry
Maudsley Hospital
DeCrespigny Park
London SE5 8AF
England

October 20, 1980

"This book arose out of collaborative work in behavioral psychotherapy when I joined Michael Gelder in 1965, at the Maudsley Hospital, London. Phobias had been in the limelight for most of this century as paradigms of neurosis. Freud cited little Hans as the exemplar for psychoanalytic theory while Watson's little Albert became a model learned phobia for conditioning theorists. Theoretical castles were built on these quicksands, undeterred by the paucity of relevant data, by the failure of attempts to replicate little Albert's experience, or by the wide gap separating etiology from treatment, whatever the ideal.

"In the 1960s the development of behavioral treatment for phobias gave them even more prominence than previously, and helped clinical psychologists to extend their professional role as therapists. Large series of treated phobic patients and fearful clients were collected at many centres, including the Maudsley. Clinical analyses showed that phobic disorders could be classified into multiple phobias like agoraphobia, which is commonly associated with many other neurotic problems like depression, anxiety, and obsessions, less diffuse social phobias, and specific phobias which tend to occur on their own. These three groups differed as regards age of onset of the phobia, sex incidence, habituation of skin conductance, and time needed for treatment. That animal phobias rarely began after age seven suggested phylogenetic influences on learning which had been ignored by general learning theorists throughout this century. The biological boundaries of learning which ethologists had long accepted, only received serious attention in the 1970s. *Fears and Phobias* is often cited in this connection. This area is a textbook illustration of fashion in science, of the rise and fall of scientific paradigms, their selective attention to certain details, and their neglect of glaring inconsistencies. Thomas Kuhn's ideas which describe the physical sciences apply equally to the behavioral sciences.

"The book reviewed the literature not only of the phenomenology but also the treatment of phobias which by 1968 was already extensive and has since mushroomed. The popularity and efficacy of behavioral psychotherapy is steadily increasing in scope. The frequency of citations of *Fears and Phobias* can be attributed to its review of (1) the undying phenomenological features of clinical problems which remain the focus of dominant though now outdated psychoanalytic and conditioning theories of neuroses, and (2) a large literature on treatments which became common in the 1960s and whose descendants are widely employed today.

"Interested readers will find more up-to-date practical information about the treatment of phobias and obsessions in my book *Living with Fear*[1] and a discussion of current theoretical issues in my forthcoming book *Cure and Care of Neurosis.*"[2]

1. **Marks I M.** *Living with fear.* New York: McGraw-Hill, 1980. 302 p.
2. --------------. *Cure and care of neurosis.* New York: Wiley. In press, 1981.

CC/NUMBER 36
SEPTEMBER 5, 1983

This Week's Citation Classic

Zola I K. Culture and symptoms—an analysis of patients' presenting complaints. *Amer. Sociol. Rev.* **31**:615-30, 1966.
[Department of Sociology, Brandeis University, Waltham, MA]

There is a selective process in the differing complaints which a group of Italian and Irish patients bring to the doctor for the same physical disorder. It may be this process rather than etiological ones which account for many of the previously unexplained epidemiological differences between societies and even between subgroups within a society. [The *Social Sciences Citation Index*® (*SSCI*®) indicates that this paper has been cited in over 160 publications since 1966.]

Irving Kenneth Zola
Department of Sociology
Brandeis University
Waltham, MA 02254

June 22, 1983

"When I was a graduate student in the late 1950s in the department of social relations, Harvard University, one of the most lively debates concerned the definition of 'normality.' In research this suspicion emerged as an increasing dissatisfaction with how problems were conceptualized. For example, suppose you accepted that the standard by which one was labeled 'deviant' was objective and scientific. To investigate such concerns you then got two populations—one possessed of the 'deviant' characteristic and one not—and then asked how these groups differed. The usual focus was on how one became 'deviant' more than on how one remained 'conformist.' Since many of us had interests in the mental health area, it was here that our discussions were most informed. We were intrigued by new findings which showed how widely mental illness varied not only in social prevalence and incidence, but also in perception in cultures around the world as well as within our own.

"And yet we shared some concerns about mental illness as the linchpin in this debate, particularly about the objectivity of conceptions and measurements of psychological functioning. For me the answer came one night at a graduate student party. In answer to some probably unasked question, I blurted out, 'We need to find some form of deviance which everyone accepts as real, objective, scientific, and then show how that is socially conditioned.' 'Like what?' asked someone. 'Like physical disease,' I replied.

"The next day my insight still felt right, and I shared it with my medical colleagues. It was easy to apply the findings and controversies about mental illness to the field of physical illness: the so-called 'objectivity' of signs and symptoms not only influenced how we delivered our services (i.e., if anyone was sick enough they would eventually be seen), but also how we did any patient research (i.e., we inevitably studied people's *information* about specific diseases, rarely if ever their attitude or perception of them). Specifically, I decided to investigate how someone decided that 'the trouble' they had was 'important enough' to make them seek medical aid, how they presented these troubles, and whether or not these 'decisions' and 'presentations' varied by ethnic group and by their objective physical condition.

"This research resulted in many papers of which 'Culture and symptoms' is clearly the most well known. Although I recognize its academic quality, it is by no means my favorite article. Moreover, I have always been more interested in decision making[1] than in symptomatology. I did realize, however, that this article provided the scholarly, empirical legitimation for much of my later work. Yet professional acceptance was neither swift nor easy, even for this so-called 'classic.' When I first presented the findings, some accused me of being racist because the results could be used to perpetuate ethnic stereotypes. Even fellow sociologists were rather critical, and the paper required considerable revision before the *American Sociological Review* deemed it worthy of publication.

"It is now well over 20 years since this research was first undertaken and it still seems to warrant citation, reprinting, and discussion. Though flattered, I have over the years become concerned that part of the reason is not the brilliance of the article but the state of the art or at least the state of the audience which reads it. And so when recently offered the opportunity to speculate on this question, I did so and wrote 'Oh where, oh where has ethnicity gone?' "[2]

1. **Zola I K.** Pathways to the doctor—from person to patient. *Soc. Sci. Med.* 7:677-89, 1973.
2. ------------. Oh where, oh where has ethnicity gone? (Gelfand D & Kutzik A, eds.) *Ethnicity and aging.* New York: Springer, 1979. p. 66-80.

Chapter

8

Social Psychology

General / 217

Attitudes / 218–222

Attribution / 223–230

Interaction and groups / 231–241

Psychological effects of social situations / 242–245

CC/NUMBER 7
FEBRUARY 16, 1981

This Week's Citation Classic

Brown R. *Social psychology.* New York: Free Press, 1965. 785 p.

Evidence is presented that group decisions involving risk become riskier following discussion of individual recommendations because each individual has intended to take a bold risky stand but has not known how to do so until the range of individual stands was made known. [The *Social Sciences Citation Index® (SSCI™)* indicates that this book has been cited over 735 times since 1965.]

Roger Brown
Harvard University
Department of Psychology
and Social Relations
Cambridge, MA 02138

January 12, 1981

"I wrote the book, *Social Psychology*, after teaching a course with that title for ten consecutive years, first at Harvard, then at MIT, and then at Harvard again. The course was never twice the same. I maintained a continuing search for topics in social psychology that I could teach with enthusiastic interest. In addition, there was a continuing effort with each topic to find a mode of exposition that would lay bare the issues and quickly engage student interest. There is, I think, no forcing the discovery of good expository structure. It does not come without thorough familiarity with the subject, but even then, it is a blessing that cannot be guaranteed. One is grateful when it happens.

"I felt minimal concern for 'coverage' of social psychology, as conceived in 1965, because it is not a definable theoretical term anyway, but just an educational expedient, and so I added some interesting things not usually included (e.g., the development of intelligence and of moral reasoning) and dropped some things usually included but, to my mind, dull.

"Although *Social Psychology* was marketed as a textbook I did not hesitate to put forward new theoretical ideas. The explanation of the shift-to-risk in group decision making (see abstract) is the principal cause of the book's frequent citation in scientific articles. The gist of the theory is that, in a wide range of decisions, moderate risk is valued in this culture and that value becomes salient in group discussion.

"The book includes anecdotes and jokes and is sometimes written in the first person, and readers who like the book occasionally think they like it for these qualities. I doubt that these qualities, which are easily adopted, are very important. What mattered most, I think, was the structure which gave direction and some drama to each chapter, and these are, I am sure, more important contributors to 'readability' for adults than are high word frequencies or simple sentence structures or sensational content.

"The book has no illustrations, except for a couple of diagrams which I drew myself; it has no guide to students and no guide to teachers and no associated book of readings. Its level of difficulty is high. I should not say so myself, but I think the book is honest science. It is not pretentious and in content it favors cognitive topics rather than sizzling social issues. It went almost directly from my pencil to the printer and was written about as fast as my pencil could move because, of course, it had all been composed in advance in the antecedent ten years of teaching.

"Nothing derived from my scientific work but extrinsic to it has given me as much pleasure as the letters students have generously written me saying that the book meant something important to them.

"A recent summary of this line of work has been published by D.G. Myers and H. Lamm."[1]

1. **Myers D G & Lamm H.** The group polarization phenomenon. *Psychol. Bull.* **83**:602-27, 1976.

This Week's Citation Classic

Sherif C W, Sherif M & Nebergall R E. *Attitude and attitude change. The social judgment-involvement approach.* Philadelphia: W. B. Saunders, 1965. 264 p. [Inst. Group Relations and Dept. Speech, Univ. Oklahoma, OK]

Social judgment theory relates involvement of self to the situational contexts for communication. Predictions about assimilation–contrast effects in judgments of communications and attitude change on issues varying in personal importance are tested through research findings derived through multiple and innovative methods. [The *Social Sciences Citation Index®* *(SSCI™)* **indicates that this book has been cited over 190 times since 1966.]**

Carolyn Wood Sherif
Department of Psychology
Pennsylvania State University
University Park, PA 16802

October 24, 1980

"Sherif and Hovland[1] proposed a theory of social judgment to clarify apparent contradictions in attitude change research. This book elaborated the theory and presented an enlarged data base, especially from a joint project on reactions to communications on 1960 presidential campaign issues. M. Sherif and I collected data while visiting the University of Washington, returning to the University of Oklahoma with data in one car and three children in another. R.E. Nebergall, then in Oklahoma's speech department (now at University of Illinois), had collected data in several southwestern states.

"Testing the theory required new procedures for assessing attitudes. Two distinct methods were presented (method of ordered alternatives and the own categories technique). A person's attitude was conceived as a set of categories enabling discrimination and evaluation of communications on an issue. Attitude was measured as the latitudes (ranges) of advocated positions acceptable and objectionable to the person, with positions neither acceptable or objectionable composing the latitude of noncommitment. The three latitudes vary in structure with the degree of the person's involvement in accepted positions. With higher involvement, the rejected latitude broadens while noncommitment all but disappears.

"To the degree that acceptable positions define one's self, the more those positions serve as standards for sizing up messages on the issue. Messages close to the internal standard are assimilated (the differences minimized), but messages increasingly different are contrasted (differences exaggerated).

"Propensity for attitude change by individuals varying in involvement forms a series of curvilinear functions, when plotted against positions advocated in communications increasingly different from the acceptable latitude. Probability of change increases with small to moderate message differences, but decreases with larger discrepancies, declining to no change and finally change opposed to the advocated position. The range for message assimilation and increasing change is greater with less personal involvement. This book introduced problems concerning degrees of involvement in various issues which became central in subsequent research.[2]

"The extensive research support for the theory is one reason for the citations. The novel research procedures are another. Finally the timing may have been right. Communication researchers were becoming aware that degree of involvement is critical in practical problems of attitude change. After one printing, the publisher was absorbed by the Columbia Broadcasting System, which axed 'small titles.' It is gratifying that the book has been cited despite the publisher."

1. **Sherif M & Hovland C I.** *Social judgment. Assimilation and contrast effects in communication and attitude change.* New Haven: Yale University Press, 1961. 218 p.
2. **Sherif C W.** Values, attitudes, and involvement of the self. (Howe H & Page M, eds.) *Attitudes and values.* Lincoln, NE: University of Nebraska Press, 1980. 365 p.

CC/NUMBER 38
SEPTEMBER 21, 1981

This Week's Citation Classic

Fishbein M. An investigation of the relationships between beliefs about an object and the attitude toward that object. *Hum. Relat.* **16**:233-9, 1963.
[University of California, Los Angeles, CA]

This paper provides support for the hypothesis that attitudes toward an object are a function of (1) salient beliefs about the object and (2) the evaluative aspects of those beliefs. It also provides evidence for the validity of a measure of belief strength and demonstrates that descriptive beliefs are important determinants of attitude. [The *Social Sciences Citation Index*® (*SSCI*®) indicates that this paper has been cited over 150 times since 1966.]

Martin Fishbein
Department of Psychology
University of Illinois
Champaign, IL 61820

July 8, 1981

"Many different factors contributed to the development of the theory of the relations between beliefs and attitudes presented in this paper. The paper was based on my doctoral dissertation and, not surprisingly, it reflects the theoretical and research interests of my two major advisors: Bertram H. Raven and Irving Maltzman. Bert, a social psychologist, was, at the time, excited and intrigued by Leon Festinger's *A Theory of Cognitive Dissonance*.[1] Thus, my first job as Bert's research assistant was to develop a measure of belief strength that could be used as the dependent variable in an experiment testing Festinger's model of 'forced compliance.' Although this seemed like a reasonable request at the time, Bert and I quickly discovered that no generally accepted measures of belief strength existed. However, Charles Osgood's *The Measurement of Meaning*[2] had also just been published and it seemed to me that the 'semantic differential' technique could be used to measure beliefs as well as attitudes. These notions eventually led to the development of the AB Scale.[3]

"Although the AB Scale appeared to have both reliability and validity, it led to the finding that there was no necessary relation between beliefs in the existence of an object (e.g., ESP) and the attitude toward that object. This finding was contrary to most social psychological theory since beliefs had traditionally been viewed as a part of attitude. It therefore became necessary to not only distinguish between beliefs in the existence of an object and beliefs about an object, but also to better understand the relations among beliefs about an object and the attitude toward that object. Existent theories were based on notions of consistency, congruence, or balance but I had trouble accepting the notion of a need or drive toward consistency. In particular, I thought it was perfectly reasonable for someone to hold some negative beliefs about an object yet to generally evaluate that object positively.

"It was here that Maltzman's influence came into play. Maltzman, an experimental psychologist, had been applying Hull-Spence learning theory to an analysis of thinking. I found that by conceptualizing a belief system as a habit-family-hierarchy of responses and by relying on notions of mediated generalization, I could account for the relations among beliefs and attitude without having to incorporate a need or drive for consistency. My doctoral dissertation was an attempt to articulate the theory in both S-R and social psychological terminology, to further validate the B Scale, and to provide an empirical test of the theory.

"I feel that I was very fortunate in being able to work under two men with radically different views of psychology. More important, I am grateful that they both provided the support and encouragement for me to pursue my own ideas. The fact that my dissertation has now become a *Citation Classic* is a tribute to both of them.

"I believe that this article has become a *Citation Classic* because of (a) the general interest in the attitude concept by investigators in a variety of disciplines and (b) the fact that the paper describes a relatively simple operational procedure for identifying and assessing the cognitive structure underlying attitudes toward any object. For a more recent discussion of the model and its application to behavioral prediction in a variety of content domains see *Understanding Attitudes and Predicting Social Behavior*."[4]

1. **Festinger L.** *A theory of cognitive dissonance.* Evanston, IL: Row Peterson, 1957. 291 p.
2. **Osgood C E, Suci G J & Tannenbaum P H.** *The measurement of meaning.* Urbana, IL: University of Illinois Press, 1957. 342 p.
3. **Fishbein M & Raven B H.** The AB scales: an operational definition of belief and attitude. *Hum. Relat.* **15**:35-44, 1962.
4. **Ajzen I & Fishbein M.** *Understanding attitudes and predicting social behavior.* Englewood Cliffs, NJ: Prentice Hall, 1980. 278 p.

This Week's Citation Classic

Wicker A W. Attitudes versus actions: the relationship of verbal and overt behavioral responses to attitude objects. *J. Soc. Issues* **25**:41-78, 1969.
[University of Wisconsin, Milwaukee, WI]

This article reviewed the empirical research on the attitude-behavior relationship. The major conclusion was, 'It is considerably more likely that attitudes will be unrelated or only slightly related to overt behaviors than that attitudes will be closely related to actions.' [The *Science Citation Index®* **(***SCI®***) and the** *Social Sciences Citation Index™* **(***SSCI™***) indicate that this paper has been cited over 270 times since 1969.]**

Allan W. Wicker
Faculty in Psychology
Claremont Graduate School
Claremont, CA 91711

July 27, 1979

"This article was, to a considerable extent, the result of a personal need I felt in the late 1960s to establish the social significance of the attitude concept and related research. I had completed in 1965 an MA thesis that compared the accuracy of prediction of two models of attitude change, and was somewhat disillusioned by the experience. Attitude changes of small magnitude were relatively easy to obtain from undergraduates in the laboratory, but I doubted that the changes had much enduring significance. I began to wonder whether people's attitudes were, in fact, influential guides to their everyday actions, as many social psychologists seemed to assume.

"I decided to explore the issue more systematically. One of the ten propositions that I formulated for my PhD oral examination asserted that the criteria routinely applied to measures of attitudes (such as sensitivity, reliability, and validity) ought also to be applied to overt behaviors.

"A research grant from the Graduate School of the University of Wisconsin-Milwaukee, where in 1967 I took my first faculty position, allowed me to pursue this interest further. With the help of two undergraduates, I searched the social science literature for studies in which individuals' attitudes and overt behaviors toward the same object had been measured on separate occasions. I excluded from the review studies in which self-reports were the sole behavioral measures. The criteria were rather stringent, but were in keeping with the prevailing assumption about attitudes.

"The manuscript was published in the second journal to which it was submitted. The editor of the leading psychological journal which published literature reviews rejected it on the advice of two reviewers.

"I can think of several possible reasons why the paper has been frequently cited: 1) Its major conclusion challenged an implicit assumption held by many social psychologists; 2) it provided the first systematic review of the literature in this area; and 3) shortly after it was published I mailed out several hundred unsolicited reprints to attitude researchers.

"Numerous articles have appeared on this topic since my 1969 review. Some writers have sought to defend the attitude concept; others have suggested theoretical refinements of the issue or have provided new empirical data. (An updated summary of the attitude-behavior literature is in preparation by Richard J. Hill, an early researcher in this area.[1]) Shortly after my review appeared I published an empirical paper examining the influence of selected other variables on the attitude-behavior relationship,[2] and then turned to other (less frequently cited, but more promising) research interests."

1. **Hill R J.** The attitude-behavior relationship: a review. (Rosenberg M & Turner R, eds.) *Sociological perspectives on social psychology.* New York: Basic Books. In press.
2. **Wicker A W.** An examination of the "other variables" explanation of attitude-behavior inconsistency. *J. Personal. Soc. Psychol.* **19**:18-30, 1971.

Strickland B R. The prediction of social action from a dimension of internal-external control. *J. Soc. Psychol.* **66**:353-8, 1965.
[Department of Psychology, Emory University, Atlanta, GA]

In the spring of 1963, the Rotter IE Scale was administered to 53 black social activists and a control group of 105 black students. A significant relationship was found between internal expectancies and behavioral commitment to civil rights activism. [The *Social Sciences Citation Index*® (*SSCI*®) indicates that this paper has been cited in over 120 publications since 1966.]

Bonnie R. Strickland
Department of Psychology
University of Massachusetts
Amherst, MA 01003

December 27, 1983

"As a displaced Southerner in the clinical program at Ohio State University in the early 1960s, I followed the events of the civil rights movement with great interest. A number of us worked with Julian Rotter*, Doug Crown, and Shep Liverant to revise and improve the early assessment instruments of internal *versus* external control of reinforcement expectancies (IE). This was particularly exciting in that IE beliefs were predictive of behavior not only in experimental laboratories but in real life as well. In learning laboratories, internals gave different extinction curves following acquisition than did externals. In prisons and hospitals, internals were more knowledgeable about situational events, such as opportunities for parole or health care. The willingness of internals to involve themselves in social action was an obvious question of interest.

"Pearl Gore-Dansby and Rotter completed the first study on IE and attempts to change racial practices in the South.[1] Internal black college students were significantly more likely than externals to commit themselves to social action such as signing petitions, participating in mass rallies, or taking 'freedom rides' across the South. A limitation of the findings was that while written responses were available, no actual behavioral indexes were gathered.

"In 1962, I returned to Atlanta, the center of organized civil rights activities at that time. In the spring of 1963, the Southern Student Non-Violent Coordinating Committee (SNCC) held a conference there. Fifty-three SNCC members and selected civil rights activists agreed to complete the Rotter IE Scale plus several other questionnaires. We ran into one minor difficulty. We asked respondents to note their race since we planned to use data only from black activists. Some participants responded 'human' and could not be placed according to ethnic background.

"SNCC activists were predominantly involved in voter registration in rural areas of the Southeast. They lived in conditions of poverty with physical harassment and threats of violence. The mean number of arrests was five with one respondent having been jailed 62 times. One hundred and five black college students who had not been so involved in dramatic social action served as a control group. Black students were difficult to identify who had not, at the least, participated in street demonstrations, but generally the control students had not made a full-time commitment to civil rights. As expected, SNCC activists were significantly more internal than matched college students. No sex differences were evident.

"Events surrounding civil rights activities, of course, changed rapidly during the 1960s, especially in regard to debates about civil disobedience and confrontational techniques. As some activists began to espouse violence, Sank and I found militants to be more external than moderate activists.[2] Surely some of our early findings are now as dated as the language we used (Negroes, White Citizen Councils, etc.). Still and all, I suspect that the importance of this article had to do with the fact that this was one of the first studies in which an individual difference variable predicted an important social action."

1. **Gore P M & Rotter J B.** A personality correlate of social action. *J. Personality* **31**:58-64, 1963. (Cited 195 times.)
2. **Sank Z B & Strickland B R.** Some attitudinal and behavioral correlates of a belief in militant or moderate social action. *J. Soc. Psychol.* **90**:337-8, 1973.
***Rotter J B.** See Citation Classic. Commentary on "Generalized expectancies for internal versus external control of reinforcement." *Psychol. Monogr.* 80:1-28, 1966.
Current Contents/Social & Behavioral Sciences **14**(5):20, 1 February 1982.

NUMBER 7
FEBRUARY 12, 1979

This Week's Citation Classic

Byrne D. Interpersonal attraction and attitude similarity. *J. Abnormal Soc. Psychol.* **62**: 713-5, 1961.

College students examined an attitude scale purportedly filled out by an anonymous fellow student. It was found that as subject-stranger attitude similarity increased, the stranger was linked better and evaluated as being more intelligent, more knowledgeable about current events, more moral, and better adjusted. [The *Science Citation Index*® *(SCI*® *)* and the *Social Sciences Citation Index™ (SSCI™)* indicate that this paper has been cited 209 times since 1961.]

Donn Byrne
Department of Psychological Sciences
Purdue University
West Lafayette, IN 47907

January 20, 1978

"This relatively simple experiment turned out to be the beginning of an active research program that has stretched over almost two decades. The methodology, the procedures, and most important, the theoretical interpretation of the relationship have influenced my research as well as that of my students and numerous colleagues. Some of the research by others was designed expressly in the futile (in my opinion) attempt to disconfirm the findings and/or my interpretation of their meaning.

"The paper in question was a slender reed on which to build the ensuing empirical and theoretical structure. The conceptualization of attraction as a function of reinforcement and of similar attitudes as one class of reinforcers was provided in a 1956 paper by Theodore Newcomb that I read and was impressed by as a graduate student.[1] Then, during my first year as an Assistant Professor at the University of Texas, the notion of operationalizing those constructs in a particular way (adapted from some earlier work by Anthony Smith) and of testing the hypothesized effect experimentally was developed. The work was planned while lying painfully in bed on a Saturday morning following a long-lasting Friday evening party.

"This research has undoubtedly been cited a great deal not for its intrinsic merit but primarily because it was the prototype of a great deal of subsequent work. I believe that there are three major reasons that this approach to attraction proliferated. First, the methodology of the attitude similarity studies is straightforward, easy to utilize, and inexpensive. These pragmatic concerns tend, reasonably enough, to influence many behavioral scientists and their graduate students. Second, the results were powerful both in a statistical sense and in terms of the obvious emotional impact on the subjects. For those among us who are familiar with weak relationships and marginal results, a blockbuster effect is a powerful motivator to pursue a particular line of inquiry. Third, the reinforcement conceptualization (proposed several years before there was any direct confirmatory evidence) served to initiate research among that tiny band of social psychologists who find learning theory intellectually compatible *and* among that much larger group who find such an approach anathema.

"As an illustration of the tenacity of an ideational system, it might be of interest to note that the basic constructs that were developed to explain interpersonal attraction have more recently been expanded to account for human sexual behavior and, in a final burst of grandiosity, to serve as the basis for a forthcoming theory of personality. But for that party in Texas, the psychological world might have been spared these various excesses."

Reference

1. **Newcomb TM.** The prediction of interpersonal attraction. *Amer. Psychol.* **11**:575-86, 1956.

CC/NUMBER 22
MAY 28, 1984

This Week's Citation Classic™

Storms M D. Videotape and the attribution process: reversing actors' and observers' points of view. *J. Personal. Soc. Psychol.* **27**:165-75, 1973.
[Department of Psychology, Yale University, New Haven, CT]

Sets of two unacquainted college students (actors) met for brief 'getting acquainted' conversations while two other students observed. One actor was videotaped and the tape was replayed to all four subjects. Actors who viewed themselves on tape made stronger personal attributions for their behavior during the conversation while actors who viewed the other actor on tape attributed their own behavior more to the situation. Observers' attributions about the two actors' behavior were similarly influenced by whom they saw on the videotape replay. [The *Social Sciences Citation Index*® (*SSCI*®) indicates that this paper has been cited in over 325 publications since 1973.]

Michael D. Storms
California School of Professional Psychology
2235 Beverly Boulevard
Los Angeles, CA 90057

April 12, 1984

"During my last year of graduate school at Yale University, I had planned and started an applied social psychology dissertation at a local factory. Several weeks into the study, and after I had collected pretest data, the factory went out of business and I was left stranded without a dissertation. In desperation I approached every faculty member I knew and begged for a dissertation idea. One of my professors, Dick Nisbett, mentioned a theoretical paper he had just completed with Ed Jones[1] in which they argued that people tend to attribute the cause of their own behavior more to situational factors while they tend to attribute the cause of others' behavior more to personality factors—a phenomenon they called the 'actor/observer effect.' Dick thought I might be able to find some kind of dissertation idea in that paper.

"Meanwhile, I had also become fascinated by the emerging technology of videotape recording. This was in the late 1960s, and few people had seen themselves on tape. In the process of taping several of my friends and colleagues and showing the tapes back to them, it occurred to me that when people see themselves on videotape for the first time, they are put in the unique position of being observers of their own actions. Would that then lead them to make more observer-like attributions about their behavior?

"Thus, the idea was born for a very simple dissertation in which two strangers would meet and converse for five minutes, one participant in the conversation would be taped, and the tape would be replayed immediately after the conversation. As hypothesized, the actor who saw him/herself on tape made more personal attributions for his/her own behavior during the conversation.

"It is hard to say why a particular study becomes frequently cited in psychology. I suspect this study has gained some attention because it makes a very simple point about the influence of salience and attention on higher-order cognitive processes—when my subjects saw themselves on videotape, information about themselves became more salient and more likely to become grist for their attribution mills. The field of social cognition and attribution theory has since spawned much more sophisticated analyses of the influence of salience, attention, perception, and 'point of view,' such as the acclaimed work of Shelley Taylor (e.g., reference 2). Dick, whose influential theoretical work provided the basic idea for my dissertation, has continued to publish insightful papers on how people's cognitive maps are influenced by the ways they process the data available to them (e.g., reference 3)."

1. **Jones E E & Nisbett R E.** *The actor and the observer: divergent perceptions of the causes of behavior.* Morristown, NJ: General Learning Press, 1971. 16 p.
2. **Taylor S E & Fiske S T.** Salience, attention, and attribution: top of the head phenomena. (Berkowitz L, ed.) *Advances in experimental social psychology.* New York: Academic Press, 1978. Vol. 11. p. 249-88.
3. **Nisbett R E & Ross L.** *Human inference: strategies and shortcomings of social judgment.* Englewood Cliffs, NJ: Prentice-Hall, 1980. 334 p.

This Week's Citation Classic

Jones E E & Davis K E. From acts to dispositions: the attribution process in person perception. *Advances in experimental social psychology.* (L. Berkowitz, ed.) New York: Academic Press, 1965. Vol. II, p. 219-266.
[Duke University, Durham, NC]

A theory is proposed to account for an observer's attribution of personal dispositions upon the perception of an act. Informative ('correspondent') dispositions will be inferred to the extent that there are few distinctive reasons for the act and these reasons have low 'prior probability.' [The *Science Citation Index®* *(SCI®)* **and the** *Social Sciences Citation Index*™ *(SSCI*™*)* **indicate that this paper has been cited over 295 times since 1965.]**

Edward E. Jones
Department of Psychology
Princeton University
Princeton, NJ 08540

January 17, 1978

"This integrative theoretical paper originated in a very simple notion I had used in explaining to undergraduates how we perceive and make inferences about other people: strong and confident dispositional inferences are drawn about a person when we see him or her act under conditions of high choice. To me this was a relatively self-evident proposition that nevertheless had didactic value precisely because students would readily recognize its common sense validity.

"When I was invited to prepare a paper for *Advances in Experimental Social Psychology,* I thought I would try to formalize this notion and thus provide a framework for discussing my own and others' person perception research. After several discussions with Keith Davis, a former student whom I much admired, a theory of 'correspondent inference' emerged that was considerably more complicated than its animating notion. Although the theory seemed to flow naturally from a careful consideration of the conditions and consequences of perceived choice, I recall being quite nervous about the resulting essay. At times I wondered whether we had concealed a banal truth in some new and pretentious jargon. At other times I began to wonder whether we had merely re-invented information theory and shown its utility in the person perception context. When I discussed the ideas with my immediate colleagues, their reactions were politely supportive, but I remained uncertain of the value and clarity of our formulation.

"In order to understand why the original paper has been so often cited, it is necessary to consider the *zeitgeist* in the middle and late 1960s. A number of independent efforts were beginning to crystallize into an 'attributional approach' to interpersonal relations. Our paper was one of the first systematic attempts at an attribution theory. It was not particularly acclaimed or widely cited soon after its publication, but as the attribution movement gathered influence in the late 1960s, the paper was resurrected and became a standard reference in social psychology textbooks.

"It is not clear to me how much the paper was a stimulus for the development of today's omnipresent attributional perspective in social psychology and how much it was merely a reference swept up in the enthusiasm generated by the work of others such as Fritz Heider[1] and Harold Kelley.[2] I like to believe that the staying power of the essay reflects its utility as a framework for housing past experimental results and for generating new research."

1. **Heider F.** *Psychology of interpersonal relations.* New York: Wiley, 1958. 322 p.
2. **Kelley H H.** Attribution theory in social psychology. *Nebraska symposium on motivation.* (Levine D., ed.), Lincoln, NE: Univ. Nebraska Press, 1967, p. 192-240.

CC/NUMBER 41
OCTOBER 8, 1984

This Week's Citation Classic™

Miller D T & Ross M. Self-serving biases in the attribution of causality: fact or fiction? *Psychol. Bull.* **82**:213-25, 1975.
[University of Waterloo, Ontario, Canada]

Research demonstrates that people accept more responsibility for their successes than for their failures. The traditional explanation for this asymmetry focuses on people's need to think well of themselves. It can also be explained, however, by implicating various cognitive processes, such as expectancies and covariation detection. [The *Social Sciences Citation Index®* (*SSCI®*) indicates that this paper has been cited in over 240 publications since 1975.]

Dale T. Miller
Department of Psychology
Simon Fraser University
Burnaby, British Columbia V5A 1S6
Canada

July 27, 1984

"Attribution theory was a very 'hot' research area in social psychology during the 1970s, so in my last year in graduate school at the University of Waterloo, I occasionally attended a seminar on this subject taught by Michael Ross. The topic on one of the days I visited the seminar was people's causal attributions for positive and negative outcomes. Near the end of the seminar, the idea emerged that the tendency of people to take credit for success and to deny responsibility for failure may have its roots in cognitive processes rather than motivational ones, as had generally been assumed. I was intrigued by this idea and, since I was quick to seize any opportunity to divert myself from the writing of my dissertation, I spent some time in the library closely examining the relevant studies.

"My review of the literature and a subsequent discussion with Ross convinced me that there were alternative cognitive explanations for what we were later to term the 'self-serving attributional bias.' Ross and I both were busy with other projects at the time, however, and we did not discuss the idea further. Indeed, the paper would not have been written (by us, at least) if it were not for the fact that a couple of months later our respective travel plans for the Christmas vacation fell through, leaving us both with an unexpected block of uncommitted time. We agreed that our misfortune provided us with an ideal opportunity to delve into the question of self-serving attributions. By the end of the holidays, we had completed a rough draft of the paper.

"There are probably a number of reasons this paper is so highly cited. One reason is simply that this article reviewed a body of literature that had not been reviewed previously and that continues to grow. The most important reason, however, is that the argument that attributional biases reflect features of information processing rather than the perceiver's needs or wishes was consistent with a dominant theme in the rapidly expanding area of social cognition. A major tenet of the cognitive 'revolution' that has swept social psychology is that most inferential errors and biases have cognitive rather than motivational origins.

"Since the publication of our paper, research on this topic has continued at a brisk pace. Much of this research has sought stronger evidence for the role of motivation in causal attribution.[1,2] We now know much more about the factors that influence the attributions people make for positive and negative outcomes. However, an understanding of the precise interplay of cognitive and motivational factors in this process still eludes us."[3]

1. **Miller D T.** Ego involvement and attributions for success and failure. *J. Personal. Soc. Psychol.* **34**:901-6, 1976. (Cited 80 times.)
2. **Sicoly F & Ross M.** Facilitation of ego-biased attributions by means of self-serving observer feedback. *J. Personal. Soc. Psychol.* **35**:734-41, 1977.
3. **Tetlock P & Levi A.** Attribution bias: on the inconclusiveness of the cognition-motivation debates. *J. Exp. Soc. Psychol.* **18**:68-88, 1982.

CC/NUMBER 11
MARCH 15, 1982

This Week's Citation Classic

Feather N T. Attribution of responsibility and valence of success and failure in relation to initial confidence and task performance.
J. Personal. Soc. Psychol. **13**:129-44, 1969.
[Flinders Univ. South Australia, Bedford Park, South Australia]

This paper showed that subjects were more likely to attribute success or failure to luck rather than to ability when the outcome was unexpected than when it was expected. They were also more satisfied with the unexpected success and more dissatisfied with the unexpected failure than when their expectations were confirmed by the outcome. [The *Social Sciences Citation Index*® (*SSCI*®) **indicates that this paper has been cited over 155 times since 1969.]**

N.T. Feather
Department of Psychology
School of Social Sciences
Flinders University of South Australia
Bedford Park 5042
South Australia

January 20, 1982

"I collected the data for this study in 1968. I had spent 1967 at the Institute of Social Research in Ann Arbor working with Jack Atkinson on research into achievement motivation. I also remember meeting Bernie Weiner at UCLA and talking with him about achievement motivation and possible research on causal attribution just before I left the US. On the long sea voyage home to Australia, I spent some of the time thinking about the psychological processes that might underlie how a person makes causal attributions for success and failure and also about the variables that might affect a person's judgments about the attractiveness or aversiveness (positive/negative valence) of achievement-related outcomes. These ideas jelled soon after my arrival at Flinders to take up the foundation chair in psychology, and the study was quickly designed and completed in my first year there.

"It would be wrong, however, to see this study as an excursion into a completely new area. For many years prior to the research I had been involved in applying the expectancy-value approach to the study of human motivation, especially in relation to achievement behavior. I had also been interested in how balance theory could be applied to model both the cognitive effects of communication between source and receiver and the effects of attitude on the selective recall of arguments.

"The study reported in the 1969 article brought some of these strands together. The paper attempted to achieve a nice balance between theory and empirical findings. I received thoughtful and encouraging comments from Bill McGuire who was then editor of the journal in which the paper was published.

"The article appeared at an opportune time and anticipated a period of active interest in attribution theory among psychologists. It was a forerunner in the attribution field and I think that that is one reason why it is so often cited. The fact that the paper was multifaceted is probably another reason for its frequent citation. The different themes (e.g., attribution, valence, expectancy, balance theory, sex differences) were such as to interest a wide range of psychologists. Indeed, the article is cited in many different contexts that include attribution theory, expectancy models, cognitive theories of human motivation, the analysis of job satisfaction, and the psychology of sex differences.

"I have continued to do research into causal attribution, valence, and expectancy theory since 1968. My recent book, *Expectations and Actions: Expectancy-Value Models in Psychology*, contains a chapter in which the earlier research, including the 1969 study, is reviewed and brought up to date.[1] A theoretical paper provides a conceptual integration of my applications of balance theory to the analysis of communication effects, attribution behavior, and selective recall.[2] And a recent article presents a theoretical analysis of the conditions under which values may spill over into action, again taking expectations and valences into account.[3] The general question of the interrelationships between cognition, affect, and behavior continues to engage me, and the 1969 article was an important step in the development of my ideas."

1. **Feather N T.** Actions in relation to expected consequences: an overview of a research program. (Feather N T, ed.) *Expectations and actions: expectancy-value models in psychology.* Hillsdale, NJ: Lawrence Erlbaum Associates, 1982. p. 53-95.
2. ----------------. Organization and discrepancy in cognitive structures. *Psychol. Rev.* **78**:355-79, 1971.
3. ----------------. Human values and the prediction of action: an expectancy-valence analysis. (Feather N T, ed.) *Expectations and actions: expectancy-value models in psychology.* Hillsdale, NJ: Lawrence Erlbaum Associates, 1982. p. 263-89.

This Week's Citation Classic

McArthur L A. The how and what of why: some determinants and consequences of causal attribution. *J. Personal. Soc. Psychol.* **22**:171-93, 1972.
[Brandeis University, Waltham, MA]

Kelley's attribution theory was supported. Behaviors that were nondistinctive and/or nonconsensual were attributed to causes in the actor, while distinctive and/or consensual behaviors were attributed to causes in a target stimulus. Behaviors that were inconsistent over time were attributed to circumstantial causes. [The *Social Sciences Citation Index*® **(***SSCI*®**) indicates that this paper has been cited in over 180 publications since 1972.]**

Leslie Ann Zebrowitz McArthur
Department of Psychology
Brandeis University
Waltham, MA 02254

February 17, 1983

"It was 1968, my third year in graduate school at Yale University. Having completed a pre-dissertation research requirement, I had a year to do whatever research I liked before embarking on my dissertation. In a seminar taught by Chuck Kiesler during the preceding semester, I had read a paper by Harold Kelley[1] that I found a refreshing change from dissonance theory which so dominated the recent literature. Whereas dissonance theory viewed people as 'rationalizing creatures' and systematically demonstrated how they rather foolishly changed their beliefs in order to justify their behavior, Kelley's attribution theory viewed people as 'naive scientists' who logically weighed information in order to make correct inferences about the causes of their own and others' behavior. This view of human thought was more in keeping with my own 'naive psychology' than the dissonance view, and I decided to test it.

"The method that I chose was inspired by a questionnaire methodology that my adviser, Bob Abelson, had developed to study inductive and deductive inference.[2] It was easily adapted to attribution theory questions, and permitted a comprehensive test of Kelley's model within a single experiment. After collecting the data and performing some cursory statistical analyses that revealed strong support for Kelley's model, I put this research aside and began planning my dissertation research.

"Like most graduate students, I wanted my dissertation to be earthshaking...and I didn't really think that my test of Kelley's theory was sufficiently exciting. In consultation with the requisite three faculty advisers, I designed and executed my intended *magnum opus*. The results I obtained were confusing, at best. Having approved my research design, my advisers could not reject this work simply because the results were disappointing. But I hated to write a lengthy dissertation that culminated in such meager findings. So, I asked if I might submit my earlier study testing Kelley's model as my dissertation research. Thanks to the willingness of my committee to bend the rules, this study became my 'adopted' dissertation, and I gave it much more time and thought than I would otherwise have done. Indeed, had my 'real' dissertation panned out, it is possible that this much cited study would never have been published. But certainly someone would eventually have published data supporting Kelley's model. While I like to think that the extensive citation of my experiment does reflect its merits, I know that it also reflects my good fortune to have done the right thing at the right time.

"Attribution theory's time had come. In rapid succession was the publication of not only Kelley's theory but also the attribution theories of Jones and Davis[3] and Bem.[4] These works have inspired researchers for more than a decade, during which time attribution theory has come to dominate the field as dissonance theory did before it. Oddly enough, however, what first drew me to attribution theory—its conceptualization of human thought as rational—no longer typifies attribution research. Most current work stresses the errors and biases in causal thinking, not the essential logic."[5]

1. **Kelley H H.** Attribution theory in social psychology. *Nebr. Symp. Motiv.* **15**:192-238, 1967.
[The *SCI* indicates that this paper has been cited in over 795 publications since 1967.]
2. **Abelson R P & Kanouse D E.** The subjective acceptance of verbal generalizations. (Feldman S, ed.) *Cognitive consistency: motivational antecedents and behavioral consequents.* New York: Academic Press, 1966. p. 171-97.
3. **Jones E E & Davis K E.** From acts to dispositions: the attribution process in person perception. (Berkowitz L, ed.) *Advances in experimental social psychology.* New York: Academic Press, 1965. Vol. 2. p. 219-66.
4. **Bem D J.** Self-perception: an alternative interpretation of cognitive dissonance phenomena. *Psychol. Rev.* **74**:183-200, 1967.
5. **Nisbett R E & Ross L.** *Human inference: strategies and shortcomings of social judgment.* Englewood Cliffs, NJ: Prentice-Hall, 1980. 334 p.

This Week's Citation Classic

Deaux K & Emswiller T. Explanations of successful performance on sex-linked tasks: what is skill for the male is luck for the female. *J. Personal. Soc. Psychol.* **29**:80-5, 1974. [Purdue University, Lafayette, IN]

Explanations for an equivalent successful performance by a male and a female were found to differ, with males being credited with relatively more ability than luck and females seen as luckier than males. These differences were found only when the task was masculine in content. [The *Social Sciences Citation Index*® *(SSCI*®) **indicates that this paper has been cited in over 170 publications since 1974.]**

Kay Deaux
Department of Psychological Sciences
Purdue University
West Lafayette, IN 47907

May 4, 1983

"After fairly traditional work on attitudes as a graduate student and as an assistant professor at Wright State University, I arrived at Purdue University looking for an area of research that was less charted and potentially more involving. Prompted by the rising feminist movement, I began to consider how social psychology might be applied to gender-related issues. My initial inquiries were rather simple (and not heavily cited)—a modest revelation that results obtained with male subjects and male stimulus persons do not necessarily hold true if women are included,[1] and a demonstration, similar to Goldberg's,[2] that male and female performances are not rated equally.[3] Although such demonstrations were important, I felt it was necessary to adopt a more theoretical approach to the issues of sex discrimination.

"Attribution theory appeared to offer a suitable framework. Drawing from the fertile ideas of Fritz Heider,[4] investigators such as Bernard Weiner[5] and Norman Feather[6] had begun to explore the explanations that people offer for their success and failure. Applying this framework to the case of sex discrimination, I predicted that different expectations for male and female performance would result in different explanations for their respective success.

"Joined by Tim Emswiller, a creative and energetic undergraduate (whose peripatetic post-Purdue career has included a stint as a theater costumer at Yale University, graduate work in social psychology at the City University of New York, and, at last report, marketing research for American Express), I designed the study cited here. The results were as expected when the task had masculine associations; however, the feminine task, perceived without cause as easier, did not elicit differential attributions.

"I believed the study to be an important step forward in understanding sex discrimination. The *Journal of Personality and Social Psychology* reviewer, while voicing a few concerns, seemed to agree, recommending acceptance for a study that was the 'first of its type' with 'interesting' results. The editor was less impressed. Although acknowledging it to be 'a good idea and a nice study,' he found the interpretation 'a bit cloudy' and elected to reject the article. Unwilling to accept this verdict, I wrote what I hoped was a persuasive (and, in retrospect, was a somewhat testy) letter to the editor asking for reconsideration. He did indeed reverse his decision, accepting the manuscript with no revision.

"The high citation rate of this article seems attributable to its location at the junction of two major trends during the 1970s. First, research on attribution processes dominated that decade, subsumed only recently in the more general concern with social cognition. Secondly, the 1970s saw a tremendous growth in research on gender-related issues, a surge that continues in the 1980s. In 1976, I reviewed a number of studies in this area and attempted to provide a more detailed, theoretical framework.[7] More recent research, while improving the methodology and qualifying some of the conditions under which this particular phenomenon occurs, has verified its existence and persistence."

1. **Deaux K.** To err is humanizing: but sex makes a difference. *Represent. Res. Soc. Psychol.* **3**:20-8, 1972.
2. **Goldberg P.** Are women prejudiced against women? *Transaction* **5**:28-30, 1968.
3. **Deaux K & Taynor J.** Evaluation of male and female ability: bias works two ways. *Psychol. Rep.* **32**:261-2, 1973. [The *SSCI* indicates that this paper has been cited in over 55 publications since 1973.]
4. **Heider F.** *The psychology of interpersonal relations.* New York: Wiley, 1958. 322 p.
5. **Weiner B, Frieze I, Kukla A, Reed L, Rest S & Rosenbaum R.** *Perceiving the causes of success and failure.* Morristown, NJ: General Learning Press, 1971. 26 p.
6. **Feather N T.** Attribution of responsibility and valence of success and failure in relation to initial confidence and task performance. *J. Personal. Soc. Psychol.* **13**:129-44, 1969. [Citation Classic. *Current Contents/Social & Behavioral Sciences* **14**(11):24, 15 March 1982.]
7. **Deaux K.** Sex: a perspective on the attribution process. (Harvey J, Ickes W J & Kidd R F, eds.) *New directions in attribution research.* Hillsdale, NJ: Lawrence Erlbaum Associates, 1976. Vol. 1. p. 335-52.

CC/NUMBER 49
DECEMBER 8, 1980

This Week's Citation Classic

Weiner B & Kukla A. An attributional analysis of achievement motivation.
J. Personal. Soc. Psychol. **15**:1-20, 1970.
[University of California, Los Angeles, CA]

The determinants of achievement evaluation were examined. Effort expenditure, as well as outcome, are most influential in determining the performance evaluation of others. Low ability-high effort-success leads to most reward, while high ability-low effort-failure begets most punishment. [The *Social Sciences Citation Index® (SSCI™)* **indicates that this paper has been cited over 210 times since 1970.]**

Bernard Weiner
Department of Psychology
University of California
Los Angeles, CA 90024

October 9, 1980

"I feel somewhat embarrassed (and delighted) about replying to this request, for I do not consider this paper either an empirical or a theoretical 'landmark' for the field of psychology. It did, however, contribute to some later advances in attribution theory as well as provide a foundation for my personal theoretical developments. The reasons for its popularity are that some of the first investigations applying attribution theory to the achievement domain are reported, and attribution theory subsequently gained ascendance in psychology. In addition, the contents are relevant to a wide variety of issues both in psychology and education.

"My research collaborator at the University of California, Los Angeles, was Andy Kukla, a graduate student who contributed to all phases of the research. The investigations were undertaken at a time when the concept of locus of control was beginning to sweep psychology. People were classified as 'internal' or 'external' in locus of control, and placement on this personality dimension of perceived self versus environmental causation was related to all kinds of psychological indexes. But I was concerned about the lack of differentiation among the possible perceived causes of success and failure.

"A study conducted by Schmitt provided a necessary insight.[1] In that investigation punishments were allocated when an individual committed an immoral act either because the person was unable (he did not have the money to repay a debt) or because he was unwilling to pay. I remember having the simple and obvious insight (previously attained by many others) that the internal factors of ability and effort must be distinguished in the achievement domain. This certainly does not sound profound, but had far-reaching consequences for the development of an attributional theory of achievement strivings.

"The research in the article primarily examined allocation of rewards and punishments in achievement situations where the outcomes were ascribed to various levels of ability and effort. The major findings were that effort, as well as outcome, are the most influential in determining evaluation of others. Further, a low ability-high effort-successful person is especially rewarded (consider the handicapped person completing a marathon race), while a high ability-low effort-failing individual is particularly punished (think of your reaction toward a bright student failing because of a lack of effort). Three additional experiments examined other issues related to the antecedents and the consequences of the allocation of causality.

"The six experiments presented in the paper were not reported in the order in which they were conducted. The work made more sense after it was completed than during the process. As I recall, the manuscript was rejected (or provisionally accepted) on one or two occasions and extensive revisions were required. The editor at that time generally wrote comments that were somewhat longer than the submitted papers. By the time I had read and digested his comments, another study was completed and inserted into the manuscript."

1. **Schmitt D R.** The invocation of moral obligation. *Sociometry* **27**:299-310, 1964.

This Week's Citation Classic

Pheterson G I,[1] Kiesler S B[2] & Goldberg P A.[3] Evaluation of the performance of women as a function of their sex, achievement, and personal history. *J. Personal. Soc. Psychol.* **19**:114-18, 1971.
[Univ. California, Riverside, CA;[1] Univ. Kansas, Lawrence, KS;[2] and Connecticut Coll., New London, CT[3]]

This study investigated the conditions under which women are prejudiced against women. Female entries in a painting contest were evaluated less favorably than identical male entries, but female winners equally to identical male winners. Women were therefore prejudiced against female attempts but not against female successes. [The *Social Sciences Citation Index*® (*SSCI*®) indicates that this paper has been cited in over 155 publications since 1971.]

Gail I. Pheterson
Institute of Clinical Psychology and Personality
University of Utrecht
3512 JK Utrecht
The Netherlands

August 24, 1983

"The above study was conducted while I was a senior undergraduate student at Connecticut College for Women. In retrospect, I imagine the research to reflect my emerging consciousness of prejudices against women in society at large as well as my concern about the effect of those prejudices on female self-evaluation. In addition, the research likely reflects a personal preoccupation with, and perhaps anxiety about, the future of a woman 'entry' such as myself. Apparently, my beginning consciousness and accompanying concern were shared by many, or so it seems from the interest in my article. It is ironic that this student research project which supported the hypothesis that entries encounter more prejudice than prizewinners should have earned me 'honors in psychology,' a sort of prize in itself.

"The research was conducted with amazingly little obstruction. In fact, all the data were collected late one evening by going from dormitory to dormitory with a slide projector and research booklets. Students were buzzed in their rooms and asked to help with my senior research project by coming downstairs, looking at slides, and answering questions in a booklet, all of which would take less than 15 minutes. This was surely one case in which a peer relationship facilitated efficiency and cooperation between researcher and subject. The research design and data analysis required more time and contemplation than the data collection. As for the design, I am indebted to one of my professors, Phil Goldberg, for the model used in his earlier study on women's prejudice against women's journal articles.[1] The actual conduct of the study was accomplished in close cooperation with another professor, Sara Kiesler, whose expertise (and grant support) were invaluable. For me, the research was significant both as a first step in original scholarship and as a first fascination with female psychology.

"It can be argued that for research to contribute to liberation struggles, it must expose oppression, examine the effects of oppression, and eventually explore processes of change. This study started from the assumption of societal prejudice against women (one aspect of oppression) and proceeded to examine the effects of that prejudice on women. The research has been frequently cited both to further explore those effects and also to examine strategies of combating both institutionalized and internalized prejudice.

"It is now 14 years later. I am still involved in research related to analyzing and eliminating prejudice against women. My prime focus remains the social conditions affecting women's attitudes toward other women. Although I didn't perceive it in context at the time, my initial article was one of many snowballs propelling a broad range of attention to women's position in society. That attention brought about what continues to be the second wave of feminism in this century."

1. **Goldberg P.** Are women prejudiced against women? *Trans-action* 5:28-30, 1968.

NUMBER 9
FEBRUARY 26, 1979

Argyle M & Dean J. Eye-contact, distance and affiliation. *Sociometry* 28:289-304, 1965.

It was postulated that approach and avoidance forces produce an equilibrium level of eye-contact and physical proximity, and that if one of these is disturbed compensatory changes will occur in the other. It was found that eye-contact and length of glance were shorter the closer two people were placed together. [The *Science Citation Index®* (*SCI®*) and the *Social Sciences Citation Index* ™ (*SSCI* ™) indicate that this paper has been cited 239 times since 1965.]

Michael Argyle
University of Oxford
Department of Experimental Psychology
Oxford OX1 3UD
UK

January 6, 1978

"Every psychologist is aware of the importance of perception, and knows that visual perception involves looking. Yet until the early 1960s social psychologists had paid no attention to gaze as a feature of social behaviour. For some years I had wanted to study social interaction at the level of the detailed moves and signals involved, but didn't know how to do this. Discussion with a colleague working in motor skills, E.R.F.W. Crossman, led to the formulation of the motor skills model of social behaviour; this model led us to think about gaze. A research student, Adam Kendon, did frame-by-frame analysis of conversations, and found that glances were closely linked with utterances.[1] I had been interested in George Miller's analysis of approach-avoidance conflicts, and thought that they applied to proximity—there seemed to be pushes and pulls towards an equilibrium distance. Similar considerations perhaps applied to gaze, and therefore to both taken in combination, so that one variable might compensate for the other. I suggested this to Janet Dean, an Oxford undergraduate, for her third year project, and various experiments were run in our first social psychology lab using cumulative stop watches. It became immediately clear that gaze increased with distance. So we ran several replications of the basic experiment.

"The paper then had a rather curious history. It was ill-received in the Oxford Psychology Department, who found the discussion of gaze rather embarrassing; it was attacked by the leading social psychologist of the day at a European conference, rejected by *Nature*, and rejected by the *Journal of Abnormal and Social Psychology* on the grounds that the main variable (gaze) was unfamiliar. After it had been published in *Sociometry*, a number of papers appeared attacking it on various methodological grounds. However later papers by ourselves and others confirmed the original results. The main amendment and extension to be made came from Patterson, who suggested that under some conditions there is reciprocity rather than equilibrium maintenance.[2]

"We were not aware that Ralph Exline at Delaware had been doing research on gaze before us, though John Lanzetta, then the ONR Liaison Officer in London, put us in touch. Since our early papers, over 500 studies on gaze have been published. Our paper perhaps became known because (1) it was one of the first to report findings about an important and totally overlooked phenomenon, (2) it demonstrated that gaze was a variable that was subject to empirical laws, (3) we were lucky in obtaining very clear results, and (4) these have been easy to replicate. There has been an increased awareness of the importance of non-verbal communication in general during recent years, though most recent discussion still misses one of the essential points—that gaze functions simultaneously as both a channel and a signal."

References

1. **Kendon A.** Some functions of gaze direction in social interaction. *Acta Psychologica*,26:1, 1-47, 1967.
2. **Patterson M L.** An arousal model of interpersonal intimacy. *Psychol. Rev.* 83:235-45,1976.

This Week's Citation Classic

Kendon A. Some functions of gaze-direction in social interaction. *Acta Psychologica* **26**:22-63, 1967. [Institute of Experimental Psychology, Oxford, England]

Films of two-person conversations were transcribed and analyzed from the point of view of how gaze direction is related to utterance and silence. It was found that patterns of looking were systematically related to features of talk and could be accounted for in terms of the monitoring functions of gaze. At the same time, evidence was presented that suggested that gaze direction may also play a role in the regulation of turn-taking in conversation. [The *Social Sciences Citation Index*® (*SSCI*®) **indicates that this paper has been cited over 180 times since 1967.]**

Adam Kendon
Department of Anthropology
Connecticut College
New London, CT 06320

August 30, 1981

"In 1963 E.R.W.F. Crossman, then at Oxford, proposed that behavior in social interaction could be analyzed as if it were a perceptuo-motor skill. Together with Michael Argyle he established the Social Skills Project at the Institute (now Department) of Experimental Psychology at Oxford. At that time I had just completed my D. Phil. thesis on the temporal organization of talk in conversation, based on work I had done with Eliot Chapple at Rockland State Hospital, Orangeburg, New Jersey, and there I had proposed a very similar approach. Accordingly, I was invited to join Crossman and Argyle's project. Crossman proposed that we film some conversations so that we could examine the behavior involved and find out what the elements of action in social interaction might be. He proposed this method on analogy with the method followed in the analysis of perceptuo-motor skills: first film a skilled operator to see what patterns of action are followed. After developing a suitable apparatus, we filmed a number of pairs of undergraduates who, meeting for the first time, were simply asked to 'get acquainted.' After some months of work on these films, in which I was joined by Jacques Ex of Nijmegen, who was in the institute as a visiting fellow, a workable transcription system was devised which made it possible to write down gaze direction, facial expression, head position, and body posture, frame by frame. All this was done in ignorance of Birdwhistell[1] and Scheflen,[2] whose work subsequently has greatly influenced me.

"With these detailed transcriptions we attempted to see what regularities there might be. Initial analyses, conducted without any hypothesis, were not very successful. One day, however, I was watching an interview from behind a one-way mirror and I was struck by the way the interviewee consistently looked away as he began his answers and looked back at the interviewer as he came to the end of his utterance. From my previous work on the timing of utterances in conversation, I had become interested in how smooth turn-taking might be achieved, and upon observing how gaze direction was patterned in this interview, it occurred to me that it might serve as a coordinating signal. With this idea in mind, I examined gaze direction in relation to speech in the filmed conversations and the findings led to the paper here being discussed.

"This paper has been cited frequently in part because it was one of the first to demonstrate that detailed descriptive analysis of behavior in social interaction could provide evidence for the role visible behavior plays in the interactive process. Since 1967, there has been a huge growth in work on gaze in social interaction.[3] Despite the frequency with which my paper has been cited, however, it is striking that no direct attempt to follow up on my findings was published until 1978."[4]

1. **Birdwhistell R L.** *Kinesics and context; essays on body motion communication.* Philadelphia, PA: University of Pennsylvania Press, 1970. 338 p.
2. **Scheflen A E.** *Communicational structure: analysis of a psychotherapy transaction.* Bloomington, IN: Indiana University Press, 1973. 378 p.
3. **Argyle M & Cook M.** *Gaze and mutual gaze.* Cambridge: Cambridge University Press, 1976. 210 p.
4. **Beattie G.** Floor-apportionment and gaze in conversational dyads. *Brit. J. Soc. Clin. Psychol.* **17**:7-16, 1978.

This Week's Citation Classic

Duncan S, Jr. Nonverbal communication. *Psychol. Bull.* **72**:118-37, 1969.
[University of Chicago, IL]

Research is reviewed on the communicative functions of nonlanguage behaviors, such as voice quality (paralanguage), body motion (kinesics), touch, and use of personal space (proxemics). A major distinction is drawn between structural and external-variable research in this area. [The *Social Sciences Citation Index*® (*SSCI*®) **indicates that this paper has been cited in over 125 publications since 1969.]**

Starkey Duncan
Department of Behavioral Sciences
University of Chicago
Chicago, IL 60637

November 2, 1982

"In 1967, I joined the faculty of the University of Chicago. Intending to do research on the 'nonverbal' (and verbal) aspects of face-to-face interactions, I sent off a set of grant applications. But what to do until the grant (if any) was awarded? Beyond keeping myself occupied and out of trouble, a comprehensive review of the literature seemed useful prior to undertaking a major research effort in the area.

"In addition to simply pulling together the rather skimpy literature available at that time, the review had three main purposes. (a) The main areas of nonverbal-communication research were enumerated with basic references for each, including available transcription systems. (b) The potential value of nonverbal actions for various areas of psychological research was suggested, along with the advantages of variables based on these actions over other, more familiar variables in psychology. (c) I wanted to communicate to psychologists the ideas underlying an approach to studying the interaction process developed by anthropologists and linguists. In this 'structural' approach, interaction is viewed as a rule-governed phenomenon; research is aimed at discovering and documenting these rules, much as linguists seek to formulate a grammar for a language. More familiar to psychologists was the 'external variable' approach in which nonverbal actions, such as gaze direction, were related to individual difference variables, such as affiliativeness. The definition of this approach has since been modified.[1]

"The paper had, if nothing else, excellent timing. *Post hoc*, but surely not *propter hoc*, there was an enormous surge of research on nonverbal communication beginning in the 1970s—and with good reason. The more concrete nonverbal actions had a great advantage as raw data over the more traditional—and inferential—content categories for describing interaction, such as 'shows solidarity' or 'empathic response.' Researchers using variables based on nonverbal actions easily obtained excellent reliability and were typically rewarded with strong, replicable results. But I fear that many investigators were just as intrigued with the possibility that observing these actions would provide a relatively direct window on the subjects' inner feelings—a notion shamelessly exploited in the popular books on the subject. A rather more complex view is generally held today.

"My effort to generate interest in structural research among psychologists proved to be a dud. As the nonverbal-communication literature grew exponentially, few studies took a structural approach. However, in announcing their topic to be some aspect of nonverbal communication, many investigators cited the review as a way of identifying the field. And the review may have contributed to general acceptance of the term 'nonverbal communication,' as opposed to about a half-dozen others current at the time."

1. **Duncan S D, Jr. & Fiske D W.** *Face-to-face interaction: research, methods, and theory.* Hillsdale, NJ: Lawrence Erlbaum Associates, 1977. 361 p.

Mehrabian A. *Nonverbal communication.*
Chicago, IL: Aldine·Atherton, 1972. 226 p.
[Department of Psychology, University of California, Los Angeles, CA]

Nonverbal communication involves a large number of *symbols* (gestures, expressions) that are difficult to conceptualize. This volume presents a system for description and integration of findings in this field based upon a succinct conceptualization of the *referents* in this communication process. The three fundamental dimensions of reference are positiveness, potency or status, and responsiveness (later described as pleasure-displeasure, dominance-submissiveness, and level of arousal). [The *Science Citation Index*® (*SCI*®) and the *Social Sciences Citation Index*® (*SSCI*®) indicate that this book has been cited in over 280 publications since 1972.]

Albert Mehrabian
Department of Psychology
University of California
Los Angeles, CA 90024

August 6, 1984

"When I began my studies on nonverbal communication, I was overwhelmed by the diversity of bodily and vocal cues, each of which could have a particular significance, and possibly a different significance in different contexts. Typical studies during the 1960s tended to focus on a very few of these cues and attempted to detail the significance of each cue in terms of arbitrarily selected concepts that suited the particular investigator. Thus, integration of the available findings within a coherent framework was extremely difficult.

"Having come into psychology with an engineering background, I tended to conceptualize psychological phenomena in terms of variables and their interrelationships. Also, I appreciated the importance of concise and systematic description as the foundation of any scientific activity. Factor analyses of some of the data from my studies in which numerous nonverbal behavioral variables had been scored and from other studies that had identified relationships between groups of cues and referents of those cues were helpful.[1,2] I was led to the idea that nonverbal communication essentially has a limited set of referent dimensions dealing with expression and communication of feelings and attitudes. Thus, instead of focusing on the numerous behavioral cues, I analyzed the referents of nonverbal communication to try to achieve a system of organization.

"Emotions were easily analyzed in terms of three basic and independent dimensions, pleasure-displeasure, arousal-nonarousal, and dominance-submissiveness (although these were labeled differently in earlier studies). Attitudes (e.g., like-dislike, preference, approach-avoidance) were in turn analyzed in terms of emotions—once again, though, these relationships were clarified in our studies from the mid- to late 1970s. For example, a strong positive attitude entails pleasure plus arousal; a strong negative attitude involves displeasure and arousal. Eye contact generally implies liking and preference, although there are important exceptions. When displeasure cues (e.g., words, bodily tension) accompany eye contact, they imply a strong negative attitude. So eye contact essentially implies communicator arousal and, depending on its association with pleasant and unpleasant verbal or nonverbal cues, serves to intensify the communication of positive *versus* negative attitudes.

"Once this framework for conceptualizing referents of nonverbal communication was in place, it was an easy matter to summarize the existing literature and to generate studies that would explore systematically important phenomena in the field (e.g., status communication, deceit, persuasion) that had been neglected or studied only minimally. *Nonverbal Communication* summarized about 10 years of my studies based on the above framework, and perhaps this emphasis on organization and concise description explains its value to other researchers and students.

"Almost 10 years later, I wrote a new (second) edition of *Silent Messages*[3] that was written more informally and primarily as a text, but that nevertheless updated the framework in terms of many new findings that had become available in the meantime. The conceptual analysis of nonverbal communication in *Silent Messages* also helps clarify some puzzling and apparently inconsistent findings in the literature."

1. **Mehrabian A & Ksionzky S.** Categories of social behavior. *Comp. Group Stud.* 3:425-36, 1972.
2. **Mehrabian A.** Verbal and nonverbal interaction of strangers in a waiting situation. *J. Exp. Res. Pers.* 5:127-38, 1971. (Cited 30 times.)
3. ------------------. *Silent messages: implicit communication of emotions and attitudes.* Belmont, CA: Wadsworth, 1981. 196 p.

This Week's Citation Classic

CC/NUMBER 37
SEPTEMBER 15, 1980

Deutsch M & Gerard H B. A study of normative and informational social influences upon individual judgment. *J. Abnorm. Soc. Psychol.* **51**:629-36, 1955. [Research Center for Human Relations, New York University, New York, NY]

The effects of two different types of social influence upon individual judgment were investigated: normative and informational. Prior studies of 'group' influence were shown to involve only incidentally the type of influence most specifically associated with groups, normative influence. The role of normative influence in buttressing as well as undermining individual experience was also investigated. [The *Social Sciences Citation Index® (SSCI™)* **indicates that this paper has been cited over 190 times since 1966.]**

Morton Deutsch
Department of Psychology
Teachers College
Columbia University
New York, NY 10027

July 16, 1980

"Gerard and I were intrigued by the Asch situation: a situation in which a naive subject makes judgments about which of three lines is most similar in length to a standard line after being exposed to false, but unanimous, judgments by three accomplices of the experimenter. It was a very popular paradigm for doing research on the effects of social influence upon individual judgment prior to our study. Gerard thought he could develop a simple apparatus which would make it easier to conduct and record the results of an Asch-type experiment and I thought that the term 'group influence' was being misused to characterize the social psychological processes in the usual Asch-type experiment. Normally, the subject was not given experimental instructions which made him feel that he was a member of a group faced with a common task requiring cooperative work for its most effective solution. Gerard and I joined efforts, using his neatly-designed apparatus, to show what would happen when we either enhanced or diminished the 'groupiness' of the people in the experimental situation. We labeled the type of social influence most associated with groups as 'normative social influence' and distinguished this from 'informational social influence' which does not require groups. We also designed the experiment so as to have relevance to other basic issues; most notably, to demonstrate that normative social influence could buttress as well as undermine individuality in judgment. That is, the norms of a group could strengthen an individual's resolve to express his personal views or they could pressure him to conform to majority opinion.

"The distinction between 'normative' and 'informational' social influence caught on and has been widely employed; the methodology has been adopted and improved by others; and some of its other ideas have also stimulated research by others. When I wrote the paper, I did not think that it was a particularly important one. For me, it was mainly a common-sense protest against some intellectual sloppiness about 'group' influences. It was outside my primary stream of theoretical and experimental work. I have been surprised by its popularity. I have written other papers and books on cooperation and competition and also on conflict resolution which seems to me to be of considerably greater significance, theoretically and practically, than this one. Although these works are well known, they appear to have been cited less often. I am not sure why. But I suspect that our '*Citation Classic*' paper offered cogent criticisms of some basic ideas, as well as methodological innovations, in a 'trendy' research area."

CC/NUMBER 24
JUNE 13, 1983

This Week's Citation Classic

Sommer R. Studies in personal space. *Sociometry* **22**:247-60, 1959.
[Saskatchewan Hospital, Weyburn, Saskatchewan, Canada]

Patterns of interaction in *face-to-face* groups were mapped as a function of table arrangement, group size, gender, and mental status. Corner locations were favored for group interaction and neighboring chairs preferred over distant chairs. Schizophrenic individuals showed an impaired concept of social distance. [The *Social Sciences Citation Index*® (*SSCI*®) indicates that this paper has been cited in over 160 publications since 1966.]

Robert Sommer
Department of Psychology
University of California
Davis, CA 95616

March 3, 1983

"I was working as a psychologist in a large isolated mental hospital in Western Canada. The interior of the building was cavernous, poorly lit, with long corridors, institutional colors, inadequate ventilation, and little soundproofing. The building violated Florence Nightingale's first canon that a hospital do the sick no harm. The superintendent, Humphry Osmond, and I decided that changes in the physical milieu would benefit both patients and staff. When we attempted to learn about the connection between architecture and behavior, we were surprised to find out how little information was available. More was known about the design of zoo cages and chicken coops than about the design of hospital wards. We therefore embarked on a research program to investigate human spatial behavior. We wanted to identify those physical arrangements that would increase social interaction and those which could increase privacy. The studies began on the wards themselves, using patients and staff as subjects, and then were extended into other locations using experimental procedures.

"The article begins with natural observations of groups of people conversing in natural settings. Certain key principles of spatial behavior were identified. To control for the effects of extraneous factors, including previous level of contact, experimental studies were subsequently undertaken in which groups of people were asked to converse at different layouts of tables and chairs. We wanted to determine how group size, gender, and table arrangement would affect spatial relationships. Goals of the study were both practical in seeking to improve ward design and theoretical in investigating human spatial behavior.

"The reasons why the study was so frequently cited relate to the newness of the topic being investigated. The work filled a gap in social psychological theory which tended to overlook the physical conditions under which interaction takes place. The study also filled a need in architecture and the other design fields for behavioral data. Designers were eager for information that could help them create more effective and humane interior spaces. The study also had relevance to the growing interest in nonverbal communication.

"It was not easy to publish the results back in 1959. The editor of the major social psychological journal commented that the paper was 'interesting' and he enjoyed reading it, but he did not feel that the results had anything to do with social psychology. This was true, of course, since social psychological theory and research were dominated by laboratory experimentation and neglectful of the context of interaction. Fortunately, Dick Hill, editor of *Sociometry*, a publication of the American Sociological Association, recognized the importance of the topic and accepted the paper, along with several subsequent articles clarifying and extending the original findings. Looking back, I am pleased to observe how well the results have held up over the years. The study has been replicated and extended and a large body of literature in this area has accumulated. More than a thousand papers on personal space have been published since the original article appeared. I remain interested but not current with the work and occasionally undertake some small study typically motivated by student interest in some specific issue. The research laid the basis for a book published ten years after the original article[1] and numerous talks to audiences of architects, planners, and psychologists. The term 'personal space' entered popular usage and is included in the 1980 edition of *Bartlett's Quotations*. More recent reviews of work in the field can be found in Altman[2] and Holahan."[3]

1. **Sommer R.** *Personal space: the behavior basis of design.* Englewood Cliffs, NJ: Prentice-Hall, 1969. 177 p.
2. **Altman I.** *The environment and social behavior.* Monterey, CA: Brooks/Cole, 1975. 256 p.
3. **Holahan C J.** *Environmental psychology.* New York: Random House, 1982. 422 p.

This Week's Citation Classic

Stoner J A F. Risky and cautious shifts in group decisions: the influence of widely held values. *J. Exp. Soc. Psychol.* **4**:442-59, 1968. [Massachusetts Institute of Technology, Cambridge, MA]

In an experiment comparing individual and group decisions involving risk, group decisions tended to be more cautious on items where widely held values favored the cautious alternative and individuals considered themselves relatively cautious. Group decisions tended to be more risky when the converse of these conditions existed. [The *Social Sciences Citation Index*® (*SSCI*®) indicates that this paper has been cited in over 110 publications since 1968.]

James A.F. Stoner
Joseph A. Martino Graduate School
of Business Administration
Fordham University at Lincoln Center
New York, NY 10023

November 12, 1982

"Late in 1960, I was 'shadowing' General James M. Gavin (ret.), president of Arthur D. Little. I was working on a group term project for Warren Bennis's leadership seminar at the Massachusetts Institute of Technology's management school. Gavin observed, *en passant*, that councils of war were abandoned during the Civil War because the group process yielded excessively cautious decisions...and fighting wars requires taking risks. His comment struck a responsive chord: I was frequently frustrated by the cautiousness of groups in which I worked.

"Earlier that year, I had decided to do my master's thesis with Donald G. Marquis, a fabulous thesis adviser.[1] Comparing individual and group decisions involving risk eventually became our topic. Michael Wallach granted permission to use the 12-item Wallach-Kogan choice dilemma questionnaire and MIT graduate management students were our subjects.

"Rather than being more cautious than individuals as we had predicted, the groups were more risky on the questionnaire as a whole. On only one item were they more cautious. Marquis was in Russia when the results came in and Wallach was quite helpful in guiding the analysis and early write-up.

"The thesis was widely replicated and a mini risky-shift-studying industry grew in the 1960s.[2] Many studies used choice dilemma items, but most ignored a 1962 master's thesis by Frode Nordhϕy under Marquis. Building on the single cautious shifting item, Marquis and Nordhϕy demonstrated that other cautious shifts could occur.[3,4]

"In 1964, I started doctoral work at MIT. Marquis felt researchers were missing the boat by concentrating on risky shifting items and ignoring Nordhϕy's work. He said, 'If you want to understand a phenomenon, look where it does not occur.' An independent study project with Marquis turned into the doctoral thesis which became the *Citation Classic* article. We showed that groups could be more cautious or more risky and predicted when that would occur—consistent with Nordhϕy.

"There were no obstacles to publishing the doctoral article, but G.C. Hoyt and James F. Burns provided crucial support to me in surviving the thesis-writing process. The master's article I drafted in Africa a few months after the thesis defense was never published. When I returned from Africa in 1963, an embarrassed Marquis reported that the committeeman who took responsibility for getting it published had never submitted it to the agreed journal. Fortunately for me, Marquis had shared the research with Roger Brown, who built the group dynamics chapter of his excellent social psychology textbook around my and Nordhϕy's theses.[4] I started the doctoral program as a minor celebrity—discoverer of the risky shift.

"I think the doctoral article is widely cited because the risky and cautious shifts were (1) counterintuitive, (2) easily replicated for research or classroom demonstration, and (3) prominently discussed in Brown's widely adopted text. Perhaps some researchers cite it as a 'proxy' for the unpublished master's thesis. Finally, it may have helped move the research momentum from replicating and extending the risky shift to investigating a broader 'choice shift' perspective."

1. **Stoner J A F.** *Marquis' "laws" of dissertations.* New York: Fordham University, November 1982, Faculty of Business Working Paper #82-5.
2. **Cartwright D.** Determinants of scientific progress: the case of research on the risky shift. *Amer. Psychol.* **28**:222-31, 1973.
3. **Nordhϕy F.** *Group interaction in decision-making under risk.* Master's thesis. Cambridge, MA: Massachusetts Institute of Technology, School of Industrial Management (Sloan School of Management), 1962.
4. **Brown R.** *Social psychology.* New York: Free Press, 1965. 785 p. [Citation Classic. *Current Contents/Social & Behavioral Sciences* **13**(7):16, 16 February 1981.]

 CC/NUMBER 34
AUGUST 20, 1984

Tuckman B W. Developmental sequence in small groups.
Psychol. Bull. **63**:384-99, 1965.
[Naval Medical Research Institute, Bethesda, MD]

Based on a review of 50 articles describing stages of development in therapy, T-, natural, and laboratory groups, a model of small group development is proposed. Four stages, covering both group interpersonal and task activities are described and labeled 'forming,' 'storming,' 'norming,' and 'performing.' [The *Science Citation Index*® (*SCI*®) and the *Social Sciences Citation Index*® (*SSCI*®) indicate that this paper has been cited in over 165 publications since 1965.]

Bruce W. Tuckman
College of Education
Florida State University
Tallahassee, FL 32303

June 4, 1984

"My first professional job was as part of a small group of social psychologists in a think tank setting studying small group behavior as the US Navy prepared for a future of small crew vessels and stations. Nine of us at the Naval Medical Research Institute were busy studying small groups from all perspectives and under all conditions. I was fortunate to have an experienced and talented boss by the name of Irwin Altman, who had been collecting every article he could find on group development. He turned his collection over to me and suggested that I look it over and see if I could make anything out of it.

"The collection contained 50 articles, many of which were psychoanalytic studies of therapy or T-groups. The task of organizing and integrating them was challenging. After separating out two realms of group functioning, namely, the interpersonal or group structure realm and the task activity realm, I began to look for a developmental sequence that would fit the findings of a majority of the studies. I hit on four stages going from (1) orientation/testing/dependence, to (2) conflict, to (3) group cohesion, to (4) functional role-relatedness. For these I coined the terms: 'forming,' 'storming,' 'norming,' and 'performing'—terms that would come to be used to describe developing groups for the next 20 years and which probably account for the paper's popularity.

"There still remained the task of getting the paper published and that was no mean feat. Lloyd Humphreys, then editor of the *Psychological Bulletin*, turned it down, offering me constructive editorial criticism but concluding that the reviewed studies themselves were not of sufficient quality to merit publication. I was persistent, though, and rewrote the manuscript per his recommendations and sent it back to him despite his initial outright rejection. I pointed out that I was not trying to justify the collected articles but to draw inferences from them. Humphreys did a complete about-face and accepted my argument and my manuscript and, in short order, it appeared in print.

"I ordered, thanks to the Navy, 450 reprints and used them all to fill requests within the first three or four years after the article appeared. Requests came from all over the world and from a wide range of disciplines and I have saved some of the more exotic ones. Almost yearly, I receive a request from someone to use parts of the article or at least the terms 'forming,' 'storming,' 'norming,' and 'performing' in print. Again, quotability may be the key to success.

"In 1977, I published, by invitation, an update of the model in a journal called *Group & Organization Studies*—in collaboration with Mary Ann Jensen.[1] We reviewed 22 studies that had appeared since the original publication of the model and which we located by means of the *Social Sciences Citation Index*. These articles, one of which dubbed the stages 'Tuckman's hypothesis,'[2] tended to support the existence of the four stages but also suggested a fifth stage for which a perfect rhyme could not be found. We called it 'adjourning.'"

1. **Tuckman B W & Jensen M A.** Stages of small-group development revisited. *Group Org. Studies* **2**:419-27, 1977. (Cited 5 times.)
2. **Runkel P J, Lawrence M, Oldfield S, Rider M & Clark C.** Stages of group development—an empirical test of Tuckman's hypothesis. *J. Appl. Behav. Sci.* **7**:180-93, 1971.

CC/NUMBER 42
OCTOBER 15, 1984

This Week's Citation Classic™

Amir Y. Contact hypothesis in ethnic relations. *Psychol. Bull.* **71**:319-42, 1969.
[Department of Psychology, Bar-Ilan University, Ramat-Gan, Israel]

Research regarding the effect of intergroup contact on ethnic relations was reviewed, categorizing the variables under numerous topics, primarily those related to producing positive as compared to negative effects. Some generalizations and practical applications were suggested. [The *Social Sciences Citation Index*® (*SSCI*®) indicates that this paper has been cited in over 160 publications since 1969.]

Yehuda Amir
Department of Psychology
Bar-Ilan University
Ramat-Gan 52100
Israel

July 19, 1984

"My interest in ethnic contact originated from my PhD dissertation at New York University that dealt with this topic. Only 10 years later, this article was published in *Psychological Bulletin*. The idea of writing such an article followed a meeting in 1967, initiated by Israel's Minister (Secretary) of Education and Culture. At this meeting, a number of social scientists from Israeli universities were asked to evaluate possible outcomes of the newly planned policy of ethnic school desegregation (i.e., contact). Interestingly enough, social scientists could not come to any clear conclusions on this matter. Thus, on my way back from that meeting, I decided to read the relevant literature on ethnic contact and see whether more clear-cut recommendations could be made. This venture lasted for a whole year and, consequently, the *Bulletin* article was published.

"Three major reasons come into my mind to account for the large number of citations to the article. First, ethnic contact, like the weather or living with a spouse, belongs to that category of events that fits the idea of 'you can't live with it, but it's sure difficult to live without it.' Where other approaches, such as education or the mass media, have failed, ethnic interaction is still the one technique that holds some promise to reduce prejudice and produce better intergroup relations. This, too, is not easy to achieve. Yet, as we are dealing here with a major social issue relevant today in many countries of the world, interest in this topic is still high, especially with regard to ethnic contact in the schools, international student exchange, cross-cultural training, dyadic relations, and so on. Second, the article, though not basically theoretical, provided researchers with a broad taxonomy and categorization of independent and dependent variables related to the topic. And finally, no basically new comprehensive summary on ethnic contact has been published since, leaving social scientists no alternative but to quote this article. The only exception to this may be in the field of ethnic contact in the schools (i.e., school desegregation), which has been widely studied and summarized in the 1970s and 1980s, including a recent summary by me.[1]

"What will the future tell? As we are dealing with a major social issue, we shall probably see more research on this topic. What is much needed is an article dealing with this topic on a purely theoretical basis involving theory and ideas from different disciplines in the social sciences, such as psychology, sociology, anthropology, education, political science, and geography. This is especially important because our present-day information in this area is primarily geared to concrete and applied rather than to theoretical and basic knowledge. Whoever will deal successfully with this aspect of ethnic contact may be next on the list of the most-quoted articles in the social sciences."

1. **Amir Y, Sharan S & Ben-Ari R,** eds. *School desegregation: cross-cultural perspectives.* Hillsdale, NJ: Erlbaum, 1984. 300 p.

CC/NUMBER 5
FEBRUARY 2, 1981

This Week's Citation Classic

Darley J M & Latané B. Bystander intervention in emergencies: diffusion of responsibility. *J. Personal. Soc. Psychol.* 8:377-83, 1968. [New York Univ. and Columbia Univ., New York, NY]

When a group of people is confronted with an emergency, a diffusion of responsibility process can interfere with an individual's responsiveness. *Not* **'getting involved' in an emergency can be more easily rationalized when other potential sources of help are available. [The** *Social Sciences Citation Index® (SSCI™)* **indicates that this paper has been cited over 160 times since 1968.]**

John M. Darley
Department of Psychology
Princeton University
Princeton, NJ 08544

January 14, 1981

"A woman had been stabbed to death. Sadly, this was not a rare event in New York City in the late 1960s. But following a tip from police investigators, *New York Times* reporters discovered something quite shocking about the incident: the woman had been murdered in the courtyard of her apartment building while 38 of her neighbors watched the incident unfold. None had given assistance, even such low-risk assistance as telephoning the police.

"The outcry over this was enormous. Newspapers were filled with condemnation of the neighbors. Many analysts, including social scientists, contributed instant diagnoses of the source of their inhumanity: some suggested alienation, others apathy, still others dehumanization. Social psychologists, however, tend to be suspicious of analyses of human actions, even shocking or immoral actions, that automatically attribute those actions to some personality deficit or moral deficiency in the actor. Instead, we are much more likely to look at the specifics of the situation to try and determine from the actor's perspective how he analyzes the situation, and how his responses flow from his analysis.

"Discussing the Kitty Genovese murder, Bibb Latané and I realized that a social-psychological analysis could be made. The analysis suggested several subtle ways in which the presence of a group of witnesses can influence any individual witness, and that those influences frequently work together to produce widespread *in*action on the part of the group.

"This paper represents the first of many studies we did on bystander responses to emergencies. It demonstrated experimentally that the presence of others reduced an individual's feelings of personal responsibility in an emergency situation. In another study,[1] we showed that the startling inaction of a bystander to an emergency is often seen by other bystanders to be reflecting a decision that whatever is taking place is *not* an emergency. This definition is communicated to another bystander, and his inaction communicates it back. A kind of 'anti-panic mob' is formed in which individuals do not respond because they define the situation as no emergency.

"Latané and I went on to do other studies on this topic; many of these studies are reported in our book, *The Unresponsive Bystander: Why Doesn't He Help?*[2] winner of the 1968 Socio-Psychological Prize of the American Association for the Advancement of Science and the Century Psychology Prize for 1968. Other researchers joined in (a recent review indicates over 400 pre-1975 articles[3]), and a research area came into being. This, of course, is the primary reason the article has been so highly cited. A second reason is that research in this area provides a useful example of the social-psychological analysis of a problem. Thus the article is frequently cited in textbooks as an example of this analysis, and because these studies demonstrate that genuine experimental research can be done on important social topics."

1. **Latané B & Darley J M.** Group inhibition of bystander intervention in emergencies. *J. Personal. Soc. Psychol.* **10**:215-21, 1968.
2. ----------------------------. *The unresponsive bystander: why doesn't he help?* New York: Appleton-Century-Crofts, 1970. 131 p.
3. **Lau S & Blake B F.** Recent research on helping behavior: an overview and bibliography. *Catalog of selected documents in psychology* **6**:69, 1976. Journal Supplement Abstract Service, MS. 1289.

This Week's Citation Classic

Bryan J H & Test M A. Models and helping: naturalistic studies in aiding behavior. *J. Personal. Soc. Psychol.* 6:400-7, 1967.
[Northwestern University, Evanston, IL]

Four experiments concerned with helping behavior were conducted. Three addressed the effects of altruistic models upon helping, while one was concerned with the impact of the solicitor's race upon donations. [The *Social Sciences Citation Index*® (*SSCI*®) **indicates that this paper has been cited over 130 times since 1967.]**

James H. Bryan
Department of Psychology
Northwestern University
Evanston, IL 60201

June 5, 1981

"The experiments reported in the article reflected my interest in the nature of altruistic or helping behaviors, an interest traceable to the trial of Adolf Eichmann. The trial of this agent of the holocaust apparently stimulated a speech by Rabbi Schulweiss which in turn prompted remembrances by the Christian rescuers of Jews, in addition to reflection upon the atrocities. Perry London of the University of Southern California then encouraged me to collaborate with him in the study of the Christians who had rescued Jews. David Rosenhan joined the collaborative efforts and addressed some of the variables associated with participation in the early freedom rides involving the desegregation of the South. One of the early hypotheses generated from what were mainly interview studies of rescuers and freedom riders was the importance of adult exemplars or models in affecting the participation of those who observe the model.

"While Eichmann and Schulweiss indirectly, and London directly, affected the nature of my interest, another group of colleagues, all then located at Northwestern University, shaped the methodology employed. Webb, Campbell, Sechrest, and Schwartz were then in the midst of writing what now must be considered a classical book in psychology, *Unobtrusive Measures.*[1] There was considerable encouragement within the department to extend experiments and studies from the laboratory to other perhaps less esoteric settings. Mary Ann Test, then a graduate student, was particularly interested in naturalistically based studies and, in a sweet and gentle fashion, insisted that our work on helping be conducted in natural settings.

"In summary then, the topic addressed was altruism; the site of the experiments was outside the milieu of the psychologist. While only God knows, my guess as to factors contributing to the article's popularity involves both the topic and the experimental sites. The work on altruistic and helping behavior was rather sparse when the article was published but several social scientists from prestigious universities were involved in such work. Thus, Berkowitz and colleagues[2] and Latané and Darley[3] had either published or were about to publish important works in the area. Additionally, the field would soon become increasingly enthusiastic, rightly or wrongly, about extending investigations from the laboratory to other settings. Our experiments simply, unwittingly, and luckily exploited two features of the *zeitgeist*, one involving a substantive area, the other a methodology. For further work in the study of development of helping behavior see *Positive Social Behavior and Morality*."[4]

1. **Webb E J, Campbell D T, Schwartz R D & Sechrest L.** *Unobtrusive measures: nonreactive research in the social sciences.* Chicago: Rand McNally, 1966. 225 p.
2. **Berkowitz L & Daniels L.** Responsibility and dependency. *J. Abnormal Soc. Psychol.* 66:429-36, 1963.
3. **Latané B & Darley J M.** Social determinants of bystander intervention in emergencies. (Macaulay J & Berkowitz L, eds.) *Altruism and helping behavior.* New York: Academic Press, 1970. p. 13-28.
4. **Staub E.** *Positive social behavior and morality.* New York: Academic Press, 1979. Vol. 2.

This Week's Citation Classic

CC/NUMBER 29
JULY 21, 1980

Katz D & Kahn R L. *The social psychology of organizations.* New York: Wiley, 1966. 489 p. [Dept. Psychol. and Survey Research Center, Univ. Michigan, Ann Arbor, MI]

A description of theoretical models of organizations and of research results bearing on processes of organizational functioning and change is presented. [The *Social Sciences Citation Index® (SSCI™)* **indicates that this book has been cited over 960 times since 1966.]**

Daniel Katz
Department of Psychology
University of Michigan
Ann Arbor, MI 48104

January 29, 1980

"*The Social Psychology of Organizations* was written as a theoretical treatise for students in the social studies and health sciences interested in an analysis of the phenomena of organized groups. Though most of our lives are spent within the confines of organizations, most psychological treatments emphasize an individual psychology and few social psychological approaches go beyond the family or the small informal group. On the other hand, the conventional accounts of sociologists or economists tend to leave out people in their explanations of social structure. Between the micro approach of the psychologist and the macro account of the sociologist there is a need for a bridge to interrelate the concepts of the two levels. Our book was an attempt to apply such a bridge through the framework of open system theory. Open system theory had proved useful at the biological level and its major conceptualizations of input, throughput, and output, of negative entropy, of system boundaries and interdependence with the environment, seemed capable of application to complex social phenomena.

"Specifically, open system theory suggested two important lines of attack. One derived from the notion of systems and suggested that the problems of organizations could be viewed as a function of the type of structuring in which they occurred. For example, a peaceful outcome to differences between labor and management in a company marginal to the industry might be due to this marginal position in which neither could afford a costly strike. The second line of attack is the search for social dynamics in the interdependence of organization and environment as the organization relies upon energic and informational input from its surround and processes this input to achieve a product which the larger society needs. Organizations are not self-contained, though they seek to control their environs and extend their boundaries.

"Organizations which have received the most study are industrial in nature and our book utilized investigations in this field to illustrate how open system theory could be tied to research. Previously, organizational and industrial psychology had been linked with the scientific management of Taylor[1] or the classic bureaucracy of Weber,[2] which accepted the existing structures as givens and did not deal adequately with problems of restructuring or social change. Open system theory, with its emphasis upon openness to new inputs, therefore, had an advantage. Students in areas other than business administration and industrial psychology, such as educational organization, social work, hospital administration, and public administration, were quick to utilize the approach of open system theory. Its usefulness to so many types of social scientists has justified a revision to take account of development in the field over the past 12 years—a revision which appeared in the late spring of 1978."[3]

1. **Taylor F W.** *Principles of scientific management.* New York: Harper, 1923. 144 p.
2. **Weber M.** *Theory of social and economic organization.* New York: Free Press, 1947. 436 p.
3. **Katz D.** *The social psychology of organizations.* New York: Wiley, 1978. 838 p.

This Week's Citation Classic

Milgram S. The experience of living in cities. *Science* **167**:1461-8, 1970.
[Graduate Center, City University of New York, New York, NY]

The individual experiences the density, large numbers, and heterogeneity of city life as overloads which require adaptive adjustments. These adjustments create the distinctive norms and behaviors characteristic of city life. Experiments comparing small town and city behavior test the overload hypothesis. [The *Science Citation Index*® **(***SCI*®**) and the** *Social Sciences Citation Index*® **(***SSCI*®**) indicate that this paper has been cited over 260 times since 1970.]**

Stanley Milgram
Department of Psychology
Graduate School
City University of New York
New York, NY 10036

September 25, 1981

"I was pleased to learn this paper had become a *Citation Classic*, and believe the following personal and *zeitgeist* factors should be mentioned in connection with it. First, the personal. For many years I lived in New York, Boston, and Paris. The contrast between these cities, and my experiences in small towns, stimulated an interest in 'urban atmosphere.' But it was not until the mid-1960s, while teaching a tutorial at Harvard University on urban psychology, that I tried to analyze experimentally what made the 'atmosphere' of a city such as New York differ from that of other communities.

"Although research into urban questions had a well-entrenched history in sociology, the social psychologist, with his characteristically experimental bent, had not yet thought of 'the city' as a manageable topic for scientific investigation. Sociological theorists such as Georg Simmel[1] and Louis Wirth[2] had speculated on the consequences urban circumstances had for the mental and social life of city inhabitants, and provided rich hypotheses, but these had not yet come under experimental scrutiny.

"For example, we have long heard that big cities are 'fast' while small towns are slower in pace. But what exactly did this mean? Did it imply, for example, that people in the city walk faster than small towners? One of the first studies carried out in my Harvard tutorial dealt with the measurement of walking speeds in downtown Boston, compared to the pace in the small town of Concord, Massachusetts. We found city people walked about ten percent faster. Since then, more systematic studies have been carried out on this topic (e.g., Bornstein[3]) and the results hold up well.

"In subsequent years, my students at the City University of New York carried out a grab bag of experimental studies on city *vs.* small town behavior, but one limitation became apparent: because there are so many specific phenomena one could study in a city, it was important to bring the investigations under a more rigorous theoretical discipline. This was provided by the systems theory notion of *overload* (in which the individual is seen to make adaptive adjustments in the face of environmental demands on his attention, decisions, and actions). Thus, an integrative concept was added to the diverse experimental studies to produce a more systematic presentation of findings and issues. And that is more or less how the article came about.

"Why is the article heavily cited? Probably because questions of environmental quality were just beginning to take hold in the late-1960s, and the article linked this general concern to a specific sociopsychological method and theory for investigating the quality of city life. It helped make the city a fit subject for experimentation."

1. **Simmel G.** The metropolis and mental life. (Wolf K W, ed.) *The sociology of Georg Simmel.* New York: Free Press, 1950. p. 409-24.
2. **Wirth L.** Urbanism as a way of life. *Amer. J. Sociol.* **44**:1-24, 1938.
3. **Bornstein M H & Bornstein H G.** The pace of life. *Nature* **259**:557-9, 1976.

CC/NUMBER 9
MARCH 1, 1982

This Week's Citation Classic

Griffitt W & Veitch R. Hot and crowded: influences of population density and temperature on interpersonal affective behavior.
J. Personal. Soc. Psychol. **17**:92-8, 1971.
[Department of Psychology, Kansas State University, Manhattan, KS]

This paper demonstrates that high temperature and high population density evoke negative affective states in humans. It also demonstrates that these negative affective states exert negative effects on feelings about other people and about the nonsocial environment. [The *Social Sciences Citation Index*® **(***SSCI*®**) indicates that this paper has been cited over 160 times since 1971.]**

William Griffitt
Department of Psychology
Kansas State University
Manhattan, KS 66506

January 7, 1982

"The experiment reported in this paper resulted from the convergence of two of my major areas of interest at the time it was conducted. First was my interest in interpersonal attraction stimulated by my major professor, Donn Byrne. In what ultimately became known as a 'reinforcement-affect model of attraction,'[1] our view was that *in*terpersonal liking and disliking resulted from *intra*personal positive and negative feelings that might be evoked in a variety of ways. Second was an interest in the popular, but untested, assumption that uncomfortable environmental conditions such as high temperatures, high noise levels, crowding, and the like contribute to interpersonal dislike, hostility, and even violence. To the extent that such environments evoke negative feelings, it seemed theoretically and logically likely that social behaviors would be negatively affected by negative environments. Thus, we set out to examine the effects of high temperatures and high population density on liking and disliking others.

"Our attraction methodology was well established and it seemed a relatively simple matter to manipulate the human population density of a given space. Manipulating temperature precisely, however, posed other problems. One needs to control, or at least take into account, humidity and airflow even as the number of people in a room changes radically.

"We were fortunate to have access to laboratory space devoted to studies of the effects of temperature extremes on performance, comfort, and animal behavior. In our 'hot' condition, subjects participated at an *effective temperature* of 93.5° F (109° F, 46 percent relative humidity) and in the 'normal' condition at an effective temperature of 73.4° F (74° F, 93 percent relative humidity). Experiments were run either in high density conditions (4.06 square feet per person) or low density conditions (12.73 square feet per person). After 45 minutes in such conditions, subjects were provided with information about an anonymous person and recorded their feelings about the person. They also recorded their moods and feelings about various aspects of the experiment and environment. As expected, subjects in the 'hot and crowded' conditions reported more negative feelings and moods, reacted to the other person more negatively, and evaluated the experiment and experiment room more negatively than those in the normal temperature and low density conditions. With perspiration flowing, makeup smearing, and clothing soaked, some subjects in the 'hot and crowded' conditions even became verbally abusive toward the experimenter, the psychology department, and the university. We were eminently successful in demonstrating the potential for unpleasant environments to provoke negative social behavior.

"I believe that this article has become a *Citation Classic* because it was the first, using rather tight experimental controls, to demonstrate the potentially negative impact of high temperatures and high population density on social behavior. It also had the benefit of timing. It appeared when serious concern was growing over the 'population explosion,' ghetto living conditions, and when 'environmental psychology' was in its seminal stages."

1. **Clore G L & Byrne D.** A reinforcement-affect model of attraction. (Huston T L, ed.) *Foundations of interpersonal attraction*. New York: Academic Press, 1974. p. 143-70.

Adams J S. Toward an understanding of inequity. *J. Abnormal Soc. Psychol.* **67**:422-36, 1963. [General Electric Company, Crotonville, NY]

A theory of inequity is presented. The theory specifies the conditions under which perceived inequity will arise and the means by which it may be reduced or eliminated. Field studies supporting the theory and laboratory experiments designed to test certain aspects of it are reported. [The *Social Sciences Citation Index®* **(***SSCI®***) indicates that this paper has been cited over 215 times since 1966.]**

J. Stacy Adams
Graduate School of Business Administration
University of North Carolina
Chapel Hill, NC 27514

August 24, 1981

"This paper was the product of the felicitous interaction of several influences in the 1960-1961 period. The *zeitgeist* was heavily laden with concern for civil rights and social justice and provided a fertile seedbed in which ideas about the nature of social exchanges, especially employer-employee monetary exchanges, might germinate.

"My attention was originally drawn to inequity problems by a number of phenomena. First, a large proportion of employment dissatisfaction, grievances, and industrial strikes appeared to result from employee perceived wage inequities. Furthermore, intriguing anecdotal evidence suggested that wage dissatisfaction remained among some employees following substantial wage increases. Second, distressful interpersonal social relationships in nonwork situations reportedly often involved perceived inequities, as in child-parent, student-teacher, and marital exchanges. Third, the early 1960s was suffused by concern for civil rights and social justice—matters of equity. Despite the pervasiveness of these phenomena and their economic and social costs, there was little understanding of either the antecedents or the behavioral consequences of perceived inequity, especially of the latter, although Homans[1] had provided seminal insights into causes.

"It seemed to me highly improbable that persons who experienced inequity in their transactions with others would merely feel and manifest dissatisfaction, whatever its emotional coloration and intensity. Indeed, Festinger's theory of cognitive dissonance[2] and an abundant body of related research predicted and provided evidence that imbalanced cognitions held by people led them to behave in several distinct ways to redress the imbalance.

"The article provided a theoretical structure that specified the conditions under which perceived inequity in social exchanges occurs and the conditions that lead to differing modes of inequity reduction, both cognitive and behavioral. It was then possible to hypothesize rigorously and test empirically a wide variety of behaviors in different social exchange situations. Indeed, behaviors that defied conventional wisdom were deducible from the theory. For example, it was predictable that overpaid employees would increase their unit work output if paid by the hour, whereas overpaid piece workers would decrease unit output and increase output quality.

"The response of academic researchers and industrial relations practitioners to this paper has been very gratifying since its publication. Some years later, following 12 years of research on inequity by approximately 170 different researchers, a review of the literature bearing directly on equity theory, as it came to be called, revealed four general phenomena.[3] First, the annual growth rate of publications was exponentially increasing. Second, the number of *new* researchers working on inequity was also increasing exponentially, albeit at a lower rate. Third, from an initial emphasis on salary and wage inequity, research expanded to equity problems in the domains of child development, coalition formation, bargaining, social protest, conflict resolution, interpersonal relationships, and the social psychology of victimization. Finally, major derivations from the original theory were tested, with the consequence that the theory was sustained or modified in part, expanded, and made relevant to a broader spectrum of social phenomena. This continues today."

1. **Homans G C.** *Social behavior: its elementary forms.* New York: Harcourt, Brace & World, 1961. 404 p.
2. **Festinger L.** *A theory of cognitive dissonance.* Evanston, IL: Row Peterson, 1957. 291 p.
3. **Adams J S & Freedman S.** Equity revisited: comments and annotated bibliography. (Berkowitz L & Walster L, eds.) *Advances in experimental social psychology.* New York: Academic Press, 1976. Vol. 9. p. 43-90.

Chapter

Psychotherapy

General / 249–256

Reports on specific methods / 257–269

Evaluation of therapies / 270–275

This Week's Citation Classic

Bergin A E & Garfield S L. (eds.) *Handbook of psychotherapy and behavior change: an empirical analysis.* New York: Wiley, 1978 (1971). 957 p. [Dept. Psychol., Brigham Young Univ., Provo, UT and Dept. Psychol., Washington Univ., St. Louis, MO]

An interdisciplinary group of thirty-five authors and editors contributed to this comprehensive review, evaluation, and synthesis of empirical literature on all aspects of psychotherapy. It attempted to place each aspect of clinical change within a context of scientific evaluation. [The *Science Citation Index*® *(SCI*®*)* **and the** *Social Sciences Citation Index*™ *(SSCI*™*)* **indicate that this book has been cited over 255 times since 1971.]**

Allen E. Bergin
Values Institute and
Department of Psychology
Brigham Young University
Provo, UT 84602

August 8, 1979

"During six years together at Teachers College, Columbia University, where Sol Garfield was director of the Clinical Psychology program, we developed a fruitful collaboration from which I benefited greatly. Before Garfield went to Washington University (St. Louis) and I to BYU, we had the pleasure of completing our finest joint project, the *Handbook*. It was an attempt to bring order out of a bewildering array of claims and counterclaims in the field of psychotherapy. We decided that the clinical issues could best be addressed by establishing as clearly as possible the empirical status of each question. Unlike many fields, this one is greatly influenced by unverified but strongly held opinions. We wanted to clarify how the field could advance by bringing it solidly within a research as opposed to a purely clinical framework. Among some professionals this goal was controversial. The result far exceeded our expectations.

"We have been surprised and pleased to find that the book became a standard text and reference in the US and many parts of the world, as well as gaining acceptance among disciplines as diverse as social work, psychiatry, and school counseling. It clearly filled a need and apparently its empirical framework proved persuasive. We have often remarked upon the fact that this synthesis of other people's research has had far more influence than any of the original data-gathering projects we conducted and published. It seems that the time was ripe for a vigorous attempt to separate wheat from chaff.

"One thing that made the *Handbook* such a frequent reference source was the original way in which some of the chapters were written. More than good reviews of the literature, they creatively reassessed large domains of inquiry, rearranged existing data, and came forward with new empirically-based implications for practitioners and original hypotheses for further study. Each was reviewed by both editors and an outside reviewer, and was revised from one to four times. Some authors became bitter over our obsessionalizing and expressed feelings toward us that are not printable, but ultimately all were reconciled and proud of the final product.

"Due to the multifaceted and expansive literature in the field, we depended upon the expertise of many distinguished collaborators who share our empiricist philosophy and whose creative contributions we gratefully acknowledge. They are: Albert Bandura, Richard Bednar, H.R. Beech, Gerald Davison, H.J. Eysenck, Donald Ford, Jerome Frank, Jack Gibb, Arnold Goldstein, Kenneth Heller, Leonard Jacobson, Donald Kiesler, Leonard Krasner, Peter Lang, Frank Lawlis, Arnold Lazarus, Eugene Levitt, Lester Luborsky, Gerald Marsden, Ruth Matarazzo, Joseph Matarazzo, Philip May, Kevin Mitchell, Edward Murray, Roger Myers, Gerald Patterson, Sheldon Roen, Arthur Shapiro, Norman Simonson, Donald Spence, Hans Strupp, Charles Truax (deceased), and Hugh Urban."

CC/NUMBER 8
FEBRUARY 23, 1981

This Week's Citation Classic

Strupp H H & Bergin A E. Some empirical and conceptual bases for coordinated research in psychotherapy: a critical review of issues, trends, and evidence. *Int. J. Psychiat.* 7:18-90, 1969.
[Vanderbilt Univ., Nashville, TN and Teachers College, Columbia Univ., New York, NY]

The article was perhaps the first comprehensive critical review of the psychotherapy research literature. It was part of a larger effort to explore whether large-scale collaborative studies by independent investigators were feasible, and it proposed several possible research studies for investigation. Since that time the field has undergone considerable growth and development, based in part on our effort to synthesize results and point new directions. [The *Science Citation Index®* **(***SCI®***) and the** *Social Sciences Citation Index®* **(***SSCI™***) indicate that this paper has been cited over 210 times since 1969.]**

Hans H. Strupp
Department of Psychology
Vanderbilt University
Nashville, TN 37240

February 3, 1981

"The history of psychotherapy research, which began in the 1940s, was significantly influenced by three National Institute of Mental Health-sponsored national conferences, held respectively in 1957, 1961, and 1966. Following the third conference in Chicago, a small informal committee of prominent researchers, chaired by Joseph D. Matarazzo, was formed for the purpose of exploring the feasibility of collaborative research among independent investigators. Would researchers collaborate? Was the field sufficiently developed to make collaborative efforts productive at that time? The committee judged that exploration of the problem called for a major commitment and that no single person was likely to be equal to the challenge.

"With the active support of A. Hussain Tuma and Donald Oken, representing the Clinical Research Branch of the NIMH, the committee invited a behaviorally and client-centered researcher (Allen E. Bergin) and a psychodynamically oriented researcher (myself) to undertake, as a first step, the task of critically reviewing the extensive research literature. The result was the subject review article, in which we interpreted the empirical status of the field and outlined several possible collaborative projects that might significantly advance knowledge of therapeutic effects. Additional products were invited critiques by recognized researchers[1] and a comprehensive bibliography.[2]

"Phase 2 involved a more intensive exploration of the feasibility issue. It encompassed traveling nationwide to visit research centers, consult with a sizable group of experts, draft discussion papers, and eventually formulate a set of recommendations. Our main conclusion,[3,4] as of 1970, was essentially negative. (A decade later, however, NIMH launched the first large-scale collaborative study in psychotherapy, aimed at the treatment of major depressions.)

"Our collaboration was a tremendously enriching personal and professional experience, an opportunity that comes one's way perhaps once in a lifetime. Our odyssey was enormously exciting. Best of all, we became close friends and our friendship has endured. We remain grateful to Matarazzo, whose vision brought us together, to Tuma, and to many other colleagues who broadened our horizons. It is deeply gratifying that our own collaboration has apparently stimulated the thinking of numerous colleagues and thus played a part in furthering research in this important area. Psychotherapy research has clearly ceased to be an esoteric pursuit by a few specialists; it has become a respectable area of scientific investigation."

1. *Critical evaluations of:* Some empirical and conceptual bases for coordinated research in psychotherapy: a critical review of issues, trends, and evidence. *Int. J. Psychiat.* 7:116-68, 1969.
2. **Strupp H H & Bergin A E,** eds. *Research in individual psychotherapy: a bibliography.* Bethesda, MD: NIMH, 1969. 167 p.
3. **Bergin A E & Strupp H H.** New directions in psychotherapy research: a summary statement. *J. Abnormal Psychol.* 76:13-26, 1970.
4. -------------------------------. *Changing frontiers in the science of psychotherapy.* Chicago: Aldine-Atherton, 1972. 468 p.

This Week's Citation Classic

CC/NUMBER 10
MARCH 7, 1983

Stokes T F & Baer D M. An implicit technology of generalization.
J. Appl. Behav. Anal. **10**:349-67, 1977.
[Univ. Manitoba, Winnipeg, Manitoba, Canada and Univ. Kansas, Lawrence, KS]

An effective therapeutic behavior change often must occur over time, persons, and settings, and the effects of the change sometimes should spread to related behaviors. This generalization of behavior change does not always occur automatically, and frequently needs to be actively programmed as part of a treatment intervention. The research literature relating to the technology of generalization promotion was reviewed. [The *Social Sciences Citation Index*® (*SSCI*®) indicates that this paper has been cited in over 165 publications since 1977.]

Trevor F. Stokes
Department of Psychology
West Virginia University
Morgantown, WV 26506

December 1, 1982

"In 1971, I was a junior psychology major at the University of Western Australia in Perth. One day I was at the library coffee shop with a friend, Milton McGhee, who was a graduate student in social work. We talked about some of his practicum experiences with juvenile delinquents, noting the fact that initial behavior changes could be accomplished readily, for the most part, within the controlled confines of a secure institution. Unfortunately, however, these newly learned skills often were not used after release to a competing environment containing multiple reinforcers for deviant as well as nondeviant life-styles. We sat there, in our temporary escape from the books upstairs, pondering the need for development of additional treatment procedures to accomplish this needed generalization of behavior change.

"Around this same time, I was in the throes of deciding upon the topic for a senior honors thesis. I had heard that a distinguished American psychologist, Donald Baer, would soon be at the university on sabbatical. I therefore took the bold step of writing to recruit his assistance as the supervisor of the project. With little regard to the extant literature, I proposed 'examining something dealing with generalization.' My prudent solicitations were handsomely rewarded. In July of 1971, I received a letter from Baer. He suggested we get to work shortly after his arrival in Perth, 'assuming minimal culture shock.' Baer's letter ended in his usual charming style by noting, 'The problem you cite is an excellent one, and could prove reinforcing to us both. Let's hope so.' So began our positive and productive collaboration, beginning with my senior honors thesis.[1]

"Following the completion of my bachelor's degree, I ventured to Kansas to attend graduate school and study further with Baer. We continued collaborative research on issues in the development of a technology of generalization. In addition, we commenced a systematic review of the research and treatment literature in that area. An initial draft was produced within a year, followed by two years of discussion, review, and refinement of our ideas. Finally, we succumbed to the pressure of academic life and publication priorities and submitted the paper before someone else responded to the current concerns about generalization by producing a similar analysis and discussion.

"I believe that the paper is widely cited because it discusses one of the major issues in behavior analysis and modification. As the treatment intervention techniques have become more sophisticated and effective with a diversity of behavior problems, so the need to establish and document generalized behavior changes has become much greater. The paper makes a number of suggestions for the clinician to incorporate into interventions. It also critiques a number of promising areas in the technology of generalization promotion and provides a general categorization of techniques designed to assess or program generalization. It was our hope that the field would regard the discussion as a useful organization and conceptualization of generalization and its programming."

1. **Stokes T F, Baer D M & Jackson R L.** Programming the generalization of a greeting response in four retarded children. *J. Appl. Behav. Anal.* 7:599-610, 1974.

D'Zurilla T J & Goldfried M R. Problem solving and behavior modification. *J. Abnormal Psychol.* **78**:107-26, 1971.
[Department of Psychology, State University of New York, Stony Brook, NY]

Problem-solving theory and research were reviewed for possible applications in behavior modification. 'Real life' problem solving was conceptualized as a five-stage cognitive-affective-behavioral process that is important for social competence. Guidelines for the clinical application of problem-solving training were discussed. [The *Social Sciences Citation Index*® shows that this paper has been cited in over 240 publications, ranking it among the top 10 ever published in this journal.]

Thomas J. D'Zurilla
Department of Psychology
State University of New York
Stony Brook, NY 11794

October 11, 1984

"The subject of this paper occurred to me during the late 1960s. At that time, Marv Goldfried and I were working on a research project in which we were attempting to develop a behavioral method for assessing social competence.[1] Our subject population for the study was college freshmen. We were identifying problematic situations related to college life and work and asking subjects to report their likely responses to these situations. We were struck by the wide differences among subjects in the effectiveness of their responses and speculated that some of the freshmen were better problem solvers than others.

"Although it is obvious that humans are problem solvers, we realized that this fact had been sorely neglected in our theories of social competence and psychological adjustment. Moreover, the potential value of training in problem-solving skills as a means of facilitating social competence and psychological adjustment had not been recognized in the field of behavior modification. We decided then to prepare a paper that we hoped would help bridge the gap between problem-solving research and applied behavior modification.

"We wanted to reach as many empirically oriented clinical psychologists as possible, so we submitted the paper to the *Journal of Abnormal Psychology*. We were nearly frustrated in our efforts to get the paper published in the *Journal* but were saved by the good judgment and foresight of the new editor-elect, Donald R. Peterson. The paper was first sent to two reviewers, both of whom returned it after some delay saying that they would be unable to review it. A third reviewer commented that the article was very interesting and stimulating, but since it was devoid of data it was inappropriate for a prime data journal. Fortunately, Peterson disagreed and decided to publish it anyway.

"I think that the paper has been cited so often because it was published at a time when mental health professionals were beginning to explore ways in which clinical interventions might be improved through placing a greater emphasis on facilitating the social competence of persons who seek help in dealing with emotional or adjustment problems. It was also a time when the *Zeitgeist* within behavior modification was beginning to shift from *therapist*-controlled, *behavioral* interventions, to *self*-controlled, *cognitive-behavioral* interventions. A quote from Michael Mahoney in 1974 reflects the excitement that developed within the field of behavior modification about the potential value of problem solving: 'The potential relevance of problem solving to both clients and therapists needs little elaboration. In terms of adaptive versatility and the ability to cope with an ever-changing array of life problems, these cognitive skills may offer an invaluable personal paradigm for survival. Their potential contribution to therapeutic efficacy and independent self-improvement will hopefully become an issue of priority in future empirical scrutiny.'[2]

"In a recent book chapter, Arthur Nezu and I have reviewed empirical studies on the outcome of problem-solving training over the past 10-15 years that contribute support for this approach as a treatment technique, a maintenance strategy, and a prevention method."[3]

1. **Goldfried M R & D'Zurilla T J.** A behavioral-analytic model for assessing competence. (Spielberger C D, ed.) *Current topics in clinical and community psychology*. New York: Academic Press, 1969. Vol. 1. p. 151-96.
2. **Mahoney M J.** *Cognition and behavior modification*. Cambridge, MA: Ballinger, 1974. p. 212.
3. **D'Zurilla T J & Nezu A.** Social problem solving in adults. (Kendall P C, ed.) *Advances in cognitive-behavioral research and therapy*. New York: Academic Press, 1982. Vol. 1. p. 201-74.

CC/NUMBER 25
JUNE 23, 1980

Wolpe J. *Psychotherapy by reciprocal inhibition.*
Stanford, CA: Stanford University Press, 1958. 239 p.

This book describes how the anxiety central to experimental neuroses is lastingly eliminated by the competition of feeding responses. On the basis of this finding, methods emerged for eliminating human neuroses, using the calming effects of muscle relaxation, anger, sexual arousal, and other competitors with anxiety. [The *Social Sciences Citation Index® (SSCI™)* **indicates that this book has received over 1340 citations since 1966. The** *Science Citation Index® (SCI®)* **indicates that this book has received over 160 citations since 1961.]**

Joseph Wolpe
Department of Psychiatry
Health Sciences Center
School of Medicine
Temple University
Philadelphia, PA 19129

July 20, 1979

"This book's story began in 1943 when I was a medical officer in the South African Medical Corps, stationed at a base hospital in Kimberley that received soldiers disabled in the North African campaign. Many were cases of battle neurosis. A popular treatment in those days was narcoanalysis. It was believed that in the stuporous state induced by intravenous thiopentone, recovery should result from the emergence of painful 'repressed' battle memories. In fact, it became apparent after a few months that narcoanalysis was providing practically no lasting results at all.

"This, coupled with the knowledge that the Russians had never accepted psychoanalysis, caused me to explore the possibility that neurosis might be a phenomenon of emotional conditioning. I immersed myself in the conditioning literature, and wrote commentaries on all Pavlov's experiments published in English. I paid particular attention to the experimental neuroses which Pavlov was the first to report,[1] and which were later produced by several experimenters in the United States. What I found extraordinarily instructive was Masserman's studies of experimental neuroses in cats,[2] even though he steadfastly psychoanalyzed his animals instead of learning from their behavior.

"Upon my discharge from the army in June, 1946, I began experiments to clarify the nature of neurotic behavior of cats. I was able to show that experimental neuroses were actually conditioned anxiety-response habits, and that they could be eliminated by systematic programs of counterconditioning, using feeding as the counter-anxiety behavior. On the basis of these experiments, I wrote a thesis to obtain an advanced degree in psychiatry.[3] In 1949, Leo J. Reyna persuaded me to revise and expand my thesis for possible publication. Late that year, I sent the revision to Clark L. Hull at Yale for his advice, since my work owed much to his. He suggested that I offer the manuscript to Appleton-Century, but neither that publisher, nor, later, McGraw-Hill, judged it suitable for publication.

"Subsequently, several of the theoretical parts of the thesis appeared in *Psychological Review*,[4-10] and the main findings of my work on experimental neurosis in the *British Journal of Psychology*.[11] The derived clinical methods first entered the psychiatric scene in 1954.[12] A fellowship at the Center for Advanced Study in the Behavioral Sciences in 1957-58 made possible the preparation of this book, which combined the substance of the previous publications and greatly extended the clinical ramifications of the reciprocal inhibition principle which continues to be the main source of behavior therapy techniques."

1. **Pavlov I P.** *Conditioned reflexes and psychiatry.* New York: International Publishers, 1941. 199 p.
2. **Masserman J H.** *Behavior and neurosis.* Chicago: University of Chicago Press, 1943. 269 p.
3. **Wolpe J.** *An approach to the problem of neurosis based upon conditioned responses.* Unpublished PhD thesis. Johannesburg, South Africa: University of Witwatersrand, 1948.
4. -----------. An interpretation of the effects of combinations of stimuli (patterns) based on current neurophysiology. *Psychol. Rev.* **56**:277-83, 1949.
5. -----------. Need-reduction, drive-reduction, and reinforcement: a neurophysiological view. *Psychol. Rev.* **57**:19-26, 1950.
6. -----------. Primary stimulus generalization: a neurophysiological view. *Psychol. Rev.* **59**:8-10, 1952.
7. -----------. The neurophysiology of learning and delayed reward learning. *Psychol. Rev.* **59**:192-9, 1952.
8. -----------. Formation of negative habits: a neurophysiological view. *Psychol. Rev.* **59**:290-9, 1952.
9. -----------. Learning theory and "abnormal fixations." *Psychol. Rev.* **60**:111-6, 1953.
10. -----------. Theory construction for Blodgett's latent learning. *Psychol. Rev.* **60**:340-4, 1953.
11. -----------. Experimental neuroses as learned behavior. *Brit. J. Psychol.* **43**:243-68, 1952.
12. -----------. Reciprocal inhibition as the main basis of psychotherapeutic effects. *Arch. Neurol. Psychiat.* **72**:205-66, 1954.

This Week's Citation Classic

CC/NUMBER 2
JANUARY 14, 1980

Tharp R G & Wetzel R J. *Behavior modification in the natural environment.* New York: Academic Press, 1969. 236 p.
[Dept. Psychol., Univ. Hawaii, Honolulu, HI and Dept. Psychol., Univ. Arizona, Tucson, AZ]

The application of behavior modification procedures by significant adults in the families and schools of problem children is suggested and exemplified; also, a theory is developed. Outcome data are presented. [The *Science Citation Index*® **(***SCI*®**) and the** *Social Sciences Citation Index*™ **(***SSCI*™**) indicate that this book has been cited over 240 times since 1969.]**

Roland G. Tharp
Department of Psychology
University of Hawaii
Honolulu, HI 96822

July 19, 1979

"Dissatisfaction with psychotherapy, its frequent disruptive effects on social relationships, and the failure of therapeutic gains to survive into natural environments were issues which led me through several years work in natural-group treatments, such as marriage and family therapy, and the therapeutic community. When Ralph Wetzel, who had been trained at the University of Washington, which was a seedbed of the behaviorist movement, became my colleague at Arizona, we joined forces and theories.

"Wetzel was himself dissatisfied with the state of behavior modification, largely limited then to institutional applications. Then, as now, behavior improvements did not seem to generalize to environments or relationships beyond the one of treatment. We reasoned that pro-social behavior would be maintained only if the natural environments of children—their families and schools—could be altered to support the desired behavior. Therefore the actual targets of behavior change must be the parents, teachers, siblings, aunties, etc., of referred problem children.

"To make the demonstration more dramatic, we did not contact the children themselves whatsoever, beyond a very brief period of initial assessment. Over a four-year period, we consulted the 'natural environments' of 77 delinquent and pre-delinquent children, helping them to create and maintain programs of contingent reinforcement. At that time, the 'deprofessionalization' of helping relationships was much in the wind. Our demonstration staff consisted entirely of baccalaureate-level young men and women whom we trained and supervised. This produced the 'triadic model' of intervention, in which the expert worked indirectly with parent or teacher 'mediators,' who in turn worked directly with the 'target' children. This, hopefully, produces a changed social environment, not dependent on continued professional counseling.

"The outcome data were quite favorable. The demonstration opened up behavior modification into the real world, and suggested operations which have now become routine for mental health workers.

"I believe the continued frequent citation of the book is due to two features. First, it contains a clear theory and a practical manual. Second, though, is the full discussion of problems, and ultimate limitations of the approach; for this focus, Wetzel is primarily responsible. Gaylord Thorne, who was the on-site director of the project, was unable to participate in the authorship, but he made great contributions from his background in probation and community psychology work.

"During the project, we encountered enormous resistance from the establishment of psychiatry and clinical psychology. Now, 15 years later, applied behavior modification has become the establishment itself. My current work is directed toward correcting some of its excesses."

This Week's Citation Classic

CC/NUMBER 11
MARCH 17, 1980

Ullmann L P & Krasner L, eds. *Case studies in behavior modification.* New York: Holt, Rinehart & Winston, 1965. 401 p. [Univ. Illinois, IL and State Univ. New York, Stony Brook, NY]

This is the first book to use the words 'behavior modification' in its title. It has 85 pages of introductory material and 50 reprinted clinical/experimental papers. It brought together widely separated material and provided a workable alternative to psychoanalytic theories. [The *Science Citation Index*® **(***SCI*®**) and the** *Social Sciences Citation Index*™ **(***SSCI*™**) indicate that this book has been cited over 480 times since 1965.]**

Leonard P. Ullmann
Department of Psychology
University of Hawaii
Honolulu, HI 96822

February 1, 1980

"Because of crowding, Len Krasner, as training unit chief, and I, as coordinator of a research project, were placed in an isolated Quonset hut at Palo Alto VA. We combined his work on verbal conditioning (independent variable) and my work on emotional expressiveness (dependent variable) and found that we could obtain effects on major indicants of schizophrenia that were rapid and superior to then current treatments. The direct alteration of behavior and its salubrious effects ran directly counter to disease theories of 'mental illness.' A series of speakers, which included Bandura, Bijou, Ferster, Goldiamond, Kanfer, Patterson, Sarbin, and Staats, confirmed and broadened our thinking.[1] In our teaching, we found that the approach illustrated and made relevant basic psychological principles that students previously thought academic. In our clinical work, we found increased effectiveness.

"The introductory material was written during the 1963 Christmas vacation after I had taught a seminar on the topic at the University of Illinois. Hobart Mowrer, Wesley Becker, Sid Bijou, Gordon Paul, Douglas Bernstein, Dan O'Leary, Don Meichenbaum, Tom Borkovec, Ed Craighead, and George Allen were some of the faculty and students at Illinois, while Alan Ross joined Krasner at Stony Brook where Gerry Davison and Terry Wilson later graduated. In short, we were lucky to be where we were when we were.

"The book has been highly cited because it presents an integrated, scientifically verifiable alternative to psychoanalysis, covering the development, maintenance, and intervention of changeworthy behaviors. It tells what, how, when, where, and why.

"Some matters were ironic. For one, we thought the term 'behavior modification,' which we adapted from Carl Rogers, was more neutral than 'behavior therapy,' and quite the reverse has been true in the popular press. For another, we used a broad range of psychological and sociological concepts.[2,3] We found ourselves criticized by some for overlooking hypothesized functions, while others thought we had 'deviated' towards mushiness. My son asked me, 'Dad, are you a real behaviorist?' "

1. **Krasner L & Ullmann L P, eds.** *Research in behavior modification: new developments and implications.* New York: Holt, Rinehart & Winston, 1965. 403 p.
2. **Krasner L & Ullmann L P.** *Behavior influence and personality: the social matrix of human action.* New York: Holt, Rinehart & Winston, 1973. 560 p.
3. **Ullmann L P & Krasner L.** *A psychological approach to abnormal behavior.* Englewood Cliffs, NJ: Prentice-Hall, 1969. 687 p.

This Week's Citation Classic

Krasner L & Ullmann L P, eds. *Research in behavior modification: new developments and implications.* New York: Holt, Rinehart & Winston, 1965. 403 p. [State Univ. New York, Stony Brook, NY and Univ. Illinois, IL]

This was the first book to bring together the research/applications of a group of clinical/experimental psychologists under the label of behavior modification. The work of the contributors has been seminal in the subsequent growth of the behavioral field. [The *Social Sciences Citation Index*® (*SSCI*®) **indicates that this book has been cited over 190 times since 1966.]**

Leonard Krasner
Department of Psychology
State University of New York
Stony Brook, NY 11794

January 1, 1982

"*Research in Behavior Modification* grew out of a series of lectures presented within the context of the psychology training program, of which I was the coordinator, at the Veterans Administration Hospital in Palo Alto, California, in the early-1960s. At that time, I was also doing research on two aspects of the exciting new field of applying learning theory of experimental psychology to clinical problems: namely, verbal conditioning analogs of psychotherapy with Leonard Ullmann, and establishing a token economy on a psychiatric ward with Jack Atthowe.[1]

"My goal was to present to our clinical psychology trainees those investigators who were involved in the basic experimental research and clinical applications of a behavioral/social learning model of human behavior. In those ancient days it was possible to keep up with most developments in psychology and to be in contact with virtually everyone in a scientific network who was doing important things in our area of interest. With the cooperation of Tom Kennelly, director of the psychology services, we invited those investigators who were doing relevant research to visit the VA Hospital in Palo Alto and to participate in the monthly lecture series which ran for a period of about two years. Whenever possible the various investigators attended each others' presentations or listened to tape recordings to facilitate discussion and ideas.

"In this volume, Ullmann and I brought together the papers presented by the participants in the lecture series into a theoretical framework. Our related volume, *Case Studies in Behavior Modification*,[2] which was published at the same time, included virtually all of the literature illustrating this new approach to changing human behavior which we labeled 'behavior modification.' These were the first books to utilize that term in their titles. Within this rubric we emphasized clinical techniques based on 'laboratory-tested procedures' such as positive reinforcement, modeling, vicarious reinforcement, the use of peers as reinforcers, and the programming of parents. The major theoretical commonality among these investigators was that their approach to maladaptive behavior was through a psychological rather than a medical model. Behavior modification deals directly with behavior rather than with a hypothesized underlying disease or pathology that causes 'symptoms.'

"This book has been widely cited because it offered a rationale, with research and clinical applications, for a social reinforcement model of human behavior that was to expand and grow rapidly during the 1960s and 1970s until it was to become the predominant view in the field.[3] Virtually every contributor to this volume has been a major influencer in the behavioral field. We take special note of the contributions of the late Charles Ferster, whose research on autistic children, self-control and depression, and theoretical formulations (of behavioral pathology, chapter 2) was to have considerable impact on the subsequent development of the behavior modification field. We miss him."

1. **Atthowe J M, Jr. & Krasner L.** Preliminary report on the application of contingent reinforcement procedures (token economy) on a "chronic" psychiatric ward. *J. Abnormal Psychol.* **73**:37-43, 1968. [Citation Classic. *Current Contents/Social & Behavioral Sciences* **13**(28):18, 13 July 1981.]
2. **Ullmann L P & Krasner L,** eds. *Case studies in behavior modification.* New York: Holt, Rinehart & Winston, 1965. 401 p. [Citation Classic. *Current Contents/Social & Behavioral Sciences* **12**(11):18, 17 March 1980.]
3. **Krasner L & Ullmann L P.** *Behavior influence and personality: the social matrix of human action.* New York: Holt, Rinehart & Winston, 1973. 560 p.

This Week's Citation Classic

CC/NUMBER 28
JULY 13, 1981

Atthowe J M, Jr. & Krasner L. Preliminary report on the application of contingent reinforcement procedures (token economy) on a "chronic" psychiatric ward. *J. Abnormal Psychol.* **73**:37-43, 1968.
[College of San Mateo, CA and State Univ. New York, Stony Brook, NY]

Chronic backward patients received tokens for performing desirable behaviors (self-care, participating in activities, interacting with others, demonstrating responsibility, etc.). Tokens could be exchanged for those things that patients desired (cigarettes, passes, etc.). Results indicated a significant increase in the performance of desirable behavior. [The *Science Citation Index*® **(***SCI*®**) and the** *Social Sciences Citation Index*® **(***SSCI*®**) indicate that this paper has been cited over 160 times since 1968.]**

John M. Atthowe, Jr.
Department of Psychiatry
Rutgers Medical School
College of Medicine and Dentistry
of New Jersey
Piscataway, NJ 08854

May 25, 1981

"The impetus for this investigation developed along the banks of the Tennessee River in the late 1950s while trying to persuade Tom Gilbert that operant conditioning was not effective with humans. A few years later I was to see firsthand the ineffectiveness of the then treatment programs for hospitalized mental patients. In 1962, after corresponding with Len Krasner at the VA Hospital in Palo Alto about the possible use of behavior modification techniques with mental patients, I accepted what was to be the first postdoctoral internship in behavior modification in the VA.

"Under the preceptorship of Krasner, I proposed and received in 1963 a two year research associate grant to study contingency management (token economy) in a hospital ward. There was much opposition to the use of these 'overly simplified, animal procedures' with human beings. With Krasner and especially Tom Kennelly, chief of psychology, running interference, I was finally allowed to start a contingency management program on one of the forgotten back wards.

"The hospital was dominated by the 'medical model' in which the physician made all the decisions. Nursing personnel were committed to this model as well as the principle of noncontingent 'tender loving care.' In order to carry out this investigation I needed to make the day to day decisions, and I had to have a staff that would go along with changes I introduced. For four months Kennelly played politics and Krasner and I sold behavior modification to both the professional and nonprofessional staff. The result was the verbal recognition of the program goals by the hospital and ward staff.

"We started to collect baseline data for two months which was extended to six months as we were forced to change key personnel without upsetting individual services. It had become very apparent that the staff could sabotage the program at any time. I had learned that to do research in large social systems, you needed to continually reinforce the mediators of change (staff) even more than patients.

"As the program developed, I was faced with many unpopular decisions. One actively delusional patient earned enough tokens for an extended pass. He had not been out of the hospital for 44 years; yet, he decided to see his old neighborhood in Texas. As we said good-bye to him, most people felt we would never see him again. However, he returned on time after sleeping in the Fort Worth bus depot. His old neighborhood was now concrete.

"The study was published at the beginning of a widespread and very prolific applied behavior modification movement. Clinicians and researchers in the mental health and retardation field, in prisons, and in school settings throughout the world found token reinforcement a useful adjunct to treatment. At about the same time, National Educational Television filmed the program adding to its publicity. Its inclusion in *Great Cases in Psychotherapy*[1] suggests its strong clinical flavor. One of the most scholarly reviews of the field is *The Token Economy* by Alan Kazdin."[2]

1. **Wedding D & Corsini R J,** eds. *Great cases in psychotherapy.* Itasca, IL: Peacock, 1979. 314 p.
2. **Kazdin A E.** *The token economy.* New York: Plenum, 1977. 327 p.

This Week's Citation Classic

CC/NUMBER 39
SEPTEMBER 29, 1980

Kazdin A E & Bootzin R R. The token economy: an evaluative review. *J. Appl. Behav. Anal.* **5**:343-72, 1972.
[Penn State Univ., University Park, PA and Northwestern Univ., IL]

The token economy is a technique widely used in treatment, rehabilitation, and educational settings. The paper reviewed applications for a variety of treatment populations. Problems associated with achieving durable therapeutic changes and with conducting research on token economies are discussed. [The *Science Citation Index®* *(SCI®* **) and the** *Social Sciences Citation Index® (SSCI™)* **indicate that this paper has been cited over 210 times since 1972.]**

Alan E. Kazdin
Department of Psychiatry
Western Psychiatric Institute & Clinic
University of Pittsburgh
School of Medicine
Pittsburgh, PA 15261

July 10, 1980

"While a graduate student in the late 1960s, I worked part-time at a facility for emotionally disturbed and mentally retarded children and adults. My task was to develop treatment programs that would direct adults toward community placement. It appeared that an incentive system, referred to as a *token economy,* might be suitable to this end. A token economy is a reward system where some medium of exchange (e.g., stars, points, tickets), referred to as *tokens,* are delivered for client behaviors. Tokens can be exchanged for a variety of events (e.g., prizes, privileges) in the way that money can be exchanged in national economies.

"Although the use of tokens had been demonstrated in several studies, much of the information was unpublished. I collected this information and prepared an overly lengthy paper evaluating the current status of token economies. The paper was prepared while I was a graduate student. Richard Bootzin, the coauthor of the paper and one of my mentors, volunteered to edit the manuscript so that it might be fit for public consumption and publication.

"The bases for the frequent citation of the paper are a matter of surmise. Perhaps significance should be attached to the fact that the paper: was the first to review applications of the token economy across a wide range of treatment populations; encompassed several unpublished papers not widely available; was fortunate to appear in a prominent journal; and was made into a separate monograph. Overall, the paper served as a reference for articles applying the technique or addressing the problems that were likely to be encountered.

"After approximately five years elapsed, the field had expanded tremendously so I wrote a book on the same topic.[1] The token economy had been greatly extended to new populations and research questions and problems addressed in the original article had been illuminated greatly. The book, when compared to the earlier article, provided a much more comprehensive evaluation of the area and its problems. Unfortunately, the book was not very successful and did not capture the attention of those who faithfully cited the original paper. Indeed, if *Current Contents®* develops a 'nonclassics section for noncited texts,' I would expect my book to be a leading contender."

1. **Kazdin A E.** *The token economy: a review and evaluation.* New York: Plenum Press, 1977. 342 p.

This Week's Citation Classic

Phillips E L. Achievement Place: token reinforcement procedures in a home-style rehabilitation setting for "pre-delinquent" boys. *J. Appl. Behav. Anal.* **1**:213-23, 1968. [University of Kansas, Lawrence, KS]

Token reinforcement procedures were used to reduce antisocial behaviors and increase prosocial behaviors of delinquent adolescents in a treatment-oriented group home. Clinical responsibility for the program rested with a highly trained husband-wife team ('teaching-parents') who lived full-time in the home. [The *Social Sciences Citation Index*® (*SSCI*®) indicates that this paper has been cited in over 145 publications since 1968, making it the 13th most-cited paper published in this journal.]

Elery L. Phillips
Boys Town USA Department
Father Flanagan's Boys' Home
Boys Town, NE 68010

April 21, 1983

"This paper consisted of a series of experiments that formed part of my master's degree work at the University of Kansas. My wife Elaine and I had started a group home for delinquents, and our early attempts to codify a systematic program were unique enough at the time that much of our research contributed to our graduate degrees. Modifying token economy techniques for our setting and population, we demonstrated that antisocial youth behaviors (e.g., aggressive statements) could be improved without interfering with the clinical relationship between ourselves and the boys in our home.

"In retrospect, I suspect one of the reasons the work continues to be cited is that it was a blending of several trends that have influenced current work with delinquents. In the late-1960s, it was uncommon to find a residential treatment program for delinquents that was in a neighborhood home, used a token economy, and employed a research orientation in a humanistic manner. The fledgling field of applied behavior analysis formed the scientific framework and the paper was published in the founding year of the field's journal.

"Of course, looking back on this early work highlights the simplicity of the youth behaviors we addressed; but, since then, my work and that of numerous colleagues has moved to far more complex human enterprise. We realized early on that, if we were going to seriously attempt to help the hundreds of thousands of troubled youngsters who need it, we must provide a 'package' that others could use, including necessary staff training, program evaluation, and management systems in addition to the psychological youth treatment techniques.[1] Further, we realized that we must borrow concepts from the business world (e.g., marketing) and find ways to communicate what we learn to others.[2] As part of this effort, we started in the mid-1970s to adapt the community-based model at the large institution[3] of Boys Town, since many youths will continue to be served in such established settings. In the 16 years since the paper was published, several hundred more papers, manuals, films, and related materials have been produced by colleagues using the same model (now called the Teaching-Family Model) as we have begun working with new populations. Currently, over 180 homes in 18 states follow the same approach started years ago at our home in Kansas.

"Although trained as psychologists, we have come to appreciate the benefits of borrowing elements from other fields to construct a human service program that seems to do well in different locales, with different staff working with different populations, and funded from different sources—with comparable effects for the clients no matter where they are. We have learned from political science, management, training and development, personnel, communications, computer science, and other disciplines.

"I have been fortunate in my associations with colleagues such as my wife Elaine, coworkers Dean Fixsen, Montrose Wolf, and numerous others who remain friends as well as professionals committed to helping today's youth. We've learned that it takes far more than small-scale research projects... but that's where it started."

1. **Phillips E L, Fixsen D L, Phillips E A & Wolf M M.** The Teaching-Family Model: a comprehensive approach to residential treatment of youth. (Cullinan D & Epstein M H, eds.) *Special education for adolescents: issues and perspectives.* New York: Charles E. Merrill, 1979. p. 203-33.
2. **Phillips E L, Phillips E A, Fixsen D L & Wolf M M.** Behavior shaping works for delinquents. *Psychol. Today* 7:75-9, 1973.
3. **Coughlin D D, Maloney D M, Baron R L, Dahir J, Daly D L, Daly P B, Fixsen D L, Phillips E L & Thomas D L.** Implementing the community-based Teaching-Family Model at Boys Town. (Christian W P, Hanna G T & Glahn T J, eds.) *Programming effective human services: strategies for institutional change and client transition.* New York: Plenum Press. In press, 1983.

CC/NUMBER 22
MAY 30, 1983

This Week's Citation Classic

Foxx R M & Azrin N H. The elimination of autistic self-stimulatory behavior by overcorrection. *J. Appl. Behav. Anal.* **6**:1-14, 1973.
[Anna State Hospital, Anna, IL]

Self-stimulatory behavior is a common problem of retarded and autistic individuals. Yet, no method was in general usage and of demonstrated effectiveness in eliminating it. Overcorrection procedures eliminated the self-stimulatory behaviors of a variety of individuals and these effects endured. [The *Social Sciences Citation Index*® **(***SSCI*®**) indicates that this paper has been cited in over 170 publications since 1973.]**

Richard M. Foxx
Department of Treatment Development
Anna Mental Health and
Developmental Center
Anna, IL 62906

March 23, 1983

"In the early years of my research career in California institutions, I had been looking for logical, natural consequences to use in reducing the maladaptive behaviors of retarded individuals rather than more traditional or 'artificial' behavioral consequences. My feeling was that artificial consequences might make normalization[1] more difficult whereas natural negative consequences might enhance it and thereby help close the gap between the behavior of mentally handicapped individuals and normals. In late-1970, I left California to pursue a PhD at Southern Illinois University and to work at the Anna State Hospital Research Lab which was directed by N.H. Azrin. This *Citation Classic* resulted from our research on developing new treatment strategies or rationales.

"The overcorrection rationale originated during the development of a toilet-training program for retarded individuals.[2] We decided to discourage accidents by requiring soiled individuals to clean the floor and themselves and then repeatedly practice the proper sequence of toileting. These natural, negative consequences effectively eliminated toileting accidents and appeared to make more sense than such traditional negative consequences as time-out. The treatment rationale that emerged was that individuals should assume responsibility for their inappropriate acts by undoing or correcting the effects of these acts by restoring the situation to a vastly improved state from that which existed prior to the act and by practicing overly correct forms of relevant behavior in those situations where the act commonly occurred.

"After refining and expanding the rationale, we began applying it to other maladaptive behaviors. In our first effort, we successfully treated aggressive-disruptive behaviors.[3] Initially, we labeled the method restitution, but soon rejected it because it was less descriptive than the term overcorrection.

"We then decided to use the rationale to develop effective consequences for self-stimulatory behavior. Self-stimulation consists of repetitive, stereotyped behavior that has no apparent functional effects on the environment and is a serious problem of retarded and autistic individuals since it interferes with learning adaptive skills. At the time of our study (which was my dissertation with Azrin serving as adviser), the only successful procedures for eliminating self-stimulation involved the use of physical punishment by a slap or contingent electric shock. For obvious reasons, neither had received widespread usage. Specific overcorrection procedures were developed for the specific self-stimulatory behaviors of retarded and autistic children and compared with several alternative procedures including punishment by a slap. The overcorrection procedures rapidly eliminated self-stimulation, were more effective than the alternative procedures, and produced long-lasting suppressive effects. Even so, the paper received mixed reviews. Fortunately, the editor (Ivar Lovaas) decided it merited publication.

"Our study has been cited so often because it: 1) described the successful and acceptable treatment of a widespread difficult problem; 2) was the first time that the overcorrection rationale had been fully delineated; 3) described a new treatment strategy that was applicable to a wide range of maladaptive behaviors; and 4) raised a number of conceptual issues that spurred other researchers."[4]

1. **Wolfensberger W.** *The principle of normalization in human services.* Toronto: National Institute on Mental Retardation, 1972. 258 p.
2. **Foxx R M & Azrin N H.** *Toilet training the retarded: a rapid program for day and nighttime independent toileting.* Champaign, IL: Research Press, 1973. 141 p.
3. ------------------------------. Restitution: a method of eliminating aggressive-disruptive behavior of retarded and brain damaged patients. *Behav. Res. Ther.* **10**:15-27, 1972.
4. **Foxx R M & Bechtel D R.** Overcorrection. (Hersen M, Eisler R & Miller P, eds.) *Progress in behavior modification.* New York: Academic Press, 1983. Vol. 13. p. 227-88.

CC/NUMBER 20
MAY 16, 1983

This Week's Citation Classic

Stuart R B. Behavioral control of overeating. *Behav. Res. Ther.* 5:357-65, 1967.
[School of Social Work, Univ. Michigan, Ann Arbor, MI]

A logic for the functional analysis and control of eating behavior is presented along with case data on the efficacy of highly structured intervention methods with eight moderately obese women. Treatment involves identification and change of chains of eating-related behaviors. [The *Social Sciences Citation Index*® **(***SSCI*®**) indicates that this paper has been cited in over 220 publications since 1967.]**

Richard B. Stuart
Department of Family and
Community Medicine
University of Utah
Salt Lake City, UT 84112
and
Weight Watchers International, Inc.
Manhasset, NY 11030

March 1, 1983

"For many years, obesity had been regarded as an intractable if not untreatable disorder. While clearly attributable to a positive energy balance, it had long been assumed that the control system of the urge to overeat was neuroanatomical, neurochemical, or psychodynamic. Therapeutic approaches therefore characteristically ignored the focal problem—eating too much while expending too little energy—in favor of focusing on hypothetical underlying mechanisms.

"At the time when efforts were first being made to apply laboratory-derived techniques for the functional analysis of behavior to humans, I was just beginning to do clinical research at the University of Michigan. Overeating appeared to be a suitable therapeutic objective because it was measurable, could be assessed promptly, and seemed related to such other problems of behavioral excess as smoking, substance abuse, and alcoholism. Therefore, I contracted to work with a 40-year-old woman seeking a weight loss of 47 pounds. Through the course of five months, an effective program was developed for her use. Seeing her weight loss, the three other members of her duplicate bridge game presented for treatment. Their success was noted by various physicians in Ann Arbor, and they, in turn, began referring patients to what became an eating disorders clinic.

"Adaptations and expansion of the methods described in this paper resulted in the publication of a book[1] which described a three-stage program of change in behavior, nutrition, and activity patterns. This manual served as the basis for several hundred investigations which generally proved to be more effective than alternative approaches to the management of mild to moderate obesity.[2]

"Unfortunately, further investigation revealed that changes achieved through these direct methods were not long-lasting. It appeared as though the urge to overeat was an outgrowth of life-style patterns that resulted in strong negative moods like depression, anxiety, boredom, or anger. These moods were the immediate precursors to most problem-eating incidents. The long-term control of obesity depended upon a two-phase approach in which eating urges were controlled through life-style change and eating behavior was then directly attacked through the techniques originally described.[3] It is regrettable that papers using the more narrow approach still appear, and I can only hope that citation of the newer, more effective methods will supplant mention of the earlier effort.

"Two things happened simultaneously to create a fertile ground for this paper. First, the results of epidemiological studies such as the Framingham series heightened awareness among public health professionals about the association between obesity, hypertension, and related cardiovascular diseases. Second, human applications of behavior change technology were beginning to receive positive clinical attention. This paper provided public health professionals with a previously unavailable means of promoting weight loss at the same time that it gave behavior modifiers an opportunity to apply their evolving technology to a clinically relevant problem with precisely measurable outcome."

1. **Stuart R B & Davis B.** *Slim chance in a fat world: behavioral control of obesity.* Champaign, IL: Research Press, 1972. 240 p.
2. **Stuart R B, Mitchell C & Jensen J A.** Therapeutic options in the management of obesity. (Prokop C K & Bradley L A, eds.) *Medical psychology: contributions to behavioral medicine.* New York: Academic Press, 1981. p. 321-53.
3. **Stuart R B.** The chances of keeping it off after taking it off: the maintenance of weight loss. (Davidson P O, ed.) *Behavioral strategies for lifestyle change.* New York: Brunner/Mazel, 1979. p. 151-94.

This Week's Citation Classic

CC/NUMBER 23
JUNE 7, 1982

McFall R M & Lillesand D B. Behavior rehearsal with modeling and coaching in assertion training. *J. Abnormal Psychol.* **77**:313-23, 1971. [University of Wisconsin, Madison, WI]

Nonassertive college students were taught to be more assertive about refusing unreasonable requests. Training was provided through two sessions of role playing, with the treatment program administered via prerecorded audiotape. Variations in treatments across subjects assessed the contributions of specific components. [The *Social Sciences Citation Index*® *(SSCI*®*)* **indicates that this paper has been cited over 190 times since 1971.]**

Richard M. McFall
Psychological Clinic
Indiana University
Bloomington, IN 47405

March 16, 1982

"As a graduate student of George A. Kelly,[1] I was interested in exploring the potential psychotherapeutic benefits of role playing techniques. After joining the faculty of the University of Wisconsin, I began looking for a psychological problem for which role playing might be a sensible treatment method. Joseph Wolpe and Arnold Lazarus[2] had reported successfully using 'behavior rehearsal,' a form of role playing, to teach socially anxious clients to behave more assertively; therefore, I decided to evaluate experimentally the value of role playing methods for 'assertive training.'

"My first experiment[3] (with Albert R. Marston) convinced me that the prevailing conception of assertiveness was too ambiguous to be measured satisfactorily. Since my primary interest at the time was in assessing the treatment effects of role playing, I decided to finesse the definitional problem by focusing on an extremely narrow but reliably measurable subtype of assertive behavior—namely, the refusal of unreasonable requests. At times I have regretted choosing such a narrow and negative referent for assertive behavior, as it has contributed to the tendency for people to equate assertion with abrasive, aggressive, and self-centered behavior. Nevertheless, from a research perspective, it proved to be a good decision.

"The next experiment (with Diane Bridges Lillesand) became this *Citation Classic*. Generally, I think the study was influential because it provided other investigators in the area with a fresh experimental paradigm and a set of novel measures that resolved several assessment problems. The experimental treatments and behavioral measures were prerecorded on audiotape, which enabled other laboratories to replicate our work. The study also happened to be one of the first controlled experiments on 'assertive training,' which was destined to become a popular topic in the 1970s.

"Although the study initially received mixed reviews, the editor (Donald Peterson) fortunately decided to publish it. He suggested a change in terms—from 'assertive training' (Wolpe and Lazarus's term) to 'assertion training'—for grammatical reasons. Subsequently, this change provided an unintended gauge of the study's impact; one could monitor the spreading use of the revised term.

"In recent years my research focus has evolved from the original narrow interests in role playing and assertion to a broader and more basic interest in the relationships among social competence, social skills, and psychopathology."[4]

1. **Kelly G A.** *The psychology of personal constructs.* New York: Norton, 1955. 2 vols.
2. **Wolpe J & Lazarus A A.** *Behavior therapy techniques.* Oxford: Pergamon Press, 1966. 198 p.
3. **McFall R M & Marston A R.** An experimental investigation of behavior rehearsal in assertive training. *J. Abnormal Psychol.* **76**:295-303, 1970.
4. **McFall R M.** A review and reformulation of the concept of social skills. *Behav. Assess.* **4**:1-33, 1982.

CC/NUMBER 39
SEPTEMBER 26, 1983

This Week's Citation Classic

Wolf M, Risley T & Mees H. Application of operant conditioning procedures to the behaviour problems of an autistic child. *Behav. Res. Ther.* **1**:305-12, 1964. [Univ. Washington, Seattle, and Western State Hospital, WA]

This paper describes one of the earliest attempts to apply behavioral procedures to autistic children, to evaluate the effects of time-out on children, to use single-subject evaluation and measurement procedures in a naturalistic setting for children, and to employ behavioral procedures in a comprehensive manner that included the training of parents, institutional staff, and teachers. [The *Social Sciences Citation Index*® (*SSCI*®) indicates that this paper has been cited in over 290 publications since 1966.]

Montrose M. Wolf
Department of Human Development and Family Life
University of Kansas
Lawrence, KS 66045

July 25, 1983

"In the early 1960s, there was much excitement about the application of the principles of behavior to clinical and educational problems. Sidney W. Bijou and Donald M. Baer, University of Washington, gathered together a vigorous group interested in these applications.

"Soon after I had arrived, as a new and not very self-confident postdoc, Bijou described an interesting case and an unsettling challenge. The director of the children's unit at the local mental hospital had said to Bijou, something like, 'I understand that you guys think you can teach anyone to do anything. Let's see if you can teach a little, three-and-a-half-year-old autistic boy with severe self-destructive tantrums, sleeping problems, and no normal language how to wear his glasses. Because of cataracts in his eyes, both lenses have been removed. For the past year, we and his parents have tried without success to get him to wear his glasses. The ophthalmologist predicts that unless the boy begins wearing his glasses within the next six months, he will permanently lose his macular vision. Let's see you guys teach this boy to wear his glasses!'

"Todd Risley, Hayden Mees, and I found that we were able to develop procedures that dealt effectively with the tantrums, self-destructive behavior, sleeping and eating problems, and that also established the wearing of glasses, and some appropriate language and social behavior. For the two years following the boy's seven-month stay at the institution, we and our colleagues developed procedures for teaching him several other appropriate social and self-care behaviors.[1] He recently graduated from high school. By all accounts, except for his abnormally thick glasses, he has the appearance and style of a typical adolescent.

"This paper may have been widely cited for several reasons. It describes the earliest attempt to apply and to evaluate systematically the effects of brief time-out on child behavior. O'Leary and Carr[2] have suggested that this paper became a model for future studies in the field because of its emphasis on parent and teacher training, early intervention, and systematic follow-up to ensure maintenance of treatment gains as well as continued acquisition of new behaviors. The research was also an early example of the application of single-subject research methodology in a naturalistic setting. Behavioral data were collected in order to evaluate the effectiveness of almost all of the procedures that were used. It was not until a few years later that some of us formalized our notions regarding single-subject experimental design and measurement procedures. These were described in a paper by Baer, Risley, and myself[3] which was recently selected as a *Citation Classic.*

"A final reason for the paper's frequent citation may be the fact that the procedures it described became part of a major body of behavioral technology for treating autistic children. Most of the described procedures have been successfully replicated in research with other autistic children. We replicated most of these procedures ourselves and evaluated their effectiveness using single-subject research methodology.[4] Other researchers have also replicated these procedures, adding their own important additions and refinements. Some have evaluated this evolving technology using elegant and carefully controlled comparison group experimental designs."[5,6]

1. **Wolf M M, Risley T R, Johnston M K, Harris F R & Allen K E.** Application of operant conditioning procedures to the behavior problems of an autistic child: a follow-up and extension. *Behav. Res. Ther.* **5**:103-11, 1967.
2. **O'Leary K D & Carr E G.** Childhood disorders. (Wilson G T & Franks C M, eds.) *Contemporary behavior therapy: conceptual foundations of clinical practice*. New York: Guilford Press, 1982. p. 445-504.
3. **Baer D M, Wolf M M & Risley T R.** Some current dimensions of applied behavior analysis. *J. Appl. Behav. Anal.* **1**:91-7, 1968. [Citation Classic. *Current Contents/Social & Behavioral Sciences* **14**(46):14, 15 November 1982.]
4. **Risley T R & Wolf M M.** Establishment of functional speech in echolalic children. *Behav. Res. Ther.* **5**:73-88, 1967.
5. **Lovaas O I, Koegel R L, Simmons J Q & Long J S.** Some generalization and follow-up measures of autistic children in behavior therapy. *J. Appl. Behav. Anal.* **6**:131-65, 1973.
6. **Hemsley R, Howlin P, Berger M, Hersov L, Holbrook D, Rutter M & Yule W.** Treating autistic children in a family context. (Rutter M & Schopler E, eds.) *Autism*. New York: Plenum Press, 1978.

CC/NUMBER 47
NOVEMBER 21, 1983

This Week's Citation Classic

Cautela J R. Covert sensitization. *Psychol. Rep.* **20**:459-68, 1967.
[Boston College, Chestnut Hill, MA]

Covert sensitization is a technique designed to increase an avoidance response. When covert sensitization is employed, the client is asked to imagine a target behavior to be avoided and then imagine an aversive consequence such as vomiting or being disgraced. Applications of covert sensitization to maladaptive approach behaviors such as excessive alcohol intake, overeating, or stealing are described. [The *Social Sciences Citation Index*® (*SSCI*®) indicates that this paper has been cited in over 250 publications since 1967.]

Joseph R. Cautela
Department of Psychology
Boston College
Chestnut Hill, MA 02167

October 3, 1983

"When I attended Wolpe's first Behavioral Institute at the University of Virginia in 1965, I was impressed by the efficiency and wide applicability of the desensitization procedure. In this procedure, imagery is manipulated to reduce an avoidance response. It was Wolpe's contention that, not only could desensitization be applied to maladaptive avoidance behaviors due to anxiety, but that maladaptive approach behaviors, such as alcoholism, obesity, or sexual deviations, could be treated successfully by desensitization. His assumption was that these maladaptive approach behaviors were elicited by anxiety-producing stimuli. Therefore, if the client was desensitized to these anxiety components, then the maladaptive approach behavior would be eliminated.

"After I left the training institute, I began to employ desensitization in treating both maladaptive avoidance and approach behaviors. At one particular period in my clinical practice, I was treating a female for alcoholism and another female for obesity. After the behavioral analysis in both these cases, I desensitized both clients for all the possible antecedent conditions that appeared to trigger the maladaptive approach behaviors. After concluding that my examination of relevant antecedent conditions was thorough, I began to speculate that perhaps I should focus on having the clients imagine appropriate consequences to reduce the frequency of the behaviors.

"In the literature at that time there was some evidence that employing aversive stimulation was successful in the elimination of some faulty approach behaviors, e.g., papers by Thorpe, Schmidt, and Castell[1] and Marks, Rachman, and Gelder.[2] Therefore, I reasoned, why not have individuals imagine they were receiving aversive consequences since Wolpe's desensitization procedure was successful by having the clients focus on imagining antecedent conditions?

"I decided to apply the imagining of aversive consequences to the two cases mentioned here. I chose vomiting as the aversive consequence, probably because the cases each concerned oral behavior. Fortunately, these clients began to improve after the application of the new procedure.

"After the success of these two cases, I began to apply covert sensitization to quite a variety of maladaptive approach behaviors. The publication of the procedure resulted in many clinical case illustrations and experimental investigations, e.g., Barlow, Leitenberg, and Agras.[3]

"My original conceptualization of the covert sensitization process was vague. It wasn't quite clear to me whether I was dealing with mere contiguity, since the target behavior overlapped the aversive scene—or was it due to operant features? With the success of covert sensitization, I concluded that since clients could imagine aversive consequences to reduce behaviors, they could imagine reinforcing consequences to strengthen or increase behaviors. This led to the development of covert reinforcement. Establishing the covert reinforcement procedure made it obvious to me that I was dealing with a kind of covert operant conditioning. This, then, was the beginning of the development of the covert conditioning model."[4,5]

1. **Thorpe J G, Schmidt E & Castell D.** A comparison of positive and negative (aversive) conditioning in the treatment of homosexuality. *Behav. Res. Ther.* **1**:357-62, 1963.
2. **Marks I M, Rachman S & Gelder M G.** Methods for the assessment of aversion treatment in fetishism with masochism. *Behav. Res. Ther.* **3**:253-8, 1965.
3. **Barlow D H, Leitenberg H & Agras W S.** Experimental control of sexual deviation through manipulation of the noxious scene in covert sensitization. *J. Abnormal Psychol.* **74**:597-601, 1969. (Cited 80 times.)
4. **Cautela J R.** Covert conditioning: assumptions and procedures. *J. Ment. Imagery* **1**:53-64, 1977.
5. **Cautela J R & McCullough L.** Covert conditioning: a learning-theory perspective on imagery. (Singer J, ed.) *The power of human imagination.* New York: Plenum Press, 1977. p. 227-50.

CC/NUMBER 46
NOVEMBER 14, 1983

Gelder M G, Marks I M & Wolff H H. Desensitization and psychotherapy in the treatment of phobic states: a controlled inquiry.
Brit. J. Psychiat. **113**:53-73, 1967.
[Institute of Psychiatry and Maudsley Hospital, London, England]

A clinical trial of desensitization and two forms of psychotherapy for phobic outpatients is described. Results were compared over two years, throughout treatment and follow-up. Ratings were made of symptoms and social adjustment. All three raters agreed that desensitization led to the greatest improvement in phobias. [The *Science Citation Index*® (*SCI*®) and the *Social Sciences Citation Index*® (*SSCI*®) indicate that this paper has been cited in over 180 publications since 1967.]

M.G. Gelder
Department of Psychiatry
Warneford Hospital
University of Oxford
Oxford OX3 7JX
England

July 29, 1983

"My interest in behaviour therapy began in 1962 at Maudsley Hospital, when I shared in the care of a phobic patient with Victor Meyer, a member of the psychology department who was using the new methods. Sir Aubrey Lewis encouraged me to find out more about behavioural treatments, and to try to devise a way of evaluating them. I read the literature on the evaluation of psychotherapy and was soon convinced of the difficulties of assessing the effects of any kind of psychological treatment. However, it seemed possible that some of these difficulties could be avoided in an investigation of behaviour therapy. First, it would be possible to study only patients who shared a single diagnosis—phobic disorder—because advocates of behaviour therapy were making specific claims about their ability to treat such cases. If this was done, assessment would be simplified because it could concentrate on phobic symptoms, which are easier to rate than the intrapsychic changes which are the concern of psychotherapists. Secondly, the new methods of behaviour therapy were only likely to be adopted in preference to brief psychotherapy if they led to substantially better results; and this question should be answerable with the existing, rather insensitive, assessment procedures provided that they could be shown to be reliable.

"Although these judgements proved to be largely correct, the research success of the research depended on three pieces of good fortune. The first was the presence in London at the time of Joseph Wolpe, the originator of the form of behaviour therapy I was proposing to study (*viz.*, systematic desensitization). Wolpe was extremely generous in advising me about his treatment. The second piece of good fortune concerned Heinz Wolff, a consultant psychotherapist at Maudsley Hospital. He immediately saw the potential importance of the investigation and agreed to supervise the psychotherapy which was to be the treatment against which the behaviour therapy was to be tested. The third stroke of luck concerned Isaac Marks. With the help of Lewis, I had obtained financial support from the Medical Research Council to pay for a research worker who was to join me in carrying out the project. Marks was available at the time and accepted the post. In this way, a long and fruitful collaboration began. With this team, and with the help of many other doctors working at Maudsley, the trial proceeded without any major problems, and the resulting paper was accepted for publication.

"I think that the work has been cited frequently because it was one of the first attempts to compare behaviour therapy with brief psychotherapy in patients with clinically significant problems. Also, despite many shortcomings inherent in a study carried out with few resources, the results showed that clinical trial methodology could be used to evaluate behaviour therapy. Moreover, in discussing the results, it was emphasized that although we had been evaluating behaviour therapy and brief psychotherapy as alternatives, we saw no reason why they should not be used together in selected cases. This statement, together with Wolff's direct involvement in the research, helped to initiate a more constructive exchange of ideas between psychotherapists and behaviourists.

"Subsequent progress in the behavioural treatment of phobic disorders has been reviewed in the monographs by Mathews *et al.*[1] and by Marks."[2]

1. **Mathews A M, Gelder M G & Johnston D W.** *Agoraphobia, nature and treatment.* New York: Guilford Press, 1981. 233 p.
2. **Marks I.** *Care and cure of neuroses: theory and practice of behavioral psychotherapy.* New York: Wiley, 1981. 331 p.

CC/NUMBER 25
JUNE 22, 1981

Wahler R G, Winkel G H, Peterson R F & Morrison D C. Mothers as behavior therapists for their own children. *Behav. Res. Ther.* **3**:113-24, 1965. [University of Washington, Seattle, WA]

Three children, referred for psychological treatment, were observed interacting with their mothers in a clinic playroom. Based on the observational findings and a social learning theory conception of childhood behavior problems, the mothers were taught to change their reactions to the children's behaviors. In each of the three cases, these planned shifts in mother reactions were shown to produce therapeutic changes in the children. [The *Social Sciences Citation Index*® *(SSCI*®) **indicates that this paper has been cited over 150 times since 1966.]**

R.G. Wahler
Department of Psychology
Child Behavior Institute
University of Tennessee
Knoxville, TN 37916

May 21, 1981

"This study represents one of the early developments in the field of clinical behavior modification. As such, it was a logical extension of already published experimental analyses of child social interchanges.[1] These studies in nursery school and institutional settings documented the dramatic power of adult social attention as a class of reinforcers for children's desirable and deviant behavior. In my clinical position at the University of Washington, Seattle, such findings came to mind whenever I was called on to provide help to behaviorally disturbed children. In essence, it appeared to me that the mothers of these children were highly responsive to the children's deviant actions and less attentive to their more adaptive behaviors. Thus, it seemed reasonable to assume that the mothers may have been maintaining these problem behaviors through differential reinforcement. If this were indeed the case, then teaching the mothers to shift their attention contingencies to the children's desirable behaviors ought to produce therapeutic benefits.

"The above formulation was easier said than done. The notion that pathology inducing parents might serve as therapists for their own children was contrary to standard clinical practice—and contrary to the expectations of the parents and children. The latter expectations turned out to be our greatest obstacles to the new clinical practice. Mothers felt we were shirking our responsibilities as 'doctors' and the children sometimes felt that we were siding against them. For example, in one exceptionally difficult case, the mother was learning to use a procedure called 'time-out.' This technique required the mother to briefly isolate her five-year-old son in a playroom whenever he violated a rule. At first, the mother insisted that I step in and isolate her boy, 'because you're the doctor.' Then, after she finally accepted the responsibility and began to use the procedure correctly, her son initiated a new ploy directed to me. Whenever the mother placed him in time-out, he began a mournful wail heard throughout the clinic: 'Save me, Dr. Wahler, save me!' Needless to say, I was not a very popular person with him, his mother to some extent, and even the secretarial staff of the clinic. But, as the observational findings eventually proved, this youngster developed some remarkable changes in his referral problems. At the conclusion of treatment he even said he liked me.

"I believe the popularity of this study was due to its new look at the old problem of how to effect therapeutic change in troubled children. In essence, the new look argued that if parents are part of the problem why not teach them the necessary skills to remediate that problem? See my recent article in the *Journal of Applied Behavior Analysis* for further work in this field."[2]

1. **Allen K E, Hart B M, Buell J S, Harris F R & Wolf M M.** Effects of social reinforcement on isolate behavior of a nursery school child. *Child Develop.* **35**:511-18, 1964.
2. **Wahler R G.** The insular mother: her problems in parent-child treatment. *J. Appl. Behav. Anal.* **13**:207-19, 1980.

Hawkins R P, Peterson R F, Schweid E & Bijou S W. Behavior therapy in the home: amelioration of problem parent-child relations with the parent in a therapeutic role. *J. Exp. Child Psychol.* **4**:99-107, 1966. [University of Washington, Seattle, WA]

The negative relationship between an 'unmanageable' four-year-old and his mother was systematically assessed and modified in its natural environment, the home, with the mother as 'therapist' and using a functional analysis of the various stimuli and behaviors. Effects were evaluated experimentally, with follow-up 24 days after termination. [The *Social Sciences Citation Index*® *(SSCI™)* indicates that this paper has been cited over 140 times since 1966.]

Robert P. Hawkins
Department of Psychology
West Virginia University
Morgantown, WV 26506

April 7, 1981

"On finishing my PhD I had the opportunity to teach psychology at the University of Washington and work in the child development laboratory, directed by Sid Bijou. That lab's atmosphere facilitated highly creative work with normal, retarded, and maladjusted children, including some excellent parent training in the child development clinic by Bob Wahler and colleagues.

"Bob Peterson was my graduate assistant, and he had worked with Wahler training parents. We agreed to continue this work, but when a real case of a naughty four-year-old with a distraught mother came along, I felt that we should take our parent training out of the laboratory and into the home.

"I had worked a year in an excellent child guidance clinic and was convinced that their traditional manner of treating children's problems was largely fruitless. Assessment ('diagnosis') of the problem was done in the clinic—using parents' verbal reports and various tests that had little to do with the problem presented—while the real problem behavior and its causes were in the daily home, school, or community of the child. The clinicians' interventions consisted of little more than patient listening and the making of vague suggestions as to how the parent might behave differently toward the child. And the effectiveness of this treatment was evaluated primarily in terms of how the parent *said* the child was changing, which was probably more influenced by the parent's desire to please the clinician (or terminate treatment), than by the child's real behavior. This whole process of therapy by *talking* in a clinician's *office* seemed highly questionable.

"Bob and I decided to carry out both the assessment and the treatment in the child's home and to document the results objectively, and Bijou agreed. Edda Schweid, a graduate student, agreed to help us. Our assessment was a 'functional analysis' of the behavior of mother and son, like those in Ulrich, Stachnik, and Mabry,[1] and the intervention was similarly based.

"The results were excellent, and we experimentally demonstrated that they were due to our intervention. We went back and took data 24 days later for three sessions and found the effects lasting. About four years later I talked with the mother by telephone and found that she'd had no recurrence of the problems. Peterson was at least as responsible for the research as I.

"This research, along with work by a few others, has led to thousands of parent training programs around the nation, to a greater appreciation for intervening in 'the natural environment,' and to a large body of applied research[2] which accounts for much of the citation of this study. Our following up the case after intervention was over, our measuring some of the mother's behavior, and our direct involvement in the home are other reasons.

"Having seen the myriad 'mistakes' we parents make in child-rearing, I became convinced that enough is now known about the culturally *critical* job of parenting that we should require high school training in the practical skills of that job, and I wrote a few articles to that effect.[3] The idea now seems accepted by most educated people in our country, but there are few such programs thus far, and they seldom include the 'laboratory' experience that makes the difference between learning *about* something and learning *to do* something. Yet it is a beginning.

"I am now developing a program in which trained, closely supervised foster parents clinically treat a severely maladjusted youth in their own home."

1. **Ulrich R, Stachnik T & Mabry J.** *Control of human behavior.* Glenview, IL: Scott, Foresman, 1966. Vol. 1.
2. **Graziano A M.** Parents as behavior therapists. (Hersen M, Eisler R M & Miller P M, eds.) *Progress in behavior modification.* New York: Academic Press, 1977. Vol. 4.
3. **Hawkins R P.** It's time we taught the young how to be good parents (and don't you wish we'd started a long time ago?). *Psychol. Today* **11**:28-40, 1972.

This Week's Citation Classic™

Harris M B. Self-directed program for weight control: a pilot study.
J. Abnormal Psychol. **74**:263-70, 1969.
[Stanford University, CA]

A behavioral weight control program using self-monitoring, positive reinforcement, stimulus control, modification of the act of eating, and aversive counterconditioning led to weight loss for all participants with no undesirable side effects. Control group subjects tended to gain weight. [The *Science Citation Index*® (*SCI*®) and the *Social Sciences Citation Index*® (*SSCI*®) indicate that this paper has been cited in over 145 publications since 1969.]

Mary B. Harris
Department of Educational Foundations
College of Education
University of New Mexico
Albuquerque, NM 87131

December 7, 1983

"Even counting my unpublished undergraduate thesis, this paper was only the third research study I had ever done. In 1966-1967, I was a second-year graduate student at Stanford University, inspired by the new techniques for behavior modification and discouraged by my own upwardly mobile weight, when I began the research described herein. Ferster, Nurnberger, and Levitt[1] had suggested many of the procedures which I used or modified but had provided no data to substantiate them. Stunkard[2*] had provided a rationale for the importance of research in the area by summarizing the dismal results of previous research on weight control programs. My adviser, Albert Bandura, provided useful advice and the facilities for the program, and my own naivete and enthusiasm provided the belief that if people are taught behavioral techniques which can lead to permanent habit change, attainment and maintenance of weight loss should be relatively simple.

"With this goal in mind, I attempted to devise a behavioral program that would include a little bit of everything, from self-monitoring to positive reinforcement to stimulus control to altering the actual chain of behaviors involved in eating. In addition, I used an aversive counterconditioning procedure with one group of subjects and learned far more about individual variations in the subjective experience of nausea than I ever cared to know. By following this program, all subjects, as well as I, lost weight, with no apparent undesirable side effects. The control group subjects tended to gain weight. To top it off, the paper was accepted by the editor of the *Journal of Abnormal Psychology* **with a very kind letter within two weeks. Needless to say, I have never received such a speedy response, even a rejection, from any journal since.**

"I would guess that this article is widely cited because it was one of the first to use behavioral techniques for weight control in a well-designed study. Since its appearance, I have conducted a number of other studies on behavioral weight control, stressing exercise as well as eating behaviors. However, I have come to realize that even the most effective programs rarely lead to attainment and maintenance of socially ideal weights, and so I have turned more to studying social attitudes toward obesity and the pressures which lead people to feel that they must be thin to be attractive and/or happy.[3,4] I now feel that 'overweight' people would be best advised to focus on developing healthful eating and exercise behaviors and to be less concerned about their weight. However, I must admit that doing research on obesity is an excellent way to maintain one's weight at a socially acceptable level."

1. **Ferster C B, Nurnberger J I & Levitt E B.** The control of eating. *J. Mathetics* 1:87-109, 1962. (Cited 175 times.)
2. **Stunkard A J.** The management of obesity. *NY State J. Med.* **58**:79-87, 1958.
3. **Harris M B.** Eating habits, restraint, knowledge and attitudes toward obesity. *Int. J. Obesity* 7:271-86, 1983.
4. **Harris M B & Smith S D.** The relationships of age, sex, ethnicity and weight to stereotypes of obesity and self-perception. *Int. J. Obesity* 7:361-71, 1983.

*See also **Stunkard A J.** Citation Classic. Commentary on The results of treatment for obesity: a review of the literature and report of a series. *Arch. Intern. Med.* **103**:79-85, 1959.
Current Contents/Clinical Practice **11**(47):24, 21 November 1983.

This Week's Citation Classic™

Wollersheim J P. Effectiveness of group therapy based upon learning principles in the treatment of overweight women. *J. Abnormal Psychol.* **76**:462-74, 1970.
[University of Illinois, Urbana, IL]

This study evaluated the effectiveness of a behavior therapy group treatment program in helping overweight college women lose weight. The design of the study and the highly positive results established a cause-effect relationship between the treatment program and weight loss. [The *Social Sciences Citation Index*® (*SSCI*®) indicates that this paper has been cited in over 155 publications since 1970.]

Janet P. Wollersheim
Department of Psychology
University of Montana
Missoula, MT 59812

February 8, 1964

"Being a graduate student of Gordon L. Paul,[1] I was interested in treatment outcome research as a dissertation topic. In 1967, when I conceived of the study, behavior therapy was beginning to receive much attention as a set of treatment procedures in clinical psychology. I wanted to conduct a treatment study using these procedures together with an index of change that was objective, valid, and easily measured. At this same time, as a graduate student in clinical psychology, I was treating clients in the psychology department's clinic as part of my training requirements. One of these clients was extremely obese. It occurred to me that body weight would be an objective, valid, and easily measured dependent variable in a treatment study focused upon reducing obesity.

"After designing the study, I feared I might not obtain enough subjects to volunteer in response to an announcement of the program's availability in the university newspaper and on bulletin boards. Much to my surprise, not only did many overweight women seek entrance into the program, but so did a large number of normal weight and underweight women. This was the era of Twiggy, the anorexic-looking model of the 1960s. I came to appreciate more fully how much our society had come to value the trim figure.

"Several thoughts occur to me as to why the study has been so widely cited. While my work expanded and modified behavior therapy weight reduction procedures published by Ferster, Nurnberger, and Levitt,[2] and by Goldiamond,[3] it was the first group psychotherapy study concerning weight reduction designed with the controls necessary to establish cause-effect relationships between therapeutic techniques and treatment outcome. The results were among the most favorable reported in the weight reduction literature, a literature characterized by poorly designed research and extremely discouraging results. This work helped extend the applicability of behavioral principles to a new problem area, that of obesity. Additionally, the treatment package was specified in detail in a manual[4] which has been used extensively by others in the field.

"Reflecting upon this work, I often wonder why another study[5] reporting a longer follow-up period with these subjects is not cited more often. Then, too, although I believe that this publication was among the first coining the term, 'cognitive-behavioral,' later publications are credited with devising the term. Perhaps my article was not written in such a way as to highlight usage of this new term. I tend to think that publication of this work was one important factor involved in my being awarded Fellow status in the American Psychological Association in 1980.

"Today, we know that behavior therapy procedures are effective in promoting weight loss *if implemented*. The major problem revolves around motivating clients to initiate such programs, maintain them, and suffer the hardships of caloric restriction. A book edited by Wolman and DeBerry[6] is one of several covering more recent work in the area."

1. **Paul G L.** *Insight vs. desensitization in psychotherapy: an experiment in anxiety reduction.* Stanford, CA: Stanford University Press, 1966. 148 p. (Cited 600 times.)
2. **Ferster C B, Nurnberger J I & Levitt E B.** The control of eating. *J. Mathetics* **1**:87-109, 1962. (Cited 170 times.)
3. **Goldiamond I.** Self-control procedures in personal behavior problems. *Psychol. Rep.* **17**:851-68, 1965. (Cited 130 times.)
4. **Wollersheim J P.** Obesity: behavioral treatment manuals. *Catalogue of selected documents in psychology.* Washington, DC: American Psychological Association, 1975. Vol. 5. p. 237.
5. ------------------. Follow-up of behavioral group therapy for obesity. *Behav. Ther.* **8**:966-8, 1977.
6. **Wolman B B & DeBerry S,** eds. *Psychological aspects of obesity: a handbook.* New York: Van Nostrand Reinhold, 1982. 318 p.

CC/NUMBER 1
JANUARY 4, 1982

This Week's Citation Classic

Breger L & McGaugh J L. Critique and reformulation of "learning-theory" approaches to psychotherapy and neurosis. *Psychol. Bull.* **63**:338-58, 1965. [Univ. Oregon, Eugene, OR and Univ. California, Irvine, CA]

'Learning theory' explanations of neuroses and treatment techniques based on conditioning models were critically reviewed. The theories of learning used by behavior therapists were shown to be invalid and out of date. Their claims for the success of treatment were vitiated by a variety of uncontrolled and biasing factors. [The *Science Citation Index®* (*SCI®*) **and the** *Social Sciences Citation Index®* (*SSCI®*) **indicate that this paper has been cited over 185 times since 1965.]**

Louis Breger
Division of Humanities and Social Sciences
California Institute of Technology
Pasadena, CA 91125

October 14, 1981

"In the early-1960s, my colleague James McGaugh and I were both teaching in the psychology department of the University of Oregon. Jim was trained in the Tolman tradition at the University of California, Berkeley; he was an experimental psychologist with a deep appreciation of the complexities of human learning and memory. I was a psychoanalytically oriented clinical psychologist, interested in psychological disturbance and psychotherapy. At that time, several of our colleagues began to espouse the virtues of the 'new' behavior therapy, both that stemming from Wolpe, Eysenck, and their ilk, and the Skinnerian operant conditioning approach. At first we found their enthusiasm hard to comprehend; they seemed to have rediscovered just those aspects of John B. Watson's behaviorism that had long been proven inadequate (by Karl Lashley in the 1930s for instance). Our discussions failed to persuade them and behavior therapy seemed to be growing, so we decided to do a thorough review of the area and detail our findings in an article.

"What we found in the literature was worse than we anticipated. What was called 'modern learning theory' consisted of an amalgam of outmoded classical conditioning models. Learning was equated with peripheral response acquisition and all the laboratory work that demonstrated the necessity of central mediators (schemas, plans, cognitive maps) was ignored. The behavior therapists were using a model of learning to explain complex human behavior that could not explain the behavior of rats in mazes. We presented all this and argued strongly for a cognitive or schema theory.

"In addition to the theoretical inadequacies, the behavior therapy movement was characterized by a curious contrast between claims to scientific status, on the one hand, and grossly unscientific procedures (loose and shifting use of concepts, poorly controlled studies), on the other. We pointed out that simply using *words* like 'objective,' 'experimental,' and 'controlled' did not make one's work scientific and we called on those in the field to live up to their own standards.

"As one might expect, our article aroused a good deal of controversy. There were rebuttals and counterrebuttals, the hard-liners ignored it (or didn't understand the argument), and those already suspicious of behavior therapy welcomed it. And there were a number of people working within the behaviorist movement who were strongly influenced by our arguments. Theory has clearly moved toward a cognitive model and claims for success are more temperate.

"My own subsequent work has continued along two of the lines laid down in the article. I have used a cognitive or schema model—for instance in my paper on dream function in information processing terms[1]—a model which then expanded into a wider concern with symbolism, meaning, and the interpretation of human experience. And I continue to analyze theory from an outside or critical perspective, most recently in my book on Freud."[2]

1. **Breger L.** Function of dreams. *J. Abnormal Psychol.* **72**:1-28, 1967.
2. ------------. *Freud's unfinished journey: conventional and critical perspectives in psychoanalytic theory.* London: Routledge & Kegan Paul, 1981. 145 p.

CC/NUMBER 2
JANUARY 9, 1984

This Week's Citation Classic™

Hogarty G E, Goldberg S C & the Collaborative Study Group. Drug and sociotherapy in the aftercare of schizophrenic patients: one-year relapse rates. *Arch. Gen. Psychiat.* **28**:54-64, 1973.
[Social Science Res., Friends Medical Science Res. Ctr., Inc., Baltimore, and Psychopharmacology Br., Natl. Inst. Mental Health, Rockville, MD]

Following hospital discharge, 374 schizophrenic patients admitted to three participating clinics were randomly assigned to one of four treatment groups: placebo alone, placebo and a special therapy, drug alone, and drug plus social therapy. Patients were treated under these controlled conditions for two years or until relapse. Differential relapse rates were reported. [The *Science Citation Index*® (*SCI*®) and the *Social Sciences Citation Index*® (*SSCI*®) indicate that this paper has been cited in over 205 publications since 1973.]

**Gerard E. Hogarty
Department of Psychiatry
Western Psychiatric Institute and Clinic
University of Pittsburgh
Pittsburgh, PA 15213**

December 2, 1983

"When this study was first conceived in the late 1960s, enthusiasm for the community treatment of the seriously ill schizophrenic patient had already crested. While the number of resident schizophrenic patients in public mental hospitals was decreasing dramatically, relapse and rehospitalization were increasing proportionately. Maintenance neuroleptic treatment seemed to forestall relapse, but rates differed widely among centers and investigators. Psychosocial forms of aftercare treatment had rarely been subject to experimental control, and most reports in the literature read like uncritical theater reviews. No aftercare study had controlled for both drug and psychosocial treatment in the posthospital maintenance of these patients. Prevention of relapse and enhancement of personal and social adjustment were the two important outcome criteria, parameters which continue to be the subject of our investigations to this day.

"What I find somewhat perplexing is that this very preliminary report on relapse rates in the first year has been so widely cited. In the following year,[1,2] for example, and in subsequent years,[3,4] our final results which describe the effects of drug and psychosocial treatment on relapse and adjustment over the entire two-year period were published. While drug was enormously superior to placebo in forestalling a relapse, nonetheless nearly 50 percent of patients eventually relapsed on drug in two years. (Subsequent studies, which assured the receipt of medication via parenteral administration, yielded similarly high relapse rates, precipitating research for predictors of relapse other than drug noncompliance.[5]) Further, certain schizophrenic patients who were exposed to our intensive efforts at social restoration seemed to relapse earlier. For those who 'survived' on social therapy and placebo, their adjustment was markedly impaired relative to patients able to survive on placebo alone! The combination of drug and social therapy ultimately proved to be the treatment of choice.

"To me, this study has served as a testimonial to the dedication, motivation, personal sacrifice, and suffering of over 30 staff and nearly 400 patients and their families. The cost involved in undertaking these long-term maintenance trials, both human and financial, probably accounts for their rare appearance in the literature. The exacting price of this early study created something of a moral charge not only to publish and implement results whenever possible, but to build on these early gains and failures through continued, systematic study.

"In the decade since this study first appeared, other investigations have also indicated that certain schizophrenic patients might be sensitive to the overstimulation of their therapeutic environment...while other investigations have shown that overstimulation from the *natural* environment is adversive as well.[6] These observations, coupled with an extensive literature in psychophysiology, indicate that many schizophrenic patients might have profound deficits in the regulation of sensory input which could be exploited in the form of psychotic relapse by environmental stimuli. This model of pathogenesis has contributed to the development of a new series of investigations which utilize a more rational prescription of drug and psychological treatment in the long-term maintenance of schizophrenic disorders."[6]

1. **Hogarty G E, Goldberg S C & Schooler N R.** Drug and sociotherapy in the aftercare of schizophrenic patients: II. Two-year relapse rates. *Arch. Gen. Psychiat.* **31**:603-8, 1974. (Cited 140 times.)
2. --. Drug and sociotherapy in the aftercare of schizophrenic patients: III. Adjustment of nonrelapsed patients. *Arch. Gen. Psychiat.* **31**:609-18, 1974. (Cited 75 times.)
3. **Goldberg S C, Schooler N R, Hogarty G E & Roper M.** Prediction of relapse in schizophrenic outpatients treated by drug and social therapy. *Arch. Gen. Psychiat.* **34**:171-84, 1977. (Cited 70 times.)
4. **Hogarty G E & Ulrich R F.** Temporal effects of drug and placebo in delaying relapse in schizophrenic outpatients. *Arch. Gen. Psychiat.* **34**:297-301, 1977. (Cited 20 times.)
5. **Hogarty G E, Schooler N R, Ulrich R, Mussare F, Ferro P & Herron E.** Fluphenazine and social therapy in the aftercare of schizophrenic patients: relapse analyses of a two-year controlled study of fluphenazine decanoate and fluphenazine hydrochloride. *Arch. Gen. Psychiat.* **36**:1283-94, 1979. (Cited 35 times.)
6. **Anderson C M, Hogarty G E & Reiss D J.** Family treatment of adult schizophrenic patients: a psycho-educational approach. *Schizophrenia Bull.* **6**:490-505, 1980.

This Week's Citation Classic

Smith M L & Glass G V. Meta-analysis of psychotherapy outcome studies. *Amer. Psychol.* **32**:752-60, 1977. [University of Colorado, Boulder, CO]

The outcome of 375 studies, in which clients who received psychotherapy were compared with untreated persons, were quantified and statistically summarized. Findings showed psychotherapy to be effective and that the different varieties of therapy do not produce differential effects. Both good and poor designs produced positive effects. [The *Science Citation Index*® (*SCI*®) **and the** *Social Sciences Citation Index*® (*SSCI*®) **indicate that this paper has been cited in over 180 publications since 1977.]**

Mary Lee Smith
and
Gene V. Glass
University of Colorado
Campus Box 249
Boulder, CO 80309

January 20, 1983

"For 30 years, scholars have argued over questions such as, 'Does psychotherapy work better than the mere passage of time or the kind attention of another person in alleviating psychological maladjustment and distress?' 'What form of therapy (behavioral, cognitive, psychodynamic, drug) is the most efficacious?' 'How scientifically rigorous are the studies that demonstrate the effectiveness of psychotherapy?'

"Individual researchers by the hundreds have addressed these questions, and research reviewers have summarized the studies to arrive at overall conclusions. The conclusions have been energetically rebutted by scholars representing adversarial philosophies and interests. Perhaps we were naive to believe that by applying a new set of procedures for extracting the meaning from large collections of studies—procedures that are quantified, replicable, and objective—that we would settle the controversy. We were wrong, a fact which is not in itself interesting, but which certainly explains the selection of the article as a *Citation Classic*. The work has been praised by advocates and vilified by opponents of psychotherapy as well as those who advocate specific forms of therapy such as psychoactive drugs or behavioral treatments. The latter groups have a stake in the aggrandizement of their therapies over competitors' and therefore were displeased by the finding of no differential efficacy among the forms of therapy. The work has been called everything from 'mega-silliness' and 'blossoming nose blemish' to a 'classic of social science.' The work has also attracted considerable attention, both positive and negative, from research methodologists because it was an early example of the technique of meta-analysis (the quantitative synthesis of results of extant research studies). Researchers who have subsequently applied the technique to other bodies of literature have cited the article. These facts explain the citation rate, which, as anyone can see, is a mixed blessing.

"Originally, the psychotherapy outcome literature was selected as an appropriate test of meta-analysis. Funding was received from the Spencer Foundation for the years 1975-1976. The findings were first presented as part of Glass's presidential address to the American Educational Research Association. Submitted to the *American Psychologist*, the manuscript was accepted with minor revisions. What followed were the reactions noted above, the reprinting of the article in several books, and renewed funding from the Spencer Foundation. During 1977-1978, we added nearly 100 studies of psychotherapy effectiveness and a separate meta-analysis of research on the effectiveness of drugs compared with psychotherapy. Eventually these analyses were transformed into a book manuscript[1] which also documented the history of the controversy as well as the methodological arguments about controlled studies of psychotherapy and meta-analysis. Since then, we have evoked more variegated reactions, several successful replications,[2] a follow-up of later studies,[3] and considerable methodological work on meta-analysis."[4]

1. **Smith M L, Glass G V & Miller T I.** *Benefits of psychotherapy.* Baltimore, MD: Johns Hopkins University Press, 1980. 269 p.
2. **Landman J T & Dawes R M.** Smith and Glass' conclusions stand up to scrutiny. *Amer. Psychol.* **37**:504-17, 1982.
3. **Shapiro D A & Shapiro D.** Meta-analysis of comparative therapy outcome studies: a replication and refinement. *Psychol. Bull.* **92**:581-604, 1982.
4. **Glass G V, McGaw B & Smith M L.** *Meta-analysis in social research.* Beverly Hills, CA: Sage, 1981. 279 p.

NUMBER 36
SEPTEMBER 3, 1979

Lazarus A A. *Behavior therapy and beyond.* New York: McGraw-Hill, 1971. 306 p.

Follow-up studies revealed that traditional behavior therapy techniques may achieve rapid but not necessarily lasting therapeutic results. Additional procedures, especially methods of 'cognitive restructuring,' are necessary for durable clinical results. This book describes broad-spectrum methods of behavioral assessment and therapy for overcoming 'neurotic' disorders. [The *Science Citation Index®* **(***SCI®***) and the** *Social Sciences Citation Index™* **(***SSCI™***) indicate that this book has been cited over 375 times since 1971.]**

Arnold A. Lazarus
Graduate School of Applied and
Professional Psychology
Rutgers University
Piscataway, NJ 08854

July 10, 1979

"As a practicing therapist, I found it discouraging to help someone overcome his or her anxieties, sexual problems, phobias, compulsions, and other miseries, only to find that person troubled again by the same difficulties a year or two later. I had long been disillusioned with psychoanalytic methods and had switched to 'behavior therapy' (a term I introduced into the scientific literature in 1958). As I carried out more extensive follow-ups, I realized that while behavioral methods often achieved rapid results, long-lasting gains were more elusive.

"My critics claimed that their results with purely behavioral techniques were both rapid and durable. They cast aspersions on my clinical competence, but offered only anecdotal rebuttals. Undaunted, while embracing a philosophy of 'technical eclecticism,' I continued searching for treatment methods that would prove to be more efficient and effective.

"In the late 1960s I started adding 'cognitive' methods to the more objective behavioral techniques and found a synergistic outgrowth. Thus, *Behavior Therapy and Beyond* was one of the first books on (what has since been termed) 'cognitive behavior therapy.' The main intent of the book was to expand the legitimate base of behavioral operations. Thus, in addition to the more usual behavioral methods such as systematic desensitization, graded sexual assignments, and assertiveness training, a variety of cognitive methods and other innovative techniques were carefully described. More recently, my book *Multimodal Behavior Therapy* has further refined and amplified these cognitive-behavioral procedures.[1]

"Many people—students and practitioners—have told me that *Behavior Therapy and Beyond* made them realize that one can practice 'behavior therapy' in an entirely 'humanistic' manner. The most frequent comment I have received since the book was published is that people who were antagonistic to the very idea of 'behavior therapy' emerged feeling very positive about the fact that coercive and manipulative methods were conspicuously absent. Indeed, dehumanization was strongly opposed and condemned. Regarding the intrinsic value of adopting a broad behavioral orientation, many people were willing to re-examine their own prejudices."

1. **Lazarus A A.** *Multimodal behavior therapy.* New York: Springer, 1976. 241 p.

This Week's Citation Classic

Luborsky L, Chandler M, Auerbach A H, Cohen J & Bachrach H M. Factors influencing the outcome of psychotherapy: a review of quantitative research. *Psychol. Bull.* 75:145-85, 1971. [Dept. Psychiatry, Univ. Pennsylvania, Philadelphia, PA; Univ. Rochester; and New York Univ., NY]

The article reviewed the patient, therapist, and treatment factors influencing the outcomes of psychotherapy in 166 studies, and then offered a plan for a systematic multivariate crossvalidation study of the most promising factors. The review identified among the main factors psychological health-sickness of the patient and similarities of patient and therapist. [The *Science Citation Index*® *(SCI*®) **and the** *Social Sciences Citation Index*® *(SSCI*®) **indicate that this paper has been cited in over 250 publications since 1971.]**

Lester Luborsky
Department of Psychiatry
Hospital of the University of Pennsylvania
Philadelphia, PA 19104

September 20, 1982

"The review was done by the Penn Psychotherapy Project which is still engaged in the same research although with new members added: Jim Mintz (UCLA); Marjorie Cohen (Penn); Paul Crits-Christoph (Yale); Leslie Alexander (Bryn Mawr); A. Thomas McLellan, George E. Woody, and Charles P. O'Brien (Penn and Philadelphia VA Medical Center); Marilyn Johnson (Rush University); Thomas Todd (Harlem Valley Psychiatric Center); and Stanley Greenspan and William Polk (NIMH). The review was a preliminary to a proposal for a crossvalidation. NIMH obliged by awarding a five-year grant (1968-1973). Ever since, we have been analyzing the data on 73 patients in moderate length, psychoanalytically oriented psychotherapy.

"Part of the review's popularity was its position as the first comprehensive review of the topic. Those who investigate the topic of the kinds of patients who benefit from psychotherapy—an increasing number of investigators—therefore begin by citing our first review. An updated version of it is in our forthcoming book (below).

"The results of the crossvalidation are now being assembled in a book, *Psychotherapy: Who Benefits and How?* which is in two parts: part one, what can be predicted based on the patient and therapist before treatment; part two, what can be predicted based on the treatment. Part one shows that most patients benefited from psychotherapy, but in terms of predicting the benefits, only a few patient variables were significant, and these were at a modest level. The Prognostic Index Interview[1] variables did best; e.g., emotional freedom composite predicted .30 ($p < .05$) and a crossvalidation on 30 patients yielded .39 ($p < .05$). Psychological health-sickness was a pretreatment predictor at the same level. We are proceeding with investigations of psychological health-sickness; e.g., the 'Six programs for substance abuse study' (McLellan *et al.*, in preparation) showed the level of prediction was even better for psychological severity than for drug severity. Neither the therapist measures nor most of the treatment measures predicted significantly.

"In part two of the book considerable attention is devoted to the 'helping alliance.' It is defined as the patient's experience of the treatment or the therapist as providing or being able to provide the needed benefits to fulfill the patient's goals in treatment. We found that measures of the early helping alliance offered comparable or better prediction of treatment outcome than a range of pretreatment measures.[2-4] Research at other centers on helping alliance measures has mushroomed with measures being developed in Toronto, San Francisco, British Columbia, and Nashville.

"What made the present phase of our research possible was the foresighted, but expensive, decision to collect tape recordings of all psychotherapy sessions for all 73 patients. Since these were on seven-inch reels, as was the custom in those days, we now have a roomful.

"I will end with one tidbit of recent findings about an important correlate of the helping alliance—it is basic background similarities between patient and therapist, e.g., age and religious activity. The sum of ten such similarities correlated with the helping alliance measure about .6! Apparently these similarities foster the capacity of the patient to experience being helped."

1. **Auerbach A & Luborsky L.** *A Prognostic Index for psychotherapy.* Unpublished paper, 1966.
2. **Luborsky L, Mintz J, Auerbach A, Christoph P, Bachrach H, Todd T, Johnson M, Cohen M & O'Brien C P.** Predicting the outcomes of psychotherapy—findings of the Penn Psychotherapy Project. *Arch. Gen. Psychiat.* **37**:471-81, 1980.
3. **Morgan R, Luborsky L, Crits-Christoph P, Curtis H & Solomon J.** Predicting the outcomes of psychotherapy by the Penn Helping Alliance Rating Method. *Arch. Gen. Psychiat.* **39**:397-402, 1982.
4. **Luborsky L.** Helping alliances in psychotherapy: the groundwork for a study of their relationship to its outcome. (Claghorn J L, ed.) *Successful psychotherapy.* New York: Brunner/Mazel, 1976. p. 92-116.

This Week's Citation Classic

CC/NUMBER 32
AUGUST 11, 1980

Eysenck H J. The effects of psychotherapy: an evaluation.
J. Consult. Clin. Psychol. **16**:319-24, 1952.
[Inst. Psychiatry, Maudsley Hosp., Univ. London, London, England]

It used to be assumed that treatment of neurotic disorders by psychoanalysis or psychotherapy was instrumental in producing cures. However, there is a strong spontaneous remission effect. An analysis of reported effects of psychoanalysis, psychotherapy, and spontaneous remission shows that the different varieties of treatment fail to show any better results than that produced by spontaneous remission. [The *Science Citation Index® (SCI®)* **and the** *Social Sciences Citation Index® (SSCI™)* **indicate that this paper has been cited over 275 times since 1961.]**

H.J. Eysenck
Department of Psychology
Institute of Psychiatry
De Crespigny Park
Denmark Hill
London SE5 8AF
England

July 3, 1980

"In 1949 I was sent to the USA to study American practices of clinical psychology, preparatory to launching the first department to teach the subject in the UK, and establishing this new profession over here. As an experimentalist I was extremely critical of the unproven assumptions made by American clinicians, including the use of projective tests for diagnosis, and the use of psychotherapy and psychoanalysis for treatment. I concluded from a survey of the literature that there was no evidence for the validity of the former, or for the efficacy of the latter. This was regarded as heresy when I advanced these views in lectures all over the USA, but I decided nevertheless to publish a short paper on psychotherapy, partly in order to elicit criticisms that might prove me wrong.

"These arrived in great number, and have continued ever since; unfortunately they were based on a misunderstanding of the syllogism underlying my argument. I had reviewed studies of neurotic disorders in which there had been no form of psychological treatment; two out of three of the severely ill patients were cured or very much improved after two years. I then argued that (1) if there is no adequate study of psychoanalytic therapy showing a better improvement rate, then there is no firm evidence that the therapy is therapeutically effective. (2) A review of existing studies showed that indeed there did not exist any such adequate study. (3) Consequently, I concluded that there was no evidence of therapeutic success for psychoanalysis (or more general methods of psychotherapy, which I also analysed in a similar manner).

"Critics argued that my paper did not prove that psychoanalysis was useless, a conclusion I had never suggested; it needed a philosopher, E. Erwin, to resurrect the correct syllogism in his discussion of the great debate.[1] He agreed that my conclusion was valid then, and still continues to be valid. A large-scale review of the by now immense literature by Rachman and Wilson came to the same conclusion.[2]

"As far as I personally am concerned the outcome was that I was ostracised by the clinical fraternity, had efforts to establish alternative methods of treatment (behaviour therapy) blocked by psychiatrists, was refused research grants by embattled psychoanalysts on grant-giving bodies, and was generally treated as an outcast and a pariah. Even friends who agreed with me privately refused to commit themselves in public, and although developments since have proved that my argument was correct, and that the new methods I advocated were demonstrably superior, denigrations and erroneous statements of the original arguments still appear in textbooks, articles, etc. Efforts were made to terminate my appointment, and quite generally I was made to feel that one does not oppose the *Zeitgeist* with impunity, however correct the argument. *Exoriare aliquis nostris ex ossibus ultor !*"

1. **Erwin E.** Psychoanalytic therapy: the Eysenck argument. *Amer. Psychol.* **35**:435-43, 1980.
2. **Rachman S & Wilson T.** *Effects of psychological therapy.* London: Pergamon, 1980. 99 p.

Chapter

10

Sociology

Theoretical studies and issues / 279–287

Organizational analysis / 288–294

Class, race, and mobility / 295–301

Social problems / 302–305

This Week's Citation Classic

CC/NUMBER 32
AUGUST 8, 1983

Wrong D H. The oversocialized conception of man in modern sociology. *Amer. Sociol. Rev.* **26**:183-93, 1961.
[Brown University, Providence, RI]

To the Hobbesian question of how humans become tractable to social controls, sociology has provided an answer that doubts the very possibility of their being anything but thoroughly socialized creatures and thus denies the reality of the question. The Freudian view of man, on the other hand, which sociologists have misrepresented, sees man as a *social* though never a fully *socialized* being. [The *Social Sciences Citation Index*® (*SSCI*®) indicates that this paper has been cited in over 180 publications since 1966.]

Dennis H. Wrong
Department of Sociology
New York University
New York, NY 10003

May 24, 1983

"In the early 1960s, the most admired sociologists tended to hold a view of society as a smoothly running, well-integrated machine or organism which succeeded without coercion in shaping individuals to play the parts, or 'roles,' required to keep it operating. The 'conservative' implications of this conception were already being widely criticized by my former teacher, C. Wright Mills, among others, for minimizing group conflicts and eschewing a critical, even political, challenge to existing beliefs and institutions. I had myself previously engaged in such criticism. However justified, it nevertheless seemed to me that it too assumed the extreme malleability of individuals even though it stressed their class and subgroup attachments rather than presupposing the unity of the whole society. The experience of inner psychic conflict, of the pain and sacrifice involved in conforming to social demands, of what philosophers and literary artists had called 'the tragic sense of life,' seemed to be suppressed in nearly all prevailing sociological viewpoints.

"I had earlier been exposed to studies of 'culture and personality' influenced by a neo-Freudian social psychology holding that individual personality was the product of culture and social structure in opposition to Freud's alleged biologism. In the 1950s, a number of literary and social critics, including Trilling, Riesman, Marcuse, Rieff, and Norman Brown, had made Freud more accessible, separating his ideas from therapeutic concerns. I now saw in Freud a deep awareness lacking in the neo-Freudians of how the interaction of infant experience and social life created a common human nature underlying the cultural variations of time and place.

"Curiously, 'The oversocialized conception of man in modern sociology' combined the pessimism and stoicism of the intellectual climate of the 1950s with the insistence on the costs of conformity and the justice of protests against social fate rooted in the body and sexuality which became so central a few years later to the ethos of the 'counterculture.' The latter emphasis undoubtedly accounted for the favorable reception of the article, which is still often read as a celebration of individual creativity and rebellion against social constraints. Younger sociologists understood the article as a defense of voluntarism and 'free will' against the determinism of conventional or 'mainstream' sociology.

"Such a reading was also in line with the emergence within academic sociology of new anti-positivist perspectives that often singled out Talcott Parsons, the thinker I had most fully criticized, as their major target. Yet this reading ignored the specifically Freudian grounding of my argument. Freud was hardly a voluntarist nor a believer in the infinite variety and perfectibility of humankind. My version of the inevitable tension he saw between human nature and society gave the article a less time-bound interest and appeal.

"Two recent books have been published."[1,2]

1. **Lasch C.** *Haven in a heartless world: the family besieged.* New York: Basic Books, 1977. 230 p.
2. **Endleman R.** *Psyche and society.* New York: Columbia University Press, 1981. 465 p.

Gouldner A W. The norm of reciprocity: a preliminary statement. *Amer. Sociol. Rev.* **25**:161-78, 1960. [Washington University, St. Louis, MO]

The manner in which the concept of reciprocity is implicated in functional theory is explored, enabling a reanalysis of the concepts of 'survival' and 'exploitation.' The need to distinguish between the concepts of complementarity and reciprocity is stressed. Distinctions are also drawn between 1) reciprocity as a pattern of mutually contingent exchange of gratifications, 2) the existential or folk belief in reciprocity, and 3) the generalized moral norm of reciprocity. Reciprocity as a moral norm is analyzed; it is hypothesized that it is one of the universal 'principal components' of moral codes. [The *Science Citation Index*® **(***SCI*®**) and the** *Social Sciences Citation Index*™ **(***SSCI*™**) indicate that this paper has been cited over 290 times since 1960.]**

Alvin W. Gouldner
Department of Sociology
Washington University
St. Louis, MO 63130

October 10, 1979

"Appearing historically near the end of the 'silent generation' of college and university students, 'The norm of reciprocity' was an early articulation of growing disenchantment in the sociological ranks with the dominance of functionalist theory. The paper was completed shortly after my arrival at Washington University from the University of Illinois in the Fall of 1959. Its rapid completion and the timing of its submission for publication were, as I recall, motivated by my desire to inform colleagues of my new academic residence and interests. At that time I had recently finished up work in the area of industrial and organizational sociology and had begun to concern myself more and more with general sociological theory. Increasingly central in my thinking were what I perceived to be a number of outstanding functionalist omissions. 'The norm of reciprocity', in particular, was directed toward the failure of functionalism to effectively deal with problems of power and unequal exchange or exploitation.

"The article can best be understood—both historically and intellectually—alongside its sister pieces, 'Reciprocity and autonomy in functional theory'[1] and 'The importance of something for nothing' (completed in final form and only published much later in my *For Sociology*).[2] Initially these papers arose out of, and served as the theoretical warrant for, a number of empirical studies undertaken at the University of Illinois in the middle and late 1950s. That work, which by and large remains dormant, included theses by Richard A. Peterson and Kenneth Downey, who were, among others at that time, engaged in factor analyses of the basic components of moral systems. The exposure to that rich empirical context and the enormous body of data was integral to my growing critique of the work of Talcott Parsons[3] and of the functionalist paradigm articulated by my former teacher Robert K. Merton.[4]

"In effect 'The norm of reciprocity' and its companion work presage the neo-Marxist critique of functionalism which I later developed more fully in *The Coming Crisis of Western Sociology*.[5] In retrospect it seems clear that this earlier work arose both from a specific empirical environment and my own thinking through of problems beginning to fester in the sociological milieu. Given that it was published during a period marking the initial stage of considerable intellectual transition, frequent citation of this paper is in part a measure of its anticipation of a changing mood and of its role as an analytical document in that change."

1. **Gouldner A W.** Reciprocity and autonomy in functional theory. (Gross L Z, ed.) *Symposium on sociological theory.* Evanston, IL: Row, Peterson, 1959. p. 241-70.
2. -------------------. The importance of something for nothing. *For sociology.* London: Allen Lane, 1973. p. 260-99.
3. **Parsons T.** *The social system.* Glencoe, IL: Free Press, 1951. 575 p.
4. **Merton R K.** *Social theory and social structure: toward the codification of theory and research.* Glencoe, IL: Free Press, 1949. 423 p.
5. **Gouldner A W.** *The coming crisis of western sociology.* New York: Basic Books, 1970. 528 p.

CC/NUMBER 37
SEPTEMBER 13, 1982

This Week's Citation Classic

Seeman M. On the meaning of alienation. *Amer. Sociol. Rev.* **24**:783-91, 1959. [University of California, Los Angeles, CA]

Alienation is examined as a pervasive theme in classical and modern sociology. An organized view of alternative meanings of alienation is presented, in a form oriented toward their modern empirical use. Five varieties of alienation are identified: powerlessness, meaninglessness, normlessness, isolation, and self-estrangement. [The *Social Sciences Citation Index®* **(***SSCI®***) indicates that this paper has been cited in over 350 publications since 1966.]**

Melvin Seeman
Department of Sociology
University of California
Los Angeles, CA 90024

May 24, 1982

"Three personal aspects of this work might be of interest: (1) it documents the often-praised interplay between teaching and research; (2) it was a successful example (rarer than one might think) of interdisciplinary collaboration; and (3) it illustrates how a work's success can bring irritation as well as pride.

"My concern for clarifying the meaning of alienation began when I taught a course on 'prejudice and personality.' My text was the then new *The Authoritarian Personality*,[1] and I soon recognized the cloudiness of both the text and my teaching when it came to explicating the section on alienation as a source of anti-Semitism. My dissatisfaction led me to struggle with an idea which was, at that time, essentially being 'rediscovered' (not only through the long-lost Marxian Paris manuscripts, but also in Durkheim, de Tocqueville, Weber, and others).

"Since a key element in my developing schema involved the sense of powerlessness, I readily found a congenial parallel in Julian Rotter's embryonic concern about 'internal *vs.* external control' (I-E). Rotter, the late Shephard Liverant, and I constituted ourselves as a team at the Second Interdisciplinary Conference at the University of New Mexico, and it was there that much of the conceptual work was accomplished on what was eventually to appear as the well-known I-E scale.[2] My parallel work on the alienation concept profited more than is commonly appreciated from this collaborative work (e.g., though there is a good deal more to 'alienation' than powerlessness, my conception of the latter is thoroughly consistent with the distinction between internality and externality).

"Though I am naturally pleased that this paper has been influential, I confess to a certain irritation when (not too rarely) this paper, now two decades old, is cited in splendid isolation as though it is the late word on alienation, ignoring subsequent conceptual refinements and empirical applications. My purpose in elaborating the varieties of alienation as I did was, above all, to make the classic idea more useful in empirical studies of contemporary society. Hence, for me, the publications that *followed* the 1959 piece—e.g., the studies of social learning in hospitals, prisons, and politics; or the studies of alienation in work—are as important as the original conceptualization (if not more so). The recent summary reviews of research in this field are equally cases in point,[3,4] since they clarify some issues that were not aptly treated in the original work (e.g., how to deal with the dimension of 'social isolation').

"Finally, why has the paper been so frequently cited? Perhaps because it really didn't settle anything. It dealt with a concept that was central to the then reemerging Marxist perspective in the social sciences, and it appeared at a time of discontent and transition that suited the idea of alienation (the turbulent 1960s). That it didn't settle anything helped in that the paper became a counterfoil for those who opposed its empiricism and its separation of social critique from demonstration. I certainly can't say that it was successful because of its immediately recognizable excellence: indeed, it drew an unenthusiastic evaluation from an important referee for *American Sociological Review*. Perhaps there is a message there of sorts for critics who would judge too harshly: the unimpressed reviewer finally decided that perhaps others would find the analysis useful and (wisely in retrospect?) recommended its publication despite his doubts."

1. **Adorno T W, Frenkel-Brunswik E, Levinson D J & Sanford R N.** *The authoritarian personality.* New York: Harper & Row, 1950. 990 p.
2. **Rotter J B, Seeman M & Liverant S.** Internal versus external control of reinforcement: a major variable in behavior theory. (Washburne N F, ed.) *Decisions, values and groups.* London: Pergamon Press, 1962. Vol. 2. p. 473-516.
3. **Seeman M.** Alienation studies. *Annu. Rev. Sociol.* **1**:91-123, 1975.
4. **--------------.** Alienation and engagement. (Campbell A & Converse P E, eds.) *The human meaning of social change.* New York: Russell Sage Foundation, 1972. p. 467-527.

This Week's Citation Classic

CC/NUMBER 45
NOVEMBER 10, 1980

Dean D G. Alienation: its meaning and measurement. *Amer. Sociol. Rev.* **26**:753-8, 1961. [Denison University, Granville, OH]

Alienation was conceptualized as having three major components: powerlessness (P), normlessness (N), and social isolation (SI). Constructed scales intercorrelated .41 to .67 (N 384). A low but significant correlation was found between P, N, and SI and occupational prestige, education, income, and rural background; there was a small positive correlation with advancing age. [The *Social Sciences Citation Index®* *(SSCI™)* **indicates that this paper has been cited over 220 times since 1966.]**

Dwight G. Dean
Department of Sociology and Anthropology
Iowa State University
Ames, IA 50011

August 14, 1980

"My interest in studying political apathy as a dissertation area was stimulated by the potential of the concept of alienation as an explanatory variable, which was suggested by my major professor, Melvin Seeman (then at Ohio State and at UCLA for many years). He conceptualized alienation as a syndrome consisting of five subtypes: powerlessness, normlessness, social isolation, meaninglessness, and self-estrangement. I developed scales for only the first three components, since the latter two seemed to me really to be a form of powerlessness. The scales intercorrelated from .41 to .67 (Columbus, Ohio, stratified sample of 384 respondents). A low but significant correlation was found between these three scales and occupational prestige, education, income, and rural background; a small positive one between alienation and advancing age.

"In another article,[1] I reported that the hypothesized negative correlations between the alienation components and non-voting in a presidential election were not sustained. I suggested that (1) alienation might be related to 'protest' voting, and (2) whereas the scales referred to society as a whole, alienation more likely would be experienced in more personal circumstances, e.g., work, home,[2] etc.

"While the 'worth' of these articles was not at the outset recognized by journal editors (may younger authors be encouraged), the eventual publication of these studies dealing with the measurement of alienation coincided with a period of intense interest in the subject. For some years attention to the topic increased and a plethora of articles appeared, most of them empirical and utilizing one of two or three scales in existence. Then for a period of time scholarly interest waned to such an extent that an 'obituary' article appeared in the literature. Recently there has been a renewed interest in the area, and an international journal devoted to alienation is being established. Other than the good fortune of publishing an article dealing with the measurement of a popular concept, I suspect scholars have sensed an advantage in using a common scale in order to compare results across a wide range of social circumstances.

"As to difficulties: I remember the struggle to reduce the theoretical abstractions to the empirical level, the search for key ideas which could become questionnaire items, the validation of these by independent judges/experts, the pretesting—but I suppose this process is always the most difficult part of research.

"Since graduate days my research and teaching interests have been in the field of the family, and I have only occasionally utilized the concept of alienation. We have recently reported one study[3] which found a negative correlation between alienation and emotional maturity—a subject that I hope to pursue in the future."

1. **Dean D G.** Alienation and political apathy. *Soc. Forces* **28**:185-9, 1960.
2. **Lee G R.** Marriage and anomie: a causal argument. *J. Marriage Fam.* **36**:523-32, 1974.
3. **Dean D G & Lewis A K.** Alienation and emotional maturity: a preliminary investigation. *Psychol. Rep.* **42**:1006, 1978.

This Week's Citation Classic

Ryder N B. The cohort as a concept in the study of social change. *Amer. Sociol. Rev.* **30**:843-61, 1965. [University of Wisconsin, Madison, WI]

The arrival of a new birth cohort each year permits the society to persist despite mortality. Each new cohort is simultaneously a threat to stability and an opportunity for societal transformation. The congruence of social change and cohort differentiation suggests measuring the former by the latter. [The *Social Sciences Citation Index*® *(SSCI*®*)* **indicates that this paper has been cited over 180 times since 1966.]**

Norman B. Ryder
Office of Population Research
Princeton University
Princeton, NJ 08544

September 25, 1981

"When I first became obsessed with the subject of cohorts, in graduate school at Princeton in the late-1940s, there was appreciable awareness of the idea in formal demography, but little application, for want of lengthy time series of data. When the baby boom made a mockery of population projections, the cohort approach offered a way of at least reformulating the problem. It proved to be the right idea at the right time, although it was bound to develop in due course.

"On my dissertation examination, I was asked why one should make cohort calculations at all, and the best answer I could muster at the time was that that was the way people lived, aging *pari passu* with time. With the degree out of the way, I spent the next 15 years trying to come up with a less banal answer. A not entirely random search of the literature revealed the same idea in many guises and fields. As a measurement problem, it turns up wherever there is interest in the life cycle characteristics of our long-lived species. From a mathematical standpoint, the basic idea is that, if one visualizes a surface as cut by a series of parallel plane sections at one angle, and again at another angle, the formal relationships between comparable parameters of the two series of plane section illuminate the distinction between longitudinal and cross-sectional data sets.

"Although some facility with such technical questions may have justified my employment, I felt obliged, as a member of a sociology department (at the University of Wisconsin, Madison) to talk sociology as well as demography. Accordingly, I tried to think of such technical questions in concert with a quite disparate body of writings consisting of theoretical and philosophical speculations in political and cultural history (characterized by names like Karl Mannheim and José Ortega y Gasset). Neither the technicians nor the theorists seemed aware of the existence of their counterparts, despite their common problem.

"In the past several decades, the cohort approach has grown into an indispensable part of the process of demographic measurement. Although my article may have helped accelerate the development a little, I suspect that the main stimulus was the progressive lengthening of the available time series of reliable population data. For sociologists and others, it may have provided some insight into how to think demographically about non-demographic subjects. At least it focused attention on the peculiarly complex problems of studying cultures during an era of rapid social change, and on one direction in which that complexity can be reduced. In addition to myself, several researchers have recently published work in this field."[1-4]

1. **Glenn N D.** *Cohort analysis.* Beverly Hills, CA: Sage Publications, 1977. 72 p.
2. **Hastings D W & Berry L G,** eds. *Cohort analysis: a collection of interdisciplinary readings.* Oxford, OH: Scripps Foundation for Research in Population Problems, 1979. 349 p.
3. **Esler A.** *Generational studies: a basic bibliography.* Williamsburg, VA: College of William and Mary, 1979. 314 p.
4. **Ryder N B.** *The cohort approach: essays in the measurement of temporal variations in demographic behavior.* New York: Arno Press, 1980. 206 p.

CC/NUMBER 22
MAY 31, 1982

This Week's Citation Classic

Davies J C. Toward a theory of revolution. *Amer. Sociol. Rev.* **27**:5-19, 1962. [California Institute of Technology, Pasadena, CA]

Revolution is most likely to occur when a prolonged period of rising expectations (material and nonmaterial) and rising gratifications is followed by a short period of sharp reversal, during which the gap between what people want and what they get quickly widens and becomes intolerable. [The *Social Sciences Citation Index*® *(SSCI®)* **indicates that this paper has been cited over 195 times since 1966.]**

James C. Davies
Department of Political Science
University of Oregon
Eugene, OR 97403

November 12, 1981

"In the mid-1950s I was teaching political psychology and American history at the California Institute of Technology and was nurturing an interest in the causes of civil disturbances (strikes, riots, full-scale revolutions). Looking for antecedents of the 1894 Pullman strike in the Chicago area, I found in the US Bureau of Census' *Historical Statistics of the United States, 1789-1945* that real wages rose steadily during the post-Civil War period, until the 1894 recession. Then working people were suddenly out of jobs or had much lower take-home pay. I drew an inverted J on a piece of paper and left the idea to simmer on a back burner of my mind.

"Using such data as were available, I found that the phenomenon of suddenly frustrated rising expectations appeared in major revolutions like the Russian of 1917, the Egyptian of 1952, and very likely the American of 1775 and the French of 1789. In a seminar I taught on revolution at the University of California at Berkeley in 1959, one student found that the J-curve fit Dorr's Rebellion in Rhode Island in 1842—and another could get no significant quantified data about China before its 1949 revolution. But the idea did fit events preceding Leisler's Rebellion in New York in 1689. The idea seemed so elementary and so universal that I hurried to be the first to spell it out, in June 1960. It took me three days to give birth to a brainchild that had gestated about four years. It took almost two years to get its legitimacy acknowledged by publication.

"Most statistics I could find pertained to material goods, to prices, and to wages and hours. For this reason, and because the inference gap is greater when interpreting the nonmaterial wants of people (like social and political equality)—and because I really feared that editors would reject as out of hand a psychologically based theory that related basic human wants to political behavior—I phrased the original abstract in socioeconomic rather than overtly psychological terms. For similar reasons, I introduced the essay by integrating some of the complementary theorizing of Marx and de Tocqueville, on the suggestion of Seymour Martin Lipset.

"I like to think that the article is cited because the J-curve is simple, goes to the heart of those causes of revolution that 'start' in people's minds, and is neither so holistic as to be banal nor so vague as to be mystical and untestable. While no theory can be definitively verified, the invalidations of it that I have thus far seen have been sadly unsystematic, either because they confused expectations and gratifications or because they showed no understanding of cycles. In a 1969 article,[1] I established 1940 as the starting point for the final long rise of expectations of black people in the US, when blacks were afforded more equal economic opportunity in war industries and when lynchings were rapidly declining. Three people in 1977 wrote an article in which they said the J-curve didn't fit the Black Rebellion, because their data, for the years 1956-1968, showed no J-curve. Without saying why, they started their cycle 16 years later than I did, apparently because that was when their data commenced.[2-5] But the J-curve remains testable, and thanks to over 25 editors and authors who have presented the theory, it also remains alive, well, and visible."

1. **Davies J C.** The J-curve of rising and declining satisfactions as a cause of some great revolutions and a contained rebellion. (Graham H D & Gurr T R, eds.) *The history of violence in America: historical and comparative perspectives.* New York: Praeger, 1969. p. 690-730.
2. **Miller A H, Bolce L H & Halligan M.** The J-curve theory and the black urban riots; an empirical test of progressive relative deprivation theory. *Amer. Polit. Sci. Rev.* **71**:964-82, 1977.
3. **Miller A H & Bolce L H.** Letter to editor. (Reply to Crosby.) *Amer. Polit. Sci. Rev.* **73**:818-22, 1979.
4. **Crosby F.** Letter to editor. (Rejoinder.) *Amer. Polit. Sci. Rev.* **73**:822-5, 1979.
5. **Davies J C.** Letter to editor. (Comment by Davies.) *Amer. Polit. Sci. Rev.* **73**:825-30, 1979.

CC/NUMBER 21
MAY 26, 1980

This Week's Citation Classic

Merton R K. *Social theory and social structure.* New York: Free Press, 1949. 423 p. [Columbia University, New York, NY]

This book codifies structural and functional analysis which is then utilized in studies of social structure, the sociology of knowledge, and the sociology of science. [The *Social Sciences Citation Index® (SSCI™)* **indicates that this book has received over 2,970 unique citations since 1966. The** *Science Citation Index® (SCI®)* **indicates that this book has received over 175 unique citations since 1961.]**

Robert K. Merton
Department of Sociology
Columbia University
New York, NY 10027

February 9, 1980

"I am not at all sure of the reasons for *Social Theory and Social Structure (STSS)* still being cited 30 years after its first appearance. To answer that question with reasonable assurance would require a detailed citation analysis and readership study, hardly worth the effort. My own guess is that this results from a continuing, perhaps enlarged interest in the sort of theoretical 'paradigms' (in a pre-Kuhnian sense) introduced in the book for the analysis of cultural and social structures.

"Part of the book is given over to the structural analysis of classes of substantive problems which also happen to be of enduring interest. For example, as March, Simon, and Guetzkow note in their book *Organizations*[1]—itself a '*Citation Classic*'[2]—my focus on 'unanticipated consequences' led to a model of bureaucratic structures designed to complement the classical Weberian model. So, too, I have the impression that the several hundred theoretical and empirical papers drawing upon the paradigm of anomie-and-opportunity structure for the analysis of structurally induced deviant behavior more often cite the book rather than the paper which appeared in the late 1930s.

"Perhaps a bare inventory will be enough to indicate some of the sociological themes that continue to elicit interest: the systematizing of reference-group theory to consolidate sociological and psychological orientations; the concepts of local and cosmopolitan 'influentials' designed to differentiate flows of communication and influence in social systems; the concept of 'the self-fulfilling prophecy' as a special type of recurrent 'unanticipated consequences' which, especially in the last decade, has been investigated in diverse domains of social, political, economic, educational, and scientific behavior. Also, an explicit 'Paradigm for the Sociology of Knowledge,' dating back to the mid-1940s, which relates to the lately expanded interest in this field of inquiry, and, finally, a batch of early papers in the sociology of science, a field which has clearly taken off in the last 20 years or so.

"This inventory does not, of course, begin to account for these themes apparently remaining of interest to sociologists and other social scientists as well. I suspect that the continuing citations to a book become venerable through its advanced age may also reflect the possibly lower frequency in the social than in the biological and physical sciences of a pattern described in *STSS*[3] and elsewhere[4,5] as obliteration by incorporation (OBI). OBI is the obliteration of the source of ideas, methods, or findings by their incorporation into currently accepted knowledge. But since we don't yet know whether OBI is in fact less common in the social sciences, this only succeeds in explaining one unknown by another. And, as the ancients warned us all, that is not the best of explanatory practices."

1. **March J G, Simon H & Guetzkow H.** *Organizations.* New York: John Wiley, 1958. 262 p.
2. **Simon H.** Citation Classic. *Current Contents/Social & Behavioral Sciences* (40):12, 1 October 1979.
3. **Merton R K.** *Social theory and social structure.* New York: Free Press, 1968. p. 25-38.
4. **Garfield E.** The 'obliteration phenomenon' in science—and the advantage of being obliterated! *Current Contents* (51/52):5-7, 22 December 1975. (Reprinted in: **Garfield E.** *Essays of an information scientist.* Philadelphia: ISI Press, 1980. Vol. 2. p. 396-8.)
5. **Messeri P.** Obliteration by incorporation. Unpublished manuscript. Columbia University, 1978.

This Week's Citation Classic

Riesman D, Denney R & Glazer N. *The lonely crowd: a study of the changing American character.* New Haven, CT: Yale Univ. Press, 1950. 386 p.

This book was one of the first to reflect a self-conscious society. Using materials from philosophy, history, popular culture, psychoanalysis, as well as sociology, gave it an audience among educated people generally. [The *Social Sciences Citation Index® (SSCI™)* **indicates that this book has been cited over 635 times since 1966.]**

David Riesman
Department of Sociology
Harvard University
Cambridge, MA 02138

January 9, 1980

"*The Lonely Crowd* was the outcome of an invitation from Yale University's Committee on National Policy to spend two six-month leaves of absence from the University of Chicago in 1948 and 1949 to do research at Yale. I recruited Nathan Glazer to work with me there; his collaboration and that of Reuel Denney at the University of Chicago were essential in the creation of the book. Glazer brought to bear his wide knowledge of the social sciences; Denney, a former professor of the humanities with a keen interest in popular culture, was a late convert to the social sciences.

"The book reflects the interest, after the Second World War, in linking sociology, on the one hand, with psychoanalytic psychology and characterology and, on the other, with social history. Our study was an ambitious effort at synthesis (including demography) which would be far more difficult to undertake within the more specialized subdisciplines of today.

"Glazer and I read interviews in public opinion surveys, seeking to understand how so many respondents had opinions on so many subjects—how very few (ten percent or less) answered, 'Don't know,' when asked about something outside their own knowledge or experience. We then began to do our own interviewing to gain a better sense of individual character from the nuances of interviews—a diagnostic approach illustrated in the companion volume Glazer and I published in 1952, *Faces in the Crowd.*[1]

" 'Research' is almost too formal a term for the speculative essay *The Lonely Crowd* turned out to be, covering many facets of American experience from children's fairy stories to mass media and to the 'veto groups' which we saw as dominating our political life.

"The book made its way slowly; the late Lionel Trilling, discovering it and writing an essay about it in a book club journal, *The Griffin,* he was editing at that time, helped launch the book and give it visibility. Trilling saw in this book that social science might take the place of novels as a vehicle for understanding society. He also saw the value of our creation of new terminology which quite rapidly entered the common language. However, the terms 'inner direction' and 'other direction' *as applied to individuals* have been misused by people, who like to 'type' themselves and others in a dichotomous way, whereas the book sought to make clear that the labels were rather broad descriptions of 'ideal types' in Max Weber's sense of that term.

"The book first took off in an Anchor paperback edition,[2] then returned to Yale,[3] and eventually sold over a million copies in the United States and in many foreign countries. I wrote two prefaces to Yale paperback editions—one in 1960, another in 1969—in which I cautioned readers against over-interpretation of the book, and against certain erroneous assumptions (for example, that we were entering an era of unparalleled affluence)."

---

1. **Riesman D & Glazer N.** *Faces in the crowd.* New Haven, CT: Yale University Press, 1952. 751 p.
2. **Riesman D.** *The lonely crowd: a study of the changing American character.* Garden City, NY: Doubleday, 1953. 359 p.
3. ---------------. *The lonely crowd: a study of the changing American character.* New Haven, CT: Yale University Press, 1961. 315 p.

This Week's Citation Classic

CC/NUMBER 45
NOVEMBER 8, 1982

Toffler A. *Future shock.* New York: Random House, 1970. 505 p.

Future Shock **argues that people overwhelmed by change suffer not only concrete biochemical consequences, but also marked psychological distress—disorientation, confusion, occasionally lapsing into violence or apathy. It analyzes the social, psychological, and political implications of accelerating change and recommends changes in education, control of technology, and a new form of political process termed anticipatory democracy. [The** *Science Citation Index®* **(***SCI®***) and the** *Social Sciences Citation Index®* **(***SSCI®***) indicate that this book has been cited in over 1,195 publications since 1970.]**

Alvin Toffler
40 East 78th Street
New York, NY 10021

September 13, 1982

"*Future Shock*[1] is a book of social analysis and criticism. Its subject is change, the acceleration of change, and our attempts to cope with it. Rapid technological and social change translates into more transience, novelty, and diversity in the environment. In turn, this places heavy pressure on people to adapt.

"Yet, there are, at any time, certain biological and cultural limits to the speed and complexity of our adaptive decision-making. When accelerating technological, social, and cultural changes demand too many (or too complex) adaptive decisions in too short a time, our decision-making competence deteriorates. We may become 'irrational.'

"In writing not merely on the effects of social and technological change on individuals and organizations, but more specifically on the effects of the *acceleration* of change, *Future Shock* approached the question of human adaptation in a novel way.

"The problems of maladaptation to rapid change first came to my notice in the late-1950s when I was a political correspondent in Washington. It became clear to me that the government lacked adequate sensing mechanisms with which to monitor and cope with rapid change.

"In 1965, I was invited by *Horizon* magazine to write an article about our unreadiness for the future. In preparation, I began reading about 'culture shock'—the dislocation travelers experience when suddenly plunged into an alien culture. An analogy occurred to me: if people could be, so to speak, dislocated in space, why not in time? If accelerating techno-social change was creating an alien society in our very midst, perhaps much of the widespread disorientation, alienation, psychological stress, and even breakdown we see is the result of adaptational failure. Perhaps people could suffer from 'the premature arrival of the future' and go into 'future shock.'

"This analogy started me and my wife (who is also my colleague, editor, and intellectual companion) on five years of research.

"*Future Shock* first appeared in July 1970 and clearly struck a very raw nerve. Since then, some 7,000,000 copies have been sold in more than 50 countries, and it has been translated into two score languages from Arabic and Hebrew to Greek, Chinese, Polish, Rumanian, Finnish, as well as, of course, French, Spanish, Japanese, and German. It is now used in hundreds of university courses in many different disciplines from sociology to biology, religion, jurisprudence, philosophy, and experimental psychology. Numerous experiments have been triggered by it. It has been quoted by presidents and prime ministers, as well as scientists. Many periodicals have commented on it, from scientific journals in the US to *Pravda* in Moscow and *Le Monde* in Paris. The term 'future shock' has also made its appearance in various recent dictionaries, and the book has won the Prix du Meilleur Livre Étranger as well as the McKinsey Foundation Book Award for its 'distinguished contribution to management literature.'

"I suspect there are several reasons why *Future Shock* has been so widely cited in the scientific literature. First, it is interdisciplinary. Second, the issues it deals with are inherently international. Third, it looks at the problems of change and adaptation in a novel way—cutting across conventional lines of analysis. And finally, the basic phenomenon—accelerative change—is felt strongly in science itself, so that many scientists have a personal experience of the very process described."

1. **Toffler A.** *Future shock.* New York: Bantam Books, 1981. 517 p.

This Week's Citation Classic

Rizzo J R, House R J & Lirtzman S I. Role conflict and ambiguity in complex organizations. *Admin. Sci. Quart.* **15**:150-63, 1970.
[Dept. Management, Western Michigan Univ., Kalamazoo, MI and Bernard M. Baruch College, City Univ. New York, NY]

The literature indicates that dysfunctional consequences result from the existence of role conflict and role ambiguity in complex organizations. Yet systematic measurement and empirical testing of these role constructs are lacking. This study describes the development and testing of questionnaire measures of them. [The *Social Sciences Citation Index*® (*SSCI*®) **indicates that this paper has been cited in over 175 publications since 1970.]**

John R. Rizzo
Department of Management
College of Business
Western Michigan University
Kalamazoo, MI 49008

December 10, 1982

"Several years prior to this article, my coauthors and I were actively involved in organizational development consultation and research. One client organization in particular stimulated us into this study. Interviews with dozens of managers revealed many of them to be experiencing role conflict and/or ambiguity. Despite little evidence of malicious behavior, it was an achievement oriented climate with considerable pressure to produce. Yet there was a lack of support and direction, and an insufficiency of policies or goals to guide work. Coupled with a blame orientation, many managers were under stress. R.J. House (now at the University of Toronto) and I even found ourselves interviewing a local minister who was counseling a large number of managers who were seeking help in connection with job induced problems! The organization permitted us to do questionnaire surveys of a large sample of managers, giving us the opportunity to develop several measures that were both useful for survey feedback to the organization and needed in the management literature. Credit must be given to House for his ability to link the literature and needs of the field to practical situations of the kind we faced. We divided the work of acquiring and developing survey instruments, did much work together, and rotated senior authorship on several new measures. One was the Organizational Practices Scale[1] and another the Role Conflict and Ambiguity Measure.

"For the role measures, we drew on the work of Kahn *et al.*[2] and Gross *et al.*[3] to write items representing the constructs. We were later pleased to find, with the help of S.I. Lirtzman, that there was clean factorial separation of role conflict from role ambiguity and that the measures correlated in expected directions with other independent and dependent variables.

"The Kahn *et al.*[2] work must have helped to generate interest, for we had requests for the scale before it was published. The frequent use and citation of the scale are probably attributable to its anticipated explanatory power and to the fact that role conflict and ambiguity are often experienced in complex organizations. They represent types of behavior relevant to widely acknowledged organization principles and practices such as formalization, task expectations, communication requirements, and performance appraisal, to name a few. It appeared we were onto something, for while we went on to different pursuits, other researchers apparently needed the scale and have used it often. Unfortunately, not all have administered the entire scale or contributed to its further development, although several, including House,[4] have recently done so. Research has tended to uphold the factorial integrity of the two constructs. Yet, more work needs to be done. In their review of the literature on role constructs, Von Sell, Brief, and Schuler[5] found moderate consistency in the forms and results of relevant research. The framework they provide for organizing research in this area should help us move toward learning more. If the popularity of these measures continues, I am sure it is attributable to the pervasiveness of role conflict and ambiguity as phenomena we all experience in complex organizational life."

1. **House R J & Rizzo J R.** Toward the measurement of organizational practices: scale development and validation. *J. Appl. Psychol.* **56**:388-96, 1972.
2. **Kahn R L, Wolfe D M, Quinn R P, Snoek J D & Rosenthal R A.** *Organizational stress: studies in role conflict and ambiguity.* New York: Wiley, 1964. 470 p.
3. **Gross N, Mason W S & McEachern A W.** *Explorations in role analysis: studies of the school superintendency role.* New York: Wiley, 1958. 379 p.
4. **House R J, Levanoni E & Schuler R S.** *An empirical examination of the construct validity of the Rizzo, House, and Lirtzman role scales: toward a clarification of the nature of role conflict.* Paper presented at the Midwest Academy of Management Meeting, Columbus, Ohio, 1982.
5. **Von Sell M, Brief A & Schuler R S.** Role conflict and role ambiguity: integration of the literature and directions for future research. *Hum. Relat.* **34**:43-71, 1981.

CC/NUMBER 39
SEPTEMBER 24, 1984

This Week's Citation Classic™

Pelz D C & Andrews F M. *Scientists in organizations: productive climates for research and development*. New York: Wiley, 1966. 318 p.
[Survey Research Center, Inst. for Social Research, Univ. Michigan, Ann Arbor, MI]

In 11 R&D settings in industry, government, and academia, the technical performance of scientists and engineers was related to the nature of their interactions with colleagues and superiors, type of work, autonomy, influence, and motivations. [The *Science Citation Index*® (*SCI*®) and the *Social Sciences Citation Index*® (*SSCI*®) indicate that this book has been cited in over 435 publications since 1966.]

Donald C. Pelz
Center for Research on Utilization
of Scientific Knowledge
Institute for Social Research
University of Michigan
Ann Arbor, MI 48109

July 6, 1984

"This book grew out of a project commissioned by the National Institutes of Health (NIH) in the early 1950s. NIH was expanding rapidly and had added a clinical center, and its directors wanted to assess staff morale and productivity. Of particular interest were results on technical performance of intramural scientists as judged by panels of peers. Would similar factors relate to performance in university and industrial laboratories? F.M. Andrews joined me in the late 1950s for a study of 11 organizations—5 industrial and 5 government labs, and several departments of a university—resulting in the 1966 book.

"Many parallels appeared for basic and developmental laboratories, and for PhDs and non-PhDs. When I sought to extract some basic principles for an article in *Science*[1] (which became the introduction for a revised version of the book 10 years later[2]), technical performance appeared to flourish in the presence of conditions that seemed antithetical—hence the concept of 'creative tensions' or 'creative contradictions.' Effective scientists and engineers needed both some source of 'security' or *protection* from external disruption and some source of 'challenge' or *exposure* to external demands. Security could be provided by autonomy, influence, or specialization; challenge by frequent communication, multiple R&D functions, or colleague diversity. I was reminded of a passage in Emerson's essay on 'Self-Reliance' a century earlier: 'It is easy in the world to live after the world's opinion; it is easy in solitude to live after our own; but the great man [read: effective scientist] is he who in the midst of the crowd keeps with perfect sweetness the independence of solitude.'

"Why has the book been frequently cited? In part, we suspect, because of its timing. It pioneered in the postwar and post-Sputnik wave of concern for the management of research and development. We like to think, too, that the format helped. The book presented a complex matrix of factors in a clear and readable manner, with meaningful charts and simple tables, and concluded each chapter with a dialogue between the authors and a hypothetical reader on practical implications.

"The book has been translated into Japanese and Russian, and, we are told, it has been widely read in both areas. In the early 1970s, it stimulated a cross-national study of research teams under UNESCO auspices. Andrews served as technical adviser for the first round in six European countries—Austria, Belgium, Finland, Hungary, Poland, and Sweden—and edited a book.[3] In second and third rounds, the methodology was extended to South America, Africa, Asia, and Russia—a total of 16 countries, including some repeats. The series will be the subject of a conference in January 1985 in Rio de Janeiro. Andrews found keen interest in the research results among an audience of several hundred in a 1983 visit to Beijing.

"The UNESCO studies have sustained many of the findings from the American data, even though the UNESCO studies focus on performance of R&D *teams* rather than on individuals as in the initial study. The UNESCO data found performance to be higher under conditions of strong personal dedication, diversity in several factors (number of roles, projects, skill areas, funding sources, and disciplines), and frequent communication with many colleagues. Groups were more effective when their members had high influence but moderate autonomy, and were comprised of four to six people who had worked together about 7 to 10 years. In short: conditions governing technical contribution appear to transcend cultural boundaries and political systems."

1. **Pelz D C.** Creative tensions in the research and development climate. *Science* **157**:160-5, 1967. (Cited 30 times.)
2. **Pelz D C & Andrews F M.** *Scientists in organizations: productive climates for research and development*. Ann Arbor, MI: Institute for Social Research, 1976. 401 p. (Cited 55 times.)
3. **Andrews F M,** ed. *Scientific productivity, the effectiveness of research groups in six countries*. Cambridge, England: Cambridge University Press, 1979. 469 p.

CC/NUMBER 19
MAY 9, 1983

This Week's Citation Classic

Blau P M. A formal theory of differentiation in organizations. *Amer. Sociol. Rev.* **35**:201-18, 1970. [University of Chicago, IL]

Organizational size and differentiation are positively related, but the two have opposite implications for administrative overhead: differentiation increasing it, and size decreasing it, contrary to the bureaucratic stereotype. The growth of differentiation with increasing size occurs at decelerating rates, which can be explained by the feedback effect of complexity's administrative cost. [The *Social Sciences Citation Index*® (*SSCI*®) indicates that this paper has been cited in over 180 publications since 1970.]

Peter M. Blau
Department of Sociology
Columbia University
New York, NY 10027

March 14, 1983

"Until a quarter of a century ago, most sociological research on organizations involved either case studies or surveys of individuals in organizations. I was one of the first—I thought I was the first, being unaware of concurrent studies in England—to design research on a sufficient number of organizations to permit quantitative analysis. Preliminary results of the first major study of government agencies showed an organization's size to be strongly related to most of its other features, particularly to all aspects of differentiation—the division of labor, hierarchical levels, number of branches, number of major departments, number of sections per department, etc. My first reaction was to dismiss this as uninteresting and try to devise procedures to get rid of the influence of size to examine the independent effects of other conditions—by residualizing, using ratios, or always controlling size. It was only after some months that I decided that such a dominant influence cannot be dismissed as uninteresting but must be taken seriously.

"I then developed the simple theoretical model in the *Citation Classic*, centering on two major effects of size. Assuming the causal sequence size-differentiation-administration, size has a direct effect, reducing administrative overhead, which reflects an economy of scale, but it also has an indirect effect, enlarging administrative overhead, because the more differentiated structure it produces requires more administrative coordination. The coordination problems engendered by increasing differentiation act as a brake slowing down further increases in differentiation with expanding size, which explains the curvilinear relationship.

"This theory is the central part of a book on these government agencies coauthored with Schoenherr.[1] Subsequent studies of numerous other kinds of organizations—other government agencies, department stores, universities and colleges, factories—all corroborated the basic model of the relationships between size, differentiation along various lines, and ratio of administrative personnel. Although I have in recent years turned away from the study of formal organizations, I have continued to analyze the significance of size differences, size distributions, and differentiation for social structures.

"One reason that this paper has been often cited may be that it represents a simple theory that is quite close to the empirical data that it explains and that can test it, in contrast to many sociological theories, which are using such vague concepts and so few unequivocal hypotheses that it is not clear what they can explain or how they could be tested. There may be another reason: it represents a scientific approach in sociology, and it tends to be cited by those who adopt a humanistic approach as a horrible example of what sociology should not be like."

1. **Blau P M & Schoenherr R A.** *The structure of organizations*. New York: Basic Books, 1971. 445 p.

This Week's Citation Classic

CC/NUMBER 32
AUGUST 9, 1982

Hickson D J, Pugh D S & Pheysey D C. Operations technology and organization structure: an empirical reappraisal. *Admin. Sci. Quart.* **14**:378-97, 1969. [Industrial Admin. Res. Unit, Univ. Aston, Birmingham, England]

Technology is not the primary influence upon organization structure which many believed it to be following Woodward's[1] pioneering research. A multivariate study of diverse organizations in England shows it to be related only to variables directly impinged upon by the work flow, and not to the wider administrative structure. [The *Social Sciences Citation Index®* (*SSCI®*) **indicates that this paper has been cited in over 185 publications since 1969.]**

David J. Hickson
Organizational Analysis Research Unit
University of Bradford Management Centre
Bradford BD9 4JL
England

April 22, 1982

"An open question in the 1960s was whether the technology of a firm, indeed of any kind of organization, is primary in shaping how it is set up and run. This was a provoking possibility. If by just knowing a firm's production technology its management structure could be predicted then two sweeping consequences followed. First, researchers would hold a ready key to understanding. Second, teaching should be specific to each technology and not be about 'organizations' or 'management' in general, a teaching revolution.

"The question had arisen from the pioneering research of Woodward[1] in Britain. This interested me, but it was not the focus of the Aston Programme of research in Birmingham, under the leadership of Derek Pugh. This aimed at testing a multivariate explanation of organization structure.

"The team worked at desks all together in the same room; physical proximity and an understanding that publications would be multiauthored being designed to maximise collective commitment. The team process is described in the introductions to the series of Aston Programme volumes commencing with that of Pugh and myself.[2] At the time of the work on technology some of the members in addition to Pugh and myself were Kerr Inkson, Roy Payne, and Diana Pheysey.

"As drafts of journal papers began to take shape it was agreed to concentrate them (if accepted) in a single journal, the then quite new *Administrative Science Quarterly*. As there were several simultaneously being worked on we came to know them by numbers, *ASQ* 0 (in 1963),[3] *ASQ* 1 (in 1968),[4] *ASQ* 2 and 3 (in 1969),[5,6] and eventually *ASQ* 4. This last was the technology paper.

"The other papers dealt with theory and results generally, indicating the balance of predictive capability between a range of 'contextual' variables including technology. *ASQ* 4 singled out that variable. This was because of my interest, which was shared by Pheysey, but also because the results contradicted my expectations, if not everyone's. I had thought that with better samples and methods we would 'prove Woodward right' on the primacy of technology. As it turned out, our results did nothing of the sort. Disconcerted, we examined them every way round we could think of, with me hoping that we had overlooked something. What this forced thoroughness led to was a paper that may have been widely cited because it is an example of careful step-by-step analysis and point-by-point buildup of argument. My name went first because of my particular interest but it was very much a joint effort. The results qualified the assumptions that had been derived from Woodward's work. They suggested that technology has notable effects on only aspects of organization most immediate to it, and that over the wider organization its influence is overwhelmed by other factors. This is an outcome supported by numerous researchers since, so that it puzzles me how frequently textbooks reference the paper and yet continue to deal with technology as if the view that others had taken from Woodward had never been modified.

"The most lasting impression on me was that here were results that were persistently opposite to what I hoped for: it is not so that social science results can always be twisted to anything the researcher wants them to be."

1. **Woodward J.** *Industrial organization: theory and practice.* London: Oxford University Press, 1965. 281 p.
2. **Pugh D S & Hickson D J.** *Organizational structure and its context: the Aston Programme I.* Farnborough, England: D.C. Heath, 1976. 231 p.
3. **Pugh D S, Hickson D J, Hinings C R, Macdonald K M, Turner C & Lupton T.** A conceptual scheme for organizational analysis. *Admin. Sci. Quart.* **8**:289-315, 1963.
4. **Pugh D S, Hickson D J, Hinings C R & Turner C.** Dimensions of organization structure. *Admin. Sci. Quart.* **13**:65-105, 1968.
5. --. The context of organization structures. *Admin. Sci. Quart.* **14**:91-114, 1969.
6. **Pugh D S, Hickson D J & Hinings C R.** An empirical taxonomy of structures of work organizations. *Admin. Sci. Quart.* **14**:115-26, 1969.

This Week's Citation Classic

Emery F E & Trist E L. The causal texture of organizational environments. *Hum. Relat.* **18**:21-32, 1965.

The further development of the open system thinking propounded by von Bertalanffy[1] and Prigogine[2] requires us to characterize the environments within which open systems are functioning. Four levels of environmental organization can be distinguished in terms of their causal texturing. [The *Social Sciences Citation Index*® (*SSCI*™) **indicates that this paper has been cited over 220 times since 1966.]**

F. E. Emery
Australian National University
P.O. Box 4
Canberra, ACT 2600
Australia

October 30, 1980

"The line of thinking that led to this paper arose from an extracurricular interest in the postwar debate about appropriate divisional structures for the nuclear battlefield. I gained a great deal of inspiration from Wynne's analysis of the evolution of the Western Front, 1914-18.[3]

"Coming out from an academic cocoon to work at the Tavistock Institute in London I found myself trying to comprehend the behavior of very large organizations in the face of very devastating winds of change. The gestation period from marginal notes and backs of envelopes was no more than 18 months. The opportunity to test the reality of these ideas was provided by an 'invisible college' that emerged in Europe at this time. This was the 11 to 13 member 'Informal European Group,' which met for a couple of days and nights every nine months or so in secluded retreats. Its only business was that of hashing over embryonic ideas.

"We struck a sticky patch in trying to label the different environments. My predilection was to simply number them as a series. My colleague, Eric Trist, convinced me that people would need more descriptive labels in order to handle the ideas. The labelling of the type IV environment as a 'turbulent environment' certainly seems to have caught the eye, if not much more. Perhaps this explains some of the citations. However, I think that by the late 1960s, with burning US cities, the Beatles, and the Paris students, very many analysts sensed that their social ground was moving in turbulent ways.

"When Trist and I presented the paper to the International Congress of Psychology, Washington, 1963, we were dumbfounded by the total lack of reaction. Many months later we received a very apologetic letter from the chairman of our session, himself in the forefront of organizational theorizing in the US, to the effect that it was only after the conference that the penny had dropped for him.

"The conceptual developments in that paper have continued to play a considerable role in my subsequent thinking. That has been a very satisfactory reward. I would not, however, quite think that it has attracted any award or honor. My fullest development of that conceptual framework, and its integration with my work on purposeful and ideal-seeking systems, was published in 1977.[4] That publication helped my last university to not renew my research contract as it could not find a place for, to quote, 'my systems cum futures' studies.

"I do not find this surprising, nor particularly bothersome. Those who want to play with, and cite, new ideas are not usually those who have to face the awesome problems of allocating resources to competing educational and research ends. Perhaps, though, some significant degree of social turbulence has to be experienced before any conceptual analysis of turbulence takes on significance. Perhaps I should have thought more deeply in terms of my own theory of environments before deciding to travel homewards."

1. **Bertalanffy L von.** The theory of open systems in physics and biology. *Science* **111**:23-9, 1950.
2. **Prigogine I.** *Introduction to thermodynamics of irreversible processes.* Paris: Dunod, 1968. 147 p.
3. **Wynne G C.** *If Germany attacks: the battle in depth in the West.* London: Faber and Faber, 1940. 343 p.
4. **Emery F E.** *Futures we are in.* Leiden: Martinus Nijhoff, 1977. 230 p.

This Week's Citation Classic

NUMBER 40
OCTOBER 1, 1979

March J G, Guetzkow H & Simon H. *Organizations.*
New York: John Wiley & Sons, 1958. 262 p.
[Graduate School of Industrial Administration, Carnegie Institute of Technology, Pittsburgh, PA]

Organizations **provides a theoretical framework for knowledge about human behavior in organizations, and reviews the empirical evidence for the propositions that make up the theory. The theory emphasizes the motivations for organizational participation and the processes of decision making within organizations. [The** *Science Citation Index® (SCI®)* **and the** *Social Sciences Citation Index ™ (SSCI ™)* **indicate that this book has been cited over 950 times since 1961.]**

H. Simon
Department of Psychology
Carnegie-Mellon University
Pittsburgh, PA 15213

July 16, 1979

"In 1949 a new business school, the Graduate School of Industrial Administration, was created at Carnegie Institute of Technology. The faculty of the new school proposed to build business education on a solid social science foundation. Organization theory was selected as a major focus of research, and a program of empirical studies of managerial decision making processes was launched. I was a member of the original faculty of the school, Guetzkow joined in 1950, and March in 1953.

"At this time, the Ford Foundation decided to commission a series of 'propositional inventories' in the behavioral sciences. The idea was to 'propositionalize' the theory of some domain, and then to summarize the empirical evidence relevant to each proposition. We agreed to take on such an inventory for the Foundation.

"The product of our undertaking, *Organizations,* does not really look very much like a 'propositional inventory,' although the first five chapters conform more closely to that model than the last two. The difficulties were numerous. A body of scientific theory is not a set of isolated propositions, nor can particular pieces of evidence be matched to particular propositions. Moreover, much of the empirical work in organization theory takes the form of case studies, which are difficult to handle according to customary criteria of objectivity and encodability. We discussed alternative frameworks for organization theory in the opening chapters, then devoted the remainder of the book to motivation and decision-making theory.

"*Organizations* is still in print, without revision, after twenty years. Its references are now badly out of date, but its theoretical structure does not appear to have been superseded by any subsequent work, and indeed has obtained considerable new empirical support.

"Whether the book's durability is a tribute to our foresight or to the slow development of the field, is best judged by others. The work was simply one step along the route of the authors' continuing research in organizational behavior. In the ensuing twenty years, their work has taken divergent paths. March went on, with R. Cyert, to produce their equally 'classic' *Behavioral Theory of the Firm.*[1] Guetzkow focussed more and more upon the simulation of decision making in international relations.[2] My own research has led me into the study of problem solving processes, and to the work with A. Newell that is summarized in our *Human Problem Solving.*[3]

"Organizations and families are the most important environment of human behavior. My greatest personal satisfaction from our book was the knowledge that it helped to establish organizational behavior as a basic domain of the social sciences."

1. **Cyert R M & March J G.** *A behavioral theory of the firm.* Englewood Cliffs, NJ: Prentice-Hall, 1963. 332 p.
2. **Guetzkow H, Alger C F, Brody R A, Noel R C & Snyder R C.** *Simulation in international relations: development for research and teaching.* Englewood Cliffs, NJ: Prentice-Hall, 1963. 248 p.
3. **Newell A & Simon H A.** *Human problem solving.* Englewood Cliffs, NJ: Prentice-Hall, 1972. 920 p.

CC/NUMBER 14
APRIL 6, 1981

This Week's Citation Classic

Perrow C. A framework for the comparative analysis of organizations. *Amer. Sociol. Rev.* **32**:194-208, 1967. [University of Wisconsin, WI]

The structure of an organization depends upon the kind of task it typically performs. Routine tasks suggest specialization, formalization, hierarchy, and centralized power; nonroutine tasks are better performed under the opposite conditions. Tasks are defined cognitively as search procedures and exceptions encountered. [The *Social Sciences Citation Index*® *(SSCI*™*)* **indicates that this paper has been cited over 210 times since 1967.]**

Charles B. Perrow
Department of Sociology
State University of New York
Stony Brook, NY 11794

March 23, 1981

"This article was one of three independent statements in 1967 of what came to be called 'contingency theory.'[1,2] It held that the structure of an organization depends upon (is 'contingent' upon) the kind of task performed, rather than upon some universal principles that apply to all organizations. The notion was in the wind at the time.

"I think we were all convinced we had a breakthrough, and in some respects we did—there was no one best way of organizing; bureaucracy was efficient for some tasks and inefficient for others; top managers tried to organize departments (research, production) in the same way when they should have different structures; organizational comparisons of goals, output, morale, growth, etc., should control for types of technologies; and so on. While my formulation grew out of fieldwork, my subsequent research offered only modest support for it. I learned that managers had other ends to maximize than efficient production and they sometimes sacrificed efficiency for political and personal ends. That gave me considerable pause and while I gave the theory a big play in a 1970 book,[3] I downplayed it considerably in a 1972 book.[4] But it wasn't until I read Harry Braverman[5] and others that I realized how much of a mystification the theory was. The historical record showed that bureaucracies were set up to control the work force without any change in the technology initially, and only after a compliant, wage dependent work force was assembled were technologies created to fit this favorable structure. At the macro level at least, the causal direction could be reversed, and go from structure to technology.

"In its limited way, my article is reasonably useful and accurate, but only if we assume there was no better way industrial development could proceed and only if we ignore other types of efficiency, e.g., for employees, the community, and the society. If we note how the technologies we favor reproduce authoritarian and exploitative structures, then the theory is of limited normative value indeed, and falsely suggests an evolutionary inevitability.

"I hope the citations to it and similar works fall off rapidly and citations to a much more power-relevant and politically sophisticated view of organizations will increase. Far more than at any other time, organizational theory is bursting with new ideas and much more awareness of pervasive biases, as a new edition of my 1972 book shows.[6] The field has grown far beyond contingency theory; that theory has a very limited and not very interesting application."

1. **Lawrence P & Lorsch J.** *Organization and environment.* Cambridge, MA: Harvard University Press, 1967. 279 p.
2. **Thompson J D.** *Organizations in action.* New York: McGraw-Hill, 1967. 192 p.
3. **Perrow C.** *Organizational analysis: a sociological view.* Belmont, CA: Wadsworth, 1970. 192 p.
4. ------------. *Complex organizations: a critical essay.* Glenview, IL: Scott, Foresman, 1972. 224 p.
5. **Braverman H.** *Labor and monopoly capital: the degradation of work in the twentieth century.* New York: Monthly Review Press, 1974. 465 p.
6. **Perrow C.** *Complex organizations: a critical essay.* Glenview, IL: Scott, Foresman, 1979. 270 p.

CC/NUMBER 50
DECEMBER 13, 1982

This Week's Citation Classic

Sewell W H, Haller A O & Portes A. The educational and early occupational status attainment process. *Amer. Sociol. Rev.* **34**:82-92, 1969; and **Sewell W H, Haller A O & Ohlendorf G W.** The educational and early occupational status attainment process: replication and revision. *Amer. Sociol. Rev.* **35**:1014-27, 1970. [Univ. Wisconsin, Madison, WI]

A social psychological model for explaining the relationship between social origins and later educational and occupational achievements is presented, tested, and revised using samples of young men from various community size categories. The 'Wisconsin Model' has since been replicated and modified by scholars in the US and abroad. [The *Social Sciences Citation Index*® **(***SSCI*®**) indicates that these papers have been cited in over 170 and 185 publications respectively.]**

William H. Sewell
Department of Sociology
University of Wisconsin
Madison, WI 53706

October 28, 1982

"These articles are from a long series of publications based on a longitudinal study,[1] begun over 25 years ago, with the continuous support of NIMH, which examines the influence of social psychological factors on the educational and occupational aspirations and achievements of a large sample (10,000) of Wisconsin high school seniors. The earlier papers focused on the influence of community, neighborhood, and school contexts and of significant others (parents, teachers, and peers) on aspirations and achievements, while holding constant sex, intelligence, and socioeconomic status. In the first papers, building on the influential work of Blau and Duncan,[2] my colleagues and I developed a social psychological model to elaborate and explain the effects of socioeconomic background and ability on the educational and occupational achievements of a subsample of farm males. The model posited that background influences are mediated by academic achievements in high school, significant others' encouragement, and by educational and occupational aspirations. The second paper further tested and modified this model using men from a wide range of community size categories.

"The model, commonly called the 'Wisconsin Model,' has since been replicated in a number of studies here and abroad. It also has stimulated critical comment and attempts at modification and improvement. Our own subsequent work has resulted in the disaggregation of the indexes of socioeconomic status and significant others' influence; the inclusion of other background, social structural, and achievement variables;[3] and the application of these more complex models to explain differences between the mid-career achievements of the sexes.[4] Most recently, in as yet unpublished research, a still more complex model has been developed that takes into account the effects of measurement error. The results of this analysis further indicate the essential soundness of the ideas that were the basis of the original model. We now have information from interviews with a large sample of the siblings of our original informants and are currently examining the educational, occupational, and family formation processes of same and opposite sex pairs of siblings. This will permit us to measure and interpret the total effects of family background, not merely of socioeconomic origins, on these processes.

"Why have these papers been cited so often? Possibly, because they appeared soon after the Blau and Duncan book which had demonstrated the potential usefulness of linear causal models in explaining socioeconomic achievements. Possibly, because our model was based on longitudinal rather than cross-sectional data, thus making causal inferences more plausible. But more probably, it was because the model established and explicated the crucial mediating role of social psychological variables in the complex process by which social origins affect later socioeconomic achievements."

1. **Sewell W H & Hauser R M.** The Wisconsin longitudinal study of social and psychological factors in aspirations and achievements. (Kerckhoff A C, ed.) *Research in sociology of education and socialization.* Greenwich, CT: JAI Press, 1980. Vol. 1. p. 59-99.
2. **Blau P M & Duncan O D.** *The American occupational structure.* New York: Wiley, 1967. 520 p.
3. **Sewell W H & Hauser R M.** *Education, occupation and earnings: achievement in the early career.* New York: Academic Press, 1975. 237 p.
4. **Sewell W H, Hauser R M & Wolf W C.** Sex, schooling and occupational status. *Amer. J. Sociol.* **86**:551-83, 1980.

This Week's Citation Classic

CC/NUMBER 31
AUGUST 1, 1983

Rosen B C. Race, ethnicity, and the achievement syndrome. *Amer. Sociol. Rev.* **24**:47-60, 1959. [University of Connecticut, Storrs, CT]

A differential psychocultural orientation toward achievement helps explain why some ethnic and racial groups are more upwardly mobile than others. Achievement motivation, achievement values, and educational-occupational aspirations form an achievement syndrome that affects both the goals individuals set for themselves and their strivings to attain these goals. [The *Science Citation Index*® (*SCI*®) **and the** *Social Sciences Citation Index*® (*SSCI*®) **indicate that this paper has been cited in over 205 publications since 1961.]**

Bernard C. Rosen
Department of Sociology
Cornell University
Ithaca, NY 14853

May 20, 1983

"The Russian rocket *Sputnik* put this paper into orbit, in a manner of speaking, and it has been kept there by a recognition among social scientists that despite the melting pot, many Americans maintain their ethnic cultures and identities even after several generations in this country. The space competition with the Russians ignited the nation's interest in achievement, and the black liberation movement's struggle for equality and advancement evoked similar concerns among other racial and ethnic groups. Looking back, I can see that it was my good fortune to study the linkages between race, ethnicity, child-rearing, personality, and social mobility at a time when international and national forces converged to heighten interest in all these subjects. For an account of more recent research, see reference 1.

"My interest in ethnic cultures undoubtedly stemmed from personal factors and had already surfaced in a dissertation on Jewish adolescents (later published as a book[2]) before I began work on achievement. The achievement research bégan when I joined a research project at Yale University in 1952 on the effects of ethnic culture on adolescent academic performance. At Yale, I encountered the new work on the achievement motivation and began to wonder if group differences in personality might not help explain class, racial, and ethnic differences in social mobility. It was only a short step from speculating about ethnicity and achievement to research on the subject, but it was a long haul before I completed the two projects that undergird this article. I had to acquire some skill in using the Thematic Apperception Test (TAT), administer it to hundreds of adolescents in the northeastern US, and then interview their mothers—an exhausting job since I had no funds to hire help. Fortunately, students, a wife, and friends helped with the fieldwork and in scoring the TAT protocols. The data analysis was also time-consuming and tedious. In the pre-computer age, we had to depend on card sorters and desk calculators, and even doing a simple two-way analysis of variance took many hours, particularly when I would come up with a statistically impossible negative sum of squares—an easy mistake to make when working with a large sample.

"What particularly intrigued me about this study, apart from its confirmation of my hunches about ethnic effects on achievement, was the nice way achievement motivation, achievement values, and aspiration levels hung together, empirically and theoretically. But what was I to call this cluster? A complex? No, there were too many complexes around and besides that seemed too clinical. Syndrome seemed a better word. I remember turning to the dictionary for a precise meaning of the term. Syndrome seemed to suit, and I coined the term 'achievement syndrome' to describe this cluster of motives, values, and aspirations. To my surprise the term seems to have caught on."

1. **Fyans L F, Jr.**, ed. *Achievement motivation: recent trends in theory and research.* New York: Plenum Press, 1980. 471 p.
2. **Rosen B C.** *Adolescence and religion: the Jewish teenager in American society.* Cambridge, MA: Schenlaman, 1965. 218 p.

This Week's Citation Classic

Lenski G E. Status crystallization: a non-vertical dimension of social status. *Amer. Sociol. Rev.* **19**:405-13, 1954.
[University of Michigan, Ann Arbor, MI]

Individuals whose relative status in terms of income, education, occupation, and ethnicity varied substantially were more likely to favor liberal causes and vote Democratic than one would predict from a simple additive model in a random sample of Detroiters. [The *Social Sciences Citation Index*® (*SSCI*®) indicates that this paper has been cited in over 240 publications since 1966.]

Gerhard E. Lenski
Department of Sociology
University of North Carolina
Chapel Hill, NC 27514

October 25, 1982

"This paper grew from an interest in social stratification that had its origins in military service in World War II. I became interested in the impact of the military rank system on behavior, and especially in the responses of individuals to discrepancies between prior civilian status and military status.

"Later, on entering graduate school, I discovered that there was a specialty within sociology devoted to the study of stratification and quickly gravitated toward it. One thing that disturbed me, however, was the unidimensional nature of the major paradigms. They seemed to be oversimplifying the real world.

"After moving to Michigan, I met others who were thinking along the same line, especially Werner Landecker. Soon thereafter, Ronald Freedman obtained funding for the Detroit Area Study and Landecker and I were invited to participate.

"Landecker and I collaborated on the design of a part of the first survey and I assumed we would publish our results jointly. However, because Landecker's interests were much more structural than mine at this point, we decided on a division of labor. I focused on the social psychological problem of 'status' crystallization, while he tackled the structural problem of 'class' crystallization.[1]

"The frequency of citation of this paper probably reflects three things: 1) a recognition of the inadequacy of the unidimensional model, 2) the ease with which the concept of status crystallization could be tested with existing data, and 3) the ambiguity of later findings (partly due to the failure of later researchers to replicate strictly).

"My chief disappointment with subsequent research has been the failure of others to pick up on the idea that multiple responses are possible to the stress generated by status inconsistency and that tests should check out *simultaneously* as many of them as possible and not base conclusions on any one alone. I have also been disappointed by the failure of many to pick up on the early finding that inconsistencies between ascribed and achieved ranks are especially potent."

1. **Landecker W S.** *Class crystallization.* New Brunswick, NJ: Rutgers University Press, 1981. 255 p.

CC/NUMBER 51
DECEMBER 22, 1980

This Week's Citation Classic

Wilensky H L. The professionalization of everyone? *Amer. J. Sociol.* **70**:137-58, 1964. [Department of Political Science, University of California, Berkeley, CA]

The traditional model of professionalism emphasizes autonomous expertise and the service ideal. Historical data show a typical process by which the established professions have arrived; deviations are explained by power struggles common to all occupations. Other data suggest that (1) bureaucracy enfeebles the service ideal more than it threatens autonomy; and (2) a client orientation undermines colleague control. The main theme: very few occupations will achieve the authority of the established professions. [The *Social Sciences Citation Index® (SSCI™)* **indicates that this paper has been cited over 195 times since 1966.]**

Harold L. Wilensky
Department of Political Science
University of California
Berkeley, CA 95720

November 7, 1980

"The ideas were developed in the 1950s in my courses on industrial and occupational sociology and in a little noticed book.[1]

"I had long felt that talk of 'the expert society' or the 'technocratic society' was misleading. In their enthusiasm about the upgrading of skills in modern society some students had even written of 'the professionalization of labor.' Such notions are still prominent in social science. For instance, Kenneth Galbraith's 'techno-structure'[2] and Daniel Bell's 'post-industrial society'[3] depict a vast expansion in numbers and power of professionals and scientists.

"For many decades ideological passion and intellectual mood have burdened discussions of professionalism. Such theorists as Parsons accent the service ideal and technical knowledge as bases of professional practice.[4,5] However, critics such as C. Wright Mills sound a skeptical note: the established professions, they argue, display the venality and fakery of a used car dealer while professional knowledge is often mystification in the service of monopoly privilege.[6]

"My article discounts both views, provides an empirical test of ideas about the process of professionalization, and synthesizes findings on the structural and personal roots of three role orientations (discipline-professional, careerist, missionary). By analyzing barriers to professionalization, I suggest that future occupational groups will combine elements from professional and bureaucratic models; the average professional will combine professional and nonprofessional orientations; and the typical occupational association will be a hybrid—neither a trade union nor a professional association.

"Perhaps the article is cited frequently because it (1) succinctly covers issues important for both social theory and public policy; (2) provides simple measures of typical orientations of professionals toward their work; and (3) shows that although some growth in professionalization continues, there are profound limits to the achievement of both an exclusive jurisdiction and a credible moral claim like those of medicine, law, or the clergy (and even their authority is not secure).

"I was surprised that my measures of role orientations and summary of received notions about professionalism have been cited far more than what I consider the most original and subtle theme: that the ideal base for a claim to exclusive jurisdiction and professional authority is knowledge that is neither too general and vague (thereby familiar to laymen) nor too narrow and specific (thereby easily programmed). What makes long training necessary and persuades the public of the mystery of the craft is both intellectual and practical knowing, some explicit (learned from books and demonstrations), some implicit (intuitive understanding acquired from supervised practice and observation).

"I was astonished by the number of professional association leaders who read it and asked me to solve their problem of achieving professional status—an invitation I have resisted.

"An alert reader caught a minor statistical error. See an exchange between Richard J. Hill and myself where I show that correcting the error leaves the conclusions intact."[7,8]

1. **Wilensky H L.** *Intellectuals in labor unions: organizational pressures on professional roles.* New York: Free Press, 1956. 336 p.
2. **Galbraith K.** *The new industrial state.* New York: New American Library, 1968. p. 282-95.
3. **Bell D.** *The coming of post-industrial society: a venture in social forecasting.* New York: Basic Books, 1973. p. 136-7, 143-5, 374.
4. **Parsons T.** *The social system.* Glencoe, IL: Free Press, 1951. p. 433-9, 454ff.
5. -------------. Propaganda and social control. *Essays in sociological theory.* Glencoe, IL: Free Press, 1954. p. 142-76.
6. **Mills C W.** Old professions and new skills. *White collar.* New York: Oxford University Press, 1953. p. 112-41.
7. **Hill R J.** The professionalization of everyone? Reply to Wilensky H L. *Amer. J. Sociol.* **71**:84-6, 1965.
8. **Wilensky H L.** Reply to Hill R J. *Amer. J. Sociol.* **71**:84-6, 1965.

This Week's Citation Classic

CC/NUMBER 18
MAY 5, 1980

Dahrendorf R. *Class and class conflict in industrial society.* Stanford, CA: Stanford University Press, 1959. 336 p.

While building on Marx, social conflict theory has to substitute relations of power for property as the cause of conflict and explore the intensity and violence of conflicts as variable rather than linear. Thus, conflict gives rise to changes of differing degrees of radicalness and rapidity. In this form, the theory is applicable to capitalist as well as post-capitalist society. [The *Science Citation Index®* **(***SCI®***) and the** *Social Sciences Citation Index®* **(***SSCI™***) indicate that this book has been cited over 625 times since 1961.]**

Ralf Dahrendorf
University of London
London School of Economics
and Political Science
London WC2A 2AE
England

February 4, 1980

"When I wrote the first (German)[1] version of *Class and Class Conflict in Industrial Society* in 1956-57, conflict was still a rare and distant, indeed for many an objectionable, notion in social science. The original book was submitted as a thesis for admission to the senior teaching staff (*Habilitationsschrift*) at the University of Saarbrücken, and in the disputation which accompanied the process, a senior professor evoked the mirth of his colleagues when he said: 'If your thesis is correct that there is conflict in all organisations, then there would have to be conflict in universities too....' Perhaps the fact that 10 years after the original publication few doubted that this was the case has contributed to the success of the book.

"In 1957-58, I spent a memorable year at the Center for Advanced Study in the Behavioral Sciences in Palo Alto. Talcott Parsons was at the Center during that year, and in the course of a 'Conflict Seminar,' he, the senior and distinguished theorist, and I, the young and perhaps slightly prepotent social scientist, had several disputes. Their central subject was the question of how one would go about explaining social processes—by assuming the essential cohesiveness of an integrated social system and looking at change as disturbance, deviance, and dysfunction, or by regarding society as held together by constraint, and thus assuming the built-in conflictuality of social life. It was during that year, and on the basis of lively discussions at the Center, that I began to translate, or rather rewrite, the book. Its English version, first published in 1959, is the only authentic version and the one which has met with much comment, both critical and appreciative.

"Digging a little deeper, however, my motives were neither the continuing debate with Parsons, nor above all any desire to be original. They were, rather, to look at Marx's theory of social change with the eyes of someone who believed that Popper's strict concept of theory could be applied in the social sciences as well. Obviously, Marx had been wrong so far as explaining social processes in industrialized societies was concerned. Why? And what kind of approach promised more explanatory power?

"The approach suggested in *Class and Class Conflict* is in many ways rather formal. The elements of a theory of change which the book suggests are concerned above all with the rate of social change, that is, with its tempo and its depth. Since then, much of my thought has been devoted to the more difficult question of the direction of change and thus the substance of social conflict. But that is another story.

"The book, being an early contribution to conflict theory, became a college textbook and thus a starting point for further development: this above all is why it was widely cited."

1. **Dahrendorf R.** *Soziale Klassen und Klassenkonflikt in der industriellen Gesellschaft.* Stuttgart: F. Enke, 1957. 270 p.

This Week's Citation Classic

NUMBER 18
APRIL 30, 1979

Coleman J S, Campbell E Q, Hobson C J, McPartland, J, Mood A M, Weinfeld F D & York R L. *Equality of Educational Opportunity.* Washington, DC: US Department of Health, Education & Welfare. Office of Education (OE-38001 and supp.), 1966. 548 p.

[The *Science Citation Index®* *(SCI®)* **and the** *Social Sciences Citation Index™* *(SSCI™)* **indicate that this monograph has been cited over 875 times since 1966.]**

James S. Coleman
University of Chicago
Department of Sociology
Chicago, IL 60637

January 3, 1978

"This research originated in a way that was more unusual in 1964 than it is now: It resulted from an explicit directive to the U.S. Commissioner of Education in the Civil Rights Act of 1964. A section (402) of the Bill stated:

> The Commissioner shall conduct a survey and make a report to the President and the Congress, within two years of the enactment of this title, concerning the lack of availability of equal educational opportunities for individuals by reason of race, color, religion or national origin in public education institutions at all levels in the United States, its territories and possessions, and the District of Columbia.

"This was one of the first forays of Congress into mandating research related to policy. It was met with some confusion at the Office of Education, because that agency had not before gathered direct information from students or even schools, but only from school districts, primarily reports on school finances.

"However, the Commissioner, Francis Keppell, and the Assistant Commissioner for Educational Research, Alexander Mood, determined to break this pattern to meet the directive, and to obtain extensive information from students, teachers, and schools. Mood asked Ernest Campbell and me to co-direct the survey, to be carried out both in higher educational institutions and at the elementary and secondary level. The initial, and perhaps most critical, task was to determine the intent of Congress; to learn what Congress meant by 'lack of availability of equal educational opportunities,' and what parties had interests in the information to be obtained. To do this, we examined the Congressional Record, and we interviewed representatives of various civil rights and minority groups. No single definition of equal educational opportunity emerged, but several, in two broad classes. One was equal opportunity as defined by the inputs to education: facilities, teachers, materials, curriculum. A second was equal opportunity as defined by educational outputs: the growth in achievement in basic skills and acquisition of knowledge.

"A major reason for the later impact of the report was that it attempted to examine equality of educational opportunity in both of these ways. This had the effect of directing attention to the output definition, for most earlier research had limited itself to inputs as measures of inequality of educational opportunity.

"Data collection and data processing for the research was contracted to Educational Testing Service, which gathered data on about 800,000 public school students and smaller numbers of college students in the fall of 1965 and had the data ready for analysis by early spring of 1966. The analysis was carried out and the report written to meet the Congressional deadline of July 2, 1966.

"The report at first attracted little attention, primarily because it had no immediately apparent policy implications, and because its results were somewhat negative. It showed fewer inequalities of inputs for minorities than expected (smaller, for example, than regional or urban-rural inequalities), and it showed that the traditional input measures of school quality were not strongly related to achievement of students.

"However, for primarily three reasons, the report subsequently gained attention. One was the very finding of lack of relation between traditional input measures and school achievement, a result which disturbed conventional wisdom, and generated a number of attempts at reanalysis to find such effects. A second was that one result of the research, showing that backgrounds of fellow-students in the school were related to achievement, came to be useful for, and used by, the growing push toward affirmative racial integration of the schools. Thus the report came to be used in school board deliberations, in court decisions, and by local educational administrators to aid in the argument for increasing school integration. A third reason was that the report was an early example of a new genre: social research on a large scale directed to issues of social policy. Thus it attracted attention among practitioners of social research both as an illustration of how such research may be done and as an illustration of various pitfalls of such research."

This Week's Citation Classic

CC/NUMBER 1
JANUARY 7, 1980

Glazer N & Moynihan D P. *Beyond the melting pot: the Negroes, Puerto Ricans, Jews, Italians, and Irish of New York City.* Cambridge, MA: MIT Press, 1970 (1963). 363 p.

The book studies the role of ethnicity in the politics, economy, and culture of New York City, by way of profiles of the five largest groups. It argues that the ethnic group in New York, and the United States, is not a survival, but a new creation, each shaped by a distinctive history, culture, and American experience, which gives each group a distinctive role in the life of the city. [The *Science Citation Index®* **(***SCI®***) and the** *Social Sciences Citation Index*™ **(***SSCI*™**) indicate that this book has been cited over 380 times since 1969.]**

Nathan Glazer
Graduate School of Education
Harvard University
Cambridge, MA 02138

September 13, 1979

"I had, since the mid-1940s, been studying and writing about American ethnicity, an interest spurred by my work as an editor of *Commentary* magazine. I had already written a book about American Jews,[1] and another book on the American Communist Party,[2] which interpreted it more as an expression of ethnic rather than of class interests. The genesis of *Beyond the Melting Pot* was an idea of James Wechsler, editor of the *New York Post,* and Irwin Ross, for a series in the newspaper on the ethnic groups of the city. Daniel Bell suggested me as the person to write it. I expanded the idea into a book, which was modestly supported by the New York Post Foundation. Martin Meyerson, then director of the Joint Center for Urban Studies of Harvard and MIT, was also interested in my work on ethnicity, and the support was funneled through the Center.

"My approach to American ethnic groups was influenced by R.E. Park,[3] who traced the changes affecting ethnic groups objectively and sympathetically, avoiding the competing ideologies of Americanization and cultural maintenance; and by the social anthropologists who emphasized the wholeness of a culture, and the significance of family and child-rearing patterns for a people. I thought it essential that the analysis of each group should be grounded in its history and its economic role. What emerged from these orientations as somewhat original was the idea that the ethnic group was not only a survival from the age of mass immigration, but something of a new creation, and thus we could expect not rapid assimilation but an extended persistence, even as each group underwent change.

"My original intention was to have each ethnic group studied by a scholar from that group, who combined the empathy and understanding one might expect on the basis of origin and intimate experience, an objective perspective, and a willingness to participate in the project. The combination, in 1959, was hard to find. The only collaborator was Daniel P. Moynihan, a young political scientist suggested by Irving Kristol. Moynihan wrote the section on the Irish and brought to the book unexcelled knowledge of the political role of ethnicity in New York City.

"The book's impact, I believe, was based on the fact that it took ethnicity seriously at a time when most thinking people considered it a survival from the age of mass immigration and of decreasing importance. It turned out we—in America and the rest of the world—were due for a revival of ethnic interests, loyalties, and attachments in the later 1960s and 1970s, accompanied by considerable social research on ethnicity. A good deal of that research takes off from—or against—some point or hypothesis in *Beyond the Melting Pot.*"

1. **Glazer N.** *American Judaism.* Chicago: University of Chicago Press, 1972 (1957). 210 p.
2. ----------. *The social basis of American communism.* New York: Harcourt, Brace & World, 1961. 244 p.
3. **Park R E.** *The immigrant press and its control.* New York: Harper, 1922. 487 p.

CC/NUMBER 38
SEPTEMBER 22, 1980

This Week's Citation Classic

Hirschi T. *Causes of delinquency.*
Berkeley, CA: University of California Press, 1969. 309 p.

Using a large sample of adolescents, the predictions of three major theories of delinquency are tested for consistency with the data. Social control theory, the traditional theory of sociological analysis, consistently outperforms its modern competitors. [The *Social Sciences Citation Index® (SSCI™)* **indicates that this book has been cited over 215 times since 1969.]**

Travis Hirschi
School of Criminal Justice
State University of New York
Albany, NY 12222

August 12, 1980

"I suspect this book is cited for four distinct reasons: the theory of delinquency it advocates, its findings on the correlates of delinquency, the set of data on which it is based, and for the methodology it employs. In any event, my recollections of how the book came to be are compartmentalized along these lines.

"The ideas in the book were common in the literature of sociology and criminology at the time (1964) I decided to order them in some systematic fashion for a dissertation at Berkeley. I had been familiar with these ideas for some time. I had learned to respect them because they had been deemed worthy of explication by David Matza, Irving Piliavin, Erving Goffman, and Neil Smelser, among others.

"The central findings in the book had been reported in the criminological literature over a period of many years. I was familiar with these findings because I had by then been working for several years with Hanan Selvin on a methodological critique of delinquency research.

"My initial plan was simply to put the ideas and the research findings together. With this plan in mind, I went on the job market. I came home from my first trip east convinced there were more important things than regular employment. The ideas I found exciting and obviously consistent with available data had been treated as contrary to fact, passé, and even appalling. The only way to remedy this situation, it seemed, was to show the ability of the ideas to account for a single body of relevant data.

"Despite the efforts of my dissertation advisor, Charles Y. Glock, I was unable to obtain data for secondary analysis. (In those days, large scale data sets were rare and investigators were perhaps understandably reluctant to release them before they had been thoroughly exploited.) Glock then put me in touch with Alan B. Wilson, whose Richmond Youth Project was just getting underway at the Survey Research Center. Wilson agreed to let me add items to the research instruments in exchange for work on the project. (A NIMH predoctoral fellowship precluded gainful employment and provided large amounts of poverty-induced leisure.) Although I eventually became deputy director of the project, my contributions were mainly clerical (and physical—boxes of questionnaires are heavy), rather than intellectual.

"The key to the book is the body of data on which it is based. I know from experience that the ideas could not otherwise have been sharpened sufficiently to impress sociologists. I know that most of the findings were available (though often ignored) before my work was published. I know too that the statistical analysis is not sufficiently sophisticated by itself to attract more than negative attention. It is therefore fitting that many of the citations to my work stem from the fact that it contains a convenient description of the Richmond Youth Project. Thanks to Wilson's generosity, the Richmond data have been available for secondary analysis of delinquency-related issues almost from the day they were transportable. In fact, my work was cited before it appeared in print in an article based on secondary analysis of the Richmond data."[1]

1. **Jensen G.** "Crime doesn't pay": correlates of a shared misunderstanding. *Soc. Probl.* **17**:189-201, 1969.

This Week's Citation Classic

Glaser D. *The effectiveness of a prison and parole system.* Indianapolis: Bobbs-Merrill, 1964. 596 p. [University of Illinois, Urbana, IL]

This work presents data on prison and parole experiences, their statistical relationships to recidivism rates, and methods of guiding parole decisions actuarially. Its conclusions stress the variability of offenders, their problems of postprison employment, and ways of helping them acquire legitimate occupations. [The *Science Citation Index®* **(***SCI®***) and the** *Social Sciences Citation Index™* **(***SSCI™***) indicate that this book has been cited over 285 times since 1964.]**

Daniel Glaser
Department of Sociology
and Social Science
Research Institute
University of Southern California
Los Angeles, CA 90007

December 17, 1979

"In 1957, when I was an assistant professor at the University of Illinois and only three years beyond the PhD, the assistant director of the Bureau of Prisons, Frank Loveland, invited me to Washington to discuss a major study of the federal correctional system. He had gotten my name from Lloyd Ohlin, then at Columbia and now at Harvard.

"After discussing research possibilities, Loveland and I joined James Bennett, head of the Bureau for over two decades, and an older man, Francis B. Sayre, who, I learned, had proposed this project. Sayre (now deceased) had left the Harvard law faculty around 1930 to reorganize the Massachusetts prisons. Later, under President Franklin Roosevelt, he was undersecretary of state, then the last US-appointed governor of the Philippines under the independence plan that he fathered, and in 1942 fled the Japanese in a submarine with General MacArthur. When he finally retired, he renewed his interest in prisons. After Sayre and Bennett accepted our ideas, they perused annual reports of foundations to determine which members of boards of directors they should phone. Some months later, following formal proposal writing, I had a quarter million dollars from the Ford Foundation. Grant-getting has never been the same for me since.

"I ran the study from Urbana, placing research assistants for a year in five Midwest federal prisons, and for a year in federal probation offices to contact parolees from these institutions. Our advisory board, chaired by Sayre, included federal and state correctional officials as well as academicians from several disciplines. Meeting quarterly at first, the board's non-researchers wanted conclusive answers to all questions, immediately if not sooner. Much of my time was spent in diminishing their expectations. They made our range of inquiry too broad, but they also made us focus on policy-relevant problems (to which I tried to apply abstract theory and reproducible research methods). Our concern was with remediable conditions that foster a prisoner's postrelease unemployment and recidivism. Our data have been repeatedly cited to justify expansion of halfway houses, financial aid to inmates at release, meaningful work and educational opportunities in prison, and fewer restrictions on letters and visits to prisoners. In 1965 this study earned me the John Howard Association's Annual Award, presented by the Governor of Illinois. Because the 1964 book seemed too technical to officials, the abridged 1969 edition was prepared.[1]

"In reacting to crime, many academicians join politicians in glib generalization. Neither their promised panaceas nor their laments that 'nothing works' are justifiable. Instead, we need: (1) more application of our most adequately established knowledge on what works best for whom; (2) monitoring of such applications to assure that they are what we expect; and (3) continued evaluation and experimentation to expand this knowledge. If such efforts are well-grounded in theory, both pure and applied science, as well as the general public, will benefit.

"That this work has been highly cited reflects the persistence of the problems it addresses and the constant return to research after the failure of simple solutions."

1. **Glaser D.** *The effectiveness of a prison and parole system.* Indianapolis: Bobbs-Merrill, 1969. 345 p.

This Week's Citation Classic

Donabedian A. Evaluating the quality of medical care.
Milbank Mem. Fund Quart. **44**:166-206, 1966.
[School of Public Health, Univ. Michigan, Ann Arbor, MI]

This paper is a review of quality assessment methods, which discusses what to assess, where the information comes from, the nature of the criteria and standards, the sampling of care, and the reliability and validity of the measurement scales. Future work is proposed. [The *Science Citation Index*® (*SCI*®) and the *Social Sciences Citation Index*® (*SSCI*®) indicate that this paper has been cited in over 205 publications since 1966.]

Avedis Donabedian
School of Public Health
University of Michigan
Ann Arbor, MI 48109

November 29, 1982

"When a student at the Harvard School of Public Health, I wrote a paper on quality assessment for my teacher Franz Goldmann. Soon afterward, I became a rather junior participant in a research effort, led by Leonard Rosenfeld, to develop indicators of need and unmet need for medical care in the Boston area. A study of the quality of hospital care was one part of this program of studies. Though I was not, myself, involved in this, I heard a lot about the study, and must have become intrigued by the subject. I was, therefore, well primed when, some years later, I was asked, I believe at Rosenfeld's instigation, to review and evaluate the then rather limited literature on quality assessment.

"My contribution was to be only part of an ambitious project initiated by the Health Services Research Study Section of the US Public Health Service under the chairmanship of Kerr L. White. Almost the entire field of health services research was to be scrutinized, using for the purpose a series of 15 commissioned papers, each by an expert in some designated part. I did not see myself as an expert in quality assessment, and it became apparent at the planning meetings of the group of authors and administrators that few others did. I had been selected perhaps because no one else was available, and there was even some doubt as to whether or not the job could be done at all. I remember Richard Weinerman detailing the many pitfalls that I was about to face, and asking how I proposed to handle them. 'By not falling into them,' I said, throwing caution to the wind. Saved by laughter.

"The paper came at a critical juncture. Efforts to assess the quality of medical care were beginning to gather strength. In another few years, the federal government was to throw its full weight behind the enterprise. And yet, there was at the time no well-organized picture of what quality assessment meant. The paper supplied the much needed organizing framework for past and future studies of quality, and it provided the nomenclature that permitted intelligent discussion. Much of the current language of quality assessment has its roots in this paper, even though many who use the language are not aware of what a recent invention it is.

"With two major exceptions, the paper proved to have been conceptually comprehensive as well. At that time, quite by design, I took the relationship between good care and its outcomes as a given, and I excluded a consideration of monetary cost. I have since added these two components to a more comprehensive model."[1]

1. **Donabedian A, Wheeler J R C & Wyszewianski L.** Quality, cost, and health: an integrative model. *Med. Care* **20**:975-92, 1982.

This Week's Citation Classic

CC/NUMBER 49
DECEMBER 3, 1979

Muth R F. *Cities and housing: the spatial pattern of urban residential land use.* Chicago, IL: University of Chicago Press, 1969. 355 p.

This book analyzes the workings of the price system in urban housing markets and investigates the determinants of the spatial structure of urban areas and the growth of cities. It contrasts and tests alternative theories of housing quality in inner-city areas. [The *Science Citation Index*® *(SCI*®*)* **and the** *Social Sciences Citation Index* ™ *(SSCI*™*)* **indicate that this book has been cited over 345 times snce 1969.]**

Richard F. Muth
Department of Economics
Stanford University
Stanford, CA 94305

July 17, 1979

"My work in this field began over 20 years ago while at Resources for the Future in Washington, DC. One day while reading a book by a good friend and colleague, I came across the claim that the rental value of farmland is determined without reference to external markets. Thinking this to be surely incorrect, I sat down to work out what I thought to be a correct analysis of how markets determine land values, especially in a spatial context. Much of this was worked out over a two day period while more-or-less confined to my apartment by a severe snowstorm. It resulted in my first paper on the subject.[1]

"Roughly six months later I was visiting at the department of economics, Vanderbilt University, Nashville, Tennessee. I was chatting with my former teacher Milton Friedman, who had come down from Chicago to give a public lecture and several seminars. After describing my recent work, I mentioned that under certain circumstances, it implied that urban population densities would decline negative exponentially with distance from the city center. Milton remarked that Colin Clark had found this to be the case empirically in a paper published eight years earlier,[2] of which I had previously been unaware. Finding true confirmation of the analysis, I determined to pursue it further.

"Shortly thereafter I accepted an appointment in the Graduate School of Business at the University of Chicago. My position was supported by a grant from the RELM Foundation, which wanted to sponsor research related to the new federal urban renewal program. On moving to Chicago in the summer of 1959, I read everything I could find in Rockefeller Library on urban land and housing markets and on real estate. I concluded that we then understood very little about these markets and that some basic research had to be done before tackling applied questions such as urban renewal. Richard A. Ware, secretary of the RELM Foundation, quite graciously encouraged me to do so. As described in the preface of my book, I set myself the first task of developing further the theory of city structure and land use. Almost all of the research for the book and the writing of the first draft was done before I left Chicago for Washington five years later.

"The one feature of the book that has seemed to me to inspire more professional attention than any other is Chapter 2 on the spatial equilibrium of the household. This analysis resulted largely from earlier conversations with Lowdon Wingo in Washington and reviewing his manuscript[3] for publication. It had seemed to me then that the appropriate way to determine how the price of housing and/or urban land varies is to consider the maximization of household utility as constrained by income less transport costs. The other feature of my book that seems to distinguish it from other contributions to the same subject at about the same time is its extensive empirical work."

1. **Muth R F.** Economic change and rural-urban land conversions. *Econometrica* **29**:1-23, 1961.
2. **Clark C.** Urban population densities. *J. Roy. Statist. Soc. Ser. A* **114**:490-6, 1951.
3. **Wingo L, Jr.** *Transportation and urban land.* Washington, DC: Resources for the Future, Inc., 1961. 132 p.

Chapter

11

Economics

Novel perspectives / 309–316

Efficiency studies / 317–319

Behavior of prices / 320–322

This Week's Citation Classic

CC/NUMBER 16
APRIL 21, 1980

Theil H. *Economics and information theory.* Amsterdam: North-Holland, 1967. 488 p. [Center Math. Stud. Business Econ., Univ. Chicago, Chicago, IL]

This book describes applications of information theory to problems in economics, such as the measurement of income inequality, industrial concentration, concentration in international trade, and the fit of allocation models. [The *Science Citation Index® (SCI®)* **and the** *Social Sciences Citation Index™ (SSCI™)* **indicate that this book has been cited over 270 times since 1967.]**

Henri Theil
Center for Mathematical Studies
in Business and Economics
University of Chicago
Chicago, IL 60637

February 14, 1980

"The origin of this book is clear in my mind, although I cannot pinpoint the year in which it happened (it must have been in the early 1960s). I was working in consumption theory and obtained unfamiliar expressions such as $\Sigma_i w_i \log w_i$, where w_i is the budget share of good i (the share of this good in the consumer's total expenditure). Leafing through my father's encyclopedia in Utrecht, the Netherlands, I found that this expression had something to do with the entropy measure in physics. That came as a great surprise, because I vividly remembered that when I was a graduate student at the University of Amsterdam around 1950, my statistics teacher David van Dantzig had assured me that the entropy concept would be important in economics also.

"These developments were encouraging and potentially exciting, but they did not enable me to do very much because most of the relevant literature is in physics and electrical engineering, and I was not an expert in either of those areas (nor am I now). The breakthrough came when I found Koopman and Kimball's paper on information theory, which is formulated largely in mathematical terms.[1] Thereafter I derived numerous applications of informational concepts in economics. Perhaps the best known application is that to the measurement of income inequality, thus accounting for the book's high citation. In this book I proposed two informational inequality measures, both of which have attractive decomposition properties. Recently Bourguignon proved that these two measures are the only ones which have these properties.[2]

"To a large extent, the appearance of the book in its present form was caused by my move from Rotterdam to Chicago in 1966. I recognized that the large-scale applicability of informational concepts to economics was mainly caused by the frequent occurrence of 'shares,' or allocation proportions which are nonnegative and add up to 1, and I also recognized that economics is not the only social science in which such proportions play a prominent role. However, extending these approaches to other social sciences was something that I could do only after I had settled in Chicago."[3]

1. **Koopman B O & Kimball G E.** Information theory. (Assembled by the Operations Research Center, MIT) *Notes on operations research 1959.* Cambridge, MA: Technology Press, MIT, 1959. p. 188-210.
2. **Bourguignon F.** Decomposable income inequality measures. *Econometrica* **47**:901-20, 1979.
3. **Theil H.** *Statistical decomposition analysis with applications in the social and administrative sciences.* Amsterdam: North-Holland, 1972. 337 p.

CC/NUMBER 15
APRIL 9, 1984

This Week's Citation Classic™

Stigler G J. The economics of information. *J. Polit. Econ.* **69**:213-25, 1961.
[University of Chicago, IL]

The amount of information that economic actors collect before making decisions, and the principles on which they collect the information, are investment acts, to be studied by standard economic theory. Rules for the efficient collection of information are derived using the statistical theory of extreme values. An application is made to advertising. [The *Social Sciences Citation Index*® (*SSCI*®) indicates that this paper has been cited in over 370 publications since 1966.]

George J. Stigler
Center for the Study of the Economy
and the State
University of Chicago
Chicago, IL 60637

February 20, 1984

"Economists almost invariably assumed that the individuals with whom their theories were concerned possessed complete information on the things they dealt with: prices and technologies. One corollary was that there would be only one price for a commodity in a market: no buyer would pay more than the lowest price offered by sellers, and no seller would offer his good at less than the highest price offered by a buyer. Yet there is a dispersion of prices at a given time in almost every market. The dispersion is small when the product is standardized and when it is quoted on an organized exchange, for example, shares in IBM. The dispersion is wider for new automobiles, and wider still for workers' wages.

"These facts led me to propose a theory of the economic determination of the amount of information people would possess. For example, an individual will search more (learn more price offers) if he spends more on the good, or if the dispersion of prices among sellers is larger, or if he is a regular patron (rather than, say, a tourist) in a market.

"I may quote my Nobel Lecture—the award was based largely on the work—on the reception of the paper.

" 'The proposal to study the economics of information was promptly and widely accepted, and without even a respectable minimum of controversy. Within a decade and a half, the literature had become so extensive and the theorists working in the field so prominent, that the subject was given a separate classification in the *Index of Economic Articles*, **and more than a hundred articles a year are now devoted to this subject.**

" 'The absence of controversy certainly was no tribute to the definitiveness of my exposition. I had chosen fixed sample rather than sequential analysis, which a majority of later economists prefer. I had not presented a general equilibrium solution in which the behavior of both sides of a market is analyzed, and that step proved difficult to take. I had done little with information on quality and other variables, in contrast to price, although I soon extended the approach to a different kind of information in the theory of oligopoly. I had not applied the theory to the problem of unemployment, a literature initiated by an important paper by Armen Alchian.[1] All I had done was to open a door to a room that contained many fascinating and important problems.

" 'The absence of controversy was due instead to the fact that no established scientific theory was being challenged by this work: in fact, all I was challenging was the neglect of a promising subject. Moreover, the economics of information was susceptible to study by quite standard techniques of economic analysis. The theory immediately yielded results which were intuitively or observationally plausible. Here was a Chicago theory that didn't even annoy socialists!' "[2]

1. **Alchian A.** Information costs, pricing, and resource unemployment. (Phelps E S, ed.) *Microeconomic foundations of employment and inflation theory.* New York: Norton, 1970. p. 27-52.
2. **Stigler G J.** The process and progress of economics. *Les prix Nobel 1982.* Stockholm, Sweden: Almqvist & Wiksell, 1983. p. 253-72.

CC/NUMBER 8
FEBRUARY 20, 1984

This Week's Citation Classic™

Sandmo A. On the theory of the competitive firm under price uncertainty. *Amer. Econ. Rev.* **61**:65-73, 1971.
[Inst. Economics, Norwegian Sch. Economics and Business Administration, Bergen, Norway]

The standard model of the competitive firm is based on the assumption that demand conditions are known at the time when the production decision is made. This paper develops the theory under the alternative assumption that the firm only knows the probability distribution of the price and that it is averse to risk. [The *Social Sciences Citation Index*® (*SSCI*®) indicates that this paper has been cited in over 150 publications since 1971.]

Agnar Sandmo
Institute of Economics
Norwegian School of Economics and
Business Administration
5000 Bergen
Norway

January 2, 1984

"The foundations for a theory of economic behaviour under uncertainty had been available at least since the late 1940s, but it was not until several years later that economists began to apply the foundations to analyses of specific economic problems. Stimulated to a large extent by the work of Kenneth Arrow of Stanford University, I had written several papers on aspects of consumer behaviour under uncertainty, exploring the implications of the so-called expected utility theorem for theories of saving and portfolio choice. As a next step, it was natural to turn one's attention to firm behaviour and study the production decisions of firms when demand conditions were known only in a probabilistic sense. I started to work on this problem in Bergen in the summer of 1969, and completed the paper at the Center for Operations Research and Econometrics at the University of Louvain, Belgium, where I spent the following academic year on leave of absence.

"This kind of research was very much in the air at the time, and several other people, notably Baron[1] and Leland,[2] were doing related work taking a similar approach. Many more were following the new developments in the area, and for that reason it was a rewarding problem to be working on; it was easy to find people to talk to who had a serious interest in this kind of research.

"I do not myself consider this article to be my best paper, and it is natural to speculate on why it has come to be cited so often. One reason is surely purely historical: it happened to be one of the first papers in a new area, and a reference to it therefore describes in a convenient way the author's own approach to the subject. Apart from that, the attraction of the paper probably lies in its simplicity. New ideas about modelling attitudes to risk were just in the process of being absorbed into the economics profession, but many probably felt that the ideas were difficult to understand and evaluate in the abstract; my article presented them with an application to one of the simplest of all economic models, known to all economists since their first year of study. Moreover, the paper did not push the subject very far, indicating a number of problems to which the analysis could be extended, and a large number of papers have been written on this and related topics since then. Much of this work has been surveyed by Hey.[3]

"One of the less satisfactory features of the paper is its assumption that the firm as such has well-defined attitudes to risk, and that its behaviour is governed by risk aversion. On the one hand, this formulation disregards the fact that a firm consists of a group of individuals, whose personal attitudes to risk may not easily be aggregated. On the other hand, the formulation does not take into account the possibility of sharing risks through the stock market. These features may have accounted for some critical references, but I still feel that there is something to be said for my own approach in terms of descriptive realism."

1. **Baron D P.** Price uncertainty, utility and industry equilibrium in pure competition. *Int. Econ. Rev.* **11**:463-80, 1970. (45 cites.)
2. **Leland H E.** Theory of the firm facing uncertain demand. *Amer. Econ. Rev.* **62**:278-91, 1972. (Cited 110 times.)
3. **Hey J D.** *Uncertainty in microeconomics.* Oxford, England: Martin Robertson, 1979. 261 p.

CC/NUMBER 6
FEBRUARY 9, 1981

This Week's Citation Classic

Edwards W. The theory of decision making. *Psychol. Bull.* **51**:380-417, 1954. [Johns Hopkins Univ., Baltimore, MD]

This article introduces psychologists to economic theories about theories that focus on the ideas of utility and rationality. It also reviews psychological and other empirical data bearing on those theories as descriptions of human decision making, comments on the theories and data from a psychologist's perspective, and suggests additional studies. Topics covered include utility maximization, indifference curves, risky choices, transitivity, and multi-person games. [The *Science Citation Index® (SCI®)* **and the** *Social Sciences Citation Index® (SSCI™)* **indicate that this paper has been cited over 250 times since 1961.]**

Ward Edwards
Social Science Research Institute
Department of Psychology
University of Southern California
Los Angeles, CA 90007

January 22, 1981

"As a graduate student, in one week in 1949, I read an article about level of aspiration by Kurt Lewin[1] and a number of his former students, and attended a colloquium by Fred Mosteller reporting his experimental application of von Neumann-Morgenstern's ideas about utility measurement. The obvious similarity of the ideas from such dissimilar roots stimulated me, and interacted with knowledge of economic theory obtained both because my father was a prominent economist and because I had taken many economics courses as an undergraduate. This confluence of ideas (which in fact, as I learned much later, converged earlier in Berlin in 1928) led to my PhD thesis and to my lifelong research interest in decision making.

"At Johns Hopkins, in my first post-PhD job, I decided that I could not afford my existing state of ignorance about the literature of decision making, then mostly a topic in economics and statistics. Since I had to read the stuff anyhow, I chose to get a publication out of it by writing a review. So I borrowed for three months an office in the library of the economics department, holed up all day, every day, and emerged with 'The theory of decision making' in virtually final-draft form.

"The article correctly reflected the literature of its time, but seems extraordinarily naive today. For some reason, I had never anticipated what its impact would be. The topic of decision making apparently was not salient in psychological thinking as available for research and theorizing; this article made it so. That is why it has been so frequently cited. Economists, too, found it useful; they had not considered the possibility that the assertions about individual behavior and rationality that make up the main content of microeconomics were readily subject to experimental test, and that some such tests had been performed, with dubious results.

"In 1960, I reviewed the field again, this time for the *Annual Review of Psychology*. The title of that review, 'Behavioral decision theory,'[2] has served as a name for the field ever since. Other reviews have appeared at intervals since then, in the *Annual Review of Psychology*[3] and elsewhere. Today, behavioral decision theory is a lively sub-field within cognitive psychology.

"The worst failure of 'The theory of decision making' was my inability to anticipate the important applications that such a theory could have. It should have been obvious, but wasn't, that a good theory of how decisions should be made was certain to impact the world of non-academic decision makers. I didn't start to see that point until 1958, and it didn't become highly visible in technical literature until Howard Raiffa, Ronald A. Howard, and I started making it so in the mid- to late-1960s under the label of decision analysis. It is fun, though fruitless, to speculate what the intellectual and organizational condition of decision analysis would be if I had been as interested in applications in 1954 as I am now."

1. **Lewin K, Dembo T, Festinger L & Sears P S.** Level of aspiration. (Hunt J M, ed.) *Personality and the behavior disorders.* New York: Ronald, 1944. Vol. 1. p. 333-78.
2. **Edwards W.** Behavioral decision theory. *Annu. Rev. Psychol.* **12**:473-98, 1961.
3. **Slovic P, Fischhoff B & Lichtenstein S.** Behavioral decision theory. *Annu. Rev. Psychol.* **28**:1-39, 1977.

NUMBER 46
NOVEMBER 12, 1979

This Week's Citation Classic

Cyert R M & March J G. *A behavioral theory of the firm.* Englewood Cliffs, NJ: Prentice-Hall, 1963. 332 p. [Graduate School of Industrial Administration, Carnegie Institute of Technology, Pittsburgh, PA]

A Behavioral Theory of the Firm **attempts to integrate the theory of the firm and organization theory. It relates internal factors such as organizational structure and decision-making processes to economic actions such as pricing. The theory also emphasizes such factors as organizational learning and organizational slack to the economic decisions of the firm. [The** *Science Citation Index® (SCI®)* **and the** *Social Sciences Citation Index™ (SSCI™)* **indicate that this book has been cited over 770 times since 1963.]**

Richard M. Cyert
Office of the President
Carnegie-Mellon University
Pittsburgh, PA 15213

July 24, 1979

"The work on *A Behavioral Theory of the Firm* began in 1952, although at that time we did not know that the product would be *A Behavioral Theory of the Firm.* I had been at Carnegie since 1948, and James March had just arrived. I was an economist, and he, a political scientist. My interest was in oligopoly theory and his, in organization theory. I had been concerned that economic theory concentrated on variables outside the firm in developing solutions to the oligopoly problem. Assumptions were made about the way in which one firm would react to another firm's actions, particularly with respect to price changes. In discussing this problem, Jim and I came to the conclusion that it would be fun to explore the possibility of integrating organization theory and oligopoly theory.

"Since both of us carried our lunches, we agreed to conduct a series of (brown bag) seminars with only ourselves there. We concentrated on studying the variables within an organization that might affect important economic decisions such as pricing. In particular, we looked at the various ways in which biases could enter the information transmittal process within an organization. This paper was eventually published in the *American Economic Review.*[1]

"That work and the publication of the paper launched us into a whole series of activities. We talked at a large number of conferences, continued to publish papers, and involved a number of graduate students in our research. At the same time, each of us was working on other projects and was publishing papers and books in different areas.

"As we began to accumulate and publish papers and as interest built up in our work, we conceived the idea of integrating our studies in the form of a book and of utilizing the work of students and former students who had done related work.

"As is inevitable, our lives became more complicated, and it was difficult to work without interruption in our offices. We searched for a place that might give us more privacy and found an unfinished room over the auditorium in the Graduate School of Industrial Administration. We moved a couple of tables and two chairs into the room and named it *'A Behavioral Theory of the Firm* Room.' We worked together and separately in that room for a couple of years, finishing additional papers and putting the book in final form.

"Part of the pleasure of doing research is having co-authors whom one can enjoy as friends. Both Jim and I liked baseball, and we were able to indulge ourselves occasionally with ease because the Pittsburgh Pirates then played at Forbes Field, only a few blocks from campus. On those rare days when a day game was played, we would wander over to the field and sit in the bleachers and watch a ball game. I do not think any of the ideas of *A Behavioral Theory of the Firm* can be directly traced to those 'seminars,' but they were enjoyable times—particularly in 1960 when the Pirates won the pennant and the World Series."

1. **Cyert R M & March J G.** Organizational structure and pricing behavior in an oligopolistic market. *Amer. Econ. Rev.* **45**:129-39, 1955.

CC/NUMBER 27
JULY 5, 1982

This Week's Citation Classic

Baumol W J. *Business behavior, value and growth.* New York: Macmillan, 1959. 164 p. [Princeton University, Princeton, NJ]

In standard models the sole objective of the business firm is profit maximization. But evidence suggests businesspeople pursue other objectives, including sales volume and growth. This book shows how such alternative models are constructed and analyzed and yield behavioral theorems relevant for theory and practice. [The *Social Sciences Citation Index®* **(*SSCI®*) indicates that this book has been cited over 370 times since 1966.]**

William J. Baumol
Department of Economics
Princeton University
Princeton, NJ 08544

March 15, 1982

"When initially serving as a consultant to business firms on problems upon which economic theory promised to shed some light, my training in standard analysis led to recommendations based on the hypothesis that the businessperson's only goal in life is to earn the most profits. However, when the recommendations received only a mixed reception, I was forced to rethink matters. For example, when it was pointed out to a firm that certain segments of its business demonstrably cut into profits and were likely to do so for the indefinite future, I expected the management to rejoice at this opportunity to increase profits by eliminating the unremunerative portion of sales. Though many of my recommendations were received with some degree of enthusiasm, the sort of proposal just described only elicited an embarrassing silence.

"It soon became clear that management often valued an increased scale of activity as an end in itself, whether or not it increased profits or even if it involved a limited sacrifice of earnings.

"This led me to inquire why classical economic models assumed profits were the firm's only goal. Obviously, there is nothing inherently 'irrational' about the choice of alternative objectives. It became clear that the profit maximization prêmise had been selected by economists because it was so tractable analytically and yielded so many fruitful theorems. Indeed, other economists had previously produced empirical evidence suggesting that businesses have other aims,[1] but they were apparently unable to construct rigorous and tractable models corresponding to this evidence.

"I therefore devoted myself to the construction of such alternative models and after the usual period of frustrations and blind alleys, finally came up with what has since come to be called the 'sales maximization' model. This has subsequently served as a prototype for still other constructs by other economists[2,3] which have contributed to our understanding of the way in which firms actually work and has enabled economists to improve the advice they offer to industry.

"No doubt, the ease with which the analysis lent itself to modification, the opportunities it offered for empirical testing, and the new range of insights it offered account for the frequency with which the work has been cited."[4]

1. **Lanzillotti R F.** Pricing objectives in large companies. *Amer. Econ. Rev.* **48**:921-40, 1958.
2. **Williamson O E.** *The economics of discretionary behavior: managerial objectives in a theory of the firm.* Englewood Cliffs, NJ: Prentice-Hall, 1964. 182 p.
3. **Marris R.** *The economic theory of managerial capitalism.* London: Macmillan, 1964. 346 p.
4. **Williamson O E.** The modern corporation: origins, evolution, attributes. *J. Econ. Lit.* **19**:1537-68, 1981.

This Week's Citation Classic™

Gordon H S. The economic theory of a common-property resource: the fishery.
J. Polit. Econ. **62**:124-42, 1954.
[Carleton College, Ottawa, Ontario, Canada]

The economic theory of common-property resources is developed showing that in cases like the fishery a behavioral equilibrium occurs which dissipates the net output value of the industry through misallocation of production factors. [The *Social Sciences Citation Index*® (*SSCI*®) indicates that this paper has been cited in over 225 publications since 1966. There have been 20 additional cites in *SCI*®.]

H. Scott Gordon
Department of Economics
Indiana University
Bloomington, IN 47405

December 8, 1983

"After I became a faculty member at Carleton College (now University) in Ottawa in 1948, I began to do occasional work for the Canadian Department of Fisheries. (Though my academic interests were in economic theory, this work on fisheries economics was extremely practical and empirical.) Fisheries economists and biologists had frequently noted that though ocean resources are very rich, fishermen seldom earn more than a meager income. Biologists usually attributed this to depletion of fish stocks through 'overfishing,' but no satisfactory theory existed to explain why this should occur in the fishery but not other renewable natural resource industries like agriculture. One day, in casual conversation with two fisheries economists, I suggested that the essential problem was a discrepancy between the *equilibrium* use of fishing location and its *optimum* use. Challenged to justify this, I constructed a model of fisheries exploitation in which this discrepancy results from the lack of private property rights in marine resources, unlike land ownership in agriculture. I then looked at other natural resource industries with similar 'common-property' characteristics, and the few marine industries with private property arrangements. The experience in these was consistent with my model. The cited paper presented a general economic theory of common-property resources with main reference to the fishery.

"For several years the paper was cited occasionally, but I had no reason to think that it was regarded as especially significant. In the 1960s, notice of it accelerated, partly, I think, due to realization by economists that property-ownership arrangements play a central role in economic phenomena that had not hitherto been effectively delineated and partly because of increased interest in the economic theory of natural resource exploitation. Since then, the 'fisheries model' has been applied to a wide variety of cases, and has been elaborated upon a great deal (see, for example, reference 1).

"I learned from a recent journal that I was not the first to understand the source of the fisheries problem. A Danish economist, Jens Warming, captured the essentials of my model in a nonrigorous form in a paper written in 1911.[2,3] No matter, being correct is better than being original, in science at least.

"Though my model is very simple, I had considerable difficulty formulating it. At one point, in frustration, I put it aside altogether for three months and, when I returned to it, the parts fell into place in a few minutes. Since then, I have had a number of similar experiences, and am a great believer in allowing a problem to simmer for a while on the back burner of the mind—not for too long though!"

1. **Mirman L J & Spulber D F,** eds. *Essays in the economics of renewable resources.* Amsterdam: North-Holland, 1982. 287 p.
2. **Warming J.** Om grundrente af fiskegrunde. *Nat. Tidsskr.* **49**:499-505, 1911.
3. **Andersen P.** 'On rent of fishing grounds': a translation of Jens Warming's 1911 article, with an introduction. *Hist. Polit. Econ.* **15**:391-6, 1983.

This Week's Citation Classic

CC/NUMBER 20
MAY 14, 1979

Hardin G. The tragedy of the commons. *Science* **162**:1243-7, 1968.
[University of California, Santa Barbara]

When resources are scarce, free access to common property—meadows, ocean fisheries, or pollution-sinks like the atmosphere—is ruinous. Those who restrain their demands because of long-term bad effects lose out in competition with short-term maximizers. This perverse logic makes ruin inevitable. [The *Science Citation Index®* *(SCI®)* **and the** *Social Sciences Citation Index™ (SSCI™)* **indicate that this paper has been cited over 270 times since 1961.]**

Garrett Hardin
Department of Biological Sciences
University of California
Santa Barbara, CA 93106

June 30, 1978

"As the retiring president of a scientific association I was required to give a public address: this paper was the result. By this time in my career writing was pretty easy for me; but I was not prepared for the agony of writing this essay. Over a period of two months one draft followed another, and they were strikingly different. I wrote a total of seven drafts, as I recall. After the address was delivered I sent it to *Science*. Three months passed, and then the editor made two comments: we accept the paper, but it is too long. Out came the scissors; I cut out the first half, wrote a few introductory sentences for the remainder, and the job was done.

"Why was the writing so difficult? Principally because I was reaching conclusions that repelled me, and I tried desperately to avoid them. Freedom in an unmanaged commons leads inevitably to ruin. In a crowded world our only real freedom lies in joining with others in choosing and implementing the forms of coercion—mutual coercion, mutually agreed upon—which describes the result of any law in a democracy. Voluntarism will not save the whales or keep the skies unpolluted. Neither will it make possible population control by purely personal birth control in a welfare state: in this case, the compassionate rule of welfare, 'to each according to his need,' creates a commons, with the usual prognosis of ultimate ruin.

"I did not work out the full theory until the publication, in 1977, of my book *The Limits of Altruism.*[1] Glimpses of the theory are found as far back as Aristotle. A. N. Whitehead said, 'We give credit for an idea not to the first man to have it, but to the first one who takes it seriously.' On that basis I think I deserve credit; I did take the idea seriously, developing many of its ramifications. Not all at once, however. Applications to foreign aid and immigration I delayed for six years, when my 'Living on a lifeboat' evoked considerable opposition.[2]

"As for methodology, I think my work points to the importance of abandoning the melioristic assumptions encased in Adam Smith's 'invisible hand' in favor of the pejoristic ones of Gresham's Law. Pure technological optimism has had its day: a search for the pathologies of man-nature systems now pays off better—such is the thrust of my 1976 essay, 'Pejorism: the middle way.'[3] Time will tell if I am right."

1. **Hardin G.** *The limits of altruism: an ecologist's view of survival.* Bloomington, IN: Indiana Univ. Press, 1977. 154 p.
2. ------------. Living on a lifeboat. *Bioscience* **24**:561-8, 1974.
3. ------------. Pejorism: the middle way. *N. Amer. Rev.* **261**:9-14, 1976.

This Week's Citation Classic

Leibenstein H. Allocative efficiency vs. "X-efficiency."
Amer. Econ. Rev. **56**:392-415, 1966.
[Department of Economics, University of California, Berkeley, CA]

X-efficiency theory challenges the maximization postulate of standard economic theory. This paper shows that X-inefficiency is, at times, as much as 30 times greater than allocative inefficiency and suggests reasons for the existence of X-inefficiency—i.e., (a) incomplete employment contracts, (b) discretionary effort, and (c) nonmaximization of profits. [The ***Social Sciences Citation Index®*** **(*SSCI®*) indicates that this paper has been cited in over 270 publications since 1966. This paper is the 4th most cited in this journal, 1969-80.]**

Harvey Leibenstein
Department of Economics
Harvard University
Cambridge, MA 02138

May 7, 1982

"X-efficiency theory is concerned with the underutilization of resources available. It seems appropriate that my work began as a consequence of the availability of underutilized research assistance. We, my assistant and I, investigated a body of literature that was normally overlooked by economists—literature containing direct or indirect reports of management consultants or technical aid teams operating in various parts of the world. We found that, with a fairly high degree of consistency, these teams reported instances in which labor, machinery, or raw materials were either not used to their full capacity, or were used in extremely wasteful ways. They reported that managers of business enterprises, presumably reasonable men, often had apparently costless improvements suggested to them, yet the improvements were never introduced. This behavior clearly contradicted standard economic theory, which holds that enterprises minimize costs. I felt the need to examine, measure, and explain this phenomenon.

"I think I can guess at some reasons for the popularity of this article. First, it makes a basic and simple point that deviates from conventional thinking in the field. Second, the point is backed up by a lot of data from widely varying sources. Finally, ideas are presented in relatively simple form making it easily understood by students at various levels. In the subsequent decade and a half I have written a number of papers and three books spelling out X-efficiency theory, its applications, and the circumstances under which X-inefficiency would be greater or smaller.[1-3]

"While the initial article was easily published, later related articles introducing an important postulate—the 'partial non-maximization' postulate—proved to be highly controversial.[4-7] This last was frequently resisted by referees. Economists generally resist the relaxation of the maximization postulate.

"My experience has been that while non-economists find it difficult to accept the notion that people *always* do as well as they can, economists seem to feel equally strongly that maximization is the essential postulate for economic theorizing.[3] In recent years there has been a gradual, if slight, increase in tolerance toward alternative postulates.[4] Needless to say, I look upon this movement as healthy, and a necessary one for any developing science."

1. **Leibenstein H.** *Beyond economic man: a new foundation for economics.* Cambridge, MA: Harvard University Press, 1976. 297 p.
2. ------------------. *General X-efficiency theory and economic development.* London: Oxford University Press, 1978. 189 p.
3. ------------------. *Inflation, income distribution, and X-efficiency theory.* London: Croom Helm, 1980. 122 p.
4. ------------------. Aspects of the X-efficiency theory of the firm. *Bell J. Econ.* **6**:580-606, 1975.
5. ------------------. A branch of economics is missing: micro-micro theory. *J. Econ. Lit.* **17**:477-502, 1979.
6. ------------------. On bullseye painting economics. *J. Post Keynesian Econ.* **4**:460-5, 1982.
7. ------------------. The prisoners' dilemma in the invisible hand. *Amer. Econ. Rev.* In press, 1982.

 NUMBER 17
APRIL 23, 1979

Arrow K J, Chenery H B, Minhas B S & Solow R M. Capital-labor substitution and economic efficiency. *Rev. Econ. Statist.* **43**:225-50, 1961.
[Stanford University, Stanford, CA]

The way in which capital and labor cooperate in production is of basic importance for economic development. Previous analysis had been largely based on a linear logarithmic relation. The empirical data has disconfirmed this simple view and more flexible forms have been found, in which the elasticity of substitution between capital and labor was no longer restricted to one, but could be any constant. These new production functions have proved to allow for simple and yet flexible research, confirmed on several different bodies of data. [The *Science Citation Index®* *(SCI®)* **and the** *Social Sciences Citation Index ™ (SSCI ™)* **indicate that this paper has been cited over 260 times since 1961.]**

Kenneth J. Arrow
Department of Economics
Harvard University
Cambridge, MA 02138
December 27, 1977

"Output can be thought of as a function of capital labor and technological knowledge. For a single country the latter variable could be approximated by time; we can also consider different countries representing varying technical levels. Decomposition about the changes into these factors had been begun by Tinbergen and Solow. However, they have been constrained, in order to achieve manageable formulas, to use a Cobb-Douglas production function, in which output is linear-logarithmic in capital and labor. This implied that the value shares of the two factors were in constant proportion over time.

"I had speculated that the decomposition might be faulty if the wrong production function were used, but I had done little about it. Chenery had been collecting a great deal of data about different countries. In particular, a then graduate student at Stanford, Bagicha Minhas, now a professor at the Indian Statistical Institute in Delhi, had been doing careful cross-country comparisons and held that the share of labor in value added for a given industry was not constant across countries. Specifically they found that value added per worker had a good linear logarithmic fit to the wage rate, but the coefficient for many industries was less than one, where the Cobb-Douglas assumption would imply a coefficient of one. They discussed this problem with me, and after a couple of wasted weeks I realized that their findings could be rationalized by the assumption of a production function with an elasticity of substitution different from one but constant. It turned out that Solow had in fact suggested just such a production function in a theoretical paper.[1]

"It turned out that constant elasticity-of-substitution-in-production-function had implications which were relatively easy to fit, being linear in form. As a result, we were able to test our hypothesis on a wide variety of data and attained some interesting results.

"Subsequent work has gone still further, but the impulse to find useable new production functions was released by our paper and resulted in a flood of subsequent work. Our original incentive to confine ourselves to functions giving relatively simple derived forms has probably been made obsolete by the improvements in computer technology, which make fitting complex nonlinear forms much chapter. Our paper now is probably of historical significance in pointing to a more general methodological approach."

1. **Solow R M.** A contribution to the theory of economic growth. *Quart. J. Econ.* 65:65-94, 1956.

Jorgenson D W. Capital theory and investment behavior. *Amer. Econ. Rev.* **53**:247-59, 1963. [Department of Economics, University of Chicago, Chicago, IL]

This paper presents an econometric model of investment behavior based on the neoclassical theory of optimal capital accumulation. The paper incorporates tax policy as a determinant of investment expenditures through the rental price of capital services. [The *Social Sciences Citation Index*® (*SSCI*®) indicates that this paper has been cited in over 195 publications since 1966.]

Dale W. Jorgenson
Department of Economics
Harvard University
Cambridge, MA 02138

August 4, 1982

"This paper is the progenitor of a series of 25 papers I have written on the econometrics of investment behavior. Much of this work was carried out in collaboration with my graduate students at the University of California, Berkeley, including Sidney S. Handel, M. Ishaq Nadiri, Calvin D. Siebert, and James A. Stephenson, and with one undergraduate student, Robert E. Hall. Results published through 1971 were summarized in my review article in *Journal of Economic Literature*.[1]

"My *American Economic Review* paper has been widely cited because it contains three original ideas that have been extensively developed by myself and my students, and by others. First, there is the idea of incorporating price effects into the econometric modeling of investment behavior through the rental price of capital services. This idea was the key to treating investment behavior as part of the economic theory of producer behavior and has been employed in almost all subsequent work on the econometrics of investment. I have published a more detailed treatment of this idea in two articles that appeared in 1967 and 1973.[2,3]

"The second key idea in my article is the use of rational distributed lag techniques in modeling economic behavior. At the time my article was published, this idea represented a considerable advance in statistical technique for analyzing economic time series. I later published a more detailed treatment of the technique in a paper that appeared in *Econometrica* in 1966.[4]

"The third idea presented for the first time in my paper is the incorporation of the impact of tax policy on investment behavior through the rental price of capital services. This technique has now become standard in the economics of public finance. Closely related ideas have been used in analyzing a wide range of economic behavior, including savings, labor supply, and demand for specific commodities.

"My paper and the research that followed it resulted in my receiving the John Bates Clark Medal of the American Economic Association in 1971. This medal is awarded every two years to a person under 40 who has made a contribution to economics. The citation for my award reads in part: 'His prolonged exploration of the determinants of investment spending, whatever its ultimate lessons, will certainly long stand as one of the finest examples of the marriage of theory and practice in economics.' "

1. **Jorgenson D W.** Econometric studies of investment behavior: a survey. *J. Econ. Lit.* **9**:1111-47, 1971.
2. --------------------. The theory of investment behavior. (Ferber R, ed.) *The determinants of investment behavior.* New York: Columbia University Press, 1967. p. 129-56.
3. --------------------. Technology and decision rules in the theory of investment behavior. *Quart. J. Econ.* **87**:523-43, 1973.
4. --------------------. Rational distributed lag functions. *Econometrica* **34**:135-49, 1966.

CC/NUMBER 33
AUGUST 13, 1979

This Week's Citation Classic

Sharpe W F. Capital asset prices: a theory of market equilibrium under conditions of risk. *J. Finance* **19:**425-42, 1964.
[Department of Operations Research, University of Washington, Seattle, WA]

Given homogeneous probabilistic predictions of the joint distribution of security returns, capital asset prices will adjust in equilibrium so that expected returns will be linearly related to security risks, where the risk of each security is measured by its beta value, indicating the sensitivity of the security's return to changes in the return on an efficient portfolio. [The *SCI*® indicates that this paper has been cited over 425 times since 1964.]

William F. Sharpe
Graduate School of Business
Stanford University
Stanford, CA 94305

January 9, 1979

"I began to work on portfolio theory and capital asset prices in 1960; the initial results were contained in my dissertation, completed at the University of California, Los Angeles in June, 1961. In it I explored normative aspects of portfolio construction and developed a positive model for the determination of capital asset prices under conditions of risk, using the very strong assumption that the risk of a security can be dichotomized into: (1) a part due to correlation with all other securities, and (2) a part due to factors completely unique to the security in question. This assumption (which I called the diagonal model, but is now usually termed the single index model) is obviously a simplification of reality. We now know that it is a great oversimplification. However, it does allow great reductions in the cost of solving the quadratic programming problem associated with efficient portfolio construction. An algorithm designed to exploit its characteristics, developed in my dissertation, was published in 1963.[1]

"Shortly after completing the dissertation, I set out to see if the strong single-index model assumption could be relaxed when building a positive model of capital asset pricing. Happily I found that the key results could all be obtained without the assumption (although some still mistakenly believe that it is needed). I first presented this much more general model at the University of Chicago in January, 1962, and submitted a written version to the *Journal of Finance* shortly thereafter. The usual refereeing process and other editorial matters delayed publication until September, 1964.

"A few months later, John Lintner's more extensive analysis was published.[2] It started from a different point and for a while both John and I believed that our models had reached different conclusions and were inconsistent with each other. After the usual confusion (some of it in print), it is now well established that the two approaches are completely compatible. A third model was developed by Mossin.[3] Although he initially interpreted one of his results differently, his approach has been shown to be fully compatible with the other two.

"The resulting theory is usually termed the Sharpe-Lintner or Sharpe-Lintner-Mossin Capital Asset Pricing Model (CAPM). While much has been done to extend it, the basic ideas remain at the core of much of modern finance theory and practice. I suspect that this stems in part from the fact that the results are both reasonable (although not intuitively obvious) and practical. Moreover, the results are not wildly inconsistent with empirical evidence, and this has undoubtedly helped them gain acceptance as well."

1. **Sharpe W F.** A simplified model for portfolio analysis. *Manage. Sci.* **9**:277-93, 1963.
2. **Lintner J.** The valuation of risk assets and the selection of risky investments in stock portfolios and capital budgets. *Rev. Econ. Statist.* **47**:13-37, 1965.
3. **Mossin J.** Equilibrium in a capital asset market. *Econometrica* **34**:768-83, 1966.

This Week's Citation Classic

Rosen S. Hedonic prices and implicit markets: product differentiation in pure competition. *J. Polit. Econ.* 82:34-55, 1974.
[University of Rochester, NY and Harvard University, Cambridge, MA]

The equilibrium structure of price and quality variation in differentiated product markets is revealed as a marriage problem between attributes of buyers and sellers. The theory interprets empirical price-quality regressions and suggests new methods for obtaining complete structural and behavioral information from the data. [The *Social Sciences Citation Index*® (*SSCI*®) **indicates that this paper has been cited in over 170 publications since 1974.]**

Sherwin Rosen
Department of Economics
University of Chicago
Chicago, IL 60637

November 3, 1982

"My work on this topic was stimulated by many empirical studies relating price variation of differentiated products to performance measures and other characteristics. While the intuitive basis for these methods was clear, they did not square well with available economic theory because the problem of quality determination in markets had been largely ignored and there was no rigorous theory of product differentiation in a market setting. Substantial attention had been devoted to finding theoretical structures that would support the empirical studies and explain their findings, but I was dissatisfied with those attempts because they did not adequately deal with the full market equilibrium aspects of the problem.

"The innovation of my work was conceptual. It showed how the empirical results could be interpreted in terms of an unfamiliar type of spatial equilibrium. I think its appeal was to combine familiar elements from several different branches of economics into a new package that gave a reasonably precise, but straightforward and accessible, interpretation of well-known results found by others. It also suggested some new methods for obtaining more information from the data, which subsequent investigators have found interesting.

"The work itself is a development of the ancient theory of equalizing differences generalized with modern technical apparatus to multiple dimensions and to a much wider class of problems. That theory was well known to me from my training as a labor economist, but apparently was unfamiliar to others working on the problem. I owe much in the development of these ideas to a lengthy correspondence with H. Gregg Lewis on one of my first publications.[1] It gradually dawned on me that the approach we had argued so much about earlier had greater generality than the specific point at issue. In particular, it showed how cross-sectional price variation could be sustained as an equilibrium phenomenon in many market settings. However, I did not at all anticipate many of the areas in which this framework would find application in subsequent work.

"My results have been used mostly for interpreting empirical work and for thinking about how to formulate empirical procedures in many practical problems that have spatial elements, where 'space' is interpreted broadly to include the latent characteristics of goods (or, in the labor market, jobs). The theoretical description of equilibrium has proved to be reasonably complete and durable, but far less work has been done on developing econometric methods for extracting all of the structural information on preferences and technologies from the data. I conjectured some methods in the article that are now understood to be incomplete and difficult to apply in practice, so that problem remains very much on the research agenda."

1. **Rosen S.** On the interindustry wage and hours structure. *J. Polit. Econ.* 77:249-73, 1969.

This Week's Citation Classic

Mandelbrot B. The variation of certain speculative prices. *J. Business* **36**:394-419, 1963.
[Harvard University, Cambridge, MA and Research Center, International Business Machines Corp.]

Changes of commodity and security prices are fitted excellently by the Lévy-stable probability distributions. Their parameter, α, is the intrinsic measure of price volatility. The model also accounts for the amplitudes of major events in economic history. An unprecedented feature is that price changes have an infinite population variance. [The *Social Sciences Citation Index*® **(*SSCI*®) indicates that this paper has been cited over 150 times since 1966.]**

Benoit B. Mandelbrot
Thomas J. Watson Research Center
IBM
Yorktown Heights, NY 10598

March 3, 1982

"Early in 1961, while on my way to a seminar, I stepped into the office of my host, a Harvard economist. On his blackboard, I noticed a diagram nearly identical to one I was about to draw. His diagram referred to a topic of which I knew nothing: records of the price of cotton. My host had given up his attempt to model this phenomenon, and he challenged me to take over.

"In a few weeks, I had succeeded by introducing a radically new hypothesis. I preserved the *random walk* hypothesis, that the market is like a lottery or a casino, with prices going up or down as if determined by the throw of dice. I also preserved the *efficient market* hypothesis, that the market's collective wisdom takes account of all available information, hence, the price tomorrow and on any day thereafter will *on the average* equal today's price. The third basis of the usual model is the hypothesis that price changes follow the Gaussian distribution. All these hypotheses, due to Louis Bachelier,[1] were first faced seriously in 1960. The resulting theory, claiming that price (or its logarithm) follows a Brownian motion, would be mathematically convenient, but it badly fails to fit the data. First of all, the records of throws of a die appear unchanged statistically, but in comparison, the records of competitive price changes 'look *non*stationary'; they involve countless configurations that seem too striking to be attributable to mere chance. A related observation: the histograms of price changes are very far from the Galton ogive; they are long-tailed to an astonishing degree, due to large excursions whose size is obviously of the highest interest.

"My model replaces the customary Gaussian hypothesis with a more general one, while allowing the population variance of the price changes to be infinite. The model is time-variant, but it creates endless configurations; it accounts for all the data, including both the seemingly nonstationary features, and the seemingly nonrandom large excursions.

"A visiting professorship of economics at Harvard, 1962-1963, was triggered by a preprint that covered cotton and diverse commodities and securities. Also, my paper was immediately reprinted in Cootner's book along with two discussions of it[2-4] and must have affected my becoming Fellow of the Econometric Society. However, after a few further forays[5] my interest was drawn irresistibly away from economics, and toward the very different task of creating the new fractal geometry of nature.[6,7] Having learned to live with the unprecedented infinite variance syndrome had trained me to identify telltale signs of divergence in the most diverse other contexts, and to account for them suitably.

"By its style, my work on prices remains unique in economics: while all the other models borrow the final formulas of physics, I lean on its basic mental tool (invariance principles) and deduce totally new formulas appropriate to the fact that prices are not subjected to inertia. My work is also unique in its power: the huge bodies of data that it fits involve constant jumps and swings, but I manage to fit everything without postulating that the rules themselves shift and change. Thus, my models are acknowledged as having opened a path toward a new and more realistic economics. Nevertheless, the progress of this new economics is slow, due to inherent mathematical difficulties and to my failure to push its development. All too often (though with notable exceptions[8,9]), a publication devoted to the totally discredited Gaussian model quotes my work to show the author's awareness of his work's limitations, and possibly to assuage his conscience."

1. **Bachelier L.** Théorie de la spéculation. *Ann. Sci. École Norm. Supér.* **III-17**:21-86, 1900.
2. **Mandelbrot B.** The variation of certain speculative prices. (Cootner P H, ed.) *The random character of stock market prices.* Cambridge, MA: MIT Press, 1964. p. 307-32.
3. **Fama E F.** Mandelbrot and the stable Paretian hypothesis. (Cootner P H, ed.) *The random character of stock market prices.* Cambridge, MA: MIT Press, 1964. p. 297-306.
4. **Cootner P H.** Comments on the variation of certain speculative prices. (Cootner P H, ed.) *The random character of stock market prices.* Cambridge, MA: MIT Press, 1964. p. 333-7.
5. **Mandelbrot B B.** Forecasts of future prices, unbiased markets, and "martingale" models. *J. Business* **39**:242-55, 1966.
6. --------------------. *Fractals: form, chance & dimension.* San Francisco, CA: W.H. Freeman, 1977. 365 p.
7. --------------------. *The fractal geometry of nature.* San Francisco, CA: W.H. Freeman. In press, 1982.
8. **Samuelson P.** Efficient portfolio selection for Pareto-Lévy investments. *J. Finan. Quant. Anal.* **2**:107-22, 1967.
9. ----------------. Efficient portfolio selection for Pareto-Lévy investments. (Stiglitz J E, ed.) *The collected scientific papers of Paul A. Samuelson.* Cambridge, MA: MIT Press, 1972. Vol. 3. p. 861-76.

Chapter

12

Law and Political Science

Constitutional issues / 325–328

Power / 329–330

Public policy / 331–332

This Week's Citation Classic

CC/NUMBER 39
SEPTEMBER 27, 1

Fiss O M. Racial imbalance in the public schools: the constitutional concepts. *Harvard Law Rev.* **78**:564-617, 1965.
[Harvard Law School, Cambridge, MA]

This paper provides a framework for analyzing the constitutional issues relating to so-called *de facto* school segregation. It explains why school boards may use racial assignments in order to eliminate the segregation, and why they are sometimes constitutionally forbidden to use geographic criteria as a method of school assignment. [The *Social Sciences Citation Index®* (*SSCI®*) indicates that this paper has been cited in over 185 publications since 1966.]

Owen M. Fiss
Yale Law School
New Haven, CT 06520

August 3, 1982

"Looking back, I am above all struck by the date: the paper was written in the fall of 1963, and published in January 1965. The date explains the genesis of the paper, the character of the analysis, and maybe even the source of its significance.

"In 1963, the civil rights movement was the most dominant force in American political life and posed the most serious challenge to the legal system. The focus was on the South, and the effort to desegregate schools of that region, but it was becoming increasingly clear that the implications of *Brown v. Board of Education* could not be contained. The movement was beginning to turn to the North and West, and though there were only a few litigated cases at that time, political controversies over school desegregation were raging in most of the major cities of the nation, looking to a judicial settlement.

"It also happened that in 1963 I was a third-year student at the Harvard Law School, enrolled in a seminar on constitutional litigation. The instructor was Paul Freund. It might have seemed, given the political events that I have described and my personal commitments,[1] that northern school desegregation would be an obvious paper topic for that seminar. The process of selecting a topic was complicated, however, by the peculiar intellectual milieu of the Harvard Law School in the early-1960s, which was not hospitable to *Brown* and the developments that it triggered. Conversation was dominated by a famous article by Herbert Wechsler, which attacked *Brown* as 'unprincipled.'[2] Most constitutional law courses were preoccupied with the case-or-controversy requirement, and other devices for limiting the judicial power. They referred to *Brown* only to demonstrate its problematic character.

"I first presented myself to Freund as a student interested, as best I can remember, in writing a paper on the concept of 'standing' in litigation involving foreign affairs. He looked at me with a measure of disbelief. I wore my passions on my sleeve. He asked what I was truly interested in and in response, almost reading off the headlines of the day's newspapers, I spoke of civil rights and the emerging crisis over northern school desegregation. He told me, as a professor sometimes should, and with the appropriate degree of indirection, that should be the subject of my paper. In the first footnote I expressed my appreciation to Freund for his help in selecting the topic and his support and advice in bringing the paper to fruition; years later, in a brief submitted in a case involving the Cincinnati schools, I was criticized for this expression of gratitude. The lawyer said that I was trying to appropriate Freund's stature in the profession in order to lend a measure of plausibility to what was but a student's dream.

"The paper was an early statement, not just for me (over the past decade I returned to the subject a number of times[3-7]), but also for the history of school desegregation law, and that might account for some of its rough edges and also for its place in the law. It was written before the Warren Court and *Brown* had been fully accepted into the professional and academic culture as legitimate; before the Supreme Court had elaborated on the substance of *Brown*; before a significant body of case law had been developed on the subject even by the lower courts; before the major civil rights legislation of the 1960s had been enacted; before a literature had been generated on the subject. At a very early point, the article provided a conceptual framework for understanding *Brown* and it identified the path the law must take in order to realize the full promise of that decision. We were on that path until 1974, though the present Supreme Court seems to be leading us in another direction altogether."

1. **Fiss O M.** A vision of the Constitution. *Harvard Civil Rights-Civil L.* **13**:243-6, 1978.
2. **Wechsler H.** Toward neutral principles of constitutional law. *Harvard Law Rev.* **73**:1-35, 1959.
3. **Fiss O M.** The Charlotte-Mecklenburg case—its significance for northern school desegregation. *Univ. Chicago Law Rev.* **38**:697-709, 1971.
4. ------------. School desegregation: the uncertain path of the law. *Phil. Publ. Aff.* **4**:3-39, 1974.
5. ------------. The jurisprudence of busing. *Law Contemp. Prob.* **39**:194-216, 1975.
6. ------------. Groups and the equal protection clause. *Phil. Publ. Aff.* **5**:107-77, 1976.
7. ------------. Inappropriateness of the intent test in equal protection cases. *Fed. Rules Decisions* **74**:276-81, 1977.

This Week's Citation Classic

Van Alstyne W W. The demise of the right-privilege distinction in constitutional law. *Harvard Law Rev.* **81**:1439-64, 1968. [Duke Law School, Durham, NC]

A critical review is presented of a century-old paradox: How can a government barred by the Bill of Rights from directly abridging basic freedoms nonetheless require a waiver of those freedoms by those with whom it deals as employer, contractor, licensor, and welfare administrator? [The *Science Citation Index*® *(SCI*®*)* **and the** *Social Sciences Citation Index*™ *(SSCI*™*)* **indicate that this paper has been cited over 265 times since 1968.]**

William Van Alstyne
College of William and Mary
Marshall-Wythe School of Law
Williamsburg, VA 23185

March 17, 1978

"This article has been cited a good deal most probably because it is short, published in the most widely-circulated law journal in this country, and deals with a constitutional issue affecting a vast number of people in this new age of The Administrative State. It was written as one of several pieces during a 'year off' as a faculty fellow at the Yale Law School. I wrote it from some professional concern with the importance of the issues it addresses, but I became interested principally from a sense of delight with the contradictory nature of several Supreme Court cases that seemed to be all riddle and no answer—a carryover from undergraduate preoccupations as a philosophy major.

"These ten years later, I have picked up the remaining pieces of the constitutional puzzle to write about a closely related problem: When (if ever) must government provide some kind of hearing to those with whom it deals through its manifold administrative powers? This article is probably better than the *Harvard Law Review* piece and is fully as important as that piece. Because it is longer, however, and because it appears in a journal of slightly less distinction (*The Cornell Law Review*), it shall surely not become a 'Citation Classic.'[1]

"After seventeen years of teaching, I find that my own best writing results from subjects I regularly teach in an institution whose ambience stimulates one's writing without demanding or quantifying it—in the 'inefficient' tradition which most people outside universities regard as indefensible and wasteful. They are quite wrong. The best work still comes from conditions of freedom, choice, and encouragement—rather than from direction, duress, and anxiety."

1. **Van Alstyne W W.** Cracks in "the new property": adjudicative due process in the administrative state. *Cornell Law Rev.* **62**:445-93, 1977.
[The *SSCI* indicates that this paper has been cited 18 times since 1977.]

This Week's Citation Classic

CC/NUMBER 37
SEPTEMBER 14, 1981

Emerson T I. Toward a general theory of the First Amendment.
Yale Law J. **72**:877-956, 1963.
[Yale Law School, New Haven, CT]

This article analyzes the values underlying the First Amendment and the goals sought to be achieved by that constitutional guarantee; discusses the role of law and legal institutions in maintaining a system of free expression; and attempts to formulate a comprehensive legal doctrine by which the First Amendment can be applied in various concrete situations. [The *Social Sciences Citation Index*® (*SSCI*®) indicates that this paper has been cited over 360 times since 1966.]

Thomas I. Emerson
Yale Law School
New Haven, CT 06520

June 23, 1981

"When I first came to teach at Yale Law School, after 13 years in various legal posts in the federal government, I was very much interested in the relation of the individual citizen to the government. Together with David Haber, I began offering a seminar in political and civil rights. The central role played by the First Amendment in our system of individual rights soon became apparent and I began to concentrate in that area.

"At that time, no legal scholar had undertaken to write a general survey of the First Amendment since Zechariah Chafee's *Free Speech in the United States*, published in 1941.[1] I decided to fill this gap. In 1960, I had a sabbatical year and went to Washington to work on the project. I started at the beginning, that is, with the historical background of the First Amendment. After months of work, mainly in the Library of Congress, Leonard Levy's *Legacy of Suppression* appeared in the bookstores.[2] The Levy book covered the same ground as my research, and I was clearly preempted. I went back to New Haven virtually empty-handed.

"Since my next sabbatical was not due for six years, I decided to prepare the introductory chapter of my magnum opus and publish it as a law journal article. The project kept expanding in the writing but I finally finished it during the summer of 1962. To my dismay, the student editors of the *Yale Law Journal* were at first reluctant to accept the article; they thought it was 'too bland,' by which they meant not sufficiently 'legal.' In the end, however, they relented.

"I think the reason the article has been cited so frequently is that it provides a useful survey of the functions served by the First Amendment in a democratic society and offers an understandable legal theory based upon a distinction between 'expression' and 'action.' In addition, as the misgivings of the *Journal* editors suggest, the article can be understood not only by lawyers but by the general reader.

"In 1966, the article was published as a book by Random House, and it has been cited frequently in that form.[3] After another sabbatical in 1967-1968, I completed the original project, a book which treats the Supreme Court's First Amendment decisions in detail up to the end of the Warren Court. This has been published under the title *The System of Freedom of Expression*.[4]

"The original article remains current so far as the theoretical treatment of the First Amendment is concerned, but neither that article nor the *System* book keeps up with the Supreme Court decisions. For a current account of the Court's cases, the best source is Laurence Tribe's treatise, *American Constitutional Law*."[5]

1. **Chafee Z.** *Free speech in the United States.* Cambridge, MA: Harvard University Press, 1941. 634 p.
2. **Levy L W.** *Legacy of suppression.* Cambridge, MA: Harvard University Press, 1960. 353 p.
3. **Emerson T I.** *Toward a general theory of the First Amendment.* New York: Random House, 1966. 245 p. [The *SSCI*® indicates that this book has been cited over 150 times since 1966.]
4. ----------------. *The system of freedom of expression.* New York: Random House, 1970. 754 p.
5. **Tribe L H.** *American constitutional law.* Mineola, NY: Foundation Press, 1978. 1204 p.

CC/NUMBER 52
DECEMBER 26, 1983

This Week's Citation Classic™

Galanter M. Why the "haves" come out ahead: speculations on the limits of legal change. *Law & Society Review* **9**:95-160, 1974.
[Faculty of Law and Jurisprudence, State University of New York, Buffalo, NY]

Patterns of litigation, legal services, legal institutions, and legal rules are traced to the pervasive effects of differences in the capabilities of disputing parties—especially the differences between recurrent (usually organizational) users of the system and occasional (usually individual) users. [The *Social Sciences Citation Index*® (*SSCI*®) indicates that this paper has been cited in over 155 publications since 1974, making it the most-cited article published in this journal to date.]

M. Galanter
Law School
University of Wisconsin
Madison, WI 53706

November 22, 1983

"This paper was the serendipitous product of a delightful semester in 1970 when I was a fellow of Yale Law School's short-lived but amazingly productive soft-money Program on Law and Modernization. The original crystal of this paper—a juxtaposition of observations from the handful of then available empirical studies of litigation—came to me while having a drink with some colleagues before an evening meeting. I stopped by my office and typed a couple of pages of notes. These grew into a well-received seminar presentation. The paper seemed to strike a responsive chord; many readers brought me examples and suggested extensions. All sorts of observations seemed to attach themselves to the crystal. (The ambitious theoretical piece on different kinds of legal knowledge that I expected to complete that semester was put aside. It's still unfinished—I periodically resolve to return to it!)

"As this paper went through successive drafts over the next couple of years, it was rejected by all the leading law reviews and a couple of political science journals as well. (Just recently I met a prominent scholar who told me appreciatively how he assigned this paper to his students every year. He was disbelieving when I reminded him that as an editor of a renowned law review, he had rejected it. I recalled his letter especially because he had written that 'although fascinating and well written' the paper controverted 'what we can observe' about the legal system.)

"I was about to take over as editor of the *Law & Society Review*. Even my predecessor diplomatically said the paper was too long to consider during his final year. Although I would have preferred that it appear independently of my editorship, I knew the *Review* would be a good place for it and wondered how I might get it in. A wise friend suggested that I invite a guest editor to organize a symposium into which this paper would fit. That's how it got published. The symposium on litigation and dispute processing, by the way, turned out to be pathbreaking and influential in focusing research on this area.

"When I began this paper, I had just started to do some teaching about American law. For a dozen years, almost all of my research and writing had been on India. Although India is hardly mentioned in the paper, my Indian work was a real, if ghostly, presence in it. My years of immersion in Indian law, I like to think, emboldened me to discard much of the received view of how legal systems work and to develop a fresh perspective from which to view the legal process in America.

"This paper is often cited to acknowledge the terms 'repeat player' and (less often) 'one shotter' that have been widely used to refer to recurrent and occasional users of legal process. There have been a number of attempts to test hypotheses drawn from the paper. I've seen it cited for various general and specific observations about the legal system. Often, I suspect, citation is a shorthand invocation of an approach that emphasizes the capabilities and goals of the 'customers' who use legal institutions, rather than the concerns of the professionals who staff them.

"Occasionally, I'm frustrated to see it cited rather than other work of mine more relevant to the matter at hand. But I am naturally pleased at the continuing appeal of this paper even as litigation studies have become more sophisticated.[1] The ideas it elaborates continue to animate my work (see, for example, reference 2). (I have become aware of its flaws and have considered improving and enlarging it. I had a contract to turn it into a small book but delayed so long that I ended up returning the advance. So this may never get done.)"

1. **Grossman J B & Trubek D M,** eds. Special issue on dispute processing and civil litigation. (Whole issue.) *Law & Society Review* **15**(3-4), 1980-81. 529 p.
2. **Galanter M.** Justice in many rooms: courts, private ordering, and indigenous law. *J. Legal Pluralism* **19**:1-47, 1981.

CC/NUMBER 14
APRIL 5, 1982

Bachrach P & Baratz M S. Two faces of power. *Amer. Polit. Sci. Rev.* **56**:947-52, 1962. [Bryn Mawr College, Bryn Mawr, PA]

One face of power is participation in decision making, in resolution of political issues. The second face is the capability, primarily through manipulation of the prevailing mobilization of bias, to keep grievances about the current allocation of values from becoming political issues. [The *Social Sciences Citation Index®* **(*SSCI®*) indicates that this paper has been cited over 170 times since 1966.]**

Peter Bachrach
Department of Political Science
Temple University
Philadelphia, PA 19122
and
Morton Baratz
26745 New Hampshire Avenue
Brookville, MD 20833

February 2, 1982

"The joint effort that led to 'Two faces of power' and beyond began inauspiciously. Although each of us had read a substantial portion of the relevant literature and had added something to it, each was only semiliterate in the other's primary discipline; one was more interested in what 'ought to be' and the other in what 'is,' and each was inclined to defend stubbornly his positivist or normative predilections. Moreover, unlike so many other scholarly collaborators who join for the explicit purpose of producing published research, we formed our federation primarily to teach ourselves as well as our students. In other words, our initial objective copied that self-described by Robert A. Dahl and Charles E. Lindblom[1] at the start of their collaboration in the late-1940s: we aim to teach one another enough about our respective disciplines so that either could thereafter teach the course alone.

"In the process of teaching the course the second time we decided to try to put on paper what we had learned in the classroom. In no period before or since that time has either of us experienced such intellectual excitement, such joy of discovery. Prodding each other in and out of the classroom (often reducing our students to mere spectators), we formulated careful distinctions among power and its several correlates; enlarged and reformulated the concept 'mobilization of bias' as a principal source for nondecision making (which constitutes the 'second face of power'); and showed by reference to their own writing that pluralists such as Dahl and 'elitists' such as Floyd Hunter and C. Wright Mills had overlooked evidence that, because it confirmed the existence of *both* faces of power, denied their own conclusions.

"Beginning the day after commencement, we needed fewer than 30 calendar days to write the final version of the article. Most of its substance had already been assembled in our minds. To flesh out the argument we drew upon both the scholarly literature and our personal experience in the political microcosm that was Bryn Mawr College. One key illustration in the article is based upon what actually happened to one of us during a faculty meeting.

"We are unable to say with certainty why the article has attracted so much attention, although we felt certain when it was published that it would draw notice after the passage of a few years. That forecast proved accurate for a reason we could not predict: the middle- and late-1960s were a time of intense intellectual and political ferment at home and abroad. For many persons, covering a variety of political persuasions, 'Two faces of power' effectively explained certain events and, just as importantly, certain nonevents.

"Perhaps our greatest satisfaction about the article is that it provoked sharp criticism from pluralists (for example, the *American Political Science Review* thought it appropriate to publish criticisms of the article, all from a pluralist perspective, three different times, over the course of several years) and from the left by both Marxists and non-Marxists. From this body of criticism has evolved a deeper and more useful conception of political power, as is evidenced by Steven Lukes's *Power: A Radical View*[2] and John Gaventa's *Power and Powerlessness*."[3]

1. **Dahl R A & Lindblom C E.** *Politics, economics, and welfare.* Chicago: University of Chicago Press, 1976. p. xvi.
2. **Lukes S.** *Power: a radical view.* New York: Macmillan, 1974. 64 p.
3. **Gaventa J.** *Power and powerlessness.* Oxford: Clarendon Press, 1980. 267 p.

CC/NUMBER 45
NOVEMBER 7, 1983

This Week's Citation Classic

Lindblom C E. The science of "muddling through."
Public Admin. Rev. **19**:79-88, 1959.
[Yale University, New Haven, CT]

Incremental decision making (consisting of a specified set of interlocked strategies) is contrasted with decision making as envisaged by conventional (at that date) decision theory. Incrementalism is argued to be feasible and useful; the ideologized decision making of conventional theory is not. [The *Science Citation Index*® (*SCI*®) and the *Social Sciences Citation Index*® (*SSCI*®) indicate that this paper has been cited in over 490 publications since 1961.]

Charles E. Lindblom
Institution for Social and Policy Studies
Yale University
New Haven, CT 06520

October 6, 1983

"In *Politics, Economics, and Welfare,* R.A. Dahl and I in 1953 had introduced incremental decision making as an only moderately significant concept for understanding a method of decision making, an aspect of politics, and especially a key feature of democratic politics.[1] In doing so, we were influenced—more than we realized at the time, I would now guess—by Karl Popper's concept of piecemeal social engineering.[2] If I recall correctly, my subsequent interest in returning to the concept and making more of it was stimulated by a 1956 conference in which conferees tried to explain national differences in antitrust policy, to which discussion I offered the explanation that incremental policy-making ties each nation to its own peculiar past. Stimulated by that discussion, I tried my hand at an academic article or two on incrementalism[3] and was then invited by William B. Shore, executive editor of the *Public Administration Review,* to develop the concept less academically for his readers.

"I thank Shore for two contributions that account in some large part for the success of the article. He urged me to write what I had to say as simply and clearly as possible and with less of the abstraction that characterized my more academic paper(s) that he had seen on the subject. He also proposed the remarkable title under which the paper was published in *Public Administration Review.*

"Another explanation for the success of the article was—and is—the state of social science then and now. Although the reception of my work on incrementalism gives me pleasure, what I wrote represents no great discovery or insight. Incrementalism is a common, though not universal, obvious feature and useful method of policy-making, as well as personal decision making. Only a careless—at the same time overly tidy—and pretentious social science could have developed a conventional view of decision making so naive that incrementalism could strike many as a great clarification of decision strategies. I believe that none of my children saw anything noteworthy in the article or in the concept of incrementalism until their education had confused their earlier commonsense insights.

"Professional discussion of incrementalism, from my hand or from anyone else's, though never ending, has rarely been distinguished on any account. In particular, scholars have attributed to me a variety of forms of the concept of incrementalism strange to me (for which I am foolishly grateful despite irritation that they write before reading). I have tried to straighten out confusions in the literature, including large ones of my own making, in 'Still muddling, not yet through,'[4] invited by the editor of the journal to celebrate the twentieth birthday of the original article."

1. **Dahl R A & Lindblom C E.** *Politics, economics, and welfare: planning and politico-economic systems resolved into basic social processes.* New York: Harper, 1953. 557 p.
2. **Popper K R.** *The open society and its enemies. Volume 1. The spell of Plato.* Princeton, NJ: Princeton University Press, 1963. 351 p.
3. **Lindblom C E.** The handling of norms in policy analysis. *The allocation of economic resources: essays in honor of Bernard Francis Haley.* Stanford, CA: Stanford University Press, 1959. p. 160-79.
4. ------------------. Still muddling, not yet through. *Public Admin. Rev.* **39**:517-26, 1979.

This Week's Citation Classic

Lineberry R L & Fowler E P. Reformism and public policies in American cities. *Amer. Polit. Sci. Rev.* **61**:701-16, 1967.
[University of Texas, TX and York University, Toronto, Ontario, Canada]

Municipal reform created institutions (chiefly manager government, nonpartisan elections, and at large constituencies) designed to change the relationship between citizens and policymaking. Using various measures, we found that the 'responsiveness' of city governments with reformed institutions to socioeconomic cleavages in the population is lower in cities with reformed than in cities with unreformed institutions. [The *Social Sciences Citation Index*® **(***SSCI*®**) indicates that this paper has been cited in over 160 publications since 1967. Of the many papers published in this journal, this one ranked 4th in the** *SSCI* **analyses covering 1969-80.]**

Robert L. Lineberry
Office of the Dean
College of Liberal Arts and Sciences
University of Kansas
Lawrence, KS 66045
and
Edmund P. Fowler
Glendon College of York University
Toronto, Ontario M4N 3M6
Canada

March 25, 1982

"In the fall of 1965 we were enrolled in a graduate seminar at the University of North Carolina, Chapel Hill, taught by Robert Daland. Dawson and Robinson's 1963 article[1] on state spending and political climate, and Banfield and Wilson's 1963 book, *City Politics*,[2] had attracted our attention, and the idea of doing a quantitative analysis of urban policy 'outputs' attracted us. We asked Daland if we could do a joint paper. Daland liked the results and advised submission to *American Political Science Review.* Just before we had finalized our revision, though, *American Political Science Review* published a paper by Wolfinger and Field which traveled much similar ground.[3] A little discouraged, we went back to the computer for more analysis. (Then, computer based research in political science was primitive and 'turnaround times' of 36-48 hours were not uncommon.)

"The political science department at Chapel Hill was located in the old medical school; graduate student offices were in the old cadaver rooms and dog runs. Working there late one night poring over sets of multiple regressions, we noticed that 'multiple R's' between socioeconomic variables and spending-taxing levels were consistently higher in unreformed than reformed cities. One of us remarked: 'That's just the way the reformers would have wanted it.' Thus, serendipitously was born the idea that reforming local governments was associated with lessened 'responsiveness' to their populations. Rewritten, the paper went off to *American Political Science Review.*

"Three reviews came back. One reviewer simply said that it was one of the best papers he had seen in years; another wrote ten pages of detailed and bitter criticism; the third was dispassionate and recommended publication after minor revisions. Editor Austin Ranney tentatively accepted it and we went back to our revision, our job searches, and our dissertations. After the paper came out, Ranney sent us a letter from Wolfinger, critical to the core, which he planned to publish, and invited our response. 'Never fear,' his cover letter noted to these young scholars being attacked by one of the major figures in empirical political science, 'of such exchanges is fame constructed.'

"The article struck a responsive chord and (to our surprise) became a *Citation Classic* because it dealt with an important theoretical issue in the field—the impact of reformism—using the quantitative techniques which captured the imagination of, even dazzled, political scientists at the time. It melded, one might say, historicism with empiricism. The article was far from favorably received; many theoretical and methodological critiques were launched against it, some very well taken. Despite its many weaknesses, we should still be willing to argue that it was right, even if sometimes for the wrong reasons. Perhaps sometime in our careers, we might produce something else as widely cited as what came to be called in the urban politics field 'LineberryandFowler.' "

1. **Dawson R E & Robinson J A.** Inter-party competition, economic variables, and welfare policies in the American states. *J. Politics* **25**:265-89, 1963.
2. **Banfield E C & Wilson J Q.** *City politics.* Cambridge, MA: Harvard University Press, 1963. 362 p.
3. **Wolfinger R & Field J O.** Political ethos and the structure of city government. *Amer. Polit. Sci. Rev.* **60**:306-26, 1966.

CC/NUMBER 15
APRIL 11, 1983

This Week's Citation Classic

Lowi T J. *The end of liberalism: ideology, policy, and the crisis of public authority.* New York: Norton, 1969. 322 p.
[University of Chicago, IL]

A new liberal state was established during and after the New Deal, and it grew immensely in size and presence but without self-examination. Its particular way of using government, through broad delegation and interest representation, is undermining liberalism itself. What is left is a powerful apparatus run by career administrators and controlled by special interests hiding behind an optimistic but increasingly irrelevant liberal rhetoric. It is the second republic of the US, and in character it is 'a state of permanent receivership.' [The *Social Sciences Citation Index* **(***SSCI*®**) indicates that this book has been cited in over 615 publications since 1969.]**

Theodore J. Lowi
Department of Government
Cornell University
Ithaca, NY 14853

February 23, 1983

"This was not the book I set out to write. In 1964, I had published a book[1] on New York City in which I proposed a theory of politics critical of the liberal pluralist model prevailing at that time. I argued that analysis must begin with the institutions of government ('the state') and move out from there to politics. The politics of groups and interests, I argued, takes its shape from the state, not the other way around. I had located three (eventually four) distinct areas of government activity (types of public policy), and I was able to show that some important political attributes were distributed very differently from one area to the other. I called my theory 'arenas of power' and argued that in any political system there will be several areas of government activity; that each will develop its own distinctive arena of power; and that of the four identified in US contexts, only one arena fit the classical pluralist model.

"To pursue the theory further, I turned from cities to national policies and published several articles advancing the theory and reporting empirical results. By 1967, more convinced than ever that a theory of politics must begin with 'the state,' or its policies, I took leave on a Guggenheim and set out for Paris—where else?—to write *Arenas of Power*. As the writing progressed, I discovered that the liberal administrations of the 1930s and 1960s had a definite preference in their use of the state, that this preference shaped their choice of policies, and that their policies were producing forms of politics antagonistic to their own goals. That is to say, I was getting a confirmation of my theory that the state creates its own politics, but I was becoming so alarmed by the real world it was revealing to me that I abandoned the analytic book in favor of the normative, critical essay that became *The End of Liberalism*.

"I have continued to work on *Arenas of Power*. Since the articles published from it have been widely cited,[2,3] *Arenas of Power* has become one of the best-known unpublished books in political science. And I continue to see *The End of Liberalism* as volume II of this endeavor. I cannot explain why *The End of Liberalism* is widely cited; my publisher tells me it is something of an underground best-seller. (A new edition of the book appeared in 1979.[4]) My guess is that it hit a highly responsive chord because it was one of the first books of its time to discover, or rediscover, 'the state' as a real political force. America had for 150 years been a stateless society. American political science had developed around a stateless political theory, and this was the essence of realism only as long as reality continued to be relatively stateless. Reality changed after the 1930s. I suppose I helped bring political science around to the realization."

1. **Lowi T J.** *At the pleasure of the mayor: patronage and power in New York City, 1898-1958.* New York: Free Press of Glencoe, 1964. 272 p.
2. ----------. American business, public policy, case-studies, and political theory. *World Polit.* **16**:677-715, 1964. [The *SSCI* indicates that this paper has been cited in over 220 publications since 1966.]
3. ----------. Four systems of policy, politics, and choice. *Public Admin. Rev.* **32**:298-310, 1972. [The *SSCI* indicates that this paper has been cited in over 60 publications since 1972.]
4. ----------. *The end of liberalism: the second republic of the United States.* New York: Norton, 1979. 331 p.

Chapter

13

Miscellaneous

This Week's Citation Classic

NUMBER 42
OCTOBER 15, 1979

Berelson B & Steiner G A. *Human behavior: an inventory of scientific findings.* New York: Harcourt, Brace & World, 1964. 712 p.

This book is a comprehensive attempt to summarize those findings of the behavioral sciences for which some substantial body of scientific evidence exists, by current standards. The findings are arranged in 1-2-3-4 order, and organized by the major topics of the field. Most findings have supporting evidence and illustrations. [The *Science Citation Index® (SCI®)* **and the** *Social Sciences Citation Index ™ (SSCI ™)* **indicate that this book has been cited over 330 times since 1964.]**

Bernard Berelson
7 Ardsley Terrace
Irvington on Hudson
New York, NY 10533

August 6, 1979

"In effect, this book was born at a lunch at the University of Chicago in Fall 1957, when Allen Wallis, then dean of the Business School, was formally introducing me to social science colleagues as a new member of the School's faculty. Someone asked what it was exactly that I was going to do in a business school—certainly not my field—and before I could reply Allen said: 'He's going to tell us what's true in the behavioral sciences.' That was such a shocker that there was no need for any further response from me, but on the way back to the office I kept thinking: Why not?

"That was the genesis of the idea. I began experimental work on the sociological side, and with the help of James Lonie at the School, found my way to Gary Steiner, who immediately saw the challenge and joined up to cover the psychological material.

"I have always believed that such a book could be done, indeed conceived, only by people like us who were marginal to the disciplines covered. I was a trained librarian, of all things, without a single formal course in any behavioral science let alone a degree. Gary was an authentic Ph.D. in psychology but he had 'gone downtown' into a commercial career. If a proper disciplinarian worked along this line, the outcome would be the traditional text—whose subject is the discipline rather than the behavior.

"That was also reflected in the use of the book, predicted by both the publishers and ourselves. Namely, that it would have difficulty in displacing the traditional disciplinary text by some form of 'survey' course but that it would do well in the 'marginal' settings of professional schools and junior colleges, not to mention as a trade book, where the interest was less on the discipline as such than on the (more or less) verified and communicable knowledge. (I used to hear of hard-pressed university lecturers withholding the book from students but using it themselves, but much of that must have been apocryphal!)

"By now the book is long out of print, and surely out of date (though a few years ago the chairman of a major department told me that in his discipline the bibliography would change but not the findings!). In the original volume (not the summary version), there were 1,045 findings about human behavior that we thought had some decent claim to substantiation. (In early talks about the book, having already compressed a gigantic literature, I used to offer a 3-proposition grand summary: (1) some do, some don't; (2) the differences aren't very great; and (3) it's more complicated than that.) The book has been cited, I suppose, because it provides an easy way to refer to material, particularly from a neighboring field."

CC/NUMBER 11
MARCH 12, 1984

This Week's Citation Classic™

Annett M. A classification of hand preference by association analysis. *Brit. J. Psychol.* **61**:303-21, 1970.
[Department of Psychology, University of Hull, UK]

An association analysis was made of the responses of young adults to a hand preference questionnaire. Many patterns of preference were distinguished and there were no marked differences between adjacent classes. These findings are believed to demonstrate that hand preference is distributed continuously and not discretely. When it is necessary to classify handedness, the preference continuum can be divided at several levels of discrimination. A second study of hand preference and manual speed showed that it is possible to order the main preference groups for asymmetry of manual skill. Some of the problems in studies of laterality are examined as possible consequences of the treatment of a continuous distribution as if it were discrete. [The *Social Sciences Citation Index*® (*SSCI*®) indicates that this paper has been cited in over 185 publications since 1970.]

Marian Annett
Department of Applied Social Studies
Coventry (Lanchester) Polytechnic
Coventry CV1 5FB
UK

December 30, 1983

"My research on laterality began almost by accident when my plans to continue doctoral work on conceptual thinking were not supported. It was relatively easy to collect data on hand preference by questionnaire on an occasional and part-time basis when my children were small, and my husband's developing career enabled me to collect data in several places: Oxford, Sheffield, Aberdeen, and Hull. At the University of Hull, I was appointed honorary research associate and offered the facilities necessary for seeking external funding. The cited work was supported by the Medical Research Council, UK.

"During the 1960s, I used whatever opportunities came my way to collect data from large and complete samples of students, schoolchildren, and recruits, in groups where volunteer effects would be absent or minimal. I wanted to know what proportion of the population is consistently left-handed for all important actions and what proportion is mixed-handed, preferring the right hand for some and the left hand for other actions. About 30 percent of subjects in several samples were found to be mixed-handed, and three to four percent consistently left-handed. It seemed to me extraordinary, and it still does, that the fact that about one-third of the population is mixed-handed is generally ignored in laterality research.

"By the late 1960s, with questionnaire data on over 2,000 subjects, an analysis could be made of patterns of mixed-handedness. The question was whether it is possible to make clear distinctions between mixed-handers, to say that some are *really* right-handers and some are *really* left-handers. At the suggestion of J.P.N. Phillips, the technique used was association analysis, as developed by botanists[1,2] interested in meaningful distinctions in plant ecology. A computer program was written for me by M.J. Norman, of the University of Hull, Sub-Department of Computation. The analysis produced a multitude of patterns, and no evidence of any hitherto obscure subdivision. The item most correlated with all others turned out to be hammering, with writing only just behind.

"The analysis was an important stage in the development of my Right Shift Theory,[3] since it convinced me that hand preferences are distributed continuously, and it led to the discovery that the continuum of preference can be reliably coordinated with the continuum differences between the hands in skill. The coordination, first demonstrated in the cited paper, was confirmed in later work, and is the foundation of several further discoveries, summarized in a book just completed.[4]

"The paper is most often cited for its appendix, the questionnaire. It is occasionally cited as evidence for the continuity of the hand preference distribution, but this uncomfortable fact is still not accommodated in most current approaches to laterality."

1. **Williams W T & Lambert J M.** Multivariate methods in plant ecology. I. Association-analysis in plant communities. *J. Ecology* **47**:83-101, 1959.
2. **Williams W T.** Citation Classic. Commentary on *J. Ecology* **47**:83-101, 1959. *Current Contents/Agriculture, Biology & Environmental Sciences* **13**(16):16, 19 April 1982.
3. **Annett M.** The distribution of manual asymmetry. *Brit. J. Psychol.* **63**:343-58, 1972. (Cited 100 times.)
4. ------------. *Left, right, hand and brain: the Right Shift Theory.* Submitted for publication.

CC/NUMBER 37
SEPTEMBER 12, 1983

This Week's Citation Classic

Keele S W. Movement control in skilled motor performance.
Psychol. Bull. **70**:387-403, 1968.
[University of Oregon, Eugene, OR]

The duration of target directed movements depends on several factors including distance and accuracy and is described by Fitts's law.[1] The law depends on the accuracy of component movements and the time to process visual feedback. Series of movements are controlled by motor programs. [The *Science Citation Index*® (*SCI*®) and the *Social Sciences Citation Index*® (*SSCI*®) indicate that this paper has been cited in over 160 publications since 1968.]

Steven W. Keele
Department of Psychology
University of Oregon
Eugene, OR 97403

June 30, 1983

"The successful scientist is usually regarded as one who makes an important theoretical or empirical discovery. But sometimes a timely review, bringing the ideas of others to the attention of a wider body of scientists, makes a useful contribution. This was the case with my review. I started the paper at Michael Posner's suggestion when I was a postdoctoral fellow just out of Wisconsin and studying with him at the University of Oregon. The time was right for a review of motor control. Motor control research was on the verge of resurgence, but many interested parties were unaware of important background work.

"The area was just emerging from domination by behaviorism and neobehaviorism. Those schools concerned themselves with factors that influence motor learning (e.g., distribution of practice), but were little concerned with the *processes* of motor control. Although very early psychologists, such as Woodworth (1899),[2] were concerned with motor processes, their analyses fell to the wayside only to reemerge in the 1950s and 1960s with development of an information processing orientation throughout psychology. In the motor domain it was led by people like Paul Fitts[1] and E.R.F.W. Crossman.[3] Psychologists needed to know about the dormant ideas of important investigators working around the turn of the century and the recent reawakening of the process view. The timeliness of my review was a major reason for its success.

"Rather shocking to most authors, I am sure, is how little readers may extract from a long labor of love and how, eventually, the memory of an article (or even a book) becomes reduced to a catchy phrase or two. This happened with my article. I emphasized the concept of a motor program—the concept that a pattern of motor activity could be centrally represented and activated without the absolute necessity of peripheral feedback. The majority of people citing the article quote a single sentence that summarized the program concept. Despite the compression to a single sentence, the program concept marked a dramatic departure from conditioning and reflex conceptions of motor control.

"However, a number of people did attend to other issues in the review. Of particular interest was Fitts's description of how movement time increased logarithmically with both movement distance *and* movement precision. Recently many theories have been invoked to explain Fitts's law. Interestingly, most of them make reference to a seminal theory by Crossman which was never published and might have gone largely unnoticed were it not in my review. The review also showed how estimates of processing time for visual feedback, investigated by Posner and myself, meshed very nicely with Crossman's theory. On rarer occasions yet, some people discovered a few other gems in the historical literature as a result of the review.

"Keeping one's eyes open to important discoveries of others and helping publicize them is still a useful contribution. Thirteen years after the original review, I again reviewed much of the field of motor control from a psychologist's viewpoint,[4] and another more up-to-date but somewhat different review will soon appear."[5]

1. **Fitts P M & Peterson J R.** Information capacity of discrete motor responses. *J. Exp. Psychol.* **67**:103-12, 1964.
2. **Woodworth R S.** The accuracy of voluntary movement. (Whole issue.) *Psychol. Rev. Monogr. Suppl.* (13),1899. 114 p.
3. **Crossman E R F W & Goodeve P J.** Feedback control of hand-movement and Fitts' Law. Paper presented at the meeting of the Experimental Psychology Society, Oxford, July 1963. *Quart. J. Exp. Psych. A—Hum. Exp. P.* **35**:251-78, 1983.
4. **Keele S W.** Behavioral analysis of movement. (Brooks V B, ed.) *Handbook of physiology. Section 1: The nervous system. Vol. II. Motor control, part 2.* Bethesda, MD: American Physiological Society, 1981. p. 1391-414.
5. --------------. Motor control. (Boff K R, ed.) *Handbook of perception and performance.* New York: Wiley. To be published.

CC/NUMBER 16
APRIL 19, 1982

This Week's Citation Classic

Locke E A. Toward a theory of task motivation and incentives. *Organ. Behav. Hum. Perform.* **3**:157-89, 1968. [American Institutes for Research, Washington, DC]

This paper summarizes research on the relationship between goals and task performance. The results indicate that hard goals lead to a higher level of performance than easy goals and that specific, hard goals lead to better performance than 'do your best' goals. It is also argued that money, time limits, feedback, participation, and praise may affect performance through their effects on goal setting. [The *Social Sciences Citation Index®* **(***SSCI®***) indicates that this paper has been cited over 175 times since 1968.]**

Edwin A. Locke
College of Business and Management
and
Department of Psychology
University of Maryland
College Park, MD 20742

February 18, 1982

"I was fortunate to work in graduate school (at Cornell University) with T.A. Ryan and Patricia C. Smith, who had argued that the simplest way to look at work motivation was to view it as regulated by 'tasks,' i.e., goals. At that time, the early-1960s, there had been very little research on the effects of different goals on task performance. Therefore, I decided to do my doctoral thesis on this topic. The results were very positive, and I continued this line of research after I got my first job at the American Institutes for Research, supported by a grant from the Office of Naval Research.

"Again the results were very positive. My main problem at that time was getting the research published, since psychology was still dominated by behaviorism which asserted that behavior could be understood without reference to the mind. I recall one editor (of the *Journal of Experimental Psychology*) turning down a goal setting article on the alleged grounds of an inadequate experimental design. I then redesigned the study, did it over, got the same results, and resubmitted it. It was turned down again on the grounds that psychology had given up old-fashioned 'mentalistic' concepts (like 'goal') long ago. I then sent the editor the original rejection letter to show him the contradiction; he angrily evaded the whole issue and that was the last time I sent anything to that journal.

"Other journals, however, were more open to ideas that challenged the status quo. And each published article made it easier to get subsequent ones published. The 1968 article was written after more than a dozen successful goal setting studies had been conducted and published and was based on these studies plus the few others that I could find. The article has been widely cited because it was the first to extensively document the efficacy of the technique of goal setting. The result was an explosion of research on goal setting (summarized most recently by myself, Shaw, Saari, and Latham[1]) which has shown it to be one of the most robust and dependable of motivational phenomena. The basic findings have been replicated numerous times. Goal setting is now an element of Bandura's[2] social learning theory. The relation of goal setting to incentives (such as money and feedback) has been found to be more complex than was originally envisioned, however.

"Perhaps one of the greatest ironies in terms of consequences is that behaviorists, in a last desperate attempt to avoid extinction as a result of the cognitive revolution in psychology, are now using the very technique that they once tried to ban from the journals! They have relabeled it, of course, to try to pretend that they were for it all along. They call it 'organizational behavior modification' but the major technique they use is to assign goals and provide feedback regarding performance in relation to the goals."

1. **Locke E A, Shaw K N, Saari L M & Latham G P.** Goal setting and task performance: 1969-1980. *Psychol. Bull.* **90**:125-52, 1981.
2. **Bandura A.** *Social learning theory.* Englewood Cliffs, NJ: Prentice-Hall, 1977. 247 p.

This Week's Citation Classic

CC/NUMBER 3
JANUARY 18, 1982

Deci E L. Effects of externally mediated rewards on intrinsic motivation. *J. Personal. Soc. Psychol.* **18**:105-15, 1971. [University of Rochester, Rochester, NY]

Monetary rewards were found to decrease intrinsic motivation for the rewarded activity—puzzle solving in a laboratory experiment and headline writing in a field experiment. By contrast, positive performance feedback enhanced intrinsic motivation for the target activity in a laboratory experiment. [The *Social Sciences Citation Index*® **(***SSCI*®**) indicates that this paper has been cited over 170 times since 1971.]**

Edward L. Deci
Department of Psychology
University of Rochester
Rochester, NY 14627

November 6, 1981

"In a graduate seminar at Carnegie-Mellon University, Vic Vroom was discussing 'insufficient justification' research[1] when I realized how interesting it might be to consider the effects of different levels of justification on tasks of varying levels of initial interest. I remember being terribly excited by the question, though I did nothing with it for a year. Somewhat later Vic and I were writing the introduction for a book of readings that we were preparing for Penguin.[2] In it we were considering the motivational assumptions that underlie different theories of management. Scientific management, for example, is very extrinsic, whereas participative management is primarily intrinsic, and we raised the possibility of combining the better elements of each approach. That led to the question of whether the two types of motivation are additive; the question interested me very much.

"A few weeks later I was startled by the realization that the two questions were really the same question. With that realization came a rush of excitement and a flood of ideas. I was nearing the end of my second year of graduate school and was ready to start my dissertation; I knew then that I had found the idea and the basic structure for studying it. I did three studies that explored the question, and they were published together as the article cited above.

"I think there are several reasons why the paper has been widely cited. For one thing, it explored an idea whose time had come. Quite independently, two other groups of researchers headed by Arie Kruglanski at Tel Aviv University and Mark Lepper at Stanford University were exploring the same question. The fact that we were all working on the same question at that time was an important factor in helping to generate interest in the area. I also think the concept of intrinsic motivation is a very compelling one that has a lot of relevance to people's lives. Rich Ryan and I are finishing a book[3] in which we discuss the relevance of this area of research for education, psychotherapy, child rearing, and management. In addition, the findings from the research appeared to be contradictory to some basic tenets of the conditioning theories that were so central to psychology at that time, so a considerable controversy began. Finally, I think psychology is ready for a new field of human motivation, and the concept of intrinsic motivation holds promise. The area of research which arose following the publication of this article can be related to expectancy theory and attribution theory, which are of wide interest, but it also provides the basis for going beyond cognition to a level of analysis that is deeper in the individual and encompasses a wider range of human functions.

"Three years ago Ryan and I reviewed 50 studies on intrinsic motivation[4] that had been done since this article was published. The book we are now finishing reviews twice that number."

1. **Festinger L & Carlsmith J M.** Cognitive consequences of forced compliance. *J. Abnormal Soc. Psychol.* **58**:203-10, 1959.
2. **Vroom V H & Deci E L,** eds. *Management and motivation.* Baltimore, MD: Penguin, 1970. 399 p.
3. **Deci E L & Ryan R M.** *Intrinsic motivation and human behavior.* New York: Plenum. To be published.
4. ------------------------------. The empirical exploration of intrinsic motivational processes. (Berkowitz L, ed.) *Advances in experimental social psychology.* New York: Academic Press, 1980. Vol. 13. p. 39-80.

CC/NUMBER 12
MARCH 22, 1982

This Week's Citation Classic

Easterbrook J A. The effect of emotion on cue utilization and the organization of behavior. *Psychol. Rev.* **66**:183-201, 1959.
[Institute of Psychiatry, University of London, London, England]

This review argued that emotional arousal acts consistently to reduce the range of cues an organism uses, and that reductions in range of cue utilization from this and other causes serve to organize or disorganize action depending on the behavior observed. [The *Social Sciences Citation Index®* (*SSCI®*) **indicates that this paper has been cited over 260 times since 1966.]**

J.A. Easterbrook
Department of Psychology
University of New Brunswick
Fredericton, New Brunswick E3B 5A6
Canada

January 21, 1982

"As our 'chutes opened, our bodies swung, and the fellow from the starboard door hit my helmet with his boots. Stunned, I made a bad landing and hit my head on the ground. My 'spatio-temporal field' shrank and slowly expanded. I swear I stopped to observe this phenomenon and mark its psychological significance!

"This accident influenced the empirical generalization Dick Solomon permitted me to publish six years later. Of course, the mind had been prepared, and more work was to follow. In particular, my MA thesis research had served to generalize some observations made by D.R. Davis,[1] with G.C. Drew and others, using 'the Cambridge cockpit' during World War II—including one which I encoded in the general statement, 'Marginal acts drop out under stress.' And I had often been reminded of that notion during later field studies of military problems. For instance, people found it hard to notice or remember what had to be done outside a warm tent when -40°F air was moving at 40 mph.

"Back at university in 1957, I found the psychological literature had advanced 15 years in seven. A lot of reading was required, so I worked out a schedule. Sticking to it was difficult though. Reports touching on the 'marginal omissions' notion kept diverting me. Sometimes they linked up with one another and that excited me. Before long, I deduced that I was interested in this subject matter, should cease treating it as intrusive, and consider working on it for my doctorate. So I wrote it up and passed it on to Hans Eysenck as an introduction to a thesis proposal.

"Economic events worked out so that I never got around to testing the propositions of this paper, but did my doctorate on alcohol in relation to stress. Maybe that was for the best. Others were able to design clever tests which had not occurred to me. A character in 'Pogo' once said something like, 'You must always word the answer so as not to spoil the question.' My wording may have spoiled the questions for me.

"Apparently this was an essay whose time had come. It seems to have stimulated research and to have introduced the term 'cue utilization' into our jargon. Psychology in the late-1950s seems to have been ready for a behavioristic analysis of attention which had some compatibility with the dominant Hullian learning theory. Perhaps we also had a fondness for simplicity.

"But I think the paper also contained a kernel of truth. No doubt its proposition about proficiency needed modification to accommodate Kahneman's[2] points about in-task learning and arousal. Perhaps the implicit model also needed revision to account for voluntary attention, as Wachtel[3] suggested and Kahneman implied. In any case, such considerations finally penetrated my better judgement, and helped motivate preparation of my recent book on voluntary behavior."[4]

1. **Davis D R.** *Pilot error.* London: HMSO, 1948. Air publication 3139A.
2. **Kahneman D.** *Attention and effort.* Englewood Cliffs, NJ: Prentice-Hall, 1973. 246 p.
3. **Wachtel P L.** Anxiety, attention, and coping with threat. *J. Abnormal Psychol.* **73**:137-43, 1968.
4. **Easterbrook J A.** *The determinants of free will: a psychological analysis of responsible adjustive behavior.* New York: Academic Press, 1978. 259 p.

This Week's Citation Classic

Moyer K E. Kinds of aggression and their physiological basis.
Commun. Behav. Biol. Pt. A **2**:65-87, 1968.
[Department of Psychology, Carnegie-Mellon University, Pittsburgh, PA]

The physiological bases of aggressive behavior have been reviewed and the concept has been developed that aggression is not a unitary phenomenon. The following classes are tentatively suggested: predatory, inter-male, fear-induced, irritable, territorial, maternal, and instrumental. The physiological basis of each of these classes of aggression is examined. [The *Science Citation Index*® (*SCI*®) and the *Social Sciences Citation Index*® (*SSCI*®) indicate that this paper has been cited in over 320 publications since 1968.]

K.E. Moyer
Department of Psychology
Carnegie-Mellon University
Pittsburgh, PA 15213

June 3, 1983

"My concern with the problem of aggressive behavior began in 1966 in an attempt to understand what appeared to me to be a significant increase in senseless violence. That was the year that Richard Speck killed eight young women in a nurses' residence in Chicago; Charles Whitman climbed to the top of the clock tower of the University of Texas with a high-powered rifle and shot innocent passersby, killing 14 and injuring 31 more; and Robert Smith, a high school senior, coolly and without apparent motive shot five women and two children through the head after forcing them to lie on the floor in the form of a cartwheel.

"Initially, my motive was to find out what was known about the physiology of this bizarre hostile behavior in order to determine whether the field of physiological psychology (broadly defined) could make any contribution to the control of irrational aggressive tendencies. It can, as a later publication has shown.[1] Two descriptors characterized much of the literature on aggression at that time: confusion and contradiction. Many studies could not be replicated and results, sometimes from the same laboratory, were contradictory. There was little precise theorizing in the field partly because it was so difficult to reconcile diverse findings. It seemed clear that experimenters and theorists alike were observing quite different behaviors and referring to them as aggressive.

"The attack of a predator on its prey was labeled aggressive, as was the ritualistic contest between two males in the establishment of a dominance relationship. It was generally agreed that these two behaviors differed on a number of dimensions in spite of the fact that they were both given the same label. It became obvious that there was a need for a studied differentiation among the various aggression types.

"There were early attempts to define types of aggression by Scott[2] and Valzelli.[3] The reasons that these classifications of aggression were infrequently referred to by researchers are not clear. It may have been because the papers were not in journals in the mainstream. Thus there continued to be a need for a set of useful definitions differentiating among the various behaviors labeled aggressive. The paper 'Kinds of aggression and their physiological basis' appears to have filled that need. In general, when a concept appears at the right time and in the right place it will be frequently cited.

"A final note on the fallibility of journal editors and their boards may be in order. This paper was rejected by the editors of two major psychological journals before its eventual publication."

1. **Moyer K E.** *The psychobiology of aggression*. New York: Harper & Row, 1976. 402 p.
2. **Scott J P.** *Aggression*. Chicago: University of Chicago Press, 1958. 148 p.
   [The *SCI* and the *SSCI* indicate that this book has been cited in over 180 publications since 1961.]
3. **Valzelli L.** Drugs and aggressiveness. *Advan. Pharmacol.* **5**:79-108, 1967.
   [The *SSCI* indicates that this paper has been cited in over 55 publications since 1967.]

CC/NUMBER 2
JANUARY 11, 1982

This Week's Citation Classic

Buss A H. *The psychology of aggression.* New York: Wiley, 1961. 307 p.
[Department of Psychology, University of Pittsburgh, Pittsburgh, PA]

Aggression was construed as a subclass of punishment, and antecedents and consequences were examined. Angry aggression and instrumental aggression were distinguished, which clarified the role of frustration as a cause of aggression. An apparatus-procedure was devised for studying human aggression in the laboratory. [The *Social Sciences Citation Index*® *(SSCI*®) **indicates that this book has been cited over 450 times since 1966.]**

Arnold H. Buss
Department of Psychology
University of Texas
Austin, TX 78712

October 5, 1981

"In the 1950s while at the University of Pittsburgh, I found that there was no book on the psychology of human aggression, a topic on which I was doing research. I distinguished between angry and instrumental aggression. When angry, we are rewarded by the pain or discomfort of the victims of our aggression. When not angry, our aggression is rewarded by any of the many reinforcers that occur in everyday life (money, status, and so on); the aggression achieves the same rewards that nonaggressive responses achieve, hence the term *instrumental* aggression. Frustration, which is one of the minor causes of aggression,[1] usually leads to angry aggression. Thus the above distinction and other theoretical analyses helped to put the frustration-aggression hypothesis in proper perspective.

"I developed a new paradigm to study aggression in the laboratory. The real subject played the role of an experimenter who used electric shock to correct the mistakes of a 'learner' (ostensibly another subject but in reality a confederate who never received any shock). The real subject might use so low an intensity of shock that it would not hurt (nonaggression) or a level that would hurt (aggression). This paradigm was ethical in that it offered the subjects a rationale for aggressing (thus denying the possibility of guilt), and it was also practical and yielded quantitative data. I called it the *aggression machine.*

"Using this paradigm, I demonstrated the expected gender difference (men aggress more intensely than women) and also that male targets receive more intense aggression than do female targets. These two gender differences were especially evident in the aggression that can occur after harm has been done.[2] When men aggressed against men, there was no diminution in aggression intensity after they had previously harmed a target; in the other three gender combinations of aggression-target, aggression level dropped. In this experiment, the only one on the effect of previous harm, the subjects had no particular reason to aggress against their targets.

"In another experiment,[3] which also seems to be unique, I studied the effect of firing a target pistol on subsequent aggression (using the aggression machine). Firing a weapon had no effect on subsequent aggression, nor were people who like and use guns more aggressive than those who do not like or use guns. Guns are, of course, dangerous to have around, but evidently they do not cause *further* aggression.

"Why has the book been cited frequently? The main reason appears to be the aggression machine, which has enjoyed wide use both in its original form and in several modifications. My theoretical analysis of aggression and its causes and consequences is also well known. Finally, my book was one of the very few available on human aggression at the time."

1. **Buss A H.** Physical aggression in relation to different frustrations. *J. Abnormal Soc. Psychol.* **67**:1-7, 1963.
2. ------------. The effect of harm on subsequent aggression. *J. Exp. Res. Personal.* **1**:249-55, 1966.
3. **Buss A H, Booker A & Buss E H.** Firing a weapon and aggression. *J. Personal. Soc. Psychol.* **22**:296-302, 1972.

CC/NUMBER 25
JUNE 21, 1982

Costin F, Greenough W T & Menges R J. Student ratings of college teaching: reliability, validity, and usefulness.
Rev. Educ. Res. **41**:511-35, 1971.
[Dept. Psychology, Univ. Illinois at Urbana-Champaign, Champaign, IL]

Student ratings can provide reliable and valid information on the quality of college instruction. Such information can be useful for departmental evaluation and for helping teachers improve their performance. Various factors other than student ratings must also be considered when appraising the effectiveness of teaching. [The *Social Sciences Citation Index*® (*SSCI*®) **indicates that this paper has been cited over 195 times since 1971.]**

Frank Costin
Department of Psychology
University of Illinois
Champaign, IL 61820

March 12, 1982

"Academicians do not generally greet their departmental committee appointments with enthusiasm, especially since they often perceive them as unwelcome intrusions to scholarly activities. The circumstances under which this *Citation Classic* was conceived are therefore rather unusual, for they grew out of a committee assignment.

"In the spring of 1969 I was asked by Morton Weir, then head of the department of psychology at the University of Illinois, to chair a committee whose charge was to review critically the research on student ratings of instruction and to present conclusions concerning the usefulness of this mode of evaluation. It was anticipated that such information could help the faculty make rational decisions about the worth of student ratings, not only for improving one's teaching but also for purposes of salary increases and promotion. Joining me in the enterprise were my two colleagues, William Greenough and Robert Menges. They became valuable members of the team.

"The committee's task was timely, for much debate had been going on among our faculty concerning appropriate ways of obtaining students' opinions of instruction and its worth. Furthermore, students' demands that they be given a voice in evaluating their teachers were increasing, reflecting a national trend consistent with students' growing concern about the quality of college instruction. As elsewhere, informal, 'unofficial' student ratings of instruction were being circulated in a kind of 'underground press.' A significant number of faculty members felt that since students were already publicizing their appraisals of teaching, the use of a more systematic, research-based approach should be considered.

"Once into our task, we discovered a wealth of material for critical analysis, not only that which had already been reviewed by others but also much that had not yet been considered in any systematic fashion. It was probably inevitable that as our work progressed we began to raise questions and seek answers that went beyond our original charge. For example, although we concluded that student ratings could be reasonably reliable and that useful information concerning the teaching process could be derived from well-conceived rating systems, we also emphasized that many other factors should be considered in dealing with the broad problem of evaluating instruction. (Our article summarizes these on page 531.)

"The committee report was well received and apparently influenced a significant number of our colleagues to regard more positively the potential usefulness of student ratings of instruction and to take a greater interest in developing appropriate instruments.

"Having completed the report we decided that we had already gone a considerable distance toward filling a gap in the literature on student evaluation of instruction. Several months later, after expanding its scope, the work was accepted for publication in the *Review of Educational Research.*

"The numerous citations resulting from this publication reflect not only the concerns many college teachers and researchers have about the use of student ratings but also the importance of making available a comprehensive and critical analysis of both their advantages and limitations. The widespread and continuing interest in what we did is gratifying testimony to what a committee appointment can sometimes lead to! More recent work in the field has been reported by myself and others."[1,2]

1. **Costin F.** Do student ratings of college teachers predict student achievement? *Teach. Psychol.* **5**:86-8, 1978.
2. **Braskamp L A, Caulley D & Costin F.** Student ratings and instructor self-ratings and their relationship to student achievement. *Amer. Educ. Res. J.* **16**:295-306, 1979.

This Week's Citation Classic

CC/NUMBER 21
MAY 23, 1983

Averill J R. Personal control over aversive stimuli and its relationship to stress. *Psychol. Bull.* **80**:286-303, 1973.
[Department of Psychology, University of Massachusetts, Amherst, MA]

Three main types of control were distinguished: behavioral control (direct action on the environment), cognitive control (reducing uncertainty and imposing meaning on events), and decisional control (having a choice among alternative courses of action). Each type of control is related to stress in a complex fashion, sometimes increasing it, sometimes reducing it, and sometimes having no influence at all. [The *Science Citation Index®* **(*SCI®*) and the** *Social Sciences Citation Index®* **(*SSCI®*) indicate that this paper has been cited in over 195 publications since 1973.]**

James R. Averill
Department of Psychology
University of Massachusetts
Amherst, MA 01003

March 1, 1983

"It has long been recognized that having control over an aversive situation may mitigate stress reactions, e.g., a nervous passenger may become carefree and even reckless when behind the wheel. There are, however, several problems with this simple observation. For one thing, the concept of control is exceedingly vague. For another thing, having control does not always reduce stress; for some people on some occasions, personal control may actually have the opposite effect. The *Citation Classic* article was written to address these two issues. The original impetus for the article was a study by me and Rosenn,[1] in which complex relationships were observed among coping strategies (listening or not listening for a warning signal), the availability of a control response (being able to avoid an aversive stimulus), and anticipatory stress reactions.

"A review of other research quickly revealed that personal control sometimes has detrimental as well as beneficial effects. But with few exceptions (e.g., the famous 'executive monkeys' studied by Brady, Porter, Conrad, and Mason[2]), this fact has received relatively little attention in the psychological literature. There is a general cultural bias (which I share) that personal control is a good thing; and, according to a rather simplistic line of reasoning, what is good should not have any bad consequences, except perhaps under pathological conditions. After publication of the *Citation Classic* article, one disgruntled reader suggested that I was fostering reactionary political tendencies by insinuating that personal control can have stressful consequences. Unfortunately, this reader's reaction is not exceptional. Furedy[3] has also noted a strong bias in the psychological literature which supports the generalization that people show a strong preference for warning signals (a form of cognitive control); he cites a number of examples in which evidence contrary to this generalization has been ignored, while supporting evidence has been emphasized.

"I mention the above not simply because it illustrates a conflation of ideological and psychological issues, for that is not the major source of difficulty. Stress is a factor of considerable practical importance, e.g., in susceptibility to and recovery from illness. Strong incentives therefore exist to develop simple interventions for the alleviation of stress. The provision of personal control, even if only illusory, is one such intervention; and its beneficial effects are sometimes dramatic. However, in the rush for application, there has been a tendency to gloss over numerous ambiguities and counterinstances. One of the major ambiguities has to do with the very meaning of 'personal control.'

"Why has the *Citation Classic* article been cited so frequently? Largely, I believe, because it provides a simple scheme for organizing the various ways the concept of control has been operationalized by psychologists. Three major kinds of control were distinguished: behavioral, cognitive, and decisional or volitional. Subsequent research (e.g., Cornelius and myself[4]) has shown that these various kinds of control are not substitutable, nor are their effects additive. Rather, the various kinds of control can interact in complex ways, with one type enhancing, nullifying, or even reversing the effects of another, depending on the circumstances."

1. **Averill J R & Rosenn M.** Vigilant and nonvigilant coping strategies and psychophysiological stress reactions. *J. Personal. Soc. Psychol.* **23**:128-41, 1972.
2. **Brady J V, Porter R W, Conrad D G & Mason J W.** Avoidance behavior and the development of gastroduodenal ulcers. *J. Exp. Anal. Behav.* **1**:69-72, 1958.
3. **Furedy J J.** An integrative progress report on information control in humans: some laboratory findings and methodological claims. *Aust. J. Psychol.* **27**:61-83, 1975.
4. **Cornelius R R & Averill J R.** The influence of various types of control on psychophysiological stress reactions. *J. Res. Personal.* **14**:503-17, 1980.

Index of Authors

All authors of Citation Classics are listed. An asterisk after a page number indicates that a commentary by the author appears on that page.

Adams JS 245*
Adorno TW 194
Albert J 138
Allen KE 184*
Amir Y 239*
Amsel A 125*, 131*
Anderson JR 91*
Andrews FM 289
Anger D 132*
Annett M 336*
Argyle M 231*
Arrow KJ 318*
Atkins AL 165
Atthowe JM Jr 257*
Attneave F 135*
Auerbach AH 274
Averill JR 344*
Azrin NH 119*, 120, 260

Bachrach HM 274
Bachrach P 329*
Baer DM 108*, 251
Bailey MM 182
Bakan P 71*
Baltes PB 193*
Bamber D 79*
Bandura A 143*, 145*
Baratz MS 329*
Barker RG 106*
Barrish HH 110*
Bastien S 10
Battig WF 159*
Baumol WJ 314*
Bell RQ 19, 189*
Bellugi U 176
Bem SL 23*
Berberich JP 206
Berelson B 335*
Bergin AE 249*, 250
Berry JW 84*
Bieber I 212*
Bieber TB 212
Bieri J 165*
Bijou SW 267
Birdsall TG 81
Birley JLT 27
Blau PM 290*
Block J 198
Bolles RC 115*
Bootzin RR 258
Bousfield AK 8
Bousfield WA 8*
Bower GH 91, 142*, 147
Bowers KS 109*
Bowlby J 183*
Breger L 270*
Breitmeyer BG 80*
Briar S 165
Broadbent DE 98*, 136*
Bronfenbrenner U 190*
Brophy JE 155*
Brown R 93*, 175*, 176, 217*
Brown SC 52
Bryan JH 241*
Buchsbaum MS 209*
Buell JS 184
Buss AH 342*
Byrne D 222*

Campbell EQ 300
Carlton PL 69*
Carroll JB 157*
Catania AC 116*
Cattell RB 34*
Cautela JR 264*
Chall JS 86
Chandler M 274
Chapman JP 211*
Chapman LJ 211*
Chernery HB 318
Chow GC 39*
Clayton PJ 210
Cohen J 40*, 274
Coleman JS 300*
Collaborative Study Group 271
Cooper FS 90
Cooper JE 27
Corrigan B 45
Costin F 343*
Costner HL 36*
Cox VC 67
Craik FIM 92*
Crespi LP 127*
Crowder RG 88*
Crowne DP 24*
Cyert RM 313*

Dahrendorf R 299*
Dain HJ 212
Dale E 86*
Darley JM 240*
Davies JC 284*
Davis KE 224
Davison GC 118*
Dawes RM 45*
Day D 138
DeLo JS 10
Dean DG 282*
Dean J 231
Deaux K 228*
Deci EL 339*
Dember WN 130*
Denney R 286
Deutsch D 140*
Deutsch JA 140*
Deutsch M 235*
Dince PR 212
Donabedian A 304*

Douglas RJ 64*
Douglas VI 205*
Draper NR 41*
Drellich MG 212
Droppelman LF 18
Duncan S Jr 233*
Dunham PJ 117*
Dunn LM 202*
Dyk RB 169
D'Zurilla TJ 252*

Earl RW 130
Easterbrook JA 340*
Edwards W 48*, 312*
Emerson TI 327*
Emery FE 292*
Emswiller T 228
Epstein AN 66
Exline RV 85*
Eysenck HJ 275*

Falk JL 128*
Farrar DE 38*
Faterson HF 169
Feather NT 226*
Ferster CB 105*
Fishbein M 219*
Fiss OM 325*
Flavell JH 204
Fowler EP 331*
Foxx RM 260*
Fraser C 176*
Frenkel-Brunswik E 194

Gagné RM 154*
Galanter M 328*
Galassi JP 10*
Galassi MD 10
Ganz L 80
Garfield SL 249
Geer JH 15*
Geisser S 49
Gelder MG 265*
Gelman R 147
Gerard HB 235
Gergen KJ 58*
Gibson EJ 148*
Glaser D 303*
Glass GV 272
Glauber RR 38
Glazer N 286, 301*
Goldberg LR 51*
Goldberg PA 230
Goldberg SC 271
Goldfried MR 252
Good TL 155
Goodenough DR 169
Goodman J 177
Goodman LA 35*
Gordon HS 315*
Gorham DR 26
Gouldner AW 280*
Graham P 27
Grand HG 212
Granger CWJ 42*
Gray D 85
Greenhouse SW 49*
Greenough WT 343
Greenspoon J 129*
Griffitt W 244*
Groves PM 72*
Guetzkow H 293
Gundlach RH 212

Haan N 198*
Hake DF 119
Hall RV 158*
Haller AO 295
Halwes TG 204
Hardin G 316*
Harlow HF 151*
Harris DB 22*
Harris FR 184
Harris MB 268*
Hart B 184
Hatanaka M 42
Hawkins RP 267*
Hebb DO 68*
Herrnstein RJ 111*
Herron EW 25
Herzberg F 199*
Hess RD 179*
Heston LL 207*
Hickson DJ 291*
Hilgard ER 142
Hirschi T 302*
Hobson CJ 300
Hogarty GE 271*
Holland JL 200*
Holmes TH 30*
Holtzman WH 25*
House RJ 288
Howard IP 82*
Hudson L 171*
Hunt JM 180*
Hutchinson RR 119

Isaacs AD 27

Jackson D 158
Jacobson L 156
Jensen AR 3*
Johnson NS 101
Johnston J 46*
Jones EE 224*
Jorgenson DW 319*

Kagan J 138*, 191*
Kahn RL 242
Kahneman D 166*
Kaiser HF 33*
Kakolewski JW 67
Kalat JW 126*
Kanner L 203*
Kaplan A 60*
Karp SA 169
Katkin ES 113*
Katz D 242*
Katz MM 28*
Kazdin AE 258*
Keele SW 337*
Kendall LM 13
Kendon A 232*
Kiesler SB 230
Kimble DP 63*
Kimura D 65*
Kintsch W 149*
Kiresuk TJ 29*
Kirk RE 55*
Kirk SA 12*
Kirk WD 12
Kogan N 170
Kolin EA 14
Kosslyn SM 163*
Krasner L 255, 256*, 257
Kremer MW 212
Kruskal JB 7*
Kruskal WH 35*
Kuethe JL 168*
Kukla A 229

Latané B 240
Lazarus AA 273*
Leaman RL 165
Lefcourt, HM 197*

Leff JP 208
Leibenstein H 317*
Lenski GE 297*
Levinson DJ 194
Liberman AM 90*
Lichtenstein S 139
Lillesand DB 262
Lindblom CE 330*
Lindman H 48
Lineberry RL 331*
Lirtzman SI 288
Locke EA 338*
Lockhart RS 92
Lorr M 18
Lovaas OI 206*
Lowi TJ 332*
Luborsky L 274*
Lund D 158
Lyerly SB 28
Lykken DT 44*

MacKinnon DW 181*
Mackintosh NJ 152*
Mandelbrot B 322*
Mandler JM 101*
March JG 293, 313
Marcia JE 188*
Marks IM 213*, 265
Marlowe D 24
Massaro DW 87*
Mausner B 199
McArthur LA 227*
McCarthy J 12
McFall RM 262*
McGaugh JL 270
McNair DM 18*
McNeill D 93
McPartland J 300
Mees H 263
Mehrabian A 234*
Meichenbaum DH 177*
Menges RJ 343
Merton RK 285*
Meyer DE 141*
Milgram S 114*, 243*
Miller DT 225*
Miller H 165
Minhas BS 318
Mitchell RF 4
Moely BE 204*
Montague WE 159
Mood AM 300
Morrison DG 43*, 266
Morton J 88, 137*
Moss HA 191
Mowrer OH 144*, 146*
Moyer KE 341*
Moynihan DP 301
Murray EN 113
Muth RF 305*

Nebergall RE 218
Newell A 167*
Nunnally JC 47*

Ohlendorf GW 295
Olson DR 161*
Olson FA 204
Oltman PK 5*
Orne MT 56*
Overall JE 26*

Paivio A 162*
Patterson JR 20
Pearlstone Z 100
Pelz DC 289*
Perloff BF 206
Perrow C 294*
Peterson DR 185*
Peterson LR 94*
Peterson MJ 94
Peterson RF 266, 267
Pheterson GI 230*
Pheysey DC 291
Phillips EL 259*
Phillips W 138
Pomerantz JR 163
Portes A 295
Posner MI 4*
Poulton EC 83*
Price DJD 59*
Price L 14
Pugh DS 291
Pylyshyn ZW 164*

Rahe RH 30
Rao CR 50*
Rathus SA 9*
Reese HW 178*
Reich T 210
Rescorla RA 107*
Reynolds GS 116*
Riesman D 286*
Rifkin AH 212
Rimland B 201*
Risley T 108, 263
Rizzo JR 288*
Roenker DL 52*
Rohwer WD Jr 3
Rokeach M 196*
Ropartz P 121*
Rosen BC 296*
Rosen S 321
Rosenthal R 54*, 156*
Rosman BL 138
Ross M 225
Rotter JB 112*
Rozin P 126*
Ryder NB 283*

Sachs JS 99*
Sandmo A 311*
Sanford RN 194*
Saunders M 110
Savage LJ 48
Schachter S 160*
Schaefer ES 19*
Schaeffer B 206
Schaie KW 57*
Schmidt RA 153*
Schooler C 187*
Schuette D 85
Schvaneveldt RW 141*
Schweid E 267
Scott JP 122*
Scott WA 53*
Seeman M 281*
Seligman MEP 150*
Sewell WH 295*
Shankweiler DP 89, 90
Sharpe WF 320*
Sheehan PW 21*
Shepard RN 6*
Sherif CW 218*
Sherif M 218
Sherman RE 29
Shipman VC 179
Silverman J 209
Simmelhag VL 124
Simon H 167, 293*
Singer J 160
Skinner BF 105*
Slamecka NJ 96*
Slovic P 139*
Smith H 41
Smith MB 198

Smith ML 272*
Smith PC 13*
Snyder M 195*
Snyderman BB 199
Solow RM 318
Sommer R 236*
Spencer WA 73
Sperling G 78*
Staddon JER 124*
Stein AH 182
Steiner GA 335
Stigler GJ 310*
Stokes TF 251*
Stoner JAF 237*
Storms MD 223*
Strickland BR 221*
Strupp HH 250*
Stuart RB 261*
Studdert-Kennedy M 89*, 90
Swartz JD 25
Swets JA 81*

Tanner WP Jr 81
Teitelbaum P 66*
Templer DI 17*
Templeton WB 82*
Terrace HS 123*
Test MA 241
Tharp RG 254*
Thayer RE 11*
Theil H 309*
Thompson CP 52
Thompson RF 72, 73*
Thomson DM 97*
Thorpe JS 25
Toffler A 287*
Trabasso T 147*
Tripodi T 165
Trist EL 292
Tuckman BW 238*
Tulving E 97, 100*
Tversky A 166*
Tversky B 95*

Ullmann LP 255*, 256
Ulrich RE 120*

Vaillant GE 192*
Valenstein ES 67*
Van Alstyne WW 326*
Vanderwolf CH 70*
Vaughn CE 208*
Veitch R 244

Wahler RG 266*
Wallach MA 170*
Walters RH 145
Warren JR 186*
Weiner B 229*
Weinfeld FD 300
Wetzel RJ 254
White MJ 77*
Wicker AW 220*
Wilbur CB 212
Wilensky HL 298*
Wilson GD 20*
Wing JK 27*
Winkel GH 266
Winokur G 210*
Witkin HA 169*
Wolf MM 108, 110, 184, 263*
Wolff HH 265
Wollersheim JP 269*
Wolpe J 253*
Woods PJ 115
Wrong DH 279*

York RL 300

Zellner A 37*
Zola IK 214*
Zoob I 14
Zuckerman M 14*, 16*

Index of Subjects

Achievement orientation in females 182
Activation, measurement through self-report 11
Adaptation (*see* Development of adaptation)
Adjustment (*see* Measurement of personality and adjustment)
Affects (*see* Measurement of affects)
Aggressive behavior
- agonistic behavior of mice and rats 122
- extinction-induced 119
- physiological basis of 341
- psychology of 342
- reflexive fighting in response to aversive stimulation 120
- relation to olfactory stimulation 121

Alienation, meaning of 281, 282
Androgyny, measurement of 23
Anxiety, measurement of 16, 17
Applied regression analysis 41
Assertion training, behavioral rehearsal with modeling and coaching in 262
Assertive behavior, measurement of 9, 10
Association, measures of 35, 36
Association analysis, classification of hand preference by 336
Association and regression analysis
- applied regression analysis 41
- criteria for measures of association 36
- estimating seemingly unrelated regressions and tests for aggregation bias 37
- measures of association for cross classification 35
- multicollinearity in regression analysis 38
- multiple regression as a general data-analytic system 40
- scree tests for the number of factors 34
- tests of equality between sets of coefficients in two linear regressions 39
- varimax criterion for analytic rotation in factor analysis 33

Associative learning, mental imagery in 162
Attachment theory 183
Attention, some theoretical considerations 140
Attitudes
- attitude and attitude change 218
- attitude similarity and interpersonal attraction 222
- attitude-behavior relationship 220
- prediction of social action from a dimension of internal-external control 221
- relationships between beliefs about an object and attitude toward that object 219

Attitudes and attributes (*see* Measurement of attitudes and attributes)
Attribution
- attribution process in person perception 224
- determinants and consequences of causal attribution 227
- in analysis of achievement motivation 229
- in evaluation of performance of women 230
- of success and failure in relation to expected outcome 226
- of successful performance on sex-linked tasks 228
- self-serving biases in the attribution of causality 225
- videotape and the attribution process 223

Auditory perception (*see also* Speech perception)
- precategorical acoustic storage 88
- preperceptual images, processing time, and perceptual units in 87

Autism (*see* Childhood disturbances)
Autistic child, application of operant conditioning procedures to problems of 263

Bayesian approach to the study of information processing in judgment 139
Bayesian statistical inference for psychological research 48
Behavior
- biological bases of (*see* Biological bases of behavior)
- brain areas and (*see* Brain areas and behavior)

Behavior *(continued)*
brain mechanisms and (*see* Brain mechanisms and behavior)
learning theory and 146
measurement of (*see* Measurement of behaviors)
Behavior modification
case studies in 255
developments and implications of research in 256
in the natural environments 254
of children by parents 266, 267
principles of 143
problem solving and 252
Behavior problems of middle childhood 185
Behavioral research
experimental design procedures for 55
experimenter effects in 54
methodology for 60
Behavioral sciences, inventory of scientific findings on 335
Behavioral theory, historical decay of 58
Behaviorism and neo-behaviorism
agonistic behavior of mice and rats 122
analysis of exploratory, manipulatory, and curiosity behaviors 130
behavioral study of obedience 114
concepts and methods for studying the environment of human behavior 106
contrasted conditions of reinforcement 117
current dimensions of applied behavior analysis 108
dependence of interresponse times on relative reinforcement of different interresponse times 132
discrimination learning with and without errors 123
effects of a "Good Behavior Game" 110
extinction-induced aggression 119
frustrative nonreward in partial reinforcement and discrimination learning 131
generalized expectancies for internal versus external control of reinforcement 112
implications of the superstition experiment for principles of adaptive behavior 124
instrumental conditioning of autonomically mediated behavior 113
ontogeny of behavior in the albino rat 115
Pavlovian conditioning and its proper control procedures 107
production of polydipsia in normal rats by an intermittent food schedule 128
quantitative variation of incentive and performance in the white rat 127
reflexive fighting in response to aversive stimulation 120
reinforcing effect of two spoken sounds on the frequency of two responses 129
relation between olfactory stimulation and aggressive behavior 121
responding maintained by interval schedules of reinforcement 116
role of frustrative nonreward in noncontinuous reward situations 125
schedules of reinforcement 105
situationism in psychology 109
specific hungers and poison avoidance as adaptive specializations of learning 126
strengthening behavior by reinforcement 111
systematic desensitization as a counterconditioning process 118
Betts' Questionnaire upon Mental Imagery, shortened form of 21
Biological bases of behavior
behavioral effects of hippocampal damage 63, 64
cerebral dominance and the perception of verbal stimuli 65
cholinergic mechanisms in control of behavior by the brain 69
drives and the conceptual nervous system 68
dual-process theory of habituation 72
hypnotizability, laterality of eye movements and 71
lateral hypothalamic syndrome 66
limbic-diencephalic mechanisms of voluntary movement 70
mechanism of habituation 73
role of the hypothalamus in motivation 67
Birth order and social behavior 186, 187
Brain areas and behavior
behavioral effects of hippocampal damage 63, 64
cerebral dominance and the perception of verbal stimuli 65
drives and the conceptual nervous system 68
lateral hypothalamic syndrome 66
role of the hypothalamus in motivation 67
Brain mechanisms and behavior
cholinergic mechanisms in the control of behavior 69

dual-process theory of habituation 72
habituation as a model phenomenon for study of neuronal substrates of behavior 73
hypnotizability and functional brain asymmetry 71
limbic-diencephalic mechanisms of voluntary movement 70
Brief Psychiatric Rating Scale 26

Category norms for verbal items in 56 categories 159
Childhood disturbances
acquisition of imitative speech by schizophrenic children 206
autistic disturbances of affective contact 203
in foster home reared children of schizophrenic mothers 207
infantile autism 201
influence of family and social factors on course of psychiatric illness 208
problem of sustained attention and impulse control 205
production deficiency in young children's clustered recall 204
special education for the mildly retarded 202
Children, information processing in 138
Children's drawings as measures of intellectual maturity 22
Cholinergic mechanisms in the control of behavior 69
Chronometric analysis of classification 4
Cities, reformism and public policies in 331
Class and class conflict in industrial society 299
Clinical judgments, research on 51
Clustering in free recall, estimation of 52
Cognition (*see* Memory and recall)
Cognitive processes (*see* Higher cognitive processes, Information and information processing, Intelligence, Learning)
College Self-Expression Scale for measuring assertiveness 10
Color-word test for perception and recall 3
Community mental health programs, method for evaluating 29
Conservatism, new measure of 20
Constitutional issues
demise of the right-privilege distinction 326
racial imbalance in public schools 325
speculations on the limits of legal change 328
toward a general theory of the First Amendment 327
Content analysis, reliability of 53
Creative talent, nature and nurture of 181
Creativity-intelligence distinction 170
Cross classification, measures of association for 35
Culture related to presenting complaints of patients 214

Death Anxiety Scale, construction and validation of 17
Decision making
in economics 312
linear models in 45
research on clinical judgments 51
Decision processes in perception 81
Delinquency, causes of 302
Demand characteristics and their implications 56
Design issues
demand characteristics and their implications 56
experimenter effects in behavioral research 54
measures for estimation of clustering in free recall 52
model for study of developmental problems 57
procedures for the behavioral sciences 55
reliability of content analysis 53
research on clinical judgments 51
Development of abilities
early experience and the socialization of cognitive modes in children 179
intelligence and experience 180
nature and nurture of creative talent 181
socialization of achievement orientation in females 182
Development of adaptation
attachment theory 183
behavior problems of middle childhood 185
birth order and social behavior 186, 187
development and validation of ego identity status 188
direction of effects in studies of socialization 189
effects of social reinforcement on isolate behavior of a nursery school child 184

Development of language (*see* Language development)
Developmental problems, general model for study of 57
Developmental sequences
  adaptation to life 192
  study of age and generation effects 193
  study of psychological development 191
  toward an experimental ecology of human development 190
Discriminant analysis, interpretation of 43
Discriminant learning
  frustrative nonreward in 131
  with and without "errors" 123
Disturbance syndromes
  analysis of patients' presenting complaints 214
  disordered thought in schizophrenia 211
  fears and phobias 213
  manic depressive illness 210
  psychoanalytic study of homosexuality 212
  stimulus intensity control and the cortical evoked response 209
Disturbances (*see* Childhood disturbances)
Drives and the conceptual nervous system 68

Econometric methods 46
Economic time series, spectral analysis of 42
Economics
  applications of information theory to problems in 309
  behavior of prices (*see* Prices, behavior of)
  behavioral theory of the firm 313
  business behavior, value, and growth 314
  efficiency studies (*see* Efficiency studies)
  of information 310
  theory of common-property resources 315
  theory of decision making 312
  theory of the competitive firm under price uncertainty 311
  tragedy of the commons 316
Educational opportunity, equality of 300
Efficiency studies
  allocative efficiency versus X-efficiency 317
  capital theory and investment behavior 319
  capital-labor substitution and economic efficiency 318
Emotion, effect on cue utilization and the organization of behavior 340
Emotional state, cognitive, social, and psychological determinants of 160
Ethnicity
  and the achievement syndrome 296
  role in New York City 301
Experimenter effects in behavioral research 54
Eye-contact
  functions in social interactions 232
  relation to distance 231

Factor analysis
  scree test for the number of factors 34
  varimax criterion for analytic rotation in 33
Fear
  development of a scale to measure 15
  treatment of 213

Goal attainment scaling 29
Goals, effect on task motivation 338
Goodenough draw-a-man test, revision and extension of 22
Group decisions, influence of widely held values on 237
Groups (*see* Interaction and groups)

Habituation
  as a model phenomenon for study of neuronal substrates of behavior 73
  dual-process theory of 72
Hand preference, classification by association analysis 336
Higher cognitive processes
  category norms for verbal items in 56 categories 159
  cognitive determinants of emotional state 160
  cognitive theory of semantics 161
  critique of mental imagery 164
  development of psychological differentiation 169
  discimination of behavioral information 165
  human problem solving 167
  imagery, propositions, and the form of internal representations 163
  judgmental heuristics 166
  mental imagery in associative learning and memory 162
  social schemas 168
Hippocampus, behavioral effects of damage to 63, 64
Holtzman Inkblot Technique 25
Homosexuality, psychoanalytic study of 212

Human behavior, inventory of scientific findings on 335
Hyperactive children, problem of sustained attention and impulse control in 205
Hypnotizability, relation of laterality of eye movements to 71
Hypothalamus
  recovery of feeding and drinking after lateral damage to 66
  role in motivation 67

Illinois test of psycholinguistic abilities 12
Imagery, shortened questionnaire for measuring 21
Infantile autism (*see* Childhood disturbances)
Information, economics of 310
Information and information processing
  Bayesian and regression approaches to the study of information processing in judgment 139
  application of information theory to psychology 135
  attention, some theoretical considerations 140
  information processing in the child 138
  interaction of information with word recognition 137
  perception and communication 136
Information theory, applications to problems in economics 309
Inkblot perception and personality 25
Intelligence
  and experience 180
  contrary imaginations 171
  study of the creativity-intelligence distinction 170
Interaction and groups
  bystander intervention in emergencies 240
  contact hypothesis in ethnic relations 239
  developmental sequence in small groups 238
  eye-contact, distance and affiliation 231
  functions of gaze-direction in social interaction 232
  influence of widely held values on group decisions 237
  naturalistic studies in aiding behavior 241
  nonverbal communication 233, 234
  normative and informational social influences on individual judgment 235
  studies in personal space 236
Job satisfaction and dissatisfaction 199
Judgment process
  clinical and social 165
  under uncertainty 166

Language development
  control of grammar in imitation, comprehension, and production 176
  early stages of 175
  training impulsive children to talk to themselves 177
  verbal mediation as a function of age level 178
Law and political science
  constitutional concepts of racial imbalance in public schools 325
  demise of the right-privilege distinction in constitutional law 326
  end of liberalism 332
  reformism and public policies in American cities 331
  science of muddling through 330
  speculations on the limits of legal change 328
  toward a general theory of the First Amendment 327
  two faces of power 329
Learning
  attention in learning 147
  causes and consequences of teacher-student relationships 155
  conditions of 154
  effect of teacher attention on study behavior 158
  effect of teacher expectation on 156
  facilitation in recognizing pairs of words 141
  formation of learning sets 151
  generality of the laws of 150
  learning, memory, and conceptual processes 149
  learning theory and behavior 146
  learning theory and personality dynamics 144
  model of school learning 157
  principles of behavior modification 143
  principles of perceptual learning and development 148
  schema theory of discrete motor skill learning 153
  selective attention in animal discrimination learning 152

Learning *(continued)*
social learning and personality development 145
theories of 142
Liberalism, end of 332
Linear models in decision making 45
Linear statistical inference and its applications 50

Manic depressive illness 210
Measurement of affects
construction and validation of a Death Anxiety Scale 17
development of a scale to measure fear 15
manual for the profile of mood states 18
measurement of anxiety 16
Measurement of attitudes and attributes
development of a parental attitude research instrument 19
extension of the Goodenough draw-a-man test 22
measurement of psychological androgyny 23
new measure of conservatism 20
new scale of social desirability 24
shortened form of Betts' Questionnaire upon mental imagery 21
Measurement of behaviors
assessing assertive behavior 9, 10
construction of unambiguous anchors for rating scales 13
development of a sensation-seeking scale 14
Illinois test of psycholinguistic abilities 12
measurement of activation through self-report 11
Measurement of perception and recall (*see* Perception and recall)
Measurement of personality and adjustment
Brief Psychiatric Rating Scale 26
evaluating community mental health programs 29
Holtzman Inkblot Technique 25
measuring adjustment and social behavior in the community 28
Present State Examination 27
Social Readjustment Rating Scale 30
Medical care, evaluating the quality of 304
Memory and recall
associative encoding and retrieval 97
availability versus accessibility of information 100
discussion of work on 149
examination of trace storage in free recall 96
for syntactic and semantic aspects of connected discourse 99
human associative memory 91
levels of processing 92
mental imagery in 162
pictorial and verbal encoding in a short-term memory task 95
role of auditory localization in attention and memory span 98
short-term retention of individual verbal items 94
story structure and recall 101
"tip of the tongue" phenomenon 93
Mental imagery 162, 163, 164
Mood states, manual for the profile of 18
Motivation
effect of rewards on 339
role of the hypothalamus in 67
Motivation and incentives, toward a theory of 338
Motivation to work 199
Motor performance, movement control in 337
Muddling through, science of 330
Multicollinearity in regression analysis 38
Multidimensional scaling
by optimizing goodness of fit to a nonmetric hypothesis 7
with an unknown distance function 6
Multiple regression as a general data-analytic system 40
Multivariate statistical regression model 37

Nonverbal communication 233, 234

Obedience, behavioral study of 114
Organizational analysis
causal texture of organizational environments 292
comparative analysis of organizations 294
formal theory of differentiation in organizations 290
human behavior in organizations 293
operations technology and organization structure 291
productive climates for research and development 289
role conflict and ambiguity in complex organizations 288

Parental attitude research instrument, development of 19

Pavlovian conditioning and its proper control procedures 107
Perception (*see* Auditory perception, Perception and recall, Speech perception, Visual perception)
Perception and recall
  chronometric analysis of classification 4
  measurement of clustering and of sequential constancies in repeated free recall 8
  multidimensional scaling by optimizing goodness of fit to a nonmetric hypothesis 7
  multidimensional scaling with an unknown distance function 6
  portable rod-and-frame apparatus 5
  Stroop color-word test 20
Personality
  authoritarian 194
  internal-external control of reinforcement 197
  making vocational choices 200
  moral reasoning of young adults 198
  motivation to work 199
  nature of belief systems and personality systems 196
  self-monitoring of expressive behavior 195
Personality and adjustment (*see* Measurement of personality and adjustment)
Personality development, social learning and 145
Personality dynamics, learning theory and 144
Phobias
  desensitization and psychotherapy in treatment of 265
  treatment of 213
Poison avoidance as an adaptive specialization of learning 126
Political science (*see* Law and political science)
Polydipsia, production in rats by an intermittent food schedule 128
Population density, influence on interpersonal affective behavior 244
Power, two faces of 329
Present State Examination, reliability of 27
Prices, behavior of
  product differentiation in pure competition 321
  theory of market equilibrium under conditions of risk 320
  variation of certain speculative prices 322
Prison and parole system, effectiveness of 303
Problem solving
  and behavior modification 252
  general theory of 167
Profile data, methods in the analysis of 49
Psychiatric disorders, describing and classifying 27
Psychiatric illness (*see* Childhood disturbances, Disturbance syndromes)
Psychological differentiation, development of 169
Psychological experiment, social psychology of 56
Psychological research
  Bayesian statistical inference for 48
  statistical significance in 44
Psychology, applications of information theory to 135
Psychometric theory 47
Psychopathology, Brief Rating Scale for characterizing 26
Psychotherapy
  application of contingent reinforcement on a chronic psychiatric ward 257
  application of operant conditioning to problems of an autistic child 263
  bases for coordinated research in 250
  behavior modification (*see* Behavior modification)
  behavior rehearsal with modeling and coaching in assertion training 262
  behavior therapy in the home 267
  behavioral control of overeating 261
  by reciprocal inhibition 253
  covert sensitization 264
  effectiveness of group therapy in weight control 269
  elimination of autistic self-stimulatory behavior by overcorrection 260
  empirical analysis of psychotherapy and behavior change 249
  evaluation of effects of 275
  evaluative review of the token economy 258
  factors influencing the outcome of 274
  follow-up studies on 273
  implicit technology of generalization 251
  in aftercare of schizophrenic patients 271
  in the treatment of phobic states 265
  learning-theory approaches to 270
  meta-analysis of outcome studies 272
  mothers as behavior therapists for their own children 266
  self-directed program for weight control 268

Psychotherapy *(continued)*
- token reinforcement procedures for pre-delinquent boys 259

Race and the achievement syndrome 296
Racial imbalance in public schools, constitutional concepts of 325
Readability, formula for predicting 86
Recall (*see* Memory and recall, Perception and recall)
Reciprocity, norm of 280
Regression analysis (*see* Association and regression analysis)
Regression approach to the study of information processing in judgment 139
Reinforcement
- contrasted conditions of 117
- effects of a "Good Behavior Game" 110
- generalized expectancies for internal versus external control of 112
- instrumental conditioning of autonomically mediated behavior 113
- schedules of 105, 116
- strengthening behavior by 111

Revolution, toward a theory of 284
Rod-and-frame apparatus, portable 5

Schizophrenia, disordered thought in 211
Schizophrenic children, acquisition of imitative speech by 206
Schizophrenic mothers, psychiatric disorders in children of 207
Schizophrenic patients, drug and sociotherapy in aftercare of 271
Science, quantitative methods in the analysis of 59
Scree test for the number of factors 34
Semantics, cognitive theory of 161
Sensation-seeking scale, development of 14
Sequential constancies in repeated free recall 8
Social behavior in the community, methods for measuring 28
Social desirability, new scale of 24
Social learning and personality development 145
Social problems
- causes of delinquency 302
- effectiveness of prison and parole system 303
- evaluating the quality of medical care 304
- spatial pattern of urban residential land use 305

Social psychology
- history 58
- attitudes (*see* Attitudes)
- attribution (*see* Attribution)
- experience of living in cities 243
- influences of population density and temperature on interpersonal affective behavior 244
- interaction and groups (*see* Interaction and groups)
- of organizations 242
- risks of group decisions 217
- theory of inequity 245

Social Readjustment Rating Scale 30
Socialization, direction of effects in studies of 189
Sociology
- achievement by occupations of status as professions 298
- class and class conflict in industrial society 299
- cohort as a concept in the study of social change 283
- educational and early occupational status attainment process 295
- equality of educational opportunity 300
- future shock 287
- meaning of alienation 281, 282
- norm of reciprocity 280
- organizational analysis (*see* Organizational analysis)
- oversocialized conception of man in modern sociology 279
- race, ethnicity and the achievement syndrome 296
- role of ethnicity in New York City 301
- social problems (*see* Social problems)
- social theory and social structure 285
- status crystallization 297
- study of the changing American character 286
- toward a theory of revolution 284

Spectral analysis of economic time series 42
Speech perception (*see also* Auditory perception)
- hemispheric specialization for 89
- perception of the speech code 90

Statistics, design, and general methodology
- Bayesian statistical inference for psychological research 48

applied regression analysis 41
criteria for measures of association 36
demand characteristics and their implications 56
econometric methods 46
experimental design for the behavioral sciences 55
experimenter effects in behavioral research 54
interpretation of discriminant analysis 43
linear models in decision making 45
linear statistical inference and its applications 50
measures for the estimation of clustering in free recall 52
methodology for behavioral science 60
methods in the analysis of profile data 49
model for the study of developmental problems 57
multicollinearity in regression analysis 38
multiple regression as a general data-analytic system 40
psychometric theory 47
quantitative analysis of historical and modern science 59
reliability and validity of clinical judgments 51
reliability of content analysis 53
scree test for the number of factors 34
social psychology as history 58
spectral analysis of economic time series 42
statistical regression model 37
statistical significance in psychological research 44
tests of equality between sets of coefficients in two linear regressions 39
varimax criterion for analytic rotation in factor analysis 33

Stress, relationship of personal control over aversive stimuli to 344
Stroop color-word test 3
Student ratings of college teaching, reliability of 343
Systematic desensitization as a counterconditioning process 118

Task motivation and incentives, toward a theory of 338
Teacher-student relationships, causes and consequences of 155
Teaching, reliability of student ratings of 343
Temperature, effect on interpersonal affective behavior 244
Token economy, evaluative review of 258
Token reinforcement procedures for pre-delinquent boys 259

Urban residential land use, spatial pattern of 305

Varimax criterion for analytic rotation in factor analysis 33
Verbal behavior, modifiability of 129
Verbal stimuli, cerebral dominance and the perception of 65
Visual perception
decision processes in perception 81
formula for predicting readability 86
human spatial orientation 82
information available in brief visual presentations 78
laterality differences in 77
models for magnitude estimation 83
reaction times and error rates for same-different judgments 79
Temne and Eskimo perceptual skills 84
theories of visual pattern masking, saccadic suppression, and information processing 80
visual behavior in a dyad as affected by interview content and sex 85
Vocational choices 200
Voluntary movement, limbic-diencephalic mechanisms of 70

Weight control
behavioral control of overeating 261
effectiveness of group therapy in 269
self-directed program for 268
Witkin's rod-and-frame test, portable version of 5
Word recognition
facilitation in recognizing pairs of words 141
interaction of information with 137

Index of Institutions

The institutions listed are those at which the work reported in the Citation Classic was done.

Adelphi College, Garden City, New York 14
Albert Einstein Medical Center, Philadelphia, Pennsylvania 14
American Institutes for Research, Washington, DC 338
Anna State Hospital, Anna, Illinois 119, 120, 260

Bar-Ilan University, Ramat-Gan, Israel 239
Baylor University, Waco, Texas 55
Beaver College, Glenside, Pennsylvania 199
Bell Telephone Laboratories, Murray Hill, New Jersey 6, 7, 99, 141
Bethlem Royal Hospital, London, England 213
Boston College, Chestnut Hill, Massachusetts 264
Boston University, Boston, Massachusetts 18
Bowling Green State University, Bowling Green, Ohio 122
Brandeis University, Waltham, Massachusetts 214, 227
Brigham Young University, Provo, Utah 249
Brown University, Providence, Rhode Island 279
Bryn Mawr College, Bryn Mawr, Pennsylvania 329

California Institute of Technology, Pasadena, California 284
California State College, Long Beach, California 11
Cane Hill Hospital, Coulsdon, England 27
Carleton College, Ottawa, Canada 315
Carnegie Institute of Technology, Pittsburgh, Pennsylvania 293, 313
Carnegie-Mellon University, Pittsburgh, Pennsylvania 167, 341
Catholic University of America, Washington, DC 18
City University of New York, Brooklyn, New York 165
City University of New York, New York, New York 243, 288
College of San Mateo, San Mateo, California 257
College Student Personnel Institute, Claremont, California 186
Columbia University, New York, New York 43, 123, 194, 240, 250, 285
Connecticut College, New London, Connecticut 230
Cornell University, Ithaca, New York 13, 39, 150, 190

Dalhousie University, Halifax, Canada 117
Denison University, Granville, Ohio 282
Duke Law School, Durham, North Carolina 326
Duke University, Durham, North Carolina 124, 170, 224

Educational Testing Service, Princeton, New Jersey 170
Emory University, Atlanta, Georgia 221

Fels Research Institute, Yellow Springs, Ohio 67, 138, 191
Flinders University of South Australia, Bedford Park, South Australia 226
Florida State University, Tallahassee, Florida 154
Friends Medical Science Research Center Inc., Baltimore, Maryland 271

General Electric Company, Crotonville, New York 245
George Peabody College for Teachers, Nashville, Tennessee 202

Harvard Business School, Cambridge, Massachusetts 38
Harvard Law School, Cambridge, Massachusetts 325
Harvard University, Cambridge, Massachusetts 54, 78, 93, 105, 111, 132, 156, 157, 175, 176, 192, 217, 301, 321, 322
Harvard University School of Public Health, Boston, Massachusetts 128
Haskins Laboratories, New Haven, Connecticut 89
Haskins Laboratories, New York, New York 90
Hebrew University, Jerusalem, Israel 95, 166
Hennepin County General Hospital, Minneapolis, Minnesota 29
Hollins College, Virginia 115

IBM Thomas J. Watson Research Center, Yorktown Heights, New York 322
Illinois Wesleyan University, Bloomington, Illinois 120
Indian Statistical Institute, New Delhi, India 50
Indiana University, Bloomington, Indiana 94, 129
Indiana University Medical Center, Bloomington, Indiana 105
Institute of Experimental Psychology, Oxford, England 232
Institute of Pennsylvania Hospital, Philadelphia, Pennsylvania 21
Institute of Psychiatric Research, Indianapolis, Indiana 16
Institute of Psychiatry, London, England 208, 213, 265, 275, 340

Johns Hopkins Hospital, Baltimore, Maryland 203
Johns Hopkins University, Baltimore, Maryland 163, 168, 200, 312

Kansas State University, Manhattan, Kansas 52, 244

Massachusetts Institute of Technology, Cambridge, Massachusetts 38, 237
Massachusetts Mental Health Center, Boston, Massachusetts 56
Maudsley Hospital, London, England 27, 207, 213, 265, 275
McGill University, Montreal, Canada 65, 68, 205
Medical Research Council, Cambridge, England 83, 98, 136, 137
Medical Research Council, London, England 208
Michigan State University, East Lansing, Michigan 71
Montclair State College, Montclair, New Jersey 9
Montreal Children's Hospital, Montreal, Canada 205

National Institute of Mental Health, Bethesda, Maryland 49, 187, 209
National Institute of Mental Health, Rockville, Maryland 19, 28, 189, 191, 271
Naval Medical Research Institute, Bethesda, Maryland 238
New York University, New York, New York 40, 116, 235, 240, 274
Northwestern University, Evanston, Illinois 241, 258
Norwegian School of Economics and Business Administration, Bergen, Norway 311

Ohio State University, Columbus, Ohio 24, 86
Ontario Institute for Studies in Education, Toronto, Canada 161
Oregon Research Institute, Eugene, Oregon 45, 51, 139

Pennsylvania State University, University Park, Pennsylvania 22, 182, 258
Princeton University, Princeton, New Jersey 127, 314
Proctor and Gamble 41
Purdue University, Lafayette, Indiana 228

Queens College, City University of New York, Flushing, New York 89

Rutgers University, Piscataway, New Jersey 273

San Francisco Unified School District, San Francisco, California 156
Saskatchewan Hospital, Weyburn, Canada 236
Society of Medical Psychoanalysts, New York, New York 212

Squibb Institute for Medical Research, New Jersey 69
Stanford Medical Center, Stanford, California 64
Stanford University, Stanford, California 23, 79, 80, 91, 140, 142, 143, 145, 147, 253, 268, 299, 318
State University of New York, Buffalo, New York 15, 113, 188, 328
State University of New York, Stony Brook, New York 118, 142, 252, 255, 256, 257
State University of New York College of Medicine, New York, New York 169
State University of New York Downstate Medical Center, Brooklyn, New York 5
Swarthmore College, Swarthmore, Pennsylvania 58

Tavistock Clinic, London, England 183
Tavistock Institute, London, England 292
Tulane University, New Orleans, Louisiana 125

US Naval Personnel Research Laboratory, San Diego, California 201
Universität des Saarlandes, Federal Republic of Germany 193
Université Louis Pasteur, Strasbourg, France 121
University of Arizona, Tucson, Arizona 254
University of Aston, Birmingham, England 291
University of Buffalo, Buffalo, New York 178
University of California, Berkeley, California 3, 165, 181, 194, 198, 298, 302, 317
University of California, Irvine, California 72, 270
University of California, Los Angeles, California 147, 206, 219, 229, 234, 281
University of California, Riverside, California 230
University of California, San Diego, La Jolla, California 101, 116
University of California, Santa Barbara, California 316
University of Cambridge, Cambridge, England 171
University of Canterbury, Canterbury, New Zealand 20
University of Chicago, Chicago, Illinois 35, 47, 179, 233, 290, 305, 309, 310, 319, 332, 335
University of Colorado, Boulder, Colorado 149, 272
University of Connecticut, Storrs, Connecticut 8, 89, 112, 296
University of Delaware, Newark, Delaware 85
University of Durham, Durham, England 82
University of Edinburgh, Edinburgh, Scotland 84
University of Hawaii, Honolulu, Hawaii 254
University of Houston, Houston, Texas 80
University of Hull, Hull, England 336
University of Illinois, Urbana, Illinois 33, 34, 144, 146, 185, 255, 256, 269, 303, 343
University of Kansas, Kansas City, Kansas 158
University of Kansas, Lawrence, Kansas 106, 108, 110, 230, 251, 259
University of Kentucky, Lexington, Kentucky 24
University of London, London, England 275, 340
University of Manitoba, Winnipeg, Canada 251
University of Massachusetts, Amherst, Massachusetts 344
University of Michigan, Ann Arbor, Michigan 48, 53, 60, 81, 130, 242, 261, 289, 297, 304
University of Minnesota, Minneapolis, Minnesota 44, 195, 204
University of Missouri, Columbia, Missouri 155
University of Nottingham, Nottingham, England 42
University of Oklahoma, Norman, Oklahoma 218
University of Oregon, Eugene, Oregon 4, 45, 51, 63, 135, 270, 337
University of Oregon Medical School, Eugene, Oregon 73, 207
University of Oxford, Oxford, England 152, 231, 232
University of Pennsylvania, Philadelphia, Pennsylvania 21, 66, 107, 126, 274
University of Pittsburgh, Pittsburgh, Pennsylvania 342
University of Rochester, Rochester, New York 274, 321, 339
University of Southern California, Los Angeles, California 153
University of Tennessee, Knoxville, Tennessee 18

University of Texas, Austin, Texas 25, 155, 165, 222, 331
University of Toronto, Scarborough, Canada 124
University of Toronto, Toronto, Canada 92, 100, 131
University of Vermont, Burlington, Vermont 96
University of Washington, Seattle, Washington 36, 184, 263, 266, 267, 320
University of Washington School of Medicine, Seattle, Washington 30
University of Waterloo, Waterloo, Canada 109, 145, 177, 225
University of Western Ontario, London, Canada 70, 162, 164
University of Wisconsin, Madison, Wisconsin 37, 41, 46, 87, 151, 211, 262, 283, 294, 295
University of Wisconsin, Milwaukee, Wisconsin 220

Vanderbilt University, Nashville, Tennessee 250
Victoria University of Wellington, Wellington, New Zealand 77

Washington University, St. Louis, Missouri 17, 249, 280
Washington University School of Medicine, St. Louis, Missouri 210
West Virginia University, Morgantown, West Virginia 10, 57, 193
Western Michigan University, Kalamazoo, Michigan 288
Western Reserve University, Cleveland, Ohio 199
Western State Hospital, Seattle, Washington 263

Yale Law School, New Haven, Connecticut 327
Yale University, New Haven, Connecticut 59, 88, 91, 97, 114, 223, 286, 330
Yeshiva University, New York, New York 165
York University, Toronto, Canada 331